W9-BNG-247

# Ethnicity in Contemporary America

# Ethnicity in Contemporary America,

## A Geographical Appraisal

### Second Edition

Jesse O. McKee, Editor

ROWMAN & LITTLEFIELD PUBLISHERS, INC.
*Lanham • Boulder • New York • Oxford*

Samford University Library

ROWMAN & LITTLEFIELD PUBLISHERS, INC.

Published in the United States of America
by Rowman & Littlefield Publishers, Inc.
4720 Boston Way, Lanham, Maryland 20706
http://www.rowmanlittlefield.com

12 Hid's Copse Road
Cumnor Hill, Oxford OX2 9JJ, England

Copyright © 2000 by Rowman & Littlefield Publishers, Inc.

*All rights reserved.* No part of this publication may be reproduced,
stored in a retrieval system, or transmitted in any form or by any
means, electronic, mechanical, photocopying, recording, or otherwise,
without the prior permission of the publisher.

British Library Cataloguing in Publication Information Available

**Library of Congress Cataloging-in-Publication Data**
Ethnicity in contemporary America : a geographical appraisal / Jesse O. McKee, editor.—
2nd ed.
    p.  cm.
  Includes bibliographical references and index.
  ISBN 0-7425-0034-9 (cloth : alk. paper)
  1. Ethnology—United States.  2. United States—Emigration and immigration.  3. United
States—Population.  4. United States—Ethnic relations.  5. Minorities—United States.  I.
McKee, Jesse O.

E184.A1 E885 2000
305.8'00973—dc21                                                                99-088089

Printed in the United States of America.

♾™ The paper used in this publication meets the minimum requirements of American
National Standard for Information Sciences—Permanence of Paper for Printed Library
Materials, ANSI/NISO Z39.48-1992.

E
184
.A1
E885
2000

# Contents

# Figures and Tables

# Preface

*Ethnicity in Contemporary America* is intended to serve as a text or supplementary reading book for college-level courses in ethnic or multicultural studies or other appropriate courses. This multiauthored text was first published in 1985. For the revised edition, the outline of the text and the table of contents have remained. But each chapter has been thoroughly revised and updated, is an original contribution, and is written specifically for this text. Although each chapter follows a rather flexible structured outline—that is, to discuss each ethnic group as to its origin, diffusion, socioeconomic characteristics, and settlement patterns—each chapter's outline of topics discussed varies somewhat with each ethnic group and is an expression of that group's historical development and the author's interpretation of that minority group.

A *minority*, in a general sense, means a number forming less than one-half of the whole. When applied to ethnic or social relations, several characteristics appear. First, being a member of a minority indicates that one is a member not only of a social group but frequently of a political unit as well. A dominant group in society normally shares a host of common traits such as language and religion, a common value system and history, and a common physical appearance or an identifiable "biological visibility." Cultural traits, value systems, and physical appearance of a minority are frequently devalued by the dominant group. Minorities are also conscious of themselves as a group and usually resist intermarriage.

*Ethnic* is a term frequently used to refer to minority or racial groups. The word is derived from the Greek word *ethnos*, meaning a "people" or "nation."[1] It is a very popular term that emphasizes the cultural ethnos of a group and to a lesser degree its physiognomic (racial) traits. An *ethnic group* has been defined as a group of people "of common ancestry and cultural tradition, living as a minority in a larger or host culture."[2] "A strong feeling of group identity, of belonging, characterizes ethnicity."[3] "*Ethnic Geography* is the study of the spatial and ecological aspects of ethnicity."[4] Unlike a nationality group, an ethnic group usually does not possess a strong loyalty to a former nation-state. Usually, *nationality* also includes such meanings as the individual's place of birth, citizenship of the individual or group, or the ancestor's place of birth. Frequently, different ethnic groups may base their identity on different traits. For the Amish, it is religion; African Americans identify with race; the French Canadians use the mother tongue; Jews use religion; and folk culture is utilized by Appalachian Southerners.

*Race* is used to refer to a group of persons connected by common physical and/or biological characteristics that are transmitted in descent. It is a term full of misunderstandings and myths. *Race* is not to be confused with *culture* or *nationality*. *Culture* is learned behavior, and the use of the term *nationality* may infer cultural traits. In a strict sense, *race* infers a biological connotation only, but use of the term frequently emphasizes the barriers often placed on a minority race by a dominant group. For purposes of this book, the use of the term *race* has not been emphasized in favor of the more comprehensive and less discriminatory concept of ethnic minority. The ethnic groups discussed in this book provide a sampling of some of the major ethnic minority groups in the United States.

In Part I, the opening chapter discusses migration theory and acculturation processes. The next chapter discusses the immigration history of the United States from 1607 to the present, including major U.S. immigration legislation, and provides a background as to the time of entry, volume, and spatial distribution of various immigrant groups. Separate chapters then follow in Part II on selected ethnic minorities that include the Native Americans, African Americans, Mexican Americans, Cuban Americans, Puerto Ricans, Jews, Japanese, Chinese, and Indochinese.

Nine chapters in Part II are devoted to specific ethnic groups, the majority of which are of non-European ancestry. Part III discusses "Rural and Urban Ethnic Islands" in which the focus is on the selection of specific immigrant groups, primarily of European heritage, and on a discussion of their various impacts on the cultural landscape of the United States. The "Rural Ethnic Islands" chapter discusses specific groups such as the Germans, Belgians, Swedes, Finns, Norwegians, Amish, Cajuns, and Mormons. Emphasis is placed on their material cultural contributions, particularly their house types and barns. The "Urban Ethnic Islands" chapter focuses on the ethnic mixes (mainly European) in selected American cities, their urban settlement concentrations, and other such features as the foreign language press, foreign language broadcasting, and ethnic festivals.

The study of ethnic minorities is interdisciplinary in nature. Anthropologists, sociologists, demographers, historians, political scientists, economists, and geographers as well as scholars in other disciplines have written extensively on the subject. Admittedly, each discipline approaches the study of ethnic groups differently. Each distinguishes itself by the questions it addresses, and not necessarily by the phenomena it investigates. This text is a geographic appraisal of ethnicity in contemporary America. Geographers not only examine the character of places and people but emphasize spatial relations of phenomena. They ask such questions as "How do humans organize their society in space to accomplish their needs and wants?" or "How are minority groups related spatially to other groups within a society?" It is hoped that scholars in other disciplines will find this approach complementary to their own research and teaching pursuits.

The editor of this volume acknowledges the cooperation extended to him by the contributors. I wish to thank chapter authors for their patience, time, and knowledge in revising this text. For each of the authors, the editor wishes to thank the various staff members and research assistants who assisted the authors at their respective universities. In addition, a word of appreciation is extended to those who helped critique the text in its early stages of development, to Marilyn Sirmon for her editorial service, and to Betty Blackledge for typing and proofreading portions of the original manuscripts. Finally, a word of thanks is extended to Susan McEachern, executive editor, and to other staff members at Rowman & Littlefield Publishers, Inc., who were involved with the production of this text.

## NOTES

1. Terry G. Jordan and Lester Rowntree, *The Human Mosaic: A Thematic Introduction to Cultural Geography*, 7th ed. (New York: Longman, 1997), 316.
2. Jordan and Rowntree, *The Human Mosaic*, 316.
3. Jordan and Rowntree, *The Human Mosaic*, 316.
4. Jordan and Rowntree, *The Human Mosaic*, 316.

# MIGRATION THEORY
# AND IMMIGRATION

# Introduction

*Jesse O. McKee*

Human beings have always tended to be rather mobile. In societies experiencing advanced economic and technological progress, particularly in transportation and communication facilities, a corresponding increase in mobility and migration occurs. This mobility of humans is evidenced by the linguistic, religious, social, and racial mixing of much of the world's population. In the United States, for example, one-fourth of its residents do not reside in the state in which they were born, and every year about one out of five American moves to a new residence.

Migration is not random, nor is it just biologically determined. It is selective—frequently influenced by such demographic characteristics as race, age, sex, and a host of other variables including educational attainment, occupation, and marital status, as well as economic and political pressures generally associated with specific geographic areas. Some migrate by free choice; others are forced. Migration is frequently thought of in terms of individuals exercising free choice, but the majority of worldwide migrations in the twentieth century have been impelled. Many persons emigrate in search of better jobs, higher wages, and general improvement in their quality of life. But by some estimates, more than 100 million persons have been forced to move because of ecological changes in their homelands, civil or international war, differences in political ideologies, or pressing economic conditions. These displaced persons or refugees are recognized as comprising a type of migratory movement different from that of those exercising free will. Some refugees realize that prospects of returning to their homelands are virtually nil and that their movements are permanent. Others see their moves as temporary and do expect to return at a future date.

Once an individual migrates, particularly to another country, there are usually enormous social and cultural adjustments to be made: job skills to be acquired, language problems, gainful employment and housing, and acceptance into the host society.

To further understand the topics of migration and assimilation of an ethnic minority, this introductory chapter provides a theoretical and conceptual framework from which to examine and evaluate migration patterns and cultural adaptations of various ethnic minority groups. The chapter also provides a frame of reference from which to view the various ethnic groups discussed in the ensuing chapters of this text.

## MIGRATION THEORY

The pioneer effort in establishing migration theory was developed and written by British demographer E. G. Ravenstein in 1885 and 1889. In his first paper, Ravenstein summarized five items. He added two more statements in his second paper. After studying migration in Britain and then adding more than twenty countries for his second article, he reached the following conclusions:[1]

1. *Migration and distance:* Most migrants travel a short distance, but those who travel farther tend to move to larger cities.
2. *Migration by stages:* Migration produces "currents of migration," and people surrounding cities move to them, leaving gaps to be filled by people from more remote districts.
3. *Streams and counterstreams:* Each main current or stream of migration produces a counterstream.
4. *Urban–rural differences:* People living in towns or urban areas are less migratory than those inhabiting rural areas.
5. *Predominance of females among short-distance migrants:* Generally, females tend to be predominant among short-distance migrants.
6. *Migration and technology:* Improvements in technology regarding transportation and industrial development encourage an increase in migration.
7. *Dominance of the economic motive:* Other variables such as climate and social and political pressures are important, but the desire to improve one's economic status is a dominant variable.

Everett S. Lee, writing in 1966, expands on some of Ravenstein's ideas. He feels that "[n]o matter how short or how long, how easy or how difficult, every act of migration involves an origin, a destination, and an intervening set of obstacles."[2] He believes that the factors that influence one's decisions to migrate can be summarized under four headings:

1. Factors associated with the area of origin
2. Factors associated with the area of destination
3. Intervening obstacles
4. Personal factors

He then summarizes three of these factors in a schematic diagram (Fig. 1). The two circles represent places of origin and destination, separated by intervening obstacles. Factors that cause potential migrants to respond favorably to an area are indicated by a plus sign; negative factors are indicated by a minus sign. Those factors to which potential migrants tend to act indifferently are indicated with a zero. Usually, before moving, a potential migrant considers the positive and negative factors at the point of origin. Family ties may be a plus, but a cold climate and being unemployed may be minuses. At the point of destination, family ties may be negative, but a warmer climate and the opportunities for a job are pluses or pull factors. Migration can be thought of in terms of pluses and minuses, or "push and pull" factors. Usually, one or more negative variables exist at the point of origin that push the migrant from the point of origin, and one or more plus variables exist at the point of destination that tip the migrant's decision-making process and pull the individual to the

**Figure 1    Origin and Destination Factors and Intervening Obstacles in Migration. Source: "A Theory of Migration" by Everett Lee, 1966. Reprinted by permission from *Demography*.**

point of destination. Once these variables are evaluated and a potential decision is made, the final act of moving cannot be pursued until the intervening obstacles are surmounted. Financial and psychic costs, together with marital status, number of dependents, educational skills, age, health, distance involved, and many other personal and possible restrictive variables, must be considered. Most moves cannot be completed until the intervening obstacles are surmounted. Even then, the decisions may not always be rational. Accidental occurrences may still account for a considerable proportion of total migrations.

Voluntary migration is selective rather than random with biological and cultural determinants, such as ethnic compositions, sex, marital status, educational attainment, and occupational skills. The interplay of these variables may shift when forced migration forces are at work, resulting in many refugees and displaced persons. Certain life cycles or stages can also affect migration. Graduation from high school or college, marriage, entrance into the labor market, divorce, death of a spouse, and retirement are all factors that may induce persons to migrate.

Lee also postulates about the volume of migration, development of streams and counterstreams, and the characteristics of migrants.[3]

## Volume of Migration

1. "The volume of migration within a given territory varies with the degree of diversity of areas included in that territory." The higher the diversity, the greater the in-migration flow.
2. "The volume of migration varies with the diversity of people." The greater the diversity, the higher the rate of migration.
3. "The volume of migration is related to the difficulty of surmounting the intervening obstacles." Fewer obstacles may permit increased migration.
4. "The volume of migration varies with fluctuations in the economy." During periods of business expansion, in-migration is likely to increase in the affected areas.
5. "Unless severe checks are imposed, both volume and rate of migration tend to increase with time." Once the set of intervening obstacles are surmounted, increasing migration is likely.
6. "The volume and rate of migration vary with the state of progress in a country or area." In developed nations people are very mobile in contrast to lesser-developed nations. When persons change residences in lesser-developed societies, frequently it is en masse and often under duress.

### Stream and Counterstream

1. "Migration tends to take place largely within well defined streams."
2. "For every migration stream, a counterstream develops."
3. "The efficiency of the stream (ratio of stream to counterstream or the net redistribution of population affected by the opposite flows) is high if the major factors in the development of a migration stream were minus factors at origin."
4. "The efficiency of stream and counterstream tends to be low if origin and destination are similar."
5. "The efficiency of migration streams will be high if the intervening obstacles are great."
6. "The efficiency of a migration stream varies with economic conditions, being high in prosperous times and low in times of depression."

### Characteristics of Migrants

1. "Migration is selective."
2. "Migrants responding primarily to plus factors at destination tend to be positively selected."
3. "Migrants responding primarily to minus factors at origins tend to be negatively selected; or where minus factors are overwhelming to entire groups, they may not be selected at all."
4. "Taking all migrants together, selection tends to be bimodal."
5. "The degree of positive selection increases with the difficulty of the intervening obstacles."
6. "The heightened propensity to migrate at certain stages of the life cycle is important in the selection of migrants."
7. "The characteristics of migrants tend to be intermediate between characteristics of the population at origin and the population at destination."

In summary, the hypotheses established by Lee regarding volume, streams and counterstreams, and characteristics of migrants are significant and provide a rather simple schema for examining migration at local, national, or international levels.

Many migration models embrace the classic "push and pull" theories. With these theories, migration is felt to occur because of a disequilibrium between countries of emigration and immigration with regard to such variables as income, availability of jobs, or perceived quality of life. Thus, migration serves to reestablish social/political order and a socioeconomic equilibrium. However, another school of thought regarding migration theory prevalent in the 1970s and 1980s is structural/conflict theories, including neo-Marxist perspectives such as world systems theory.[4] Many of these structural models, rather than explain the causes of migration in terms of "push and pull" factors, view "international migration as an integral aspect of a world capitalist system based on inequality and domination."[5] With this view, migration is seen as providing "cheap labor to capitalists in development countries,"[6] thus exploiting migrants and maintaining inequality. In the world system/dependency model, migration is seen as inherent to the world capitalist system. Support for this theoretical perspective gains credence when newcomers to the United States gain employment in low-level jobs vacated by native workers, thus reinforcing inequality between development and developing nations. In this view, migration is not perceived as a positive phenomenon. Immigrants can frequently cause competition and inequality in the labor market of the host country. For newcomers having to accept low-paying jobs, often characterized by unstable working conditions where chances for upward mobility are slim, eventual social and political integration into the host society may prove difficult. On the other hand, skilled migrants entering the host society have fewer problems acculturating into the host society.

Another school of thought, quite in vogue in the United States today, is multiculturalism (earlier known as cultural pluralism). This theory supports immigration as a positive phenomenon[7] and presumes the desirability of multiethnic societies, particularly in complex societies consisting of different ethnic and religious groups.[8] Multiculturalism is appealing as an ideology and social policy and entails the recognition and acceptance of ethnocultural minorities. Yet frequently multiculturalism is difficult to accomplish without modifying the host country's socioeconomic and political structure. Much debate exists between multiculturalism as an ideology and implementation as a governmental policy.

## TYPES OF MIGRATION

There are three basic types of migratory movement: cyclic, periodic, and migratory. *Cyclic* movements are journeys that begin and eventually terminate at the initial place of origin. Typically, the daily "journey to work," or commuting trip, is an excellent example of this type; so too are the many shopping, social, and service trips taken by most Americans on a daily or weekly basis. Another form of cyclic movement is seasonal, which may involve traveling for leisure on holidays and vacations. Although many of the aforementioned types of movement can be thought of as regular, some cyclic movements such as business trips or weekend travel may be viewed as irregular.

Another type of movement is *periodic*. This type usually involves a temporary stay away from one's normal site of residence. Examples may include persons in military service, students in college, migrant laborers, or people who move to the Sunbelt states from northern states during the winter.

The third type, *migratory* movement, involves a permanent change in residence for a substantial period of time in a new political unit. This type of movement has a spatial requirement and a time component (usually a year—but not always) and involves a territorial/administrative change in a political unit. However, further clarification is needed. People who make a permanent change in their residence are considered movers, not migrants, unless the move takes them into a new political unit (Fig. 2). Thus, all migrants are movers, but not all movers are migrants. There is little problem in understanding migration in terms of interstate or intercountry moves. However, there appears to be no general agreement as to what constitutes a political unit, particularly below the county level. So, undoubtedly some confusion will persist over when to designate specific individuals officially as migrants or movers.

In further examination of migratory movements, it is useful to think of migration in terms of *total displacement migration* and *partial displacement migration*, particularly with regard to social and cultural attachments to the place of origin and the new place of destination.[9] Total displacement involves the move to a new residence, which will

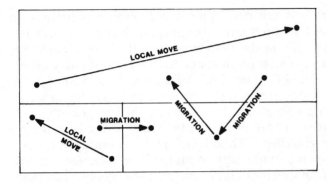

Figure 2   Migration versus Local Move. Source: Modified from G. S. Lewis, *Human Migration* (New York: St. Martin's, 1982), 10.

modify drastically the person's activity space of journey to work, school attendance, shopping patterns, and other social and leisure trips. Conversely, partial displacement allows individuals to continue to use much of their same activity space. Frequently, partial displacement is not caused by job relocation but is constrained by it. In this instance, migrants change residences but are still able to maintain many of their former activity-space ties to shopping centers, churches, and social facilities.

## CLASSIFICATION OF MIGRATION

William Petersen was one of the first to recognize most of the following different classes of migration: (1) primitive, (2) free-individual, (3) mass or groups, (4) restricted, and (5) impelled or forced.[10] *Primitive* migration involves people who are unable to cope with certain natural forces such as geophysical, meteorological, or ecological hazards related to the deterioration of their physical environment. One solution to coping or adjusting to the problem is to move.

*Free-individual/group* migration involves the movement of individuals or families acting on their own initiative without being compelled by official or governmental policy. Much of the immigration to the United States in the eighteenth, nineteenth, and early twentieth centuries might be categorized as this type.

*Mass* migration refers to a social group of persons larger than a family. Free migration can cause collective behavior, and when large numbers begin to migrate and migration streams or channels become refined and streamlined, it can be considered mass migration.

*Restricted* migration has rapidly started to replace free and mass migration. Since the early Chinese Exclusion Act of 1882, and particularly since 1921, the United States has placed restrictions on the number and ethnic composition of those seeking resident status. Similar legislation exists in most other nations. The restrictions may help to stem the tide of normal migration flows, but frequently the greatest migration problems involve refugees and displaced persons, which can play havoc with normal migration legislation and regulations.

*Impelled* or *forced* migration is the fifth category. Impelled migration includes migrants who retain some power of decision and degree of choice, whereas forced migration refers to migrants who have no control or power of decision over their moves. For those who have fled their homelands, *émigrés* regard their exile as temporary and plan to return at some date in the future, whereas *refugees* intend to settle permanently in a new country. Forced migration intended to remove a dissident population is frequently referred to as *displacement*. Although all displacement need not be forced, some is impelled. The end result is the same in that these migrants feel that they cannot safely return to their homelands.

## ACCULTURATION, ASSIMILATION, AND CULTURAL PLURALISM (MULTICULTURALISM)

### How Are Minorities Created?

A *minority* refers to people who are members of a social group that comprise less than one-half of the total population. Usually they share a host of social and cultural traits that help to bind the group together as a subordinate group in a greater complex society. Often in appearance they may be physically distinguishable, and they may possess certain physical or cultural traits that are held in low esteem by the dominant culture. Minority groups emerge through four processes: (1) voluntary migration, (2) involuntary migration, (3) annexation, and (4) colonialism.[11] With regard to the United States, many minority groups have evolved from voluntary migration, but some have been involuntary, such as African Americans, and the American Indian has been the dominant group falling under the category of annexation. Colonialism has not been a major factor in the creation of minorities within the United States.

### How Do Minorities Adapt?

The American public has always been concerned with the acculturation of minority groups into mainstream American society, particularly when the volume of migrants increases rather rapidly in a short time span. In the past, and still somewhat true today, more concern has been expressed over the willingness of these new immigrants to adopt the English language and a political ideology compatible with democratic ideals than with the religious preference of these new arrivals. Religious choice is still a highly cherished freedom in the United States. Educational attainment, health condition, and occupational status of immigrants also have been frequent areas of concern.

Three basic concepts guide the process of migrants becoming Americanized: Anglo-conformity, the melting pot, and cultural pluralism.[12] The *Anglo-conformity* concept involves keeping English as the official language and adopting Anglo-culture norms as the standard of life. The Americanization of European ethnic groups has been rather successful, but non-European immigrants have frequently been denied full assimilation into the Anglo-culture because of their skin color and visibility. For these groups, some acculturation has occurred, but structural assimilation has not taken place. Prejudice, discrimination, and even segregation have kept many of these minority groups in a subordinate position.

The *melting pot* concept assumes that as different ethnic groups come to the United States, they intermingle, thereby producing a new composite national stock and a new breed called the "American." In practice, the melting pot concept has become similar to that of Anglo-conformity. Contributions by minorities have been ignored and through time have been lost in the "pot." Thus, both of these concepts in actuality are based on "the absorption and eventual disappearance of the immigrant cultures into an overall 'American culture.'"[13] Basically, descendants of immigrants from southern and eastern

Europe who initially came to the United States in the late nineteenth and early twentieth centuries give evidence to the Anglo-conformity and melting pot theories and substantiate the idea that assimilation does occur in American society.[14]

A viable alternative to these two concepts is that of *cultural pluralism* or what contemporarily is referred to as *multiculturalism*. Cultural pluralism or multiculturalism enables a minority group to keep its identity and to maintain its culture yet participate in the dominant society. However, cultural pluralism based on prejudice and inferiority of certain ethnic groups is not a sensible substitute. A workable relationship between the dominant and subordinate cultures whereby equality is assured and some degree of collective societal goals can be agreed on is probably the best alternative. Figure 3 is a schematic diagram attempting to show that many groups have Americanized and are part of the mainstream (Canadians, Irish, Scots, etc.), whereas other ethnic groups have not been fully assimilated. They operate, rather, as subcultures in a pluralistic society (i.e., African Americans, Native Americans). Some of these subcultures function close to the mainstream; others are on the margin of plural acceptance.

Researchers have developed other theories that explain how minorities adapt to dominant–minority relationships. These theories are generally referred to as "race relations cycles." One such cycle involves the alternatives of (1) separatism, (2) accommodation, (3) acculturation, (4) assimilation, and (5) amalgamation.[15] *Separatism* refers to the geographic separation of a group so they can maintain their way of life. The early history and settlement patterns of the Mormons and the Amish exemplify this mode of adaptation quite well. Some groups, upon arrival, tend to cluster to promote self needs and security, but this clustering should not be considered the same as separatism.

In *accommodation* the minority or subordinate group must, out of necessity, adopt various traits and conform to a certain degree to the wishes and behavior of the dominant group.

*Acculturation* is the process whereby individuals adopt traits from another group. Usually the adoption of material traits, language, and secular behavior is undertaken. Certain elements of the minority culture, however, may be maintained and practiced in a subcultural fashion. Later, cultural attitudes, values, and other nonmaterial traits from the dominant culture are acquired. Most ethnic groups must acculturate to some extent

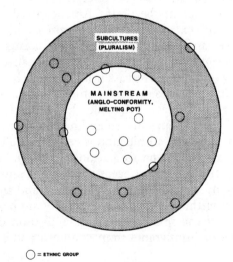

Figure 3    Degree of Americanization of Ethnic Groups.

with the dominant or host culture. In return, the dominant or host culture frequently makes accommodations and adopts some of the minority's cultural traits, thereby enabling both cultures to coexist.

*Assimilation* occurs when a minority individual or group adopts the cultural traits of the dominant group and identifies with that group, and the dominant group accepts the individual or group without discrimination. The assimilated individual must also be assured that intermarriage can occur without fear of being ostracized by the dominant group. When full assimilation occurs, the minority status ceases to exist.

*Amalgamation* is the biological merging of a distinct racial stock with the dominant racial group. Of course, some amalgamation will always take place between dominant and minority groups with or without formal approval should the two groups interact and live in close proximity to each other. This condition does not necessarily infer, however, that assimilation has occurred.

It is also quite presumptuous to infer that minority groups will follow the aforementioned five alternatives in sequential fashion. For example, acculturation is not always followed by assimilation, nor is assimilation inevitably followed by amalgamation. Some minority groups may never fully assimilate. Traditionally, in American society, it can be stated that most minority groups have tended to achieve some form of accommodation, acculturation, or assimilation. Separatism and even secession have been proposed by some groups, but this alternative has not been extremely successful.

Other types of race relation cycles have been proposed by Robert Park and Emory Bogardus. According to Park, there are four main cycles: (1) *contact*, (2) *competition*, (3) *accommodation*, and (4) *assimilation*.[16] After contact, competition between groups for jobs, land, and other goals occur; violence may even break out. One group then establishes dominance, and the groups learn to accommodate each other. Eventually, assimilation may result. Bogardus has developed seven cycles: (1) *curiosity*, (2) *economic welcome*, (3) *industrial and social antagonism*, (4) *legislative antagonism*, (5) *fair-play tendencies*, (6) *quiescence*, and (7) *second generation difficulties*.[17]

Michael Banton in his research has created six orders of race relations: (1) *peripheral contact* (in which groups remain independent), (2) *institutionalized contact and acculturation*, (3) *domination*, (4) *paternalism*, (5) *integration*, and (6) *pluralism* (Fig. 4).[18] He then establishes a developmental sequence among the orders (Fig. 5). In the United States, sequence 1 of contact, domination, and pluralism is the most appropriate model of race relations. The contact, paternalism, and integration sequence best describes the experience of European-African relations. Part of it is exemplified in the South in the United States with regard to white-black relations, but the final order, integration, has not developed. The final order in the South is better categorized as pluralism. The third sequence—contact, acculturation, and integration—has been the general one for many white migrants to the United States. Normally, except where race and/or color is a significant factor, these immigrants have become Americanized, or integrated by the third generation—the "three-generation process." However, sometimes in the third generation "the grandchildren of immigrants attempt to recover the heritage of the first generation."[19] The idea that the second generation tries to forget its heritage and the third to recover or revive it is often referred to as "Hansen's law" or thesis.[20]

For assimilation or Americanization to occur, certain key factors encourage or discourage the process. These include (1) similarity of the two groups culturally and physically, (2) the desire of the minority to assimilate and willingness of the majority to allow them to, (3) the nature of minority settlement, and (4) recentness of arrival and proxim-

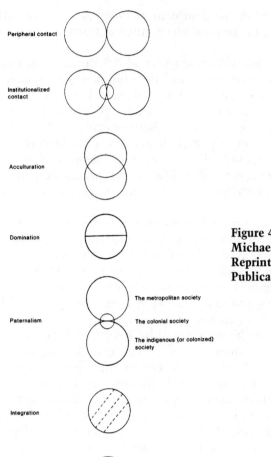

Figure 4    Six Orders of Race Relations. Source: Michael Banton, *Race Relations*, 69–75. Reprinted by permission of Tavistock Publications, Inc.

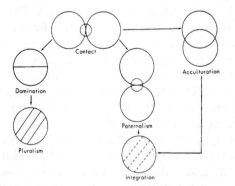

Figure 5    Sequence of Racial Orders. Source: Michael Banton, *Race Relations*, 69–75.

ity to the homeland.[21] If these factors are favorable, the Americanization process proceeds without too much complication, but for some it may not be achieved. Won Moo Hurh, in his study of Korean immigrants, develops seven critical phases in the adaptation process[22] (Fig. 6). These phases include *excitement,* followed by *exigency* or disenchantment—a critical phase because the immigrant may leave. For those who stay, a period of *resolution* is established in which the immigrant resolves to "make it." After reaching *optimism,* the immigrant may realize that he or she is being discriminated against, and an *identification crisis* emerges before the immigrant finally accepts the role between a foreigner or outsider and a fully accepted member of society—*marginality acceptance.* In this model, assimilation is obviously not achieved.

Although each migratory movement to the United States is unique and has its own historical pattern with regard to acceptance, adaptation, acculturation, or possible assimilation into American society, certain generalizations can be stated with regard to specific internal dynamics in the way migrations evolve and the acceptance, marginalization, or exclusion of specific ethnic groups by the host culture.[23] Stephen Castles and Mark J. Miller have summarized these patterns into a four-stage model:[24]

- *Stage 1:* temporary labour migration of young workers, remittance of earnings and continued orientation to the homeland
- *Stage 2:* prolonging of stay and the development of social networks based on kinship or common area of origin and the need for mutual help in the new environment
- *Stage 3:* family reunion, growing consciousness of long-term settlement, increasing orientation toward the receiving country, and emergence of ethnic communities with their own institutions (associations, shops, cafes, agencies, professions)
- *Stage 4:* permanent settlement which, depending on the policies of the government and the behavior of the population of the receiving country, leads either to secure legal status and eventual citizenship or to political exclusion, socioeconomic marginalisation and the formation of permanent ethnic minorities

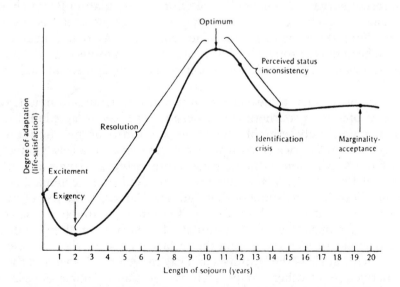

**Figure 6    Critical Phases in Adaptation Process: A Hypothetical Model. Source: Won Moo Hurh (1977), 46. Used by permission.**

This model has analytical value in examining post–World War II migrations from Latin America and Asia to the United States.

Numerous migrants from northwestern Europe, as well as other white migrant groups, have had an easier time of adapting and being accepted into the mainstream. Research efforts to document this include the use of a social distance scale, frequently referred to as the Bogardus scale.[25] The seven items used, with their corresponding distance score, are as follows:[26]

- To close kinship by marriage (1.00)
- To my club as personal chums (2.00)
- To my street as neighbors (3.00)
- To employment in my occupation (4.00)
- To citizenship in my country (5.00)
- As visitors only to my country (6.00)
- Would exclude from my country (7.00)

The survey, administered to white respondents as well as African Americans, Jews, and Asians over forty years (1926, 1946, 1956, and 1966), reveals striking similarity in the hierarchy of acceptance of various groups. Although some groups have moved up or down in the scale (i.e., Japanese, Russians, and Italians), the general order has been for white Americans and people of North European descent to be in the upper third of the distance scale. Eastern and southern Europeans occupy the middle third, and racial minorities the bottom third (Fig. 7). When certain racial (i.e., blacks) and religious (Jews) minorities have been surveyed, they place their group high (i.e., egocentric and ethnocentric tendencies), but then they tend to follow a similar hierarchy as demonstrated in Figure 7. This study is significant in trying to analyze past perceptions among various ethnic groups in the United States.

A more recent survey, conducted by the Office of Population Research at Princeton University, asked longtime resident Americans about their perceptions of various immigrant groups. Three broad conclusions emerged. One was that migrants from Latin America/Caribbean ranked somewhere near the bottom in terms of how Americans view immigrants, European immigrants were the most favored, and Asians fell in the middle of the rankings.[27]

In summary, numerous studies have shown that immigrants from northwestern Europe and later people from southern and eastern Europe have adapted into American society and may more closely resemble the Anglo-conformity or melting pot models. Conversely, many Native Americans, African Americans, and, to a lesser extent, Hispanics and Asians have had a more difficult time assimilating and may not fit the Anglo-conformity model very well. Adaptation and limited cultural, economic, and spatial assimilation may best describe some of these groups. Certainly the rise of multiculturalism has emerged as a partial result of America's failure to assimilate these groups and/or the failure of these groups to want to assimilate. In addition, multiculturalism today involves more than ethnic identity, and on the surface it appears to encompass a variety of other developments such as the feminists and gay movements as well as the recognition of the distinctiveness of other groups such as Louisiana Cajuns, Florida Jews, white Southern Baptists, the Amish, Appalachian southerners, or California Sikhs.

| I Racial distance indices given racial groups in 1926 by 1,725 selected persons throughout the U.S. | | II Racial distance indices given racial groups in 1946 by 1,950 selected persons throughout the U.S. | | III Racial distance indices given racial groups in 1956 by 2,053 selected persons throughout the U.S. | | IV Racial distance indices given racial groups in 1966 by 2,605 selected persons throughout the U.S. | |
|---|---|---|---|---|---|---|---|
| 1. English | 1.06 | 1. American (U.S. white) | 1.04 | 1. Americans (U.S. white) | 1.08 | 1. Americans (U.S. white) | 1.07 |
| 2. American (U.S. white) | 1.10 | 2. Canadians | 1.11 | 2. Canadians | 1.16 | 2. English | 1.14 |
| 3. Canadians | 1.13 | 3. English | 1.13 | 3. English | 1.23 | 3. Canadians | 1.15 |
| 4. Scots | 1.13 | 4. Irish | 1.24 | 4. French | 1.47 | 4. French | 1.36 |
| 5. Irish | 1.30 | 5. Scots | 1.26 | 5. Irish | 1.56 | 5. Irish | 1.40 |
| 6. French | 1.32 | 6. French | 1.31 | 6. Swedish | 1.57 | 6. Swedish | 1.42 |
| 7. Germans | 1.46 | 7. Norwegians | 1.35 | 7. Scots | 1.60 | 7. Norwegians | 1.50 |
| 8. Swedish | 1.54 | 8. Hollanders | 1.37 | 8. Germans | 1.61 | 8. Italians | 1.51 |
| 9. Hollanders | 1.56 | 9. Swedish | 1.40 | 9. Hollanders | 1.63 | 9. Scots | 1.53 |
| 10. Norwegians | 1.59 | 10. Germans | 1.59 | 10. Norwegians | 1.66 | 10. Germans | 1.54 |
| 11. Spanish | 1.72 | 11. Finns | 1.63 | 11. Finns | 1.80 | 11. Hollanders | 1.54 |
| 12. Finns | 1.83 | 12. Czechs | 1.76 | 12. Italians | 1.89 | 12. Finns | 1.67 |
| 13. Russians | 1.88 | 13. Russians | 1.83 | 13. Poles | 2.07 | 13. Greeks | 1.82 |
| 14. Italians | 1.94 | 14. Poles | 1.84 | 14. Spanish | 2.08 | 14. Spanish | 1.93 |
| 15. Poles | 2.01 | 15. Spanish | 1.94 | 15. Greeks | 2.09 | 15. Jews | 1.97 |
| 16. Armenians | 2.06 | 16. Italians | 2.28 | 16. Jews | 2.15 | 16. Poles | 1.98 |
| 17. Czechs | 2.08 | 17. Armenians | 2.29 | 17. Czechs | 2.22 | 17. Czechs | 2.02 |
| 18. Indians (American) | 2.38 | 18. Greeks | 2.29 | 18. Armenians | 2.33 | 18. Indians (American) | 2.12 |
| 19. Jews | 2.39 | 19. Jews | 2.32 | 19. Japanese Americans | 2.34 | 19. Japanese Americans | 2.14 |
| 20. Greeks | 2.47 | 20. Indians (American) | 2.45 | 20. Indians (American) | 2.35 | 20. Armenians | 2.18 |
| 21. Mexicans | 2.69 | 21. Chinese | 2.50 | 21. Filipinos | 2.46 | 21. Filipinos | 2.31 |
| 22. Mexican Americans | - | 22. Mexican Americans | 2.52 | 22. Mexican Americans | 2.51 | 22. Chinese | 2.34 |
| 23. Japanese | 2.80 | 23. Filipinos | 2.76 | 23. Turks | 2.52 | 23. Mexican Americans | 2.37 |
| 24. Japanese Americans | - | 24. Mexicans | 2.89 | 24. Russians | 2.56 | 24. Russians | 2.38 |
| 25. Filipinos | 3.00 | 25. Turks | 2.89 | 25. Chinese | 2.68 | 25. Japanese | 2.41 |
| 26. Negroes | 3.28 | 26. Japanese Americans | 2.90 | 26. Japanese | 2.70 | 26. Turks | 2.48 |
| 27. Turks | 3.30 | 27. Koreans | 3.05 | 27. Negroes | 2.74 | 27. Koreans | 2.51 |
| 28. Chinese | 3.36 | 28. Indians (from India) | 3.43 | 28. Mexicans | 2.79 | 28. Mexicans | 2.56 |
| 29. Koreans | 3.60 | 29. Negroes | 3.60 | 29. Indians (from India) | 2.80 | 29. Negroes | 2.56 |
| 30. Indians (from India) | 3.91 | 30. Japanese | 3.61 | 30. Koreans | 2.83 | 30. Indians (from India) | 2.62 |
| Arithmetic mean of 48,300 racial reactions | 2.14 | Arithmetic mean of 58,500 racial reactions | 2.12 | Arithmetic mean of 61,590 racial reactions | 2.08 | Arithmetic mean of 78,150 racial reactions | 1.92 |
| Spread in distance | 2.85 | Spread in distance | 2.57 | Spread in distance | 1.75 | Spread in distance | 1.56 |

**Figure 7   Changes in Social Distance, 1926–1966. Source: Bogardus (1968), 152. Used by permission.**

## How Society Removes the Minority Status

If a society recognizes the existence of minorities, then that society is confronted with the issue of possibly removing that status. Extermination, expulsion, and secession do not appear to be appropriate solutions. Assimilation, amalgamation, and Americanization may work for some groups but not all. For most minorities, participation in a pluralistic society seems to be a significant aspiration to attain. Although much of the research in the past focused on assimilation models and how immigrants became "Americanized," many contemporary studies no longer emphasize so heavily assimilation but stress "adaptation and integration" and see immigrants adapting as opposed to assimilating in a post–World War II America. Multicultural models promote ethnic and racial distinctiveness within a society and downplay assimilation and the Anglo-conformity/melting pot core.

In a pluralistic society, minority groups retain certain traditions and cultural traits with some degree of collective identity. The dominant group accepts the minority identity and assures equality and human dignity in the dominant–minority relations. The relationship between the dominant and minority groups should be agreeable to both parties involved. Thus, it may not be a desirable goal to remove the minority status from all groups. Indeed, to do so may even be an impossible objective to achieve. Minorities operating in a pluralistic society that attaches no negative stigmas to a minority status offer an achievable alternative to extermination, expulsion, secession, or Anglo-conformity. But one should recognize that there are differences between cultural and social pluralism. "Although in practice both go together, cultural pluralism refers to the maintenance of ethnic subcultures with their traditions, values, and styles,"[28] whereas "social pluralism refers to the extent that society is structurally compartmentalized into analogous and duplicatory, but culturally alike, sets of institutions and into corporate groups that are differentiated on a basis other than culture."[29]

## NOTES

1. E. G. Ravenstein, "The Laws of Migration," *Journal of the Royal Statistical Society* 48 (June 1885): 167–227. Also "The Laws of Migration," *Journal of the Royal Statistical Society* 52 (June 1889): 214–301. These two articles have been summarized by Everett S. Lee, "A Theory of Migration," *Demography* 3 (1966): 47–57. Also see D. B. Grigg, "E. G. Ravenstein and the 'Laws of Migration,'" *Journal of Historical Geography* 3 (1977): 41–54.

2. Lee, "A Theory of Migration," 47.

3. Lee, "A Theory of Migration," 52–57.

4. Barbara Schmitter Heisler, "The Future of Immigrant Incorporation: Which Models? Which Concepts?" *International Migration Review* 26 (Summer 1992): 623–645.

5. Heisler, "The Future of Immigrant Incorporation," 627.

6. Heisler, "The Future of Immigrant Incorporation," 627.

7. John Isbister, *The Immigration Debate: Remaking America* (West Hartford, Conn.: Kumarian, 1996).

8. Nathan Glazer, *We Are All Multiculturalists Now* (Cambridge, Mass.: Harvard University Press, 1997).

9. John A. Jakle, Stanley Brunn, and Curtis C. Roseman, *Human Spatial Behavior: A Social Geography* (North Scituate, Mass.: Duxbury, 1976), 151–155.

10. William Petersen, "A General Typology of Migration," *American Sociological Review* 23 (June 1958): 256–265.

11. Raymond W. Mack, *Race, Class and Power*, 2d ed. (New York: Van Nostrand, 1968), 227–228.

12. Milton Gordon, *Assimilation in American Life* (New York: Oxford University Press, 1964).

13. Harry H. L. Kitano, *Race Relations* (Upper Saddle River, N.J.: Prentice Hall, 1974), 59.

14. Stanley Lieberson, Mary C. Waters, *From Many Strands: Ethnic and Racial Groups in Contemporary America* (New York: Russell Sage Foundation, 1988).

15. Charles F. Marden and Gladys Meyer, *Minorities in American Society* (New York: American Book Company, 1962), 34–38.

16. Robert E. Park, *Race and Culture* (New York: Free Press of Glencoe, 1964).

17. Emory S. Bogardus, "A Race Relations Cycle," *American Journal of Sociology* 35 (January 1930): 612–617.

18. Michael Banton, *Race Relations* (London: Tavistock, 1967), 67–76.

19. S. Dale McLemore, *Racial and Ethnic Relations in America* (Boston: Allyn & Bacon, 1980), 5.

20. McLemore, *Racial and Ethnic Relations in America*, 5.

21. Richard T. Schaefer, *Racial and Ethnic Groups* (Boston: Little, Brown, 1979), 43.

22. Won Moo Hurh, *Comparative Study of Korean Immigrants in the United States: A Typological Approach* (San Francisco: R and E Research Associates, 1977), 46–52.

23. Stephen Castles and Mark J. Miller, *The Age of Migration* (New York: Guilford, 1993).

24. Castles and Miller, *The Age of Migration*, 25.

25. Emory Bogardus, "Comparing Racial Distance in Ethiopia, South Africa, and the United States," *Sociology and Social Research* 52 (January 1968): 149–156.

26. Schaefer, *Racial and Ethnic Groups*, 64.

27. Thomas J. Espenshade and Maryann Belanger, "U.S. Public Perceptions and Reactions to Mexican Migration," in *At the Crossroads*, ed. Frank D. Bean et al. (New York: Rowman & Littlefield, 1997).

28. Kitano, *Race Relations*, 54.

29. Kitano, *Race Relations*, 54.

# Humanity on the Move

*Jesse O. McKee*

Since the 1970s, immigration has become a critical issue in the United States. Concern over the rise of immigrants from Latin American and Asian countries, a rather steady flow in the number of undocumented workers, and the problem of refugees caused Congress and U.S. citizens to question seriously our policies on immigration and to make sweeping changes in the 1980s and 1990s. The United States is a nation of immigrants, and it basically clings to its humanitarian instincts and concern for the socially, economically, and politically depressed people in the world. Yet it must decide just how open to make its immigration policy regarding the volume, source areas, and socioeconomic and demographic characteristics of its immigrants.

Population growth is also a concern of many Americans since it is estimated that 50 percent of the national population growth is attributable to immigration. Then there is the problem of the perceived rate of acculturation into American society of many of these non-European ethnic groups. Will multiculturalism increase as a viable alternative to acculturation and assimilation? Should the United States continue to promote bilingualism or support the learning of English only?

Many questions are again being raised about current immigration in the United States that are reminiscent of the arguments presented in the early twentieth century prior to the enactment of the quota laws in 1921 and 1924. Numbers and acculturation issues, and to some extent the spatial dispersal of these immigrants, are causes for concern to the residents of the states where these people are settling. For example, in 1996, 83.9 percent of all Cubans planned to settle in Florida; 41.9 percent of all Filipinos in California; 67.6 percent of all Mexicans in California and Texas; 53.4 percent of people from the People's Republic of China in New York and California; and 51.9 percent of all Dominicans in New York.[1] It is important, therefore, to understand the present issues of immigration and to seek familiarity and an appreciation of past U.S. migration trends and immigration policies. Thus, this chapter is devoted to the historical development of immigration in the United States and will also serve as an introduction to the other ethnic groups discussed in this text.

## IMMIGRATION TO THE UNITED STATES SINCE THE SEVENTEENTH CENTURY

The chronicling of immigrants to the United States since 1607 is indeed a fascinating topic and critical to the understanding of American history and the development of American culture. The processes whereby these cultures, transplanted from the Old World (particularly Europe) to America, began to transform the landscape into something distinctively American are in themselves quite intriguing. The development processes of American culture have not been static. The nation continually changes. As new groups arrive and the exchange of cultural traits takes place, and as the acculturation process is set into motion, a slightly different America emerges. To be sure, certain groups have had more impact than others, and their imprint on the landscape has been more noticeable. Our ties to Europe are evident in our basic cultural traits of language, religion, political system, and technological achievement. The imprint of the various Asian groups, and to some extent those from Latin America, is presently developing. The contribution of these groups to American society has not yet been fully realized.

The immigration waves to America can be subdivided in many ways. A suggested division, which will be the basis for discussion in this chapter, appears in Table 1.1.

## 1607–1820: Colonial and Early U.S. Period

The settling of Jamestown marks the beginning of the stream of immigrants who eventually came to America from virtually all over the globe. In the early years (1607–1700), the English and the Welsh provided the initial wave together with Africans. Besides the Vikings, Africans may have been the first non-Indian permanent settlers in what is today the United States when some fled from a Spanish colony to the Pee Dee River area in South Carolina in 1526.[2] However, the generally accepted date of Africans in America is 1619, when "twenty Negroes were put ashore at Jamestown . . . by the captain of a Dutch frigate."[3] These early Africans were considered to be indentured servants and not slaves,

**Table 1.1    Immigration Periods.**

| | |
|---|---|
| 1607–1700: | *Initial Wave.* Strong English and Welsh, with a complement of Africans. |
| 1701–1775: | *Second Wave.* Predominantly English, Welsh, and African, with strong Teutonic and Scotch-Irish components. |
| 1776–1820: | *Third Wave.* Similar in composition of immigrants as in the second wave, but with a reduced number of arrivals. |
| 1821–1880: | *Northwest European Wave.* Heavily Irish, German, British, French, and other northwest Europeans, together with a complement from Canada, China, and the West Indies. |
| 1881–1920: | *Great Deluge.* Large numbers of southern and eastern Europeans principally from Italy, Austria, Hungary, Russia, together with those from northwest Europe, Canada, Mexico, West Indies, Asiatic Turkey, and Japan. |
| 1921–1930: | *Transition Decade.* Reduction in number, principally from Canada, Mexico, Italy, Germany, and the United Kingdom. |
| 1931–1960: | *Immigration Bust.* Principally from the Western Hemisphere nations of Canada and Mexico, northwestern Europe (Germany and Great Britain), plus Italy, and a complement of Japanese after World War II. |
| 1961–Present: | *Immigration Boom.* Largely Hispanic Americans from Mexico, Cuba, Dominican Republic, and other West Indies nations, together with Asians from the Philippines, Korea, China, India, and Vietnam. |

Source: Wilbur Zelinsky, *The Cultural Geography of the United States* (Englewood Cliffs: Prentice Hall, Inc., 1992), 23. The classificatory scheme is modified from Zelinsky.

but as their numbers grew, a Virginia slave code came into existence. As the need for laborers increased, Maryland, the Carolinas, Georgia, the Middle colonies, and New England became involved in slavery and the slave trade. By 1650 the estimated population in the colonies was 50,368, of which 1,600 were African Americans.[4]

Between 1700 and 1775, migration to the United States continued to be predominantly English, Welsh, and African, together with Teutons and Scotch Irish. Other small ethnic and religious groups of the seventeenth and eighteenth centuries included the Spanish, Dutch, French, Swedes, Flemish, Jews, and Italians; however, the British accounted for the largest number of immigrants. Their superior military, economic, and political strength enabled them to establish superiority in eastern North America. In 1790, shortly after the suspension of major movements in 1775, the census reported a population of 3,929,214 people, of which 757,208 were of African descent, with 697,624 of this number as slaves. Of the remaining population, more than 75 percent was of British origin, 8 percent was German, and the remainder was primarily Dutch, French, or Spanish. In addition, it is also estimated that more than one million Native Americans lived within the present-day borders of the United States.

Because of military conflicts in America and Europe, immigration from abroad to the United States was light between 1776 and 1820. It did not resume until after 1820. Official immigration figures for people entering the United States before 1820 are lacking, but between the end of the Revolutionary War and 1820, it is estimated that about 250,000 entered the United States. Thus, this early period (1607–1820) has three very distinct subdivisions: 1607–1700 (initial wave), 1701–1775 (second wave), and 1776–1820 (third wave).

### Early Immigration Policy

Prior to the American Revolution, the United States obviously had no immigration policy. At the time of the founding of the new nation with the signing of the Treaty of Paris in 1783, British influence was dominant, but other ethnic groups had settled, and pluralism was evident in American life.

During the 1790s, Congress was mainly concerned about regulating naturalization and citizenship. A series of acts were passed. The Naturalization Act of 1795 required a five-year residency, an oath swearing attachment to the Constitution, and satisfactory proof of good character and behavior (Table 1.2). In 1798 another Naturalization Act was passed raising the residency requirement from five to fourteen years. In that same year Congress passed the Alien Enemies Act and the Alien Friends Act. Both acts gave the president powers to deport any alien whom he considered dangerous to the nation's welfare and security. When the two alien acts expired in 1802, a new Naturalization Act was enacted reestablishing the provisions of the 1795 act.

Since the United States had not been collecting detailed and adequate data on immigrants, Congress passed a law in 1819 ("Steerage Legislation") requiring that select data be gathered on immigration by nationality, sex, occupation, and age.

### 1821–1930: Maturation of Immigration

### Source of Migrants

During this period, the number of immigrants, their country of origin, and the process of acculturation of these new arrivals differed rather vastly from the previous period when

**Table 1.2    Major Immigration Legislation.**

1795    *Naturalization Act*—required declaration of intent, five-year residency, oath swearing attachment to Constitution, satisfactory proof of good character and behavior.

1798    *Alien Enemies Act, Alien Friends Act*—President may deport any alien whom he considers dangerous to U.S. welfare.

1798    *Naturalization Act*—applicant for citizenship must reside 14 years in United States, 5 in state where naturalization is sought.

1802    *Naturalization Act*—reestablished provisions of the 1795 Naturalization Act.

1819    *Steerage Legislation*—regulated accommodations provisions; set minimum standards on transatlantic vessels; required ship captains arriving from abroad to compile lists of passengers and to designate age, sex, and occupation of each.

1875    *Immigration Act*—the first national restriction of immigration, banned prostitutes and convicts.

1882    *Immigration Act*—increased lists of inadmissibles (those considered lunatics, idiots, convicts, likely public charges) and established head tax.

1882    *Chinese Exclusion Act*—barred Chinese laborers (repealed in 1943).

1885    *Alien Contract Labor Law (Foran Act)*—barred importation of contract labor; intended to end employers practice of importing large numbers of low-paid immigrants, thus depressing the U.S. labor market.

1888    *First Deportation Law*—authorized deportation of contract laborers.

1891    *Immigration Act*—increased inadmissible classes (those considered to have loathsome or contagious diseases, and polygamists, paupers, and those guilty of moral turpitude); Act also authorized deportation of illegal aliens.

1903    *Immigration Act*—increased inadmissible classes (epileptics, those who become insane within five years of entry or have had two attacks of insanity, beggars, anarchists, and white slavers).

1906    *Naturalization Act*—made English a requirement, provided for administrative reform.

1907    *Immigration Act*—increased inadmissible classes (imbeciles, feeble minded, tubercular, suffering from physical or mental defects affecting the ability to earn a living; those admitting to crimes involving moral turpitude, women coming for immoral purposes, unaccompanied children under 16).

1917    *Immigration Act*—established literacy as basis of immigrant entry; increased inadmissible classes (those considered to have constitutional psychopathic inferiority, men entering for immoral purposes, chronic alcoholics, stowaways, vagrants, those with one attack of insanity); Asian exclusion affirmed.

1921    *Emergency Quota Act*—limited annual immigration to 3% of national origin of foreign born in United States in 1910; European immigration limited to 355,000 per year—55% from northwestern Europe and 45% from southeastern Europe.

1924    *National Origins Act*—(fully effective in 1929), assigned quotas to each nationality in proportion to its contribution to the existing U.S. population, based on 1920 census. (As an interim measure, reduced annual quota to 2% of national origin or foreign born in United States in 1890, nearly eliminating immigration from central and southern Europe.) Other provisions: aliens ineligible for citizenship excluded; total quota of 150,000, plus unlimited entry by Canadians and Latin Americans; U.S. consuls abroad to issue visas; avowed aim of act was to maintain the "racial preponderance [of] the basic strain on our people."

**Table 1.2   Continued.**

1929    *National Origins Act*—enacted quotas now to be computed according to national composition of entire U.S. population in 1920, based on 1920 census.

1942    *Bracero Program*—established bilateral agreements with Mexico, British Honduras, Barbados, and Jamaica for entry of temporary workers.

1943    *Chinese Exclusion Laws*—repealed all such laws.

1946    *War Brides Act*—facilitated immigration of foreign-born spouses and children of armed service personnel.

1952    *Immigration and Nationality (McCarran-Walter) Act*—codified immigration and naturalization statutes, national origins provisions retained; no limitations on Western Hemisphere immigration; preference system established.

1965    *Immigration and Nationality Act Amendments of 1965*—repealed national origins provisions; created annual Eastern Hemisphere ceiling of 170,000 with annual per-country limit of 20,000; new preference system with labor clearance requirement; Western Hemisphere ceiling of 120,000 with no country limitations or preference system, but with labor certification requirement.

1976    *Immigration and Nationality Act Amendments of 1976*—extended per-country limitation of 20,000 and preference system to Western Hemisphere.

1978    *Act of 1978*—established "worldwide ceiling law" and combined Eastern and Western quotas creating a worldwide ceiling of 290,000 immigrants.

1980    *Refugee Act of 1980*—allocated 50,000 visas for "normal-flow" refugees and permitted the president, after consultation with Congress, to increase the annual allocation. Reduced worldwide ceiling to 270,000 immigrants annually.

1986    *Immigration Reform and Control Act*—authorized legalization for illegal aliens who entered the U.S. before January 1, 1982, and have lived in the U.S. continuously since then. Created sanctions prohibiting employers from knowingly hiring, recruiting, or referring for a fee aliens not authorized to work in the U.S.

1990    *Immigration Act of 1990*—created a flexible annual cap of 675,000 immigrants per year beginning in 1995 to be preceded by a 700,000 level for fiscal years 1992 through 1994—the 675,000 level consists of 480,000 family-sponsored, 140,000 employment-based, and 55,000 "diversity immigrants" (the cap excludes refugee and asylee adjustments); increased the level of employment-based entries as well as family-sponsored entries; made immigrants eligible for naturalization after five years and state residency after three months.

1996    *Antiterrorism and Effective Death Penalty Act of 1996*—expedited procedures for the removal of alien terrorists and establish specific measures to exclude members and representatives of terrorist organizations.

1996    *Personal Responsibility and Work Opportunity Reconciliation Act of 1996*—established restrictions on the eligibility of legal immigrants for means-tested public assistance; broadened restrictions on public benefits for illegal aliens and nonimmigrants.

1996    *Illegal Immigration Reform and Immigration Responsibility Act of 1996*—established measures to control U.S. borders; protect legal workers through worksite enforcement and remove deportable aliens; place added restrictions on benefits for immigrants and illegal aliens.

Sources: *U.S. Immigration Policy and the National Interest,* 1981, 32–44. *Statistical Yearbook of the Immigration and Naturalization Service,* 1996, A.1-1–A.1-25.

most were from Great Britain and their cultural adjustment and acculturation processes were minimal. Most late-nineteenth- and early-twentieth-century migrants experienced more "culture shock" and had to work harder at learning the ways of life in America, frequently under difficult circumstances. Except for intermittent periods of war, economic depression, or immigration restrictions, the flow of migrants (mainly from Europe) continued to increase in numbers during most of this time period. This 110-year interval can be subdivided into three divisions: 1821 to 1880, when most migrants were from northern and western Europe; 1881 to 1920, when southern and eastern Europe predominated; and the "transition" period from 1921 to 1930, when the quota acts were put into effect and most migrants came from the Western Hemisphere nations and northwestern Europe. Figure 1.1 summarizes by decade the five countries with the highest levels of immigration to the United States from 1821 to 1978, and Figure 1.2 shows the top five immigrant source areas from 1981 to 1996.

From 1820 to 1996, sharp increases and periodic declines are readily visible (Fig. 1.3). During the 1820s and 1830s, 742,564 people immigrated to the United States.[5] The total number of immigrants for the decade of 1840 (1,713,251) was more than double that for the previous two decades. Immigration continued to increase into the 1840s as potato famines in Ireland and political unrest in Europe provided a push to emigrate to America. Immigration then declined somewhat in the late 1850s and 1860s but resumed after the Civil War.

During the period 1821 to 1880, 86 percent of the immigrants were from northern and western Europe (Fig. 1.4), mainly Germany, Ireland, and the United Kingdom, with a lesser number from Norway, Sweden, Denmark, Netherlands, Switzerland, Belgium, and France. A total of 10,181,044 people came to the United States during this period, an average of 169,684 a year. Ireland dominated the 1820s, 1830s, and 1840s. Germany dominated the 1850s, 1860s, and 1870s followed by Ireland, the United Kingdom, Canada, and Newfoundland (Fig. 1.1). Fewer than 250,000 came from Asia during this sixty-year span. Most of these Asian immigrants were Chinese. Just slightly more than 1,000 people came from Africa. The contribution from Africa was very small during this period, a situation basically attributed to the outlawing of the importation of slaves into the United States in 1808. Few Africans wished to emigrate to a nation that was still engaged in slavery.

Because of the large number of Catholic Irish immigrants, some anti-Irish feeling began to emerge in America. They were accused of bringing diseases to the United States and contributing to crime. The uproar over these immigrants spurred Protestant evangelicals and nativists to form associations and political parties such as the Native American Party in 1845 and later the American (Know-Nothing) Party in 1856 to preserve the nation's morals and ethnic purity. These groups sought to place a curb on immigration. After the Civil War, when the economy and the settlement of the West expanded, the need for labor increased and immigration rose correspondingly. Thus, these early political groups did not necessarily affect immigration policy, but they raised basic questions that Americans had to address later in the nineteenth and early part of the twentieth centuries.

This period from 1881 to 1920 is frequently referred to as the Great Deluge. And in some respects, the Great Deluge period can be extended to 1930 based on the volume of immigrants, not the composition. Although the quota acts of 1921 and 1924 slowed down immigration immensely, many people continued to come to the United States during the 1920s, particularly from the Western Hemisphere, which had no quotas (Fig. 1.3). During this time period, 1881–1920, the shift from northern and western Europe to

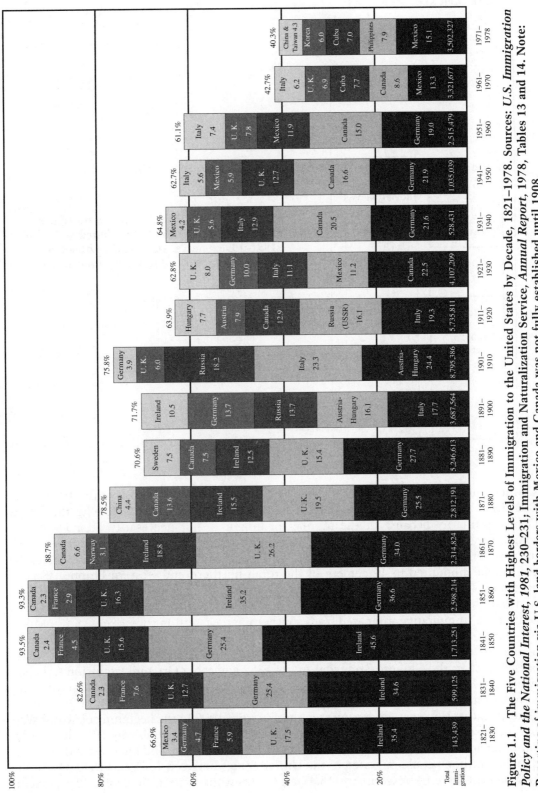

**Figure 1.1** The Five Countries with Highest Levels of Immigration to the United States by Decade, 1821–1978. Sources: *U.S. Immigration Policy and the National Interest, 1981,* 230–231; Immigration and Naturalization Service, *Annual Report,* 1978, Tables 13 and 14. Note: Reporting of immigration via U.S. land borders with Mexico and Canada was not fully established until 1908.

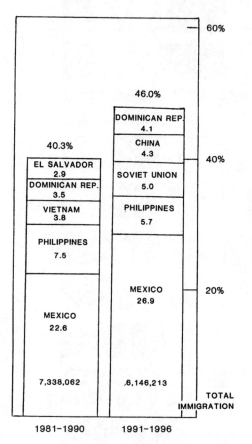

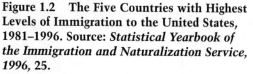

Figure 1.2    The Five Countries with Highest Levels of Immigration to the United States, 1981–1996. Source: *Statistical Yearbook of the Immigration and Naturalization Service, 1996, 25.*

southern and eastern Europe was most notable. However, if the decade of the 1920s (the Transition Decade) is included with the Great Deluge (it is included here with the Great Deluge primarily because of the number of migrants, not necessarily because of the source areas of migrants), a total of 27,572,583 immigrants entered the United States during this period, an annual average of 551,452 people. Migration from southern and eastern Europe amounted to 49 percent of the total; northern and western Europe, 35 percent; and Northern America (Canada and Newfoundland), 8 percent (Fig. 1.4). If one were to delete the decade of the 1920s from the Great Deluge period, then more than 50 percent of the immigrants originated from southern and eastern Europe.

During this period, 1881–1930, the volume of immigration varied. It declined slightly before the turn of the twentieth century when certain immigration restrictions were passed, such as the Chinese Exclusion Act of 1882 and other Oriental Exclusion Acts between 1882 and 1907. These were designed to restrict immigration of Chinese to California. Other laws prescribed immigrants' physical and mental health, morals, and financial status. However, migration rose sharply from 1900 to the beginning of World War I. It increased again in the early 1920s and then declined considerably by 1930 due to the quota act and the Great Depression. Further examination of this period reveals that more than 5.2 million people migrated to the United States between 1881 and 1890. Of these, 27.7 percent were from Germany, 15.4 percent from the United Kingdom, 12.5 percent

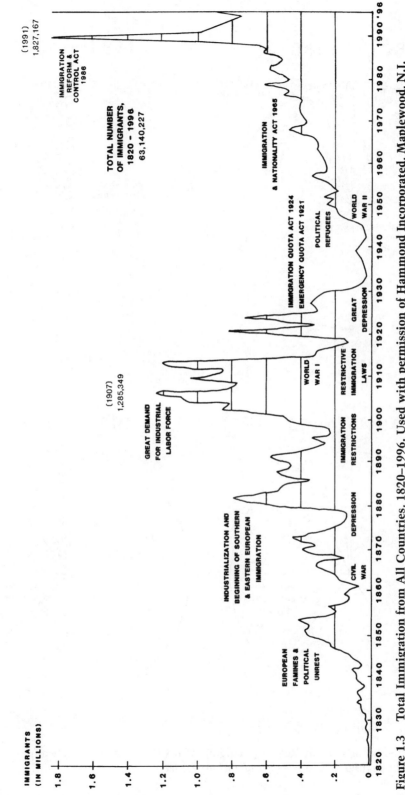

Figure 1.3  Total Immigration from All Countries, 1820–1996. Used with permission of Hammond Incorporated, Maplewood, N.J.

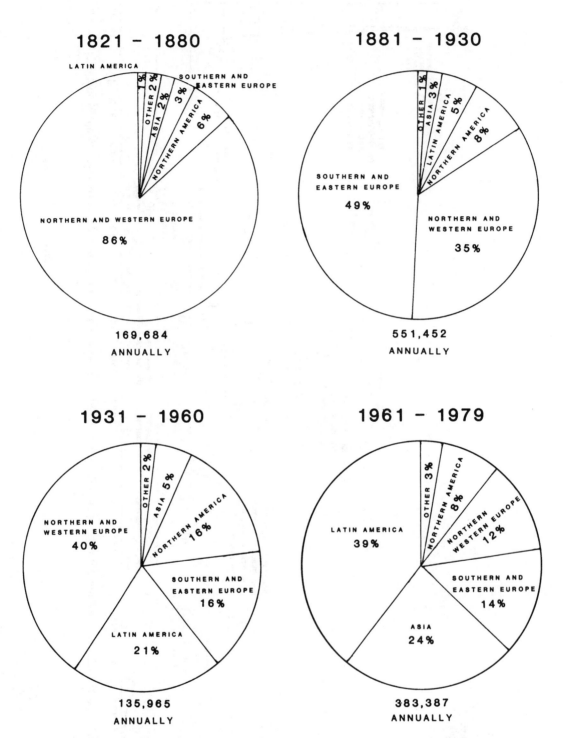

**1821 – 1880**

LATIN AMERICA

OTHER 2%

ASIA 2%

SOUTHERN AND
EASTERN EUROPE 3%

NORTHERN AMERICA 6%

1%

NORTHERN AND WESTERN EUROPE

86%

169,684
ANNUALLY

**1881 – 1930**

OTHER 1%

ASIA 3%

LATIN AMERICA 5%

NORTHERN AMERICA 8%

SOUTHERN AND
EASTERN EUROPE

49%

NORTHERN AND
WESTERN EUROPE

35%

551,452
ANNUALLY

**1931 – 1960**

OTHER 2%

ASIA 5%

NORTHERN AMERICA 16%

NORTHERN AND
WESTERN EUROPE

40%

SOUTHERN AND
EASTERN EUROPE

16%

LATIN AMERICA

21%

135,965
ANNUALLY

**1961 – 1979**

OTHER 3%

NORTHERN AMERICA 8%

NORTHERN AND
WESTERN EUROPE 12%

LATIN AMERICA

39%

SOUTHERN AND
EASTERN EUROPE

14%

ASIA

24%

383,387
ANNUALLY

Figure 1.4    U.S. Immigrants by Region of Origin, 1921–1979. Source: Compiled from *Statistical Yearbook of the Immigration and Naturalization Service, 1979.*

from Ireland, and 7.5 percent each from Canada and Sweden (Fig. 1.1). Between 1891 and 1900, more than 3.6 million immigrated, largely from eastern and southern Europe (principally Italy, Austria-Hungary, and Russia) and from Germany and Ireland.

The largest decade with regard to numbers was 1901 to 1910, when more than 8.7 million immigrants entered the United States, mainly from eastern Europe, Italy, and Russia. In 1907 alone, 1,285,349 people entered the United States, the highest of any year in U.S. history until 1991, when 1,827,167 people were admitted. The decade 1911–1920 was another period of large numbers of immigrants (more than 5.7 million), similar in source areas of the immigration of the previous decade except that a large group came from Canada and Newfoundland.

During the 1920s, after the quota acts of 1921 and 1924, the largest number of immigrants to the United States came from Canada, Newfoundland, and Mexico—nations with no quotas. These three nations contributed 33.7 percent of the immigration total. Italy, Germany, and Poland accounted for 26.7 percent. Thus, slightly more than 60 percent came from these source areas.

The settlement patterns of these immigrants, resulting from the Great Deluge and the preceding decades, are indeed intriguing. Many of them gravitated to the larger cities and to the Northeast. But many, like the Germans and Scandinavians, sought the Upper Midwest and north–central states. Very few settled in the South—the apparent explanations include an inferior array of economic opportunity, even after emancipation; a social climate that few immigrants found enticing; and a xenophobia that may have been both cause and effect of the low incidence of aliens.[6]

## Immigration Policy

During most of the 1800s, which witnessed the expansion of the western frontier, Indian removal, and the Civil War, Congress paid little attention to enacting immigration laws. From 1821 to 1880, the migrants were primarily of Irish, German, and British descent.

To help control immigration in the latter part of the 1800s against certain undesirables, Congress passed immigration acts in 1875 and 1882 to restrict the admission of prostitutes, convicts, and lunatics. Racial restrictions were incorporated into law with the passing of the Chinese Exclusion Act in 1882, which restricted Chinese laborers. (See Table 1.2 for major immigration legislation between 1881 and 1930.)

The first Chinese, arriving in the United States in 1847, were young boys brought by a missionary for schooling in Massachusetts. Between 1860 and 1880, Chinese migrants came to work on the railroads and in mining. Anti-Chinese feelings began to develop in the West as many critics felt that the Chinese were slow to assimilate.

During the 1880s, additional legislation was passed regarding immigrant laborers. The alien Contract Labor Law of 1885, which barred the importation of contract labor, attempted to end the practice of employers importing large numbers of immigrants. Then in 1888, the Deportation Law authorized the deportation of contract laborers. In 1891, another immigration act was passed that increased the list of inadmissible classes to include those having contagious diseases, polygamists, paupers, and those guilty of moral turpitude. It also provided for medical inspection of all arrivals and the deportation of illegal aliens. As immigration increased near the turn of the nineteenth century, Ellis Island was established as an immigrant processing center in 1891.

From 1881 to 1920, more than twenty-three million immigrants arrived in the United States. Much concern was expressed over the number of incoming migrants, the perceived cultural inferiority of these people, and their ability to assimilate into American society. A feeling of xenophobia gripped many Americans. Discrimination against Jews, Italians, and other southern and eastern Europeans became prevalent. Certain American groups fought to restrict open immigration. An Immigration Restriction League was formed in the mid-1890s. Many of its members centered their arguments against immigration on literacy and English-language abilities. Debate and controversy over immigration continued into the early 1900s. In 1903 and 1907, immigration acts were passed that further increased the list of inadmissible classes to include anarchists, beggars, white slavers, epileptics, imbeciles, and those who became insane within five years of entry, together with other categories relating to physical or mental defects.

In 1906, a naturalization act was passed making knowledge of the English language a requirement for citizenship. There was also widespread demand to establish a literacy test as a mechanism to screen migrants. The Dillingham Commission report published in 1911, totaling forty-one volumes, called for restrictions on eastern and southern Europeans, believing that migrants from these areas were quite different religiously, linguistically, and culturally. It also endorsed the literacy test as a way to help stifle immigration of certain undesirable ethnic groups. After several unsuccessful tries, Congress finally succeeded over presidential veto in 1917 in establishing literacy as a basis for entry. Besides establishing a literacy test, the Immigration Act of 1917 also increased its list of inadmissibles to include alcoholics, vagrants, and stowaways, and it continued to affirm exclusion of Chinese laborers and to place further restrictions on Japanese immigration. Restrictions on Japanese immigration had been earlier established by the Gentleman's Agreement established in 1907. Then with World War I and the period of isolationism in the United States, the Deportation Act was passed providing for deportation of people convicted of espionage and wartime offenses. Many communists were deported as a result of this act.

After passage of the literacy test, a concerted effort was made to Americanize the foreign born. Opinions varied on the success of these programs, and many groups called for restrictions or quotas to be placed on immigration. Finally, in 1921, Congress passed the Emergency Quota Act. This act established annual quotas principally from European countries and allotted visas to each nationality—usually defined by country of birth—corresponding to the proportion of that group already in the United States. The law permitted immigration from each European country amounting to 3 percent of the corresponding number of foreign-born people of that nationality living in the United States at the time of the 1910 census.

A few years later, in 1924, the National Origins Act was passed. It became fully effective in 1929. At the time, this was probably the most important piece of immigration legislation passed since 1795. As an interim measure, the Immigration Quota Act of 1924 made adjustments to the 1921 act by using 1890 as the base year and lowering the quota from 3 to 2 percent. It established the annual immigration quota total at 150,000 people. The result was a larger quota for groups from the British Isles and northern Europe and smaller quotas from southern and eastern Europe. But the act did not place quotas on any nations in the Western Hemisphere. Then, in 1929, when the National Origins Law was put into effect, it tied immigration quotas to nationals living in the United States, with the base year being 1920. In summary, this law numerically limited immigrants and attempted to preserve the Anglo-Saxon ethnic composition of the United States.

## 1931–1960: Immigration Bust

### Source of Migrants

During the 1930s and continuing until the end of World War II, the flow of migrants dwindled before increasing during the 1950s. The Depression and World War II, together with federal restrictions, were important factors in stemming the migration wave from Europe. It is quite possible that had the quota system not been enacted, that flow of immigrants would have ebbed on its own accord due to the somewhat sluggishness of the American "pull" in the 1920s and the 1930s for unskilled labor and the weakening "push" factors that had previously caused many people to leave Europe.

Because all these factors were at play, the number of migrants entering the United States between 1931 and 1960 was 4,078,949. The annual average declined to 135,965. Since no quota restrictions were placed on Western Hemisphere nations, the proportion of migrants from this area increased dramatically. For example, between 1931 and 1940, 528,431 people immigrated to the United States—30.2 percent were from the Western Hemisphere nations. Canada and Newfoundland accounted for the largest portion of this figure—20.5 percent—and Latin America for 9.7 percent. It should also be noted, however, that Germany accounted for 21.6 percent, the highest of any country during this decade.

Between 1941 and 1950, migration from Latin America amounted to 17.7 percent. Canada and Newfoundland accounted for 16.6 percent, for a total of 34.3 percent from the Western Hemisphere. Germany accounted for 21.9 percent and Great Britain, 12.7 percent. Because of the quota acts, it is evident that the sources of immigrants dramatically shifted back to northern and western Europe and the Western Hemisphere nations.

After the war, the migration pace quickened and a total of more than 2.5 million migrated to the United States between 1951 and 1960. The Western Hemisphere led the way with 39.6 percent of the total immigration. Latin America contributed 24.6 percent of that total, with the majority coming from Mexico and the West Indies. Germany contributed 19 percent; Great Britain, 7.8 percent; and Italy, 7.4 percent. Thus, between 1931 and 1960, data reflect a shift back to northern and western Europe and a sharp decline from southern and eastern Europe. Migrants from northern and western Europe amounted to 39.8 percent, 20.9 percent from Latin America, 16.5 percent from southern and eastern Europe, and 16.1 percent from North America (Fig. 1.4). Since the quota acts did not affect the Western Hemisphere nations, an active recruitment of Mexican workers gained momentum during the 1920s and later in the 1940s and 1950s before burgeoning in the 1960s and 1970s. As early as 1918, the U.S. government exempted Mexicans from normal immigration requirements such as the literacy test, the prohibition on contract labor, and the head tax. This decision obviously increased the active recruitment of Mexican workers and helped explain the increase from the United States' neighbor south of the border.

To be sure, in addition to the active recruitment of Mexican workers, and with the cutoff of a labor supply from Europe due to World War I and the quota acts, a move also was made by northern manufacturers to recruit African Americans from the South to help fill the void vacated by a dwindling labor supply from Europe. These variables were important "pull" factors emanating in the North. Identifiable "push" factors in the South encouraging African American migration were the mechanization of farms, changes in the managerial techniques of cotton production, the boll weevil, and a series of bad crop years. The earlier passage of Jim Crow laws and other forms of segregation, discrimination, and injustices helped contribute to the first large wave of African Americans from the South to the North from 1915 to 1925. While 89.7 percent of the African American population resided in the South in 1900, it dropped to 77 percent in 1940. Then with the second wave of African Americans migrating north after World War II, the percentage of African Americans in the South dropped to 60 percent by 1960.

### 1961–Present: Immigration Boom

#### Source of Migrants

The immigration boom period can be further subdivided into two periods, 1961–1979 and 1980–present, based on immigrant flow, not immigrant source areas. From 1961 through 1979, 7,284,352 immigrants were admitted, amounting to 383,387 annually. This period was dominated by immigration from Latin American (39.2 percent) and Asian (24.5 percent) nations. However, for the period 1980–1996, 14,014,914 immigrants (almost double that of the previous period) were admitted amounting to 824,407 annually. From 1981 through 1996, the United States admitted 13,484,275 immigrants at an annual rate of 898,952 people. During this time period, Latin America (47.8 percent) and Asia (34.2 percent) were the dominant source areas, and 12.4 percent came from Europe, 2.8 percent from Africa, and 2.1 percent from Canada and Newfoundland (Fig. 1.5).

From 1961 to 1980, countries in Latin America and Asia provided the major source of migrants to the United States. Between 1961 and 1970, 3,321,677 people entered the nation. Of these, 39.2 percent were from Latin America, 17.7 percent from northern and western Europe, 16.1 from southern and eastern Europe (which includes the former U.S.S.R.), 12.9 percent from Asia, and 12.4 percent from North America.

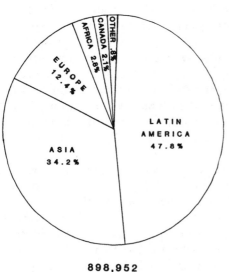

1981 – 1996

898,952
ANNUALLY

Figure 1.5   U.S. Immigrants by Region of Origin, 1981–1996. Source: *Statistical Yearbook of the Immigration and Naturalization Service, 1996.*

They entered at annual numbers of 332,167 during the 1960s. From 1971 through 1979, 3,962,675 people entered the United States, or 440,297 annually. Of these, 39.2 percent were from Latin America, 34.3 percent from Asia, 11.8 percent from southern and eastern Europe, and 6.5 percent from northern and western Europe. Although Latin American nations had the largest percentage, the 1970s can be viewed as the Asian decade since migrants from Asian countries increased from 12.9 percent to 34.5 percent from the 1960s to the 1970s. From 1971 through 1979, slightly more than 1.5 million people from Latin America entered the United States. Of this number, approximately 41 percent were from the West Indies (Caribbean) and 37 percent from Mexico. With regard to Asia in 1979, five countries accounted for 72 percent of the Asian immigrants: in rank order, the Philippines (41,300), Korea (29,248), China and Taiwan (24,264), Vietnam (22,546), and India (19,708).

From 1981 through 1996, Latin America (47.8 percent) and Asia (34.2 percent) were the dominant source areas. With regard to Latin America (47.8 percent), Mexico accounted for 24.5 percent of this total; the Caribbean countries, 11.3 percent (principally from the Dominican Republic); Central America, 6 percent; and South America, 6 percent. With regard to Asia, five countries accounted for 63 percent of the 34.2 percent immigrant total: the Philippines (6.7 percent), China (4.5 percent), India (3.5 percent), Vietnam (3.5 percent), and Korea (3.3 percent). In 1996, for example, seven countries had more than twenty-five thousand people admitted into the United States—four from Asia and three from Latin America. These leading countries included Mexico (163,572), the Philippines (55,876), India (44,859), Vietnam (42,067), the People's Republic of China (41,728), the Dominican Republic (39,604), and Cuba (26,466). Approximately 61 percent of the Mexican immigrants were admitted under the family-sponsored preferences, 34 percent were immediate relatives of U.S. citizens, and the remainder was due primarily to people still being processed for legalization under the Immigration and Reform and Control Act (IRCA) of 1986.

Reexamining Figure 1.3 will show that from 1980 to 1996, immigration numbers began to rise and they peaked in 1991 before falling (1992–1995) and then rising in 1996. From 1987 to 1996, the United States admitted slightly more than 10 million people, which is almost equal to the previous peak period decade (1905–1914) when about 10.1 million people were admitted. The previous peak immigration year was 1907 (1,285,349); this total was eclipsed in 1991 when 1,827,167 people were admitted into the United States.

This peak decade (1987–1996) can partially be explained by changes that occurred in immigration legislation. In 1986, IRCA was passed, enabling illegal aliens who had entered the United States before January 1, 1982, and had lived in the United States continuously since then to become legalized aliens. Therefore, during the years 1989–1992 (the highest peak years in immigration history), about 2.6 million[7] (48 percent) of the total admitted (5,428,551) in those years were people who became legalized as a result of the 1986 act. As a matter of fact, in the peak year (1991), when 1,827,167 people were admitted, 1,123,162 (61 percent) of those were admitted because of IRCA legalization. Also, even though the United States has a flexible annual cap of accepting 675,000 immigrants per year, as a result of the Immigration Act of 1990, immigration of immediate relatives of U.S. citizens are not subject to these numerical limits. This fact, coupled with the family-sponsored preference system, helps account for the increase in immigrant flow in 1996 after successive yearly declines since 1992.

### Undocumented Immigrants

Currently it is estimated that about five million illegal immigrants reside in the United States, and this number is growing by about 275,000 people each year.[8] This estimate of about five million "undocumented" immigrants comprises about 1.9 percent of the U.S. population. The highest number of undocumented immigrants are thought to reside in California, Texas, New York, Florida, and Illinois.

Mexico is the leading country of origin of undocumented immigrants, comprising about 54 percent of the five million total. Over 80 percent of all undocumented immigrants are from countries in the Western Hemisphere, principally Mexico, El Salvador, Guatemala, Canada, Haiti, Honduras, the Dominican Republic, Nicaragua, the Bahamas, Colombia, Ecuador, Trinidad and Tobago, and Jamaica.

### Immigration Policy since 1930

The National Origins Act, together with the Great Depression, actually resulted in a net migration loss in the United States, when emigration exceeded immigration in 1932 at the height of the Depression. The rise in the percentage of immigrants from northern and western Europe increased significantly from 1921 through 1950, although the total number of immigrants dropped drastically. World War II affected the United States in many ways, including in immigration policy changes. For example, with a labor shortage during World War II, the United States enacted the Bracero Program in 1942, which provided for the entry of temporary workers from Mexico, Belize (British Honduras), Barbados, and Jamaica and lasted until 1964. Because of our relationship with China in World War II, the Chinese Exclusion Laws were repealed in 1943.

Following the war, the problem of refugees and war brides became critical. Congress passed the War Brides Act in 1946 permitting immigration of foreign-born spouses and children of armed service personnel. Then in 1948, President Truman was very influential in getting Congress to pass the Displaced Persons Act. More than seven hundred thousand refugees and displaced people from Germany and other European nations entered the United States during the four-year program. The problem of refugees and displaced people continued into the 1950s. After the expiration of the Displaced Persons Act, Congress passed the Refugee Relief Act in 1953, and 214,000 people were admitted. Many were from eastern Europe.

The major piece of legislation passed in the 1950s, the most important act to affect immigration since the National Origins Act in 1924, was the Immigration and Nationality Act of 1952, amended in that same year by the McCarran-Walter Act. The early 1950s was the era of McCarthyism, and there was much concern over communist expansion. This anxiety concerning communism dominated American thought.

The acts referred to here preserved the national origins quota and established a system of preferences for skilled workers. They also encouraged the strengthening of family ties by giving preference to relatives of U.S. citizens. A numerical limitation of 150,000 was placed on immigration from the Eastern Hemisphere, but the Western Hemisphere remained unrestricted except for a few colonies and dependent areas. These laws also addressed two groups of refugees that were eligible to come into the United States under regular immigration procedure. First, they permitted the entry of those from "any Communist or Communist-dominated country or from any country within the general area of the Middle East."[9] Second, they eliminated the clause excluding Japanese as immigrants and established a small quota for people in the Asia-Pacific triangle. They also instituted the "parole" clause. In emergency situations, the parole clause authorized the attorney general to admit people temporarily for "emergent reasons." However, special legislation was required to grant immigration status to those so "paroled." The parole clause was used to admit more than 30,000 Hungarian refugees between 1956 and 1958, more than 650,000 anti-Castro Cubans in the early 1960s and over 100,000 in the late 1970s, thousands of Czechoslovakians in 1968 and Chileans after 1973, and more than 221,900 Indochinese as of mid-1979 following the fall of Ho Chi Minh City (Saigon) in 1975. In 1979, President Carter set the number of Indochinese to be paroled at 14,000 per month.

The problem of refugees continued to plague the United States, and the Refugee-Escapee Act of 1957 was passed to aid escapees from communist countries and the Middle East. Then in 1960, Congress passed the Refugee Fair Share Law, a temporary program to aid in the admission of World War II refugees still remaining in camps.

One of the major changes in U.S. immigration policy came with the passage of the Immigration and Nationality Amendments Act of 1965. The civil rights movement of the 1960s helped Americans and congressional leaders rethink the discriminatory national origins quota system. Also, concern over increased immigration from Latin America, particularly Mexico, together with a widening awareness of the worldwide "population explosion," helped usher in a new immigration policy. This act accomplished several goals. It abolished the National Origins Quota System and replaced it by establishing numerical restrictions and a "preference system" emphasizing family reunification, needed professions, and skilled and unskilled workers in demand in the United States. An annual ceiling of 170,000 was established for the Eastern Hemisphere with no more than 20,000 a year from any one country. The ceiling for the Western Hemisphere was set at 120,000 a year on a first-come, first-served basis, and no numerical limitations were placed on any one country. It should also be noted that the United States ended the bracero program in 1964 and that the Immigration Act of 1965 did not apply the preference system to Western Hemisphere nations.

In 1976, Congress limited the number of migrants from any Western Hemisphere nation to 20,000 and extended the "preference system" to Canada and Latin America. This action affected Mexico deeply since it had been supplying as much as 60 percent of the Western Hemisphere's ceiling of 120,000. Two years later, Congress enacted a Worldwide Ceiling Law. It set the ceiling at 290,000 annually and maintained the seven-category preferency system. In addition to the preferency system, some individuals are classified as "special immigrants" and are admitted without numerical limitation. These include such people as those who were once U.S. citizens but now desire reacquisition of citizenship or employees of the U.S. government abroad who desire to come to the United States.

In 1980, Congress again addressed the refugee problem (particularly the arrival of refugees from Southeast Asia between 1975 and 1980) and passed the Refugee Act of 1980. The act increased the "normal flow" of refugees from 17,400 to 50,000 a year. The bill also provided for "exceptional admissions" and mass admissions on an emergency basis. Should the quota of 50,000 need to be exceeded, the secretary of state and attorney general are to advise the president of such action. The president is then to consult with Congress about the number of admissions necessary above the 50,000 quota. It also broadened the definition of a refugee to include a person other than someone in a communist or communist-dominated country or from the general area of the Middle East and reduced the average ceiling of immigrants to 270,000.

In 1986, Congress addressed the illegal alien issue and passed the Immigration Reform and Control Act (IRCA). It was passed to control and deter illegal immigration. This was a major piece of legislation authorizing legalization for illegal aliens who had entered the United States before January 1, 1982, and had lived continuously in the United States since then. It also created sanctions prohibiting employers from knowingly hiring, recruiting, or referring for a fee aliens not authorized to work in the United States. As a result of this act, approximately 2.6 million people became legalized between 1989 and 1992. In 1991, for example, 1,827,167 people were admitted into the United States, the highest number of any year in U.S. history.

The Immigration Act of 1990 created a flexible annual cap of 675,000 immigrants (a change from an earlier cap of 290,000 set in 1978) per year beginning in 1995 to be preceded by a 700,000 level for fiscal years 1992 through 1994. In addition, it amended the preference system but continued the tradition of promoting family-sponsored immigrants, and it increased the level of employment-based preference entries. Thus, this act helped encourage the entry of highly skilled immigrants. With regard to the 675,000 annual cap, 480,000 were to consist of family-sponsored immigrants, 140,000 were to be employment based, and 55,000 were allocated to "diversity immigrants" (nationals of certain countries identified as being "adversely affected" by the Immigration and Nationality Act Amendments of 1965). It is also important to remember that not all immigrants are subject to the numerical cap and immediate relatives of U.S. citizens, refugees, and asylees are excluded (Table 1.3).

Antiterrorism and eligibility of immigrants for public benefits became issues in the immigration acts passed in the 1990s. The Violent Crime Control and Law Enforcement Act of 1994 and the Antiterrorism and Effective Death Penalty Act of 1996 were aimed at curbing terrorism. These acts revised deportation procedures for certain criminal

**Table 1.3  Categories of Immigrants Subject to the Numerical Cap.**

| Preference | Provision |
| --- | --- |
| **Family-sponsored preferences** | |
| First | Unmarried adult sons and daughters of U.S. citizens |
| Second | Spouses, children, and unmarried adult sons and daughters of permanent resident aliens |
| Third | Married sons and daughters of U.S. citizens |
| Fourth | Brothers and sisters of U.S. citizens (at least 21 years of age) |
| **Employment-based preferences** | |
| First | Priority workers |
| Second | Professionals with advanced degrees or aliens of exceptional ability |
| Third | Skilled workers, professionals, needed unskilled workers, and Chinese Student Protection Act |
| Fourth | Special immigrants |
| Fifth | Employment creation ("Investors") |
| **Diversity** | |

Source: *Statistical Yearbook of Immigration and Naturalization Service, 1996,* 16.

aliens and strengthened penalties for passport and visa offenses, and the 1996 act expedited procedures for the removal of alien terrorists as well as other measures regarding the exclusion of alien terrorists and representatives of terrorist organizations.

The Illegal Immigration Reform and Immigration Responsibility Act of 1996 involved more aggressive measures against illegal and legal immigrants by establishing stronger "border checks," protecting legal workers through work site enforcement and removal of deportable aliens, restricting legal immigrants' eligibility for some social programs, and strengthening rules on deportees' reentry into the United States.

### Summary: 1821–Present

The heavy immigration from Germany and northwestern Europe is evident from 1821 to 1880. From 1881 to 1920, southern and eastern Europe predominated. Beginning in the 1920s and extending to the 1960s, immigrants from the Western Hemisphere became numerous. Although the number of immigrants during the 1920s is quite high from the Western Hemisphere because of the lack of quotas, most were from Canada and Newfoundland. During the 1930s, 1940s, and 1950s, migrants continued to come from the Western Hemisphere, and immigrants from northwestern Europe accounted for a larger percentage than at any time since 1900. Since 1960, however, Latin American countries have comprised the bulk of immigration from the Western Hemisphere. The rise of migrants from Asia since the 1960s together with the decline from Europe make up another quite obvious trend. Also, the increase in the number of immigrants admitted since the middle 1960s, and particularly since the early 1980s, is also a distinguishing feature of the United States' immigration pattern as the twenty-first century begins.

## IMMIGRANTS BY TYPES OF ADMISSION

The majority (78 percent) of the immigrants entering the United States in 1996 entered as immediate relatives of U.S. citizens (33 percent) or through the preference system consisting of family-sponsored (32 percent) and employment-based (13 percent) immigrants (Table 1.4). Others entered under other categories such as refugees and asylees (not subject to a numerical cap) or under the "diversity" program or were still being processed under the IRCA for legalization.

More than one-half (56 percent) of immediate relatives of U.S. citizens admitted in 1996 were spouses (Table 1.4), whereas the majority of family-sponsored preference migrants were spouses and children of alien residents (the second preference under the family-sponsored preferences) (Table 1.3). Most of the employment-based immigrants (53 percent) entered under the third preference that includes skilled workers, professionals, and needed unskilled workers (Table 1.4).

## DEMOGRAPHIC CHARACTERISTICS OF IMMIGRANTS

In 1996, the majority (54 percent) of the immigrants were females, a sharp contrast to the first decade of this century when men accounted for 70 percent. The median age of immigrants has been increasing slightly over the past three decades, and the median age for

**Table 1.4    Immigrants Admitted by Major Category of Admission: 1996.**

| Category of Admission | 1996 |
|---|---|
| **All immigrants** | **915,900** |
| **Family-sponsored immigrants** | **594,604** |
| **Family-sponsored preferences** | **294,174** |
| Unmarried sons/daughters of U.S. citizens | 20,909 |
| Spouses & children of alien residents | 182,834 |
| Married sons/daughters of U.S. citizens | 25,452 |
| Siblings of U.S. citizens | 64,979 |
| **Immediate relatives of U.S. citizens** | **300,430** |
| Spouses | 169,760 |
| Parents | 66,699 |
| Children | 63,971 |
| **Legalization dependents** | **184** |
| **Employment-based preferences** | **117,499** |
| Priority workers | 27,501 |
| Professionals with advanced degrees or of exceptional ability | 18,462 |
| *Skilled, professionals, unskilled* | 62,756 |
| Chinese Student Protection Act | 401 |
| Needed unskilled workers | 11,849 |
| Other skilled, professionals | 50,506 |
| Special immigrants | 7,844 |
| Investors | 936 |
| **Diversity programs** | **58,790** |
| Permanent | 58,245 |
| Transition | 545 |
| **Other categories** | **144,823** |
| Amerasians | 956 |
| Children born abroad to alien residents | 1,660 |
| Parolees (Soviet & Indochinese) | 2,269 |
| *Refugees and asylees* | 128,565 |
| Refugee adjustments | 118,528 |
| Asylee adjustments | 10,037 |
| Suspension of deportation | 5,811 |
| *Total, IRCA legalization* | 4,635 |
| Resident since 1982 | 3,286 |
| Special agricultural workers | 1,349 |
| Other | 927 |

Source: *Statistical Yearbook of the Immigration and Naturalization Service, 1996,* 20.

migrants in 1996 was twenty-nine years. Fifty-four percent of the immigrants admitted in 1996 were under age thirty, and only about 5 percent were sixty-five and over.

Forty-seven percent of the immigrants admitted in 1996 between sixteen and sixty-four years old reported having an occupation at the time of entry or adjustment. The majority of the employment-based preference immigrants were professionals or skilled workers. Some of the leading occupations included nursing, engineering, social work, natural science, math and computer science, and postsecondary instruction. About 72 percent of immigrants admitted as unskilled workers reported service occupations.

## PORTS OF ENTRY AND STATES OF INTENDED PERMANENT RESIDENCE

"New arrivals" are lawful permanent resident aliens who enter the Untied States at a port of entry. These aliens are generally (there are exceptions) required to present an immigrant visa issued outside the United States by a consular officer of the Department of State. In 1996, 421,405 "new arrivals" were admitted into the United States. New York City (31 percent) was the leading port of entry, followed by Los Angeles (13 percent), El Paso (12 percent), San Francisco (8 percent), Miami (8 percent), Chicago (5 percent), and Newark (3 percent).[10] Each of these ports admitted more than 10,000 people, and these seven ports admitted 80 percent of all "new arrivals."

Since 1971, California, New York, Florida, Texas, New Jersey, and Illinois have been the top six states of intended permanent residence of immigrants. In 1996, California admitted 201,529 and New York 154,095 people (Table 1.5). California (22 percent) and New York (17 percent) accounted for 39 percent of immigrants admitted by state. Texas, Florida, New Jersey, and Illinois accounted for 29 percent. Thus, these six states admitted 68 percent of all immigrants. Nine other states admitted more than 10,000 immigrants each. Generally, the Upper Plains states (North and South Dakota), and the Mountain states (Montana, Wyoming, Idaho), the New England states (Maine, Vermont, New Hampshire), and some southern states (Mississippi, Alabama, Arkansas) admitted fewer (fewer than 2,000) immigrants. In 1996, Wyoming admitted the fewest (280) immigrants.

With regard to immigrants admitted by Metropolitan Statistical Areas (MSAs) of Intended Permanent Residence in 1996, the New York MSA admitted 133,168 immigrants (Table 1.6). Los Angeles–Long Beach (64,285), Miami (41,527), Chicago (39,989), and Washington, D.C. (34,327) each admitted more than 25,000.

**Table 1.5   Immigrants Admitted by State of Intended Residence: 1996.[1]**

| | |
|---|---|
| California | 201,529 |
| New York | 154,095 |
| Texas | 83,385 |
| Florida | 79,461 |
| New Jersey | 63,303 |
| Illinois | 42,517 |
| Massachusetts | 23,085 |
| Virginia | 21,375 |
| Maryland | 20,732 |
| Washington | 18,833 |
| Michigan | 17,253 |
| Pennsylvania | 16,938 |
| Georgia | 12,608 |
| Connecticut | 10,874 |
| Ohio | 10,237 |

[1]Includes states admitting more than 10,000 immigrants.
Source: *Statistical Yearbook of the Immigration and Naturalization Service, 1996*, 65.

**Table 1.6  Immigrants Admitted by Metropolitan Statistical Areas[1] of Intended Permanent Residence: 1996.**

| | |
|---|---|
| California | |
| Los Angeles–Long Beach | 64,285 |
| San Diego | 18,226 |
| San Francisco | 18,171 |
| Orange County | 17,580 |
| Oakland | 15,759 |
| San Jose | 13,854 |
| Riverside–San Bernardino | 10,314 |
| Sacramento | 6,953 |
| Colorado | |
| Denver | 5,698 |
| Florida | |
| Miami | 41,527 |
| Fort Lauderdale | 10,290 |
| West Palm Beach–Boca Raton | 6,553 |
| Orlando | 5,517 |
| Tampa–St. Petersburg–Clearwater | 5,010 |
| Georgia | |
| Atlanta | 9,870 |
| Hawaii | |
| Honolulu | 6,553 |
| Illinois | |
| Chicago | 39,989 |
| Maryland | |
| Baltimore | 5,429 |
| Massachusetts | |
| Boston-Lawrence-Lowell-Brockton | 18,726 |
| Michigan | |
| Detroit | 11,929 |
| Minnesota | |
| Minneapolis–St. Paul | 7,615 |
| New Jersey | |
| Newark | 17,939 |
| Bergen-Passaic | 15,682 |
| Jersey City | 11,399 |
| Middlesex-Somerset-Hunterdon | 9,286 |
| New York | |
| New York | 133,168 |
| Nassau-Suffolk | 10,594 |
| Oregon | |
| Portland-Vancouver | 5,748 |
| Pennsylvania | |
| Philadelphia | 13,034 |
| Texas | |
| Houston | 21,387 |
| Dallas | 15,915 |
| El Paso | 8,701 |
| Fort Worth–Arlington | 6,274 |

**Table 1.6** *Continued.*

| | |
|---|---|
| Virginia/Maryland | |
| Washington, DC | 34,327 |
| Washington | |
| Seattle-Bellevue-Everett | 10,429 |

[1]Includes Metropolitan Statistical Areas that admitted more than 5,000 immigrants.
Source: *Statistical Yearbook of the Immigration and Naturalization Service, 1996,* 67.

## ETHNIC REGIONS

It is estimated that more than 63 million people immigrated to the United States between 1820 and 1996, and millions more have entered illegally. It is evident that much
mixing and acculturation of these peoples have taken place. This mixing has frequently
caused many people to think of America as a "melting pot." This may not be an accurate term, however. Instead, the Unites States' ethnic mix might be likened to a "tossed
salad"—each group reflecting distinctiveness yet having overall cohesiveness within
American society. Even so, there is an overall "glue" or "salad dressing" that holds this
pluralistic American society and its culture together. The processes accounting for the
"massive transformation of Old World elements into the singular American compound"
have been summarized best by Zelinsky:[11]

1. The importation of selected individuals and, hence, selected cultural traits
2. The simple fact of long-distance transfer of people and their cultural freight
3. Cultural borrowings from the aboriginal populations
4. The local evolution of American culture
5. A continuing interchange with other parts of the world

In general terms, the sequence of migration within Europe "moved steadily outward
in wavelike fashion through time and space from a hearth area around the North Sea toward the north, east, and south."[12] "A mirror image of the migratory impulse in the European subcontinent was the spatial zonation of ethnic groups in the United States and
Canada, especially within the rural population."[13] The early arrivals in the seventeenth,
eighteenth, and early part of the nineteenth centuries tended to settle in the East. The
later arrivals in the 1800s and early 1900s tended to seek opportunities in the central and
western third of the United States, in addition to cities in the East. For example, many
Germans settled in the Upper Midwest, Scandinavians and Russians in the north–central
states, Italians in California and Nevada, and various Slavic groups in the Great Plains and
the Northwest. As the frontier moved westward and immigrant groups moved with the
frontier, change occurred in the size of ethnic blocs. Initially in New England and the
South, however, these areas were rather homogeneous in ethnic composition. Later, as settlements developed in the Midwest, rural immigrant blocs emerged together with distinct
ethnic neighborhoods in the urban centers. Finally, in the Far West, large rural blocs of a
single European ethnic group are rather rare, and group dominance within the city seldom
extends beyond a residential block.[14] In recent years, however, large urban populations of
Asians and Latin Americans have become characteristic of many southwestern cities.

There is also a distance-decay effect. The importance of relative proximity when examining the settlement of specific immigrant groups is best exemplified by the Hispan-

ics of the American Southwest, the early concentrations of the Chinese and Japanese on the West Coast, and the Cubans in Florida.[15]

Environmental affinity is another variable that may help explain the settlement patterns of some groups. For example, Scandinavians are concentrated in the north–central states, the Italians and Armenians in the Central Valley of California, the Dutch farmers in the polderizing of the Michigan marshland, the Vietnamese in the coastal Gulf regions, Greek sponge divers in the Tampa area, African Americans in areas earlier marked by the plantation system, and Cornish miners in southwestern Wisconsin. All of these examples are highly generalized but serve to provide some examples of environmental affinity.[16]

What is obvious is that some groups have tended to cluster, whereas others have mixed and internalized more for a variety of different reasons. This pattern becomes more evident when one examines the spatial distribution and regional concentration of some groups in America. There are specific core areas or regions where particular ethnic groups are clearly identifiable. Some form broad generalized geographic areas; some form rural or urban islands. These pockets of ethnic distinctiveness are readily visible and distinguishable. Some geographers have recognized this regionalization of ethnic groups as "homelands."[17] Homelands involve more than just the spatial location, clustering, or regionalization of an ethnic group; they embrace "a people's deep emotional attachment to a place that they call home."[18] Common to the development of homelands "is common ancestry [and] the emotional bonding that family, clan, and tribe imply."[19] There are five basic ingredients of a homeland: (1) a people, (2) a place, (3) a sense of place, (4) control of place, and (5) time.[20] Homelands, in some respects, are specific subtypes or more clearly defined ethnic regions. Examples of specific ethnic homelands include the New Mexico–Centered Hispano Homeland, the Louisiana–French Homeland, and the American Indian Homeland in the Four Corners area of the American Southwest.

With regard to ethnic regions, African Americans form a sizable number in the Southeast; Mexicans in the Southwest; Native Americans in Oklahoma, the Four Corners area of Colorado, Utah, Arizona, and New Mexico, and the Northern Plains and Rocky Mountain areas; Chinese and Japanese on the West Coast; Filipinos, Asian Indians, Koreans, Vietnamese, and Puerto Ricans in the urban cities of the North, principally New York and Chicago; Scandinavians in the Upper Midwest; the Germans and Slavics in the northeastern cities along with the Italians; Jews on the Eastern Seaboard; and French in New England, Michigan, and Louisiana.

### African Americans

In 1990, there were 29,986,161 African Americans in the United States, the largest ethnic minority in the nation. Approximately 50 percent of African Americans reside in the Southeast.[21] The largest number of African Americans is in New York State with 2,859,055. Fifteen other states have more than one million African Americans. In 1990, 12.1 percent of the U.S. population was of African descent. Six states are greater than 21 percent African Americans. All of these states are located in the Southeast, with Mississippi having the highest percentage (35.5 percent).

### Hispanic Americans

Hispanic Americans (22,354,059 in 1990), or Latinos, as many Hispanic Americans prefer to be called, are the second largest (9 percent) ethnic minority in the United States.[22] They are also one of the fastest-growing minorities. Hispanic Americans of Mexican and Central and South American cultural heritage are largely concentrated in the Southwest. California, Arizona, New Mexico, and Texas contain 59.5 percent of the Hispanic population. In addition, some Middle Atlantic states, Florida, and Illinois have significant proportions of Hispanics. Hispanics from the Caribbean area have tended to settle in the East. Puerto Ricans have settled mainly in New York and New Jersey, with smaller pockets in Connecticut, Massachusetts (Boston), Illinois (Chicago), and Florida (Miami). Most Cuban Americans are located in Dade County (Miami), Florida, and many Haitians, Dominicans, and Jamaicans have settled in Miami, Chicago, and New York City.

### Asian and Pacific Islanders

In 1990, 7,273,662 people or 2.9 percent of the U.S. population was of Asian or Pacific descent.[23] Forty-nine percent of Asian Americans live in California and New York, principally in Los Angeles, San Francisco, and New York. Hawaii (685,236), Texas (319,459), Illinois (285,311), New Jersey (272,521), and Washington (210,958) each have Asian populations exceeding 200,000 people.

China, the Philippines, Korea, India, Vietnam, and Japan have been the major source areas of immigrants to the United States. Many Chinese are in California, New York, Illinois, and Maryland; Indians in New York, California, Illinois, and New Jersey; Vietnamese in California, Texas, Louisiana, and Virginia; and Japanese in California and Hawaii.

### Native Americans

Native Americans totaled 1,959,324 in 1990, less than 1 percent of the U.S. population.[24] Eighty-three percent of Native Americans reside in states west of the Mississippi River and Alaska. Seven states contain 55 percent of the Native American population: Oklahoma (252,420), California (242,164), Arizona (203,527), New Mexico (134,355), Alaska (85,698), Washington (81,483), and North Carolina (80,155). Percentagewise, Native Americans had the highest proportion of total population in Alaska (15.6 percent), New Mexico (8.9 percent), Oklahoma (8.0 percent), South Dakota (7.3 percent), Montana (6.0 percent), and Arizona (5.6 percent).

### Core Areas

Core areas for five major minority groups are summarized in Figure 1.6.[25] African Americans predominate in the Southeast, Mexican Americans in the Southwest, Native Americans in the West, and Chinese and Japanese on the West Coast.

## CONCLUSION

The information in this chapter clearly indicates that the United States is a "nation of immigrants," including Native Americans (their origin can be traced to early migration across the Bering Strait). That the United States is primarily an offspring of the northwest European culture does not distract from the fact that many other ethnic groups have contributed cultural traits that have assisted in establishing a truly distinctive "American"

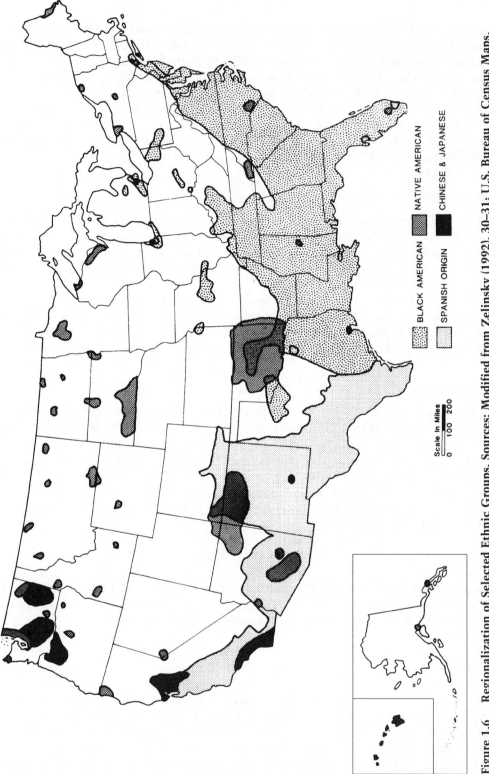

Figure 1.6   Regionalization of Selected Ethnic Groups. Sources: Modified from Zelinsky (1992), 30–31; U.S. Bureau of Census Maps, GE Series.

culture. Admittedly, the adoption of southern and eastern European cultural traits and the acceptance of these European ethnic groups into American society has been easier than for many non-European people and their cultures. For many non-European and non-white people, discrimination, prejudice, ethnocentrism, and even violence have occurred in the United States despite democratic ideals that have led to the reduction of ethnic and racial tensions.

The flow of immigrants to the United States is closely connected to the nation's immigration policy. The Quota Act in 1921, the National Origin Act in 1924, the Immigration and Nationality Act of 1952, and the Immigration and Nationality Act Amendments of 1965 have been major immigration legislative acts affecting the flow of immigrants. More recently, the Immigration Reform and Control Act of 1986 and the Immigration Act of 1990 have had major impacts on trying to control the flow of illegal and legal immigrants. The United States is a nation of immigrants, and immigrants will continue to migrate to the nation in the future. The issues, as always, have focused on the volume, source areas of new arrivals, and the amount and speed at which the acculturation process occurs.

## NOTES

1. U.S. Immigration and Naturalization Service, *Statistical Yearbook of the Immigration and Naturalization Service, 1996* (Washington, D.C.: U.S. Government Printing Office, 1997).

2. Richard A. Morrill and O. Fred Donaldson, "Geographical Perspectives on the History of Black America," *Economic Geography* 48 (January 1972): 1.

3. John H. Franklin, "A Brief History of the Negro in the United States," in *The American Negro Reference Book*, ed. John P. Davis (Upper Saddle River, N.J.: Prentice Hall, 1966), 8.

4. Karl E. Taeuber and Alma F. Taeuber, "The Negro Population in the United States," in *The American Negro Reference Book*, ed. John P. Davis (Upper Saddle River, N.J.: Prentice Hall, 1966), 100.

5. All immigration data, unless otherwise noted, were taken directly or calculated from U.S. Department of Justice, *1978 Statistical Yearbook of the Immigration and Naturalization Service* (Washington, D.C.: U.S. Government Printing Office, 1980); U.S. Department of Justice, *1979 Statistical Yearbook of the Immigration and Naturalization Service* (Washington, D.C.: U.S. Government Printing Office, 1982); U.S. Department of Commerce, Bureau of the Census, *Historical Statistics of the United States, Colonial Times to 1970, Bicentennial Edition*, 2 vols. (Washington, D.C.: U.S. Government Printing Office, 1975); U.S. Immigration and Naturalization Service, *Statistical Yearbook of the Immigration and Naturalization Service, 1996* (Washington, D.C.: U.S. Government Printing Office, 1997).

6. Wilbur Zelinsky, *The Cultural Geography of the United States* (Upper Saddle River, N.J.: Prentice Hall, 1992), 32.

7. *Statistical Yearbook of the Immigration and Naturalization Service, 1996*, 15.

8. *Statistical Yearbook of the Immigration and Naturalization Service, 1996*, 197.

9. "Humanity on the Move," in *Great Decisions 1980*, ed. Wallace Irvin, Jr. (New York: Foreign Policy Association, 1980), 53.

10. *Statistical Yearbook of the Immigration and Naturalization Service, 1996*, 60.

11. Zelinsky, *The Cultural Geography of the United States*, 5–9.

12. Zelinsky, *The Cultural Geography of the United States*, 25–26.

13. Zelinsky, *The Cultural Geography of the United States*, 26.

14. Zelinsky, *The Cultural Geography of the United States*, 26.

15. Zelinsky, *The Cultural Geography of the United States*, 29.

16. Zelinsky, *The Cultural Geography of the United States*, 29.

17. Richard L. Nostrand and Lawrence E. Estaville, Jr., "Introduction: The Homeland Concept," *Journal of Cultural Geography* 13 (Spring/Summer 1993): 1–4; Michael O. Roark, "Homelands: A Conceptual Essay," *Journal of Cultural Geography* 13 (Spring/Summer 1993): 5–11; Michael P. Conzen, "Culture Regions, Homelands, and Ethnic Archipelagos in the United States: Methodological Considerations," *Journal of Cultural Geography* 13 (Spring/Summer 1993): 13–29.

18. Nostrand and Estaville, "Introduction," 4.

19. Roark, "Homelands," 5.

20. Nostrand and Estaville, "Introduction," 1–2.

21. Mark T. Mattson, *Atlas of the 1990 Census* (New York: Macmillan, 1992), 101.

22. Mattson, *Atlas*, 97.

23. Mattson, *Atlas*, 97.

24. Mattson, *Atlas*, 125.

25. Zelinsky, *The Cultural Geography of the United States*, 30–31; James Paul Allen and Eugene James Turner, *We the People: An Atlas of America's Ethnic Diversity* (New York: Macmillan, 1988), 210.

# II

# SELECTED ETHNIC MINORITIES
# IN THE UNITED STATES

# Native Americans

*James M. Goodman and Douglas Heffington*

## THE ORIGINAL AMERICANS

The inhabitants of the Americas prior to the arrival of Europeans in the late fifteenth century are the ancestors of today's Native Americans—they were the *original Americans.* In the beginning, these natives of the New World were a majority group numbering perhaps as many as 80 to 100 million in North and South America. In the nearly five hundred years that have followed the initial European contact, Native Americans have been reduced in rank to one of the smallest of the American minorities. They constituted only 0.8 percent of the total 1990 population of the United States.

The original Americans occupied lands that now form the conterminous United States and Alaska. Most of their descendants are now either intermingled with non-Indians in urbanized landscapes or reside on reservations. These reservations represent about 2.5 percent (approximately fifty-four million acres) of the national land area. Those places where notable numbers of Native Americans live are not uniformly distributed within the nation. The modern distribution of Indian people reflects historical patterns of national growth of the United States and federal government policies that were developed to deal with its original inhabitants.

## A MINORITY AMONG MINORITIES

Native Americans are, in a modern sense, a minority among minorities. Although once the dominant population of the Western Hemisphere, disease, war, famine, and interracial mixing have reduced their numbers and diluted the purity of bloodlines. Various demographic studies estimate population of the pre-Columbian United States at nine hundred thousand to four million people. The 1990 Census of Population lists 1,959,234 American Indians, Inuits, and Aleuts. It may be concluded then that, despite the high birth rate among Indian people, drastic population reductions between the time of initial European contact and the present have resulted in a populace that is about the same size now as it was five hundred years ago. Native American populations now appear to be growing at a relatively rapid rate. When compared to other racial and ethnic minorities, however, the Native American ranks a distant fourth after Hispanics, Blacks, and Asians.

The unavoidable and most devastating impact of the peopling of the New World by Europeans was the introduction of diseases to which the Native Americans had no resistance. Smallpox, malaria, typhus fever, yellow fever, syphilis, measles, hookworm, and dysentery swept rapidly through segments of Indian populations, reducing their numbers alarmingly. Whole villages died; large regions lost as much as 75 percent of their populations. S. F. Cook estimates that the Indians of the northern San Joaquin Valley of California lost about three-fourths of their population between 1830 and 1850 due to epidemics, starvation, and exposure produced in part by warfare with non-Indians.

Endemic diseases that slowly debilitated their victims reinforced the impacts of epidemics. In some areas the result was a gradual reduction in population. These diseases, such as tuberculosis, diabetes, diarrhea, and hyperglycemia, offset the growth potential from high birthrates by reducing life expectancy. High infant mortality rates have always been common, and they continue to be so on many Indian reservations. Although most of the endemic diseases are controlled today, the social stresses of modern life make the Native American particularly susceptible to alcohol- and drug-related problems.

A reversal of population trends has come with the introduction of extensive health care and improved sanitary conditions. Diet changes have also helped. In addition, the intermarriage of Indians between tribes and between races have strengthened the genetic pool; however, at the same time it has diluted the cultural roots of each tribe. Only those Indian tribes with sizable numbers in relatively homogeneous demographic environments can hope to achieve an increased tribal population growth. Many Native American tribal elements have disappeared, or will disappear, as their numbers and the integrity of the bloodlines diminish.

## UNIQUENESS OF THE NATIVE AMERICAN MINORITY GROUP

The Native American minority group has a number of characteristics that make it distinct and unique among other minority groups in the United States. Native Americans, even five hundred years after Columbian contact, retain certain cultural traits that separate them from mainstream American society: retention of non-European languages, behavioral and religious traits that are of non–Old World origins, and ecological land use principles that are non-Anglo-American in practice.

Native Americans display great diversity in languages. About 150 different Indian languages are presently spoken. There were probably more than 200 in pre-Columbian times. Communication between Anglo-Americans, the dominant single-language minority, and the numerous Indian groups, with their complex oral (unwritten) languages, has always been difficult. Throughout the years this poor communication has resulted in faulty understanding of the social and cultural characteristics of both groups. The lack of communication between Indian groups has contributed in part to the lack of unified resistance to non-Indian aggressions in territorial expansion in the Americas. When American people speak some of the less common languages, ethnic survival becomes precarious; indeed, many groups have become extinct.

Native American religious beliefs were not compatible with the Christian ethics of European settlers. As a result Indians were frequently treated as "savages" who challenged the missionary zeal of the encroaching frontier of an expanding nation. This missionary fervor resulted in religion playing a great role in an effort to reshape the culture and social outlook of the Native Americans—in fact, a remarkable role in a nation based on the separation of church and state. The pressure to Christianize the Indian undoubtedly resulted in the disintegration of native religious identity and contributed to the demise of some Indian cultures.

The early Native Americans were settled widely over land that provided them with a rich resource base. They subsisted in a vast variety of physical environments. Some of the people maintained fixed settlements in well-defined areas; others engaged in seasonal migration within larger areas. This way of life was shattered as non-Indian Americans crowded in, pushing them into smaller and smaller land areas. Relocation frequently saw Indian people removed to areas with environments they were unfamiliar with and did not understand. The communal use of land is a common practice among Indian groups and differs greatly from the land use practices of Anglo-Americans. Individual ownership of land and the title to land are foreign ideas to the Indian, and the failure of non-Indians to understand or accept this principle resulted in loss of tribal lands. Many Native Americans were bilked out of lands that were legally assigned to them; many tribes were forced onto reservations. Those on reservations were placed in a special relationship with the federal government—a relationship that even today sets them aside as a unique communal landed minority.

## THE GEOGRAPHER'S VIEW OF THE NATIVE AMERICAN

The geographer is concerned with interactions between natural and human entities over the Earth's surface. These interactions provide a character to areas that allow the geographer to delimit and analyze regions. Regions of unique and homogeneous qualities may then be used as the space within which the perceptions and attitudes of the human inhabitant are studied. The goals, policies, and priorities developed by the governing system of the region that modify the natural environment through resource utilization can be examined as an ecological system.

The study of the Native American within the United States affords the geographer an opportunity to integrate a small, but significant, component of regional landscapes into a larger mosaic—a mosaic that frequently reveals the rich cultural diversity of a nation that also possesses a rich diversity of physical environments. Viewing Native Americans within this context aids those who seek an understanding of today's Indians and their role in American society.

The following sections will consider the origins of the modern Native Americans, the ways in which they lost their original lands, the means that the federal government developed to deal with the Indian problem, and Native Americans' demographic and socioeconomic character. The nature of modern Indian settlements will be reviewed, the character of the lands remaining to the Native American surveyed, and the nature of their resources examined.

## THE NATIVE AMERICAN: ORIGINS AND ROLES IN AMERICAN DEVELOPMENT

The people that occupied the American continents before the arrival of Europeans in the fifteenth century had a diverse origin. Archaeological, physiological, and linguistic evidence suggests that the Americas were peopled by numerous waves of immigrants from

Asia. The migrations probably occurred over thousands of years, and the migrants were unlikely to have been from the same racial stock. Physiognomic variations have suggested to some researchers that various stages in the evolution of Mongoloid stock within waves of migration that required long periods of time led to the distinctive physical types within the Native American group. Languages also display the great variety that might result from multiple origins through time and in place. These diversities were to compound the difficulties that Indians and white Americans alike experienced in their attempts at coexistence.

The initial impact of European presence in the new continent was the reduction of Indian populations due to exposure to Old World diseases. This was followed by a loss of lands due to the increasing non-Indian populations that claimed lands as a conquering nation would and later through treaties that were frequently flawed by the poor comprehension of both parties, but especially because these agreements were composed in English.

Native Americans utilized most, if not all, of the space that now constitutes the United States, but their recognition of land use rights was totally different from those that the new nation of the United States employed. Individual ownership of specifically defined plots of land was as foreign to most Indians as the communal sharing of parcels of undelimited lands was to most non-Indians. This difference in the philosophy of property rights coupled with a lack of understanding of each others land use concepts led to a series of poorly conceived "agreements" couched in the form of treaties. The treaties drafted as formal documents that registered agreement between nations were frequently misunderstood by both parties. The advantage, of course, went to those with the boldness and technological superiority to enforce their perception upon the other. The Native Americans thus saw their numbers, their lands, and their rights reduced as non-Indians flourished by asserting their treaty-gained "rights."

## The Development of Indian Lands

The Native American is the only minority that did not become an integral factor in the growth and expansion of the United States. Blacks were imported to sustain economic requirements, and, following the Civil War, a liberated but oppressed minority functioned as a subculture of the major U.S. society. Mexican and Spanish Americans were absorbed as territorial expansion occurred. Hispanics and blacks were part of the wave of immigration, whether voluntary or not, and their cultural adaptations have not placed them too far from the majority population. In contrast, the Indian was never a complement to the economic structure of the country, and when their lands were absorbed by territorial expansion, they were either relocated to undeveloped lands or confined to reserves of land (reservations) that were administered by the federal government. In the process they were disenfranchised and became wards of the state. Civil rights have always come slowly to minorities; thus, the Indians were first on this land, but they were the last to be given citizenship and voting rights.

Federal and state governments have always displayed ambiguity in the practices of dealing with the "Indian Problem." This problem is defined here as "those issues concerned with the 'proper,' i.e., ethical or moralistic, policies and methods of treating a people who occupy lands that a nation claims for its own." In essence, the problem involves the majority who wish to be fair and of good conscience in their displacement of a people who they generally view as inferior, in need of cultural and social change, or in need of protection. The Indian Problem also involves the notion that the Native American should be integrated into the society at large.

Historically, the Indian Problem involved skirmishes along a frontier that lay very close to all major settlement sites. As the frontier was pushed farther to the west and became more remote to centers of government, the sense of urgency that arose from hostile actions was reduced. Pro-Indian sentiments increased, in a general way, as the distance between Indian settled areas and the centers of the non-Indian populace increased. At a distance the Native American was sometimes viewed in an idealistic, romantic fashion; on the frontier at near range there were those who viewed Indians as a contemptuous and weak people.

In colonial times, the Native Americans were treated as members of independent states (nations) by several European countries. The British entered into trade agreements and granted individually allotted lands to Indians (in 1633) in the Massachusetts Colony. The Spanish royalty made land grants to Indians; the French treated the Indians as partners in trade. Prior to the American Revolution, the British crown established "reserved lands" for some Indians, and by 1764 it developed plans for an Imperial Department of Indian Affairs. Interestingly, concepts of reservations and special government agencies to deal with Indian affairs developed before the United States became a nation.

The northeastern quadrant of the conterminous United States was the scene of complex intrigues among two European colonial powers (France and England), the American colonists, and numerous Indian tribes. Indian tribes allied with either the French or the British in the establishment of trade areas. Frequently intertribal hostilities led to the gain or loss of trade advantages for the European competitors. Eventually, with Indian assistance, the British gained territorial supremacy, as the French were expelled from North America. During the American Revolution, Indian tribes along the western frontier of the colonies were treated with favor by the revolutionaries to prevent them from allying with the British.

Shortly after the American Revolution, the young nation of the United States looked forward to settlement beyond the Appalachian Mountain barrier that had retained its people within the littoral zone for several centuries. The Northwest Ordinance, written in 1787, stated policy toward the Indians as westward expansion started:

> The utmost good faith shall always be observed toward the Indians; their land and property shall never be taken from them without their consent; and in their property, rights and liberty, they shall never be invaded or disturbed unless in just and lawful wars authorized by Congress; but laws founded in justice and humanity shall from time to time be made for preventing wrongs done to them, and for preserving peace and friendship with them.

However, as westward expansion into the trans-Appalachian west proceeded, Indians were forcibly removed and pushed westward to the prairies west of the Mississippi River, where spatial competition arose between the displaced Indian groups. Since Indian groups were numerous and usually not unified in their dealings with the federal government, a consistency in dealing with problems associated with the settlement of non-Indians within Indian territories was never realized. In essence, however, the language of the Northwest Ordinance was ignored, and areas were removed from Indian control by military action. In some cases, Indians and their lands were absorbed and incorporated in organized territories and populaces. In most instances, Indian groups were moved en masse to other locations beyond the path of white settlement.

Prior to 1849, the military branch of the federal government, the War Department, was responsible for Indian affairs. Although interactions between Indians and non-Indians were on a frontier and did at various times involve skirmishes, some of the problems faced involved commerce and education, two areas the military was ill prepared to handle. Congress created the Department of the Interior in 1849, and Indian affairs were passed to civil control. This event corresponds with the addition of large areas to the western United States through treaties with Great Britain for the Oregon Territory and with Mexico for a large area of the southwest that became the territories of New Mexico and Utah and the state of California. At the same time, the western half of the 1803 Louisiana Purchase—that is, the Great Plains portion—was still unorganized. Thus, by the mid–nineteenth century, that section of the country that was eventually to contain most of today's Indian lands (reservations) was passed to civil control. The Department of the Interior from that time on developed the *civilizing* processes and policies that linger in Indian affairs to this day.

Pressure for land in the southeastern United States led the Congress to pass into law the Indian Removal Act of 1830. Lands of several southeastern Indian tribes were exchanged for lands west of the Arkansas Territory (organized in 1828) within the Louisiana Purchase. Although several attempts were made to organize pan-Indian resistance to land cession to the expanding United States, none were successful. Thus, by the mid–nineteenth century, all the area east of the Mississippi was organized by states. A tier of states, from Iowa southward to Louisiana, along the western edge of the eastern woodlands, represented the starting line of the race of American settlers across the grassy plains (the Great American Desert) and the Rocky Mountains, to the gold of California and the lush lands of Oregon.

The scene of Indian affairs within an expanding national territory next shifted away from the wooded landscapes of the American Midwest and South into the country of the wide-ranging, mobile plains tribes; the mountain tribes; the Pueblos, the arid and semi-arid nomadic tribes of the Southwest; and the hunters and fishers of the Pacific Coast region. A whole new set of people had to be dealt with! Some were peaceful, others were talented warriors, some were settled in fixed villages, others ranged over sizable areas, some claimed lands in well-watered sites, and others lived in arid, barren lands. Some tribes were located along the major corridors between departure points in the east and the western destination of white settlers, while other occupied areas that were relatively isolated—remote from non-Indian interests. A major factor in the treatment of the Indian Problem evolved; as the national conscience fretted with the treatment of the Indian, space for tribal relocation was diminished. The quality of that space was not capable of supporting the Native American population within an ecological subsistence system of the pre-European (American) period.

The latter half of the nineteenth century saw the further reduction of Indian lands as large areas were ceded to the United States by treaty. Indian wars continued throughout much of this time and led the federal government to adopt a policy for the achievement of peace through the restriction of Indians to reservations. The reservation concept was possible because relatively large areas of land, unattractive to non-Indians, were available in the public domain. The reservation provided a means of bringing the Indians into dependence on the United States because the land area generally would not provide the space and environment for the maintenance of traditional subsistence practices. Thus, the federal government was able to keep the tribes subservient by becoming their major source of food and other life-supporting materials. The Indians' resistance to the encroachment of non-Indians on their lands was broken for many when they became totally dependent on the United States for their subsistence.

In the closing decades of the 1800s, some reservations were dissolved by the granting of individual land titled to the heads of Indian families. This policy, referred to as *allotment,* resulted in further reduction of Indian lands and continued erosion of the traditional Indian patterns of communal land holdings. Boundaries often meant little to the Indian landowner.

From the very earliest period of contact between Europeans and Native Americans, efforts were made to modify the lifestyle of the Indians. Strong missionary leanings were common among the non-Indians, whether English, Spanish, or French. A common goal within the developing social structure of the country was to cause the Indians to abandon their traditional religious views in favor of Christianity. In doing so, the Native Americans were supposed to "rise above their savagery" and become "useful" citizens. One way this could be accomplished, according to policymakers, was to have the Indians become farmers, thus tying them to a place and occupying their time. Many Indians were, of course, successful farmers well before allotment practices were initiated, but several had never engaged in these activities. To give them a parcel of land, a plow, and a sack of seeds was no guarantee of their becoming "useful citizens"; in fact, it was a sure way to further disaster for many.

In 1924, Native Americans, in recognition of their service to the nation during World War I, were granted U.S. citizenship—the final minority group to achieve this status. At about the same time, the Meriam Report, a study by the Brookings Institute of the "Indian condition" as of the 1920s, was published. This study initiated many policy changes in the 1930s, especially the passage of the Indian Reorganization Act (IRA) of 1934. As a result, allotment policies that had reduced tribal land holdings some 60 percent, from 140 million acres in 1887 to 52 million acres in 1932, were eliminated. Procedures were developed to allow tribes a representative form of government, rather than permitting the appointment of tribal leaders by the Bureau of Indian Affairs (BIA). Investigations were set in motion that collected information on Native American culture and social conditions in the hope that there would be a more rational approach toward the improvement of the Indians' poor economic, health, and social conditions.

Just as the 1930s and 1940s were times of gain for Native Americans, the post–World War II decade of the 1950s saw attempts to reduce Indian land holdings by termination of reservations and the encouragement of Indian people, especially young and middle-aged adults, to relocate from their rural reservations and small towns to metropolitan areas where greater opportunities for employment existed. These actions, initiated by the U.S. Congress, may have represented the frustrations of government officials to the long period of the Roosevelt administration's effort to improve the Indian condition—efforts that seemed to display few tangible results despite sizable expenditures of funds and bureaucratic reorganization. Legislative reactions to these frustrations removed 1.5 million acres of land from reservations status and tried to move 11,500 Native Americans into the American mainstream as "full tax-paying citizens." However, the termination of some federal reservations, such as the Menominee Reservation in Wisconsin, worked major hardships on county and state governments. The federal government, which had hoped to be free of responsibilities, reluctantly reentered the scene by providing financial assistance to the states.

In retrospect, the complete reversal of federal Indian policy that occurred between the 1920s and 1930s and the series of legislative acts in the 1950s and 1960s demonstrate the awakening of public conscience to the Indian problems that have plagued Indian treatment from the beginning of European settlement of the Americas. Just as the Meriam Report noted the failure of allotments and led to legislative reform in the Indian Reorganization Act, the carrying forth of this law was closely monitored by a later Congress that viewed the IRA as "communistic" and "antireligionistic."

By 1970, Congress had rejected termination, and, in doing so, the Menominee Indians were restored as a tribe. Indian people were returned to conditions more favorable to survival of their cultural traditions by the passage of the Indian Self-Determination and Education Assistance Act of 1975.

The concepts of termination and assimilation that were so widely accepted in the 1950s resurfaced from time to time in the 1970s. These concepts, which are so widely opposed by Native Americans, offered a solution to the Indian Problem that would result in the loss of cultural and political identity that has nourished an American minority through centuries of severe trials. In addition, termination and assimilation violate a special relationship between Indians and the federal government that evolved through many centuries. The U.S. government pledged itself to ensure certain standards among the Indians in health and education and to assist them in the improvement of social and economic conditions.

The shifts in federal policy from Congress to Congress stymied a smooth, gradual progress toward a betterment of the Indian Problem. Given the nature of the problem, a solution may always be elusive. But therein lies one of the major traits of a minority—a trait that may be a tremendous point of pride, a strength that sustains a cultural-ethnic identity.

Native Americans today are much better educated than their predecessors. Communication problems are not nearly so common as those that their ancestors faced. Numerous men and women who are well-respected and strong spokespersons for their people are recognized today. Although progress remains to be made in many areas, the Native American is well represented and has become a visible minority. On the other hand, Native Americans are plagued by high unemployment, low educational attainment, low standards of living, and numerous social problems related to their position between traditional cultural character and a modern American lifestyle. Indians are still subject to racial and cultural prejudices. Resentment toward their "special relationship" to the federal government strongly influences political stances and attitudes of the general public. The Native American is too often viewed in stereotypical romanticism as a person who communes with nature in simple surroundings. The same view suggests to some that the person is not industrious and is content to live as a welfare recipient. These prejudices translate too frequently as "inferior" and "unequal."

## A Land-Based Minority

Native Americans have a strong cognizance of their relationship to the land. Current demographic patterns, however, indicate that the Indian has belatedly joined in the mainstream American's drift to the city. Strong attachments, nonetheless, bind them to environments that display much lower levels of human modification. Because the Indians have advanced very rapidly from a low-technology form of subsistence into an urban-industrial age, they generally retain that sentimental and emotional attachment to their place of origin.

Just as the settlement patterns of the Native American of the past have been related to federal policies related to reservations, relocations, and allotment of individually owned parcels of land, so too is the current trend of rural to urban movement of people. The federal government initiated a series of programs in the 1950s that were designed to provide Indians with employment and residences in urban areas. In part, the programs were designed to create economic improvement, but to many Indian people it was a ploy to terminate federal reservations. The immediate net outcome of the program was positive in relatively few cases. The return migration of Native Americans was great; social adjustment problems and a general lack of support systems produced by generally unenlightened planning had a severe impact on many of the people involved.

Attempts at relocation, in part, arose from the economic conditions of the Native American. Even today, unemployment on some reservations is as high as 90 percent. The attraction of the urban area is then one of economic improvement.

The disrupting effect of World War II on the populace of the United States, following a decade of economic and social despair, initiated a trend of rural to urban migration for many segments of the population, including American Indians. Early results of this migration were not favorable for those who participated in the shift. Older Indians often turned to the reservations because urban job opportunity favored younger persons. Those who remained in the new environments found themselves exploited by landlords. They lived in poor neighborhoods and mingled with other minority groups in overcrowded conditions that were worse than those they had left behind on the reservation. Help from the BIA was lacking in the preparation of Native Americans for employment in the cities. Jobs that were entered by early participants were those that allowed no opportunity for advancement.

Regardless of the many problems associated with adaptation to an urban area, the trend continues, and a greater number of individuals succeed in the rehabilitation each year. Central to the improvement of this rate of success is an ever-improving network of support factors for Indians within the cities. Indian centers now provide a means of economic and cultural support, and Indian communities within the urban complex provide a basis for emotional support. However, education, health, and housing support for a new urban Indian population has not been fully developed. Until these new support bases are developed, Native Americans will continue to have this type of massive rehabilitation of an ethnic group that represents a third world environment within the United States.

## DEMOGRAPHIC AND ECONOMIC PROFILES

Statistics on Native American populations are not reliable. There has been no commonly accepted definition of "Indian." Census data collected by enumerators suffered either because many Indians do not speak English or because many Indians are never located to be interviewed. Self-identification also has inherent problems. Data collected by mail are frequently missed because the addressee is not literate. Invariably, demographic and socioeconomic information differs from source to source.

Despite problems of reliability, some general patterns can be detected with regard to the distribution of modern Native Americans and their social and economic condition. The general population may be divided into three groups: urban, reservation, and nonurban/nonreservation. Approximately 51 percent of the 1990 Indian population lived in urban areas. Many of these urban dwellers are located in the metropolitan areas of Los Angeles, Tulsa, Oklahoma City, San Francisco and Oakland, and Phoenix. These urban locations agree closely with the states that have the largest Indian populations. The population of reservations constitutes between 20 and 25 percent of the total. The remaining population is settled in communities or on rural, nonreservation sites. These figures, however, do not reveal that many of the nonreservation dwellers maintain a strong and continuing contact with the reservation or with their former home sites that may have been on allotted land and hence former reservation sites. Native Americans generally have a much stronger place identity and sense of place than non-Indians.

Current information on a number of social and economic characteristics of the Native American is generally unavailable. However, by examining figures collected during the past decades, the following general statements can be made:

1. Incomes for Native Americans are significantly lower than those of the U.S. population at large.
2. Life expectancy has increased sharply since the establishment of the Indian Health Service in 1955.
3. Native Americans as a group are undereducated.
4. Unemployment rates run high among Indians.
5. Rural Indians, reservation and nonreservation, often live in a high degree of poverty.
6. Rural Indian women face the greatest socioeconomic difficulty.

It would be improper to suggest that all Native Americans fit the socioeconomic traits just listed. Some elements of the Indian population have achieved a typical U.S. lifestyle, hold responsible jobs, and are inconspicuous in their daily routines. Many have entered professions and serve as role models for Indian youth. But the process of transition into an effective role within the predominant Anglo-American society, while retaining cultural elements of their heritage, has made the path of Native Americans slow and difficult.

## DISTRIBUTION OF NATIVE AMERICANS

The Native American is a minority among minorities falling short of numbers generated by blacks, Hispanics, and Asians. Of the total 1990 Native American population, 1,878,285 are identified as American Indian, 57,152 as Eskimos (Inuits), and 23,797 as Aleuts. Between 1980 and 1990, the Native American population count rose from 1,366,676 to 1,959,234 (Fig. 2.1). The group's percentages shared between the same two census counts increased from 0.6 percent to 0.8 percent of the total U.S. population—hardly a major gain in percentage points, but an indication that there is growth and a higher degree of recognition.

Some Native Americans live in each of the fifty states. Their distribution is not uniform. Five states—all in the Southwest—contain 46 percent of the total Indian population. In rank order, these states are Oklahoma, California, Arizona, New Mexico, and Texas. A northern fragmented tier of states contain 15 percent of the total Native American population. These states include, in rank order, Washington, New York, Michigan, South Dakota, and Minnesota. Alaska, with its large Eskimo (Inuit) and Aleut popula-

## Native American Population
### 1890-1990

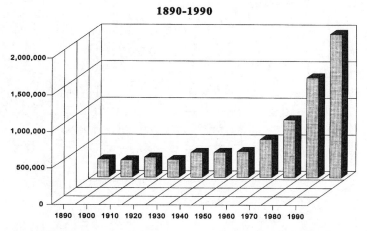

**Figure 2.1    Histogram of Native American Population from the Late 1800s to the Late 1900s.**

tion, has a little over 4 percent. The remaining Native American population is spread throughout the United States.

From a historical perspective, Native American populations have changed quantitatively and spatially. As previously noted, disease and warfare initially reduced the numbers of Indians, and later, relocation policies and practices gradually shifted the Indians to the western portions of the country. In the past several decades, Indian populations have increased, but Indian settlements remain concentrated in the western portions of the country.

In the decade beginning with 1950, the number of Indians living in rural settings dropped below 75 percent. By 1990, most Native Americans lived in areas defined by the U.S. Census Bureau as urban/suburban. At least fifty U.S. metropolitan areas are home to nearly 40 percent of the Indian people. The notion that Indians live in the "wilderness" has not been true for many years.

Native Americans can be found in all fifty United States and the District of Columbia (Fig. 2.2, Table 2.1). Data for Figure 2.2 are based on the 1990 Census Bureau information generated from self-identification. As previously stated, 1,959,234 people identified themselves as American Indian, including Alaska Natives. If broken down "ethnically," the figures are 1,878,285 Indians, 57,152 Eskimos (Inuits), and 23,797 Aleuts. All told, this represents roughly 0.8 percent of the U.S. population. These Native People's populations cluster in the southwestern United States, a fragmented northern tier of states, and Alaska.

Today, most Native Americans, like all Americans, live in urban settings. Figures 2.3 and 2.4 and Table 2.2 provide information on the top twenty metropolitan statistical areas (MSAs) with the largest Indian populations. Many of these cities, such as the Philadelphia area, greater New York City, and the Los Angeles metro area, are among our largest cities and are also MSAs with large Indian populations. As in states with high Native American counts, many of the cities with large urban Indian populations lie in the southwestern United States, that fragmented string of northern states, and Alaska.

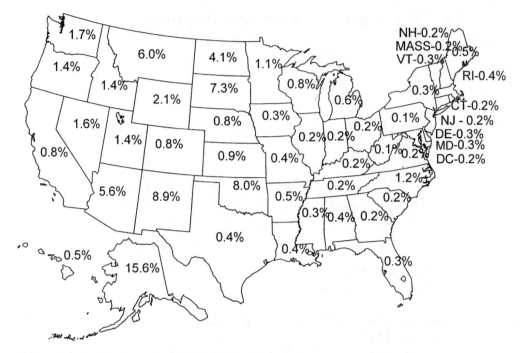

**Figure 2.2    Indian Percentage of Total State Population: 1990.**

The movement of the Native American from rural to urban environments has established a momentum that will undoubtedly continue for some time. The movement
was initiated by the federal government as an effort to improve the economic conditions
of Native Americans. The Employment Assistance Program, initiated in 1952, was designated to relocate individuals or families from reservations and rural areas to urban centers where employment opportunities existed.

The preparation of Native Americans for relocation involved some job training, financial assistance in the move, and aid in job placement. Critics of the program—and
there were many—maintained that job training resulted only in employment with minimal opportunities for advancement. Furthermore, the federal sponsors of the program
were charged with not providing adequate support for the new urban dweller: no socio-
culturally oriented counseling programs were made available, no medical subsidization
was provided once the person moved from the areas served by the Indian Health Service,
and no assistance was offered to individuals who were unfamiliar with personal financial
management and negotiations in an urban environment.

Because of the shortcomings in the early phases of the program, many Indian people
returned to their former places of residence. Those who remained in the cities experienced varying degrees of success. Some fell into deep poverty, some became derelicts,
and some succumbed to addictive drug and alcohol practices; others achieved some success in social adaptation and economic status. The last eventually became the nucleus
of a group that offered counsel and emotional support for migrants that followed. As
larger numbers of Native Americans assembled in an urban center, opportunities became
greater for a lasting migration.

**Table 2.1    Native American Population: 1990.**

| Total Population | State | Indian Population | Total Population | State | Indian Population |
|---|---|---|---|---|---|
| 4,040,587 | Alabama | 16,506 | 1,201,833 | Nevada | 19,637 |
| 550,043 | Alaska | 85,698 | 1,109,252 | New Hampshire | 2,134 |
| 3,665,228 | Arizona | 203,527 | 7,730,188 | New Jersey | 14,970 |
| 2,350,725 | Arkansas | 12,773 | 1,515,069 | New Mexico | 134,355 |
| 29,760,021 | California | 242,164 | 17,990,455 | New York | 62,651 |
| 3,294,394 | Colorado | 27,776 | 6,628,637 | North Carolina | 80,155 |
| 32,871 | Connecticut | 6,654 | 638,800 | North Dakota | 25,917 |
| 666,168 | Delaware | 2,019 | 10,847,115 | Ohio | 20,358 |
| 12,937,926 | Florida | 36,335 | 3,145,585 | Oklahoma | 252,420 |
| 6,478,216 | Georgia | 13,348 | 2,842,321 | Oregon | 38,496 |
| 1,108,229 | Hawaii | 5,099 | 11,881,643 | Pennsylvania | 14,733 |
| 1,006,749 | Idaho | 13,780 | 1,003,464 | Rhode Island | 4,071 |
| 11,430,602 | Illinois | 21,836 | 3,486,703 | South Carolina | 8,246 |
| 5,544,159 | Indiana | 12,720 | 696,004 | South Dakota | 50,575 |
| 2,776,755 | Iowa | 7,349 | 4,877,185 | Tennessee | 10,039 |
| 2,477,574 | Kansas | 21,965 | 16,986,510 | Texas | 65,877 |
| 3,685,296 | Kentucky | 5,769 | 1,722,850 | Utah | 24,283 |
| 4,219,973 | Louisiana | 18,541 | 562,758 | Vermont | 1,696 |
| 1,227,928 | Maine | 5,998 | 6,187,358 | Virginia | 15,282 |
| 4,781,468 | Maryland | 12,972 | 4,866,692 | Washington | 81,483 |
| 6,016,425 | Massachusetts | 12,241 | 606,900 | Washington, DC | 1,466 |
| 9,295,297 | Michigan | 55,638 | 1,793,477 | West Virginia | 2,458 |
| 4,375,099 | Minnesota | 49,909 | 4,891,769 | Wisconsin | 39,387 |
| 2,573,216 | Mississippi | 8,525 | 453,588 | Wyoming | 9,479 |
| 5,117,073 | Missouri | 19,835 | | | |
| 799,065 | Montana | 47,679 | | | |
| 1,578,385 | Nebraska | 12,410 | | | |

Source: Utter, 1993.

Much of the improvement in the urban environment for Native Americans, according to Indian leaders, can be traced to the development of Indian community centers or urban centers. These centers are organized by Indian groups and offer assistance ranging from advisement for job opportunities through general education, to health care and psychological support. Regardless of improvements in their conditions, however, one must be mindful of the fact that Native Americans often retain very low status in the economic and social spectrum of the city.

The continuing trend of migration to urban areas is strong evidence of the terrible economic plight of most reservations and rural areas. Unemployment is often high (frequently exceeding 50 percent of the working-age population) on Indian reservations. Nonreservation, rural-dwelling Native Americans face many of the same problems that non-Indian citizens have faced when they seek a means of support in rural environments. The stereotypical image of the quaint citizen of the wilderness is a deceiving and cruel perception of a people who have been swept into the current of abrupt social and cultural change.

**Figure 2.3    Urban Indian Population: Top 20 U.S. Cities.**

## Reservations and Allotments

The majority of nonurban Native Americans reside on lands reserved by the federal government for tribal use. Others are on lands that were allotted by the federal government to individuals and their heirs.

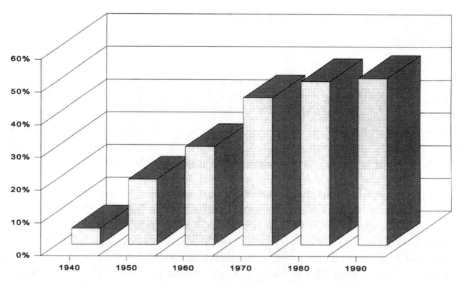

**Figure 2.4    Increasing Percentage of American Indians Living in Urban Settings. Source: Hirschfelder and de Montano (1993).**

**Table 2.2    Top 20 U.S. Metropolitan Statistical Areas with the Highest Indian Populations.**

| Rank | City | State | Population Numbers |
|---|---|---|---|
| 1 | Los Angeles–Anaheim-Riverside | CA | 87,487 |
| 2 | Tulsa | OK | 48,196 |
| 3 | New York (Long Island, CT, NJ) | NY | 46,191 |
| 4 | Oklahoma City | OK | 45,720 |
| 5 | San Francisco–Oakland–San Jose | CA | 40,847 |
| 6 | Phoenix | AZ | 38,017 |
| 7 | Seattle-Tacoma | WA | 32,071 |
| 8 | Minneapolis–St. Paul | MN/WI | 23,956 |
| 9 | Tucson | AZ | 20,330 |
| 10 | San Diego | CA | 20,066 |
| 11 | Dallas–Ft. Worth | TX | 18,972 |
| 12 | Detroit | MI | 17,961 |
| 13 | Sacramento | CA | 17,021 |
| 14 | Albuquerque | NM | 16,296 |
| 15 | Chicago | IL/IN/WI | 15,758 |
| 16 | Anchorage | AK | 14,569 |
| 17 | Denver | CO | 13,884 |
| 18 | Portland/Vancouver | OR/WA | 13,603 |
| 19 | Philadelphia | PA/NJ/DE/MD | 11,307 |
| 20 | Washington, DC | DC/VA/MD | 11,036 |

Source: Utter, 1993.

The federal government has from time to time adopted policies aimed at the reduction of Indian lands. Two of these programs, allotment and the Employment Assistance Program, have had a profound effect on the patterns of Native American land holdings and populations. Most remaining reservations and allotted lands are located in the following eleven western states: Montana, North Dakota, South Dakota, Wyoming, Utah, Colorado, Arizona, New Mexico, Idaho, Oregon, and Washington (Table 2.3).

Cartographic display of Indian land is difficult because large-scale maps are required to show the fractional nature of allotments that fall within areas depicted as reservations. Consequently, the highly generalized map of reservations (Fig. 2.5) shows only the larger reservations; some of these areas may contain a large proportion of the allotted lands listed in Table 2.3.

During the 1990 census, it was determined that slightly over 22 percent of the American Indian population lived on legally defined reservations or trust lands. This equates to 437,431 people. In Oklahoma, where a large amount of land was formerly reservation areas (known as tribal jurisdiction statistical areas, or TJSAs), another 200,789 (10 percent) Indian peoples live on these TJSAs. Tribal groups living outside Oklahoma that live on lands that are not reservations occupy what are called tribal designated statistical areas (TDSAs). These people comprise 2.7 percent of the Native American population (53,644). In Alaska, 47,244 Native peoples live on Alaska Native village statistical areas (see Table 2.3). It must be noted that not all people that live on Indian "lands" are Native peoples. The last census determined that almost 46 percent of Indian "lands" residents were non-Indians.

**Table 2.3  State Listing of American Indian and Alaska Native Areas (1990).**

| State | Type/Amount of AIANA | Level | State | Type/Amount of AIANA | Level |
|---|---|---|---|---|---|
| Alabama | AIR-1 | F | Nevada | AIR-22 | F |
| Alaska | AIR-1 | F | New Jersey | AIR-1 | S |
|  | ANVSA-217 | F |  | TDSA-1 | S |
|  | ANRC-12 | F |  |  |  |
| Arizona | AIR-23 | F | New Mexico | AIR-26 | F |
| California | AIR-99 | F | New York | AIR-8/2 | F/S |
|  | E-1 | F |  |  |  |
| Colorado | AIR-2 | F | North Carolina | AIR-1 | F |
|  |  |  |  | TDSA-5 | S |
| Connecticut | AIR-1/3 | F/S | North Dakota | AIR-5 | F |
|  | TDSA-1 | S |  |  |  |
| Florida | AIR-4 | F | Oklahoma | AIR-1 | F |
|  | E-1 | F |  | TJSA -15 | F |
|  | TDSA-1 | S |  |  |  |
| Georgia | AIR-1 | S | Oregon | AIR-8 | F |
|  |  |  |  | TDSA-2 | F |
| Idaho | AIR-5 | F | Rhode Island | AIR-1 | F |
| Iowa | AIR-2 | F | South Carolina | AIR-1 | S |
| Kansas | AIR-4 | F | South Dakota | AIR-9 | F |
|  | TDSA-1 | S |  |  |  |
| Louisiana | AIR-3 | F | Texas | AIR-2 | F |
|  | TDSA-4 | S |  |  |  |
| Maine | AIR-3 | F | Utah | AIR-7 | F |
|  | E-1 | F |  |  |  |
| Massachusetts | AIR-1 | S | Virginia | AIR-2 | S |
|  | TDSA-1 | F(pending) |  | TDSA-2 | S |
| Michigan | AIR-8/1 | F/S | Washington | AIR-27 | F |
| Minnesota | AIR-14 | F | Wisconsin | AIR-11 | F |
|  | E-1 | F |  |  |  |
| Mississippi | AIR-1 | F | Wyoming | AIR-1 | F |
| Montana | AIR-7 | F |  |  |  |
| Nebraska | AIR-5 | S |  |  |  |
|  | TDSA-1 | F |  |  |  |

AIR—American Indian Reservation  
ANVSA—Alaska Native Village Statistical Area  
ANRC—Alaska Native Regional Corp.  
F—Federal  

Entity—Trust Lands Only  
TDSA—Tribal Designated Statistical Area  
TJSA—Tribal Jurisdiction Statistical Area  
S—State  

Source: *Geographic Area Reference Manual*, Bureau of the Census, U.S. Department of Commerce, November 1994.

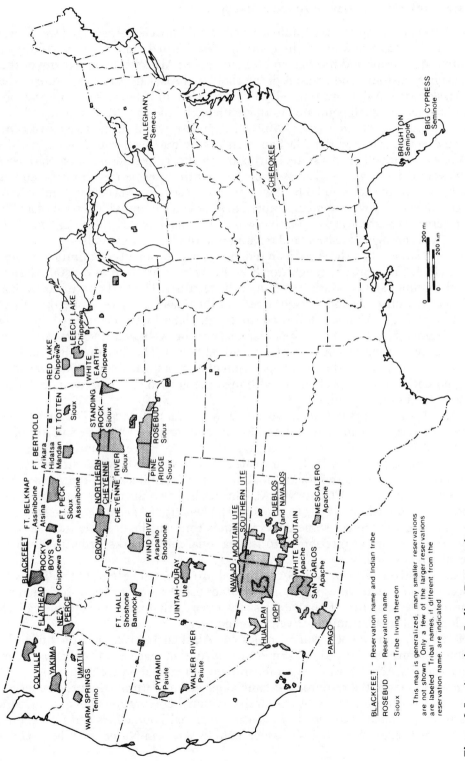

BLACKFEET – Reservation name and Indian tribe

ROSEBUD – Reservation name

Sioux – Tribe living thereon

This map is generalized, many smaller reservations are not shown. Only a few of the larger reservations are labeled. Tribal names, if different from the reservation name, are indicated.

**Figure 2.5  American Indian Reservations.**

## The Native American in Alaska: Alaskan Natives

Alaskan Natives were spared the traumatic and social impacts that affected the American Indian on the western frontier of the conterminous United States. The few numbers of non–Native Americans and the size and remoteness of Alaska sheltered many of the ancient lifestyles, customs, and cultures of the aboriginal Alaskan. Some exposure to the external Alaskan world did end tragically for some, but in a broad sense impact on the Alaskan Native was small compared to that suffered by the American Indian.

The Alaskan Native, in a sense, joined the modern world in the twentieth century. The United States acquired the Alaskan Territory by purchase from Russia in 1878; in 1959, Alaska was proclaimed a state. During the territorial period, Alaskan Natives were at times assaulted, along coastal areas by contacts with fishermen and hunters, and in the interior by gold prospectors and others who set out to develop Alaskan natural resources. Although the federal government attempted to allot lands to individual natives and to organize reservations, the Alaskan Native was never maneuvered to the extent that the American was through relocation and termination of reservation lands.

Alaskan Natives, like the American Indian, were traditionally not unified in their efforts to address the changes brought forth by Russian occupation of coastal Alaska and later by the United States' administration of the territory. The first effort at organization for political response beyond a local area was the Alaska Native Brotherhood (ANB). Founded in 1912, the ANB was followed three years later by the creation of the Alaskan Native Sisterhood (ANS). One of the chief goals of the ANB and ANS was the recognition of Alaskan Natives as citizens of the United States. The fact that the Alaskan natives retained a majority of the total population of Alaska until about 1900 allowed them a strong potential in territorial affairs, although the growth of nonnative population reduced them to a minority role.

Alaskan Native rights have been specified in several documents. The first two were the treaty between the United States and Russia and the First Organization Act of 1884. The status of Native lands was not directly confronted, however, until the period following the act of Congress in 1958 that made Alaska a state. Alaskan Natives began pursuing a series of claims to their aboriginal lands that culminated in the Alaska Native Claims Settlement Act of 1971 (ANCSA). The act had two major components: one was to protect and establish legal title to lands for the benefit of Alaskan Natives; the second was to conserve and protect some Alaskan lands through the possible inclusion—after study by the secretary of interior—into the national forest, parks, wildlife refuges, and wild-scenic river systems.

Alaskan Natives prior to ANCSA had legal or restricted title to only slightly more than twenty-four square miles in Alaska. Another 6,250 square miles were designated as reservations. The majority of Native Alaskans lived at that time on lands designated as public domain; a smaller number lived in urban areas.

ANCSA set aside 62,500 square miles for Alaskan Natives and provided almost $1 billion in return for the extinguishment of all Alaskan native land claims. One of the unique aspects of ANCSA was the establishment of regional native corporations. These organizations manage the resources—financial as well as natural—that the beneficiaries of the corporations own. Many of the twelve regional corporations have invested their monies in commercial activities beyond their regional bounds. As a result, their economic impact is extensive. Shares of stock held by Alaskan Native members (U.S. citizens with at least one-fourth Alaskan Eskimo [Inuit], Indian, or Aleut blood) of corporations have placed them squarely in the modern economic world. The process provided by ANCSA, while supplying a means of support of future generations, has thrust a people generally conditioned by subsistence activities into a state of high-finance business operations where cleavage from past cultures is sharply noticeable.

## INDIAN LANDS AND RESOURCES

About 2.5 percent of the land area of the United States is contained within Indian reservations. Reservations retain a special significance because they represent the residual or remains of a former domain of Native Americans. Since Native Americans were the only minority group to claim aboriginal lands, these parcels hold a special spiritual importance to some Indian people, a wellspring that provides an avenue to the origins of their heritage. Although these lands provide home for about one-third of the Indian population, they are worthy of consideration because they are one of the most distinctive aspects to Native Americans as a minority group.

### The Nature of Indian Lands

Indian lands that remain in tribal possession in the form of federal reservations are lands held in common for certain Indian groups.

> The United States holds legal title to Indian lands, yet those lands cannot be disposed of or managed contrary to the equitable title resting with Indians. This means that while the United States Government has the appearance of title as the nominal owner of Indian trust lands, it is actually holding title entirely for the benefit and use of the Indian owners.

Other Indian lands fall into the categories of state reservations, allotted lands, and ceded lands. State reservations form a very small fraction of the total of modern Indian land holdings. Allotted lands were issued to individual title holders, although the BIA may still hold in trust some of the titles. Much of the allotted land was purchased by non-Indians once individual Indians were given title. Most allotted lands that remain in Indian names are now shared by descendants, each with a small fraction of commonly held ownership in what was originally a plot that averaged 160 acres in size. Ceded lands were transferred from areas with vague limits that constituted the domain of the Native American to the public domain of the United States and hence to another status such as private, corporate, state, or lands administered by a federal agency.

Reservations held in trust by the federal government are, for the most part, located west of the Mississippi River. Most are in climatic zones that have deficiencies of moisture; many straddle lands that rise to high elevations. Many of these lands were undoubtedly viewed as inferior to lands settled by non-Indians. In general, the lands that became Indian reservations were barren and remote, away from well-traveled trails and major communities.

Greater than 90 percent of Indian lands reserved and allotted are located in eleven western states. Indian reservations—relatively large, contiguous areas as opposed to parcels of allotted lands—are for the most part situated within four major physical regions that lie in the interior and western portions of the United States: the Great Plains, the Rocky Mountains, the Colorado Plateau, and the Basin and Range (Fig. 2.6). Each area has a distinct set of environmental characteristics, chiefly topographic and climatic, that present certain limitations on use of the land. Many of these lands, however, contain valuable resources that may provide an economic base that has potential for the revitalization of these lands.

### Resources of Indian Lands

Indian lands generate revenues in a variety of ways. Some of the lands are mined for their minerals; other lands may be rented for agricultural use or as business sites. Still other areas are mantled by commercially important forests. Crop production is common, and livestock is grazed on much of the land. Often sizable quantities of water that flow from, across, or marginal to Indian lands have been claimed and can be used to enhance local resources or sold to consumers off the reservations.

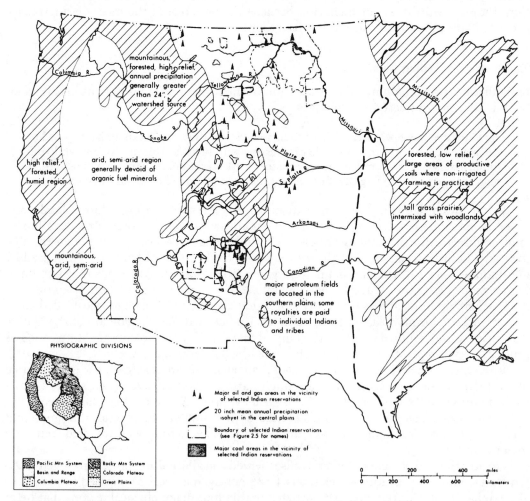

**Figure 2.6    Generalized Resource Environment in Western Indian Lands.**

Indian lands, despite their small areal extent, contain an exceptional amount of organic mineral resources, especially energy resources. Indian lands account for about one square mile of every forty square miles in the United States, yet one of every five square miles underlain by coal is on Indian land, and one of every two square miles of land containing uranium ore is on Indian land. The Indian coal reserves represent one-third of the total low sulfur strippable coal deposits in the United States. The major source of mineral production income is derived from oil and natural gas production. Indian lands have about one-twentieth of the petroleum reserves of the nation.

Organic fuel minerals are not evenly distributed on Indian lands. Some reservations have none; others are abundantly rich. As a result, some tribes derive sizable incomes from the royalties paid by production companies. The income is partially produced on reservation lands and partly on allotted lands held in trust by the BIA.

Agriculture plays a major role on many reservations in providing subsistence support or cash income support for many Native American families. Agriculture has been important to the Indian for many centuries; domestication of such plants as corn and beans occurred in the Americas well before Columbus. Many practices, developed in very early years of occupancy of the American Southwest by tribes such as the Pueblos of New Mexico and Arizona, survive today. Most Indian lands are located in areas that are either too dry or too cool to support extensive farming operations. Crop cultivation has been developed on a large-scale commercial basis in projects such as the Navajo Indian Irrigation Project in northwestern New Mexico. In this case, water impounded in the Navajo Reservoir on the upper San Juan River is distributed by canal and tunnel into a 339-square-mile development that eventually may contain nearly 200 square miles of irrigated fields, feed lots, and agribusiness operations whose profits will benefit a largely Navajo labor force and the Navajo tribal treasury. Opportunities to develop similar projects on other reservations will be expensive and will obviously require sources of water that are uncontested. Clearly, water rights are the key to any development for water is the resource on which most other land use is based.

Livestock plays a central role to many reservation economies. Too great a dependency on some range lands has resulted in a deterioration of this phase of agriculture. Overgrazing promotes soil erosion, which in turn reduces the potential of the range to recover. Livestock may be sold to provide an income, but it also serves as a subsistence base for many Indian people. Animal byproducts, such as wool, are placed in the commercial marketplace whether directly through sales of wool or indirectly through the manufacture of saleable items by Indian artisans.

Commercially significant forests thrive in some Indian country. Many of the reservations in the Rocky Mountain region, on the Colorado Plateau, and in some sections of the Basin and Range region have extensive forests of Ponderosa pine, Douglas fir, and other valuable trees. Sawmills and wood byproduct plants are located on several reservations, providing job opportunities for local residents.

The title to lands that were allotted to heads of households, and now held in trust by the BIA, have passed through generations of heirs. Many of those areas are rented for agricultural use by non-Indians. Since the ownership is so fragmented as title is passed along from generation to generation, the value to an individual is usually quite small. As time passes and future inheritances occur, these undivided interests will continue to fractionalize, and administrative costs of tracing ownership and distributing the incomes from the rentals will increase. Individual Indians will receive less and less benefit from their land.

The most important natural resources to the future economic gain of Indian tribes are the mineral resources. Most of this income is derived from energy minerals—oil, natural gas, coal, and uranium. Because of the relatively large proportion of energy reserves on Indian lands, twenty-five tribes originally joined together as the Council of Energy Resource Tribes (CERT). This group (presently more than fifty members) has organized a series of services to provide the expertise needed by individual tribes to develop their resources (Table 2.4). CERT also acts as a public relations effort between the tribes and the marketplace. Financial revenues that could be used to improve various components of tribal economy and society may be generated by these efforts.

Nonreservation tribes, such as those in Oklahoma, divide royalties paid from mineral production among qualified members of the tribe. This income is derived from retained mineral rights, a heritage of former surface lands that belonged to the tribes.

Economic opportunities are relatively limited on Indian reservations. Unemployment is often high, sometimes running in excess of 50 percent of the available labor force. Job training may be gained on the reservation or in nearby communities. Jobs are often not available, however, near a reservation home. Usually the single largest employers of the Indian is government—tribal government, the BIA, or a government-sponsored program.

In recent years, Indian gaming has become an economic asset that many tribal groups have seized upon. The Seminoles of Florida were the first Native American group to enter into the business of gaming with the opening of bingo facilities on their lands in 1979. Within three years, these bingo activities were netting the group $2.7 million annually. With this type of success, other Indian groups followed, but with this came conflict between tribal groups and state and federal governments. The result was the passing in 1988 of the Indian Gaming Regulatory Act (IGRA). The purposes of the act were to ensure fairness to players and operators, protect Indian groups from organized crime, provide a formal legislative groundwork for the operation and regulation of these gaming facilities, promote self-determination and economic development, and establish a federal agency to protect the right of the Indian group to use gaming as a way of generating revenue (this agency is known as the National Indian Gaming Commission).

With this comprehensive plan, gaming was divided into three categories: Class I gaming includes traditional and social forms of Native American games played at tribal ceremonies and powwows; Class II includes such gaming as bingo, pull tabs, and punchboards; and Class III encompasses all other forms of gaming not covered in Class I and II. Native American state gaming compacts are listed in Table 2.5 and Figure 2.7. Estimated Indian gaming revenues are graphed in Figure 2.8. This type of potential economic gain cannot help but affect the cultural landscape. For example, the newly opened Harrah's Cherokee Casino in Cherokee, North Carolina, has initiated change from a landscape that promoted pan-Indian tourist attractions and facilities to one with a more singular focus (and draw), and that is gaming (Figs. 2.9 and 2.10).

The absence of a trained labor pool to serve in a variety of labor niches is still a basic problem for many reservations. Although the number of skilled people usually increases annually, the improvement of economic opportunities on the reservation advances very slowly, if at all. Consequently, many of the young, trained Native Americans leave the reservations. The full impact that resource development on the reservation will have on economic opportunities remains to be determined.

**Table 2.4  Known and Potential Resources of Members of the Council of Energy Resource Tribes.**

| Tribe | Coal | Uranium | Geothermal | Natural Gas | Oil | Oil Shale | Gas | Lignite | Hydroelectric |
|---|---|---|---|---|---|---|---|---|---|
| Acoma Pueblo (NM) | X | | X | X | | | | | |
| Blackfeet (MT) | X | | | X | X | | | | |
| Chemehuevi (CA) | | X | | | | | | | X |
| Cherokee (OK) | X | | | X | X | | | | |
| Cheyenne-Arapaho (OK) | | | | | X | | X | | |
| Cheyenne River Sioux (SD) | X | | | | X | | X | | |
| Chippewa Cree (MT) | X | X | | | X | | X | X | |
| Coeur D'Alene (ID) | | X | | | | | | | X |
| Crow (MT) | X | | | X | X | | | | |
| Fort Belknap (MT) | | | X | X | X | | | X | |
| Fort Berthold (ND) | | | X | X | X | | | X | |
| Fort Hall (ID) | | | X | X | | | | | X |
| Fort Peck (MT) | | | X | | | | | X | |
| Hopi (AZ) | X | X | | X | X | | | | |
| Hualapai (AZ) | | X | | X | X | | | | X |
| Jemez Pueblo (NM) | | X | | X | X | | | | X |
| Jicarilla Apache (NM) | X | | X | X | X | | | | |
| Kaibab Paiute (AZ) | X | X | | X | | | | | |
| Kalispel (WA) | | X | | | | | | | X |
| Laguna Pueblo (NM) | X | X | | X | X | | | | X |
| Menominee (WI) | | | | | | | | | X |

**Table 2.4 Continued.**

| Tribe | Coal | Uranium | Geothermal | Natural Gas | Oil | Oil Shale | Gas | Lignite | Hydroelectric |
|---|---|---|---|---|---|---|---|---|---|
| Muckleshoot (WA) | X | | | X | X | | | | X |
| Navajo (AZ) (NM) (UT) | X | X | X | X | X | | | | |
| Nez Perce (ID) | | | | | | | | | X |
| Northern Cheyenne (MT) | X | | | X | X | | | | |
| Northern Ute (UT) | X | | | X | X | X | | | |
| Oglala Sioux (SD) | | X | | X | X | | | | |
| Paiute (UT) | X | X | | | X | X | X | | |
| Pauma (CA) | | | | | | | | | X |
| Pawnee (OK) | | | | | X | | X | | |
| Penobscot (MI) | | X | | | | | | | X |
| Pojoaque Pueblo (NM) | | | | | | | | | |
| Ponca (OK) | | | | | X | | X | | |
| Pyramid Lake Paiute (NV) | | | X | | | | | | |
| Rosebud Sioux (SD) | | | X | X | X | X | | | |
| Sac and Fox (OK) | | | | | X | | X | | |
| Saginaw Chippewa (MI) | | | | | X | | X | | |
| Salish & Kootenai (MT) | | | | X | | | | | X |
| San Juan Pueblo (NM) | | | | | X | | X | | |
| Santa Ana Pueblo (NM) | | | X | | | | | | |
| Seminole (FL) | | X | | X | | | | | |
| Southern Ute (CO) | X | | | X | X | | | | |

**Table 2.4 Continued.**

| Tribe | Coal | Uranium | Geothermal | Natural Gas | Oil | Oil Shale | Gas | Lignite | Hydroelectric |
|---|---|---|---|---|---|---|---|---|---|
| Spokane (WA) | X | X | | | | | | | X |
| St. Regis Mohawk (NY) | | | | | | | | | X |
| Standing Rock Sioux (ND & SD) | X | | | | X | | X | | |
| Tule River (CA) | | | | | | | | | X |
| Turtle Mountain Chippewa (ND) | X | | | X | X | | | | |
| Umatilla (OR) | | | X | | | | | | X |
| Ute Mountain Ute (CO) | X | X | | X | X | | | | |
| Walker River Paiute (NV) | | X | X | | | | | | X |
| Wichita (OK) | | | | X | X | | | | |
| Yakima (WA) | | | | X | X | | | | X |
| Zia Pueblo (NM) | | | X | X | X | | | | |

Source: Hirschfelder and Montano, 1993.

**Table 2.5   Native American State Gaming Compacts (1997).**

**Arizona—16 Tribes**

| | | |
|---|---|---|
| Ak-Chin Indian Community | Gila River Indian Community | Tohono O'Odham Tribe |
| Cocofah Tribe of Arizona | Hualapai Tribe | Tonto Apache Tribe |
| Colorado River Indian Tribes | Kaibab Paiute Tribe | White Mountain Apache Tribe |
| Fort McDowell Mohave-Apache | Pascua Yaqui Tribe | Yavapai-Apache Indian Comm. |
| Indian Community | Quechan Indian Tribe | Yavapai-Prescott Tribe |
| Fort Mojave Indian Tribe | San Carlos Apache Tribe | |

**California—5 Tribes**

| | | |
|---|---|---|
| Barona Band of the Capitan Grande of Diegueno Mission Indians | San Manuel Band of Serrano Mission Indians | Viejas Group of Capitan Grande Band of Diegueno Mission Indians |
| Cabazon Band of Cahuilla Mission Indians | Sycuan Band of Diegueno Mission Indians | |

**Colorado—2 Tribes**

| | |
|---|---|
| Southern Ute Indian Tribe | Ute Mountain Ute Tribe |

**Connecticut—2 Tribes**

| | |
|---|---|
| Mashantucket Pequot Tribe | Mohegan Indian Tribe |

**Idaho—3 Tribes**

| | | |
|---|---|---|
| Coeur D'Alene Tribe | Kootenaj Tribe | Nez Perce Tribe |

**Iowa—3 Tribes**

| | | |
|---|---|---|
| Omaha Tribe of Nebraska | Sac and Fox Tribe of Mississippi in Iowa | Winnebago Tribe of Nebraska |

**Kansas—4 Tribes**

| | | |
|---|---|---|
| Iowa Tribe of Kansas and Nebraska | Prairie Band of Potawatomi Indians of Kansas | Sac and Fox Nation of Missouri in Kansas and Nebraska |
| Kickapoo Tribe of Indians in Kansas | | |

**Louisiana—3 Tribes**

| | | |
|---|---|---|
| Chittmacha Tribe of Louisiana | Coushatta Tribe of Louisiana | Tunica-Biloxi Tribe of Louisiana |

**Michigan—7 Tribes**

| | | |
|---|---|---|
| Bay Mills Indian Community | Keweenaw Bay Indian Community | Saginaw Chippewa Indian Tribe |
| Grand Traverse Band of Ottawa and Chippewa Indians | Lac Vieux Desert Band of Lake Superior Chippewa Indians | Sault Ste. Marie Tribe of Chippewa |
| Hannahville Indian Community | | |

**Minnesota—11 Tribes**

| | | |
|---|---|---|
| Bois Forte Band of MN Chippewa (Nett Lake) | Lower Sioux Indian Community | Shakopee Mdewakanton Sioux Community |
| Fond Du Lac Band of Minnesota Chippewa | Mille Lacs Band of Minnesota Chippewa | Upper Sioux Indian Community |
| Grand Portage Band of Minnesota Chippewa | Prairie Island Community of the Minnesota Mdewakanton Sioux | White Earth Band of Minnesota Chippewa |
| Leech Lake Band of Minnesota Chippewa | Red Lake Band of Chippewa Indians | |

**Mississippi—1 Tribe**

Mississippi Band of Choctaw Indians

**Table 2.5  *Continued*.**

**Montana—5 Tribes**

Assintboine & Sioux Tribes of the Fort Peck Reservation

Blackfeet Nation

Chippewa-Cree Tribe of the Rocky Boys Reservation

Crow Tribe

Northern Cheyenne Tribe

**Nebraska—1 Tribe**

Omaha Tribe of Nebraska

**Nevada—5 Tribes**

Fort Mojave Tribal Council

Las Vegas Paiute Tribe

Moapa Band of Paiute Indians

Reno-Sparks Indian Colony

Walker River Paiute Tribe

**New Mexico—14 Tribes**

Jicarilla Apache Tribe

Mescalero Apache Tribe

Pueblo of Acoma

Pueblo of Isleta

Pueblo of Nambe

Pueblo of Pojoaque

Pueblo of San Felipe

Pueblo of San Ildefonso

Pueblo of San Juan

Pueblo of Sandia

Pueblo of Santa Ana

Pueblo of Santa Clara

Pueblo of Taos

Pueblo of Tesuque

**New York—2 Tribes**

Oneida Indian Nation

St. Regis Mohaw Tribe

**North Carolina—1 Tribe**

Eastern Band of Cherokee Indians

**North Dakota—5 Tribes**

Devils Lake Sioux Tribe

Sisseton-Wahpeton Sioux Tribe

Standing Rock Sioux Tribe

Three Affiliated Tribes of Fort Berthold

Turtle Mountain Band of Chippewa Indians

**Oklahoma—5 Tribes**

Citizen Band of Potawatomi Indian Tribe

Iowa Tribe of Oklahoma

Miami Tribe of Oklahoma

Miami-Modoc Tribes of Oklahoma

Tonkawa Tribe of Oklahoma

**Oregon—9 Tribes**

Burns-Paiute Tribe

Confederated Tribes of Coos, Lower Umpqua and Stuslaw Indians

Confederated Tribes of the Grand Ronde Comm.

Coquille Indian Tribe

Cow Creek Band of Umpqua Tribe of Indians

The Confederated Tribes of Siletz Indians of Oregon

The Confederated Tribes of the Warm Springs Reservation of Oregon

The Klamath Tribes

Umatilla Indian Tribe

**Rhode Island—1 Tribe**

Narragansett Indian Tribe

**South Dakota—9 Tribes**

Cheyenne River Sioux Tribe

Crow Creek Sioux Tribe

Flandreau Santee Sioux Tribe

Lower Brule Sioux Tribe

Oglala Sioux Tribe

Rosebud Sioux Tribe

Sisseton-Wahpeton Sioux Tribe

Standing Rock Sioux Tribe

Yankton Sioux Tribe of South Dakota

**Washington—17 Tribes**

Confederated Tribes of the Chehalis Reservation

Jamestown S'Klallam Tribe of Washington

Lower Elwha Klallam Tribe

Lummi Nation

Muckleshoot Indian Tribe

Nation Skokomish Indian Tribe

Nooksack Indian Tribe of Washington

**Table 2.5    *Continued.***

**Washington—17 Tribes *(Continued)***

| | | |
|---|---|---|
| Port Gamble S'Klallam | Quinault Indian | Tulalip Tribes of Washington |
| Puyallup Tribe of Indians | Squaxin Island Indian Tribe | Upper Skagit Indian Tribe |
| Quileute Tribal Council | Swinomish Indian Tribal Community | Yakama Indian Nation |

**Wisconsin—11 Tribes**

| | | |
|---|---|---|
| Bad River Band of Lake Superior Tribe of Chippewa Indians | Menominee Indian Tribe of Wisconsin | St. Croix Chippewa Indians of Wisconsin |
| Forest County Potawatomi Community | Oneida Tribe of Indians of Wisconsin | Sokaogan Chippewa Community |
| Lac Courte Oreilles Band of Lake Superior Chippewa | Red Cliff Band of Lake Superior Chippewa | Stockbridge-Munsee Community of Mohican Indians of Wisconsin |
| Lac Du Flambeau Band of Lake Superior Chippewa | | Wisconsin Winnebago Indian Tribe |

Source: Federal Register by Indian Gaming Management Staff, BIA, 1997.

Adjustment to nonreservation life varies from individual to individual and from generation to generation. Within urban areas there are no traditions of Indian ghettos. Individuals without peer support who arrive in an urban area face numerous difficulties in adjusting to and accepting city life. On the other hand, if one has family or relatives for emotional support, adjustment may come more easily. The relocation of Indians in the

Figure 2.7    Tribal Gaming Contracts by State.

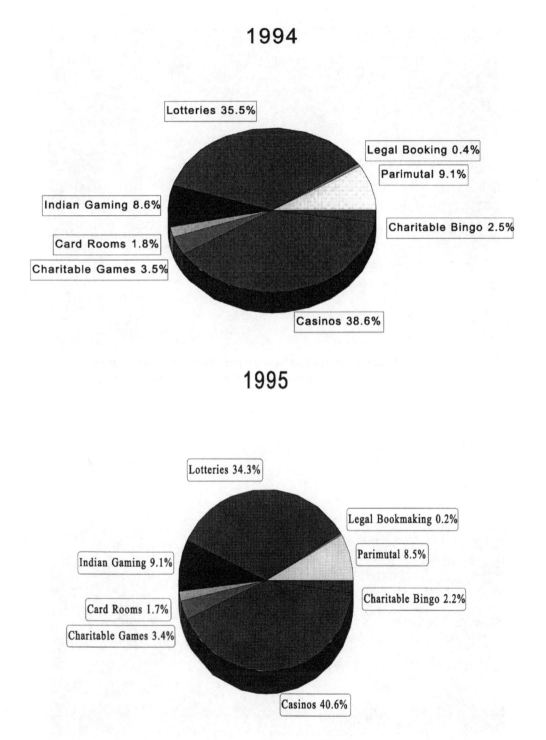

**1994**

Lotteries 35.5%

Legal Booking 0.4%

Parimutal 9.1%

Indian Gaming 8.6%

Charitable Bingo 2.5%

Card Rooms 1.8%

Charitable Games 3.5%

Casinos 38.6%

**1995**

Lotteries 34.3%

Legal Bookmaking 0.2%

Parimutal 8.5%

Indian Gaming 9.1%

Charitable Bingo 2.2%

Card Rooms 1.7%

Charitable Games 3.4%

Casinos 40.6%

**Figure 2.8    Indian Gaming Revenues for 1994 and 1995. Source:** *Gaming and Wagering Business,* **August 1994–August 1995.**

**Figure 2.9    A Pan-Indian Cultural Landscape from Cherokee, North Carolina, complete with totem poles and teepees. Source: Photo by D. Heffington.**

**Figure 2.10    The Changing Cultural Landscape of Cherokee, North Carolina, with Harrah's Newly Opened Cherokee Casino. Source: Photo by D. Heffington.**

1950s to cities was not always successful; however, in the 1990s, with better-educated individuals and more collective experiences in the urban place and the prospect of invigorated economic development with outlets such as gaming, the chances for success and successful adjustment became greater.

## NOTE

The authors wish to thank the following individuals for assistance on word processing and editing this manuscript and cartographic services: Margaret Nickell, Judy Mimbs, and Mary Goodman. Also, many thanks to Diane Wyss of the Bureau of Indian Affairs for providing the information from the Indian Gaming Commission.

## SUGGESTED READINGS

American Indian Policy Review Commission. *Final Report.* Washington, D.C.: U.S. Government Printing Office, 1977.

Deloria, V., Jr. *Behind the Trail of Broken Treaties.* New York: Delacorte, 1974.

Hamilton, C., ed. *Cry of the Thunderbird: The American Indian's Own Story.* Norman: University of Oklahoma Press, 1972.

Hirschfelder, A., and M. Kreipe de Montano. *The Native American Almanac: Portrait of Native America Today.* New York: Prentice Hall, 1993.

Josephy, A. M., Jr. *Now That the Buffalo's Gone: A Study of Today's American Indian.* New York: Knopf, 1982.

Oswalt, W. H., and S. Neely. *This Land Was Theirs: A Study of North American Indians,* 5th ed. Mountain View, Calif.: Mayfield, 1996.

Ross, T. E., T. G. Moore, and L. R. King, eds. *American Indians: A Cultural Geography,* 2d ed. South Pines, N.C.: Karo Hallow, 1995.

U.S. Civil Rights Commission. *Indian Tribes: A Continuing Quest for Survival.* Washington, D.C.: U.S. Government Printing Office, June 1981.

Utter, Jack. *American Indians: Answers to Today's Questions.* Lake Ann, Mich.: National Woodlands, 1993.

Vecsey, C., and R. W. Venables, eds. *American Indian Environments: Ecological Issues in Native American History.* Syracuse, N.Y.: Syracuse University Press, 1980.

Waddell, J. O., and O. M. Watson, eds. *The American Indian in Urban Society.* Boston: Little, Brown, 1971.

# The Evolving Spatial Pattern of Black America: 1910–1990 and Beyond

*Harold M. Rose*

The black population in the United States now numbers in excess of thirty million persons, or 12.2 percent of the nation's total population. That population is larger than was the nation's population in 1850. But what is important is the developmental sequence that has led the black population to acquire an internal identity that is rooted in a sense of peoplehood. Not only do blacks today represent a population group distinguishable in terms of a set of biological traits, but, more important, they represent a population whose experiences in America have led to the development of a unique group culture. This process has fostered not only a racial identity but an ethnic identity as well. It is not possible to indicate when an ethnic identity began to emerge, but by the close of the Civil War, it became obvious that blacks no longer represented a population group that had simply evolved from a common racial stock.

Because race in the United States has historically represented a more powerful social construct than has ethnicity, scholars have given only limited attention to the black population's ethnic qualities. This chapter will not directly address the question of ethnic status and the position of blacks in American society but will do so indirectly by highlighting those forces promoting spatial isolation during the twentieth century. The extent to which the social milieu of black Americans is severely constrained by external factors will influence the promotion and maintenance of that population's ethnic status. Therefore, a spatial-temporal treatment of how blacks have responded to the American opportunity structure during the twentieth century should provide a background for understanding the continuing evolution of an African American ethnicity.

Black Americans represent one of the original population groups involved in the making of America. Their presence in North America, according to Bennett,[1] dates back to 1619. The first blacks in the United States were indentured servants, and it was not until the middle of the seventeenth century that their status was altered to that of permanent bondage. The growth of that population was replenished through importing slaves from Africa, but after 1720 natural increase exceeded importation as the primary source of population growth.[2] Thus, the percentage of foreign-born black Americans became nominal by the end of the eighteenth century, a condition that stands in sharp contrast to the pattern of origin of America's European population.

Black Americans were introduced to the Americas as an agricultural labor source to be employed in the production of tropical and subtropical crops; thus, it was only logical that their ports of entry were basically confined to then existing southern coastal states. The introduction of blacks to the southern subtropics has been variously explained, but a more recent contention is that their immunity to selected tropical diseases to which Europeans were susceptible was the principal factor leading to their enslavement.[3] Thus, blacks were thought to represent an ideal southern labor force.

## PRE- AND POSTEMANCIPATION DISTRIBUTION: TO 1910

The spatial distribution of American blacks was essentially confined to the Chesapeake Bay area from the period of their introduction to the beginning of the nineteenth century. Virginia and Maryland were centers of concentration, with secondary centers occurring in the Carolinas. From 1790 to 1860, there was a sharp increase in the size of the black population. Johnson and Campbell[4] indicate blacks increased during this period from approximately seven hundred thousand to four million and that the increase was associated with the development of a plantation economy. Cotton, not tobacco, became the crop demanding ever-increasing quantities of slave labor.

The evolution of a system of plantation agriculture was responsible for the pattern of black population distribution that could be observed at the beginning of the twentieth century. The ever-increasing demand for cotton led to a redistribution of the slave population from the upper South to the lower South. The interregional migration of the slave population was directed to the cotton-producing states of Alabama, Mississippi, Louisiana, and Texas. By the beginning of the Civil War, the cultural hearth of the nation's black population had its boundaries fixed, boundaries that basically coincided with those of the Confederacy. Within this territorial configuration, Africans, who represented many distinctive groups, were transformed into Americans. Thus, Americanization of the nation's black population took place under the constraint of bondage associated with the labor demands of a plantation economy.

During the first 250 years that blacks were present in what now constitutes the United States, they had little control over their lives or movements. The spatial pattern of black population distribution was determined, therefore, by a set of exogenous forces dictated by labor demand. It is, however, the pattern of distribution that has emerged since 1865 that is of primary interest in this essay. Moreover, emphasis will be basically placed on the geography of black America during the twentieth century, for it is during this period that blacks had to adapt to a series of major changes in the nation's economy. These changes have subsequently had an impact on the geographic distribution of that population.

Geographers, unlike historians, have devoted only limited effort in detailing changes in the spatial distribution of black Americans, and they did not begin to show interest in the mobility characteristics of this population until after 1950. Even today sociologists conduct most migration studies that have as their focus the distribution of black Americans. Nevertheless, patterns of black migration are well documented; but the work of several geographers, including that of Calef and Nelson,[5] Hart,[6] Lewis,[7] and Morrill and Donaldson,[8] is instructive in helping us understand selected forces in the redistribution of black Americans throughout the early and mid–twentieth century. The writings of Hart and Lewis are especially instructive in allowing us to identify the cultural hearth of black Americans. The cultural hearth embraces most counties whose populations were at least 33 percent black in 1910 (Fig. 3.1).

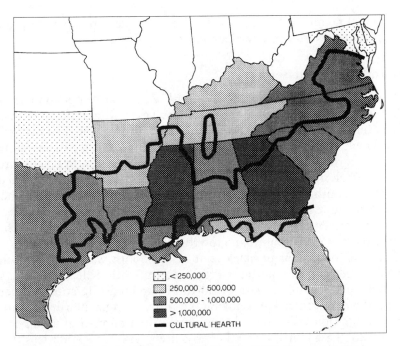

**Figure 3.1    Black Population in the South, 1910. Source: Courtesy of the University of Wisconsin–Milwaukee Cartographic Services.**

The first generation following emancipation resulted in limited interregional movement of the newly freed population. The most notable of these movements was to Kansas in the 1870s and to several northeastern states toward the end of the period. More noticeable, however, was the initiation of an urbanization process that drew blacks into both small southern towns and cities. By 1910, almost one-fifth of the region's black population could be identified as urban, whereas at the beginning of the period only 10 percent of the population resided in urban places.[9] Between 1870 and 1910, there was negligible change in the share of the black population residing in the South, with almost nine-tenths of the population present in both time periods. Thus, during the first generation following slavery, the black population evolved a pattern of redistribution within the region that led to minimum urbanization and a preponderant continued involvement in the agricultural sector.

## Incipient Regional Shifts in the Black Population

By the turn of the century, blacks had experienced one full generation as free persons, but freedom actually produced much less than it had promised. During the era following the war, the South instituted various oppressive measures that lent continuing protection to a system of white supremacy and at the same time maintained its prime agricultural workforce in place. An agricultural tenancy system continued to allow the region to satisfy a growing demand for cotton on the world market. Within this context, ex-slaves and the children of ex-slaves fashioned a bondage-free culture. But one could hardly expect the many dimensions of slave culture to disappear within a single generation. Nevertheless, within the group of counties that Lewis[10] identifies as the core of the Negro region, important aspects of twentieth-century black culture evolved.

## The Exodus from the South Begins

During the second generation following the Civil War, a pattern of population redistribution was initiated that continued for almost sixty years. Migration from the South was spurred by the termination of the massive European immigrant flow occurring as a result of the outbreak of war in Europe. Labor shortages took place in the nation's manufacturing belt when the immigrant flow was interrupted. Southern blacks already in the North, northern black newspapers distributed in the South, and labor agents encouraged blacks to leave the southern region. A steady deterioration of both social and economic conditions within the region aided and encouraged blacks to sever their ties with the South. Not all movement during the period, however, was interregional. This was also the period of takeoff in southern urban growth.

The first major movement of blacks out of the South was disproportionately confined to a selected set of core counties in the eastern South. Selected border state counties represented early leaving targets of northern-directed migrants. Numerically, the largest migrant group originated in Alabama, Virginia, Georgia, North Carolina, and Mississippi.[11] This migration was directed toward a limited number of urban centers in the Middle Atlantic and East North Central census divisions. Thus, after less than two generations following the termination of slavery, major changes took place that led to an alteration in the established pattern of black population distribution.

## The South's Pre–World War I Black Population

On the eve of the Great Migration, which was to lead to a net loss of almost a half million blacks from the region, 8.7 million of the nation's 9.8 million blacks resided in the South (Table 3.1, Fig. 3.1). More than one-third of the region's population was concentrated in Georgia, Mississippi, Alabama, and South Carolina, states where rural density reached its peak. Also in these states, the intensity of black occupancy was highest. The good cotton soils occurring in an almost continuous band from South Carolina through Mississippi

**Table 3.1    The South's Black Population in 1910.**

| Census Division | South Atlantic | | East South Central | | West South Central | |
|---|---|---|---|---|---|---|
| | Delaware | 31,000* | Kentucky | 262,000 | Arkansas | 443,000 |
| | Maryland | 233,000 | Tennessee | 473,000 | Louisiana | 714,000 |
| | Virginia | 64,000 | Alabama | 908,000 | Texas | 690,000 |
| | W. Virginia | 64,000 | Mississippi | 1,009,000 | Oklahoma | 1,984,000 |
| States | N. Carolina | 698,000 | | | | |
| | S. Carolina | 836,000 | | | | |
| | Georgia | 1,177,000 | | | | |
| | Florida | 309,000 | | | | |
| Divisional Totals: | | 4,112,000 | | 2,653,000 | | 1,984,000 |

*All values have been rounded off to the nearest 1,000.
Source: Robert B. Grant, *The Black Man Comes to the City* (Chicago: Nelson Hall Publishers, 1972), 16–17.

were responsible for providing a context in which a black core culture evolved and subsequently became diffused over a larger territory, only to be modified in the process.

Hart[12] defines black core areas in terms of intensity of occupancy at the county level. In 1910 more than one hundred counties included 50 percent or more blacks as residents. These counties represented a discontinuous band extending from the tobacco-producing regions of Virginia and North Carolina to the premier cotton counties from South Carolina through northern Louisiana. In such an intensely occupied black milieu, it is only logical to assume that aspects of black culture would originate, maintain an extended life, and diffuse outward from its origin. Movers from these core counties might be expected to engage in practices different from those developed in counties remote from the core.

Although less than 25 percent of the region's population was urban in 1910, the rise of New South industries led to urban growth in which blacks were inextricably involved. Few southern cities were less than 25 percent black at this date. By 1910, nineteen southern cities had populations of more than fifty thousand (Fig. 3.2), an urbanization level coinciding with the current metropolitan area population threshold. In environments satisfying this level of urbanization, it is appropriate to assess the existence of black territorial communities that might be viewed as possessing a ghetto or preghetto scale.

### Incipient Urban Growth

Fifteen primary black urban concentrations had evolved in the South by the early twentieth century. They were basically associated with the rise of southern commercial cen-

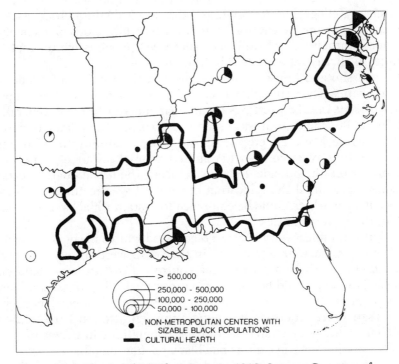

**Figure 3.2    The South's Urban System, 1910. Source: Courtesy of the University of Wisconsin–Milwaukee Cartographic Services.**

ters and therefore tended to have either river or ocean port locations. There were few exceptions to this rule, the most notable being Birmingham. Washington (94,000), New Orleans (89,000), and Baltimore (84,000) were the most populous black urban centers in the region, outstripping in size (in 1910) both the larger northern centers, New York (91,000) and Philadelphia (84,000). This set of urban centers were the first urban environments of black entry. But, given their limited size and the nature of their economies (e.g., service centers), they could hardly accommodate the vast rural populations whose economic state had changed very little since blacks were granted freedom. Rural poverty, viewed by most analysts as the chief motivation for moving out of the region, was everywhere.

The size of these larger southern urban concentrations provides one the opportunity to examine their spatial patterns as a means of addressing the validity of the notion of the existence of southern ghettos. It should be noted that the term *ghetto* was not used to describe southern black urban concentrations until recently. No doubt the absence of large southern and eastern European clusters in southern cities was responsible for the retardation in the use of this terminology to describe zones where unassimilated urban populations were concentrated. The physical character of these places as well might have led to a failure in describing them in this manner. Or, it could be that it was simply an inappropriate social construct to define settlements within the southern region.

The latter explanation appears to have greater intuitive appeal. If ghettos in the American context were viewed simply as zones where immigrants would be transformed into Americans and in the second or later generation seek their position in American society as individuals, then the concept was inappropriate. Although black residential concentrations existed in all southern cities, the spatial pattern and intensity showed much variation. Nevertheless, Kellog[13] has demonstrated that in postbellum cities black communities most often grew up on the edge of town. Moreover, numerous clusters often existed. These were not communities where blacks succeeded previous white residents but, instead, territories explicitly set aside for black occupancy.

Dog runs and shotgun houses, commonplace in the rural countryside, were often replicated in the cities. Over time, however, the urban housing stock was upgraded, and the amenities present in urban settings became far superior to those generally available in the rural South. But the central issue seems to revolve around state of permanence or transience. Immigrant ghettos were viewed by many as simply transient entities that could be expected to provide both shelter and communal resources to persons entering American society from the outside. In many respects, the urban quarters established for southern blacks represented the relocation of rural villages to the city. These zones of permanent occupancy, which could be employed to sustain a black culture, had their origins in a set of rural core counties.

Assimilation was unnecessary because blacks and whites in the South had a fixed relationship. Therefore, black urban clusters in the South were simply zones where black culture could flourish, where a set of black-controlled institutions could emerge, and where one's social world would be totally circumscribed. The contention here is that it would be inappropriate to use the term *ghetto* to describe urban black concentrations in southern cities satisfying a metropolitan population definition in 1910. Although in that year only fifteen such places existed with black populations in excess of ten thousand, numerous other southern urban centers had black populations that exceeded this threshold. Thus, sizable urban villages also existed in such places as Little Rock, Arkansas; Augusta and Macon, Georgia; Lexington, Kentucky; Charlotte, North Carolina; Columbia,

South Carolina; Chattanooga, Tennessee; and Portsmouth, Virginia. The size of the black population was partially circumscribed by the size of the total population and the center's role in the urban economy.

## FIRST-GENERATIONAL PATTERNS OF INTERREGIONAL MOVEMENT: 1910–1940

In 1910, the South's black population had a spatial pattern similar to that recorded in the 1870 census. But this date represented the eve of the beginning of a redistribution pattern that eventually led blacks to settle throughout the rest of the nation. The initial movement is generally said to have gotten under way in 1915. In just five years, approximately one-half million blacks left the South. This movement led to an intensification of the urbanization process as most blacks who left the region settled in the then largest urban centers of the Northeast and North Central regions. The process of urban ghettoization took off during this period, resulting in the formation of large contiguous spatial clusters where blacks represented the majority population.

### The Great Migration

As indicated earlier, the advent of World War I and the subsequent termination of European immigration served as the initial impetus for the Great Migration. Once under way, however, the depression of the thirties slowed down the migration flow. Blacks arriving in northern cities entered the urban economy on the lowest rung of the ladder as people from southern and eastern Europe had almost a full generation head start. This led to the latter group's more favored position in the opportunity structure once the war emergency had ended.

Blacks were especially attracted to cities where manufacturing employment was easily available. In these cities first-generation ghettos expanded abruptly, and new ghetto configurations came into being. The black population in Chicago, Detroit, and Cleveland more than doubled from 1910 to 1920, while that of New York, Philadelphia, St. Louis, Cincinnati, and Indianapolis grew at less than one-half this rate. Among the larger southern cities, only the growth rate in Houston's black community could compare favorably with the growth rate in the slower-growing northern centers. In fact, both Nashville and Louisville experienced an absolute loss in their black population during this decade. By 1920, the largest black urban concentrations were no longer in Washington, New Orleans, and Baltimore but in New York, Philadelphia, and Chicago.

It should be remembered that at this date both black and white southern populations were moving from the rural countryside to southern towns and cities. It required another twenty years, however, before the urban black population exceeded in size the rural population. Furthermore, white migrants had a greater affinity for southern cities than did blacks. Also, because blacks had been cut off from some of the skilled jobs they performed during the Reconstruction period, whites were more likely to secure the more desirable jobs. Thus, the move to southern cities, save a few, simply assured blacks continuing employment in the low-wage service economy. Even this was an inducement to move away from the almost certain poverty and fear of repression that characterized segments of the rural South.

During this period, more white southerners than blacks migrated to northern cities. Old hostilities accompanied these migrants. At this time, however, black migrants to northern cities entered occupations previously closed to them, although the jobs obtained were among the least attractive ones in the local economy. Although most emphasis has been directed to the economic factors contributing to migration, some evidence indicates that social forces played a strong secondary role[14] and were far more important than they have generally been reported.

### The Post–World War I Migrant Flows

The end of the war did not terminate the flow of black migrants to Middle Atlantic and Great Lakes cities. A speed-up in the process occurred during the twenties, when approximately twice as many migrants moved than had moved during the previous ten years. The ravages of the depression, however, led to a slowing of the rate of out-migration and subsequently to a sizable return flow;[15] but, even during the worst of times,[16] this latter movement was not sufficiently adequate to offset the continued migration of blacks out of the South. By 1940, a full generation of black movers had departed from the cultural hearth and had subsequently established a secondary black population concentration in the Northeast and in the North Central region.

From 1910 to 1940, eight southern states were sources of almost two million black migrants (Fig. 3.3). The principal contributors were Georgia and South Carolina, followed by Mississippi and Alabama. As is shown in Table 3.2, the impact on the contributing states and receiving ports of entry was substantial. The states of the South Atlantic division, de-

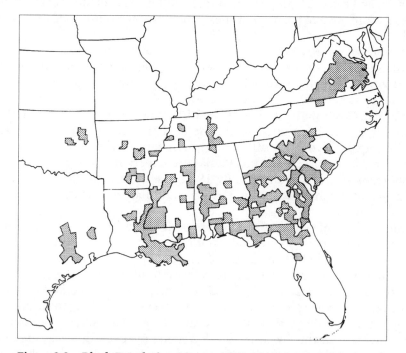

**Figure 3.3   Black Population Losses, 1910–1940. Source: Courtesy of the University of Wisconsin–Milwaukee Cartographic Services.**

**Table 3.2   Black Population in 1910 and 1940 in Primary Sending States and Primary Ghetto Centers (in 1,000s).**

| States | 1910 | 1940 | % Change 1910–1940 | Ghetto Centers | 1910 | 1940 | % Change 1910–1940 |
|---|---|---|---|---|---|---|---|
| Virginia | 671 | 661 | − 0.01 | New York | 92 | 458 | + 251 |
| North Carolina | 698 | 981 | + 40.00 | Philadelphia | 84 | 251 | + 209 |
| South Carolina | 836 | 814 | − 0.03 | Chicago | 44 | 278 | + 531 |
| Georgia | 1,177 | 1,085 | − 0.70 | Detroit | 6 | 149 | + 1,662 |
| Alabama | 908 | 983 | + 0.80 | Cleveland | 8 | 85 | + 975 |
| Mississippi | 1,009 | 1,075 | + 0.60 | Pittsburgh | 26 | 62 | + 134 |
| Arkansas | 444 | 483 | + 0.09 | Indianapolis | 22 | 51 | + 131 |
| Louisiana | 714 | 849 | + 17.00 | St. Louis | 44 | 109 | + 145 |

Source: U.S. Bureau of the Census, 1910 and 1940.

spite their high fertility, were unable to maintain their population at the 1910 level, and all except North Carolina were inhabited by fewer blacks on the eve of World War II than in the initial time period. The secondary movement from Alabama and Mississippi during this interval was not enough to prevent these states' populations from growing.

Black movement out of the South represents one of the primary movements in American migration history. Because the Depression sharply slowed black migration, the first phase of the migration movement was completed before 1940. But, during this thirty-year period, more than 1.7 million blacks had departed from the cultural hearth and were forging new lives for themselves in the Northeast and North Central part of the nation. Because prejudice was rampant and satisfactory residential accommodations were difficult to obtain, blacks encountered much difficulty in the new environment.[17] Fortunately, wages were higher and institutional constraints were lower. As a result, others were urged to join the migrants in what some were calling "the promised land."

## WORLD WAR II USHERS IN A NEW MIGRATION PHASE: 1940–1970

The advent of the second major war in this century served as the impetus that catalyzed the Depression-retarded flow of blacks from the South. The severe labor needs characterizing the period 1942–1945 did much to induce new movement. Since most of the war industries were concentrated in the American manufacturing belt, which had converted its peacetime facilities to war materials production, urban centers in the Northeast and North Central regions were again the principal targets of the migrant flows. The West, too, was a locus of aspects of war material production, especially aircraft and shipbuilding. Thus, for the first time, a sizable number of black migrants were destined for selected western urban centers (Table 3.3). Prior to 1940, only Los Angeles, among western cities, was the place of residence of more than twenty-five thousand blacks.

### The Opening of New Employment Opportunity

The distribution of employment in war-related activity did much to influence the volume and direction of migration, as can be observed in the choice of specific migration

**Table 3.3    The Destination of Southern Black Migrants from Southern Core States, 1940–1950.**

| Total Net Migrants | Northeast | North Central | West |
|---|---|---|---|
| 1,244,792 | 411,766 | 528,675 | 304,351 |

Source: Conrad Taueber and Irene B. Taueber, *The Changing Population of the United States* (New York: John Wiley & Sons, Inc., 1958).

target communities. Not only were blacks being drawn to urban centers that served as the primary ports of entry during the previous thirty years, but they were also attracted to places where there was only a nominal black presence in 1940. Cities such as San Francisco, Milwaukee, Boston, Buffalo, and Rochester were among the newer urban magnets that had not by 1940 qualified as ghetto centers. Thus, the war was primarily responsible for ushering in a third set of ghetto centers.

Although as a result of the war blacks were settling in a large number of urban centers, the primary contributors to the growth process were first- and second-generation ghetto centers. They were as a rule the largest urban centers in the nation and were subsequently able to absorb and house large numbers of migrants. But, when we consider the existence of the spatial pattern of racially restrictive covenants on housing, extraordinary pressures were placed on the housing stock in some of these centers. Seldom was housing available to blacks outside the context of racial succession in the new environments. Because of the magnitude of migration to larger urban centers and the constraints on housing access, conversions were frequently necessary to satisfy part of the housing demand.[18]

## Southern Cities Bypassed

By the end of the forties, the black population had grown to sizable levels in the traditional migration target centers. All but a select set of southern cities were bypassed in this new movement wave. As a matter of fact, net migration out of a number of leading southern cities was the rule, with selected southern coastal cities serving as the only significant regional magnets. Among the twenty-four urban centers in the nation to attract more than ten thousand black migrants during this decade (the forties), only five were located in the South: Washington (sixty-five thousand net migrants), Baltimore (thirty-five thousand net migrants), Houston (twenty-five thousand net migrants), Norfolk (eighteen thousand net migrants), and New Orleans (twelve thousand net migrants). None of the southern centers were among the primary migration target centers, although Washington was a leading secondary center. Eventually the movement that occurred during this decade led to the largest concentration ever of blacks in northern urban centers, and the subsequent decline in the relative ranking of early black urban concentrations in Birmingham, Jacksonville, Richmond, and Louisville.

Not only were the migrant destinations altered during this period, but so were migrant origins. In the decade following World War I, the South Atlantic states were the principal contributors to the South-to-North migration stream and the subsequent growth of northern urban centers along its course. Although this area maintained its relative position as a migration source region during the more recent decade, it was seriously challenged by the East South Central division, largely on the basis of massive migration from Mississippi and Alabama. The West South Central division states of

Arkansas and Louisiana also became significant contributors to regional abandonment. The contributions to migration from an expanded southern migration field were responsible for the sharp increase in the size of the black population in selected North Central and Western urban centers during the forties (Fig. 3.4).

## The Role of Agricultural Mechanization

The decline in agricultural labor demand in the cotton South, as an outgrowth of reduced crop acreage and agricultural mechanization, freed sharecroppers from the land. Fligstein specifically states, "The introduction of cotton pickers in the late 1940s made the rural non-farm population a total surplus population and left them no choice but to migrate."[19] On the other hand, tobacco production was mechanized more slowly and possibly retarded the black outflow from North Carolina's bright-leaf tobacco producing counties. It has been previously pointed out that in some North Carolina rural counties, the black population experienced an absolute increase during this decade, constituting a pattern not observed elsewhere.[20] Thus, with the expansion of opportunity in northern and western urban centers, which was motivated by the need to accelerate war production, many blacks left the South. Others left because of declining opportunity in southern agriculture, especially after the war's end. Shimkin[21] has made a distinction between persons who were pushed out of southern agriculture and persons who migrated because they perceived alternative opportunities. The former he describes as refugees. In the next decade, the number of refugees in black migration streams no doubt increased as agricultural mechanization continued apace.

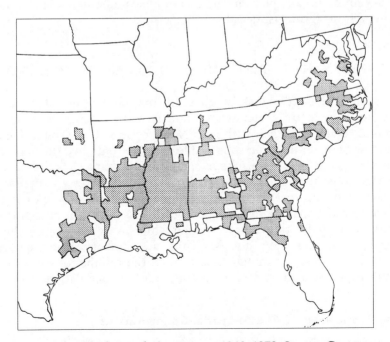

**Figure 3.4   Black Population Losses, 1940–1970. Source: Courtesy of the University of Wisconsin–Milwaukee Cartographic Services.**

## Generational Change in the National Economy

The movement that got under way during World War II continued almost unabated for thirty years. During that time, more than four million blacks left the South to settle in the large urban centers in the North and West. By the end of the period, the South's share of the nation's black population was reduced from 77 percent to 53 percent. The urban proportion of the population increased from less than 50 percent to more than 75 percent. Since the black population outside the South was already overwhelmingly urban, the percentage increase also indicates a growing southern urbanization. Needless to say, the growth of southern urban centers was adequate to stem the tide. It has been estimated that only 29 percent of southern black migrants during the fifties remained in the region, whereas 71 percent became part of interregional migration streams.[22] Thus, the decline in demand for agricultural labor, coupled with growing tensions associated with the civil rights movement concentrated in southern cities, led many to seek opportunity and equality outside the region. Nevertheless, as a result of higher than average fertility, the southern black population grew by more than two million persons from 1940 to 1970.[23]

Major economic changes were to appear in the primary target zones, the Northeast and North Central regions, before this period was to come to a close. After 1960 it was clear that manufacturing was to play a declining role in the American economy. Not only was manufacturing growth decreasing, but the manufacturing belt states were unable to capture an equitable share of incremental growth. Thus, black Americans were being attracted to manufacturing belt cities during a period when this activity was becoming relatively less important in the American economy, but at the same time manufacturing growth was beginning to take place in the region of abandonment. This did not become apparent, however, until the last decade of the period.

## GHETTO DEVELOPMENT DURING THE SECOND GENERATION: 1940–1970

Movement since 1940 has led to massive ghetto formation. By the end of the period, first- and second-generation ghetto centers were the places of residence of no fewer than two hundred thousand black residents, with both New York and Chicago black communities housing in excess of one million persons (Table 3.4). Not only had the population grown absolutely, but the proportion of blacks in the city had changed as well, most often resulting in blacks constituting a minimum of one-third of the city's population. Among first- and second-generation centers, Los Angeles represents the sole exception, with a proportional population share of less than one-fifth. However, the changing proportions were primarily associated with the rate at which whites were abandoning the city for residence in metropolitan ring communities.[24] Thus, the number of blacks entering the central city during this period was much smaller than the number of whites exiting. This movement subsequently led to a decline in both core city populations and jobs.

### The Seeming Permanence of Ghetto Spatial Configurations

Ghetto formation permitted blacks from diverse origins to develop sanctuaries in the city during their period of initial arrival, but a continuous flow of migrants resulted in

**Table 3.4   Changes in the Size of the Black Population in First and Second Generation Non-Southern Ghetto Centers: 1940–1970 (in 1,000s).**

|  | 1940 | 1970 |  | 1940 | 1970 |
|---|---|---|---|---|---|
| New York | 504 | 1667 | Cleveland | 85 | 238 |
| Philadelphia | 251 | 654 | St. Louis | 166 | 254 |
| Pittsburgh | 62 | 105 | Indianapolis | 56 | 134 |
| Newark | 52 | 207 | Cincinnati | 51 | 125 |
| Chicago | 278 | 1103 |  |  |  |
| Detroit | 149 | 660 |  |  |  |

Source: U.S. Bureau of the Census, 1940 and 1970.

ghettos becoming permanent fixtures in American urban centers. Needless to say, this statement oversimplifies the problem. Moreover, the refusal of whites to share social space with blacks and the codification of that refusal in the establishment of racially restrictive covenants are well known. The latter did much to channel growth in the first generation to a set of rigid corridors.[25] Thus, it was not until after the previous generation of migrants had carved out a residential niche for themselves that racially restrictive covenants were outlawed. But, by 1948, the year the decision was rendered, the ghetto pattern was already fully developed. Hence, a comparison of black and European ethnic ghetto development patterns prior to this period represents a comparison of an involuntary versus a voluntary development.

Throughout this period, blacks acquired housing through the racial succession process, and only recently has that pattern begun to show signs of modification. The nature and quality of the black residential environment are, therefore, a function of the nature of available housing in the wake of black expansion. During periods of surplus construction, the quality of black residential space is likely to be enhanced,[26] but during downturns in housing construction, trickle-down housing is unavailable to satisfy demand.

Unlike the fifties, the building boom in American metropolitan areas during the sixties loosened demand in core cities. Subsequently, blacks were able to upgrade their housing stock, and once this housing construction boom got under way, the transition of border markets to ghetto space accelerated. By the end of the interval, the flow of black migrants to a number of the previous target cities had slackened, but the absolute size of the black population was sufficiently large to propel expansion of ghetto space beyond the political limits of the core city. From 1965 to 1969, this spillover effect was to account for a large share of black movement to select suburban areas.

## Black Residential Development in Southern Cities

Black population growth in southern cities occurred more slowly during this developmental period. Prior to the 1950s, blacks were seldom involved in the racial residential succession process. Housing was built, rather, to satisfy the demand on a race-specific basis. At the beginning of the interval, therefore, southern cities were likely to contain a number of pockets of black residential development, with additional units often built adjacent to existing pockets. The ghettoization process did not appear to get under way in southern cities until the fifties, when economic and social changes in the

South led to modifying the racial housing allocation process. Once the modified process got under way, a filling-in of spaces separating individual pockets of black residences was initiated, and racial residential succession began.

Earlier it was indicated that the ghetto concept as employed here was inapplicable to black residential concentrations in southern cities prior to the recent period. That position was based on the general absence of racial residential turnover as the predominant mode of allocating housing to blacks. This is not to say that blacks and whites did not reside in racially segregated communities but only to point out early differences that often led to a different spatial pattern of residential segregation. In the South, moreover, social distance between blacks and whites was not determined by propinquity. As institutional barriers began to decline, however, and as the threat of institutional sharing became more prominent, convergence toward the northern pattern of black residential allocation began to appear.

From 1950 to 1956, Coe[27] reports that none of the nonwhite housing units added in Atlanta were previously occupied by whites. But by 1970, the previously existing pattern had been modified. Kenyon, writing almost two decades later, describes the Atlanta situation in the following way:

> Although Atlanta, like other southern cities, is still characterized by a number of small, as well as large black neighborhoods and communities, the rapid growth and consolidation of these sections is leading to a pattern increasingly similar to the massive ghetto belts of the large northern city.[28]

It appears currently that a mixed racial residential allocation process operates in southern cities, where both new construction in black social space and racial residential turnover are principally responsible for satisfying incremental demand. Long and Spain,[29] employing sample survey data, indicate that from 1967 to 1971, only one-sixth of black demand in southern cities was satisfied via racial succession, whereas more than two-fifths of the units occupied by blacks in the Northeast were acquired by way of racial turnover. Thus, in attempting to evaluate the impact of migration-inspired housing demand on the ghettoization process, one should be constantly aware that the housing allocation mechanism in southern and nonsouthern cities did not begin to converge until after 1950.

The slower rate of migration to southern cities generally led to less pressure on the existing housing supply. In locations where growth was rapid, however, a combination of residential turnover and new construction in black residential space satisfied demand. The strong tradition of supporting a separation of the races in the South, coupled with an absence of political clout in the black community, led new construction, whether privately or publicly financed, to take place in settings designed to attract one racial group or the other. Blacks who gained access to new housing were often better housed than people possessing similar socioeconomic rank outside the South. Under the circumstances, demand for housing in previously white areas was tempered by the lower intensity of demand and access to an alternative supply. Thus, although it is no longer improper to describe southern black communities in a metropolitan context as ghetto communities, it would be shortsighted to think of them as being historically equivalent to similar communities that have evolved outside the region. Although convergence has been under way for almost a generation, it is not yet complete.

**The Black Migrational Response to Incipient Postindustrial Development**

The last decade of the 1940–1970 period was one of great social upheaval and economic change. Older core cities were characterized by population decline and subsequent erosion of their tax base. Jobs that had been easily available during a previous period were now shifting to the suburbs, and small towns were becoming accessible by completion of the National Defense Highway System. Lower-income blacks were trapped in environments of limited opportunity, whereas their middle-income counterparts were actively involved in gaining access to housing along the white-black border.

The pattern of acquiring housing in urban centers outside the South led to a sociospatial stratification of the population within black communities, in many ways similar to that prevailing in the larger society. When the size of the black population became sufficiently large, it created the basis for extending the ghetto into contiguous suburban communities. Thus, by 1970, the largest metropolitan areas in the country, which also happened to represent the place of residence of the nation's largest black population concentrations, were also places where the largest black suburban ring populations were to be found. Needless to say, these new suburban ring populations, although much smaller in size, were almost as rigidly segregated as central city populations. Therefore, suburbanization was seldom tantamount to dispersion.

By the end of the second generation of twentieth-century black migration, the national pattern of black population distribution had been radically altered from that existing in 1910. A rural population had gone to the city with the expectation that their life chances would be improved. When blacks chose to migrate to places with income levels significantly higher than those in the area of origin, they logically expected improved wages. The nature of the economy supporting such income differences was, however, in the throes of transition toward the end of this period. The ushering in of a postindustrial economy was to have an impact on second-generation movers and their offspring in ways that could not have been foreseen in the forties or fifties. By 1970, it was evident that major changes were under way and that some black migrants who had earlier chosen to leave the South for the non-South were beginning to reverse their course.

## LARGE METROPOLITAN CENTERS AS POTENTIAL MIGRATION BASES

By 1970, the black population nationally had become overwhelmingly urban. There had developed a sizable increase in the number of blacks who were residents of the national system of ghetto centers with black populations of fifty thousand or more. Smaller ghetto centers—with fewer than fifty thousand blacks but more than twenty-five thousand blacks—were also frequently in evidence and growing. But the larger centers in this network constituted a population base that led to intermetropolitan migration becoming the modal origin and destination of black migrants. This is not to imply that nonmetropolitan to metropolitan migration was not occurring but rather to say that its contribution had been dampened. Nonmetropolitan migrants were most often destined for the largest urban centers in the nation, whereas intermetropolitan destinations were more diffuse. The growth of nonsouthern metropolitan black populations over two generations had established a migrant population base that approached the southern base in size, and this growth largely fostered the transition to intermetropolitan dominance.

## The Role of Nonsouthern Migrants on Changing Migration Patterns

An extensive literature describes both black rural to urban migration and migration from the South to the non-South. But interregional flow data emphasizing the movement pattern of black migrants of nonsouthern origin is almost nonexistent. Yet, from 1965 to 1970, nonsouthern black migrants were found to contribute substantially to the total black migration to the principal non-South migration targets. Table 3.5 compares southern migrations to the leading migrant targets of both migrant groups. In one-third of the targets, non-South migrants constitute the majority, but they account for more than two-fifths in an additional eight centers. Only in Chicago and New York did nonsouthern migrants represent as few as one-third of all migrants. Nonsouthern migrants were the predominant group in each of the western centers as they were in Columbus, Ohio, and Kansas City, Missouri. Only in centers where the vast majority of the migrants are from the South does nonmetropolitan migration origin become the dominant one. Thus, New York and Chicago continue to represent the primary target destination of migrants from states where the nonmetropolitan population continues to be larger than the metropolitan population (e.g., Mississippi and North Carolina).

The contribution of nonsouthern migrants to principal metropolitan complexes within the region is approximately 80 percent of that of southern migrants to center growth. Nonsouthern migrants, however, were far less likely to migrate to southern metropolitan areas, although Washington, Baltimore, Atlanta, Houston, Memphis, and Dallas are exceptions. Nevertheless, the volume flow from the non-South to these centers is only one-third to one-fourth as large as the southern flow. An exception is Washington, where the southern flow is only twice as large as that from the non-South. One of the problems with attempting to specify the magnitude of the nonsouthern flow is our in-

**Table 3.5    Southern and Non-Southern Contribution to Primary Non-Southern Migration Centers: 1965–1970.**

| Target Centers | Non-Southern Migrants | Southern Migrants | Non-Southern Migrants as % of Total |
|---|---|---|---|
| New York | 17,661 | 38,206 | 32.0% |
| Los Angeles | 38,575 | 34,370 | 53.0% |
| Chicago | 16,512 | 33,325 | 33.1% |
| Detroit | 22,788 | 33,081 | 40.8% |
| Philadelphia | 17,661 | 17,885 | 49.7% |
| San Francisco | 18,935 | 13,907 | 57.7% |
| Newark | 9,308 | 12,015 | 43.7% |
| Cleveland | 8,281 | 10,820 | 43.4% |
| St. Louis | 7,613 | 9,088 | 45.6% |
| Boston | 4,757 | 6,198 | 43.4% |
| San Diego | 7,150 | 5,276 | 57.5% |
| Milwaukee | 4,356 | 4,764 | 47.8% |
| Indianapolis | 4,377 | 4,411 | 49.8% |
| Columbus | 5,037 | 4,222 | 54.4% |
| Kansas City, MO | 4,416 | 4,320 | 50.5% |

Source: U.S. Department of Commerce, Bureau of the Census, *Mobility for Metropolitan Areas* (U.S. Census of Population 1970, Final Report PC[2]-2C).

ability to specify what part of this represents return migration. Returnees could seriously inflate the proportion of nonsouthern migrants destined for southern migrant targets.

## PRESENT MOBILITY STATUS

In 1990, the nation's black population totaled twenty-six million, unadjusted for the undercount. The growth rate declined from the previous decade: 20.0 percent to 17.3 percent. This change largely reflected a continuing decline in black fertility rates, with only limited change in mortality rates. The 17.3 percent increase in the black population during the decade reflected a slowing of growth among the group.

### Changing Regional Linkages

Given the observed net differences at state and county levels, some additional insights can be gained. Previous migration linkages between census division in the South and the non-South also provide clues in deducing the magnitude and direction of migration flows. What becomes clear from reviewing change at a subregional scale is the continuation of the previous pattern of net outmigration from those nonmetropolitan counties that constitute the cultural hearth. Given the general absence of economic opportunity in most of these locations, this comes as no surprise. Approximately one-fifth (3,471,906) of the nation's black population was found in this setting in 1970. Moland refers to these people as "the people left behind" and goes on to describe them as poor people who continue to suffer "unemployment, underemployment, inadequate housing, isolation from community services, and lack of access to resources and leadership to meet these and other needs."[30] But, even within this setting, differential opportunity and variations in the intensity of poverty prevail.

If size of population loss in individual nonmetropolitan counties is an index of an absence of hope, then what happens in these counties during the 1980s provides some indirect evidence of the changes that are occurring in the opportunity structure. Figure 3.5 depicts the major losing counties during the seventies. A review of the changes in volume of net migration shows that in each state there has been a sharp decline in the volume of loss from counties registering excessive losses. Only in Mississippi were losses similar to those occurring during the previous decade sustained in more than 25 percent of the losing counties. What becomes evident is, although nonmetropolitan black population are not growing as a result of net migration, they do not continue to sustain losses of the magnitude of the recent past. Only selected Delta counties in Mississippi and Arkansas have continued to have losses similar to those of the previous decade.

Are these smaller net losses the result of a continued return flow of individuals who were previous residents of the region, or is there a general retardation in leaving rates? On the basis of preliminary data, this question cannot be answered (unequivocally). In the past, Delta counties do not appear to have attracted a significant return flow when one considers the volume of out-movement. The return flow described earlier was selective in its target destination, with the principal targets being selected locations in Maryland, Virginia, North Carolina, and South Carolina.

Large net outmigration levels from the Northeast, a division with strong ties to the South Atlantic division, could possibly have led to sizable return flow to that division.

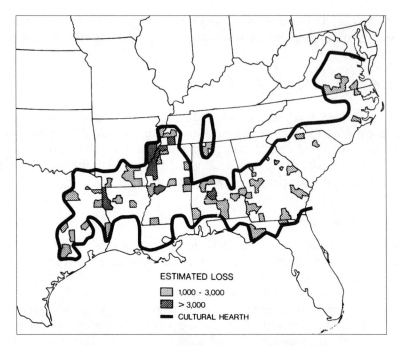

**Figure 3.5    Primary Black Population Loss in the Nonmetropolitan South during the 1970s. Source: Courtesy of the University of Wisconsin–Milwaukee Cartographic Services.**

However, the level of net migration from the North Central region was estimated to be nominal and thereby limited the magnitude of the return flow to East South Central division states. Thus, it can be deduced that there has been a slowdown in net outmigration from the South's nonmetropolitan counties in general, with only modest return flow to the previously heavy-losing Delta counties but possibly a larger return flow to counties in North Carolina, South Carolina, and Virginia.

### The Renewed Growth of Southern Urban Centers

It must be assumed that if black outmigration from nonmetropolitan counties is continuing, then intraregional metropolitan centers are serving as the locus of intervening opportunity. As older southern metropolitan areas have grown during the recent period and new ones have come into existence, they are more attractive to a segment of nonmetropolitan movers than are a growing number of urban centers outside of the region. Such a pattern can be deduced by simply observing the net migration characteristics of nonmetropolitan counties in the vicinity of southern metro areas (Fig. 3.6). In most instances, net in-migration characterizes southern central cities, whereas the surrounding nonmetropolitan field is characterized by a net outflow.

Migration to southern and western metropolitan areas during the late 1970s does much to highlight the plight of the metropolitan economy in the Northeast and North Central regions. A turnaround in migration to these regions has indeed occurred. They are becoming net migration dispensers as opposed to receivers.[31]

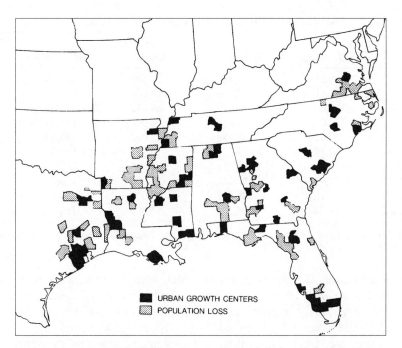

**Figure 3.6    Black Population Loss in Counties Contiguous to Urban Growth Centers, 1970–1980. Source: Courtesy of the University of Wisconsin–Milwaukee Cartographic Services.**

The primary destination of black migrants during the seventies is not easy to deduce. But if the projection method employed here does not seriously distort reality, the largest volume of net migration has been directed toward a selected set of central cities in the South and West. The primary target cities are tentatively identified in Table 3.6. Among the top ten central city targets, only Milwaukee was not located in the Sunbelt. A note of caution is, however, in order. All of the central cities shown in Table 3.6, with the probable exception of Birmingham and Oakland, have no significant metropolitan ring population. Ring growth was very sizable in some metropolitan areas; and since its origin cannot be specified, there is no way to identify its inter- and intraregional components. In some instances, people who might have in the past settled in the central cities may now be by-passing them for life in the suburban ring.

Ten years later, however, only four of these central cities continued to represent places experiencing net in-migration. Only Milwaukee, Charlotte, San Diego, and Jackson continued to serve as net in-migrant centers. This could imply that each of the remaining places were experiencing black suburbanization.

### The Relative Decline of First- and Second-Generation Ghetto Centers

As a result of altered migration patterns, first- and second-generation ghetto centers in the Northeast and North Central Census divisions have been the principal losers. This may prove somewhat misleading, however, when one views the pattern of mobility at a larger scale; that is, if one shifts to the metropolitan area rather than simply focusing at-

**Table 3.6    Primary Destination of Black Migrants to Central Cities.**

| City | 1970 Population | 1980 Population | Estimated Net Migration | 1990 Population | Estimated Net Migration |
|------|-----------------|-----------------|-------------------------|-----------------|-------------------------|
| Houston, TX | 316,551 | 440,257 | 70,000 | 458,000 | − 90,000 |
| Memphis, TN | 242,513 | 307,702 | 24,000 | 335,000 | − 14,000 |
| Milwaukee, WI | 105,008 | 146,940 | 24,000 | 191,000 | + 29,000 |
| Jackson, MS | 61,063 | 95,357 | 23,000 | 109,000 | +  1,000 |
| Dallas, TX | 210,038 | 265,594 | 20,000 | 295,000 | −  5,600 |
| San Diego, CA | 52,691 | 77,000 | 16,000 | 104,000 | + 16,000 |
| Oakland, CA | 124,710 | 159,234 | 14,000 | 163,000 | − 17,000 |
| Charlotte, NC | 72,972 | 97,627 | 12,000 | 126,000 | + 17,000 |
| Shreveport, LA | 62,152 | 84,627 | 12,000 | 89,000 | −  7,000 |
| Birmingham, AL | 126,388 | 158,223 | 11,000 | 168,000 | − 11,000 |

Source: *Data User News* (Bureau of the Census, United States Department of Commerce), October 1981 and 1990. Net migration figures derived by author.

tention on central cities, a different view emerges. Rapidly increasing black populations in these metropolitan areas (first- and second-generation centers) during the period 1940–1970 have made it virtually impossible for the central cities of these metropolitan areas to accommodate the diverse housing needs of this population and those of competing populations at the same time. Thus, during the seventies, although numerous ghetto centers experienced net outmigration from central cities, their suburban ring communities experienced net in-migration. The results of this process are highlighted in Table 3.7.

If the estimates are reasonably accurate, it becomes clear that two processes are at work. In New York, Philadelphia, Cleveland, and St. Louis, there has been a net loss of both blacks and whites from the metropolitan areas, reflecting the inability of these economies to provide the desired level of economic support. But in each instance, there was net in-migration to the suburban ring, although inadequate in volume to prevent a net loss from the metropolitan area. Nevertheless, with the exception of Houston, the scale of suburban movement in a set of predominately nonsouthern metropolitan areas

**Table 3.7    Net In- and Out-Migration Patterns within the Spatial Structure of Selected Metropolitan Areas: 1970–1980.**

| Ghetto Center | Central City Net Migration | Suburban Ring Net Migration |
|---------------|---------------------------|-----------------------------|
| New York | − 165,000 | +  43,000 |
| Newark | −  51,000 | +  50,000 |
| Philadelphia | − 125,000 | +  23,000 |
| Cleveland | −  91,000 | +  60,000 |
| Detroit | −  14,000 | +  15,000 |
| Chicago | −  93,000 | +  80,000 |
| St. Louis | −  91,000 | +  55,000 |
| Los Angeles | −  83,000 | + 157,000 |
| Washington | − 180,000 | + 194,000 |
| Baltimore | −  91,000 | +  44,000 |

Source: Estimates derived by author based on changes in size of population between 1970 and 1980.

exceeds that characterizing the leading net central city gainers. This fact reflects a difference in the stage of the mobility process that distinguishes ghetto centers on both a regional basis and age of the black community in developmental terms. Suburbanization represents the most recent stage of development and is essentially confined to first- and second-generation ghetto centers. Ghetto centers in the previously cited stage of development are beginning to manifest mobility characteristics that were previously associated with older central cities in general.

The lesser discrepancy in the magnitude of estimated net change in Detroit, Chicago, and Cleveland no doubt reflects the continuing central city in-migration to those centers, although on a much reduced scale. Under the circumstances, one can only speculate at this point about the distinguishing characteristics of movers involved in centripetal and centrifugal flows to selected ghetto centers. Implicitly these movement patterns, if they are largely characterized by suburban spillover, provide support for Deskins's[32] contention that the current stage is metropolitan ghettoization rather than the previously describe stage of central city ghettoization.

The latter stage of development reached its apex in first- and second-generation non-southern and southern border centers. This pattern is also evident in Atlanta, Miami, Richmond, and New Orleans. In most southern centers net outmigration from the suburban ring represents the modal pattern, reflecting both the more recent development of suburban ring communities in southern metropolitan areas and the presence of blacks in rural settings in metropolitan counties.

In some instances the recent rapid expansion of suburban developments in newer southern centers has led to black displacement; in other instances it has led to rural blacks in ring counties abandoning these locations for central city life. The latter pattern seems to be at work in southern counties characterized by absolute black population losses during the most recent decade when found in close proximity to counties characterized by black net in-migration. At this point, it is unclear what the role of small metropolitan centers and nonmetropolitan counties with small urban centers has been in attracting black migrants to their sphere of influence. It should be noted, however, that a small number of counties suffering absolute population losses were not located in close proximity to growth center counties. Nevertheless it is possible that smaller urban places in the South may become increasingly important as migration targets for interregional migrants.

## RECENT BLACK MIGRATION TRENDS

Black migration during the last quarter of the twentieth century began to exhibit patterns not previously observed. It had begun to slow in terms of base rates; the migrant volume had begun to subside, and the prevailing direction of migrant movement was becoming more ambiguous. Post-1970 migration behavior, while showing a break with tradition, was in fact what should have been anticipated at this stage in black migration history. By the latter part of the twentieth century, almost half of the nation's black population resided outside of the southern region, most of whom had sought refuge in the nation's largest urban centers.

This period after 1970 is viewed as a transitional one in terms of the establishment of nontraditional black cultural base. At the same time, the nation's economy was undergoing slow but continuous change. The observed economic changes would impact most harshly on poor and working-class persons residing in those urban centers to which blacks had continued to move between 1940 and 1970.

During the seventies, a reversal in black migratory behavior was observed.[33] Blacks residing in the Northeast began to seek refuge in the South. McHugh reports a large volume of black movement out of the states of New York, New Jersey, and Pennsylvania, places where the transition to postindustrialism had become most advanced. The movers from these states were most often drawn to North Carolina, South Carolina, Georgia, and Florida. The assumption is that they were essentially return movers who had linked up with kin in the area of origin, although there was a strong tendency for these migrants to settle in selected metropolitan areas.[34]

As the impact of the previously noted economic transition did not move at the same speed across the American manufacturing belt, urban centers in the Midwest did not feel the full impact of the transition before the late 1970s or the early 1980s. Thus return movement to the East South Central region did not parallel that to selected South Atlantic states. Now that two decades have passed since selected traditional migrant streams underwent major transformations, it is possible to begin to assess whether movements occurring during the 1970s represented a temporary aberration or a primary reorganization of black migratory patterns.

## Post-1980 Black Migration Patterns

The 1980s witnessed additional changes in the pattern of black migration observed during the previous decade. As recently as 1960 it was said that once blacks reached the "Promised Land," they had a strong tendency to remain there. Since 1980 the direction and volume of black migration has undergone a dramatic change. This change was first noted toward the end of the 1970s. At that time incipient evidence indicated that the South was receiving more black migrants than it was dispensing, but at that time it was uncertain if the evolving pattern represented a trend or trendlet. The evidence from the current population surveys of 1980–85 and 1990–95 and of the data produced by the U.S. Census of 1990 demonstrate clearly that the earlier data was an indication of an evolving trend. [35]

The Northeast and secondarily the Midwest became the primary dispensers of migrants. Later in the interval, the West, too, became a substantial dispenser of black migrants. Thus, the buildup of large black populations in large Northeast and Midwest urban centers over a period of two generations led to the development of a potentially large migrant pool. The economic conditions that evolved as an outgrowth of economic restructuring and the globalization of the economy established conditions that led to a reversal of migration streams.

In the interval 1985–90, the South was the destination of more than eight hundred thousand black migrants, while at the same time losing more than five hundred thousand to other regions, but mostly to the West.[36] The net gain to the South was more than three hundred thousand additional black residents. According to Frey,[37] this pattern continued during the first five years of the 1990s, when the volume of in-migration was estimated to be somewhat larger than that observed during the previous five years. The Northeast continues to represent the primary migrant source region, but the Midwest is currently dispensing numbers of migrants that bears greater similarity to the volume dispensed by the Northeast than it did earlier.

The combined forces of economic dislocation in the Northeast and Midwest and economic growth and changing social mores in the South have done much to fuel the reversal of migration patterns described here. Yet the matter is much more complex than it appears on the surface. For instance, were poor migrants more likely to be attracted to one set of destinations than nonpoor migrants, or were poor migrants likely to fit the description of linked migrants—that is, people moving into the households of relatives—than were nonpoor migrants. A number of researchers have recently begun to grapple with the above issues bearing on the makeup of migration streams.[38] Moreover, the employment of city patterns as opposed to metropolitan patterns are likely to reveal contradictory results since movers crossing a county boundary by moving from a central city to a suburb of that city qualifies to be counted as migrant. Thus, while large central cities that served as the original targets of black migration have most recently experienced net outmigration, the surrounding suburbs have often been the targets of net in-migration. When employing metropolitan data alone to reflect migration patterns, the underlying process of black suburbanization and central city decline are easily overlooked.

## THE IMPACT OF MIGRATION DECISIONS MADE BY SELECTED NONSOUTHERN CENTRAL RESIDENTS

Since most blacks at this stage in history reside in large central cities, the migration decisions that they make impact most strongly on the evolving black migration streams. It was recently noted that one-third of the black population, outside the South, resided in the twelve largest central cities in the nation.[39] With the exception of Milwaukee and San Diego, each of these were places experiencing net outmigration during the 1980s (Table 3.8). The estimates shown here demonstrate that selected nonsouthern cities that were the targets of blacks leaving the south through the 1960s had become net dispensers of black migrants. Blacks leaving these central cities were engaged in intraregional movements, interregional movements, and city-to-suburb movements.

**Table 3.8    The Black Net Migration Experience of the Nation's Largest Non-Southern American Cities during the 1980s.**

| Urban Centers | Estimates of Net Migration |
| --- | --- |
| New York | +  83,000 |
| Los Angeles | −  84,000 |
| Chicago | − 267,000 |
| Detroit | −  81,000 |
| Philadelphia | −  91,000 |
| San Francisco | −  18,000 |
| Newark | +   9,700 |
| Cleveland | −  49,000 |
| St. Louis | −  45,000 |
| Boston | +   4,300 |
| San Diego | +  16,000 |
| Milwaukee | +  25,000 |

Source: Estimates derived by the author based on changes in the size of the population between 1980 and 1990. New York, Newark, and Boston show positive net migration as a result of black immigrant flows from the Caribbean.

Large numbers of black migrants, responding to the economic downturn in rust belt cities, entered migration streams that would return them to the region of origin. Others were destined for smaller urban places within the same region, while still others moved from the central city to its suburbs. The latter move often resulted in the growth of a black metropolitan population within a specific metropolitan area, while at the same time its central city was showing a decline in its black population. But among the metropolitan areas that include the urban centers listed in Table 3.8, the volume of black movers destined for the suburbs was inadequate to prevent net losses from migration occurring in more than half of the centers listed in the table.[40] Persons leaving the above urban centers often encountered migration streams that directed them to their regions of origin. This pattern was already in evidence in the migration behavior exhibited by blacks in 1975–80. McHugh[41] demonstrated that New York State dispensed more than sixty thousand black migrants to the states of the South Atlantic division. More than half of these migrants were destined for Florida, North Carolina, and South Carolina. The largest share of these migrants were described as returnees. Most were destined for southern metropolitan areas, while others returned to the nonmetropolitan counties where they had formerly resided. The latter has been described as "homeplace migration" by Cromartie and Stack,[42] who go on to say, "When black individuals and families choose to leave cities in the North or West and migrate to the South, more often than not they follow well worn paths back to homeplaces or other locations where relatives have settled."

A number of secondary urban centers in the North and West served as primary targets of migrants leaving larger regional centers. While Chicago, New York, and Los Angeles were redistributing large numbers of blacks to selected southern urban centers, they were at the same time engaged in prompting intraregional moves. These intraregional migrants were observed to have outstripped migrants from more traditional migrant source regions. For instance, Milwaukee and Minneapolis–St. Paul were the recipients of a sizable black flow from Chicago, and Charlotte from New York City, while Las Vegas became a major destination of blacks leaving Los Angeles. Thus, nonsouthern intraregional flows had begun to take on greater importance in redistributing blacks, in some instances, to locations where they previously had only a modest presence. These, as well as a small number of additional places, constitute new migrant growth centers.

## NEW MIGRANT GROWTH CENTERS

As we enter the twenty-first century, what has apparently become more obvious is the evolution of a newer set of cities that have become targets of black migration. These new targets represent two distinct types of places: (1) intermediate-sized central cities outside the South that have long existed in the shadow of larger urban centers (i.e., Chicago, New York), the kind of places described earlier, and (2) a set of new urban growth centers in those parts of the South where economies are bustling. In the latter places, black central city growth usually outstrips black suburban growth, the inverse of the pattern that currently typifies growth in traditional migrant centers (Table 3.9). Table 3.9 illustrates both the level of net migration and the number of individuals who moved to the target center during the last five years of the decade.

**Table 3.9    Central Cities that Gained the Largest Number of Black Migrants in the 1980s.**

| Region | City | Net Gain | Resided Elsewhere in 1985 | 1990 Black Population |
|--------|------|----------|----------------------------|------------------------|
| West | San Diego | 16,000 | 25,000 | 104,000 |
| South | Charlotte | 16,000 | 15,000 | 126,000 |
| | Jacksonville | 5,000 | 22,000 | 160,000 |
| | Orlando | 10,000 | 7,400 | 44,000 |
| | Oklahoma City | 4,000 | 7,400 | 71,000 |
| Midwest | Milwaukee | 25,000 | 19,000 | 191,000 |
| | Minneapolis | 16,000 | 21,000 | 48,000 |
| Northeast | Boston | 4,300 | 17,000 | 147,000 |

Source: Social and Labor Force Characteristics of Black Persons: 1990 (Table 22), U.S. Bureau of the Census. Net gain represents the estimate of net in-migration over a ten-year period employing the national growth rate technique.

## THE ASSOCIATION BETWEEN IMMIGRATION AND CHANGING BLACK MIGRATION PATTERNS

Since 1970 immigrants to the United States from Asia, northern South America, and the Caribbean have steadily increased and currently constitute the lion's share of people entering the country from abroad. New immigrants have overwhelmingly chosen to settle in a few locations, with most choosing California, New York, Texas, Florida, Illinois, New Jersey, and Massachusetts as their destinations. In those states where new immigrants largely tend to be unskilled, it is said that they compete with American workers for low-end jobs. The influx of non-European origin immigrants to California is said to have stimulated whites to migrate elsewhere within the Pacific and Inter-Mountain region. Maharidge[43] contends that whites fear that California will soon become a state in which they no longer constitute the majority population and thus feel more comfortable by moving to states in which nonwhites constitute only a small minority in the population.

In California, where the largest number of new immigrants has settled, harsh human service policies have been introduced that are perceived to penalize new immigrants and thus discourage the current volume of flow. Clark[44] expresses doubts that the unskilled segment of the new immigrants population will be able to adapt to a rapidly changing high-tech, information-based economy and will subsequently swell the size of the underclass in the cities in which they choose to settle. Frey[45] and Roseman and Lee[46] have described the outmigration of native blacks from centers in which new immigrants have settled in large numbers (i.e., Los Angeles, New York) and suggest that these are adaptive moves made by poverty-level black migrants. Non-poverty-level black migrants, however, do not appear to be influenced by the possibility of competition with new immigrants.

The migration of blacks during the last half of the 1980s led to a redistribution away from the Northeast, the Midwest, and secondarily from the West. The South experienced major gains as a result of the reversal of traditional migration streams. A large share (≥50.0 percent) of the redistributed were moving to states from which they had originally migrated. Some, according to Stack,[47] were disgruntled with life in the urban north and yearned for what has been described as the "homeplace," generally situated in a series of high-poverty nonmetropolitan counties. Others were moving to the South for the first time. These were people who were generally better educated, some who had retired from professional jobs in the North. The better-educated and nonpoor segment of the black movers were more likely to settle in large urban centers (e.g., Atlanta, Houston, Dallas), intermediate-sized urban centers (e.g., Orlando, Charlotte, Jacksonville), and smaller southern metropolitan areas. More and more blacks who have never lived in the South are choosing to establish residence there.

Frey,[48] utilizing recently released Census Bureau estimates (1990–1996), demonstrates that the trends described here are still under way. Most new migration growth centers that evolved during the eighties continue to attract black migrants, although a few seem to have cooled down. The South continues to represent the growth pole of black migration, but net migration from poor nonmetropolitan counties in the South appears to continue to follow traditional migrant streams outside the region. Black migration today is much more complex than it was at midcentury, and attempts to explain these changes will require greater effort. But just as the South represented the core region of black settlement at the turn of the twentieth century, it will continue to perform that role as we enter the twenty-first century.

## CONCLUSION

A brief assessment of the movement pattern of black Americans focusing on twentieth-century movements illustrates one facet of economic change on the lives of the nation's largest racial minority. From 1910 to 1980, the pattern of black population distribution has undergone major change as it has shifted from a regional concentration in the South to a national distribution in which each of the nation's major regions has a significant black presence. The movement has not been uniform, however, but has been associated with major changes in national economic development.

Two major wars and changes in the structure and technology of southern agriculture provided the primary impetus for many of the moves. The pre-1910 black population was overwhelmingly southern and rural, such that more than six hundred contiguous counties, plus a few others, evolved as the cultural hearth of black America. During the twentieth century, the intensity of settlement in nonurban hearth counties continuously declined, although they have remained a seedbed for a national black population. Now, more than two generations later, secondary regional clusters have evolved that are almost totally urban, having only limited contact with the South. Only a minority of people in the North and West today were born in the South, but at the same time a growing share of the South's current black population was born outside the region.

The timing and direction of movement have led to a staged evolution in the national settlement pattern. A national system of ghetto centers has emerged as the most obvious element of recent black migration history. That system was essentially confined to the Northeast and North Central region during the first generation of movement. In the second generation, it expanded to include major urban centers in the West and secondary centers in the North. During the more recent period, the pattern of urban residence in the metropolitan South took on many characteristics of ghetto centers elsewhere. By 1980, the national network had become coextensive with the location of large and intermediate metropolitan areas.

Much of what has transpired during the first two generations of movement has been well documented, although much of that work has focused on interregional flows at the expense of intraregional and intermetropolitan flows. More important, an attempt has been made here to illustrate the importance of structural changes in the U.S. economy on the character, volume, and direction of black population movement. It is generally concluded that the United States developed into a postindustrial economy sometime after World War II. Not until the seventies, however, did black migration patterns first begin to reflect this change. Thus, a third generation of black migration got under way and is already beginning to modify the settlement system that emerged after 1910.

The principal dimensions of settlement that are beginning to emerge, reflecting both a break with the past as well as a continuation of the past, are the following:

1. Rapid suburbanization in the larger first- and second-generation ghetto centers
2. Net outmigration from the core cities in a number of first- and second-generation ghetto centers
3. Absolute population decline in selected first- and second-generation centers
4. Rapid population growth in large and intermediate-sized southern ghetto centers, as well as in intermediate-sized centers in the West and Midwest
5. The continued net outmigration from nonmetropolitan counties of the cultural hearth
6. The emergence of a strong back-to-the-South movement

Many of these changes simply represent a late response to general changes that have been under way for some time.

This essay has not explicitly grappled with the complex problems associated with the status change of blacks during this century. Implicitly, however, that is what this discussion is all about. Migration simply represents one strategy used to minimize the level of status inequality. There is little question that this strategy has produced pronounced reductions in the level of inequality, but a significant gap continues to remain. Migration can only be expected to reduce status inequality within limits established by the larger society.

Black migration and movement patterns will continue to be dominated by economic considerations with social considerations playing a secondary role. What we learned recently is that poor blacks and nonpoor blacks often choose disparate migration paths. These differences often manifest themselves in the choice of city and suburban moves, as well as moves to metropolitan versus nonmetropolitan counties. Thus, some movers exhibit characteristics of refugees, while others have been described by Shimkin[49] as purposeful movers. We have essentially overlooked the effects of gender-based migration decisions on patterns of black movement. These have been alluded to by researchers concerned with welfare migration. Although it has not been conclusively demonstrated that differential welfare payments led families with dependent children to choose one set of destinations over another, with the recent enactment of welfare reform legislation, gender-based migration decisions are likely to receive renewed emphasis.

Finally, has black migration, in the most recent interval, led to the evolution of new spatial patterns that differ from historical patterns? The one obvious change that has grown out of more recent migration decisions is settlement in intermediate-sized places where prior to 1980 blacks were only present in small numbers. What we do not know at this time is where fourth-generation ghetto centers are being formed or whether some combination of ethnic-based and non-ethnic-based communities are coming into existence. Simply put, are new movement patterns leading to greater or lessened levels of racial residential segregation or having no effect at all?

## NOTES

1. Lerone Bennett, *Before the Mayflower* (Chicago: Johnson, 1967).

2. Robert W. Fogel and Stanley L. Engerman, *Time on the Cross* (Boston: Little, Brown, 1974).

3. Kenneth F. Kiple and Virginia H. King, *Another Dimension to Black Diaspora* (New York: Cambridge University Press, 1981).

4. Daniel M. Johnson and Rex R. Campbell, *Black Migration in America* (Durham, N.C.: Duke University Press, 1981).

5. Wesley C. Calef and Howard J. Nelson, "Distribution of Negro Population in the United States," *Geographical Review* 46 (January 1956): 82–97.

6. John Fraser Hart, "The Changing Distribution of the American Negro," *Annals of the Association of American Geographers* 50 (September 1960): 242–266.

7. G. M. Lewis, "The Distribution of the Negro in the Conterminous United States," *Geography* 54 (November 1969): 410–418.

8. Richard L. Morrill and O. Fred Donaldson, "Geographical Perspectives on the History of Black America," *Economic Geography* 48 (January 1972): 1–23.

9. Daniel O. Price, *Changing Characteristics of the Negro Population* (Washington, D.C.: U.S. Bureau of the Census, 1969).

10. Lewis, "The Distribution of the Negro."

11. Johnson and Campbell, *Black Migration in America*.

12. Hart, "The Changing Distribution."

13. John Kellog, "Negro Urban Clusters in the Post-Bellum South," *Geographical Review* 67 (July 1977): 310–321.

14. Florette Henri, *Black Migration: Movement North 1890–1920* (Garden City, N.J.: Anchor Press/Doubleday, 1975).

15. Henry S. Shryock, Jr., *Population Mobility within the United States* (Chicago: University of Chicago Press, 1964).

16. Gunnar Myrdal, *An American Dilemma* (New York: Pantheon, 1972); Robert C. Weaver, *The Negro Ghetto* (New York: Harcourt, Brace, 1948).

17. Henri, *Black Migration*.

18. Paul F. Coe, "The Nonwhite Population Surge to Our Cities," *Land Economics* 35 (August 1959): 195–210.

19. Neil Fligstein, *Going North: Migration of Blacks and Whites from the South* (New York: Academic Press, 1981), 148.

20. Calef and Nelson, "Distribution of Negro Population."

21. Dimitri B. Shimkin, "Black Migration and the Struggle for Equity: A Hundred Year Record," in *Migration and Social Welfare*, ed. James W. Eaton (New York: National Association of Social Workers, 1971).

22. C. Horace Hamilton, "The Negro Leaves the South," *Demography* 1 (1964): 273–295.

23. Brinley Thomas, *Migration and Economic Growth* (Oxford: Oxford University Press, 1973).

24. Larry H. Long, "How the Racial Composition of Cities Changes," *Land Economics* 51 (August 1975): 258–267.

25. Donald R. Deskins, Jr., "Morphogenesis of a Black Ghetto," *Urban Geography* 2 (April–June 1981): 95–114; and Williard T. Chow, "The Context of Redevelopment in Oakland," *Urban Geography* 2 (January–March 1981): 41–63.

26. Brian J. L. Berry, "Short-Term Housing Cycles in a Dualistic Metropolis," in *The Social Economy of Cities*, ed. Gary Gappert and Harold M. Rose (Beverly Hills: Sage, 1975).

27. Coe, "The Nonwhite Population Surge."

28. James B. Kenyon, "Spatial Associations in the Integration of the American City," *Economic Geography* 52 (October 1976): 292.

29. Larry H. Long and Daphne Spain, "Racial Succession in Individual Housing Units," *Current Population Reports*, Special Studies, Series P-23, no. 71 (September 1978).

30. John Moland, Jr., "The Black Population," in *Nonmetropolitan American in Transition*, ed. Amos H. Hawley and Sara M. Mazie (Chapel Hill: University of North Carolina Press, 1981), 477.

31. Kevin E. McHugh, "Black Migration Reversal in the United States," *Geographical Review* 77 (April 1987): 171–182; John Cromartie and Carol B. Stack, "Reinterpretation of Black Return and Non-Return Migration," *Geographical Review* 79 (July 1989): 297–310.

32. Deskins, "Morphogenesis of a Black Ghetto."

33. Johnson and Campbell, *Black Migration in America*.

34. McHugh, "Black Migration Reversal."

35. Cromartie and Stack, "Reinterpretation of Black Return"; William H. Frey, "The New Geography of Population Shifts: Trend Toward Balkanization," in *The State of the Union: America in the 1990s*, vol. 2: *Social Trends*, ed. Reynolds Farley (New York: Russell Sage Foundation, 1995); William H. Frey, "Black Movement to the South and Regional Concentration of the Races," *Research Reports*, report no. 9412, Population Studies Center, University of Michigan, 1998; Seong Woo Lee and Curtis C. Roseman, "Independent and Linked Migrants: Determinants of African American Interstate Migration," *Growth and Change* 28 (Summer 1997): 309–334.

36. James H. Johnson, Jr., and David M. Grant, "Post-1980 Black Population Redistribution Trends in the United States," *Southeastern Geographer* 37 (May 1997): 1–19.

37. Frey, "Black Movement to the South."

38. K. Bruce Newbold, "Race and Primary Return, and Onward Interstate Migration," *Professional Geographer* 4 (1997): 1–14; Curtis C. Roseman and Seong Woo Lee, "Linked and Independent African American Migration from Los Angeles," *Professional Geographer* 50 (May 1998): 204–214.

39. Frank H. Wilson, "The Changing Distribution of the African American Population in the United States," *Urban League Review* 15 (Winter 1991–92): 53–74.

40. Frey, "The New Geography of Population Shifts"; Johnson and Grant, "Post-1980 Black Population."

41. McHugh, "Black Migration Reversal."

42. Cromartie and Stack, "Reinterpretation of Black Return," 309.

43. Dale Maharidge, *The Coming White Minority: California's Eruptions and the Nation's Future* (New York: Times Books, 1996).

44. William A. V. Clark, "Mass Migration and Local Outcomes: Is International Migration to the United States Creating a New Urban Underclass?" *Urban Studies* 35 (1998): 371–383.

45. William H. Frey, "Immigration Impacts on Internal Migration of the Poor: 1990 Evidence for U.S. States," *International Journal of Population Geography* (1995): 51–67.

46. Roseman and Lee, "Linked and Independent African American Migration."

47. Carol Stack, *Call to Home: African Americans Reclaim the Rural South* (New York: Basic Books, 1996).

48. Frey, "Black Movement to the South."

49. Shimkin, "Black Migration."

## 4

# Mexican Americans

## Daniel D. Arreola

The ancestors of Mexican Americans were the first Europeans to settle what is now the southwestern United States. A majority of their descendants still reside in the borderlands that stretch from Texas to California.

The Mexican American minority is the second largest in the United States and its numbers are growing more rapidly than the greater population. The minority today is more urban than the general population. In 1990, approximately nine of every ten Mexican Americans lived in cities, with Los Angeles being the largest single home of Mexican Americans in the United States. Cities such as San Antonio and El Paso are predominantly Mexican American.

This chapter examines the geographic evolution of the Mexican American population from the minority's origins in the borderlands to patterns of immigration, population distribution, landscape, and social characteristics. Since most of this population lives in cities, the geographic patterns of urban Mexican Americans are stressed.

## ORIGINS IN THE BORDERLANDS

Mexican American populations had their origins in the borderlands that stretch from California to Texas. Between 1598 and 1821, parts of California, Arizona, New Mexico, Colorado, and Texas were settled by Spanish-speaking peoples from New Spain, present-day Mexico. After 1821, portions of this region became part of the Republic of Mexico, and each of the settled areas developed its own regional identity. Since 1848, the major settled areas have come under Anglo influence, both political and cultural. Today, these five states remain the principal subregions where the Mexican American people are located. The transformation of these areas from Spanish outposts to Mexican provinces to Mexican American subregions represents the planting, germination, and rooting of Mexican American culture in the United States. The origins of many of the features associated with Mexican American culture from place names to architecture and numerous social customs can be traced to this early period of settlement in the borderlands.

### Patterns of Settlement

The initial settlement of the borderlands was in New Mexico (Fig. 4.1). This colonization followed the successful sixteenth-century settlement of the mining and livestock fron-

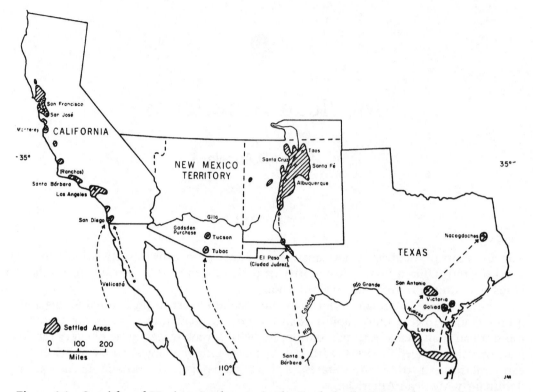

**Figure 4.1    Spanish and Mexican Settlement in the Borderlands. Source: Reprinted from Nostrand, *Annals of the Association of American Geographers* 60 (December 1970): 645, Figure 1, with the permission of the Association of American Geographers.**

tier of northern Mexico. In 1598, Juan de Oñate guided colonists to the upper drainage of the Rio Grande Valley to settle among the Pueblo Indians. In 1610, Santa Fe was founded as the provincial capital and principal center of the region. Missions and presidios were established between Taos and Socorro and downriver at Paso del Norte near present El Paso. Albuquerque was founded in 1706 following a Pueblo Indian revolt that temporarily forced the Spanish out of the northern settlements. At the close of the Spanish period in 1821, most of the borderlands population resided in New Mexico. A road connecting New Mexico with Chihuahua in northern Mexico was the principal link between the frontier and Mexico City farther south.[1]

Southern Arizona was a second region of Spanish settlement in the borderlands (Fig. 4.1). As in New Mexico, the Spanish presence in Arizona was an extension of a settlement effort that originated in Mexico. During the 1600s, Jesuit missionaries penetrated Mexico's northwest, and the few settlements established in Arizona were the northernmost reach of this frontier. Southern Arizona became known as Pimería Alta, or the upper Pima Indian area. The most successful settlements—the mission at San Xavier del Bac (1700) and the presidios at Tubac (1752) and Tucson (1776)—were situated along the Santa Cruz River. Settlements were extended to the San Pedro Valley to the east and for a short time on the Colorado River near present Yuma. In both areas, Indian hostilities prohibited successful colonization. In the Santa Cruz Valley, Apache raiding continued to be a threat to populations well into the nineteenth century. These conditions made difficult any firm footing in Pimería Alta where populations never exceeded two thousand during the Spanish and Mexican periods.[2]

Texas became a third area of Spanish settlement in the borderlands (Fig. 4.1). Colonization was prompted by the desire to confront French influence in the lower Mississippi River valley. Settlements in Texas were also an extension of the northern Mexico mining and livestock frontier. Three major mission-presidio complexes were founded in the Texas area: (1) Nacogdoches west of the Sabine River in 1716, (2) San Antonio situated between the central plateau and the gulf coastal plain in 1718, and (3) La Bahía near present-day Victoria in 1722. This last settlement was relocated to the lower San Antonio River near present Goliad in 1749. Another community, Laredo, was founded in 1755 on the north bank of the Rio Grande in the province of Nuevo Santander. By the late 1700s, San Antonio had become the major provincial settlement of Spanish Tejas (Texas). Road connections with northern Mexico and few Indian hostilities allowed for permanence in the Texas borderlands. By 1850, some fourteen thousand Mexican Americans populated the region.[3]

California was the last of the borderland outposts to witness Spanish and Mexican settlement (Fig. 4.1). Although explorations and coastal reconnoitering had taken place along the Pacific coast as early as 1542, permanent settlement did not commence for over two centuries. The threat of Russian and British intrusion into California finally led to its settlement in 1769. In that year, land and sea parties converged on San Diego where a mission-presidio complex was built. Within twenty years, additional settlements were established at the provincial capital of Monterey (1770) and in San Francisco (1776) and Santa Barbara (1782 and 1786). By the early 1800s, a chain of twenty missions connected the settlements of coastal California, including two civil communities founded at San Jose (1777) and Los Angeles (1781), the latter via overland colonization from Sonora, Mexico, by way of southern Arizona. Sea and land connections between the California settlements and an ocean link to Mexico ensured this region's viability. By 1850, over nine thousand Californios inhabited this part of the borderlands frontier.[4]

## Settlement Institutions

Spanish settlement in the borderlands, as elsewhere in the New World, was dictated by the Laws of the Indies (1573). These legal codes set forth in theory how new lands should be settled. As a result of practical problems encountered in each settlement area, not all regions of Spanish Mexican settlement complied precisely with these laws. The institutions that developed, however, were remarkably similar from one end of the borderlands to another.

The mission and presidio were the initial frontier institutions. The mission was, in essence, an extension of the religious agreement made by Spain with the Catholic Church to convert Indian populations. Missions were usually established where Indian populations were concentrated. In the borderlands, both Jesuit and Franciscan religious orders were involved in mission founding, although at different times and in different regions. The priests converted Indians to the Catholic faith, with varying degrees of success. In addition, Indians were trained to the ways of the Spaniard and employed as laborers to make the missions viable. They erected buildings, dug irrigation ditches, planted and harvested crops, cared for livestock, and performed work essential to the success of a mission (Fig. 4.2).

**Figure 4.2    Mission San Buenaventura in Ventura, California. Some colonial settlements like this one survive in the modern era as reminders of the Spanish Mexican cultural heritage of the borderlands. Source: Photo by author.**

The presidio was a military settlement or garrison. Presidios were sometimes founded in conjunction with missions. Often, they were located at strategic points along a line of transport or situated to defend a mission from native or foreign attack. Many missions and presidios were abandoned as the settlement frontier fluctuated. Some persisted and became centers of population. The presidio in Tucson, Arizona, for example, survived as a settlement through the Mexican period and today is an American city.[5]

The pueblo or town was a third Spanish settlement institution brought to the borderlands. While the mission and presidio were religious and military, respectively, the pueblo was a civil community. According to the Laws of the Indies, the civil settlement was the climax institution, whereas missions and presidios were, theoretically, only temporary frontier settlements. Pueblos were to be situated on a grant of land four square leagues, or approximately forty-two square miles. The center of the pueblo included a plaza, surrounded by government offices and a parish church. A rectangular grid of streets emanating from the plaza accommodated houses. Surrounding these were lands for cultivation, pasture, and woodland. The pueblos became major nuclei of population, attracting merchants, artisans, and farmers. Los Angeles, California, and San Antonio, Texas, for example, were founded as pueblos.[6]

A final means of settlement introduced by the Spaniards to the borderlands was the land grant. This form of settlement persisted in the border region during the Mexican period after 1821. Parcels of land were granted to private individuals. Land grants were allocated as an economic incentive to settle areas and make them productive. These lands were transformed into livestock *ranchos* where cattle and sheep became the economic mainstay of the settlement unit as in California and Texas. In other areas, where sufficient water could be controlled for irrigation, land grants became farmsteads where wheat and corn were cultivated, as in New Mexico. Today, many land grants remain as legal definitions of property in the borderlands. They persist also as place names and stand as examples of the legacy of Spanish and Mexican imprints in the border region.[7]

## The Hispanic American Borderland

After the United States–Mexico war, much of the borderland became U.S. territory. By the Treaty of Guadalupe Hidalgo, signed in 1848, many resident Mexicans of these borderlands became Mexican Americans. After the Gadsden Purchase in 1854, Arizona south of the Gila River became U.S. territory as well.

In 1850, there were perhaps eighty thousand Mexican Americans.[8] In a short time, the rapid influx of Anglos began to transform the borderlands into an American province, culturally as well as politically. The proportion of Mexican Americans to Anglos continued to decrease during the latter nineteenth century as the American population increased.

Today, the preponderance of the Mexican American minority resides in the five southwestern states that have been called the Hispanic American borderland.[9] Parts of California, Arizona, New Mexico, and Texas are the major cores of this province, but a portion of southern Colorado is also part of the region. These areas represent the early nuclei of Spanish and Mexican settlement and expanded areas of the earliest colonizations. Many of the Mexican immigrants who have entered the United States since the early twentieth century also inhabit parts of this region.

Although Mexican Americans are considered the dominant Hispanic group in this province, there are distinct regional identities. This differentiation originated with the varied periods of Spanish Mexican settlement in the borderlands and the development of separate self-referents. In Texas and California during the Mexican period, the appellations *Tejano* and *Californio* were used, respectively. In New Mexico and parts of southern Colorado, many of the Hispanic people refer to themselves as Hispano or Spanish American, not Mexican American. This subgroup claims ancestry from the earliest Spanish colonists of the region and considers itself culturally distinct from the Mexican groups that constitute the majority of the Mexican American population, such as the Tejanos in Texas.[10]

In the 1970s, *Mexican* was not only the self-referent used by Mexico-born persons in the borderlands but also the prevailing term among the native-born in much of Arizona and eastern Colorado. The primary self-referent in Texas was *Latin American* or *Latin*. In California both *Mexican American* and *Chicano* were primary terms, the latter popular among the young.[11] Today, these two terms especially have spread to other areas of the borderlands, from Arizona to Texas.

Other differences testify to the diversity of the Mexican American population in the borderlands. Foodways, religious affiliation, Spanish language retention, and music are just some of the categories that exhibit regional variation. The Hispanic American borderland is certainly the hearth area that has given rise to and continues to nourish the majority of Mexican Americans, but it is also a region that is changing as the groups that occupy it change.

## IMMIGRANTS AND IMMIGRATION

Immigration has been and continues to be an important contributor to the Mexican American population. From the middle of the nineteenth century to the present, Mexican immigrants have been an important source of labor north of the border. Their availability helped make possible the economic development of agriculture and industry in the southwestern United States, and their continued immigration, both legal and illegal, provides a labor pool to agriculture, manufacturing, and the service sector of urban economies throughout the Hispanic American borderland and beyond.

### An Immigrant Tradition

Mexican labor migration to the United States dates to the middle of the nineteenth century. The early Mexican migrants foreshadowed the coming of "wetbacks," "*braceros*," and others in the twentieth century. Together these streams have been part of a larger historical process of labor scarcity in the United States and a surplus of underemployed labor in Mexico. Scholars have argued that there has been a long tradition of a migrant subculture in Mexico, marginal populations that moved seasonally with economic opportunity.[12] When opportunity emerged in the United States, migrant Mexicans moved to satisfy the labor demand. They moved slowly at first as specific economic circumstances pulled migrants to regional nodes during the nineteenth century, then en masse during the twentieth century with the swelling of population in Mexico, changes in transport technology on both sides of the border, and the development of the southwestern United States.

Mexican immigration in this century has occurred in two distinct waves. The first took place from approximately 1900 to 1930, after which the Great Depression reduced the flow. The second was initiated by the war economy of the 1940s and continues largely undiminished to this day. Between 1910 and 1930, Mexican immigrants to the United States averaged 30,462 per year, with the greatest number (87,648) coming in 1924 and the lowest number (10,954) entering in 1913. Between 1961 and 1984, Mexico was the major sender of immigrants to the United States with nearly 1.4 million.[13]

The mining frontiers of the western United States were the first major attraction for Mexican migrant labor. Mexican laborers from the northern states of Sonora, Chihuahua, Durango, and Zacatecas responded to the demand for workers in California, Nevada, and Arizona.[14] Practically every mining community in the West had a Mexican district. Jerome and Bisbee, Arizona, for example, were copper mining towns where Mexican labor was used from the late nineteenth century to the peak of the production years just before the Depression. The towns became major destinations for Mexican immigrants and redistribution points for migration to other parts of the West. Clifton-Morenci, also in Arizona, is a copper mining town still and chiefly populated by Mexican Americans.

Railroads became the primary means for dispersing Mexican migrants in the United States. The rails bridged the expanses of the West and effectively shortened distances between population centers. In 1884, El Paso became connected by rail to Los Angeles and Chicago, and to Chihuahua and Mexico City. In the following decades, Nogales, Arizona, was linked by rail to Hermosillo, Sonora, and San Antonio and Corpus Christi were joined to Monterrey, Nuevo León, by way of Laredo. Spur lines, like capillaries, grew from these main arteries and brought Mexican migrants everywhere the railroad went. By 1930, colonies of Mexican migrants could be found in nearly every town and city along the rail

routes. The railroads were also conduits to the inner cities where migrants could be recruited by contractors who sought other types of labor.[15]

The economic development of the Southwest was facilitated by the northward drift
of Mexicans. Railroads integrated the Southwest into the nation's industrial economy,
and Mexican labor became the means for factory and mining employment as well as railroad construction and maintenance. When federal legislation encouraging western irrigation projects was passed in 1902, Mexican labor again proved important to the success
of citrus and cotton cultivation in California, Arizona, and the lower Rio Grande Valley
in Texas. The mobility of Mexican labor likewise became vital to the beet sugar industry in Colorado, Kansas, and Nebraska and to the expansion of truck farming in southern California, Arizona, and Texas.[16]

The Depression of the 1930s slowed the flow of Mexican migrants to the United
States. High unemployment north of the border initiated a reverse movement of Mexican migrants back to Mexico, including forced repatriations.[17] From 1931 to 1943, an average of 2,013 Mexicans per year migrated to the United States, representing a considerable ebbing of the previous twenty-year flow. In 1942, the American government
instituted a contract farm labor agreement with Mexico known as the Bracero Program.
Under this agreement, Mexican laborers were transported to agricultural areas in this
country to bolster the labor shortage brought on by World War II. The program served
agricultural interests well since farmers were supplied with a steady and inexpensive
source of labor. The Bracero Program also benefited Mexican migration. It pointed the
way to *el norte* (the north, or United States) and provided a view of the economic opportunities that awaited legal and illegal migrants to this country.

### Closing the "Golden Door"

In recent times, the migration of Mexicans to the United States has become a headline
issue that is especially acute during election years when politicians and others stump the
"Mexican problem." While the numbers of legal entrants have been reduced, undocumented immigrants continue to migrate to the United States. The termination of the
Bracero Program in 1964 and the quotas set for legal immigration changed the circumstances of Mexican immigration. Illegal immigration grew as a consequence of the restrictions of legal entrance. The apprehensions of Mexican illegals rose from 55,000 in
1965 to 90,000 the next year and to 200,000 by 1969. These numbers climbed to 710,000
in 1974 and 978,000 in 1979.[18]

In 1986, the Immigration and Reform and Control Act (IRCA) allowed amnesty to a
large number of illegal or undocumented immigrants. Some 1.8 million people applied
for legalization under the regular IRCA program, and an additional 1.3 million applied
under the special agricultural workers program. The majority of IRCA applicants were
Mexican, about 70 percent of the regular applicants and almost 82 percent of the special
agricultural applicants. In 1991 alone, some 893,000 Mexican applicants were granted
permanent resident status.[19]

The illegal Mexican immigrant situation has received much publicity in the borderlands and across the country. Newspapers, magazines, and television have reported count-
less times on the immigrant dilemma, and words such as *mojado* (wetback or illegal immigrant), *coyote* (illegal immigrant smuggler), and *la migra* (the Immigration and
Naturalization Service [INS]) have become part of media language. The situation has also

become heavily politicized. A frequently heard argument against illegal Mexican immigration is its alleged tendency to depress wages and increase unemployment. Undocumented or illegal Mexicans are often found performing low-skilled tasks shunned by American workers. The fact that Mexicans have little difficulty finding these jobs in the United States might suggest that they do not displace American labor to any great extent. Also, it must be remembered that illegal Mexicans do not, by themselves, depress wages. Rather, employers offer pay scales well below what U.S. citizens might accept if they were willing to work these low-skilled jobs, and illegal Mexicans and others fill the labor demand. As in other periods of American immigrant history, public pressure is usually directed against the migrant who is merely seeking to better his or her livelihood. Rarely is attention focused on the employer who hires the migrant. If illegal Mexican migration to the United States were stopped completely, one result might be higher prices for goods and services now produced by illegal workers.

A second charge against illegal Mexican immigrants is that they "freeload" on community services. This practice has not been well documented, yet the evidence suggests the contrary. Undocumented Mexican workers pay state and local taxes and must have federal income and social security taxes deducted from their earnings if they are paid a salary. Field studies suggest that illegal Mexicans make very little use of social services beyond public schools for their children who, if born here, are entitled as citizens to public education. In California and Texas, for example, undocumented Mexicans are estimated to have used public assistance services, yet they have contributed many times the amount annually to the support of such services.[20] Also, researchers have indicated that many undocumented immigrants are only here temporarily and ultimately return to Mexico. Their use of local services in many cases is occasional, whereas they contribute greatly to a fund that benefits the total population.

The total number of undocumented Mexicans in the United States is unknown. Mexico was estimated in 1992 to be the country of origin for 1.3 million undocumented immigrants, nearly 40 percent of all estimated illegals.[21] Published estimates are usually based on the apprehension of illegal aliens. These estimates may be misleading, and the basis for them varies widely among sources. Undocumented Mexican immigrants in the United States are usually located in the same areas where Mexican American populations are highest. Although illegals are likely to be in rural and suburban areas as well, they tend to concentrate in cities because Mexican American districts provide cultural familiarity and familial or friendship ties, and because jobs are more plentiful in cities. Ultimately, it is job opportunity that attracts the undocumented immigrant. Industries that often employ Mexican illegals include apparel, furniture, manufacturing, and food processing; service sector occupations in restaurants-eateries and commercial-residential cleaning are also known to be employment sheds. The INS is known to raid these industries frequently, round up illegals, and return them to Mexico. Studies have shown, however, that apprehended illegals often find their way back to similar types of employment.[22]

## A DEMOGRAPHIC PORTRAIT

The 1990 census designated Mexican Americans part of the Hispanic-origin population. The Hispanic-origin population numbered 22.3 million and included Puerto Rican, Cuban, Central and South American, Dominican, and "Other Hispanic" as well as Mexican. Mexican Americans numbered 13.5 million, or 60 percent of the Hispanic-origin group.[23] In 1980, the census counted 8.7 million people of Mexican origin or descent.[24] The difference suggests that the Mexican American population increased 4.8 million, or almost 55 percent, between 1980 and 1990. While these figures may reflect an undercount of Mexican Americans in 1980, they reveal the growth of the Mexican American population, now the second largest minority group behind African Americans.[25]

The Mexican American population is largely concentrated in the borderlands, yet areas outside this hearth region house significant numbers. The population as a whole is young, characterized by large families and rapid growth.

## Population Distribution

The Mexican American population in the borderlands totaled 11.2 million in 1990 (Table 4.1). California ranked highest in the nation with 6.1 million Mexican Americans, followed by Texas with 3.8 million. Arizona, New Mexico, and Colorado each counted less than one million Mexican Americans. Mexican Americans are located in four regional concentrations outside the borderlands: the Midwest, especially Illinois and Michigan; the West, particularly Washington; the South, focused on Florida; and the Northeast, chiefly New York (Table 4.1).

The map of Mexican American population distribution makes immediate how this pattern is tilted to the Southwest (Fig. 4.3). The borderland states accounted for 83 percent of all Mexican Americans in 1990. This percentage distribution has not changed significantly from 1980, although the absolute number of Mexican Ameri-

**Table 4.1    Mexican Americans by Region and Leading States, 1980 and 1990.**

| Region | 1990[a] | % Distribution | 1980[b] | % Distribution |
|--------|---------|----------------|---------|----------------|
| Borderlands | 11,237,325 | 83.3 | 7,227,339 | 82.7 |
| CA | 6,118,996 | | 3,637,466 | |
| TX | 3,890,820 | | 2,752,487 | |
| AZ | 616,195 | | 396,410 | |
| NM | 328,836 | | 233,772 | |
| CO | 282,478 | | 207,204 | |
| Midwest | 1,153,296 | 8.5 | 820,218 | 9.4 |
| IL | 623,688 | | 408,325 | |
| MI | 138,312 | | 112,183 | |
| West | 477,618 | 3.5 | 260,801 | 3.0 |
| WA | 155,864 | | 81,112 | |
| South | 452,703 | 3.4 | 344,305 | 3.9 |
| FL | 161,499 | | 79,392 | |
| Northeast | 174,996 | 1.3 | 87,776 | 1.0 |
| NY | 93,244 | | 29,500 | |
| Total U.S. | 13,495,938 | 100.0 | 8,740,439 | 100.0 |

Source: [a]U.S. Bureau of the Census, *1990 Census of Population and Housing*, Summary Tape File 1A.
[b]U.S. Bureau of the Census, *Census of Population: 1980, Persons of Spanish Origin by State* (Washington, D.C.: 1982).

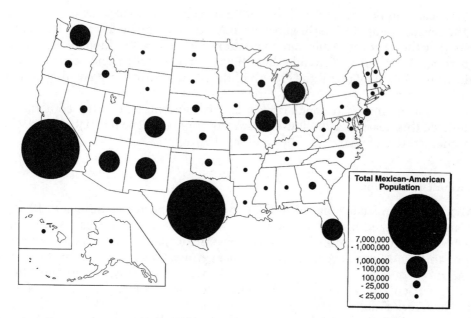

**Figure 4.3    Mexican Origin Population in the United States, 1990. Source: Compiled by author from U.S. Bureau of the Census, *1990 Census of Population and Housing*, Summary Tape File 1A.**

cans who reside in borderland states increased by some four million (Table 4.1). In the Midwest and South, Mexican Americans have also increased their presence despite losing some ground as a percentage of the total distribution. In the Northeast and West, both absolute numbers and percentages of the distribution increased from 1980 to 1990 (Table 4.1).

The absolute and percentage gains by regions notwithstanding, the concentration of Mexican Americans remains skewed to the Southwest and West of the nation. Figure 4.4 reveals the density of Mexican Americans by county and reinforces the dominance of this population in borderland counties, especially Texas. In 1990, only three counties outside Texas had greater than half of their population Mexican American: Imperial County (California), Santa Cruz County (Arizona), and Doña Ana County (New Mexico). Along the Texas border, no fewer than thirty-two counties were greater than half Mexican American population, and twenty of these were more than 70 percent Mexican ancestry.[26]

Economic opportunity first brought Mexicans to the Upper Midwest during World War I. Railroads, steel mills, and meat packing houses provided employment to these immigrants. The industries continued to draw immigrants during World War II as migrants established large permanent populations in the industrial cities of the Midwest. Unlike the Mexican migrants who moved to the cities of the Upper Midwest, Mexican American populations in the West had their origins in rural and small-town settlements. As miners, livestock herders, and agriculturalists, Mexican and Mexican Americans migrated to these areas when economic activities created a demand for their labor in the second half of the nineteenth century. Agricultural labor, again, was in high demand during the twentieth century, and Mexican migrant laborers largely filled this need. Over

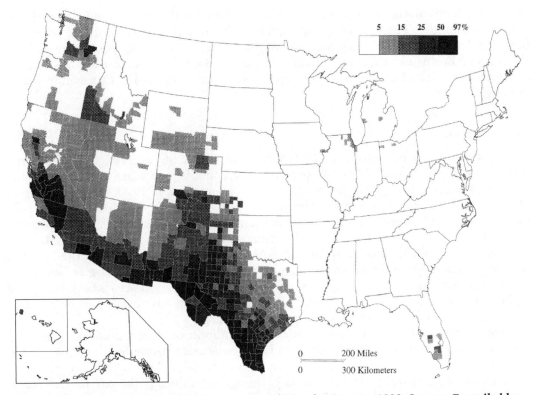

**Figure 4.4    Percentage Mexican American Population by County, 1990. Source: Compiled by T. M. Haverluk from U.S. Bureau of the Census, *1990 Census of Population and Housing*, Summary Tape File 3C, after Daniel D. Arreola and Terrence W. Haverluk, "Mexikanische Amerikaner," *Geographische Rundschau* 48 (April 1996): 213–219.**

time, temporary rural centers developed services that catered to Mexicans, and permanent populations became established. The Yakima Valley and parts of southeastern Washington, as well as the fertile Willamette Valley of Oregon, have been major agricultural districts that have accommodated Mexican migrant labor, creating satellite communities far from the borderland states (Fig. 4.4).[27]

The South grew rapidly in the decades from 1970 to 1990, and the Mexican American population expanded considerably in this region. The arc of states from Virginia to Florida, west to Louisiana, and including the states of Arkansas, Tennessee, and Kentucky (Fig. 4.3), counted 344,305 Mexican Americans in 1980 and 452,703 by 1990 (Table 4.1). Florida is the primary center among this group of states, having counted nearly eighty thousand Mexican Americans in 1980 and two times that number ten years later (Figs. 4.3 and 4.4). The reasons for the dramatic change in Mexican Americans in the South might suggest a demand for labor in extractive economies including agriculture, yet industrialization in small towns as well as cities has brought on much of the region's recent growth. The census indicates that most of the Mexican Americans in this region live in places of fewer than ten thousand people.

In the Northeast, New York has become the focus of almost one hundred thousand people of Mexican ancestry (Table 4.1). One demographer has dubbed this concentration

*"La Gran Manhatitlán"* because mostly it is an urban immigrant community on the island of Manhattan. The population appears to be clustered especially on the fringes of Black Harlem on the Upper East Side and in the Bronx, with smaller pockets in Jackson Heights and Bushwick in Queens and Sunset Park in Brooklyn. Mexican immigrants are also found in selected smaller towns in the Empire State such as the Oaxacan migrants in Poughkeepsie.[28]

## Age Structure

The Mexican-origin population in 1990 was younger, on the average, than the entire United States' population. About 42 percent were under fifteen years old, whereas only 28 percent were in this age bracket for the general population. In 1990, the median age of Mexican Americans was 23.8 years. The fertility rate, the number of births per one thousand women aged fifteen to forty-four, has been higher for Mexican American women than Anglo women since the nineteenth century; in 1995 this rate was 117 for Mexican American and 66 for all American women.[29] Also, since 1920, the growth of the Mexican stock population—native-born and foreign-born Mexican Americans—largely has been a function of natural increase.[30] High fertility rates in a population are usually evidenced by large families, and according to the 1980 data, Mexican-origin families were larger (3.8) than families of the non-Hispanic population (2.7).[31]

The character of the Mexican American population can be summarized by reading the group's age-sex population pyramid. In both the Mexican American and the general U.S. populations for 1990, females slightly outnumbered males, so that the pyramids were nearly symmetrical (Figs. 4.5 and 4.6). The age structures of the populations, however, were significantly different. The youthfulness of the Mexican American population is evident by the magnitude of the bars near the base of the pyramid. These bars mirror

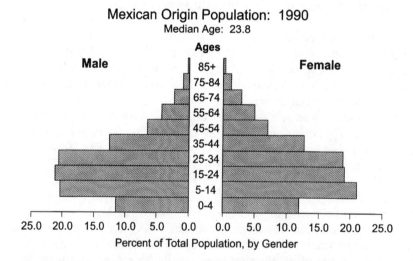

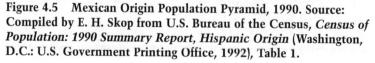

Figure 4.5    Mexican Origin Population Pyramid, 1990. Source: Compiled by E. H. Skop from U.S. Bureau of the Census, *Census of Population: 1990 Summary Report, Hispanic Origin* (Washington, D.C.: U.S. Government Printing Office, 1992), Table 1.

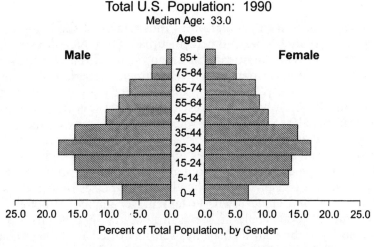

**Figure 4.6    U.S. Population Pyramid, 1990. Source: Compiled by
E. H. Skop from U.S. Bureau of the Census, *Census of Population:
1990 Summary Report, Hispanic Origin* (Washington, D.C.: U.S.
Government Printing Office, 1992), Table 1.**

the young median age of the Mexican American population compared to the U.S. population. In addition, the influence of immigration is visible in the Mexican American
pyramid by the bars associated with fifteen to twenty-four and twenty-five to thirty-four
where males outnumber females among the prime working-age groups. The narrow top
of the Mexican American pyramid suggests the relatively small elderly population when
compared to the U.S. pyramid.

What these patterns tell us is that the Mexican American population, compared to the
total U.S. population, has a much greater potential for future growth, with more than half
of its numbers in age groups under twenty-five years. The pyramids also suggest that the
dependency ratio, the number of the total population that is of working age as compared
to the number of the population that is not likely to work, is higher among the Mexican
Americans than the total population. The large numbers of dependent young as well as
old in the Mexican American population compared to smaller numbers for the U.S. population suggest the economic burden that must be assumed by the working population.

## AN URBAN PEOPLE

Despite the sometimes stereotyped rural origins of their past, Mexican Americans in
1990 were overwhelmingly an urban people. The census showed that 88 percent of persons of Mexican origin lived in metropolitan areas. This percentage was higher than the
corresponding proportion, 78 percent, for the U.S. population.[32] Moreover, about one of
every two persons of Mexican origin resided in the central cities of their metropolitan
areas. Although these areas contain large numbers of Mexican Americans, in recent
decades, there has been a population dispersion to suburban locations in some cities. In
addition, the landscapes of urban Mexican American districts can be distinguished from
other urban cultural landscapes.

**Urban Hierarchy**

In 1990, the Mexican American population in most states of the borderlands—California, Texas, Arizona, Colorado—was 90 percent urban. Only New Mexico had less than three-quarters of its Mexican Americans in urban areas. In the Northeast (94 percent), Mexican Americans were even more urban than in the borderlands, while in the Midwest (86 percent) and South (74 percent), approximately eight of every ten Mexican Americans lived in cities. Only in the West (68 percent) was the percentage living in urban areas significantly less than that for Mexican Americans overall.[33]

The cities with the greatest numbers of Mexican Americans are almost exclusively in states of the borderlands; only Chicago is outside this realm (Table 4.2). Some twenty top-ranked places are spread across the borderlands, especially in Texas and California (Fig. 4.7). New Mexico is conspicuous in the absence of places in this hierarchy emphasizing its chiefly rural and small-town settlement geography. Although New Mexico State counted some 330,000 people of Mexican ancestry in 1990, mostly in southern counties, the majority of the state's Hispanics self-identified as "Other Hispanic" in the census because most of New Mexico's Hispanic population considers itself Hispano or Spanish American, not Mexican American.[34]

Los Angeles had the greatest number of Mexican Americans, almost 1 million in the city and 3.7 million in the consolidated metropolitan statistical area.[35] The Mexican heritage of the city dates to the colonial era, and recently, Central American immigrants,

**Table 4.2    Leading Places with the Largest Absolute and Relative Mexican American Populations, 1990.**

| Largest Mexican American Population | | Highest Percent Mexican American | |
|---|---|---|---|
| City | Population | City | Percent |
| Los Angeles, CA | 936,507 | Socorro, TX | 93.0 |
| San Antonio, TX | 478,409 | Calexico, CA | 92.9 |
| Houston, TX | 358,503 | Eagle Pass, TX | 91.9 |
| Chicago, IL | 352,560 | Coachella, CA | 91.6 |
| El Paso, TX | 338,844 | Laredo, TX | 89.3 |
| San Diego, CA | 194,400 | Nogales, AZ | 87.7 |
| Dallas, TX | 185,096 | E. Los Angeles, CA | 87.5 |
| Phoenix, AZ | 176,139 | San Juan, TX | 87.2 |
| San Jose, CA | 173,803 | Mercedes, TX | 86.8 |
| Santa Ana, CA | 173,776 | Robstown, TX | 85.7 |
| Corpus Christi, TX | 118,713 | Brownsville, TX | 85.3 |
| E. Los Angeles, CA | 110,581 | Pharr, TX | 84.5 |
| Laredo, TX | 109,796 | Donna, TX | 84.1 |
| Tucson, AZ | 107,416 | San Benito, TX | 83.2 |
| Fresno, CA | 95,229 | Commerce, CA | 83.0 |
| Austin, TX | 93,323 | Edinburg, TX | 81.2 |
| Brownsville, TX | 84,448 | Douglas, AZ | 78.2 |
| Long Beach, CA | 80,523 | South El Monte, CA | 77.9 |
| Fort Worth, TX | 79,443 | Maywood, CA | 77.7 |
| Denver, CO | 74,629 | Mission, TX | 76.3 |

Source: U.S. Bureau of the Census, *1990 Census of Population and Housing*, Summary Tape File 1C.

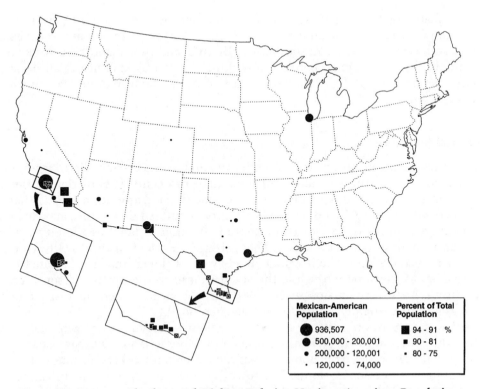

| Mexican-American Population | Percent of Total Population |
|---|---|
| ● 936,507 | ■ 94 - 91 % |
| ● 500,000 - 200,001 | ■ 90 - 81 |
| ● 200,000 - 120,001 | • 80 - 75 |
| · 120,000 - 74,000 | |

Figure 4.7    Largest Absolute and Highest Relative Mexican American Population Places, 1990. Source: Compiled by author from U.S. Bureau of the Census, *1990 Census of Population and Housing*, Summary Tape File 1C.

particularly Salvadoreans and Guatemalans, have occupied distinctive quarters in parts of the central city.[36] San Antonio, although smaller than Los Angeles, is also a recognized center of Mexican American population.[37] In fact, the Alamo City is more than half Mexican American, and, unlike Los Angeles, that population in San Antonio is not challenged by other Hispanic ethnic groups. Chicago and Houston are yet other strongholds of Mexican Americans (Table 4.2). Each of these cities became a Mexican immigrant destination during the early twentieth century. El Paso, like San Antonio and unlike Chicago, Houston, or Los Angeles, is predominantly Mexican American. Situated on the international border and across the Rio Grande from Ciudad Juárez reinforces the "Mexicanness" of the place.

Beneath these cities in rank order are five places with intermediate-sized Mexican American populations in 1990: San Diego, Dallas, Phoenix, San Jose, and Santa Ana (Table 4.2). Ten additional locations round out a secondary tier of the top twenty largest Mexican American population places, half in Texas and the remainder in California, Arizona, and Colorado (Fig. 4.7).

Yet another measure of urban hierarchy is places where Mexican Americans are a large percentage of a city's population (Table 4.2). The majority of these cities are also in the borderlands, but they are not—with the exception of East Los Angeles, Laredo, and Brownsville—the same places with the largest Mexican American populations (Fig. 4.7).

Most are places of fewer than seventy-five thousand, yet they are all places that are greater than 75 percent Mexican American (Table 4.2). More than half of these places are in south and west Texas, four in southern California, and two in southern Arizona. The proximity to the international border is a striking characteristic of nearly all these communities, reminding us of the rimland nature of most Mexican American subareas in these states (Fig. 4.7).

## Residential Structure

In most cities, Mexican Americans are a minority and live in distinct districts within the urban region.[38] Before the second half of the nineteenth century, borderland cities were predominantly Mexican, and populations were concentrated around the plazas that were established with a town's founding.[39] When railroads entered these cities and Anglo populations increased, Mexican American districts became isolated as the city expanded around or away from the old nucleus. This pattern is evident in the 1893 town plan of Tucson, Arizona (Fig. 4.8). The irregular streets west of the railroad tracks date from the early Spanish Mexican period, while the standard grid to the north and south resulted largely from Anglo subdivision after 1880. The Mexican American district became known as a *barrio*, literally translated as "neighborhood."

Barrios, sometimes referred to as *colonias* (suburbs) because they were once located far from the center of town, were also formed in the borderlands as urban expansion engulfed agricultural settlements housing Mexican American workers. In southern California, Pacoima was one such colonia. The town became enveloped by the urbanization of the San Fernando Valley, a once fertile agricultural district northwest of the Los Angeles city center.[40] Still other rural communities such as railroad worker settlements or labor camps followed a similar pattern, evolving into urban barrios. In his study of a Mexican American neighborhood in Weslaco, Texas, a lower Rio Grande Valley town, Arthur Rubel described the barrio of "Mexiquito" and its perception by residents and outsiders. The author suggests that the north and south sides of the railroad tracks are more than geographic zones; they are also societies with separate characteristics and traditions.

> New Lots [Weslaco] is a city bisected by the railway of the Missouri Pacific. In 1921, the town's first year, the north side of the tracks was allocated by municipal ordinance to the residences and business establishments of Mexican Americans, and to industrial complexes. Mexican-Americans refer to the north side of the tracks as Mexiquito, *el pueblo mexicano, nuestro lado;* even the traffic light north of the tracks is referred to as *la luz mexicana.* The other side of the tracks is spoken of as *el lado americano, el pueblo americano,* and other similar terms. Those who live south of the tracks also distinguish the two sides: "this side" and "the other side," "our side" and "their side," and "Mexican town" are all descriptive terms heard in the City of New Lots.[41]

Geographic isolation, housing restriction, and voluntary congregation have perpetuated residential segregation in the cities of the borderlands.[42] Mexican Americans are often segregated in the central cities of their metropolitan areas. There are two general explanations for this pattern. First, barrios became engulfed as the city expanded, as described earlier. A second process that helps explain the central city concentration is the filtering down of housing from one group to another. As central city areas are vacated by Anglos or other groups, lower-income populations, including some Mexican Americans,

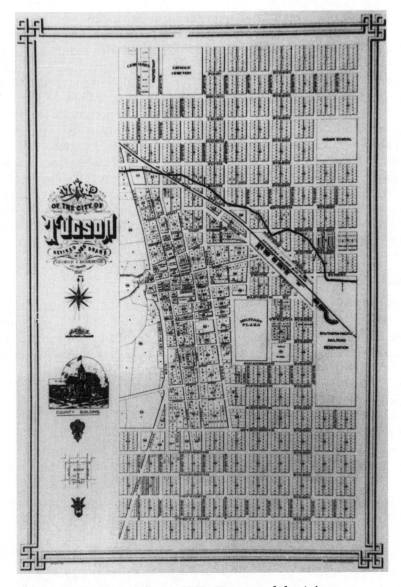

**Figure 4.8    Tucson, Arizona, 1893. Courtesy of the Arizona Historical Society, Tucson, Arizona.**

move into the inner-city neighborhoods. Many of the east side districts of Los Angeles such as Boyle Heights, City Terrace, and Lincoln Heights became populated by Mexican Americans in this manner as Jewish residents moved out of the east side to newer west side neighborhoods.[43] Similarly, in Chicago, the Mexican American population grew by 84 percent between 1960 and 1970, expanding mostly into older ethnic neighborhoods that once housed Czechs and Poles.[44] A survey of thirty-five cities in 1960 and ten in 1980 indicated that the mean index of residential dissimilarity, a measure of the degree of segregation between Anglo and Mexican American populations, was moderate.[45] Nevertheless, Los Angeles, with the nation's largest Mexican American population, is beginning to develop a "mega-barrio" of nearly two hundred square miles that contains most of the county's Hispanic population, chiefly Mexican origin but with significant Central American subgroups.[46]

Since World War II, many Mexican Americans in cities have dispersed into suburban areas. In Los Angeles County, for example, there were twenty-three municipalities in 1970 in which Mexican Americans accounted for 10 to 20 percent of the population and twenty-five cities or unincorporated areas in the county in which they made up 5 to 9 percent of the total.[47] Table 4.3 shows ten suburbs in the county where Mexican Americans increased significantly between 1960 and 1990. Similar studies in Texas and Arizona have found that dispersal from traditional barrios into the suburbs of cities escalated after World War II and the Korean War as veterans took advantage of federal legislation that allowed low interest loans and participation in the new housing market.[48] This movement to the suburbs was also an indication of the upward economic mobility achieved by Mexican Americans.

## Urban Cultural Landscapes

An axiom of human geography holds that landscape is a clue to culture.[49] Analyzing patterns of the built environment allows us to understand the social construction of a landscape and how cultures imprint space. The cultural landscapes of Mexican American barrios are distinct, differing from the landscapes of Anglo communities or those of other minority communities. Barrios surveyed in Texas, Arizona, and California include particular landscape elements—for example, brightly colored houses, fences enclosing house properties, colorful murals in residential and commercial areas, and ethnic shopping streets.

Houses are important elements of the material landscape, and they offer clues to the social groups that build and occupy them. In most barrios, Mexican Americans did not build the homes they now occupy. In fact, in many urban barrios, the housing stock is

Table 4.3    Mexican Americans in Selected Los Angeles County Suburbs, 1960–1990.

| Suburb | Percent 1960 | Percent 1970 | Percent 1980 | Percent 1990 |
|---|---|---|---|---|
| Pico Rivera | 26 | 59 | 70 | 77 |
| Huntington Park | 5 | 36 | 67 | 72 |
| Baldwin Park | 9 | 30 | 2 | 63 |
| Montebello | 18 | 44 | 90 | 60 |
| Lynwood | 4 | 16 | 38 | 59 |
| Paramount | 8 | 18 | 42 | 55 |
| Pomona | 9 | 16 | 27 | 46 |
| Norwalk | 15 | 26 | 35 | 41 |
| Alhambra | 4 | 17 | 30 | 27 |
| Monterey Park | 12 | 8 | 34 | 26 |

Sources: Francine F. Rabinovitz and William J. Siembieda, *Minorities in Suburbs: The Los Angeles Experience* (Lexington, Mass.: D. C. Heath, 1977); U.S. Bureau of the Census, *Census of Population: 1980, General Population Characteristics*, California PC80-1-B6 (Washington, D.C.: 1982), Table 16; U.S. Bureau of the Census, *1990 Census of Population and Housing*, Summary Tape File 3A.

older than in other parts of the city, passed down to numerous and different populations. Old houses, however, have not kept Mexican Americans from embellishing their residences. Houses in urban barrios are sometimes painted in bright shades of blue, pink, yellow, or green. The use of these colors appears to be a long-standing Mexican tradition. This preference has persisted and is evident in the vernacular or everyday landscapes of barrios in the borderlands.[50]

Yard fencing is another trait found in barrios. The persistent use of fences in residential landscapes has been studied in Tucson's Mexican American neighborhoods.[51] In these areas, fences and fence types were found to be keys to the identification of Mexican American households. The pattern of fence use indicates a traditional attitude about enclosed space in the urban landscape. Houses in urban Mexico in the present as well as the past have been built tight to the street with open space in the interior or back. The preference for fences as property markers in Mexican American barrios illustrates the persistence of this vernacular landscape design.

Street murals have become popular elements of the vernacular landscapes of barrios (Fig. 4.9). The street art movement in Mexican American districts started in late 1960s and spread quickly to cities with large Mexican American populations.[52] Today, highly stylized wall paintings that reflect the mural traditions of Mexico can be seen in many barrios in the borderlands. Often, the murals are created by community artists. The street art movement has heightened neighborhood identity by decorating barrio landscapes. In San Diego, murals "personalize" otherwise sterile institutional landmarks such as freeway pillars and thus mark these landscapes as symbolic places for barrio residents.[53]

**Figure 4.9    Street Mural, East Los Angeles, California. Street murals like this one decorate barrios across the borderlands and beyond, illustrating a Mexican aesthetic in the cultural landscape. Source: Photo by author.**

In many cities with large Mexican American populations, distinct immigrant quarters have become part of the cultural landscape. These smaller barrios are distinguishable from the larger Mexican American communities in that they house principally Mexican nationals or immigrants. In Los Angeles, these quarters, often a single apartment complex, have multiplied with the growth of immigrants from Mexico.[54] A Mexican immigrant colony in the San Francisco Bay area revealed a similar village atmosphere.[55] Immigrant families were found to reside on the same street or on several nearby streets. Residents maintained village social-behavioral patterns that reinforced their identity as immigrants from a particular province of Mexico, and they distinguished themselves from Mexican Americans and other Mexican immigrants. In the early morning hours, the sidewalks and street corners near these *barrioitos,* or "little barrios," are filled with Mexican men who wait to be picked up by temporary employers. These day labor pickup spots are common in many cities of the borderlands.

Another landscape that has become common in cities and suburbs where Mexican nationals, including Mexican Americans, concentrate is the Mexican Latin shopping street. Typically, this street is one that has been abandoned by Anglo or non-Hispanic merchants who relocate to suburban shopping centers. Mexican and Latino tenants rent/lease the retail spaces, and what emerges is a kind of Mexican downtown. Broadway in downtown Los Angeles is, perhaps, the most celebrated of this type of ethnic shopping street.[56] However, many other downtowns in communities from McAllen, Texas, to Huntington Park, California, have been witness to a similar transformation. In McAllen, regarded as the retail center of the lower Rio Grande Valley, the traditional Anglo main street shopping district was converted to a Mexican downtown when upscale retail fled to suburban malls. In 1997, some 149 commercial properties existed in a six-block-long area. Nearly half of the establishments were clothing and jewelry retailers. Another 22 percent were discount variety stores that market inexpensive goods, and electronics stores. These retail types have been identified as diagnostic of Mexican American shopping districts in south Texas.[57]

## SOCIAL AND ECONOMIC GEOGRAPHY

The social and economic character of the Mexican American population differed from the total U.S. population in 1990. Family income and educational attainment was lower, on the average, than that of the majority of Americans. However, indices of income and employment also vary among Mexican Americans across the country. Average incomes for Mexican Americans were higher in the Midwest than average incomes among Mexican Americans in most of the borderlands. The measurement of these characteristics combined with other population and education indices can be mapped to show the variability among Mexican American subgroups. These patterns illustrate a regional social and economic geography for the Mexican American population.

### Economic and Education Patterns

In 1994, the median income of Mexican American families, $23,609, was nearly $17,000 less than that of all white families, $40,884. At the low end of this scale, 12 percent of Mexican American families had incomes below $10,000 compared to only 4 percent for all white families in the United States. At the highest income levels, roughly 17 percent of

Mexican American families had incomes above $50,000; for all white Americans more than twice this percentage of families were in the upper income levels.[58]

Compared to the occupational status of all Americans, Mexican Americans were underrepresented in managerial, professional, technical, and administrative jobs in 1991 (Table 4.4). On the other hand, Mexican Americans were overrepresented in farming, forestry, and fishing as well as operator, fabricator, and laborer occupations. These associations mirror many decades of labor sector imbalance for the minority.[59] Like the U.S. population as a whole, however, Mexican American women significantly overrepresent men in managerial, professional, technical, administrative, and service occupations.

Mexican American occupational status suggests a pattern of low educational attainment. In 1996, only 47 percent of Mexican Americans graduated from high school and just 7 percent from college; the comparable figures for all Americans were 82 and 24 percent, respectively. While the average years of schooling completed has risen for Mexican Americans since 1960, they still have the lowest educational attainment of all U.S. Hispanic ethnic groups, below Cuban, Central/South American, Other Hispanic, and Puerto Rican.[60]

## Regional Variations

As we have seen, the distribution of the Mexican American population has been a function of historical inertia and migrations to areas of economic opportunity. The borderland states and outlier communities of Mexican Americans have evolved under different social and economic circumstances and at different times in the four hundred years of Hispanic occupancy in North America. This differential process of social adaptation and economic development has resulted in varied population groups within the Mexican American minority. Thus, Mexican Americans in south Texas are somewhat different from Mexican Americans in Chicago, and in turn, both are different from the Mexican Americans in Oregon and California.[61]

The patterns of social and economic diversity among these various Mexican American subgroups were regionalized in 1970.[62] This study was based on a sample of Mexican Americans in U.S. counties and analysis of six major socioeconomic variables. These included median personal income, percentage of the population that was steadily employed, mean highest educational level, fertility ratio, percentage of the population over fourteen born in another state, and percentage of foreign-born population. Analysis revealed seven separate population area types, and these were mapped accordingly (Fig. 4.10).

**Table 4.4    Mexican American Occupational Status by Percentage, 1991.**

| Occupation | Mexican Origin Male–Female | Americans Male–Female |
|---|---|---|
| Managerial-Professional | 8.9–14.1 | 26.3–27.2 |
| Technical-Administrative Support | 13.0–38.9 | 20.5–44.1 |
| Service | 15.0–26.9 | 10.4–17.6 |
| Precision Production, Craft, Repair | 18.8–3.2 | 18.8–2.2 |
| Operators, Fabricators, Laborers | 32.1–14.9 | 19.9–8.1 |
| Farming, Forestry, Fishing | 12.2–2.0 | 4.1–0.9 |
| Total | 100.0–100.0 | 100.0–100.0 |

Source: Marlita A. Reddy, ed., *Statistical Record of Hispanic Americans* (Detroit: Gale Research, 1993), 507–508.

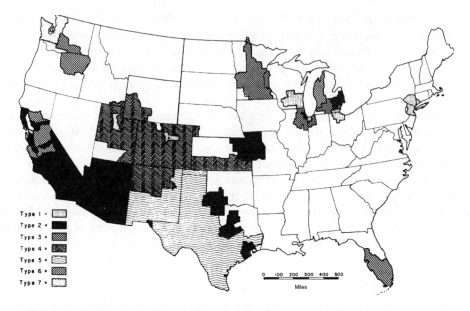

Type 1 =
Type 2 =
Type 3 =
Type 4 =
Type 5 =
Type 6 =
Type 7 =

0   100  200  300  400  500
Miles

**Figure 4.10    Area Types for People of Mexican Origin, 1970. Source: Reprinted from Boswell and Jones, *Geographical Review* 70 (January 1980): 94, Figure 2, with permission of the American Geographical Society.**

This regionalization shows the subgroups of Mexican American populations that existed in 1970, when measured by key social and economic variables. Two area types, 2 and 5, accounted for almost 86 percent of the Mexican American population in 1970, most of which was concentrated in the borderland states. The Mexican Americans in type 2 areas generally ranked higher in all categories, except fertility, than their counterparts in type 5 areas. Roughly the same numbers of Mexican Americans resided in type 1 and 4 areas as lived in areas designated type 6. However, the type 1 populations were urban and scored higher than either type 4 or 6 area populations by the variables measured. Finally, type 3 and 7 areas combined for approximately 3 percent of the population in 1970 and ranked nearly comparable by the social indicators.

Although this regional analysis was performed almost three decades ago, regional diversification of Mexican Americans is still evident by other more contemporary studies. Recent sociological and economic analyses of Mexican Americans in Houston, Albuquerque, Laredo, and Tucson reveal consistent underclass characteristics, yet variability persists.[63] Geographer Terrence Haverluk compared professional, managerial, and technical occupations for Mexican Americans in Webb, El Paso, Lubbock, and Deaf Smith Counties in Texas; Fresno County in California; and Yakima County in Washington.[64] These counties represent old and new Mexican American settlements, metropolitan areas and rural small towns, and concentrations of the minority ranging from 15 to 90 percent. In five of six counties, the percentage of occupations in professional, managerial, and technical jobs increased significantly over some four decades; in Webb County the percentage grew from 1970 to 1980 but declined from 1980 to 1990. Nevertheless, by 1990 each county ranked differently on the scale of percentage of Mexican Americans in these occupations: Webb, 57; El Paso, 40; Fresno, 35; Lubbock, 34; Yakima, 25; Deaf

Smith, 23. Similar measures of Mexican American income as a percentage of mean state income and median year of schooling completed in the same counties over four decades showed comparable regional variation.

## CONCLUSION

Mexican Americans emerged in the borderlands where Spanish and later Mexican settlement made the first European imprints on the landscapes of the region. The legacy of this early colonization remains evident in California, Texas, Arizona, New Mexico, and Colorado. These borderland states contain 83 percent of the total Mexican American population. Outside the border states, Mexican Americans are concentrated in parts of the Midwest, the West, the South, and the Northeast. The Mexican American population as a whole is younger, characterized by larger families, and growing more rapidly than the U.S. population.

During the twentieth century, two major social processes were important in the spatial evolution of the Mexican American people: immigration and urbanization. Immigration has occurred in two separate phases from 1900 to 1930 and since the 1940s to the present. In both eras, Mexican immigrants have responded to the economic opportunities available in the United States. Their labor contributions to the economic development of the United States have been substantial. They continue today to provide steady and inexpensive labor in many of the cities of the West and Midwest and elsewhere across the country. Largely because of changes in legal immigration to the United States and as a result of continued underemployment in Mexico, the majority of Mexican migrants to the United States enter illegally. This situation will not likely change in the near future, unless by political agreement between the United States and Mexico. As long as Mexico's population remains chronically underemployed and American industries and service sector economies demand labor, the push-pull factors of migration will perpetuate this phenomenon.

What this continued migration portends for the United States is a greater plurality within the Mexican American minority. If large numbers of undocumented Mexicans remain in this country, they will certainly change the ratio of foreign-born Mexicans to native-born Mexican Americans. In 1996, some 32 percent of the Mexican-origin population were not U.S. citizens.[65] Over time, the children of foreign-born migrants that are born in the United States will themselves become Mexican Americans and fuel the already rapidly growing native-born population of resident Mexican Americans. It is conceivable that the nation's second largest minority could become the nation's largest minority, surging past the African American population, if population growth rates in the Mexican American group remain high and immigrants continue to contribute to this population.

Urbanization has also been an important process of change for Mexican Americans. The Mexican American population was predominantly urban in 1990. As Mexican American populations grow, they will continue to transform the ethnic character of cities. The major Mexican American cities of the country such as Los Angeles, San Antonio, Chicago, Houston, and El Paso will likely become more Mexican American. This process will probably also affect intermediate-sized and small urban areas where Mexican Americans are significant.

In many metropolitan areas with large Mexican American populations, the central cities showed the greatest concentrations of the group. In these areas, preliminary study suggests that a Mexican American landscape is evident and can be distinguished from other urban cultural landscapes. In some cities, Mexican Americans are dispersing out of traditional barrios and into suburbs. Historian and sociologist Ernesto Galarza sees this as an inevitable development of the process of cultural evolution for the Mexican American population.[66] As economic prosperity improves, the process of acculturation to the dominant Anglo society tends to accelerate, and Mexican Americans will become more like Anglo Americans in traditions and values. Further study will be necessary, however, to evaluate the relationship between changing economic status and traditional social values and landscapes in Mexican American communities before any conclusions can be reached about urbanization and the Mexican American minority.

The regional implications of these changing social processes are equally significant to the future of the Mexican American group. The survey of key economic and population variables for the minority in 1970 revealed a mosaic of area types across the country. While the majority of Mexican Americans still reside in the borderlands, the populations inside and outside of this hearth show considerable variation still in the 1990s. This variation has its roots in the early plurality of the borderlands where different settlement cores developed separate regional identities. As these regions developed differentially, the populations in some cases preserved particular folk traditions and in others more quickly adapted to changing circumstances. Thus, Mexican Americans have evolved independently in these regions. This regional variation is likely to persist into the future because Mexican Americans are not a single, homogeneous group socioeconomically or politically.[67]

Despite internal variations within the Mexican American minority, a distinct regional pattern may be evolving in the borderlands. Some scholars and writers have speculated upon the regional dimensions of the future Mexican American population. It has been suggested, for example, that the two thousand–mile–long boundary between Mexico and the United States is emerging as the main axis of a new cultural province, called "MexAmerica."[68] This hybrid area represents what geographer Richard Nostrand has called the major zone of Anglo-Latin "cultural convergence" in the hemisphere.[69] It is a region where Mexican and American cultural influences are intermingled, where Anglo traditions are spiced with Mexican traits as immigrants move into and across the borderlands. It is also a process that has been evolving over many generations. In some respects it is a kind of *mestizaje*, a blending and overlapping of races, cultures, and lifestyles.[70] The ongoing changes in the urban areas of the borderlands are likely to prove our best clue to the future population characteristics and landscape influences of the nation's soon-to-be largest minority.

## NOTES

1. Richard L. Nostrand, "Spanish Roots in the Borderlands," *Geographical Magazine* 51 (December 1979): 203–209; Arthur L. Campa, *Hispanic Culture in the Southwest* (Norman: University of Oklahoma Press, 1979); and Carl O. Sauer, *Sixteenth Century North America: The Land and the People as Seen by the Europeans* (Berkeley: University of California Press, 1971).

2. D. W. Meinig, *Southwest: Three Peoples in Geographical Change, 1600–1970* (New York: Oxford University Press, 1971); Henry F. Dobyns, *Spanish Colonial Tucson: A Demographic History* (Tucson: University of Arizona Press, 1976).

3. D. W. Meinig, *Imperial Texas: An Interpretive Essay in Cultural Geography* (Austin: University of Texas Press, 1969); Terry G. Jordan, "Population Origins in Texas, 1850," *Geographical Review* 59 (January 1969): 83–103; and Arnoldo De León, *The Tejano Community, 1836–1900* (Albuquerque: University of New Mexico Press, 1982).

4. Nostrand, "Spanish Roots"; Leonard Pitt, *The Decline of the Californios: A Social History of the Spanish-Speaking Californians, 1846–1890* (Berkeley: University of California Press, 1971); and David J. Weber, *The Mexican Frontier 1821–1846: The American Southwest under Mexico* (Albuquerque: University of New Mexico Press, 1982).

5. Nostrand, "Spanish Roots."

6. Howard J. Nelson, *The Los Angeles Metropolis* (Dubuque, Iowa: Kendall/Hunt, 1983); Daniel D. Arreola, "The Mexican American Cultural Capital," *Geographical Review* 77 (January 1987): 17–33.

7. David Hornbeck, "Land Tenure and Rancho Expansion in Alta California, 1784–1846," *Journal of Historical Geography* 4 (October 1978): 371–390; David Hornbeck, "Mexican American Land Tenure Conflict in California," *Journal of Geography* 75 (April 1976): 209–221; Terry G. Jordan, *North American Cattle-Ranching Frontiers: Origins, Diffusion, and Differentiation* (Albuquerque: University of New Mexico Press, 1993); Jack Jackson, *Los Mesteños: Spanish Ranching in Texas, 1721–1821* (College Station: Texas A&M University Press, 1986); Joe S. Graham, *El Rancho in South Texas: Continuity and Change from 1750* (Denton: University of North Texas Press, 1994).

8. Richard L. Nostrand, "Mexican Americans circa 1850," *Annals of the Association of American Geographers* 65 (September 1975): 378–390; Oscar J. Martínez, "On the Size of the Chicano Population: New Estimates, 1850–1900," *Aztlán* 6 (Spring 1975): 43–67.

9. Richard L. Nostrand, "The Hispanic-American Borderland: Delimitation of an American Culture Region," *Annals of the Association of American Geographers* 60 (December 1970): 638–661.

10. Alvar W. Carlson, *The Spanish-American Homeland: Four Centuries in New Mexico's Río Arriba* (Baltimore: Johns Hopkins University Press, 1990); Richard L. Nostrand, *The Hispano Homeland* (Norman: University of Oklahoma Press, 1992); Daniel D. Arreola, "The Texas-Mexican Homeland," *Journal of Cultural Geography* 13 (Spring/Summer 1993): 61–74.

11. Richard L. Nostrand, "'Mexican American' and 'Chicano': Emerging Terms for a People Coming of Age," in *The Chicano*, ed. Norris Hundley, Jr. (Santa Barbara, Calif.: Clio, 1975), 143–160.

12. Arthur F. Corwin, ed., *Immigrants—and Immigrants: Perspectives on Mexican Labor Migration to the United States* (Westport, Conn.: Greenwood, 1978); Harry E. Cross and James A. Sandos, *Across the Border: Rural Development in Mexico and Recent Migration to the United States* (Berkeley, Calif.: Institute of Governmental Studies, 1981); Alejandro Portes and Robert L. Bach, *Latin Journey: Cuban and Mexican Immigrants in the United States* (Berkeley: University of California Press, 1985); Douglas S. Massey, Rafael Alarcon, Jorge Durand, and Humberto Gonzalez, *Return to Aztlán: The Social Process of International Migration from Western Mexico* (Berkeley: University of California Press, 1987); Abraham F. Lowenthal and Katrina Burgess, eds., *The California-Mexico Connection* (Stanford, Calif.: Stanford University Press, 1993); Richard C. Jones, *Ambivalent Journey: U.S. Migration and Economic Mobility in North-Central Mexico* (Tucson: University of Arizona Press, 1995).

13. Rogelio Saenz and Clyde S. Greenless, "The Demography of Chicanos," in *Chicanas and Chicanos in Contemporary Society*, ed. Roberto M. De Anda (Boston: Allyn & Bacon, 1996), 9–23.

14. Carey McWilliams, *North from Mexico: The Spanish-Speaking People of the United States* (New York: Greenwood, 1968).

15. Mario T. García, *Desert Immigrants: The Mexicans of El Paso, 1880–1920* (New Haven, Conn.: Yale University Press, 1981).

16. Alvar W. Carlson, "Seasonal Farm Labor in the San Luis Valley," *Annals of the Association of American Geographers* 63 (March 1973): 97–108; McWilliams, *North from Mexico.*

17. Abraham Hoffman, *Unwanted Mexican Americans in the Great Depression: Repatriation Pressures, 1929–1939* (Tucson: University of Arizona Press, 1974); Robert R. McKay, "Mexican

Americans and Repatriation," in *The New Handbook of Texas*, vol. 4, ed. Ron Tyler (Austin: Texas State Historical Association, 1996), 676–679.

18. U.S. Bureau of the Census, *Statistical Abstract of the United States: 1981* (Washington, D.C.: 1981); Walter Fogel, *Mexican Illegal Alien Workers in the United States*, Institute of Industrial Relations Monograph Series 20 (Los Angeles: University of California, 1979); Paul R. Ehrlich, Loy Bilderback, and Anne H. Ehrlich, *The Golden Door: International Migration, Mexico, and the United States* (New York: Ballantine, 1979).

19. U.S. Bureau of the Census, *Statistical Abstract of the United States: 1996* (Washington, D.C.: 1996); Saenz and Greenless, "The Demography of Chicanos."

20. Manuel Vic Villalpando et al., *A Study of the Socioeconomic Impact of Illegal Aliens on the County of San Diego* (San Diego: County of San Diego Human Resources Agency, 1977); Sidney Weintraub and Gilberto Cardenas, *The Use of Public Services by Undocumented Aliens in Texas: A Survey of State Costs and Revenues* (Austin: Lyndon B. Johnson School of Public Affairs, University of Texas, 1984).

21. Saenz and Greenless, "The Demography of Chicanos."

22. George Vernez and David Ronfeldt, "The Current Situation in Mexican Immigration," *Science* 251 (March 8, 1991): 1189–1193.

23. U.S. Bureau of the Census, *1990 Census of Population and Housing*, Summary Tape Files 1C and 3C.

24. U.S. Bureau of the Census, *Census of Population: 1980, Persons of Spanish Origin by State*, Supplementary Report PC80-Sl-7 (Washington, D.C.: U.S. Government Printing Office, 1982), Table 1.

25. Leo Grebler, Joan W. Moore, and Ralph Guzman, *The Mexican American People: The Nation's Second Largest Minority* (New York: Free Press, 1970).

26. Daniel D. Arreola, "Mexican Texas: A Distinctive Borderland," in *A Geographic Glimpse of Central Texas and the Borderlands: Images and Encounters*, ed. James F. Peterson and Julie A. Tuason (Indiana, Pa.: National Council for Geographic Education, 1995); Arreola, "The Texas-Mexican Homeland."

27. Terrence W. Haverluk, "The Changing Geography of U.S. Hispanics, 1850–1990," *Journal of Geography* 96 (May/June 1997): 134–145.

28. "Invaden Mexicanos NY," *El Imparcial* [Hermosillo], 28 July 1997, p. 2A; William A. Bowen, "Mexican Population, New York City, 1990, New York City Ancestry," *Digital Atlas of New York City* (Internet: http://130.166.124.2/NYpage1.html); Alison Mountz and Richard A. Wright, "Daily Life in the Transnational Migrant Community of San Agustín, Oaxaca, and Poughkeepsie, New York," *Diaspora* 5 (1996): 403–428.

29. Frank D. Bean and Gray Swicegood, *Mexican American Fertility Patterns* (Austin: University of Texas Press, 1985); Jorge del Pinal and Audrey Singer, *Generations of Diversity: Latinos in the United States*, Population Bulletin 52 (Washington, D.C.: Population Reference Bureau, October 1997).

30. Thomas D. Boswell, "The Growth and Proportional Redistribution of the Mexican Stock Population in the United States: 1900–1970," *Mississippi Geographer* 6 (Spring 1979): 57–76.

31. Frank D. Bean and Marta Tienda, *The Hispanic Population of the United States* (New York: Russell Sage Foundation, 1987).

32. Saenz and Greenless, "The Demography of Chicanos."

33. Saenz and Greenless, "The Demography of Chicanos."

34. Nostrand, *The Hispano Homeland*; Carlson, *The Spanish-American Homeland*; Daniel D. Arreola, *Geography of Hispanic Americans* (Tempe: Arizona State University Document Production Services, 1997).

35. James P. Allen and Eugene Turner, *The Ethnic Quilt: Population Diversity in Southern California* (Northridge: Center for Geographical Studies, California State University, 1997).

36. Daniel D. Arreola, "Hispanic American Capitals," in *Regional Geography of the United States and Canada*, 2d ed., Tom L. McKnight (Upper Saddle River, N.J.: Prentice Hall, 1997), 44–46.

37. Arreola, *Geography of Hispanic Americans*.

38. Shirley Achor, *Mexican Americans in a Dallas Barrio* (Tucson: University of Arizona Press, 1978); Richard Griswold del Castillo, *The Los Angeles Barrio, 1850–1890: A Social History* (Berkeley: University of California Press, 1979); Julian Samora and Richard A. Lamanna, *Mexican Americans in a Midwest Metropolis: A Study of East Chicago*, Advance Report 8, Mexican-American Study Project, UCLA Division of Research, Graduate School of Business Administration (Los Angeles: University of California, 1967); Thomas E. Sheridan, *Los Tucsonenses: The Mexican Community in Tucson, 1854–1941* (Tucson: University of Arizona Press, 1986); Richard A. García, *Rise of the Mexican American Middle Class: San Antonio, 1929–1941* (College Station: Texas A&M University Press, 1991); Arnoldo De León, *Ethnicity in the Sunbelt: A History of Mexican Americans in Houston* (Houston: Mexican American Studies Program, University of Houston, 1989); Robert Lee Maril, *Poorest of Americans: The Mexican Americans of the Lower Rio Grande Valley of Texas* (Notre Dame, Ind.: University of Notre Dame Press, 1989); George J. Sánchez, *Becoming Mexican American: Ethnicity, Culture and Identity in Chicano Los Angeles, 1900–1945* (New York: Oxford University Press, 1993).

39. Nina Veregge, "Transformations of Spanish Urban Landscapes in the American Southwest, 1821–1900," *Journal of the Southwest* 35 (Winter 1993): 371–460; Gilbert R. Cruz, *Let There Be Towns: Spanish Municipal Origins in the American Southwest, 1610–1810* (College Station: Texas A&M University Press, 1988); Daniel D. Arreola, "Plaza Towns of South Texas," *Geographical Review* 82 (January 1992): 56–73.

40. Joan W. Moore and Frank G. Mittelbach, *Residential Segregation in the Urban Southwest: A Comparison Study*, Advance Report 4, Mexican American Study Project, UCLA Division of Research, Graduate School of Business Administration (Los Angeles: University of California 1966).

41. Arthur J. Rubel, *Across the Tracks: Mexican Americans in a Texas City* (Austin: University of Texas Press, 1966), 3.

42. W. Tim Dagodag, "Spatial Control and Public Policies: The Example of Mexican American Housing," *Professional Geographer* 26 (August 1974): 262–269; Ellwyn R. Stoddard, "The Adjustment of Mexican American Barrio Families to Forced Housing Relocation," *Social Science Quarterly* 53 (March 1973): 749–759.

43. Moore and Mittelbach, *Residential Segregation*.

44. Alvar W. Carlson, "A Cartographic Analysis of Latin American Immigrant Groups in the Chicago Metropolitan Area, 1965–76," *Revista Geografica* 96 (July–December 1982): 91–106.

45. Douglas S. Massey and Nancy A. Denton, "Residential Segregation of Mexicans, Puerto Ricans, and Cubans in Selected U.S. Metropolitan Areas," *Sociology and Social Research* 73 (January 1989): 73–83; Moore and Mittelbach, *Residential Segregation*.

46. William A. V. Clark, "Residential Patterns: Avoidance, Assimilation and Succession," in *Ethnic Los Angeles*, ed. Roger Waldinger and Mehdi Bozorgmehr (New York: Russell Sage Foundation, 1996), 109–138.

47. Francine F. Rabinovitz and William J. Siembieda, *Minorities in Suburbs: The Los Angeles Experience* (Lexington, Mass.: Heath, 1977).

48. Carl Allsup, *The American G.I. Forum: Origins and Evolution* (Austin: Center for Mexican American Studies, University of Texas Press, 1982); James E. Officer, "Sodalities and Systemic Linkage: The Joining Habits of Urban Mexican Americans," unpublished Ph. D. dissertation, University of Arizona, 1964.

49. Peirce F. Lewis, "Axioms for Reading the Landscape: Some Guides to the American Scene," in *The Interpretation of Ordinary Landscapes: Geographical Essays*, ed. D. W. Meinig (New York: Oxford University Press, 1979), 11–32.

50. Daniel D. Arreola, "Mexican American Housescapes," *Geographical Review* 78 (July 1988): 299–315.

51. Daniel D. Arreola, "Fences as Landscape Taste: Tucson's *Barrios*," *Journal of Cultural Geography* 2 (Fall/Winter 1981): 96–105.

52. Daniel D. Arreola, "Mexican American Exterior Murals," *Geographical Review* 74 (October 1984): 409–424.

53. Larry R. Ford and Ernst Griffin, "Chicano Park: Personalizing an Institutional Landscape," *Landscape* 25, no. 2 (1981): 42–48.

54. Michele Markel-Cohen, "Port of Entry: Sawtelle Area Carries on Long Tradition as Migrant Labor Colony in Heart of Middle-Class West L.A.," *Los Angeles Times,* 9 January 1983, part X, pp. 1 and 10.

55. Laura Zarrugh, "Home Away from Home: The Jacalan Community in the San Francisco Bay Area," in *The Chicano Experience,* ed. Stanley A. West and June Macklin (Boulder, Colo.: Westview, 1979), 145–163.

56. Curtis C. Roseman and J. Diego Vigil, "From Broadway to 'Latino Way': The Reoccupation of a Gringo Retail Landscape," *Places: A Quarterly Journal of Environmental Design* 8 (Spring 1993): 20–29.

57. James R. Curtis, "Central Business Districts of the Two Laredos," *Geographical Review* 83 (January 1993): 54–65.

58. *Statistical Abstract of the United States: 1996.*

59. Bean and Tienda, *The Hispanic Population of the United States.*

60. del Pinal and Singer, *Generations of Diversity;* Bean and Tienda, *The Hispanic Population of the United States.*

61. Vernon M. Briggs, Walter Fogel, and Fred H. Schmidt, *The Chicano Worker* (Austin: University of Texas Press, 1977); William Madsen, *The Mexican-Americans of South Texas,* 2d ed. (New York: Holt, Rinehart, and Winston, 1973); Louise Año Nuevo de Kerr, "Chicano Settlements in Chicago: A Brief History," *Journal of Ethnic Studies* 2 (Winter 1975): 22–32; Richard W. Slatta, "Chicanos in the Pacific Northwest: An Historical Overview of Oregon's Chicanos," *Aztlán* 6 (Fall 1975): 327–340; Albert Camarillo, *Chicanos in a Changing Society: From Mexican Pueblos to American Barrios in Santa Barbara and Southern California, 1848–1930* (Cambridge, Mass.: Harvard University Press, 1979).

62. Thomas D. Boswell and Timothy C. Jones, "A Regionalization of Mexican Americans in the United States," *Geographical Review* 70 (January 1980): 88–98.

63. Joan Moore and Raquel Pinderhughes, eds., *In the Barrios: Latinos and the Underclass Debate* (New York: Russell Sage Foundation, 1993), 101–128, 149–172, 173–194, 195–210.

64. Terrence William Haverluk, "A Descriptive Model for Understanding the Wider Distribution and Increasing Influence of Hispanics in the American West," Working Paper WP-04, Hispanic Research Center, University of Texas at San Antonio, August 1994.

65. del Pinal and Singer, *Generations of Diversity.*

66. Ernesto Galarza, "Mexicans in the Southwest: A Culture in Process," in *Plural Society in the Southwest,* ed. Edward M. Spicer and Raymond H. Thompson (Albuquerque: University of New Mexico Press, 1972), 261–297.

67. Walker Conner, ed., *Mexican Americans in Comparative Perspective* (Washington, D.C.: Urban Institute Press, 1985).

68. Joel Garreau, *The Nine Nations of North America* (Boston: Houghton Mifflin, 1981); Lester D. Langley, *MexAmerica: Two Countries, One Future* (New York: Crown, 1988).

69. Richard L. Nostrand, "A Changing Culture Region," in *Borderlands Sourcebook: A Guide to the Literature on Northern Mexico and the American Southwest,* ed. Ellwyn R. Stoddard, Richard L. Nostrand, and Jonathan P. West (Norman: University of Oklahoma Press, 1983), 6–15.

70. Matt S. Meier and Feliciano Rivera, *Dictionary of Mexican American History* (Westport, Conn.: Greenwood, 1981).

# 5

# Cuban Americans

*Thomas D. Boswell*

Cuban Americans[1] represent the third largest component of persons of Latin American origin living in the United States, surpassed only by Mexican Americans and Puerto Ricans. Currently, there are approximately 1.1 million Cuban Americans.[2] Although this accounts for less than one-half of 1 percent of the United States' total population, Cubans living in the United States represent a significant minority worthy of study. They are an especially interesting American ethnic group for at least seven reasons. First, the number of Cuban Americans is equal to approximately 10 percent of all Cubans currently residing in Cuba.[3] Thus, although they represent an insignificant proportion of the United States' population, this is not true with respect to the population of Cuba. Second, immigrants from Cuba have not, until recently, been representative of Cuba's total population. The earliest waves were especially selective of professionals and entrepreneurs, thereby creating a serious "brain drain" in Cuba. Such a concentration of particular socioeconomic groups intensified the impact of emigration on Cuba's population structure, beyond what normally is suggested by a figure of 10 percent. Third, the selectivity characteristics of the Cuban migrants have exhibited a dynamic quality, so that the most recent arrivals are significantly different from those who arrived earlier. Fourth, the socioeconomic concentration of Cuban migrants has been accompanied by a spatial concentration in their American destinations. Slightly more than seven out of ten live in the two large metropolitan areas of Miami–Fort Lauderdale, Florida, and New York City–northern New Jersey–Long Island.[4] In these two areas their economic, political, and social influence has been greatly amplified. Fifth, Cubans represent the first large group of refugees who have moved to the United States as their country of first asylum.[5] In the past, most other refugees have come to America indirectly, after spending time in an intervening third country. Although some Cubans have also entered this way, the vast majority have moved directly from Cuba to the United States. As a consequence, they have been accepted automatically, until recently, as refugees who have been motivated by political persecution in a communist country. This status has entitled them to federal government benefits that were not available to most other immigrant groups who migrated to the United States primarily for economic reasons. A considerable body of literature suggests that migrants who move as political refugees are often considerably different from those who move in response to economic opportunities.[6] Sixth, Cuban Americans have made remarkable progress in adjusting to living conditions in the United States. It is probably correct to say that there has never been a large non-English-speaking immigrant group in this country that has exhibited more rapid upward socioeconomic mobility than the Cubans. A seventh reason for interest in persons of Cuban descent is that their large-scale movement to the United States is of recent origin and is an ongoing event that is a newsworthy problem currently being grappled with by the United States immigration authorities, urban planners, and purveyors of social services today.

## HISTORY OF CUBAN MIGRATION TO THE UNITED STATES

The history of Cuban immigration to the United States has taken place within nine distinct ebb and flow phases. The first was represented by a trickle movement that, for all intents, began in the middle 1800s and continued until Fidel Castro's revolution in 1959. The second was a large-scale movement that occurred between 1959 and 1962, as the Castro revolution was being consolidated. The third was characterized by a hiatus in the movement that was initiated by the Cuban Missile Crisis in 1962 and lasted until 1965. During the latter year, Castro changed his migration policy and ordered that Cuba be opened once again for a fourth phase of emigration to the United States. This was to last until 1973 and became known as the period of the Freedom Flights. Again, there was a temporary interlude in the movement to the United States between 1973 and 1980 that was to represent the fifth phase. Unexpectedly, in April 1980 a veritable flood of Cuban emigration was unleashed (as the sixth phase) through the small town of Mariel, located on Cuba's northern coast, about thirty miles west of Havana. Although it lasted only five months, approximately 125,000 Cubans participated in this wave. After September 1980, emigration again declined, as both the Cuban and United States government adopted stricter migration policies. This represents the seventh phase and continued until 1991. The eighth phase was initiated in 1991 and continued until 1994, when thousands of Cubans fled the island on makeshift rafts. This was known as the *balsero* phase. Since 1994, another period of low emigration occurred, one that has continued (as the ninth phase) to the time of the writing of this chapter.

### The Early Trickle

The first year for which census data are available for determining the magnitude of the presence of Cubans in the United States is 1870 (Table 5.1). At that time there were a little over five thousand people living in the United States who were born in Cuba. By the middle 1800s there had developed a sizable exodus of Cubans in response to political turmoil on the island. Key West, Tampa, and New York City became particularly notable as places of refuge for Cuban political exiles who were plotting the overthrow of their Spanish rulers.[7] In addition, during the 1860s and 1870s, several cigar manufacturers moved their operations from Havana to these three cities, thereby providing additional employment opportunities for Cuban immigrants.[8] A slow growth pattern emerged that was temporarily interrupted by World War I and the Great Depression of the 1930s. Miami did not begin to appear as a center of Cuban influence until the 1930s when exiles fled the effects of the revolution against Gerardo Machado. Another spurt in the stream to Miami occurred from 1953 to 1959 as would-be revolutionaries fled the Batista regime.[9] From the beginning of the twentieth century until the Castro revolution in 1959, immigration fluctuated, varying with changing political and economic conditions on the island.[10]

**Table 5.1    Estimates of Cuban Americans Living in the United States: 1870–1996 (Numbers in Thousands).**

| Years | Foreign Born (Thousands) | U.S. Born (Thousands) | Total (Thousands) |
|---|---|---|---|
| 1870 | 5.3 | NA | NA |
| 1880 | 6.9 | NA | NA |
| 1890 | NA | NA | NA |
| 1990 | 11.1 | NA | NA |
| 1910 | 15.1 | NA | NA |
| 1920 | 4.9 | NA | NA |
| 1930 | 18.5 | 17.0 | NA |
| 1940 | 18.0 | NA | NA |
| 1950 | 33.7 | NA | NA |
| 1960 | 79.2 | 45.3 | 124.5 |
| 1970 | 439.0 | 122.0 | 561.0 |
| 1980 | 627.3 | 175.9 | 803.2 |
| 1990 | 754.7 | 298.5 | 1,053.2 |
| 1996 | NA | NA | 1,127 |

NA means data are not available.

For the 1870 to 1970 period the figures are derived from: A. J. Jaffe, Ruth M. Cullen, and Thomas D. Boswell, *The Changing Demography of Spanish Americans* (New York: Academic Press, 1980), 247.

For 1980 the figures comes from: U.S. Bureau of the Census, *1980 Census of Population*, "Persons of Spanish Origin by State: 1980," Supplementary Report, PC80-S1-7, p. 2; U.S. Bureau of the Census, *1980 Census of Population*, Public-Use Microdata Sample A, One-in-a-Thousand Sample for the United States, 1983; and Thomas D. Boswell and Manuel Rivero, *Demographic Characteristics of Pre-Mariel Cubans Living in the United States: 1980*. Miami: The Research Institute for Cuban Studies, Graduate School of International Studies, University of Miami, pp. 4 and 28.

For 1990 the figures are from: U.S. Bureau of the Census, *1990 Census of Population*, "Persons of Hispanic Origin in the United States," 1990-CP-3-3, Table 1, pp. 7–8.

The early experience of Cubans living in New York and Florida proved crucial for the ability of future generations of Cuban immigrants to adjust to life in the United States. Cuban history books, songs, folktales, and poetry often provided moving accounts of living conditions in America. The exiles who emigrated after the introduction of communism in Cuba were at least partially aware of the Hispanic cultural concentrations in New York and Miami and were familiar with the geographic and climatic similarities between Cuba and southern Florida.

## Period of the "Golden Exiles"

Historically throughout the Caribbean, when one dictatorship is replaced by another, especially through use of force, the opponents of the victor became political exiles. This happened many times in Cuba before the advent of the Castro regime. Therefore, it was not surprising that when Fidel Castro's forces overthrew the government of Fulgencio Batista in January 1959, an outmigration of backers of the ousted government occurred. The magnitude of this exodus, however, was not anticipated. During the twenty-two years between 1959 and 1980, approximately 794,000 Cubans emigrated to the United States (Table 5.2). Except for Puerto Rico, no other island in the Caribbean has experienced a comparable outpouring in such a short period of time.

The key to understanding the reasons behind this remarkable exodus lies in developing an appreciation for the pervasiveness and speed of the societal changes that took place

**Table 5.2    Cuban Emigration to the United States: 1959–1994.**

| Years | Numbers | Years | Numbers |
|-------|---------|-------|---------|
| 1959 | 26,527 | 1978 | 4,108 |
| 1960 | 60,224 | 1979 | 2,644 |
| 1961 | 49,961 | 1980 | 122,061 |
| 1962 | 78,611 | 1981 | 10,858 |
| 1963 | 42,929 | 1982 | 8,209 |
| 1964 | 15,616 | 1983 | 8,978 |
| 1865 | 16,447 | 1984 | 5,699 |
| 1966 | 46,688 | 1985 | 17,115 |
| 1967 | 52,147 | 1986 | 30,787 |
| 1968 | 55,954 | 1987 | 27,363 |
| 1969 | 52,625 | 1988 | 16,610 |
| 1970 | 49,545 | 1989 | 9,523 |
| 1971 | 50,001 | 1990 | 9,436 |
| 1972 | 23,977 | 1991 | 9,474 |
| 1973 | 12,579 | 1992 | 10,890 |
| 1974 | 13,670 | 1993 | 12,976 |
| 1975 | 8,488 | 1994 | 14,216 |
| 1976 | 4,515 | 1995 | 17,937 |
| 1977 | 4,548 | 1996 | 26,466 |

Note: The figures for the 1990s do not include the balseros because their immigration status had not been decided at the time these date were published.

U.S. Immigration and Naturalization Service, *Statistical Yearbook, 1991*, p. 30; *Statistical Yearbook, 1994* (issued in 1996), p. 28, U.S. Government Printing Office, Washington, D.C.; and *Statistical Yearbook, 1996* (issued in 1998), p. 33, U.S. Government Printing Office, Washington, D.C.

as Castro consolidated his power between 1959 and 1962. In contrast to all other changes in dictatorships that have taken place in the Caribbean, Castro's efforts left no social sector untouched. Fagen et al. state that the period between 1959 and 1962 can be properly termed "cataclysmic."[11] The social structure, economic life, and political institutions were radically and rapidly altered. Those who were able and willing to adjust were welcomed into the new order. Persons who could not, or would not, accommodate to the system were rudely shouldered aside and often treated harshly. A considerable amount of confusion, suspicion, and uncertainty accompanied these changes. There were many, perhaps a majority, who perceived themselves as benefiting from these changes. Included were the vast majority of the rural masses, blacks, perhaps the indoctrinated youth, and members of the new managerial and political class of elites.

More than 215,000 Cubans migrated to America between 1959 and 1962 (Table 5.2). In the beginning, the majority were members of the economic and political elite openly affiliated with the government of Batista. By the middle of 1959, members of the landholding aristocracy began to leave as an agrarian reform law was instituted in June, with the stated purpose of breaking up large land holdings. In July 1960 a law was passed authorizing the expropriation of all American-owned property. In the same year, an urban reform law was enacted in October that was designed to confiscate private rental properties in the cities.[12] By this time the Revolution was also felt by middle-class entrepreneurs, thus widening its impact. In 1960 the number leaving expanded to approximately sixty thousand.

Relations between the United States and Cuba began to cool rapidly in early 1961. On January 3, the American government broke diplomatic relations with Cuba. The ill-fated Bay of Pigs invasion was launched in April. Castro announced in December that he was a Marxist-Leninist and that Cuba was destined to become a socialist state. He placed severe restrictions on the amount of property and money that could be taken out of the country. Finally, in October 1962, the Cuban Missile Crisis resulted in termination of air traffic to the United States. Legal emigration to America remained suspended for about three years until September 1965.[13]

The 1959 to 1962 era of Cuban immigration to the United States is often referred to as the wave of "Golden Exiles." This implies that the vast majority were former members of the elite classes in Cuba. The data in Table 5.3 suggest that this concept is only partly correct. When the occupational structure of Miami Cuban refugees (at the time they left Cuba) is compared to that of the population living in Cuba (at the time of the 1953 census),[14] it is clear that the refugees were overrepresented, especially in the legal and white-collar professions. Conversely, they were underrepresented in the extractive occupations (e.g., agriculture and fishing) and in blue-collar jobs. It is also relevant, however, to note that the refugees were a highly diverse group. Virtually all occupations were represented among the immigrants. Therefore, it is incorrect to think of all of them as having been elites in Cuba prior to their arrival in Florida. In fact, less than 40 percent should be so considered. Nevertheless, it is correct to state that, when considered as a whole, the refugees for the 1959 to 1962 interval were positively selected from the entire Cuban population.

The Miami Cuban refugees were also much more likely to be from urban origins when compared with the 1953 Cuban population. For instance, 87 percent of the refugees had lived either in Havana (62 percent) or some other large city (25 percent) in Cuba be-

**Table 5.3    Comparison of the Occupational Structures of Cuba in 1953 with the Occupations of Cuban Refugees at the Time They Emigrated to Miami, Florida, between 1959 and 1963.**

| Occupations | 1953 Cuban Census Population | Percentage of Census | 1959–63 Cuban Refugees | Percentage of Refugees | Ratio: Refugees Percentage to Census Percentage |
|---|---|---|---|---|---|
| Lawyers and Judges | 7,858 | .5 | 1,695 | 3.0 | 7.8 |
| Professionals and Semi-Professionals | 78,051 | 4.0 | 12,124 | 22.0 | 5.5 |
| Managerial and Executive | 93,662 | 5.0 | 6,771 | 12.0 | 2.5 |
| Clerical and Sales | 264,569 | 14.0 | 17,123 | 31.0 | 2.3 |
| Domestic Service, Military, and Police | 160,406 | 8.0 | 4,801 | 9.0 | 1.1 |
| Skilled, Semiskilled, and Unskilled | 526,168 | 27.0 | 11,301 | 20.0 | .7 |
| Agricultural and Fishing | 807,514 | 41.5 | 1,539 | 3.0 | .1 |
| Totals | 1,938,228 | 100.0 | 55,354 | 100.0 | NA |

NA means not applicable.
Richard R. Fagen, Richard A. Broady, and Thomas J. O'Leary, *Cubans in Exile: Disaffection and the Revolution* (Stanford, Calif.: Stanford University Press, 1968), 19.

fore leaving for Florida, whereas only 31 percent of Cuba's population lived in the same areas. On the other hand, 69 percent of all Cubans resided in small towns or rural areas. The figure for the refugees was 13 percent.[15]

## Missile Crisis Hiatus

The missile crisis and United States military blockade of Cuba in October 1962 brought to an abrupt halt all direct legal transportation between the two countries. A hiatus in legal migration to the United States was to ensue for a three-year period until September 1965. This was not to be the only time that the Castro government quickly reversed its position on emigration. Rather, it was the harbinger of future similar sharp reversals in emigration policy.

Despite the fact that direct legal transportation was stopped between Cuba and the United States, it has been estimated that close to fifty-six thousand still managed to migrate. This includes about sixty-seven hundred who were able to escape in boats and a few in planes. A little over six thousand additional persons were allowed to leave directly for the United States during this period. These were former prisoners from the Bay of Pigs expedition and members of their families. They were released in exchange for a ransom consisting of shipments of badly needed medicines and medical supplies for Cuba.[16]

The vast majority of the remaining 43,300 who were able to reach the United States from Cuba during this three-year period did so indirectly through intermediate countries, most frequently through Spain or Mexico.[17] However, this was a costly and enervating process. Persons who arrived in either New York or Miami directly from Cuba were automatically granted immediate legal entry, yet those who sought entry from a third country were considered aliens by the U.S. Department of Immigration and Naturalization Service and were therefore subject to all existing immigration restrictions. Often the wait in Madrid or Mexico City lasted well over a year before clearance was obtained.[18]

## Period of Freedom Flights

On September 28, 1965, Fidel Castro announced he would permit Cubans with relatives living in the United States to emigrate beginning on the following October 10.[19] The departures would take place by boat through the small port of Camarioca on the northern coast of Matanzas Province, about sixty miles east of Havana. Immediately, hundreds of boats departed southern Florida for Cuba to pick up friends and relatives. Unfortunately, not all the craft were seaworthy, and a number of tragedies occurred. The chaos that ensued, as a result of the panicky rush and accompanying accidents, created a source of embarrassment for the Cuban government. As a consequence, United States and Cuban authorities signed a "Memorandum of Understanding" that established arrangements for an airlift between Miami and a Cuban airport located east of Havana, in the seaside town of Varadero. The agreement was organized through the Swiss Embassy in Havana, and the flights became variously known as the "Freedom Flights," "Aerial Bridge," or "Family Reunification Flights."

Air transportation was initiated on December 1, 1965, and continued until April 6, 1973. Normally two flights a day, five days per week, were operated between Miami and Havana, carrying 3,000 to 4,000 people per month.[20] It is estimated that 297,318 people arrived during the seven-year airlift. In addition, 4,993 came by boat during the two-month boatlift from Camarioca. Thus, a little over 302,000 Cubans migrated directly to the United States between October 10, 1965, and April 6, 1973.[21] A few also continued to travel indirectly from Cuba via third countries, such as Mexico and Spain, to Miami and New York.

The airlift did not result in a free exodus from Cuba. Relatives of people already living in the United States were given priority according to closeness of the family relationship. Thus, members of nuclear families were accorded the highest preference. Males of military age (seventeen to twenty-six years old) were not usually allowed to leave, and few skilled and highly trained individuals working in critical occupations were granted exit visas until replacements could be found and trained. The elderly and sick were more likely to receive clearance to leave, since there was a greater likelihood that they would become dependent on the Cuban social security system for their support. People who filed exit applications frequently lost their jobs and were required to perform agricultural labor until space aboard planes became available. It was not uncommon for an adult male to spend two or three years working in agricultural fields for minimal wages before being allowed to exit.[22]

## The Interlude from 1973 to 1980

Beginning in August 1971, the Cuban government started creating occasional interruptions in the Freedom Flights. Fidel Castro had decided by the end of May 1969 to stop accepting new applications for leaving the island. In September 1971, he announced that the list of people who had requested exit permits was getting smaller and that the exodus would end soon. It was claimed that the intention of the Memorandum of Understanding, which was to reunite separated families, had largely been fulfilled. As a result, the number of arrivals by way of the airlift began to slacken toward the end of 1971 and continued to decrease throughout 1972, until the last flight was made on April 6, 1973.[23]

From July 1, 1973, to September 30, 1979, a total of just under thirty-eight thousand Cubans arrived in the United States (Table 5.2). This was less than 13 percent of the number that arrived during the period of the Freedom Flights and the Camarioca boatlift. Those who were able to emigrate during this seven-year interlude did so primarily through third countries, just as emigrants had done during the Cuban missile crisis hiatus earlier. Again, Mexico and Spain served as the primary stepping stones on the way to the Miami or New York metropolitan areas, with smaller numbers being channeled through Jamaica and Venezuela.

The migration selectivity processes and trends that operated in earlier phases of the Cuban emigration waves were also in effect during the 1973 to 1980 interval. Studies of Cubans living in West New York[24] and Miami[25] indicate that although the new immigrants were better off in terms of their occupational and income status than the majority left behind in Cuba, the degree of positive selection was declining. As was the case during the 1965–1973 period, this most recent wave came closer to being representative of the Cuban population. It also became apparent that economic motives were beginning to play a larger role in affecting the decision to leave Cuba, certainly more so than had been the case in the early 1960s.[26]

An interesting change began to emerge during the 1970s with respect to the emigrants' origins in Cuba. As mentioned earlier, Havana had dominated as the leading sender, with Las Villas Province being a distant second. By 1979, Las Villas had surpassed

Havana as the leading origin for Cubans going to New Jersey and was apparently having more of an influence as an origin for people going to Miami as well. Furthermore, small cities, towns, and rural areas began to account for a larger proportion of the refugees. In 1968, 56 percent of the Cubans living in the community of West New York in New Jersey had come from large cities in Cuba. In 1979, the comparable figure had declined to 40 percent.[27] This general shift in origins toward smaller settlements in Cuba is part of the same trend noted previously with respect to occupation and income—namely, a tendency for the immigrants over time to take on characteristics more similar to the population living in Cuba.

## The Flood from Mariel

In April 1980, Cuban history repeated itself, as once again mass emigration was allowed to the United States in a manner reminiscent of what occurred during the boatlift from the harbor town of Camarioca in 1965. Again the mode of transportation was by sea and this time the place of departure selected by Castro was the small port of Mariel, located on the northern coast approximately thirty miles west of Havana. There was, however, one major difference between this exodus and the one from Camarioca that took place fifteen years earlier. The Camarioca boatlift lasted for about two months and involved approximately five thousand Cubans; the Mariel diaspora lasted for close to five months (April 21 to September 26, 1980) and included 124,779 people. During the single month of May, the number leaving for the United States was 86,488.[28] This was more than the number who left the island during the entire year of 1962 (78,611), which until 1980 was the year characterized by the largest outflow of Cubans to America (Table 5.2).

To understand the mechanisms behind the Mariel exodus, it is necessary to go back to December 1978, when President Castro announced that he would allow Cuban Americans to return to Cuba for one-week visits with their families.[29] Throughout 1979 and early 1980 about one hundred thousand people took part in these sojourns, spending perhaps $100 million on the island. This stream of visitors has often been referred to as being the "blue-jeans revolution" because returning migrants usually brought gifts, such as designer jeans, for their relatives living in Cuba.[30] There were at least three motives for allowing these visits. First, the money spent in Cuba by the visitors helped the ailing Cuban economy. Second, by allowing the former Cuban residents to return, Castro hoped to demonstrate that his government was in firm control and that further attempts by Cuban exiles to dislodge him from power would prove futile. Third, Castro figured that his actions would improve his government's human rights image in other countries. What Castro and his advisers did not foresee was the "demonstration effect" that the returnees would have on their relatives still living in Cuba. Suddenly, twenty years of anti-American and antiexile propaganda subsided as the visitors provided evidence of a much higher lifestyle in the United States that contrasted sharply with the austere living conditions which existed under the direction of the totalitarian government of Cuba.[31] Perhaps, the tales of opportunities and material benefits of life in the United States were sometimes overstated. Nevertheless, the effect was clearly to promote, or increase, the desire among many Cubans to leave.

In addition to the impact of the blue-jeans revolution, several other factors influenced the decision by many Cubans to migrate to the United States. Cuba's economy was experiencing a serious recession. The two major export crops, sugar and tobacco, were being riddled by diseases. Inflation and unemployment were beginning to emerge as major problems.[32] There were still many family members in Cuba who wished to join their relatives living in the United States but who were unable to do so during the earlier Freedom Flights. Some of these were males who were obliged to participate in the military services; others were people working in certain skilled occupations who were not allowed to leave until replacements could be found. Also, 1979 was a year during which political dissent increased as a result of government austerity programs. When four hundred Mariel immigrants in Miami were asked why they left Cuba, 79 percent said they did so for political reasons. Another 12 percent cited economic reasons for their decision to leave, and 6 percent claimed that family reunification was their primary goal.[33]

More than 1 percent of the Cuban population left for the United States during the Mariel boatlift. In the process, this partially relieved an acute housing shortage and the widespread unemployment that was characterizing the island at the time. Furthermore, it allowed the government to rid itself of (or identify) dissidents who were prone toward not supporting the communist regime. It also provided Castro with scapegoats who could be blamed for undermining the Cuban economy and would be used to infuse more spirit into the revolution that was showing signs of stagnation.[34] It has been estimated that more than one million additional Cubans would have left the island had Mariel not been closed by Castro in September 1980.[35]

Once it became apparent that the number of people who wanted to leave Cuba was a lot larger than the Cuban government had originally predicted, Castro tried to turn an embarrassing situation to his advantage. He decided to force many of the captains of the boats that had been sent from Florida to pick up family members also to take back to the United States many of Cuba's social undesirables. Included in this were a number of people with criminal records, homosexuals, patients from mental institutions, and even deaf-mutes and lepers. In addition to trying to rid the island of many of what were considered to be its antisocial elements, there is little doubt that the Cuban government was trying to taint the reputation of the Cuban Americans. Approximately twenty-six thousand of the Mariel refugees had prison records, but many had been jailed for political reasons or minor crimes, such as stealing food or trading on the black market for a pair of blue-jeans.[36] Although estimates vary, probably fewer than five thousand (or 4 percent) were hard-core criminals.

An opinion poll conducted by the *Miami Herald* in May 1980 determined that 68 percent of the non-Hispanic whites and 57 percent of the blacks surveyed felt that the Mariel refugees had a largely negative impact on Dade County.[37] In addition to the perception that the Mariel sealift was being used by Castro to empty his jails and mental institutions, the "Marielitos" were not welcomed upon their arrival in Florida for at least four other reasons. First, the suddenness and massive size of the influx intensified problems in helping them become settled. Many who did not have relatives or friends to help them adjust were temporarily housed in military camps in Florida, Arkansas, Pennsylvania, and Wisconsin. One estimate is that it cost the U.S. government close to $1 billion to provide for the Mariel exiles, including the budgets for the navy and Coast Guard operations that took place during the flotilla.[38] A second reason for refugees from Mariel not being welcomed is that the United States' economy in 1980 experienced a recession, accompanied by inflation. In Dade County it has been estimated that the unemployment rate jumped from about 5 percent to 13 percent, primarily due to the Mariel influx. Also, the apartment vacancy rate was reduced to less than 1 percent, creating an acute housing shortage and high rents.[39]

A third reason for the cool reception given the "Marielitos" was that by 1980 public opinion was in favor of reducing immigration, as a result of attention given by the news media to the problems encountered during the migrations of Vietnamese, Mexicans, and Haitians to the United States.[40] A fourth factor was that between 70 and 75 percent of all the Mariel émigrés settled in southern Florida, especially in Dade County. This degree of concentration was greater than for the earlier Cuban waves and thus made adjustment problems more visible and newsworthy. Had the migrants been evenly dispersed throughout the fifty states, they probably would not have been noticed. The three largest cities in Dade County all experienced increases in their Hispanic populations as a result of the Mariel flotilla. The percentage of the population of the city of Miami that was Hispanic increased from 56 to 59 percent. For Hialeah the growth was from 74 to 78 percent; for Miami Beach the increase was from 22 to 27 percent.[41]

Unfortunately, the unwelcome attitude toward the Marielitos has diffused to many of the Cuban Americans who arrived prior to 1980. It became common to hear members of the Cuban community in Miami speak in terms of "new" and "old" Cubans. The "old" Cubans are among the harshest critics of the "new" ones. This is a tendency that has been noted historically among other immigrant groups living in the United States, but it was aggravated by the special set of circumstances that accompanied the Mariel wave, particularly the forced inclusion by Castro of the criminal element.[42] Many of the "old" Cubans feared that the "new" would tarnish their reputation, just as Fidel Castro had hoped they would.

Unlike the emigrants from Cuba who preceded them, the Mariel refugees were characterized by an unbalanced sex structure. Approximately 70 percent were males. There are two reasons for the male majority. First, most of the criminals and social misfits that the Cuban government forced aboard the Mariel boats were males. Second, many of the young men who were unable to travel aboard the Freedom Flights between 1965 and 1973 because of required military service were able to leave in 1980. The Marielitos also differed from earlier streams, since a larger percentage (about 20 percent) were blacks, and a somewhat greater proportion arrived as single adults.[43] These were significant characteristics because the Cuban Refugee Resettlement Center experienced the most trouble in finding help for the settlement of single, black, adult, Cuban males.

During the Mariel flow it was widely rumored that a disproportionately large share of these new Cuban refugees were blacks. The figure that was most often speculated was 40 percent. Figures from the 1990 U.S. Census clearly show that this was a false impression. Only about 6 percent of the Mariel refugees classified themselves as being black in this census. Another 16 percent claimed to be of "other races," and it is possible that many of these people were mulattos. Still, these percentages are very similar to those for the Cubans who arrived just before and after the Mariel wave.[44] It is clear that the typical Mariel immigrant was white; only a small minority was black.

Occupationally, the Mariel flow can best be represented as a continuation of the trend previously noted during earlier Cuban emigration stages.[45] Again, there was an increase in the representation of the working classes and a decline in the percentage that were categorized as professional and managerial workers, as these emigrants came closer to being representative of the population in Cuba. Still, despite this trend and the criminal and misfit elements, the Marielitos (as a whole) enjoyed a somewhat higher socioeconomic status than the population left behind in Cuba. It is clear that these most recent emigrants were not marginal to the Cuban economy, nor were they unemployable in the United States.[46] Despite some of the problems created by a reputation sensationalized by both the Cuban and American presses, it is the collective wisdom of most who have studied them that the Mariel refugees have quickly and effectively accommodated themselves to life in the United States.

### The Ebb Period of the 1980s and Early 1990s

After the heavy flow of Cuban emigrants from Mariel during the five months between April and September 1980, immigration to the United States slackened. Still, there was always some migration taking place. Between 1981 and 1988 the total number of Cuban arrivals was about 125,619 (Table 5.2), for an annual average of a little fewer than sixteen thousand. The Cuban government and the U.S. government tried in earnest to control or regularize the emigration flow. It was in Cuba's best interest to limit the flow because large-scale emigration was an embarrassment. It was advantageous for the U.S. government to keep the flow small because lower numbers were more easily handled and less costly to relocate and support.[47]

However, the later 1980s and early 1990s proved to be a difficult time for Cuba. The communist regimes of Eastern Europe and the former Soviet Union collapsed during the 1989–1991 period, which had a disastrous impact on the Cuban economy because of the support it received from the USSR and trade that it had become dependent on with the former Eastern Block nations. At the same time, access to free media was increasing and Cubans were hearing more about life in the developed countries, especially the United States, Canada, and the countries in Europe. Radio Martí was opened in 1985, and news from the United States became abundant and easily available. The decision to allow Cuban Americans to visit Cuba (mentioned earlier) and the opening of the island to tourism caused the Cuban people to question the policy reversals of the Cuban government. The arrival of tourists made more apparent the differences in standards of living between the wealthy capitalist countries and the island. The term "tourism apartheid" was coined to describe the situation in which Cubans were restricted from shopping in stores that had been established by the Cuban government to cater to tourists in pursuit of badly needed foreign currency. As dissatisfaction increased, the rhetoric of the Cuban government changed, taking on an increasingly hostile and blaming tone toward the people. The Cuban government started cracking down and increasingly restricting civil liberties and personal rights. On August 5, 1994, Cuba experienced its first large-scale citizen riot in Havana.[48]

The Cuban government also lost support from the people through its military efforts in Angola in 1975. The poor treatment of troops upon their return from this conflict caused many young men of military age to consider emigration as an escape from military service. They did not want to die and be buried in Africa. When the troops returned, they found that there were no jobs waiting for them, and many had to perform menial labor in agriculture or work as a state security enforcer. But the event that many believe was especially important was the sacrifice of one of Cuba's highest-ranking war heroes, General Arnaldo Ochoa. He died before a Cuban firing squad in 1989 because he was accused of being involved in drug trafficking. Many felt that he had become a scapegoat for government involvement in this clandestine industry.[49]

In addition, many young Cubans began to complain more openly about a rigid system that determined the types of jobs and education they would have. The Cuban government told them where to go to school, the level of schooling they were entitled to, the major they would have if they went to a university, and the type of job they would have when they graduated. It also told them where they would live. Many young people protested that unless a person was not politically connected, all these decisions were made by the state in the state's best interest. It was against this background of disaffection and dissatisfaction that the next wave of emigration would prevail.

## The *Balseros*

The term *balseros* refers to Cubans who leave their island homeland without either American or Cuban government approval in homemade boats or rafts.[50] It derives from the Spanish word *balsa*, which means "raft." Two waves of *balseros* have occurred in Cuba. The earliest took place immediately after the Castro Revolution during the 1959–1974 period. Approximately 16,500 Cubans took part in that exodus as one component of the Golden Exiles and Freedom Flight phases mentioned earlier. The second, and the topic of this section, occurred during the 1989–1994 period and involved more than 46,500 people.

Although all leave via floating devices, the details of the mode of travel for the *balseros* varies greatly. About 5 percent travel on well-maintained motor boats, locally called "water taxis." Essentially, these are smuggling operations that involve selling passage out of Cuba. These trips normally last about twelve hours, and during the early 1990s, the cost for this form of transportation was between $2,000 and $6,000 per person. Some water taxis come from South Florida and are usually hired by relatives wanting to help their kin escape from Cuba. Others originate through smuggling rings in Cuba. Unless they are caught by Cuban or American officials, this is the safest mode of travel.

Other *balseros* build or buy their own boats and have some knowledge of sea travel and ways they may be rescued. For them the trip is less safe, but still they regard the gamble to be worth the risks involved. About 50–60 percent of all *balseros* traveled to Florida this way. Their most typical rescue strategy is to cross the Florida Straits in two jumps, stopping at the islands in the Cay Sal Bank of the Bahamas, located about halfway between the northern coast of Cuba and the Florida Keys. They hope to be discovered here by groups such as *Hermanos al Rescate* (Brothers to the Rescue), an organization formed in 1991 of mostly Cuban American pilots to hunt for and save Cuban refugees fleeing by sea. They also hope to be picked up by the U.S. Coast Guard and taken to Miami, but things are different now that the U.S. government has decreed that they will be repatriated to Cuba.

The third group of *balseros* is composed of Cubans who have little knowledge of the sea and do not own or know how to obtain a boat. They are likely to use inner tubes or rafts crudely constructed out of empty barrels, Styrofoam, and bits of canvas or plastic. They travel with little other than their determination to leave Cuba. Those who have studied them estimate that between 30 and 40 percent of the rafters travel this way. They, of course, are the least likely to survive.

Knowledgeable Cuban and U.S. sources suggest that perhaps as many as 75 percent of all *balseros* perish before getting to the United States. Among the numerous dangers that they encounter are an inability to hold a small boat or raft on course in rough seas, food and water that are washed overboard or contaminated by saltwater, hot days with intense sunlight, dehydration, hypothermia at night, shark attacks, seasickness that intensifies dehydration and food shortages, and rough seas that damage and frequently swamp the poorly constructed rafts.

As economic and social conditions deteriorated in Cuba in the later 1980s, the incidence of *balseros* slowly increased. During the six-year period of 1983–1988, only 239 rafters were reported by the U.S. Coast Guard (Table 5.4). During 1989 through 1993, the number slowly escalated to more than nine thousand. However, 1994 was the banner year for *balsero* activity. The Cuban government tried to repeat the history of the Mariel emigration phase when Fidel Castro announced on August 12, 1994, that anybody who wanted to leave the island could. No longer, he said, would officials try to stop Cubans from leaving the island. By the time 1994 ended, more than thirty-seven thousand Cubans had left for the United States. Shortly after Castro's announcement, on August 19, U.S. Attorney General Janet Reno stated that Cuban rafters would not be allowed into the United States. The next day President Clinton confirmed that rafters would be interdicted at sea by the U.S. Coast Guard and taken to the U.S. Navy Base at Guantanamo Bay, Cuba, where they would eventually be returned to Cuba. Also, the president said the monetary remittances to Cuba would be stopped, as would family visits, gift parcels, and most charter flights to the island from the United States.

With its major source of foreign income slashed, the pressure was on Cuba to resolve the situation. Unlike Mariel, the flood of refugees had been deflected to Guantanamo without causing a rift between the Cuban American community and the U.S. government. As a consequence, the Cuban and U.S. governments agreed to talks during early September. On September 9, 1994, an agreement was announced. The United States agreed to allow twenty thousand yearly visas for eligible Cubans to impede future rafters from entering the United States and to refuse parole to those who entered illegally. In turn, the Cuban government agreed to take measures to prevent future illegal departures. By December 1994, the number of rafters being picked up by the Coast Guard had declined to zero, and this eighth phase of migration was over (Table 5.4). In May 1995, President Clinton agreed to let all but a few criminals in the Guantanamo refugee camp migrate to the United States. However, he also noted that all future *balseros* would be immediately returned to Cuba upon their apprehension at sea.

The ninth phase of Cuban emigration is the one that has taken place since 1994 and is marked by another ebb in the flow of refugees to the United States at the time of the

**Table 5.4    Number of *Balseros* by Year of Arrival: 1983–1994.**

| Years | Number of Balseros |
| --- | --- |
| 1983–1988 | 239 |
| 1989 | 391 |
| 1990 | 467 |
| 1991 | 2,203 |
| 1992 | 2,557 |
| 1993 | 3,656 |
| January–July 1994 | 4,731 |
| August 1994 | 21,300 |
| September 1994 | 11,085 |
| October–December 1994 | 23 |

Holly Ackerman and Juan M. Clark, *The Cuban Balseros: Voyage of Uncertainty* (Miami: Cuban American National Council, 1995), 22.

writing of this chapter. However, it is likely that when the details of the September 9, 1994, agreement between Cuba and the United States finally get ironed out, the flow will increase once again, to perhaps as much as twenty thousand per year.

## DISTRIBUTION AND MOBILITY PATTERNS OF CUBAN AMERICANS

It has been estimated that between 85 and 90 percent of all Cubans who have emigrated since the Castro revolution in 1959 have moved to the United States.[51] If approximately one million Cubans are presently living in this country, an additional 111,000 to 176,000 must be living outside both the United States and Cuba. Other countries that have received notable numbers of these émigrés are Spain, Mexico, Puerto Rico, Canada, Venezuela, Costa Rica, and Peru.

It is reasonable to ask why the United States has become the home of the vast majority of the Cuban emigrants, rather than one of the nearby Latin American countries that has more in common with Cuba in terms of language and other cultural characteristics. The answer is found in terms of the cultural and economic ties that bound Cuba to the United States from the middle 1800s until 1959. The long-term migration of political exiles to cities such as New York City, Key West, Tampa, and later to Miami has been noted earlier in this chapter. In addition, American entrepreneurs and businesspeople played a major role in resuscitating the Cuban economy after the Spanish-American War and Cuba's independence from Spain. Between 1898 and 1959, Cuba became as economically dependent on the United States as it was dependent most recently on the former Soviet Union. Most of the clothing worn by urbane Cubans, much of the food they ate, virtually all the cars and trucks they drove, and most of the radios they listened to came from the United States. Thus, despite language differences, many Cubans acquired tastes for American life and were aware of living conditions in the United States. This was especially true of the better-educated and more highly skilled Cubans who accounted for a disproportionate share of the earliest wave of Golden Exiles. Once these people led the way, the momentum of the stream quickly became oriented in the direction of the United States.

### Concentration in a Few States and Large Cities

Cuban Americans are highly concentrated in a few areas of the United States. In 1990, 88 percent were located in four states: Florida (64 percent), New Jersey (9 percent), New York (8 percent), and California (7 percent) (Table 5.5). Furthermore, within these states they are found almost exclusively in large cities. The U.S. Census Bureau determined in 1990 that about 95 percent of all families of Cuban descent were living in metropolitan areas.[52] Estimates provided by the U.S. Bureau of the Census indicate that nine out of every ten Cuban Americans live in only sixteen metropolitan areas (Table 5.6). The growth of the Cuban population in four of Florida's largest cities is readily apparent. As a result, the state has assumed even more of a position of preeminence than it had in 1980 (Figure 5.1). Today, almost two-thirds of all Cubans live in Florida, compared with 58 percent in 1980. While the percentage of all Cubans living in Florida has increased, the comparable percentages of the other states has been declining. Florida's location close to Cuba, its climate, and its history of Cuban settlement have been influential in this regard.

**Table 5.5    Distribution by States of Cubans and Hispanics in the United States: 1990 (Percentages).**

| States | Cubans | All Hispanics |
|---|---|---|
| Arizona | .3 | 3.2 |
| California | 7.1 | 34.8 |
| Colorado | .3 | 1.8 |
| Florida | 64.1 | 7.2 |
| Illinois | 1.9 | 4.0 |
| Massachusetts | .4 | 1.1 |
| New Jersey | 8.6 | 3.2 |
| New Mexico | .1 | 2.6 |
| New York | 8.2 | 9.7 |
| Pennsylvania | .6 | 1.0 |
| Texas | 1.4 | 19.4 |
| Rest of the States | 7.0 | 12.0 |
| Totals | 100.0 | 100.0 |

Thomas D. Boswell, *A Demographic Profile of Cuban Americans* (Miami: Cuban American National Council, 1994), 11.

Within the New York–northern New Jersey–Long Island metropolitan area, northeastern New Jersey emerged as the second-leading concentration of Cuban Americans, behind metropolitan Miami. This was due to a small cluster of Cuban families who lived in the Union City–West New York metropolitan area prior to Fidel Castro's assumption

**Table 5.6    U.S. Metropolitan Areas with More than 5,000 Cuban Americans in 1990.**

| Metropolitan Areas | Cuban Americans |
|---|---|
| Miami–Fort Lauderdale, CMSA | 586,479 |
| New York–Northern New Jersey–Long Island, CMSA | 159,239 |
| Los Angeles–Anaheim–Riverside, CMSA | 60,302 |
| Tampa–St. Petersburg–Clearwater, MSA | 33,933 |
| West Palm Beach–Boca Raton–Delray Beach, MSA | 17,315 |
| Chicago-Gary–Lake County, CMSA | 16,990 |
| Orlando, MSA | 10,090 |
| Washington, D.C., MSA | 9,206 |
| Houston-Galveston-Brazonia, CMS | 8,884 |
| San Francisco–Oakland–San Jose, CMSA | 8,025 |
| Philadelphia-Wilmington-Trenton, CMSA | 7,711 |
| Boston-Lawrence-Salem, CMSA | 6,530 |
| Las Vegas, MSA | 6,122 |
| Atlanta, MSA | 5,987 |
| New Orleans, MSA | 5,785 |
| Dallas–Fort Worth, CMSA | 5,211 |
| Total for above cities | 947,809* |

*90.0% of all Cuban Americans
MSA means Metropolitan Statistical Area
CMSA means Consolidated Metropolitan Statistical Area
U.S. Bureau of the Census, *1990 Census of Population,* "Social and Economic Characteristics, United States," CP-2-1, 1993, Table 16.1.

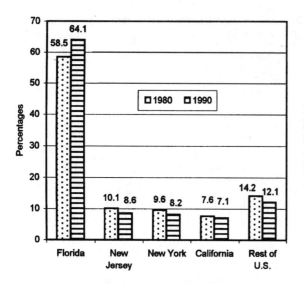

Figure 5.1    Cuban Americans in Four Key States, 1980 and 1990. Sources: U.S. Bureau of the Census, 1980 and 1990, *Census of Population,* "General Population Characteristics," Table 63, 1983, and Summary Tape File 1A, 1992.

of power in Cuba. This area is located on the western side of the Hudson River, directly across from New York City. The Cuban Americans who lived here served as an attraction for the in-migration of other Cubans coming both directly from Cuba, as well as for others moving indirectly, via a stage process, through New York City during the 1960s and 1970s.[53] By the 1970s, two-thirds of West New York's population was composed of people of Cuban descent. Here jobs were available in blue-collar occupations that provided economic opportunities, since Union City and West New York are essentially centers of light industry, warehousing, and transportation. However, population concentrations can change abruptly, as is illustrated by the fact that by the 1990s, it became apparent that the younger Cubans, especially those of the second generation who were born in the United States, were moving away from this concentration to the suburban and exurban areas of New Jersey, as they become more economically successful and affluent.

New York City's position as one of the leading cities of residence for Cuban exiles can be traced back to the nineteenth century. Its history of opportunities for immigrants from other parts of the world and its reputation as a haven for political dissidents have undoubtedly contributed to its attraction for Cuban exiles. Unlike the concentrations in Miami and Union City–West New York, Cubans in New York City have not formed any single outstanding core of settlement. Instead, they are diffused more widely throughout the city and do not dominate any particular neighborhood.

The Cuban Refugee Program has had a major effect on the distribution of Cuban émigrés outside the state of Florida. When it was established in 1961 by President Kennedy, its purpose was to help the Cuban immigrants adjust to living conditions in the United States through job placement, temporary financial assistance, and other welfare benefits. In addition, another of its primary goals was to lessen the burden of concentration on South Florida by redistributing "relocatable" Cuban families to areas outside the state. Individuals with higher education levels and skills, and those with some knowledge of English, were considered to be more easily resettled. If individuals were offered an opportunity to relocate outside of South Florida but refused to move, they were denied further federal government assistance and were considered to be on their own.[54] Of the 494,804 Cubans who registered with the Refugee Program between February 1961 and October 1981, approximately 61 percent were resettled in this manner.[55]

## Miami as a Cuban American Homeland

Although in the eyes of many Cuban Americans it is recognized that the island of Cuba is the first homeland, it can be argued that Miami has become a second homeland in absentia for most of these people. Miami is a city with a relatively short history since it was only incorporated in 1896. As a consequence, the more than thirty-five years that Cubans have been living there is a comparatively long time, especially in a city where most people have in-migrated from another country or some other place in the United States. In 1990, only about one-fourth of Dade County's population was born in the state of Florida, and probably less than 15 percent was born in metropolitan Miami.[56] Simply stated, Cubans are one of Miami's most established groups, despite the fact that they are newcomers. Many Cubans now have a sense of rootedness in Miami.[57] In fact, David Rieff goes so far as to suggest that "Cubans are probably the only people who really do feel comfortable in Dade County these days. Miami is their town now."[58] Lisandro Perez says that "Miami is the capital and Mecca for U.S. Cubans."[59]

The word *absentia* is used to describe an essential characteristic of Miami as a new homeland for Cubans. Whereas between one-third and one-fourth of most immigrants to the United States eventually return to reside in their countries of origin, probably less than one-tenth of 1 percent of Cubans have returned to live in Cuba since the revolution took place in 1959.[60] Miami Cubans find it impractical, difficult, and possibly dangerous to return to Cuba. It is impractical to return because the standard of living and the economic and educational opportunities are so much less than in the United States. It is difficult because the Cuban government carefully screens the documents of anybody entering Cuba, and they are especially suspicious of Cuban Americans returning home. Also, it can be dangerous for those Cuban émigrés who left Cuba illegally to move to the United States. For instance, if an emigrant is suspected of stealing a boat or hijacking a plane, he or she is subject to the Cuban justice system upon return to the island.

It is significant that few Cuban Americans return to live in Cuba. Because only a few return to their island origin, more return instead from elsewhere in the United States to the next best thing: Miami. Thus, Miami has become a type of surrogate homeland for many Cuban Americans.

## The Return Flow to Miami

Since the 1960s, a flow of Cubans to the Miami metropolitan area from areas outside South Florida has become apparent. At first it started as a trickle,[61] but by the middle 1970s, it became a migration stream. A survey of a sample of Cuban migrants living in Miami in 1972 determined that 27.4 percent lived elsewhere in the country before returning to Dade County. A similar survey conducted in 1977 increased the percentage to 34.6 percent.[62] In 1977, the *Miami Herald* commissioned a telephone survey that found about 40 percent of Dade County's Cubans were people who had returned from living in other parts of the country. Data from the 1980 census indicate that 55 percent of the Cubans who moved to Miami between 1975 and 1980 arrived from another state in the United States, as opposed to arriving from a foreign country.[63] During the 1980s, however, Cubans going to Miami represented only about 27 percent of all Cubans moving to Dade County. Immigration from Cuba played a larger role during the 1980s partly because of the arrival in Miami of nearly 100,000 of the 125,000 immigrants during the Mariel exodus in 1980. In addition, the Cuban government curtailed emigration to the United States during the latter half of the 1970s. Still, it is clear that migration of Cuban Americans from within the United States to Dade County played an important role in the growth of Miami's Cuban population during both the 1970s and 1980s. Both the continued immigration of Cubans to Miami and the return flow to Miami of Cubans formerly living elsewhere in the United States are reflected in the increasing concentration of Cuban Americans living in Dade County (Figure 5.2). In 1960, fewer than one in four Cuban Americans lived in Dade County. By 1990, this figure had increased to 54 percent.[64] This increasing concentration is unusual for immigrants living in the United States because usually over time most immigrants disperse to other parts of the United States, after originally concentrating in one or a few areas. The effects of the Cuban Refugee Program appear to explain this apparent paradox.

Most of the people of Cuban descent who returned to Miami from other areas in the United States were settled originally in parts of the country through the Cuban Refugee Program. Once they were able to adjust to living in the United States, save some money, and learn English, they became independent of government financial assistance. Many decided to move back to Miami, their original port of entry. When questioned about reasons for moving back to Miami, the vast majority mentioned the climate of South Florida and a desire to be near relatives and friends who were living in Dade County. Surprisingly, less than 20 percent mentioned economic opportunities as a specific motive for returning.[65]

There is a clear relationship between the states outside of Florida that received the greatest number of Cubans under the Cuban Refugee Program's resettlement efforts and the states that sent the greatest number of returnees back to Miami. For instance, between 1961 and 1981, 46.7 percent of all Cubans who resettled outside the state of Florida located in New York and New Jersey.[66] A survey conducted by the Dade County manager's office found that 61.1 percent of the returnees it questioned originated from these same states.[67] The survey undertaken by the *Miami Herald*, mentioned earlier, tends to support these findings.[68] The return of Cubans from these origins confirms the well-known proposition that for each major migration stream there develops a counterstream movement in the opposite direction.[69] Upon returning to Dade County, most settled in the western suburbs, rather than in the central city of Miami.[70] The years spent adjusting to American lifestyles outside Florida equipped these people with abilities to

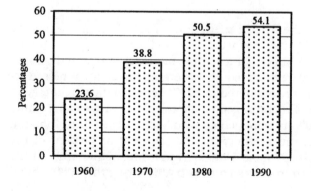

Figure 5.2    Percentage of Cuban Americans Living in Dade County, 1960–1990. Sources: U.S. Bureau of the Census, *1990 Census of Population*, Summary Tape File 1A, Washington, D.C., 1992; and Metropolitan Dade County Planning Department, Hispanic Profile: Dade County, Florida, 1986.

live comfortably near, but not in, the major Cuban concentration of Little Havana. In addition, the skills they had developed and the money they had saved enabled them to afford suburban housing.

## The Expansion and Suburbanization of Cuban American Settlement

Prior to 1959, there were no major concentrations of Hispanics living in Dade County. Although it has been estimated that approximately twenty thousand Cubans were living in metropolitan Miami at that time, they were generally a middle-class population that was scattered throughout the urban area. Once Castro seized power and began to limit severely the amount of money that Cuban emigrants could take out of the country, most of the refugees to Miami arrived virtually penniless. Despite the fact that some had relatives who could help them become established in their new homes, most resided in an area located on the southwestern edge of the city's central business district. This area had begun to deteriorate both as a residential and retail district prior to the arrival of the Cubans. Relatively inexpensive housing was available here, and the area was close to the transition zone that surrounded the central business district and contained the types of business establishments that offered the emigrants the best employment opportunities. In a short period of time, the Cubans were able to invade, and then dominate, this area through their numerical increase. As a result, it became known as "Little Havana." Its landscape acquired a definite Cuban cultural appearance, as it began to develop an improved image.[71]

The distribution of people of Cuban descent for 1990 can be seen in Figure 5.3. The original core is located in Little Havana and provides the basic function of providing cheap housing and serving as a "port of entry" for many of the more recent Latin Amer-

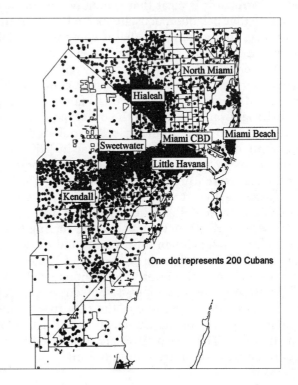

Figure 5.3   Distribution of Cuban Americans in Dade County.

ican immigrants. The areas that have the intermediate densities of Cubans (e.g., Sweetwater, Westchester, West Miami, and Virginia Gardens) are generally characterized by better-quality housing and more housing space than in the core of Little Havana. The fringe includes the outer edges of Cuban settlement in such areas as Kendall, North Miami, and Pinecrest, where Cuban families are presently invading but have not yet established numerical dominance. In these areas Cubans represent less than half of the population, and here the housing is more available and the standard of living the highest. Several outlying clusters have developed as detachments from the main body of Cuban settlement zone. The most obvious is the concentration of Cubans in Hialeah, northwest of Little Havana. This area had many of the same advantages that Little Havana originally had for Cuban settlement, and, as a result, it has developed into a second focus of Cuban activity. Hialeah is Dade County's second largest city and contains a population that was about 88 percent Hispanic in 1990. Cubans alone made up about 65 percent of Hialeah's population at that time.[72]

A study of Miami's Little Havana suggests that most of the Cuban residential areas have been expanding by a contagious diffusion process.[73] Generally, the areas closest to the main Cuban concentration of settlement are the next to be encompassed by the expansion process. One exception, of course, is the Hialeah area, which was settled by a "leapfrog" or hierarchical process. Where expansion of the Cuban ethnic area has been constrained, one of two types of barriers has been found to exist. First, neighborhoods that are dominated by blacks tend to be avoided by most Cubans, such as the gap in the growth of Little Havana to the north. Second, very wealthy areas have land values that are priced beyond the reach of most Cubans and also provide a barrier function. This has happened to the south of Little Havana in the exclusive residential areas of Coral Gables.[74] Despite these barriers, it is clear that generally a distance-decay relationship exists between the distance that neighborhoods are located away from the core of Little Havana and the proportion of their population that is composed of Cubans. Usually, the greater the distance away, the lower the percentage that is Cuban.[75]

Evidence of a suburbanization trend in the residential patterns of Cuban Americans was provided by a 1980 survey conducted by the U.S. Census Bureau. It determined that only 39.5 percent of all families of Cuban descent live in the central cities of metropolitan areas.[76] On the other hand, 57.2 percent live outside central cities but still within metropolitan areas. A panel study of a sample of newly arrived Cuban immigrants in Dade County found that in 1973, 51.7 percent lived in the central city of Miami. Six years later, in 1979, only 38.8 percent remained in the central city. Most of the rest were living in the suburbs of Hialeah or unincorporated Dade County.[77] As suggested earlier, it appears likely that the core of Little Havana served as a "port of entry" for these exiles when they first arrived, but evidence suggests that Hialeah is now serving this function also. After having lived in either Miami or Hialeah for several years, many Cuban immigrants and/or their American-born children move out to the suburban middle or fringe areas of Dade County as their economic situation improves and they can afford better housing. Figures derived from the 1990 Census of Population show that about 47 percent of all Cuban Americans live in central cities, while most of the rest live in the suburbs of American cities.[78] In Dade County, only about 25 percent of the Cubans live in the city of Miami, but another 22 percent live in Hialeah.[79] These two cities are regarded by the U.S. Bureau of the Census the "twin central cities" of metropolitan Miami.

Another study found that the suburban population of metropolitan Miami has grown primarily by two types of population infusion. The first is intraurban migration from the central city to the suburbs. The second is interurban return migration from cities outside the state of Florida to the suburbs of Dade County. Furthermore, when the socioeconomic status of suburban Dade County Cubans was compared to that of Cubans living in the central city, it was clear that (when collectively considered) the former were better off. Furthermore, the Cubans living in Hialeah appeared to occupy an intermediate position between the higher-ranking suburban Cubans and the lower-ranking Cubans who lived in Little Havana.[80]

### Ethnic Segregation

The body of literature dealing with studies of assimilation of various ethnic groups indicates that people sort themselves residentially and socially into groups that are generally homogeneous with respect to both ethnic affiliation and socioeconomic rank. This notion is known as the *ethclass* concept.[81] It has already been determined that Cubans in Dade County appear to segregate themselves from one another according to socioeconomic status within the core, middle, fringe, and outlying cluster areas. A study of Cubans living in West New York alludes to a similar finding.[82] The question that remains is, To what degree are Cubans segregated residentially from the non-Cuban population?

It has been shown that the area of Cuban residential concentration in Dade County has spread outward, from its Little Havana core, through a fringe area that is ethnically mixed. Still, considerable evidence indicates that the Cuban population is notably segregated from other ethnic classes living in metropolitan Miami. A study using 1970 census data noted that Hispanics living in Dade County were strongly segregated from blacks and Jews when considered on a census tract scale. They were also moderately segregated from non-Hispanic whites. For instance, in 1970, 86 percent of the black population would need to be redistributed among the census tracts for it to exhibit a percentage distribution identical to that of Hispanics. The comparable segregation index for Jews is 72 percent. For whites it is between 55 and 60 percent, depending on age category. The study further suggested that the differences in distribution had generally increased between 1950 and 1970.[83] A second study determined that Dade County's Cuban population was notably segregated from the county's Mexican and Puerto Rican populations in 1970. It also found that there was considerable segregation within the Cuban population according to family income classes.[84] Thus, both studies demonstrate that the concept of ethclass is generally applicable to the residential patterns displayed by Miami's Cuban Americans.

A more recent study of the segregation patterns of Cubans and other Hispanics in Miami was conducted using 1980 and 1990 census data.[85] It found that the degree of segregation of Cubans from other ethnic groups in Miami had declined slightly between 1980 and 1990 (Table 5.7). For example, the segregation index comparing Cubans with non-Hispanic whites declined from 60.0 percent to 58.7 percent, whereas the indexes for 1980 and 1990, when Cubans were compared to non-Hispanic blacks, were 86.3 percent and 81.2 percent, respectively. Clearly, the degree of segregation was greatest for Cubans when they were compared to non-Hispanic blacks. However, it is interesting to note that there is considerable segregation also when Cubans are compared to Puerto Ricans, Mexicans, and the "Other Hispanic Nationalities" shown in Table 5.7. These segregation indexes show that being Hispanic does

**Table 5.7   Indices of Segregation Comparing Cubans to Non-Hispanic Racial Categories and Hispanic National Groups Living in Dade County (Miami): 1980 and 1990.**

| Racial or Nationality Groups | Cuban Americans in Miami |
|---|---|
| Non-Hispanic White | 58.7 |
| | (60.0) |
| Non-Hispanic Blacks | 81.2 |
| | (86.3) |
| Non-Hispanic Asians | 57.8 |
| | (NA) |
| Puerto Ricans | 43.8 |
| | (46.7) |
| Mexicans | 61.8 |
| | (66.9) |
| Other Hispanic Nationalities | 29.4 |
| | (32.0) |

Figures in parentheses refer to 1980; whereas the figures without parentheses are for 1990.
NA means not available.
Thomas D. Boswell, "Racial and Ethnic Segregation Patterns in Metropolitan Miami, Florida, 1980–1990," *Southeastern Geographer*, 30 (May 1993): 101.

not mean that the various Hispanic groups are no longer aware of their national origins. Among the Hispanic national groups, Cubans are most highly segregated from the Mexican Americans. This is due to the fact that Mexicans living in South Florida tend to be the poorest of the Hispanic national groups because many work as low-paid agricultural laborers.[86]

The massive influx of Cubans to Dade County and the high level of segregation between Cuban Americans and blacks, Jews, and non-Hispanic whites has been blamed for aggravating ethnic tensions.[87] The expansion of neighborhoods dominated by families of Cuban origin has been associated with a non-Hispanic white exodus from Dade County. It has been estimated that Dade County has experienced a decline of at least 263,000 non-Hispanic whites between 1960 and 1990.[88] It is certainly too simple to blame the immigration of Cubans as the sole cause affecting the exodus of whites from greater Miami. After all, Dade County has experienced other problems during the past decade. Still, the Cuban increase is frequently stated as being one of the causes affecting the "white flight" that is helping alter radically the ethnic composition of metropolitan Miami.

## A DEMOGRAPHIC PROFILE OF CUBAN AMERICANS

The structure and composition of a population can be very revealing in providing clues about the factors that have influenced it over time. Thus, to a considerable extent the present demographic characteristics of an ethnic group provide a mirror of past historical tendencies.[89]

The demographic characteristics of Cuban Americans have been particularly influenced by the recent history of their migration to the United States. Both the emigration policies of the Cuban government and the "natural" selectivity of the types of Cubans who chose to migrate proved crucial in determining the characteristics of Cuban Americans. These can be analyzed by examining the age and sex composition; racial characteristics; employment, occupation, and income tendencies; and fertility levels of the people of Cuban descent living in the United States.

## Age and Sex Composition

When the age structure of the Cuban descent population is compared to those of the total Spanish origin and non-Spanish origin populations, some significant differences become immediately apparent (Table 5.8). The median age for the Cubans is more than thirteen years older than for the total Hispanic population and more than three years older than for non-Hispanics. Despite the fact that most have lived for a relatively short period in the United States, the age structure of the Cuban Americans more closely resembles that of non-Hispanic people than it does the Hispanic population. The fact that the Cuban origin population is considerably older in the age composition than the total Spanish-American population is related to two primary factors.[90] The first is the very low fertility patterns exhibited by the Cubans, when compared with most other ethnic components of the United States population. More will be said regarding this important tendency later in this chapter. Suffice it to say, at this point, that lower birthrates tend to depress proportional representation in the lower age classes. As a result, the population appears to "age" with declining fertility.

The second factor that helps account for the older character of the Cuban Americans has to do with the selectivity of migrants who moved from Cuba to the United States. From the earlier discussion of the history of Cuban emigration flows, it will be recalled that the Castro government was unwilling to allow most young adult males to leave the island until they had satisfied their military obligation. This was especially true during the Freedom Flights between 1965 and 1973 and helps explain why the Cuban population in Table 5.8 has a larger percentage in the sixty-five years and over age class, when compared to either the Hispanic origin or non-Hispanic populations. It was also mentioned earlier that elderly people were allowed to leave more freely because it was believed that many would become dependent on the state if they remained in Cuba.[91] This helps account for the fact that close to 19 percent of the Cuban Americans are sixty-five years of age or older, whereas only about 5 percent of the total Hispanics fall in this age class.

**Table 5.8    Age and Sex Composition of Cuban Americans, Hispanics, and Non-Hispanics in the United States: 1996.**

| Age Groups (Years) | Cuban Americans | All Hispanics | Non-Hispanics |
|---|---|---|---|
| 0–19 | 20.7% | 39.8% | 28.5% |
| 20–39 | 32.4% | 36.2% | 29.9% |
| 40–64 | 28.1% | 18.9% | 28.8% |
| 65 and Older | 18.8% | 5.1% | 12.8% |
| Median Age | 38.9 Years | 25.6 Years | 35.1 Years |
| Males | 51.3% | 50.6% | 48.7% |
| Females | 48.7% | 49.4% | 51.3% |

U.S. Bureau of the Census, *Current Population Survey, March 1996*, Washington, D.C., Internet release, February 1998.

Prior to the Mariel boatlift in 1980, a slight majority (50.2 percent) of the people of Cuban descent living in the United States were female.[92] The very minor predominance of females also was related to the migration policies of the Cuban government. The reluctance to allow males of military age to leave during the Aerial Bridge of 1965 to 1973 had an effect, as did the greater freedom for the elderly to emigrate.[93] Because women usually exhibit greater longevity, it is to be expected that they would be overrepresented in the oldest age classes. Since the Mariel exodus was heavily dominated by males, it is apparent that the balance has swung in the direction of a male predominance. By 1996, males now represent about 51 percent of the total Cuban American population (Table 5.8).[94]

## Racial Characteristics

The vast majority of Cubans living in the United States are considered to be white. The most recent year for which racial data are available for Cuban Americans is 1990. In that year, 83 percent were classified as white, with 4 percent as black, and the remaining 13 percent as other categories.[95] For the entire population of the United States, about 12 percent is black. The overwhelming proportion of the Cuban Americans who are white is not representative of the population remaining in Cuba. For instance, the 1953 Cuban Population Census shows that about 27 percent of the island's population was at that time black or mulatto. This is about seven times the percentage for the Cubans living in the United States.[96]

Five reasons have been suggested for explaining why Cuban Americans have a smaller proportion of their population as nonwhite.[97] First, the Castro revolution was designed primarily to benefit the poorer classes of Cuban society. Since blacks were more concentrated among the poor, presumably a larger percentage of them were able to obtain more opportunities under the new government. Second, the Castro government has expended major efforts to depict the United States as a racist society, as part of its anti-American propaganda policy. Third, much of the Cuban flow to the United States has been promoted and assisted through family ties with relatives already living in the United States. Fewer Cuban blacks have moved to the United States because a smaller proportion of blacks have relatives living in America on whom they can rely for assistance. Fourth, the immigration policy of the United States, since 1965, has generally favored the legal immigration of Cubans who have close family members already residing on American soil. Thus, not only were the kinship networks of whites not as readily available to them, but Cuban blacks also found that it was harder to gain entry through the American consul in Havana because of this scarcity of American relatives. Fifth, there is evidence of resentment on the part of a minority of the white Cuban American exiles living in the United States toward black Cubans because of a suspicion that many of the blacks welcomed the Castro revolution. Evidence in support of this hypothesis is manifested in Miami's Little Havana, where less than 5 percent of the resident population is black.

A comparative study of Cubans living in the metropolitan areas of Miami and Union City–West New York found that a slightly larger proportion of the latter's population was black. This difference was attributed to differing perceived levels of discrimination.[98] It has been previously noted in the literature that the majority of Cuban blacks live in the northeastern United States, where the reputation for racial tolerance is better than in the South.[99]

Earlier in this chapter it was noted that approximately 20 percent of the Cubans who immigrated via the Mariel boatlift in 1980 were black. This figure represents a proportion that is about five times higher than has been characteristic of past Cuban migration waves. But even this new figure is only about three-fourths of the percentage of the present black population in Cuba. Nevertheless, the fact that a larger proportion of blacks left Cuba during this last exodus than ever before has been heralded by some as being a sign that the Castro government is beginning to wear thin, even with the types of people it was supposed to benefit the most.

## Employment, Occupation, and Income Tendencies

When the working force and income characteristics of Cuban Americans are compared to those of all Hispanics (Table 5.9), it is clear that the Cubans have achieved a remarkably high level of socioeconomic success. This is particularly noteworthy when their relatively short length of residence in the United States is considered. In terms of occupational distribution, employment levels, and income, they are considerably better off than most other people of Hispanic origin living in America. In fact, their economic achievements approach those of the non-Hispanics in the United States. Currently

Table 5.9   Occupation, Employment, and Income Characteristics of Cuban Americans Compared to All Hispanics and Non-Hispanics in the United States: 1996 (Persons 16 Years of Age and Older).

| Categories | Cuban Americans | All Hispanics | Non-Hispanics |
|---|---|---|---|
| *Occupation Classes of Males (Percentages)* | | | |
| Managerial and Professional | 21.3 | 11.6 | 29.1 |
| Technical, Sales, and Administrative Support | 23.0 | 15.8 | 20.8 |
| Service Occupations | 14.2 | 17.5 | 9.4 |
| Farming, Forestry, and Fishing | 3.2 | 7.7 | 3.6 |
| Precision Production, Craft, and Repair | 19.0 | 18.7 | 17.8 |
| Operators, Fabricators, and Laborers | 19.3 | 28.8 | 19.3 |
| *Occupation Classes of Females (Percentages)* | | | |
| Managerial and Professional | 22.9 | 17.2 | 31.6 |
| Technical, Sales, and Administrative Support | 48.9 | 38.6 | 41.9 |
| Service Occupations | 16.6 | 26.5 | 16.7 |
| Farming, Forestry, and Fishing | .0 | 1.8 | 1.0 |
| Precision Production, Craft, and Repair | .6 | 2.5 | 1.9 |
| Operators, Fabricators, and Laborers | 11.0 | 13.5 | 6.9 |
| *Labor Force Status of Males and Females (Percentages)* | | | |
| Unemployed | 6.2 | 9.8 | 5.5 |
| Males in the Civilian Labor Force | 69.4 | 77.4 | 73.2 |
| Females in the Civilian Labor Force | 52.9 | 52.6 | 59.4 |
| *Income and Poverty Status (1995)* | | | |
| Median Income, Full-Time Employed Males | $26,245 | $20,378 | $32,383 |
| Median Income, Full-Time Employed Females | $21,879 | $17,111 | $23,110 |
| Percentage of All Persons (all ages) Living Below Poverty | 21.8 | 30.3 | 11.8 |

U.S. Bureau of the Census, *Current Population Survey, March 1996*, Washington, D.C., Internet release, February 1998.

Cuban Americans are represented by an intermediate position, in terms of their socio-economic status, between the Hispanic and non-Hispanic populations. When compared to other Hispanics, such as Puerto Ricans and Mexican Americans, it is clear that the Cubans are much better off economically.[100]

The current occupational composition of the population of Cuban Americans is a product of four major trends that have characterized the labor force history of these émigrés. The first has been the tendency, noted earlier in this chapter, for people with higher education levels and skills to be overrepresented in migration flows to the United States. Second, as also previously stated, there has been a tendency for this selection process to decline over time, so that the most recent Cuban immigrants are more similar to the population left behind in Cuba than was the case of the earlier migrants. There are a couple of reasons for the decline in the proportion of professionals among the later emigration waves. Many of the better educated and more highly skilled who wanted to leave have already done so. Thus, there are fewer remaining in Cuba to supply future streams to the United States. In addition, because the Cuban government is reluctant to see them leave, the remaining professionals have been accorded a privileged position in the socialist society of the island. Thus, they have less of an incentive to emigrate now than in the past.[101]

A third trend that has affected the occupational characteristics of Cuban Americans has been the tendency for most to experience a decline in status with their *first* job in the United States. Often they had to take whatever type of work was available when they first arrived. Their lack of facility with English was a major factor that affected their employment opportunities. In addition, many professional occupations require citizenship or formal licensing procedures that can take years to satisfy. For example, few teachers, lawyers, or doctors can practice their professions before they become certified in the United States.

A fourth factor that has affected the labor force characteristics of Cuban Americans has been their tendency toward upward mobility as their length of residence in the United States increased.[102] A study of Cubans living in the city of West New York found that although the last job held in Cuba prior to emigration had very little influence on the first job obtained in the United States, it did affect the potential for eventual upward mobility. Those who had higher-status jobs in Cuba were more likely to become upwardly mobile in the United States. In addition, younger migrants and those who were better educated have also exhibited more success in climbing the occupational ladder.[103]

## Fertility Levels

A number of fertility studies have found that middle-class families in Western societies tend to have smaller numbers of children than either the poor or wealthy classes. Wealthy couples can comfortably afford to have as many children as they want, whereas the standard of living for the very poor is not likely to be altered much through the addition of another child.[104] Given the fact that most Cuban American families are middle-class, it is reasonable to find that they have characteristically exhibited very low fertility patterns while living in the United States. In fact, Cuba has a very low birthrate.[105]

A study comparing various demographic characteristics of several components of the Hispanic American population found that the people of Cuban descent have exceptionally low birthrates.[106] In 1970, the number of births per one thousand population for the Cuban Americans was found to be sixteen. For the non-Hispanic white population of the

United States it was seventeen, whereas for Mexican Americans and Puerto Ricans living in the United States it was twenty-seven and thirty, respectively. When controlled to take into consideration such factors as older age structure of the Cuban Americans, their higher education levels, and higher female labor force participation rates, the differences became even more pronounced. When thus standardized, women of Cuban descent exhibited a fertility rate that was 23 percent lower than that of non-Hispanic white women living in the United States. When compared to Mexican American and Puerto Rican women living in the United States, the rate for Cuban women was 47 and 28 percentage points lower, respectively.[107] The study concluded by suggesting that the lower fertility performance of the Cuban descent women can be attributed to their higher education levels, higher labor force participation rates, and generally higher aspirations.

More recent data for 1990 illustrate the same principles. Cuban women who were in the thirty to forty-five year age group averaged 1.8 children. The comparable figures for all Hispanics and non-Hispanic women in the same age group were 2.6 and 1.9, respectively.[108] Clearly, Cuban American women have exceptionally low fertility when compared to most other Americans.

## CULTURAL CHARACTERISTICS OF CUBAN AMERICANS

The concept of culture is defined by social scientists to include all the learned characteristics of a given society, but only a few aspects of the culture of Cuban Americans will be discussed here. The attributes selected for discussion are those that are thought to be particularly relevant for illustrating the differences between Cuban Americans and most other Americans. Also, these are the attributes that are particularly interesting because of the ways they have been modified as a result of immigration to the United States.[109]

### The Cuban American Family

Prior to the socialist revolution in 1959, the traditional family structure in Cuba was typical of that for most of Latin America. There was a sharp distinction between the role of men and women, with a double standard being applied in work, play, and sex. The wife was expected to stay at home and attend to the running of the household and care of children. A pattern of male dominance prevailed, and the husband made most of the major family decisions. The tradition of machismo dictated that males demonstrate virility through physical strength, courage, and business success. It was common, and considered proper, for males to have extramarital affairs. Whether or not a husband had a regular mistress was frequently more affected by economics than conscience. Daughters and wives, on the other hand, were protected against temptation. A strict tradition of chaperoning was in effect for respectable, unmarried women who dated.[110]

Sociologists have developed a concept known as *resource theory* for explaining the position of decision-making power that the members of any particular family have relative to each other. An individual gains in power if the resources that he or she contributes to the family increases. These resources may be economic, intellectual, or emotional in nature.[111] Economic difficulties that many Cubans faced upon their arrival in the United States affected their adjustment. Often the husband was unable to find work or found work at a lower status level than he had experienced in Cuba. As a result, it became necessary for many wives to enter the labor force to help contribute to the support of the family. In 1990, slightly over half of all women of Cuban descent in the United States who were sixteen years of age or older were in the labor force (see Table 5.9). A survey of women in West New York found that less than one-fourth had worked in Cuba before coming to the United States.[112] Thus, as the wife's resource contribution to the family became greater through her employment, usually her power to help make decisions also increased, whereas that of her husband declined. A study of Cuban women in Washington, D.C., concluded that their entrance into the labor force is the single most important change in their lives as immigrants.[113] As a result, the traditional patriarchal family structure for Cuban Americans began to change toward greater equality in decision-making abilities for husbands and wives. Also, a lessening of the former double standard began to take place. A study of Cuban families living in Miami determined that both wives and children gained greater power in making their own decisions when they obtained employment and contributed to the family income. In addition, length of residence in the United States and degree of association with Americans were also positively associated with level of equality or independence within the family.[114] As a result, Cuban American families are less male dominated and the roles of husbands and wives are less segregated than the traditional Latin American family norm that typified Cuba before 1959.

Despite the fact that Cuban family structure has changed in the United States from what it was in Cuba, it is still different enough from the American norm to cause some conflict between the first- and second-generation Cuban Americans. Studies of acculturation stresses among Cubans living in the United States have found that the second generation, which was the first to be born in America, generally has adopted Anglo attitudes and behavior patterns more quickly than their first-generation, immigrant parents. Sometimes a crisis in authority emerges, as the parents find themselves being led and instructed in new ways by their children. Many of the traditional norms of the Cuban family became labeled "old-fashioned." Chaperoning for dating, as an example, has become a focal point of tension in many families. Many second-generation Cuban Americans feel they are caught between two cultures, by being neither completely Cuban nor American. They want to maintain selected aspects of both cultures and as a result feel that they do not belong to (or are not completely accepted by) either.[115]

Another aspect of the Cuban American family that distinguishes it from the contemporary American family is the tendency for Cuban households to include relatives in addition to members of the nuclear family. The U.S. Census Bureau indicates that about 9 percent of all people of Cuban descent live in households where there are "other relatives" (other than wife or child) of the head of the household. The corresponding figure for all Hispanics is about 10 percent; for non-Hispanics it is approximately 4 percent.[116] Often this additional relative is a widowed and dependent grandparent who came to the United States after the nuclear family had arrived. Because so many Cuban American women work, the elderly have become important as housekeepers and baby-sitters. They also have passed on elements of their culture and language to the new-generation children.[117]

One important indicator of the assimilation of an ethnic group is the degree to which it is characterized by the marriage of its members to people outside the group. For 1970, when all women of Cuban descent are considered, 17 percent had married non-Cubans.[118] However, many of the marriages to Cubans took place in Cuba before arrival in the United States. When only second-generation American-born women are considered, it was found that 46 percent of those married had married non-Spanish husbands. The comparable figures for women of Puerto Rican and Mexican descent are 33 and 16 percent, respectively.[119] Thus, second-generation Cubans have exhibited an extraordinarily high rate of out-marriage, a fact that appears to indicate a very rapid tendency toward assimilation. A comparative study of out-marriage patterns for Hispanic groups living in New York City determined that Cubans had the highest out-group marriage rates. It also found that the degree of out-marriage is much higher among second-generation, American-born children than for their foreign-born Hispanic parents. In addition, people with higher socioeconomic status, those who are older at the time they marry, and those who had been married more than once all show higher out-marriage rates. Finally, the relative degree of spatial concentration proves to be the strongest determinant of exogamous marriage rates. Groups that are more dispersed residentially throughout New York City exhibited higher out-marriage rates.[120] It was also noted that the rate of intergroup marriage is considerably higher for Cubans living in New York than for those living in New Jersey and Florida. The lower rates for the latter two states is attributed to the greater concentration of Cubans residing in the metropolitan areas of Union City–West New York and Miami.[121]

## Citizenship and Political Tendencies

Many of the Cuban refugees who arrived in the United States during the early 1960s figured that their stay in this country would be of short duration. They were convinced that Fidel Castro would soon lose control and that they would be able to return home to Cuba. As time wore on, however, it became apparent that their stay in the United States would be longer than originally expected. They began to adjust to American lifestyles and their desire and hope for returning to their island of origin decreased. Studies in both West New York and Miami clearly show that the desire to return to Cuba to live decreases as length of residence in the United States increases.[122] By the 1970s, it was clear that the vast majority of Cuban Americans planned to stay in the United States, even if the Castro government were to be overthrown.[123]

The increasing preference for remaining in the United States is paralleled by a growing desire for American citizenship. Again, length of residence is related to both achievement of citizenship and the desire to attain citizenship status. One obvious reason for the link between length of residence and becoming an American citizen is that the United States government requires that once an individual receives legal permanent residency status, a five-year wait is necessary before that person can apply for citizenship. The decision to become an American citizen is another important indicator of assimilation because it requires that the person becoming naturalized renounce any previous citizenship. To a Cuban, this usually formalizes the realization that returning to Cuba to live is no longer practical or desirable. In 1970, approximately 25 percent of all Hispanics living in metropolitan Miami were citizens of the United States. By 1978, the figure had risen to 43 percent. Furthermore, of those who were not yet citizens, 77.2 percent planned to apply for this status.[124] In West New York, none of the Cubans questioned in a 1968 survey were American citizens. At that time, 44 percent wanted to become citizens; 33.9 percent did not want citizenship status; and 22 percent could not make up their minds. In 1979, there was a dramatic change in these figures. By that time, 40.3 percent had attained citizenship status, 43.7 percent wanted to become citizens, 6 percent did not want citizenship, and 10 percent had no preference.[125] The 1990 census shows that 64.4 percent of all Cuban Americans were U.S. citizens, of whom 44.0 percent were born in the United States. Among the foreign-born Cubans, more than half (50.3 percent) were U.S. citizens.[126] It is clear that Cuban Americans are very rapidly attaining American citizenship and can be expected to continue to do so in the near future.

Once citizenship has been achieved, the political behavior of Cuban Americans can be described as being participatory, personal, anticommunist, and conservative. It is participatory in the sense that an exceptionally large percentage of Cuban American citizens both register to vote and exercise their voting rights at the polls. In 1978, 84.3 percent of the Cubans living in West New York who were eligible to vote registered to vote. In this same year, only 62.6 percent of the total eligible-to-vote population for the United States registered. In addition, the Cubans' voting participation rate was about ten percentage points higher than for the entire American population.[127] In Miami's November 1981 mayoral election, of those eligible to vote, the voter turnout rates were 58 percent for Hispanics, 38 percent for Anglos, and somewhat more than 50 percent for blacks.[128] These participatory percentages suggest that Cubans will exert even more influence in future elections in both Miami and the Union City–West New York areas as more of the people of Cuban descent become eligible to vote.

Cuban American politics are personal in the sense that most Latin American politics are personal. It represents a refusal to deal with a government that is bureaucratic and impersonal. It is a face-to-face approach, in which there is a belief that to obtain a favor a person needs to show (or have access to) a contact, someone who personally knows someone else in a position of power. In English the system is known as "power brokering"; in Spanish it is called *personalismo*. Most Cuban American politicians are well aware of the political expectations that friends and relatives have once they achieve an elected position. How they react to such pressures varies, but it is true that it helps to have friends and relatives in influential positions.[129]

People of Cuban descent tend to be both strongly anticommunist and conservative in their political learnings as a result of their experiences with the Castro government in Cuba.[130] Both tendencies favor membership in the Republican Party. A study of voting patterns in neighborhoods in Dade County, both before and after they became dominated by Cuban residents, showed a marked shift in voting preferences, first for Democratic Party candidates and later in favor of the Republican Party. In addition, a survey of over five hundred Cuban emigrants in Miami found that 73 percent supported the Republican Party and most favored conservative policies. The general preference for the Republican Party has significantly changed the reputation of Miami, which used to be known as a staunchly liberal enclave that traditionally could be counted on to vote in favor of the Democrats. The Cuban American support of Republicans has been linked to its strong feelings against communism and the Bay of Pigs fiasco. The latter was blamed on the lack of support from the Democrat presidential administration of John F. Kennedy.[131]

In 1992, the Latino National Political Survey released results of a poll it conducted throughout the United States to determine political attitudes of Cuban Americans, Mexican Americans, and Puerto Ricans living on the U.S. mainland.[132] A total of 2,817 Hispanic Americans were questioned during 1989 and 1990, as were an additional 598 non-Hispanics. This survey confirmed most of what has been said earlier in this chapter. Less than 6 percent of the Cuban Americans said they intended to return some day to live in Cuba, compared to 24 percent of the Puerto Ricans who planned to return home to Puerto Rico and 8 percent of the Mexican Americans who intended to return some day to Mexico. Cubans were more likely to characterize their political philosophy as being conservative when compared to Mexicans, Puerto Ricans, and Anglos. The Cubans were less likely to favor ethnic and racial quotas for job hiring and college admission than Mexicans and Puerto Ricans. While Mexicans and Puerto Ricans were most likely to support the Democratic Party, Cubans were most likely to support the Republicans.

## Language and Religion

Language and religion are two cultural attributes that most ethnic minorities are very reluctant to abandon. Where different from those of the host society, they increase the visibility of the minority group. The degree to which an ethnic group maintains distinct language and religious patterns is often regarded as being an important indicator of acculturation and assimilation.

### Language

Virtually all first-generation Cuban immigrants living in the United States speak Spanish as their mother tongue.[133] Like most other immigrant groups who have come to America, it is common for the first-generation Cuban Americans to teach their native language to the second generation. This is particularly the case where both parents are of Cuban origin or where one parent is from Cuba and the other is an immigrant from another Spanish-speaking country. The Spanish that is learned in the home by the second generation is usually very basic and elementary. More often than not, the second-generation children converse with neighborhood friends in a mixture of Spanish and English, called "Spanglish." In short, they learn a poor quality of Spanish that sometimes serves as a source of embarrassment for themselves and for their parents. Furthermore, their ability to speak English may also be impaired, especially if they live in a predominantly Cuban neighborhood where little English is spoken. Mixed marriages that involve an immigrant Cuban spouse and a native Anglo seldom produce children who are truly fluent in Spanish. One exception to this generalization is encountered when the mother works and the children are raised by a Spanish-speaking relative. Since by far the majority of Cuban Americans are still members of the first or second generation, it is somewhat speculative to predict the language abilities of the third generation. However, limited evidence suggests that the majority of these grandchildren of the Cuban immigrants will be fluent only in English.[134] This implies that by the third generation, facility with Spanish will be a legacy of the earlier two generations. This does not mean that Spanish will no longer be heard in areas of Cuban concentration in the near future. There are still many young first- and second-generation Spanish-speaking people of Cuban descent living in Miami, Union City–West New York, and New York City who have many years to live. It will take at least four or five more decades for the Cuban population to become assimilated linguistically. Of course, this process can be delayed even longer by any future large-scale immigration waves from Cuba.

Where Cuban Americans are heavily concentrated, as in metropolitan Miami and West New York, speaking Spanish can become an emotional issue. According to a survey conducted by the *Miami Herald,* language was the main obstacle to harmony between Anglos and Cubans living in Dade County. Some Anglos felt it was becoming necessary to be bilingual, in Spanish and English, to be in a position to compete for local jobs. They were afraid that second-generation Cubans were in a more favorable position because of their knowledge of both languages. It was widely believed that Spanish was being forced upon the Anglos by the large number of first-generation Cubans who, they thought, were not making a serious effort to learn English. The survey found that 79 percent of the non-Hispanics questioned agreed that students in Dade County schools should not be required to become proficient in Spanish. On the other hand, 70 percent of the Hispanics felt that proficiency in Spanish should be required.[135] In 1973, the Dade County commissioners passed an ordinance that officially declared the county to be bilingual. Seven years later, in November 1980, just after the Mariel exodus, the electorate of Dade County repealed the ordinance in a referendum by a voting ratio of three to two. The new ordinance stipulated that public funds were not to be used to teach languages other than English or to promote a culture other than the culture of the United States.[136] Many Miami businesspeople feared that this action may have a damaging effect on South Florida's lucrative trade with Latin America. Then in 1992 Florida voters passed a referendum that made English the official language of the state.[137] Two years later, in 1994, Dade County commissioners voted to make both English and Spanish the official languages of the county.

When asked what the most important problem posed by living in the United States is, first-generation Cubans most frequently cite the language barrier. Their lack of facility with English hinders their employment opportunities and affects their abilities to obtain government services. Since first-generation immigrants still comprise a majority among Cuban Americans, the language problem is magnified. In 1990, 68.2 percent of all Cuban Americans declared in the population census that they spoke English either very well or well. Two recent studies in Miami suggest that even though Dade County has a large Hispanic population, the greatest concern should not be that Spanish will take over as the dominant language in the county but rather that the second-generation Hispanic children are not becoming sufficiently proficient in Spanish to be able to use it to conduct business with Latin American countries.[138] Many business leaders in Miami express the strong fear that the city will lose its lead as a gateway city to Latin America if there are not enough people highly proficient in Spanish to be able to talk intelligently with business leaders from these countries. A recent survey undertaken in both South Florida and San Diego determined that 85 percent of the second-generation Hispanic children questioned said they preferred to speak in English instead of the Spanish their parents speak.[139]

### Religion

Most Cuban Americans are at least nominally Roman Catholics. Their arrival in Miami and Union City–West New York has had a major impact on the membership of many local parishes. Virtually all Catholic churches in both urban areas have priests who can give mass, hear confessions, and offer counsel in Spanish. In Cuban neighborhoods, the Catholic church has become one of the key ethnic institutions of self-identity and a center of community life.

However, some evidence indicates that the influence of Roman Catholicism has been declining among Cuban Americans. Between 1968 and 1979, the percentage of Cubans living in West New York who expressed a preference for the Catholic faith decreased from 91.5 percent to 78.3 percent, whereas those with no particular religious preference increased from 1.2 to 11.3 percent. In addition, attendance rates dropped. The proportion who attended church at least once a month went down from 79.0 percent to 47.1 percent. Those who never attended increased from 5.0 percent to 19.6 percent. Despite these declining attendance rates, almost three-quarters indicated that religion was still a very important part of their life.[140]

An explanation for the decreasing religious participation ratios of Cuban Americans is necessarily speculative. Two factors are probably involved. First, it is possible that they are being influenced by the lower participation levels of non-Hispanics, as American society is becoming increasingly secular. Second, the efforts of communism to rid Cuba of religion may have reduced the religiosity of some of the Cuban immigrants, especially those who arrived during the later waves.

In addition to those professing the Catholic faith, a sizable number of Cubans are members of various Protestant sects and a lesser number of Cuban Jews. However, one of the more unique religions practiced by Cuban Americans is an Afro-Cuban cult faith known as *Santeria*. Referred to as an Afro-Christian syncretic religion because it combines aspects of Catholicism with African magical practices, it is believed to help cure illnesses, assist in finding jobs, bring good luck, and even exorcise evil spirits.[141] Because of its magical beliefs and its practices of chanting and animal sacrifice, there is a reluctance shown by many Cubans to admit that they follow *Santeria*. Still it is believed that many use it. For instance, a survey of Cubans living in Miami and Union City found that only 1.2 percent of the households in both cities reported practicing this religion. On the other hand, 7.1 percent of the Miami respondents and 23.5 percent of the Union City respondents said they would use a *santero* (a priest for the *Santeria* faith) if they felt they needed help.[142] Practicing *Santeria* is like an insurance policy. A person hopes never to have to use it, but if needed, it can be tried out. If an important event is about to occur, everything that logically can be done to ensure a favorable outcome will be tried, and as added spiritual assistance *Santeria* may also be used.

### An Economic Enclave

There are two traditional views of the ways new immigrants are incorporated into the United States labor market. The first is called the *assimilationist view* and assumes that immigrants start in the lower-paying jobs and gradually move up the occupational ladder until they become indistinguishable, in terms of their employment characteristics, from the host population. The second perspective is termed the *internal colonialist* view. It holds that some ethnic groups are "unmeltable" and are therefore subject to exploitation in the labor market through continued employment in the lowest paying jobs with few opportunities for advancement. Versions of this latter view have most often been used as an explanation for the continued disadvantaged economic position of black Americans. They have also been applied to several other traditionally disadvantaged ethnic groups, such as the Mexican Americans and Puerto Ricans living on the mainland of the United States.

The labor force experiences of Cuban Americans who live outside of metropolitan Miami most closely fit the assimilationist model. However, the Cubans living in Miami (and to a lesser extent those who live in Union City–West New York) do not appear to parallel either of the two models. A recent study of Miami suggests that Cubans have established their own economic enclave that caters particularly to a Cuban American and Hispanic market. In this enclave it is possible to transact all business negotiations in Spanish and to use Cuban business customs, thus making it easier for newly arrived immigrants to become incorporated quickly into the economic mainstream. The initial capital and entrepreneurial skills that were used to establish the enclave were provided by the earliest waves of immigrants that left Cuba in the early 1960s. The later flows of refugees sustained its growth and allowed the enclave to reach a sufficient size for economies of scale to be developed. As the more recent waves contributed immigrants who were somewhat less educated and less skilled, they provided a cross section of laborers who allowed for a more vertically integrated local ethnic economy to develop. In this way, a laboring class of Cubans was provided to work in the Cuban-owned businesses. The return migration of Cubans, settled elsewhere in the United States through assistance provided by the Cuban Refugee Program, contributed additional capital and labor for further growth.[143]

The Cuban economic enclave in Miami does not exist independently of the rest of the American economy. In fact, the two are functionally integrated. The Cuban component has had a major impact on expanding South Florida's trade with Latin America. By 1978, the United States Custom District, in which Miami is included, accounted for 3.1 percent of all the United States' trade with Latin America. Aggregate exports from this district in 1979 amounted to approximately $6 billion, of which about 80 percent went to Latin America.[144] More recently, in 1992, Miami handled more than one-third of all U.S. trade with Latin America. Of the city's top ten trading countries, the first nine are in Latin America. About 40 percent of all U.S. trade with Central America passed through the custom district that includes Miami, and the figures for South America and the Caribbean are 17 percent and 35 percent, respectively.[145]

While most businesses in the Cuban economic enclave are small, some are large and employ hundreds of workers. Enclave firms tend to concentrate on construction, finance, textiles, leather, furniture, and cigar making. There are more than 18,000 Cuban-owned businesses in Dade County. Cuban Americans account for about 25,000 garment workers, 3,500 doctors, over 500 lawyers, and about half of the aircraft repair and maintenance labor force in Dade County. There are 16 Cuban American presidents of banks and approximately 250 vice presidents. Cubans own over 60 new and used car dealerships, about 500 supermarkets, and close to 250 drug stores. It has been estimated that the Cuban community of Dade County earns an aggregate annual income of over $2.5 billion.

## Miami's Cuban *Municipios* in Exile

Pre-Castro Cuba was divided into six provinces, which in turn were subdivided into a total of 126 *municipios*.[146] It is the *municipios* that most Cubans identify as their original homes. Administratively, Cuban *municipios* are most comparable to counties or townships in the United States. Beginning in the mid-1960s, the former residents of various *municipios* living in Miami joined together to lend assistance to new arrivals from their home areas. Through time these people expanded their activities to include social and political functions, and they established formal organizations. These units become known as *municipios en el exilio* (counties in exile).

There are 110 officially recognized *municipios* in exile in Miami. Their membership size and frequency of activities vary widely. Some of the larger *municipios*, such as those of Havana and Santiago de Cuba, have almost one thousand members and meet once a month. But most have only several hundred members and meet only a few times a year, often on the birthday of their patron saint or on dates of other holidays of special significance to their hometowns. These meetings typically take place in rented halls or restaurants, but about twenty of the *municipios* have permanent buildings. They are located primarily in Little Havana and Hialeah. The buildings are usually decorated inside with portraits of famous Cuban patriots, old photographs, flags, and assorted memorabilia from Cuba. Most of the larger *municipios* publish monthly or semiannual newsletters containing information about births, deaths, marriages, news from Cuba, and social news of interest to their members. Many, as well, provide articles and photographs dealing with the history of their *municipio* in Cuba. The presence of these *municipios* in exile is another facet that underscores Miami as being their homeland in absentia.

## CONCLUSION

The Cuban Americans have made remarkable progress in their adjustment to life in the United States. The majority of the first immigrants to arrive from Cuba after the Castro takeover in 1959 were positively selected in terms of their educational backgrounds and entrepreneurial skills. They were able to establish an economic and cultural base in the Miami and Union City–West New York enclaves that would ease the difficulties of adjustment for later waves of Cuban refugees who were not so positively selected. The Cubans who chose not to locate in the ethnic enclaves of Miami and Union City–West New York settled mainly in other large cities where they received considerable government assistance under the Cuban Refugee Program. By almost any measure, it is apparent that the Cubans are becoming rapidly acculturated to American society, although they are still readily visible as an ethnic minority.

Residentially, during the early 1960s, the Cubans living in metropolitan Miami were concentrated in the Little Havana area. By the 1990s, they had dispersed widely throughout Dade County. Although there is still a tendency for Cubans to live in Cuban-dominated neighborhoods, there are many exceptions, especially in the outer fringe of the Cuban enclave. A poll conducted by the *Miami Herald* of five hundred Hispanics and five hundred non-Hispanics living in Dade County determined that 71 percent of the non-Hispanic whites and 57 percent of the blacks lived in areas where they had Cuban neighbors.[147]

In addition to their residential patterns, Cuban Americans are also becoming more similar to Anglo-Americans in terms of their occupational patterns. After a usual decline in occupational status upon their initial arrival in the United States, most have experienced considerable upward mobility as their length of residence has increased. The younger and more highly educated Cuban immigrants have been especially successful in approaching the American occupational norms.

The fertility patterns and family structure of Cuban Americans provide further evidence of their convergence toward non-Hispanic Anglo culture. The birth rates of Cuban females are now somewhat below those of non-Hispanic white American women. The labor force participation rates for women of Cuban descent suggest that there are many working Cuban mothers, as is the case for many Anglo mothers. The patriarchal character of the traditional Cuban family is becoming weakened in the United States, as it evolves toward the American model and away from the Latin American model. American-born children of Cuban immigrants are intermarrying at exceptionally high rates with non-Hispanic whites, especially outside metropolitan Miami. This is perhaps the strongest piece of evidence of their American assimilation.

Most Cuban immigrants have given up the desire to return to Cuba, even if Cuba's communist government were to be overthrown by a democratic regime. As a result, most either have or would like to have United States citizenship status. Those who possess citizenship exhibit high levels of participation in the American electoral process. Politically, they have become very well integrated into the American system, and in Miami they have discovered the manifold advantages of "ethnic politics" that derive from their concentration in the Miami Cuban enclave.

In terms of language, Cuban assimilation appears to be occurring primarily along generational lines; that is, the second and third generations of Cuban Americans have developed the greatest facility with English. Typically, the second generation is bilingual, whereas the third usually is fluent only in English. Although the first generation is more comfortable when speaking Spanish, an increasing percentage is learning English. Their difficulties with understanding English is usually considered to be one of the most severe problems they have had to face while living in the United States. Nevertheless, there is an unmistakable drift toward the use of English and away from the use of Spanish as the generations increase.

Some studies of immigrant groups living in the United States have noted a tendency for the third generation to try to recapture some of the elements of the culture of their immigrant grandparents. The second generation often rapidly abandoned the cultural traits of their parents because they were viewed as a handicap toward their upward social mobility in American society. This tendency is embodied in the sociological concept known as the three generations concept.[148] Although the third generation of Cuban Americans is only beginning to appear, there is not much evidence to suggest that the three generations hypothesis will apply in the case of Americans of Cuban descent. All available evidence seems to indicate the opposite. The assimilation momentum built up by the first generation and increased by the second will probably be sustained during the third and subsequent generations. Of course, the rapid rate of assimilation will be retarded if there is another larger wave of cultural infusion from Cuba through renewed immigration. Where heavy concentrations of Cubans occur, as in Miami and to a lesser extent in Union City–West New York, the evidence of Cuban culture may linger, and the rate of assimilation of the first and second generation may not be quite so rapid.

Recently, some social scientists have questioned standard assimilation theory, which assumes a linear process whereby immigrants move along an inalterable course toward complete assimilation. Instead, they suggest that a segmentation process has affected the speed and direction of assimilation. In other words, not all immigrants assimilate over time at the same pace, and some of them assimilate to something other than mainstream Anglo-American norms. For example, in Miami and New York, many second-generation Haitians assimilate into American black culture. In Miami, many first-generation Nicaraguans seem to acculturate to Cuban American cultural norms.[149] While this may be true of some groups, most of the evidence regarding language use, out-marriage rates, economic advancement, occupation types, residential patterns, and demographic characteristics discussed in this chapter suggest that Cuban Americans are rapidly acculturating and assimilating into the American mainstream. In Miami the assimilation processes will probably continue to be slower than those in most other places in the United States because of the facts that almost 60 percent of Dade County's population is now composed of Hispanics and nearly half are first-generation immigrants. The Miami metropolitan area currently exhibits an amalgamation quality that is still suggestive of a pluralistic society. Like other major gateway destinations for immigration, such as Los Angeles and New York, it is likely Miami will exhibit this characteristic for a long time into the future.

Today, almost half of all Cuban Americans reside outside Miami. A recent study of Cuban American internal migration patterns within the United States during the 1985–1990 period boldly predicts that the return flow to Miami is likely to have changed during the 1990s, with the Cuban population dispersing to other cities and other states.[150] Results of the 2000 census will tell whether this prediction is correct. If it is correct, this finding will provide additional evidence in support of the hypothesis that Cubans are rapidly assimilating in the United States.

## NOTES

1. Cuban Americans are composed of people in the United States who consider themselves to be of Cuban origin or descent, regardless of whether they were born in the United States. This usage follows standard U.S. Bureau of the Census terminology. For example, all Americans were asked during the 1990 census a question about whether they considered themselves to be of "Spanish/Hispanic origin." If they answered yes to this question, they were to check one of several categories, including "Yes, Cuban." Thus, the nation's Cuban Americans classified *themselves* as being of Cuban origin. See question 7 on the 1990 Census of Population and Housing Questionnaire Form (Washington, D.C.: U.S. Bureau of the Census, 1990).

2. U.S. Bureau of the Census, *Current Population Survey, March 1996* (Washington, D.C., Internet release, February 1998).

3. The population of Cuba was estimated by the Population Reference Bureau to be 11.1 million in 1997. Population Reference Bureau, *1997 World Population Data Sheet* (Washington, D.C.: Author, 1997).

4. Thomas D. Boswell, *A Demographic Profile of Cuban Americans* (Miami: Cuban American National Council, 1994), 13.

5. Rafael J. Projias and Lourdes Casal, *The Cuban Minority in the United States: Preliminary Report on Need Identification and Program Evaluation* (Boca Raton: Florida Atlantic University, 1973), 1.

6. William S. Bernard, "Immigrants and Refugees: Their Similarities, Differences and Needs," *International Migration Review* 14 (1976): 267–280; and Egon F. Kunz, "Exile and Resettlement: Refugee Theory," *International Migration Review* 15 (Spring–Summer 1981): 42–52.

7. Patrick Lee Gallagher, *The Cuban Exile: A Socio-Political Analysis* (New York: Arno, 1980), 23–36.

8. A. J. Jaffe, Ruth M. Cullen, and Thomas D. Boswell, *The Changing Demography of Spanish Americans* (New York: Academic Press, 1980), 246–248.

9. Gallagher, *The Cuban Exile*, 34–35.

10. Lisandro Perez, "Cubans," in *The Harvard Encyclopedia of American Ethnic Groups*, ed. Stephan Ternstrom (Cambridge, Mass.: Belknap Press of Harvard University Press, 1980), 256.

11. Richard R. Fagen, Richard A. Brody, and Thomas J. O'Leary, *Cubans in Exile: Disaffection and the Revolution* (Stanford, Calif.: Stanford University Press, 1968), 100.

12. Gallagher, *The Cuban Exile*, 37–39.

13. University of Miami, *The Cuban Immigration, 1959–1966, and Its Impact on Miami–Dade County, Florida* (Coral Gables, Fla.: Research Institute for Cuba and the Caribbean, Center for Advanced International Studies, University of Miami, July 10, 1967), 1, Appendix A.

14. The 1953 Cuban population census was the one that was the most recently available at the time Fagen, Brody, and O'Leary conducted their investigation.

15. Fagen et al., *Cubans in Exile*, 1.

16. Juan M. Clark, "The Exodus from Revolutionary Cuba (1959–1974): A Sociological Analysis," Ph.D. dissertation, Department of Sociology, University of Florida, Gainesville, 1975, p. 75.

17. It has been reported that 1,612 persons (638 of whom had United States citizenship) were transported from Havana to Miami on an American Red Cross–sponsored aircraft. Virginia R. Dominguez, *From Neighbor to Stranger: The Dilemma of Caribbean Peoples in the United States*, Occasional Paper No. 5 (New Haven, Conn.: Antilles Research Program, Yale University, 1975), 22.

18. Gallagher, *The Cuban Exile*, 39–42.

19. Dominguez, *From Neighbor to Stranger*, 22.

20. Barent Landstreet, "Cuba," in *Population Policies in the Caribbean*, ed. Aaron Lee Segal (Lexington, Mass.: Lexington Books, 1975), 140–141.

21. Clark, "The Exodus," 85–98.

22. Alejandro Portes, Juan M. Clark, and Robert L. Bach, "The New Wave: A Statistical Profile of Recent Cuban Exiles to the U.S.," *Cuban Studies* 7 (January 1977): 17.

23. Landstreet, "Cuba," 141.

24. Eleanor Meyer Rogg and Rosemary Santana Cooney, *Adaptation and Adjustment of Cubans: West New York, New Jersey*, Monograph No. 5 (Bronx: Hispanic Research Center, Fordham University, 1980), 35–46 and 72.

25. Alejandro Portes, Juan M. Clark, and Manuel M. Lopez, "Six Years Later: A Profile of the Process of Incorporation of Cuban Exiles in the United States," *Cuban Studies* (July 1981): 15–57.

26. Portes et al., "Six Years Later," 2 and 30–31.

27. Rogg and Cooney, *Adaptation and Adjustment*, 18–19; and Portes et al., "Six Years Later," 11.

28. For a listing of the numbers of Cubans arriving in the United States by individual months during the Mariel boatlift, see Juan M. Clark, Jose L. Lasaga, and Rose S. Reque, *The 1980 Mariel Exodus: An Assessment and Prospect* (Washington, D.C.: Council for Inter-American Security, 1981), 5.

29. Sergio Diaz-Briquets and Lisandro Perez, *Cuba: The Demography of Revolution* (Washington, D.C.: Population Reference Bureau, April 1981), 28.

30. Guy Gugliotta, "How a Trickle Became a Flood: Origins of the Freedom Flotilla," *Miami Herald*, Special Reprint, "The Cuban Exodus" (1980), 8–10.

31. Clark et al., *The 1980 Mariel Exodus*, 2.

32. Gugliotta, "How a Trickle Became a Flood,"10.

33. Clark et al., *The 1980 Mariel Exodus*, 9.

34. Clark et al., *The 1980 Mariel Exodus*, 6.

35. Guillermo Martinez, "Mariel Refugees: A City within a City," *Miami Herald*, December 14, 1980, 1A.

36. Clark et al., *The 1980 Mariel Exodus*, 7.

37. Richard Morin, "Deluge Adds to Fear in Uneasy Miami," *Miami Herald*, Special Reprint, "The Cuban Exodus" (1980), 11. The attitudes toward the Cuban refugees who came during the twenty years before the Mariel exodus were more favorable in the same poll. About 50 percent of the non-Hispanic whites and 48 percent of the blacks felt that they had a largely positive impact on Dade County.

38. Clark et al., *The 1980 Mariel Exodus*, 15.

39. Clark et al., *The 1980 Mariel Exodus*, 12.

40. In June 1980, the Roper Poll surveyed the American public concerning its attitudes toward controlling immigration. The results showed that 80 percent agreed that the quota for legal immigration should be lowered. Furthermore, there was strong agreement among ethnic and socioeconomic groups. "What Americans Want," *The Other Side* (Newsletter of the Environmental Fund) 22 (Spring 1981): 4.

41. Fredrick Tasker, "Refugees Have Revised Census Data," *Miami Herald*, January 31, 1981, 1B.

42. Guillermo Martinez, "Cuban Miamians Prone to Highlight How They Contrast with Marielitos," *Miami Herald*, May 26, 1981, 7A; and Zita Arocha, "Mariel's Scorned, Youths Feel Sting of Rejection," *Miami Herald*, March 23, 1981, 2B.

43. Guy Gugliotta, "Who Are They? Boatloads Salted with Criminals," *Miami Herald*, Special Reprint, "The Cuban Exodus" (1980), 12.

44. Silvia Pedraza, "Cuba's Refugees: Manifold Migration," in *Origins and Destinies: Immigration, Race, and Ethnicity in America*, ed. Silvia Pedraza and Ruben G. Rumbaut (New York: Wadsworth, 1996), 274.

45. Pedraza, "Cuba's Refugees," 261–279.

46. Robert L. Bach, "The New Cuban Immigrants: Their Background and Prospects," *Monthly Labor Review* 103 (October 1980): 39–46.

47. Holly Ackerman and Juan M. Clark, *The Cuban* Balseros: *Voyage of Uncertainty* (Miami: Cuban American National Council, 1995), 22.

48. Ackerman and Clark, *The Cuban* Balseros.

49. Ackerman and Clark, *The Cuban* Balseros, 37–38.

50. Much of this section draws on the work of Holly Ackerman. See Ackerman and Clark, *The Cuban* Balseros; Holly Ackerman, "The *Balsero* Phenomenon, 1991–1994," *Cuban Studies* 26 (1996): 169–200; and Holly Ackerman, "Mass Migration, Nonviolent Social Action, and the Cuban Raft Exodus, 1959–1994: An Analysis of Citizen Motivation and International Politics," Ph.D. dissertation, Graduate School of International Studies, University of Miami, Florida, 1996.

51. Landstreet, "Cuba," 141.

52. Boswell, *A Demographic Profile*, 13.

53. Eleanor Meyer Rogg, *The Assimilation of Cuban Exiles: The Role of Community and Class* (New York: Aberdeen, 1974), 25–27.

54. Projias and Casal, *The Cuban Minority*, 102–117.

55. *Fact Sheet*, Cuban Refugee Program (Miami: U.S. Department of Health and Human Resources, October 31, 1981).

56. U.S. Bureau of the Census, *1990 Census of Population*, "Summary Tape Files, Florida," STF 3A (Washington, D.C.: U.S. Government Printing Office, 1991).

57. Lisandro Perez, "The 1990s: Cuban Miami at the Crossroads," *Cuban Studies* 20 (1990): 3.

58. David Rieff, *Going to Miami: Exiles, Tourists, and Refugees in the New America* (New York: Penguin, 1987), 224.

59. Perez, "The 1990s," 4.

60. Telephone conversation with Lisandro Perez, Department of Sociology and Anthropology, Florida International University, April 6, 1992, and U.S. Bureau of the Census, "The Hispanic Population in the United States: March, 1991," *Current Population Reports*, Population Characteristics, Series P-20, No. 455 (Washington, D.C.: U.S. Government Printing Office, 1991), 11.

61. Projias and Casal, *The Cuban Minority*, 117–120.

62. Aida Thomas Levitan, *Hispanics in Dade County: Their Characteristics and Needs* (Miami: Office of County Manager, Latin Affairs, Metropolitan Dade County, Spring 1980), 18.

63. "Latins Now Are Living All Over Dade," *Miami Herald*, July 2, 1978, 22A.

64. Thomas D. Boswell, *The Cubanization and Hispanicization of Metropolitan Miami* (Miami: Cuban American National Council, 1995), 12.

65. Levitan, *Hispanics in Dade County*, 19; and Juan M. Clark, "Los Cubanos de Miami: Cuantos Son y de Donde Provienen," *Ideal*, January 15, 1973, 17–19.

66. *Fact Sheet*, Cuban Refugee Program.

67. Levitan, *Hispanics in Dade County*, 20.

68. The *Miami Herald* survey found that 56 percent of the returnees it questioned came from the New York City–New Jersey area. "Latins Now Are Living All Over Dade," 22A.

69. Everett S. Lee, "A Theory of Migration," *Demography* 3, no. 1 (1966): 47–57.

70. Levitan, *Hispanics in Dade County*, 18; and Dade County Planning Department, "Mobility Patterns: 1969," Memorandum Report, Work Element VII, Housing in the Metropolitan Plan (Miami: Dade County Planning Department, April 1970), 43.

71. Gallagher, *The Cuban Exile,* 48–51.

72. Boswell, *The Cubanization,* 23.

73. Kimball D. Woodbury, "The Spatial Diffusion of the Cuban Community in Dade County, Florida," M.S. thesis, Department of Geography, University of Florida, 1978, 67–69.

74. Woodbury, "The Spatial Diffusion," 36.

75. Thomas D. Boswell, Afolabi A. Adedibu, and Kimberly J. Zokoski, "Spatial Attributes of Social Areas Dimensions in Miami, Florida, SMSA: 1970," *Florida Geographer* 14 (February 1980): 7–10.

76. U.S. Bureau of the Census, "Persons of Spanish Origin in the United States: March 1980," Current Population Reports, Series P-20, No. 361, May 1981 (Washington, D.C.: U.S. Government Printing Office, 1981), 5.

77. Portes et al., "Six Years Later," 5.

78. U.S. Bureau of the Census, *1990 Census of Population,* United States Summary, General Population Characteristics, "Urbanized Areas," CP1-1-1C (Washington, D.C.: U.S. Government Printing Office, 1992), Table 3.

79. Boswell, *The Cubanization,* 16 and 23.

80. Franklin P. Eichelberger, "The Cubans in Miami: Residential Movements and Ethnic Group Differentiations," M.A. thesis, Department of Geography, University of Cincinnati, 1974, 67–93.

81. Milton M. Gordon, *Assimilation in American Life* (New York: Oxford University Press, 1964).

82. Rogg, *The Assimilation of Cuban Exiles,* 136–137.

83. Morton D. Winsberg, "Housing Segregation of a Predominantly Middle Class Population: Residential Patterns Developed by the Cuban Immigration into Miami, 1950–74," *American Journal of Economics and Sociology* 38 (October 1979): 416.

84. B. E. Aguirre, Kent P. Schwirian, and Anthony J. LaCreca, "The Residential Patterning of Latin American and Other Ethnic Populations in Metropolitan Miami," *Latin American Research Review* 15, no. 2 (1980): 46, 48–49.

85. Thomas D. Boswell, "Racial and Ethnic Segregation Patterns in Metropolitan Miami, Florida, 1980–1998," *Southeastern Geographer* 33, no. 1 (May 1993): 82–109.

86. For more information on segregation patterns in Dade County as they relate to socioeconomic status, see Thomas D. Boswell and Angel David Cruz-Báez, "Residential Segregation by Socioeconomic Class in Metropolitan Miami: 1990," *Urban Geography* 18, no. 6 (1997): 474–496.

87. Morton D. Winsberg, "Housing Segregation of a Predominantly Middle-Class Population: The Case of the Miami Cubans," paper presented at the Annual Meeting of the Association of American Geographers, Los Angeles, California, April 1981.

88. Boswell, *The Cubanization,* 10.

89. The most complete discussion of the demographic characteristics of Hispanics in 1980 that allowed for comparisons of the different Hispanic American groups, including Cuban Americans, was the following: Frank D. Bean and Marta Tienda, *The Hispanic Population of the United States* (New York: Russell Sage Foundation, 1987).

90. Thomas D. Boswell, Guarione M. Diaz, and Lisandro Perez. "The Socioeconomic Context of the Cuban American Population," *Journal of Cultural Geography* 3 (Fall/Winter 1983): 29–41.

91. Diaz-Briquets and Perez, *Cuba,* 30–31.

92. U.S. Bureau of the Census, "Persons of Spanish Origin in the United States," 5.

93. Diaz-Briquets and Perez, *Cuba,* 31–32.

94. U.S. Bureau of the Census, *Current Population Survey, March 1996,* Washington, D.C., Internet release, February 1998.

95. Boswell, *A Demographic Profile,* 21.

96. Benigno E. Aguirre, "Differential Migration of Cuban Social Races," *Latin American Research Review* 11, no. 1 (1976): 104.

97. Aguirre, "Differential Migration," 111–114.

98. Boswell et al., "The Socioeconomic Context."

99. Aguirre, "Differential Migration," 115.

100. Jaffe et al., *The Changing Demography*, 51–62.

101. Gugliotta, "How a Trickle Became a Flood," 12.

102. Portes et al., "Six Years Later," 15–19.

103. Rogg and Cooney, *Adaptation and Adjustment*, 46 and 70–72.

104. William Petersen, *Population* (New York: Macmillan, 1975), 528–530.

105. Diaz-Briquets and Perez, *Cuba*, 12–24. In 1981, Cuba's crude birthrate was fifteen births per one thousand persons and Cuba was tied with that of Canada as being the lowest in the Western Hemisphere. Population Reference Bureau, *1997 World Population Data Sheet*.

106. Jaffe et al., *The Changing Demography*, 40–51 and 252–254.

107. Jaffe et al., *The Changing Demography*, 40–41.

108. U.S. Bureau of the Census, *1990 Census of Population*, "Persons of Hispanic Origin in the United States," 1990-CP-3-3, Table 1, pp. 2, 3, and 7.

109. For an entertaining account of the contributions made to American popular culture by Cuban Americans, see Gustavo Perez Firmat, *Life on the Hyphen: The Cuban-American Way* (Austin: University of Texas Press, 1994).

110. Marie LaLiberte Richmond, *Immigrant Adaptation and Family Structure among Cubans in Miami, Florida* (New York: Arno, 1980), 33–39.

111. R. O. Blood and R. L. Hamblin, "The Effect of the Wife's Employment on the Family Power Structure," *Social Forces* 36 (May 1957): 347–352; and S. J. Bahr, "Comment on the Study of Family Power Structure: A Review 1960–1969," *Journal of Marriage and the Family* 34 (May 1972): 239–243.

112. Rogg and Cooney, *Adaptation and Adjustment*, 4.

113. Margaret Stanley Boone, "Cubans in City Context: The Washington Case," Ph.D. dissertation, Department of Anthropology, Ohio State University, 1977, 18.

114. Rogg, *The Assimilation of Cuban Exiles*, 134; and Rogg and Cooney, *Adaptation and Adjustment*, 4.

115. John Dorschner, "Growing Up Spanglish in Miami," *Miami Herald*, Tropic Magazine, September 11, 1977, G13.

116. U.S. Bureau of the Census, *1990 Census of Population*, "Persons of Hispanic Origin in the United States," 1990-CP-3-3, Table 2, pp. 40, 41, and 45.

117. Perez, "Cubans," 259.

118. Joseph P. Fitzpatrick and Douglas T. Gurak, *Hispanic Intermarriage in New York City: 1975*, Monograph No. 2 (Bronx: Hispanic Research Center, Fordham University, 1979), 23–25.

119. Jaffe et al., *The Changing Demography*, 63–68.

120. Fitzpatrick and Gurak, *Hispanic Intermarriage*, 83–86.

121. Fitzpatrick and Gurak, *Hispanic Intermarriage*, 24–25.

122. Rogg, *The Assimilation of Cuban Exiles*, 37–138; and Gallagher, *The Cuban Exile*, 72–79.

123. Rogg and Cooney, *Adaptation and Adjustment*, 18; Portes et al., "Six Years Later," 10; and Levitan, *Hispanics in Dade County*, 20

124. Levitan, *Hispanics in Dade County*, 23.

125. Rogg and Cooney, *Adaptation and Adjustment*, 29.

126. U.S. Bureau of the Census, *1990 Census of Population*, "Persons of Hispanic Origin in the United States," 1990-CP-3-3, Table 1, pp. 7 and 8.

127. Rogg and Cooney, *Adaptation and Adjustment*, 29.

128. "Trouble in Paradise: South Florida Is Hit by a Hurricane of Crime, Drugs, and Refugees," *Time*, November 23, 1981, 23–32.

129. William R. Amlong, "Politics Cuban-Style Rule Miami," *Miami Herald*, May 5, 1981, 1B.

130. For information on the politics of Cuban Americans directed toward Cuba and Fidel Castro, see Maria Cristina Garcia, *Havana USA: Cuban Exiles and Cuban Americans in South Florida, 1959–1994* (Berkeley: University of California Press, 1966), 120–168.

131. Paul S. Salter and Robert C. Mings, "The Projected Impact of Cuban Settlement on Voting Patterns in Metropolitan Miami, Florida," *Professional Geographer* 24 (May 1972): 123–131.

132. Rudolfo O. de la Garza, Angelo Falcón, F. Chris Garcia, and John A. Garcia, *Latino National Political Survey: Selected Statistics* (New York: Institute for Puerto Rican Policy, 1992).

133. For the purposes of this discussion, first-generation Cuban Americans are all those persons of Cuban origin living in the United States who were born in Cuba, regardless of their age upon arrival in America. Their American-born children are regarded as the second-generation Cuban Americans. Some researchers also refer to a hypothetical "1.5 generation." These are persons who were born in Cuba but moved to the United States before they were ten years old.

134. Alejandro Portes and Ruben G. Rumbaut, *Immigrant America: A Portrait* (Berkeley: University of California Press, 1996), 195–231.

135. Sam Jacobs, "Language: Main Obstacle to Harmony," *Miami Herald*, July 3, 1978, 1A.

136. Diaz-Briquets and Perez, *Cuba*, 35.

137. Max J. Castro, "The Politics of Language in Miami," in *Miami Now! Immigration, Ethnicity, and Social Change*, ed. Guillermo J. Grenier and Alex Stepick (Gainesville: University Press of Florida, 1992), 109–132.

138. Sandra H. Fradd, *The Economic Impact of Spanish-Language Proficiency in Metropolitan Miami* (Miami: Cuban American National Council, 1996); and Sandra H. Fradd and Thomas D. Boswell, "Spanish as an Economic Resource in Metropolitan Miami," *Bilingual Research Journal* 20, no. 2 (Spring 1996): 283–337.

139. Fabiola Santiago, "Children of Immigrants Embrace Ethnicity," *Miami Herald*, June 14, 1997, 1A.

140. Rogg and Cooney, *Adaptation and Adjustment*, 25–26.

141. James R. Curtis, "*Santeria:* Presistence and Change in an Afrocuban Cult Religion," in *Objects of Special Devotion: Fetishes and Fetishism in Popular Culture*, ed. Ray Browne (Bowling Green, Ohio: Bowling Green University Popular Press, 1982); and James R. Curtis, "Miami's Little Havana: Yard Shrines, Cult Religion and Landscape," *Journal of Cultural Geography* 1 (Fall/Winter 1980): 1–15. Also, see chap. 7 in Thomas D. Boswell and James R. Curtis, *The Cuban-American Experience: Culture, Images and Perspectives* (Totowa, N.J.: Rowman & Allanheld, 1984).

142. Guarione M. Diaz, ed., *Evaluation and Identification of Policy Issues in the Cuban Community* (Miami: Cuban National Planning Council, 1981), 123–124.

143. The Cuban Refugee Program has spent approximately $1.6 billion on its assistance for Cuban refugees. Antonio Jorge and Raul Moncarz, *International Factor Movement and Complementarity: Growth and Entrepreneurship under Condition of Cultural Variation*, REMP Bulletin, Supplement 14 (The Hague: Research Group for European Migration Problems, 1981), 14–17.

144. Jorge and Moncarz, *International Factor Movement*, 1–25 and 56.

145. Jan Nijman, "Breaking the Rules: Miami in the Urban Hierarchy," *Urban Geography* 17 (1996): 5–22.

146. This section draws heavily from Boswell and Curtis, *The Cuban-American Experience*, 175–178; and Thomas D. Boswell, "The Cuban-American Homeland in Miami," *Journal of Cultural Geography* 13, no. 2 (Spring/Summer 1993): 133–148.

147. Morris S. Thompson, "Cubans Fare Better, Black Family Says," *Miami Herald*, July 5, 1978, 1A and 20A.

148. Bernard Lazerwitz and Louis Rowitz, "The Three Generations Hypothesis," *American Journal of Sociology* 69 (March 1964): 529–538.

149. Portes and Stepick, *City on the Edge*.

150. Kevin E. McHugh, Emily H. Skop, and Ines M. Miyares, "The Magnetism of Miami: Segmented Paths in Cuban Migration," *Geographical Review* 87, no. 4 (1997): 504–519.

## 6

# Puerto Ricans Living in the United States

*Thomas D. Boswell and Angel David Cruz-Báez*

Puerto Ricans represent the second largest contingent of people of Latin American origin living in the United States. In March 1996, the U.S. Bureau of the Census estimated that there were 3.1 million people of Puerto Rican descent living in this country, outside of the Commonwealth of Puerto Rico. This number represented 11 percent of the United States total Latin American population, second in number only to the Mexican Americans (eighteen million).[1] The Population Reference Bureau estimated the 1997 population of the island of Puerto Rico to be 3.8 million.[2] Since all Puerto Ricans, whether living in Puerto Rico or in one of the fifty United States, are American citizens, the total Puerto Rican American population amounts to almost seven million, with 45 percent living on the U.S. mainland and the remaining 55 percent residing in Puerto Rico.

Although the number of Puerto Ricans living in the United States represents only about 1 percent of the country's total population, their significance is greater than their numbers alone might suggest for at least five major reasons. First, they are the only large group of people to come to the United States as American citizens from a distinctly different cultural background. Because of this, they have complete freedom to move back and forth between Puerto Rico and the United States mainland without being affected by immigration restrictions. Therefore, they are the only Latin American component of the U.S. population that does not contain a significant element of illegal aliens.[3]

A second important distinguishing characteristic of Puerto Ricans living in the United States is that they represent the first large group of American immigrants who are predominantly of mixed black and white racial background. Puerto Ricans span the racial continuum between black and white. Some exhibit totally Caucasian characteristics, others are almost of pure black descent, but the largest percentage have some mixture of the two. In addition, a few exhibit Indian features. Some researchers have suggested that the experience of the Puerto Rican tolerance for social differences may be one of their major and enduring contributions to American society.[4]

A third crucial characteristic of Puerto Rican migration to the U.S. mainland is that it represents the first large airborne movement of people from abroad. Because most travel by air from San Juan to New York City, the trip is only a 3.5-hour journey and represents an investment of an average of about one week's pay. It is a fact that a person can travel from Puerto Rico to New York City in less time than it took a New Yorker to travel from

Coney Island to Times Square in New York City a century ago.[5] Thus, the physical act of moving to the United States is relatively easy and cheap, especially when compared to most other immigration waves that have characterized much of American history. Some writers have suggested that traveling between Puerto Rico and the United States is physically more like commuting rather than immigrating. Such ease of movement promotes a greater magnitude of migration and makes it easier for Puerto Ricans living in the United States to return home for visits, thereby strengthening the maintenance of cultural ties with the island and promoting the additional migration of friends and relatives.

A fourth way in which Puerto Rican migration experiences are different from those of other migrants to the United States has to do with the role that the Puerto Rican government has played in facilitating moves to the mainland. Once it became apparent that the rapid increase in migration after World War II caused serious problems of adjustment, the Puerto Rican government created a Migration Division within its Department of Labor.[6] This agency maintains offices in a number of cities in the United States and serves as an employment and orientation office for new migrants. It negotiates contracts for Puerto Ricans traveling seasonally to work in American agriculture and has been concerned with helping organize Puerto Rican communities on the mainland. It also became involved in public relation efforts to supply information and correct misconceptions about Puerto Ricans living in the United States. In addition, it supplies information to Puerto Ricans who are contemplating a move to the United States and provides counseling services to those already living there.[7] There is no doubt that this agency helped migrants from Puerto Rico adjust to the American ambiance. On the other hand, there are some researchers who suggest that this paternalistic guidance, although well intended, helped retard the development of powerful grass-root organizations among the Puerto Rican Americans, such as those that developed historically among a number of other American immigrant groups.[8]

A fifth distinguishing feature of the Puerto Rican migration experience involves the changing characteristics of the New York metropolitan area, historically the primary destination for most Puerto Rican immigrants. Although a number of other immigrant groups selected New York City as their first area of concentration, the environment of this city has changed a great deal from what it was seventy-five years ago when large numbers of Irish, Italians, and Jews arrived. Automation has created a new type of economy that relies less on the unskilled and blue-collar labor that was furnished by the earlier immigrants. Urban renewal and public housing projects constructed during the past forty years have made it difficult for Puerto Ricans to establish the degree of numerical dominance in New York City neighborhoods that typified some of the earlier arrivals. In addition, Puerto Ricans have arrived when the city and federal governments have been providing a wide range of services, such as health and welfare benefits, that did not exist seventy-five years ago. As a result, although there are some similarities, the Puerto Rican experience is not a simple repetition of the past experiences of other ethnic groups who earlier moved to the United States.[9]

## MIGRATION TO THE UNITED STATES

One of the strategies that many Puerto Ricans have employed in an attempt to increase their economic opportunities is to migrate to the mainland of the United States. In doing so, they have carried the experiences and cultural baggage acquired while living on the island. Where they come from in Puerto Rico can have a major influence in their adjustment to life on the continent. For instance, a Puerto Rican who grew up in the metropolitan area of San Juan is likely to face somewhat different problems adjusting to living in New York City or Chicago than one who originated from a rural barrio in the coffee region of the western mountains. Of course, some of the problems faced will be similar. Both will have to adjust to the cold winters and will find it useful to become familiar with the new language. Although most Puerto Rican immigrants will have witnessed some of the processes of modernization prior to their move, they will find that the pace of life and competition for jobs are considerably different in large American cities. If they faced an identity problem in Puerto Rico because of the conflict in the political philosophies of those supporting statehood, independence, or commonwealth status, they are likely to be further confused by being a member of a disadvantaged minority living on the U.S. mainland. With these thoughts in mind, the next topic covered in this chapter will be the history, causes, and consequences of the mass migration of close to half of Puerto Rico's population to the United States.

**Early Migration History**

Some Puerto Ricans like to say that Ponce de León, who founded the initial European settlement in Puerto Rico in 1508 and then searched for "The Fountain of Youth" in Florida, was the first Puerto Rican to migrate to the United States. Certainly, Puerto Ricans have been living in New York City since the 1830s. During the latter half of the nineteenth century, a few students from wealthy Puerto Rican families attended universities on the mainland. In addition, there was a handful of Puerto Rican revolutionaries periodically living in New York City and plotting (often with Cuban exiles) against the Spanish government that then controlled Puerto Rico.[10] Shortly after the beginning of the American occupation of the island in 1898, Puerto Ricans were recruited to work in the sugar cane fields of Hawaii. By 1901, there were six thousand of these people. Some subsequently resettled in California and New York.[11]

The first year in which the U.S. Bureau of the Census listed Puerto Ricans as a separate group in its publications was 1910 (Table 6.1). At that time there were just over fifteen hundred people who were born in Puerto Rico and living in the United States, with 37 percent of them residing in New York City. Between 1910 and 1920, about ten thousand more were added to the U.S. population. There are two reasons that more did not migrate during this decade. One is that it was still difficult and expensive to travel the 1,662 miles to New York City from San Juan. Second, this was a period of heavy immigration to the United States from Europe, and blacks were beginning to move northward out of the South, both of which increased the competition for available jobs. Emigration to the mainland picked up during the 1920s when about forty-one thousand new Puerto Rican residents were added to the U.S. population. The economic boom that followed the end of World War I and the strong curtailment of European immigration through enforcement of the United States Immigration Act of 1924 were factors prompting this surge. The 1930s witnessed a significant decline in the flow of Puerto Rican immigrants. During this period, the Puerto Rican component increased by slightly over seventeen thousand people. The rate of increase in the mainland Puerto Rican population for the 1920s was 347 percent, while for the 1930s it was only 33 percent. This decline in the

**Table 6.1    The Puerto Rican Population Living in the United States: 1910–1996.**

| Year | Born in Puerto Rico | Born in United States | Total | Percent Born in Puerto Rico |
|------|---------------------|-----------------------|-------|------------------------------|
| 1910 | 1,513 | NA | 1,513 | NA |
| 1920 | 11,811 | NA | 11,811 | NA |
| 1930 | 52,774 | NA | 52,774 | NA |
| 1940 | 69,967 | NA | 69,967 | NA |
| 1950 | 226,110 | 75,265 | 301,375 | 75.0% |
| 1960 | 615,384 | 272,278 | 887,662 | 69.3% |
| 1970 | 675,320 | 716,143 | 1,391,463 | 48.5% |
| 1980 | 832,920 | 1,181,080 | 2,014,000 | 41.4% |
| 1990 | 1,134,009 | 1,593,991 | 2,728,000 | 41.6% |
| 1996 | NA | NA | 3,123,000 | NA |

NA means information not available.

The figures for 1910–1960 come from Kal Wagenheim, *A Survey of Puerto Ricans on the U.S. Mainland* (New York: Praeger Publishers, 1975), 71; the figures for 1970–1990 come from Francisco L. Rivera-Batiz and Carlos Santiago, *Puerto Ricans in the United States: A Changing Reality* (Washington, D.C.: National Puerto Rican Coalition, 1995); and the figure for 1996 comes from United States Bureau of the Census, *Current Population Survey, March 1996,* Internet release, February 3, 1998, Table 1, "Selected Social Characteristics of All Persons and Hispanic Persons, by Type of Origin."

rate was caused by a decrease in the number of job opportunities as a result of the Great Depression. In fact, between 1931 and 1934, there was a net return migration of 8,694 people to Puerto Rico.[12]

By 1940, New York City had established its maximum degree of dominance as the primary residence for Puerto Ricans living on the mainland. At that time, 88 percent of all the people born in Puerto Rico but living on the mainland were residing in this city.[13] Between 1940 and 1945, the rate of flow picked up somewhat (Table 6.2) because of jobs created by the effects of World War II. The rate of flow was not greater because most Puerto Ricans traveled by boat to New York, and the Atlantic was patrolled by German ships that posed a dangerous threat to their safe passage.

When compared to the heavy European immigration that influenced United States history from the 1800s to the early 1920s, Puerto Rican movements were insignificant until 1946. Immediately after World War II, however, the flow of Puerto Ricans grew rapidly. There were a number of reasons for the tremendous increase that was to follow. First, there was a backlog of people who would like to have moved from the island during the early 1940s but could not because of the war. Second, many Puerto Rican men had fought in World War II and had been trained in the United States and, as a result, had developed an awareness of the opportunities on the mainland. Third, by 1946, there were already over one hundred thousand Puerto Rican–born residents on the mainland who served as a "family intelligence service" for friends and relatives back home. They provided information, helped find jobs, and frequently offered a place to stay and food for the new migrants. Fourth, as mentioned earlier in this chapter, the Puerto Rican government created a Migration Division within its Department of Labor that facilitated movement to the mainland and assisted the new arrivals in making the necessary adjustments. Fifth, the cost and effort of traveling to New York City were drastically reduced. By boat, the trip had formerly taken a minimum of four days and cost close to a month's pay. After the war, surplus aircraft were available and air fares were lowered to as little as $35 for a six-hour, one-way trip, closer to a week's salary. Furthermore, financing was fre-

**Table 6.2    Net Passenger Movements from Puerto Rico to the United States Mainland: 1940–1997.**

| Year | Annual Net Migration | Decade Totals | Year | Annual Net Migration | Decade Totals |
|---|---|---|---|---|---|
| 1940 | −1,008 | | 1969 | −11,582 | −221,763 |
| 1941 | −500 | | 1970 | −74,529 | |
| 1942 | −928 | | 1971 | −16,615 | |
| 1943 | −2,601 | | 1972 | 21,297 | |
| 1944 | −8,088 | | 1973 | −45,558 | |
| 1945 | −11,003 | | 1974 | −41,865 | |
| 1946 | −24,621 | | 1975 | −35,495 | |
| 1947 | −35,125 | | 1976 | 5,230 | |
| 1948 | −27,872 | | 1977 | −23,058 | |
| 1949 | −34,061 | −145,807 | 1978 | −32,317 | |
| 1950 | −37,697 | | 1979 | −25,404 | −268,314 |
| 1951 | −43,145 | | 1980 | −49,322 | |
| 1952 | −60,394 | | 1981 | −27,612 | |
| 1953 | −76,252 | | 1982 | −52,149 | |
| 1954 | −45,089 | | 1983 | −54,379 | |
| 1955 | −31,230 | | 1984 | −50,708 | |
| 1956 | −56,740 | | 1985 | −49,292 | |
| 1957 | −46,760 | | 1986 | −60,184 | |
| 1958 | −24,658 | | 1987 | −47,429 | |
| 1959 | −35,292 | −457,275 | 1988 | −59,945 | |
| 1960 | −23,501 | | 1989 | −39,572 | −490,592 |
| 1961 | −16,818 | | 1990 | −50,091 | |
| 1962 | −11,950 | | 1991 | −33,202 | |
| 1963 | −9,499 | | 1992 | −29,210 | |
| 1964 | −14,350 | | 1993 | −51,650 | |
| 1965 | −15,940 | | 1994 | 3,177 | |
| 1966 | −39,012 | | 1995 | −1,654 | |
| 1967 | −47,220 | | 1996 | −55,283 | |
| 1968 | −31,891 | | 1997 | −32,952* | −250,865** |

Note: These figures derive from net passenger movements between Puerto Rico and the U.S. mainland and should only be used as rough estimates of the emigration of Puerto Ricans to the mainland because they also include a significant number of Cubans and Dominicans who resided on the island before moving to the United States. A negative value signifies that more passengers left Puerto Rico for the U.S. mainland than returned that year. Conversely, a positive value means more passengers arrived in Puerto Rico from the U.S. mainland than traveled from the island to the mainland.

\* Means this is a preliminary figure.

\*\*Means this figure is for 8 years.

Source: Gerardo E. Sánchez-Duvargé, Bureau of Economic Analysis, Puerto Rico Planning Board, San Juan, Puerto Rico, April 1998.

quently available so passengers could make a $5 down payment, and the rest could be paid through installments after their arrival in New York. Sixth, heavy population growth in Puerto Rico was creating population pressure and heavy strains on the island's labor force capacity. Seventh, a shift was beginning to take place that would significantly alter the island's occupational structure during the 1950s and 1960s. As a result, agricultural employment was about to experience a radical decline. Both the increasing population pressure and declining agricultural employment provided strong incentives to leave the island, especially from its rural areas. In conclusion, each of these seven factors promoted emigration, especially when it is recalled that (1) since Puerto Ricans are U.S. citizens, they have freedom to move to the mainland without any legal restrictions, and (2) there was a very large gap between the economic opportunities that prevailed on the mainland and in Puerto Rico at this time.[14]

The net passenger flows shown in Table 6.2 provide some indication of the migration of people between Puerto Rico and the United States.[15] However, it should be noted that these provide only a rough estimation of the emigration of Puerto Ricans to the mainland because they also include the Dominicans and Cubans who resided in Puerto Rico before traveling to the mainland. It is important to note this because there may be significantly large movements of these two groups through Puerto Rico to the United States.[16] From 1946 to 1950, the number of Puerto Rican emigrants in the United States increased by 121,679 people (Table 6.2). Furthermore, by 1950 it became apparent that a second generation of Puerto Ricans born on the mainland was becoming numerically significant (Table 6.1). Even so, 75 percent of all mainland Puerto Ricans were born in Puerto Rico.

## The Migration Stream Matures

The 1950s represents one of the two periods of heaviest flow toward the United States. The total net movement to the U.S. mainland between 1950 and 1960 was 457,275 people (Table 6.2). In 1953 alone, 76,252 Puerto Ricans moved to the mainland, representing the heaviest flow to the mainland for any year.

During the 1960s and the 1970s, the rate of flow to the mainland began to ease (Table 6.2). Between 1960 and 1970, the net flow was 221,763, whereas between 1970 and 1980, it was 268,314 people. There are three main reasons for this decline: (1) the income differentials between the United States and Puerto Rico narrowed; (2) the "push" factors in Puerto Rico that helped motivate emigration were reduced as per capita income and the standard of living on the island rapidly improved, primarily as a result of the efforts of Operation Bootstrap; and (3) a significant amount of return migration to Puerto Rico from the mainland developed that partially offset the emigration in the opposite direction.[17]

However, the 1980s saw an increase once again in the emigration of Puerto Ricans to the U.S. mainland, as a net flow of close to half a million occurred (Table 6.2), which was the most for any decade. Some of the people involved in this migration may have included migrants from the Dominican Republic and other Caribbean neighbors of Puerto Rico who illegally immigrated to the island first and then traveled to the mainland. Research covering this period has clearly shown that both wage differentials between the island and the mainland and differing unemployment levels have played a role in this renewal of heavy emigration to the United States.[18] As the economic gap between the island and the mainland widened, certain groups of emigrant Puerto Rican workers, such as nurses and engineers, particularly benefited from this divergence when they moved to the United States.[19] It also has been demonstrated that Puerto Rican migration is sensitive to variations in the island's minimum wages.[20] Changes in the United States statutory minimum wage, when extended to Puerto Rico, have had considerable impact on the Puerto Rican labor market. The higher wages slowed employment growth, which had the effect of keeping unemployment rates high on the island and dampening the labor force participation rates, all of which further encouraged emigration during the 1980s.[21] Overall, the 1980s constituted a period of significant economic growth on the mainland, a pace that was not matched on the island. Although the Puerto Rican economy expanded during the second half of the decade, this growth was not as strong as that experienced in the United States. Economists Rivera-Batiz and Santiago summarize this decade by saying:

> As a result, wage and unemployment differentials between the island and mainland generally increased in the 1980s. For instance, in 1980, the annual earnings of male workers in New York City were on average 2.5 times those of male workers in Puerto Rico, and the earnings of female workers in New York City were 1.9 times those of female workers in Puerto Rico. This earnings gap widened during the decade, and by 1990, the average annual earnings of New York City male workers had risen to 2.8 times those of Puerto Rican workers; the earnings of New York City female workers were 2.4 times higher than those of female workers in Puerto Rico. A gap in unemployment rates also persisted. In 1980, the unemployment rate in Puerto Rico was twice that in New York City for both men and women. This gulf widened during the decade. While the unemployment rate dropped to below 5 percent in some areas of the United States in the late 1980s, especially in the North East, Puerto Rico's unemployment rate hovered around 20 percent.[22]

The first eight years of the 1990s again witnessed a slowing of the rate of emigration to the U.S. mainland (Table 6.2). The 1990s will probably be recorded in history as being similar to the experience of the 1970s. It seemed to experience a decline in the outflow of Puerto Ricans to the mainland. It is possible that some of this decline can be attributed to Puerto Rican officials and the U.S. Coast Guard who worked hard to curtail the illegal immigration of Dominicans to Puerto Rico, many of whom would then move again to the United States. Still, the net flow of Puerto Ricans exceeded a quarter of a million during this period.

The data in Figure 6.1 indicate the numerical importance of emigration for Puerto Rico. This chart shows that the growth of Puerto Rico's population has been linearly upward, from a little more than one million in 1940 to almost four million in 1996. By 1997, the island's population had reached a density of 1,119 people per square mile, compared to 76 people per square mile in the United States.[23] However, had the emigration to the United States not occurred, there would have been almost seven million people

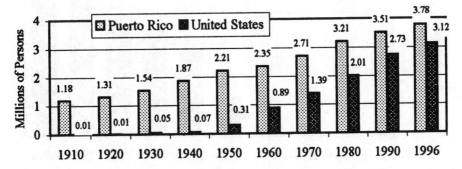

Figure 6.1    Puerto Ricans Living in Puerto Rico and the United States, 1910–1996. Sources: U.S. Bureau of the Census, *Census of Population for the United States and Puerto Rico* (Washington, D.C.: U.S. Government Printing Office, 1910, 1920, 1930, 1940, 1950, 1960, 1970, 1980, 1990); Population Reference Bureau, *1996 World Population Data Sheet* (Washington, D.C.: U.S. Government Printing Office, 1996); and U.S. Bureau of the Census, *Current Population Survey, March 1996*, released on the Internet in 1998.

residing on the island. The trends in heavy emigration of Puerto Ricans suggested by the net passenger movements shown in Table 6.2 are verified by figures representing Puerto Ricans living in the United States in Figure 6.1. By 1996, the number of Puerto Ricans living on the mainland was approaching the number living in Puerto Rico. When the percentages of all Puerto Ricans living in the United States are calculated for the decades since 1910 (Fig. 6.2), the relative importance of this movement is emphasized. As recently as 1940, less than 1 percent of all Puerto Ricans lived on the mainland. By 1996, this figure had grown to more than 45 percent.

Two other trends are worth noting that became apparent during the 1960s and 1970s regarding the mainland Puerto Rican population. First, the domination of New York City as the home of most Puerto Ricans in the United States has declined as this population disperses to other cities and states (Fig. 6.3). From a high of almost 88 percent in 1940, the percentage of mainland people who were born in Puerto Rico and living in New York City decreased to about 70 percent in 1960 and then to about 40 percent in 1996. The second trend that can be identified is that by 1970, the second and third generations of Puerto Ricans living in the United States (all of whom were born in the United States) were beginning to approach the size of the immigrant component (Table 6.1). In that year 48 percent of all people who identified themselves as being of Puerto Rican descent for the 1970 population census were of a second or subsequent generation. By 1990, almost six out of every ten Puerto Ricans living on the mainland were born in the United States. Furthermore, it is also clear that the majority of the numerical increase in the mainland Puerto Rican population is now due to natural increase (the excess of births over deaths), despite the fact that immigration continues from the island to the mainland. This is an important point because it is well known that second-generation mainland Puerto Ricans generally enjoy higher socioeconomic status than that of their immigrant parents, as has been the case historically with virtually all other American immigrant groups.[24]

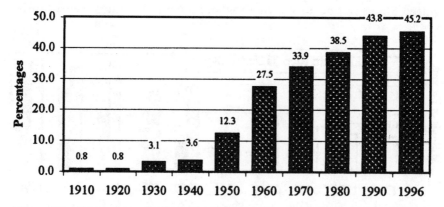

Figure 6.2    Percentage of All Puerto Ricans Living in the United States, 1910–1990. Sources: U.S. Bureau of the Census, *Census of Population for the United States and Puerto Rico* (Washington, D.C.: U.S. Government Printing Office, 1910, 1920, 1930, 1940, 1950, 1960, 1970, 1980, 1990); Population Reference Bureau, *1996 World Population Data Sheet* (Washington, D.C.: U.S. Government Printing Office, 1996); and U.S. Bureau of the Census, *Current Population Survey, March 1996*, released on the Internet in 1998.

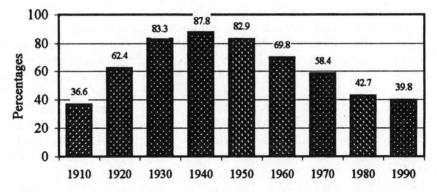

Figure 6.3    Puerto Ricans in New York State as a Percentage of All Puerto Ricans Living in the United States, 1910–1990. Sources: U.S. Bureau of the Census, *Census of Population for the United States and Puerto Rico* (Washington, D.C.: U.S. Government Printing Office, 1910, 1920, 1930, 1940, 1950, 1960, 1970, 1980, 1990).

## Selectivity of Puerto Ricans Emigrating to the United States

Migrants in free societies almost never are representative of the populations they left behind. Thus, the importance of a mass migration flow goes well beyond the significance of only the numbers. In addition to adding people to the destination's population and subtracting people from the origin, migration also affects the composition of the population involved. This section will compare the characteristics of two classes of Puerto Ricans: (1) immigrants living on the U.S. mainland and (2) the nonmigrant population residing in Puerto Rico. Data from the 1990 Census of Population show that about 202,868 migrated from Puerto Rico to the U.S. mainland between 1985 and 1990. Among these people, 72 percent were born in Puerto Rico, 20 percent were born on the mainland but had been living in Puerto Rico in 1985, and the remaining 8 percent were people born mainly in Cuba and the Dominican Republic but who were living in Puerto Rico in 1985.[25]

### Sex Structure

In 1960, the Puerto Rican migrant population living in the United States was almost exactly equally divided between males and females. However, it has not always shown this balance. A study in 1948 of New York City's Puerto Rican migrants found that 61 percent of its sample was composed of females.[26] The 1940 population census for the United States shows that at that time about 52 percent of the nation's Puerto Ricans were female. In 1950, the percentage figure was the same. Thus, there was a slight predominance of females in the migration flow up to 1950. For the males to catch up with the females by 1960 implies that there was a slight male dominance during the emigration of the 1950s. By 1970, there was again a slight female majority of 52 percent. By 1980, the majority climbed to approximately 56 percent. The 1990 census for the United States shows that among the Puerto Ricans who recently migrated to the mainland between 1985 and 1990, about 53 percent were female.[27] Thus, there has been a double turnaround in the selection process. The reason for the female dominance before 1950 is likely related to the fact that most migrants before this time came from urban areas in

Puerto Rico, and the urban areas had a slight female majority. During the 1950s, the migration stream became characterized by a dominance of rural residents who had a slight male majority and who, in turn, produced a male majority of migrants. The switch back to a slight female majority from 1960 to 1990 was probably a function of occupational changes in New York City and other cities located in the northeastern United States that tend to favor the employment of Puerto Rican women. For instance, between 1969 and 1974, this city lost 194,000 jobs in manufacturing, while it gained many clerical and secretarial jobs that usually favor females. By 1990, the sex composition of the recent emigrant population to the mainland (those who moved between 1985 and 1990) and the population remaining in Puerto Rico were virtually identical, both having a slight female majority of about 52 percent.[28]

### Age Structure

The median age for people living in Puerto Rico in 1960 was 18.5 years, whereas for Puerto Rican migrants living in the United States it was 27.9 years, and for return migrants (returning from having lived on the mainland) it was 30.1 years.[29] The lower average age for Puerto Rico was a result of two factors: (1) high fertility, which created a large proportion of children, thus drawing down the average for the total population, and (2) emigration to the U.S. mainland, which was selective of young adults. It has been estimated that 85 percent of all Puerto Rican emigrants during the 1940s and 1950s were in the fifteen- to forty-five-year age class, with a majority being in the twenty- to twenty-four-year group.[30] It is also apparent that the selectivity of emigration accounts for the older average age of the migrant population living on the mainland. As the adolescent and young adult migrants left for New York, they lowered the average age of the population in Puerto Rico and increased it for the migrants living on the mainland. It is reasonable that return migrants would be the oldest of the three populations being compared because, by definition, they must have spent some time on the mainland prior to their return to the island. One researcher found that the average stay on the mainland for his sample of return migrants was almost six years.[31]

The age characteristics of the nonmigrant, migrant, and return migrant populations suggest that the typical return migration sequence is related to stages in the family formation cycle. People traveling north from Puerto Rico to live on the mainland for the first time tend to be adolescents or young single adults. On the mainland, they form families by getting married and begin childbearing. If they return to Puerto Rico, they often do so in their late twenties or early thirties, during the childbearing phase of their family cycle.[32]

What has just been described is a generalized model to which there will be many individual exceptions. For instance, quite a number of people who migrate to the mainland do so after they have already started their families. Sometimes the whole family moves together, but often either the husband or wife will go first and try to establish a household base and secure a job before the rest of the family moves. Occasionally, children will be sent back to Puerto Rico to be raised by relatives. This practice is especially prevalent when the wife works and the mainland neighborhood lived in is characterized by crime and drug problems. Another exception to the model occurs because there is a moderate bulge near the top of the age pyramid caused by the return flow to Puerto Rico of people who have reached their sixties and are entering retirement. In any case, the model is a general description of the relationships among age, family cycle stages, and migration behavior existing for the majority of the migrants.

Data from the 1990 census for the United States allow for a more current view of the age distribution of recent emigrant Puerto Ricans (who lived in Puerto Rico in 1985) and those remaining on the island in 1990. The immigrants to the United States had 58 percent of their population being in the sixteen- to forty-four-year age group, compared to 43 percent for those remaining on the island. Conversely, Puerto Ricans living in Puerto Rico in 1990 had a somewhat larger proportion of their population being both less than sixteen years of age (29 percent vs. 26 percent) and sixty-five years of age and older (9 percent vs. 4 percent) when compared to those who emigrated to the mainland.[33] Again, this is a reflection of the selective nature of emigration that favors young adults over children and the elderly. However, it is important to note that this selectivity is apparently less extreme than it was earlier in the history of Puerto Rican movements to the mainland. In other words, although there are differences in the age structures of those who moved to the United States and those who remained in Puerto Rico, these differences are less extreme than they were during the 1940s and 1950s, as noted earlier. The reason that these differences are less pronounced is that moving to the mainland has become easier than it was during earlier decades. Transportation has become easier and is cheap, and most Puerto Ricans now have either relatives or friends already living in the United States who can serve as their hosts until they can acclimate to living in the United States.

### Socioeconomic Characteristics

Among Puerto Ricans, there is a perception that migration to the American mainland has recently caused a significant "brain drain" on the human capital of Puerto Rico. It is widely believed that from the 1940s through the 1960s most Puerto Ricans who emigrated were young adults with only limited skills and education. During the 1980s, a shift in migrant selectivity was thought to have occurred, whereby the new emigrants were more highly trained and more often college educated than was the case for emigrants during earlier periods. It was frequently suggested that by the 1980s more of the migrants were professionals and people with technical skills that were badly needed at home in Puerto Rico.[34]

A preliminary look at census data suggests this thinking may have been correct, that there may have been an increase in the degree to which some of the island's most capable young people were selected for emigration to the United States. Among emigrants who left for the mainland during the 1955–1960 period, 86 percent had not completed high school. The comparable percentages declined during the next three decades to about 40 percent for emigrants who left the island between 1985 and 1990. There is no question that the more recent Puerto Rican emigrants are better education today than they were in the past.[35]

However, it is also true that the average education levels of Puerto Ricans remaining on the island have likewise increased. Fewer island-residing Puerto Ricans today are high school dropouts and more are college graduates, compared to earlier decades. For a true educational "brain drain" to have taken place, it is necessary to be able to demonstrate that the emigrants are significantly better educated and more skilled than the population remaining in Puerto Rico. When the raw (unstandardized for age) census data are analyzed, it looks as though this has been the case because a smaller percentage of the emigrants to the United States are high school dropouts and a larger percentage are college educated when compared to those who remained on the island in 1990.

However, there is more to this story. It has already been shown in this chapter that Puerto Ricans who emigrate to the American mainland are most strongly selected from the young adult age group. It is well known that younger adult Puerto Ricans generally have higher education levels than older ones. Therefore, to obtain a clearer picture of the comparative education levels of emigrant and nonemigrant Puerto Ricans, these two subpopulations should be standardized, so they theoretically have the same age structures. When this is done, it is clear that most of the educational differences between the emigrants and nonemigrants disappear. For example, the age-standardized percentages for emigrant and nonemigrant Puerto Ricans who have not completed high school are 49 percent and 50 percent, respectively. Conversely, the percentage who have completed college are virtually identical at 14 percent.[36] Therefore, it is not correct that Puerto Rico recently has been losing its best-educated young people to the American mainland.

Further evidence of the fallacy of the "brain drain" hypothesis is provided by a comparison of the occupational structures of migrants who left Puerto Rico during the 1985–1990 period and those who remained on the island. The working emigrants had a lower percentage employed in white-collar occupations than did the labor force remaining in Puerto Rico (44 percent vs. 51 percent), and the emigrants were more represented in blue-collar jobs (56 percent vs. 49 percent). Therefore, these findings can be summarized by stating that both age-standardized education levels and the occupation structures suggest that the notion of a brain drain is a myth when comparing emigrant and nonemigrant Puerto Ricans.[37] If anything, the emigrants may have slightly lower socioeconomic status when compared to the nonemigrants who remained at home.

## Return Migration to Puerto Rico

It is a well-known fact that many mainland immigrant Puerto Ricans desire to go back to the island, at least for a visit, if not to stay permanently. A New York City study conducted in 1948 found that 22 percent of a sample of Puerto Rican migrants expressed some desire to return to live on the island.[38] Another study conducted in the 1960s noted that 34 percent planned to return.[39] Hernandez-Alvarez estimated that in 1960 there were 75,000 return migrants from the mainland living in Puerto Rico, representing about 3 percent of the island's population. For 1965 he estimated that the number had grown to 145,000, or 5 percent of the island's inhabitants.[40] The 1970 population census for Puerto Rico indicated that 13 percent of all those fourteen years of age or older had been living on the mainland in 1965.[41] Another estimate for 1972 indicates that 372,000, or 14 percent of the island's population, were return migrants.[42] Clearly, the trend has been upward since 1955, indicating that return migration is becoming increasingly important, at least until the 1970s.

A recent study has found that the number of Puerto Rican emigrants to the United States who returned to their island origin increased from 34,000 for those who moved during the 1955–1960 period to 137,474 for those who migrated during 1975–1980. However, there was a decline in the number of migrants returning to Puerto Rico ten years later during the 1985–1990 period to 79,956, which probably reflected the widening gap between economic opportunities in Puerto Rico and the United States. This same study determined that the returning migrants were somewhat less well educated and had slightly lower occupational status when compared to the nonemigrant population living in Puerto Rico. The authors interpreted this to mean that the market for unskilled labor in the United States during the 1970s and 1980s pushed blue-collar, unskilled, and more poorly educated Puerto Rican emigrant laborers to return to their island of origin.[43]

However, other older studies have noted evidence that suggests that migrants who return home to Puerto Rico do not do so primarily for economic reasons.[44] A study of prospective return migrants in New York City found that the most attractive qualities that they perceived in Puerto Rico, when it was compared to New York City, were friends, home life or family, climate, and neighbors.[45] Other factors that have also been mentioned as being influential in motivating a return are (1) retirement, (2) a desire to raise one's children in the more wholesome environment of Puerto Rico, (3) a desire to escape the drug and crime problems encountered in large mainland cities, (4) the more personal atmosphere of the island, (5) an inability to cope with American lifestyles, (6) the changing job situation on the mainland, especially in New York City, (7) a belief that skills acquired on the mainland will make it easy to find a job in Puerto Rico, and (8) homesickness.[46]

### Circular Migration and Migrant Farm Labor

Circular migration can be defined as migration between Puerto Rico and the United States that took place sometime during the 1980–1990 period and lasted at least six months, but then involved a return to Puerto Rico before the 1990 census enumeration. According to this definition, there were 130,355 such circular migrants during the decade of the 1980s according to census figures. These data show that 24 percent of these circular movers remained in the United States for less than one year. Another 22 percent stayed on the mainland for one to two years. The average length of time that these movers stayed on the mainland was somewhere between three and four years.[47]

One interesting type of circular migration that has been especially significant historically is the movement of Puerto Rican laborers to work in American agriculture. Except for working in the Hawaiian sugar cane fields at the turn of the century, Puerto Ricans did not begin to play a significant role in American agriculture until the early 1940s. With the manpower shortage created by World War II, American employers started recruiting Puerto Ricans to work on mainland farms. The American agricultural season fits in well with that of Puerto Rico because the island's sugar cane season normally lasts from January to June. During the rest of the year, many Puerto Rican cane cutters are out of work. On the island this period is known as the *tiempo muerto*, or "dead time." Since this is the period of maximum activity on farms located in the American Midwest and Northeast, the recruitment of Puerto Ricans helped the island during its season of highest unemployment and provided low-cost labor for American farms when it was most needed.

Seasonal agriculture has almost always had a tainted reputation for labor abuse in the United States, and by the mid-1940s, reports began to be heard about this in Puerto Rico. As a consequence, the Puerto Rican government passed a law that required all mainland farm employers who wanted to recruit laborers on the island to do so through use of a contract that was approved by the Puerto Rican Department of Labor. The contract contains provisions that guarantee such benefits as transportation to and from the farm, a 160-hour work month, suitable housing, food, health care, insurance, and death benefits.[48] This program was run through the Labor Department's Migration Division.

As recently as the early 1970s, an average of close to twenty thousand seasonal farm laborers were coming from Puerto Rico to work under contracts on American farms. It has been estimated that an additional twenty thousand to thirty thousand came on their own as the result of the confidence and trust they had for specific farmers.[49] They helped harvest sugar beets in Michigan and tobacco in Connecticut; tended vegetable production in New Jersey; cultivated potatoes on Long Island; and picked a range of crops north from Virginia to Massachusetts and west to Illinois. Many of these seasonal laborers eventually became permanent residents on the mainland. Some of the original Puerto Rican communities located in the American Northeast started out as clusters of farm contract laborers who stayed on the mainland. Examples of this are the Puerto Rican communities of Camden and Trenton, New Jersey; Springfield, Massachusetts; Detroit, Michigan; and Rockland County and eastern Long Island, New York.[50]

Since the mid-1960s, the contract labor program has come under attack from radical, and often militant, Puerto Ricans who charge that it is another manifestation of a colonial capitalistic system.[51] They claim that it is a way of providing cheap labor for American agriculturists. The Puerto Rican government, they charge, uses it as a way of exporting their unemployment problem rather than making the structural changes in the island economy that would create greater equality. Demonstrations have been directed against the government's Migration Division both in New York City and on the island. Most of the participants are supporters of the small, but vocal, Puerto Rico independence movement. By the 1990s, the movement of Puerto Ricans to the United States to work in agriculture had greatly diminished. In 1990, the number of workers had dropped to 2,117; by 1997, the figure was down to 918.[52]

Puerto Rican migrant labor is no longer very significant in American agriculture for several reasons. First, agriculture pays low salaries to the workers who pick the crops. Second, the rise in salaries in Puerto Rico, even though they are lower than on mainland, has made Puerto Ricans less desperate to work in agriculture. Third, working as an agricultural laborer has low prestige value among Puerto Ricans, just as it does among Americans. Fourth, laborers can be imported from Mexico who will work for lower wages than Puerto Ricans. Fifth, as agricultural employment has drastically declined in Puerto Rico, fewer laborers are available on the island to take advantage of the Puerto Rican *tiempo muerto* to work on American farms.

## Conclusions Regarding the Migration Processes

The migration of Puerto Ricans to the United States has been a dynamic process affected by a variety of factors. The movements have ebbed and flowed as conditions have changed. However, it was not until 1946 that conditions fell into line so that a mass migration developed. During the 1940s and 1950s, the stream reached a high level. Then it progressively declined during the 1960s and 1970s. One of several factors that prompted this decline was a sizable amount of return migration to Puerto Rico that became significant around 1955. After this date, it became apparent that there were significant differences between the migrant Puerto Rican population living on the mainland and the return migrants to the island. The migration to the mainland was primarily motivated by the availability of economic opportunities. Noneconomic factors seemed to be more important to the return migrants, although evidence also indicates that more recently, many returning Puerto Ricans came from blue-collar occupations that were particularly and adversely impacted by the restructuring of American manufacturing. Still, there is little doubt that noneconomic factors are also important. For instance, when a group of New York City Puerto Ricans who planned to return to the island to live were interviewed, 92 percent said they thought more job opportunities existed in New York City than in Puerto Rico. Even so, they wanted to go home.[53]

Migration to the mainland surged once again during the 1980s as the American economy boomed and the gap between wages and economic opportunities in Puerto Rico and the mainland widened. During this same period, the number of return migrants declined. The migrants who did return were more inclined to be blue-collar workers, with lower education and skill levels. Emigration to the mainland has had a major impact on the economy and demographic structure of Puerto Rico. If the 45 percent of all Puerto Ricans who currently live on the mainland were to return to Puerto Rico, its population would climb from slightly less than four million to about seven million, an increase of almost 83 percent! In the process its population density would increase from a little more that one thousand to almost two thousand people per square mile, giving it one of the world's highest densities. If the United States had a density this high, it would contain more than twice the world's current population.

A study of the impact of emigration to the mainland on the economy of Puerto Rico, during the 1940–1960 period, when the rate of flow was at one of its highest levels, reached some interesting conclusions. Had emigration not occurred, the population would have had an additional 1.3 million people and the annual growth rate would have been 3 percent, instead of the recorded 1 percent in 1960. In fact, during the 1950s, it would have been 4 percent. Such a growth rate, if continued into the future, would have resulted in a doubling of the population in less than eighteen years. Emigration reduced the island's population growth rate both directly by subtracting migrants who moved and indirectly by helping reduce the birthrate since most of the migrants were young adults in their potentially fertile years. Another benefit, derived from the age selectivity that characterized the migrants, was that the size of the labor force was reduced by almost 50 percent. With emigration, the island unemployment rate averaged about 13 percent during the twenty-year period. Without it, unemployment would have been somewhere between 25 and 33 percent. Furthermore, emigration to the mainland also helped improve the quality of the Puerto Rican labor force, since many of the migrants were working in agriculture and as unskilled laborers in other jobs prior to their departure for the mainland. Partly as a result of this, the ratio of unskilled to skilled workers decreased from 5.0 to 2.1. The addition of return migrants who (at that time) were also selected from the higher-status occupation categories also helped continue this trend.[54]

## DISTRIBUTION OF PUERTO RICANS IN THE UNITED STATES

Like virtually all immigrant groups in the United States, Puerto Ricans are highly concentrated in a few areas. Considered collectively, the eleven states with the largest Puerto Rican populations contained 91 percent of all mainland Puerto Ricans in 1990 (Fig. 6.4).[55] The largest single concentration is in the Northeast, with New York and its neighboring states of New Jersey, Massachusetts, Pennsylvania, and Connecticut forming the main cluster (Fig. 6.5). Together, these five states contain about two-thirds (68 percent) of all mainland Puerto Ricans. Clearly, New York is by far the leader, by itself

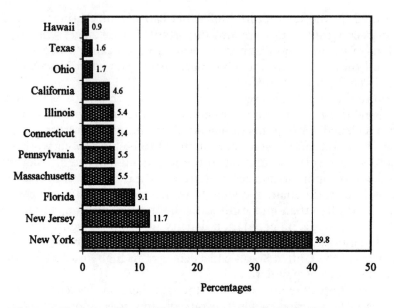

**Figure 6.4    Puerto Ricans Living in States of the United States, 1990. Source: U.S. Bureau of the Census, *1990 Census of Population* (Washington, D.C.: U.S. Government Printing Office, 1993), Summary Tape File 1A.**

containing 40 percent of all mainland Puerto Ricans. A second cluster is found in Florida, the state with the third largest Puerto Rican population. This is the state that has experienced the largest growth during the 1980s. In 1970, Florida ranked only seventh among all states in its Puerto Rican residents. The largest clusters of Puerto Ricans in Florida

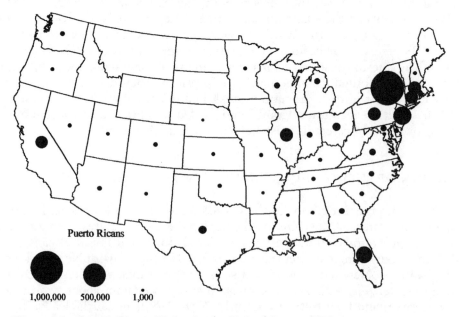

**Figure 6.5    Puerto Ricans Living in the United States, 1990.**

are found in three general areas: southeastern Florida (including Miami-Dade, Broward, and Palm Beach Counties), the center of the state focusing on Orange County (Orlando), and the metropolitan area of Tampa and St. Petersburg. Illinois ranks as the sixth leading state with Puerto Ricans. By far the majority of this state's Puerto Ricans are concentrated in the industrial corridor of the metropolitan area of Chicago and adjacent northwestern Indiana. California's (the seventh ranking state) Puerto Ricans are concentrated in the metropolitan areas of Los Angeles, San Francisco, and San Diego.[56] In fact, there is no state in the United States that is completely without Puerto Ricans. Still, the figures in Table 6.3 clearly indicate a particularly heavy concentration in the area surrounding New York. A statistical study of the distribution of Puerto Ricans living in the United States determined that the greatest numbers lived in states that (1) had higher per capita incomes, (2) were located close to either New York City or Miami, both of which served as ports of entry, and (3) had large total populations.[57]

Figure 6.6 presents the 1990 distribution by counties of Puerto Ricans living in the five states of the Northeast in which they are concentrated. It particularly shows a pattern of clustering in cities. New York's Puerto Ricans are concentrated in New York City, with much smaller accumulations in Buffalo and Rochester. In New Jersey, the two main clusters are in the northeastern corner of the state, adjacent to New York City, and in Camden County, near Philadelphia. Massachusetts's Puerto Ricans are concentrated in the metropolitan area of Boston and Hampden County, which contains the twin industrial cities of Springfield and Holyoke in the Connecticut River valley next to the state's southern border. Connecticut's Puerto Ricans cluster in Hartford, Bridgeport, Waterbury, and New Haven. In Pennsylvania, they are concentrated in the metropolitan area of Philadelphia and in the state's southeastern cities, such as Allentown, Harrisburg, Reading, and Lancaster.

Table 6.3    Metropolitan Areas with More than 20,000 Puerto Ricans in 1990.

| Metropolitan Areas* | Population Size |
| --- | --- |
| New York–Northern New Jersey–Long Island CMSA | 1,236,084 |
| Chicago-Gary–Lake County CMSA | 153,265 |
| Philadelphia-Wilmington-Trenton CMSA | 149,728 |
| Miami–Fort Lauderdale CMSA | 94,668 |
| Boston-Lawrence-Salem CMSA | 75,251 |
| Los Angeles–Anaheim–Riverside CMSA | 65,048 |
| Hartford–New Britain–Middletown CMSA | 56,634 |
| Orlando MSA | 51,703 |
| Springfield, Massachusetts MSA | 40,312 |
| San Francisco–Oakland–San Jose CMSA | 33,999 |
| Tampa–St. Petersburg–Clearwater MSA | 33,741 |
| Cleveland-Akron-Lorain CMSA | 33,070 |
| New Haven–Meridian MSA | 22,349 |
| Rochester MSA | 20,388 |
| Allentown-Bethlehem-Easton MSA | 20,149 |
| Washington, D.C. MSA | 20,092 |
| Total Population for All 16 Metropolitan Areas | 2,106,481 |

*These metropolitan areas contain 77.2 percent of the mainland Puerto Rican population.
CMSA means Consolidated Metropolitan Statistical Area.
MSA means Metropolitan Statistical Area.
Source: U.S. Bureau of the Census, *1990 Census of Population*, "Social and Economic Characteristics, United States," CP-2-1, Washington, D.C., 1993.

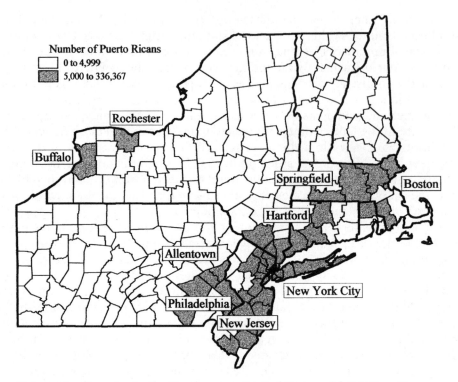

**Figure 6.6   Counties in the Northeastern United States with 5,000 or More Puerto Ricans, 1990.**

Clearly, the U.S. mainland Puerto Rican population is a decidedly urban one. In 1990, about 96 percent of all mainland Puerto Ricans lived in urban places. Furthermore, 93 percent lived in large urbanized areas (metropolitan areas with fifty thousand or more population), and 71 percent lived in the central cities of these large urban areas. Nearly 22 percent lived in the suburbs of these metropolitan areas. Only 4 percent lived in rural areas. As a standard for comparison, 75 percent of all Americans lived in urban places, 64 percent lived in large urbanized areas, 32 percent lived in the central cities of urbanized areas, 32 percent lived in the suburbs, and 25 percent lived in rural areas.[58] In Puerto Rico, 73 percent of the population lives in urban places, a figure that is very similar to that for the American population.[59] Clearly, mainland Puerto Ricans are much more highly urbanized than either the rest of Americans or Puerto Ricans living on the island.

Table 6.3 shows the sixteen metropolitan areas with twenty thousand or more Puerto Ricans. Nine of these are in the Northeast; three are in Florida; two each are in the Midwest and California. Analysis of the growths of the Puerto Rican populations living in the central cities of these metropolitan areas that took place between 1980 and 1990 reveals that the heaviest increases took place away from the traditional concentration in cities of the Northeast. Two scholars who have extensively studied Puerto Ricans living in the United States conclude that this suggests that there is "a dual pattern of Puerto Rican population growth: on the one hand, a movement away from traditional areas of settlement and large urban centers and, on the other hand, a continuous process of concentration in midsize cities within traditional areas of settlement—in this case the Northeastern

United States."[60] However, this remark may be somewhat of an overstatement because much of the growth in the Puerto Rican population in the traditional large urban centers has spilled over from the central cities and into the nearby suburbs of their metropolitan areas. Furthermore, the large percentage growth of some of the smaller and newer areas of concentration are caused by only modest absolute number increases. For example, Worcester, Massachusetts, experienced a 125 percent increase in its Puerto Rican population, but its absolute increase was less than seven thousand. Conversely, New York City's Puerto Rican population increased by only 4 percent, but its absolute numerical increase was more than thirty-six thousand.

Appropriately 83 percent of the state of New York's Puerto Ricans live in New York City. It was pointed out earlier in this chapter that the New York metropolitan area has played a dominant role throughout much of the history of Puerto Rican migration to the United States. The main attraction that it originally held was economic opportunity in the form of jobs and higher wages, just as it did for many immigrant groups who came before them. In 1910, only 554 Puerto Ricans were living in New York City.[61] It was not until World War I that the Puerto Rican element became noticeable in the city's population. The first settlement with significant numbers occurred in the area of Brooklyn Heights, next to the Brooklyn Navy Yard, in response to a demand for workers during the war years. At about the same time, a cluster of Puerto Ricans also began to develop in southern Harlem, just to the north of Central Park and east of Morningside Park.

By 1930, the number of Puerto Ricans in New York City had increased to almost forty-five thousand, with southern Harlem clearly emerging as the leading concentration with approximately 80 percent of the city's Puerto Ricans. The area around Brooklyn Heights was second with about 16 percent. Migration slowed during the depression years of the 1930s and almost stopped during World War II. After the war, it again picked up very rapidly. Quickly the population overflowed from southern Harlem to East Harlem and across the Harlem River to the South Bronx. From Brooklyn Heights, the growth spread northward to Williamsburg and southward to South Brooklyn.[62]

In 1940, about 70 percent of New York's sixty-one thousand Puerto Ricans lived in Manhattan, with the largest concentration being in East Harlem. The latter became known as *El Barrio* ("The Neighborhood"). Puerto Rican organizations sprang up in this area, as had happened with the German, Irish, Italian, and Jewish immigrants who preceded them. An open-air market, known as *La Marqueta*, was established to supply all the ethnic goods and services that Puerto Ricans could not find elsewhere in the city. Although the Brooklyn settlement expanded simultaneously, it did not develop the distinctive ethnic flavor of East Harlem.[63]

The Puerto Rican population in New York City had grown to 245,880 by 1950, including 58,460 who were second-generation Puerto Ricans born on the mainland. By this time, however, it became apparent that a shift away from Manhattan Island was beginning to take place, as its share of the city's Puerto Rican population declined to about 56 percent.[64] This trend was even clearer in 1970 when Manhattan's share had dropped to only 23 percent. By then, the Bronx contained the largest of the city's Puerto Rican population with 39 percent. Brooklyn was second with 33 percent, and Queens and the former borough of Richmond trailed Manhattan with a combined total of 5 percent. In fact, between 1960 and 1970, the Puerto Rican community of Manhattan declined by 18 percent.[65]

While the Puerto Ricans within New York City were dispersing out of Manhattan and into the other four boroughs, they were also moving to locations outside the city. As previously mentioned, the percentage of all mainland Puerto Ricans living in New York City declined from 88 to 58 percent between 1940 and 1970. New Jersey's Puerto Rican population more than doubled between 1960 and 1970, with notable communities developing in such cities as Newark, Jersey City, Patterson, Camden, and Passaic. In most cases, the Puerto Rican settlements that have developed outside New York City have exhibited a similar evolutionary process. Usually, they started out as very small settlements of migrants born in Puerto Rico who were recruited from the island or New York City to work in factory jobs or as migrant laborers. A small base was then established that provided information for friends and relatives back home, who were soon to follow through chain migration. A community began to develop with a definite Puerto Rican flavor, called a *colonia* (colony). In the beginning this was primarily composed of first-generation migrants, but as it began to mature, a second generation of American-born Puerto Ricans became conspicuous. These people were often more upwardly mobile, in a socioeconomic sense, than their immigrant parents. As the second generation became adults, some left the *colonia* to become residentially more integrated with the rest of the city's population. This dispersion to areas outside the *colonia* has sometimes been termed a diaspora.[66]

Puerto Ricans represented a little over 10 percent of the total New York City population in 1970. In addition, they comprised about two-thirds of the city's total Hispanics[67] and were the city's third largest minority, following Jews and blacks. Their presence, however, is of greater significance than their numbers might suggest, primarily because of their disadvantaged position in a highly competitive society. Even more than blacks, they were forced to take low-level jobs because of their limited education and their lack of ability to speak English. As a result of their youthful age structure and high fertility, their children accounted for about one-fourth of the city's public school enrollment. It has been estimated that 40 percent of the recipients of welfare in the form of Aid to Dependent Children and close to one-fourth of the heroin addicts were Puerto Rican in 1970.[68]

The Puerto Ricans who have migrated to New York City are probably similar, in terms of their educational and occupational profiles, to the majority of European immigrants who arrived in the city during the early part of this century. However, such a comparison is virtually meaningless since the situation is so different today from what it was then. When immigrants from eastern and southern Europe were arriving, they found both employment opportunities and available housing conveniently located in the central city. Conversely, since the later 1950s, Puerto Ricans have encountered more competition for housing, particularly from blacks in-migrating from the southern states. In addition, many of the types of jobs for which Puerto Ricans might best be able to compete were moving out of the central city and into the suburbs. In part, these were being replaced in the inner city by white-collar occupations that had higher skill requirements.[69]

The 1990 distribution of Puerto Ricans living in New York City is very similar to what it was in 1970, except there are more of them (Fig. 6.7). By the latter date, the Puerto Rican population had increased to 896,763, an increase of 4 percent from what it was in 1980, as stated earlier.[70] The proportionate decline of the city's Puerto Ricans living in Manhattan continued to 17 percent. The Bronx contained 39 percent, just as it did in 1970. Brooklyn's share hovered around 31 percent, while the percentages residing in Queens and Staten Island were 11 percent and 2 percent, respectively.[71]

A more detailed investigation of the distribution of Puerto Ricans in New York City reveals three interesting attributes. First, the primary areas of concentration tend to be adjacent to the major areas of black settlement within the city. In fact, one researcher

Figure 6.7    Census Tracts with 1,000 or More Puerto Ricans in New York City, 1990.

has hypothesized that nonwhite Puerto Ricans may link the black and Puerto Rican clusters.[72] Clearly, the residential proximity of blacks and Puerto Ricans is a reflection of their disadvantaged economic state and consequent need to compete for the city's lowest-quality housing.

Second, Puerto Ricans do not numerically dominate the neighborhoods in which they live to the same degree that other immigrant groups have in the past. In the majority of the census tracts in which they live, they make up less than 50 percent of the total population. In only a few does their percentage majority reach as high as 70 percent.[73] They have generally located in scattered housing sites, such as a block or an apartment building, rather than taking over an entire neighborhood. Moreover, they have frequently settled among other minorities, such as blacks, Italians, and other Hispanics. There are three factors that have influenced the low degree of neighborhood domination by Puerto

Ricans: (1) a general housing shortage, which makes it necessary for Puerto Ricans to live wherever there is available space which they can afford; (2) slum clearance that causes them to leave neighborhoods that they might otherwise begin to dominate; and (3) the availability of public housing, which is offered at relatively low rents to other minority groups as well as to Puerto Ricans.[74]

The third detailed attribute of Puerto Rican settlement in New York City that is of interest is the amount of segregation within the Puerto Rican population based on different levels of economic achievement.[75] Wealthier Puerto Ricans tend to live in such areas as the better suburban neighborhoods of the Bronx and Queens, whereas the poor are more concentrated in central city areas like East Harlem and the Lower East Side. This situation is not unique to New York's Puerto Ricans; it is also characteristic of the city's blacks as well as other white ethnic groups.[76]

## A DEMOGRAPHIC PROFILE OF MAINLAND PUERTO RICANS

It is relevant to note that in this section Puerto Ricans living in the United States include both Puerto Rican immigrants and Puerto Ricans born in the United States. This is important because almost 58 percent of all people who identified themselves as being of Puerto Rican descent in the 1990 population census were born in the United States. The following population components will be discussed: (1) age and sex composition; (2) education levels; (3) fertility levels; and (4) employment, occupation, and income tendencies. Also, a comparison will be made between the socioeconomic characteristics of Puerto Ricans living in a selected list of metropolitan areas in the United States to illustrate how Puerto Ricans vary regionally in the United States.

The demographic characteristics of the Puerto Ricans living on the U.S. mainland reflect three primary influences: (1) their island backgrounds, (2) migration selectivity, and (3) their mainland experiences. Earlier in this chapter a comparison was made of Puerto Ricans living in Puerto Rico with Puerto Rican immigrants living in the United States. In this section, the population characteristics of Puerto Ricans living in the United States usually will be compared with five other populations: (1) Puerto Ricans living in Puerto Rico, (2) Mexican Americans, (3) Cuban Americans, (4) Dominican Americans, and (5) non-Hispanics living in the United States. These comparisons will provide an understanding of the major contexts in which the Puerto Ricans on the mainland find themselves with respect to the rest of this country's population.

### Age and Sex Composition

The Puerto Ricans are a relatively young population when compared to the non-Hispanic population of the United States. In 1990, the median age for all mainland people of Puerto Rican descent was 25.5 years. The average for all people living in the United States who were non-Hispanics was 33.8 years. The comparable figures for Cuban Americans, Dominican Americans, and Mexican Americans were 38.9 years, 27.6 years, and 23.8 years, respectively.[77] The youthfulness of the mainland Puerto Ricans is a result of two factors: their high fertility and the age selectivity of those who have moved to the mainland. Their high fertility, which is a product of relatively low socioeconomic status, produces a population pyramid with a wide base that results from a high proportion being children. The selectivity of a majority of young adults as migrants adds an element to the population that is potentially high in fertility.

In 1980, the median age of mainland Puerto Ricans was 20.7 years,[78] which was almost five years younger than the figure for 1990. The reason for the significant increase in age between 1980 and 1990 is probably related to the fall in fertility of mainland Puerto Ricans. Figures from the *1996 Current Population Survey* indicate that in that year the median age for Puerto Ricans living in America was 25.7 years, only 0.2 of a year higher than in 1990.[79]

Approximately 51 percent of all mainland Puerto Ricans are females. This is almost identical to the gender composition of the non-Hispanic population. The comparable figures for Cuban Americans, Dominican Americans, and Mexican Americans were 51 percent, 53 percent, and 48 percent, respectively.[80] Sample figures for 1996 suggest that proportion of females among mainland Puerto Ricans has risen to almost 54 percent.[81] The higher preponderance of females among the Puerto Ricans can be explained by their selectivity as a result of the types of jobs available in New York City and other Americans cities that tend to favor the employment of women. The predominance of females, especially in New York City, has at least partly resulted from a greater percentage of mainland Puerto Rican households being headed by females. The significance of this is that women usually earn less than men, so these families are more likely to be characterized by lower incomes and higher incidences of poverty.

### Education Levels

When compared to the rest of the United States population, mainland Puerto Ricans are characterized by low education levels. In 1990, 47 percent of all Puerto Ricans twenty-five years of age or older had not completed high school, a figure that was more than twice as high as that for the country's non-Hispanics (Fig. 6.8). However, when compared

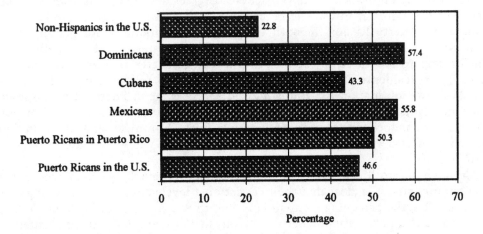

Figure 6.8   Percentage of People 25 Years of Age and Older Who Have Not Graduated from High School, 1990. Sources: U.S. Bureau of the Census, *1990 Census of Population,* "Persons of Hispanic Origin in the United States, 1990," CP-3-3, Table 3, and "Summary Social, Economic, and Housing Characteristics, 1990," CPH-5-53, Table 3.

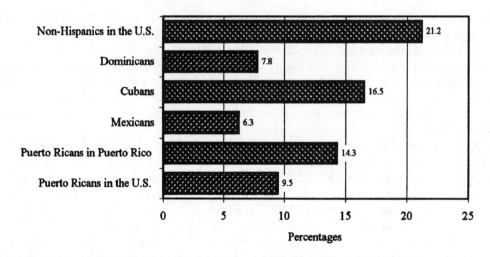

Figure 6.9    Percentage of People 25 Years of Age and Older with a B.A. Degree or Higher, 1990. Source: U.S. Bureau of the Census, *1990 Census of Population*, "Persons of Hispanic Origin in the United States, 1990," CP-3-3, Table 3.

to other Hispanics and Puerto Ricans living in Puerto Rico, the educational attainment levels of mainland Puerto Ricans were about average. Both Dominican and Mexican Americans had substantially higher high school dropout rates than Puerto Ricans, and so did island-residing Puerto Ricans. On the other hand, Cuban Americans had somewhat lower dropout rates.[82]

When considering the percentage of people twenty-five years of age and older who have graduated from four years of college, the results are very similar (Fig. 6.9). About 10 percent of the Puerto Ricans have bachelor degrees or higher, compared with about 21 percent for non-Hispanics. The percentage with bachelor degrees are higher than for mainland Puerto Ricans for both Cubans and, surprisingly, for people living in Puerto Rico.[83] The slightly higher percentage of island-residing Puerto Ricans with bachelor degrees is related to the fact that a college degree is nearly tuition-free for Puerto Rican residents attending the various branches of the University of Puerto Rico. Also, the job market for young adults is very tight in Puerto Rico, so many of those who graduate from high school continue with their education as a means of up-grading their chances for obtaining a good job. Both Dominican and Mexican Americans had a lower percentage receiving bachelor degrees, when compared to mainland Puerto Ricans.

Although Puerto Ricans living in the United States have lower than average educational attainments, it is clear that their educational levels have been improving. For example, in 1980, the percentage of mainland Puerto Ricans without high school degrees was eleven percentage points higher that it was in 1990. Similarly, the percentage with bachelor degrees was more than three percentage points lower.[84] Data for 1996 suggest that the proportion without a high school degree has fallen an additional six percentage points to about 40 percent, while the proportion with a bachelor degree has risen two more points to 11 percent.[85]

## Fertility Levels

Puerto Rican women living in the United States have high fertility rates when compared to the nation's population as a whole (Fig. 6.10). The average mainland Puerto Rican woman who is in the thirty-five- to forty-four-year age group had 2.6 children in 1990, which is about 37 percent higher than for non-Hispanic women. However, a study published in 1980, using 1970 data, determined that when the fertility rates are standardized for age structure, marital status, education level, and the degree of female participation in the labor force, the fertility performance of mainland Puerto Rican women is very similar to that of the general U.S. population.[86] In fact, one study found that, when thus standardized, mainland Puerto Rican women have about the same fertility rate as both Puerto Rican women living in Puerto Rico and non-Hispanic white women living on the mainland. The significance of this finding is that it indicates that there is nothing about Puerto Rican culture (by itself) that necessitates high fertility rates. It is clear the Puerto Rican birthrates have been declining recently on both the mainland and in Puerto Rico. The conclusion reached is that the fertility behavior of Puerto Rican women is rapidly approaching that of all white American women.[87] Still, it is likely that the higher fertility performance of mainland Puerto Rican women will continue to be felt in the cities where they are concentrated for another two or three decades, until they have reached a socioeconomic status comparable to that of the rest of the U.S. population.

## Occupation, Employment, and Income Tendencies

The labor force characteristics of mainland Puerto Ricans clearly indicate their relatively low socioeconomic status. However, it is also relevant to note that the relative economic position of mainland Puerto Ricans improved substantially during the 1980s. This finding is contrary to the findings of many other researchers who have suggested that Puerto Ricans living in the United States have been unable to improve their socioeconomic sta-

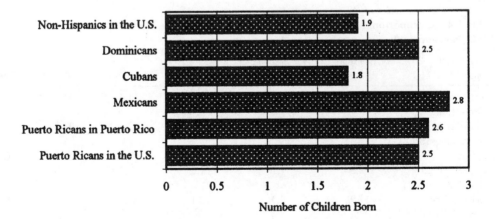

**Figure 6.10   Number of Children Born per Women 35–44 Years of Age, 1990. Sources: U.S. Bureau of the Census, *1990 Census of Population*, "Persons of Hispanic Origin in the United States, 1990," CP-3-3, Table 1, and "Social and Economic Characteristics, Puerto Rico, 1990," CP-2-53, Table 1.**

tus, while other Hispanic nationality groups have experienced more progress. In fact, it has often been suggested that mainland Puerto Ricans were becoming an "underclass" that would soon become hopelessly mired in poverty.[88] Furthermore, it was also frequently stated that Puerto Ricans were by far the poorest Hispanics living in the United States.[89] In fact, one researcher has gone so far as to say that "Puerto Ricans are the worst-off ethnic group in the United States."[90] This section will conclude that findings from the research undertaken for this chapter clearly indicate that (1) Puerto Ricans are no longer the poorest Hispanic Americans and instead are about average when compared to other Latino nationalities living in the United States; (2) Puerto Ricans have made significant economic progress during the 1980s; (3) the Puerto Rican population living in the United States has become bifurcated into two components, one of which is relatively well-off and the other of which is poor; and (4) Puerto Ricans living on the U.S. mainland are generally better off than those remaining in Puerto Rico.

## Occupational Structure

In 1990, the occupational structure of Puerto Ricans was most similar to that of non-Hispanic blacks living in the United States (Table 6.4). Puerto Ricans had a higher percentage of their labor force employed in the high-paying managerial and professional occupations and in technical, sales, and administrative support jobs than did either Mexicans or Dominicans. The Puerto Ricans also had a lower proportion employed in the operators, fabricators, and laborers category. Clearly, Puerto Ricans had higher occupational status on average than either Mexicans or Dominicans. However, it is also clear that mainland Puerto Ricans had lower occupational status when compared to Cuban Americans and non-Hispanic whites.

The occupational situation of mainland Puerto Ricans certainly improved during the 1980s. A larger percentage were working in the better-paying managerial and professional class and in the technical, sales, and administrative support category in 1990

**Table 6.4   Occupational Structures of Hispanic Groups in the United States: 1990 (Percentages).**

| Occupational Groups | Non-Hispanic Whites | Non-Hispanic Blacks | Puerto Ricans | Mexicans | Dominicans | Cubans |
|---|---|---|---|---|---|---|
| Managerial & Professional | 26.9 | 15.4 | 15.0 | 11.6 | 11.1 | 23.2 |
| Tech, Sales & Admin. Support | 31.8 | 28.7 | 32.4 | 23.6 | 26.0 | 34.1 |
| Services | 12.0 | 22.8 | 19.0 | 18.5 | 22.5 | 13.2 |
| Farming, Forestry & Fishing | 3.3 | 1.7 | 1.6 | 7.2 | 0.5 | 1.3 |
| Precision Prod., Craft & Repair | 11.9 | 0.3 | 10.1 | 14.2 | 10.5 | 11.7 |
| Operators, Fabricators & Laborers | 14.1 | 22.1 | 21.9 | 29.4 | 24.9 | 16.5 |

Source: Francisco L. Rivera-Batiz and Carlos Santiago, *Puerto Ricans in the United States: A Changing Reality* (Washington, D.C.: The National Puerto Rican Coalition, Inc., 1995), 69.

when compared to 1980. Also, a smaller percentage were working in low-paying opera-tor, fabricator, and laborers jobs.[91]

### Unemployment Rates

Mainland Puerto Ricans have a much lower unemployment rate than people living in Puerto Rico (Fig. 6.11). They also have lower unemployment than Dominicans. How-ever, at the same time, they have an unemployment rate that is more than twice that of the non-Hispanic population living in the United States. Furthermore, they have higher unemployment levels than both Cuban and Mexican Americans.

Mainland Puerto Rican unemployment has been found to be very much related to mi-grant status, educational attainment, age, and marital status.[92] Immigrants from Puerto Rico have higher unemployment rates than those born in the United States. In addition, among immigrants, those who arrived on the mainland more recently tend to have the highest unemployment rates. Puerto Ricans who are more highly educated have lower un-employment rates than those who are less well educated. For example, Puerto Ricans with a four-year college degree had an unemployment rate of 6 percent in 1990, whereas 18 per-cent of those who had not finished high school were unemployed. Age is inversely related to unemployment among mainland Puerto Rican workers. As age goes up, unemployment rates decline. Puerto Ricans in their twenties had an unemployment rate of 13 percent, whereas the rate for those in their fifties was just under 9 percent. Marital status particu-larly affects female unemployment. The highest rates of unemployment are found among Puerto Rican women who have either never married or live in female-headed households. Currently married Puerto Rican women have the lowest unemployment rates.

Between 1980 and 1990, the unemployment rate of males slightly deteriorated from 10 percent to 12 percent. For females it slightly improved from 13 percent to

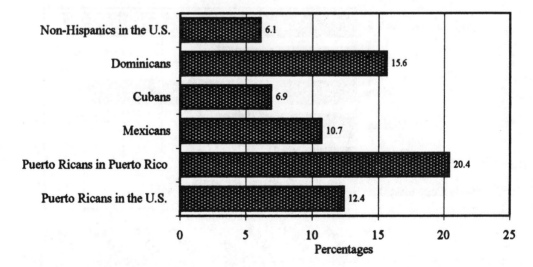

Figure 6.11    Unemployment Rates, 1990. Sources: U.S. Bureau of the Census, *1990 Census of Population*, "Persons of Hispanic Origin in the United States, 1990," CP-3-3, Table 4, and "Summary Social, Economic, and Housing Characteristics, Puerto Rico, 1990," CPH-5-53, Table 7.

12 percent.[93] The good news is that sample data for 1996 indicate that the unemployment levels for both males and females have dropped somewhat to 10 percent and 11 percent, respectively.[94]

### Income and Poverty Levels

Puerto Ricans living in the United States have a per capita income that is more than twice that of their friends and relatives remaining home in Puerto Rico (Fig. 6.12). Mainland Puerto Ricans have a higher average income than either Mexican or Dominican Americans. However, they also have a much lower average income than Cuban Americans and non-Hispanic Americans. In fact, the per capita income of mainland Puerto Ricans is only 56 percent that of American non-Hispanics. It is important to note that the current income situation for Puerto Ricans is a major improvement over what it was in 1979. For instance, by 1989, household per capita income for mainland Puerto Ricans increased 29 percent over what it was in 1980. In 1979, only Dominican Americans had lower incomes than the Puerto Ricans.[95]

The income earned by mainland Puerto Ricans is particularly sensitive to education, age, and gender. As educational attainment improves, so does income. Older Puerto Ricans generally make higher wages. Males have higher incomes than females. As the education levels of Puerto Ricans increase and as their population ages (because of declining fertility), it is reasonable to foresee a brighter future for the incomes of these people in the United States.

In 1990, almost one-third of all mainland Puerto Ricans were living in poverty. Although this was high, it was much lower than the poverty rate of Puerto Ricans living on the island (Fig. 6.13). The poverty rate of mainland Puerto Ricans is almost 2.5 times

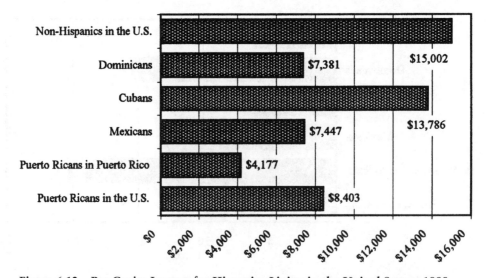

Figure 6.12    Per Capita Income for Hispanics Living in the United States, 1989.
Sources: U.S. Bureau of the Census, *1990 Census of Population*, "Persons of Hispanic Origin in the United States, 1990," CP-3-3, Table 5, and "Summary Social, Economic, and Housing Characteristics, Puerto Rico, 1990," CPH-5-53, Table 11.

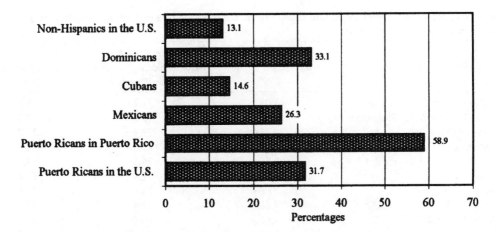

**Figure 6.13    Percentage of People Living below the Poverty Level. Sources: U.S. Bureau of the Census,** *1990 Census of Population,* **"Persons of Hispanic Origin in the United States, 1990," CP-3-3, Table 5, and "Summary Social, Economic, and Housing Characteristics, Puerto Rico, 1990," CPH-5-53, Table 11.**

as high as it is for non-Hispanics. It is 2.2 times the rate for Cubans, and it is even 20 percent higher than the prevailing rate for Mexican Americans.

Some scholars speak of the "polarization" of the mainland Puerto Ricans into two groups: one that is firmly ensconced in the American middle class and the other mired in poverty. This is the bifurcation referred to earlier in this section. The problem facing Puerto Ricans is very similar to that of blacks, who also have a "polarized" population.[96] It is the poverty component of both populations that has social scientists so concerned.

### Regional Variations in Socioeconomic Characteristics of Mainland Puerto Ricans

The major metropolitan areas in which Puerto Ricans live in the United States will be briefly discussed in this section as a means of illustrating the regional variations that exist within the mainland Puerto Rican population. This part of the chapter draws extensively from an analysis performed by economists Rivera-Batiz and Santiago using metropolitan statistical areas (MSAs) as their unit of analysis.[97] It should be noted that the cities shown in Table 6.3 are somewhat different from those displayed in Table 6.5 because the former contained a combination of metropolitan statistical areas (MSAs) and consolidated metropolitan statistical areas (CMSAs) as defined by the U.S. Bureau of the Census for 1990.[98]

The twenty-three metropolitan areas shown in Table 6.5 exhibit some interesting variations among the main states in which most of the mainland Puerto Ricans are currently living. The highest average Puerto Rican incomes tend to be found in cities located in Florida, California, and New Jersey. The lowest are found in cities located in Massachusetts and Pennsylvania. Connecticut's cities tend to be intermediate in the their income levels. New York City has the seventh highest income, but Buffalo, also located in New York, has the fourth lowest average Puerto Rican income. Chicago (with the second largest Puerto Rican population) ranks eighth from the top, and Philadelphia (with the third largest Puerto Rican population) ranks only one spot above Buffalo. The

**Table 6.5    Income, Poverty, and Unemployment Characteristics of Puerto Ricans Living in American Metropolitan Areas.**

| Metropolitan Statistical Areas (MSAs) | Mean Household Income per Person, 1989 | Percent Living in Households with Incomes Below the Poverty Level | Unemployment Rates |
|---|---|---|---|
| Los Angeles–Long Beach, CA | 12,032 | 21.2 | 8.1 |
| Tampa–St. Petersburg–Clearwater, FL | 9,267 | 19.9 | 9.3 |
| Jersey City, NJ | 9,214 | 29.8 | 13.0 |
| Trenton, NJ | 8,979 | 23.5 | 12.3 |
| Miami, FL | 8,903 | 26.3 | 8.7 |
| Newark, NJ | 8,562 | 32.4 | 12.1 |
| New York City, NY | 7,989 | 38.7 | 13.8 |
| Chicago, IL | 7,685 | 31.8 | 13.9 |
| Loraine-Elyria, OH | 7,660 | 40.1 | 13.6 |
| Bridgeport, CT | 7,549 | 33.1 | 15.8 |
| Cleveland, OH | 7,276 | 40.1 | 18.6 |
| Boston, MA | 7,186 | 43.9 | 17.1 |
| Waterrbury, CT | 6,932 | 33.1 | 14.5 |
| Rochester, NY | 6,780 | 42.8 | 15.2 |
| Allentown-Bethlehem-Easton, PA | 6,193 | 43.6 | 13.0 |
| Hartford, CT | 6,095 | 47.5 | 17.7 |
| Philadelphia, PA | 6,078 | 44.0 | 14.9 |
| Lancaster, PA | 5,409 | 45.7 | 9.0 |
| Reading, PA | 5,234 | 49.6 | 21.0 |
| Buffalo, NY | 5,194 | 51.7 | 17.1 |
| Worcester, MA | 5,142 | 55.7 | 27.7 |
| Springfield, MA | 4,658 | 56.2 | 22.6 |
| Lawrence-Haverill, MA | 4,228 | 62.0 | 31.2 |

Source: Francisco L. Rivera-Batiz and Carlos Santiago, *Puerto Ricans in the United States: A Changing Reality* (Washington, D.C.: The National Puerto Rican Coalition, Inc., 1995), 35, 48, and 73.

range in incomes among these cities is enormous. For example, the average Puerto Rican income in Los Angeles–Long Beach is nearly three times that in Lawrence-Haverill.[99]

There is a moderate association between the average incomes of Puerto Ricans and their poverty rates. Generally, the higher the average Puerto Rican income, the lower the poverty rate, but this is not a perfect one-to-one correspondence. The lowest poverty rates are found in the cities located in Florida, California, and New Jersey. The highest poverty rates are located in the cities of Massachusetts and Pennsylvania. Buffalo, New York, and Worcester, Springfield, and Lawrence-Haverill (all three in Massachusetts) have poverty rates in excess of 50 percent.[100] Unemployment rates are also related to both average incomes and poverty levels. Higher unemployment is logically associated with lower incomes and higher poverty rates. The unemployment rates for Puerto Ricans displayed in Table 6.5 range from a high of more than 31 percent in Lawrence, Massachusetts, to a low of about 8 percent in Los Angeles.

The pattern that emerges is one in which the cities of the Northeast tend to be more often associated with poor Puerto Ricans. New Jersey is a notable exception to this generalization. These are the cities that were most adversely affected by the industrial restructuring that characterized American manufacturing during the 1970s and 1980s. The new cities located in Florida, California, and New Jersey were less affected by this radical and painful industrial transformation. Also, the cities in these latter three states have been recent recipients of Puerto Ricans, most of whom are firmly members of the middle class who have in-migrated either from cities located in the Northeast or directly from Puerto Rico.

## SELECTED CULTURAL CHARACTERISTICS

Although the concept of culture embraces a wide variety of learned characteristics that typify any society, this section is selective and discusses four aspects of Puerto Rican culture that are of particular importance in establishing the character of mainland Puerto Ricans. The attributes to be studied are (1) family structure, (2) religious background, (3) language problems, and (4) attitudes toward race.

### Family Structure

Generally speaking, the family plays a more important role in the everyday events of Puerto Rican society than it does in most non-Hispanic American society. A Puerto Rican's self-confidence, sense of security, and identity are established primarily through family relationships. In contrast to other Americans, who value an individual in terms of his or her ability to compete independently for socioeconomic status, the culture of Puerto Rico views life as a network of personal relationships. Puerto Ricans rely on and trust people. They know that in times of trouble a close friend or relative can always be counted on for needed assistance. A Puerto Rican depends less on impersonal secondary relationships and generally does not trust or place much faith in large organizations. Such an attitude is not unique to Puerto Ricans but is typical of most Latin American societies.

One way in which the greater emphasis that is placed on the Puerto Rican family can be illustrated is through a description of its use of surnames. English custom in United States society dictates that family names be derived patrilineally. In Puerto Rican society, it is more common for a person to have two surnames, representing both the father's and mother's sides of the family. For instance, a man with the name Ricardo Gómez González had his name derived in the following way. His given name is Ricardo, and his two surnames are Gómez and González. Gómez was his father's family name, and Gonzáles was his mother's family name. Suppose that a woman by the name of María García Rivera married Mr. Gómez. Her new name would be María García de Gómez. She would retain her father's surname, drop her mother's name, and add her husband's father's name after the "de." In fact, for formal occasions, even more complicated combinations of names frequently are used.[101] To avoid confusion, many mainland Puerto Ricans have adopted the American custom of using only the surname of the father.

Another characteristic of Puerto Rican society that illustrates a reliance on personal relationships is the institution known as *compadrazgo*. It is somewhat similar to the tradition of godparents in the United States, except that it is usually taken more seriously in Puerto Rico and often involves a higher level of personal obligation. Under the *compadrazgo* system a set of *compadres* are selected for each child. These are best thought of as being "companion parents" with the child's natural parents. Sometimes they are selected at the time the parents were married, but they might also be decided on at the time the child is baptized or perhaps confirmed as a member of the church. The *compadres* are sometimes relatives, but often they are not. If they are not blood relatives, they become de facto members of the family upon becoming *compadres*. The purpose of a *compadre* is to offer both economic and moral assistance to the family whenever it is needed. He or she may feel freer to give advice in regard to family problems than a brother or sister of the father or mother would. It is essential that *compadres* live close to the family with which they are associated so that frequent contact can be made and the necessary obligations be honored.

The type of relationship that exists between husband and wife in a traditional Puerto Rican family is very similar to that described for the Cuban family in chapter 5. Basically, the husband is considered the superior authority. He expects to be obeyed and treated with respect by his wife and children. He often makes decisions affecting the family without consulting his wife. In addition, a double standard of morality exists regarding sexual behavior. It is regarded as normal behavior for the husband to have extramarital affairs, whereas the wife is expected to remain chaste and true to her husband. These attitudes carry over into the raising of the children. Daughters are strongly encouraged to remain virgins until they marry, and their fathers and brothers feel an obligation to protect them. When dating, a "good" girl is traditionally accompanied by a chaperone. Sons, on the other hand, are accorded much more freedom to explore their sexuality and lead much less sheltered lives. They are imbued with the spirit of machismo, which is associated with sexual prowess and influence over women and a jealous guarding of a sweetheart or wife.

The traditional Puerto Rican husband and wife relationships are changing, both in Puerto Rico and on the U.S. mainland. In both cases the main causes of change are urbanization and the emergence of a middle class. Female entrance into the labor force is perhaps the most important component of both modernization and urbanization that has influenced a redefinition of the wife's role in family decision making. This is especially true in New York City where women often have an easier time securing employment than Puerto Rican men. In addition, the modern welfare system has made it easier for women to become less dependent economically on their husbands.[102] Also, laws have now made it more difficult for husbands to abuse their wives and children physically as a way of ensuring their respect. In short, the Puerto Rican family appears to be evolving towards the American norm.

Considerable evidence suggests that Puerto Rican family bonds are weaker on the mainland than they are in Puerto Rico, because of the sometimes traumatic changes experienced with living in large American cities. In a study of fifty Puerto Rican families living in New York City slums conducted during the mid-1960s, researchers found that the percentage of couples living in free or consensual unions and the number of women who were divorced, separated, or abandoned increased in New York when compared to families living in Puerto Rican slums.[103] In 1970, about 24 percent of all mainland Puerto Rican families were headed by a woman. For the total U.S. population, the figure was close to 12 percent; for residents of Puerto Rico, it was about 16 percent. Commonly, families that are headed by a female are ones that have experienced some form of marital discord.[104] In 1979, the U.S. Bureau of the Census estimated that the proportion of mainland Puerto Rican households that were headed by a female, with no husband being present, had risen to 40 percent. As standards for comparison, the figures for all people of Hispanic origin and for Mexican Americans were 20 percent and 16 percent, respectively.[105] In

1990, the proportion of all mainland Puerto Rican families headed by a woman with no husband present was 37 percent, which was similar to the level that prevailed in 1970. The comparable figures for Mexican, Cuban, and Dominican American families were 18 percent, 16 percent, and 41 percent, respectively.[106]

One way of determining the degree to which the mainland Puerto Rican family is becoming Americanized is to look at their out-marriage rates. In 1979, about 22 percent of all husbands of Puerto Rican descent living on the mainland were married to non–Puerto Rican women, and approximately 24 percent of mainland Puerto Rican wives were married to non–Puerto Rican men.[107] The slightly higher out-marriage rate for the woman is due to the fact that more Puerto Rican females than males are living on the mainland.

Data for 1970 indicate that there is a major difference between the out-marriage rates of first- and second-generation mainland Puerto Ricans. For first-generation Puerto Rican male migrants, only 18 percent were married to non–Puerto Rican women. On the other hand, 57 percent of all second-generation males had out-married.[108] Such an intergenerational difference in out-marriage rates between first and second generations has been a common experience for most of the European immigrants who preceded the Puerto Ricans during the late 1800s and the early 1900s.

It also has been determined that there are significant differences between the out-marriage rates of second-generation Puerto Ricans living in the state of New York and the rest of the country. For instance, in 1970 about one-third of the second-generation Puerto Ricans living in New York were married to non–Puerto Ricans, whereas for the rest of the states the comparable proportion was about two-thirds.[109] The lower rate of out-marriage for New York's component is primarily a reflection of its large, concentrated Puerto Rican population, making it easier to find a spouse of Puerto Rican descent. It may also be that there is a selective outmigration of Puerto Ricans from New York City, with the more assimilated second-generation Puerto Ricans being more likely to leave the city to establish residences in other states.

## Religious Background

Religion has played a major role historically for many immigrant groups who have migrated to the United States. The congregation or parish often became the focus of social organization and provided support and security for these people, thus easing their adjustment to American society. Unfortunately, considerable evidence indicates that religion is not playing the same role for Puerto Ricans living in the United States. To understand why this is so, it is necessary to first describe the religious background in Puerto Rico. Then Puerto Ricans' experiences and adaptations on the mainland will be described.

### Religion in Puerto Rico

Three major types of religions have evolved in Puerto Rican society, all of which have been transferred to the U.S. mainland with modifications. These are (1) Catholicism, (2) Protestantism, and (3) spiritualism.

Virtually all Puerto Ricans are, at least nominally, Christians. About 80 percent are Catholic, with the remaining 20 percent being members of one of the Protestant faiths. An unknown number practice spiritualism in conjunction with either Catholicism or Protestantism.[110]

Puerto Rican Catholicism has two major characteristics that distinguish it from mainland American Catholicism: (1) a *pueblo* aspect and (2) a personal aspect. The word *pueblo* is used to refer to both a town (or city) and the people who live in it. Most settlements in Puerto Rico were established by the Spaniards according to a rigid plan that provided for a focus of activity around a central plaza. The most prominent building that faced on this plaza was the Catholic church, symbolizing the importance of the church in the social organization of the community. The entire population of the pueblo worshiped God in the same way. Virtually all festivals were religious events. Each town had its own patron saint and special holidays. Schools were run by the church, and the local priest played a prominent role in almost all events. To be Catholic was to belong to a Catholic community and was a community manifestation, not a matter of personal choice as it is in the United States.

The personal aspect of Puerto Rican Catholicism meant that religious practice was characterized by a perceived intimate relationship between individuals and their personal saints and the Virgin Mary. They were viewed as close friends who could be counted on during times of need. They were prayed to, candles were lit for them, their likenesses were carried in parades, small shrines were built to them in the home, amulets were hung around their necks, magnetic medallions were kept in their cars, and pictures were hung in their homes and places of work. These rites could be performed apart from formal worship, and at least one observer has suggested that they would continue to be practiced even if Catholicism were to suddenly disappear.[111]

Despite these overt signs of faith, many Puerto Ricans do not adhere to all the teachings of the organized church. That is, many seldom attend mass, confess, or receive communion. Many couples live in consensual unions, rather than being married by a priest. Also, perhaps one-fourth of the women of childbearing age have been surgically sterilized, which is against the teachings of the church.[112] In many cases, Puerto Ricans have a hard time identifying with the organized structure of the Catholic Church due to a number of factors. First, Catholicism has never been controlled by Puerto Ricans in Puerto Rico. During the days of Spanish rule, the majority of the priests were from Spain. Today, close to two-thirds of the clergy are from the U.S. mainland.[113] Second, Catholic schools usually charge tuition and are selective in their admission of students. This tends to limit their enrollments to students from privileged backgrounds. Most poorer children must attend public schools. Third, the church has alienated some of the population by taking an active stand against birth control through use of contraceptives, although it is less vociferous today than it was in this regard. Fourth, the official Catholic position in the 1800s was against independence from Spain and did not favor the abolition of slavery. Fifth, in 1960, the church organized a political party, called the Christian Action Party, in opposition to the island's Popular Democratic Party, the party that had created the impressive economic and social gains since the 1940s. The church's party lost badly, receiving only about 8 percent of the votes. This left Catholicism discredited not only as a political influence but also as a moral factor in public life.

Protestantism became a significant religious force in Puerto Rico after the United States took possession of it in 1898. However, of the estimated 130,000 people that are members of these sects, only about 70,000 belong to the major faiths such as the Methodists, Baptists, and Episcopalians.[114] These three religions have become popular, through American influence, primarily among the middle classes. The rest of the Protestants belong to revivalist movements such as the Pentecostals, the Seventh Day Adventists, and other Evangelical sects. The Pentecostals have proven to be particularly popular and are found widely dispersed throughout the island. They offer group singing and emotional testimony and also are strict regarding the use of language, tobacco, and alcohol. This is truly a grass-roots religion that appeals especially to the poor. It is relatively easy to become a Pentecostal minister and to open a church. Usually they are small-scale operations that are housed in storefronts in the inner city or in small houses in the suburbs or rural areas, with thirty or forty families providing their membership.

Spiritualism is practiced by many Puerto Ricans in conjunction with the more orthodox religious practices. There are many spiritist beliefs. One is that it is possible to make contact with the spirit world and that spirits can be helpful in bringing about a desired action, such as good luck for a friend or harm for an enemy. It is also believed that the spiritualist medium has the ability to contact the dead and can analyze a client's troubles. Often psychological advice is given. Closely allied with spiritualism is the practice of using herbs, oils, potions, incense, charms, and candles in a form of folk medicine. Sometimes voodoo dolls can also be bought that are thought to possess mystical qualities. These and many more items are sold in stores called *botánicas* that are widely scattered throughout the island. Spiritualism is not only practiced by the poor and uneducated; it also has quite a following among the better-educated and wealthy classes. It is treated as an insurance policy that backs up and complements traditional religious and medical practices.

### Religious Practices in the United States

Most evidence indicates that mainland Puerto Ricans are somewhat less religious than those living on the island. A study of the heads of a sample of Puerto Rican families in New York City determined that 56 percent attended church at least once a week while living in Puerto Rico, whereas only 38 percent said they attended church this often in New York. One researcher estimates that about 20 percent of New York City's Puerto Ricans are practicing Catholics and that approximately 6 percent are active followers of one of the various Protestant sects. Thus, although most of the remaining 74 percent of Puerto Ricans are nominally Catholics, they are not regular practitioners of the faith.[115]

At least two major reasons explain why Catholicism is not more widely practiced regularly on the mainland. One is that it does not have the pueblo aspect in the states that it does in Puerto Rico. Because Puerto Ricans do not generally dominate numerically the mainland neighborhoods where they live, Catholicism (and especially their type of creole Catholicism) is not a universal focus for community organization as it is in Puerto Rico. For instance, in New York City Puerto Rican festivals do not dominate the activities of any of the city's five boroughs. A second factor that limits the influence of the Catholic Church among mainland Puerto Ricans is that they have not developed "ethnic" parishes like the southern and eastern European immigrants before them did. Instead, the Catholic Church has adopted a policy of attempting to serve the religious needs of Puerto Ricans through the use of "integrated" parishes. For example, when the Italians and Irish were immigrating in large numbers to the United States, the Catholic Church made major efforts to import an Italian and Irish clergy to service them. Since 1939 in New York City, the policy has been to accommodate all new immigrant groups with the clergy and facilities that are already in place. One reason for this is that there were not any spare Puerto Rican priests to bring to New York City, since only one-third of the clergy on the island were natives of Puerto Rico. Also, it was found that by the third generation, most people of southern and eastern European descent no longer spoke the native language, and most had adopted American customs and were moving out of their former neighborhoods. As a result, clusters of old ethnic churches were left behind serving only a handful of members. These could be used more efficiently if they were re-cycled for use by the new immigrant groups. A third factor that made it inefficient to pro-vide Puerto Ricans with their own churches was their dispersed settlement among other minorities. These other groups also have to be served, so the Catholic Church tries to serve them all together. The result is that services may be conducted in several different languages. Often the services in Spanish for the Puerto Ricans are held in a basement chapel, school hall, or a small chapel somewhere else in the parish. Thus, the Puerto Ri-cans do not feel that they have their own church, and the Catholic faith has not become a major force in maintaining their cultural identity while living on the mainland.

The major Protestant denominations have experienced many of the same problems as the Catholic Church. A major exception, however, are the Pentecostal churches which are flourishing. One writer has estimated that perhaps as much as 10 percent of all Puerto Rican families in New York City belong to, and help support, one of the Pentecostal churches.[116] They are attractive on the mainland for the same reasons that they are in Puerto Rico. In addition, because they are small-scale operations, they have no trouble ac-commodating small clusters of Puerto Rican families. There may be several in a given neighborhood operating out of small storefront chapels. In addition, they are almost al-ways directed by a minister who was born in Puerto Rico. Often families coming from the same town or neighborhood in Puerto Rico will attend the same chapel in New York City. Thus, the Pentecostal churches have been successful in being able to satisfy some of the needs for security and cultural maintenance that the Catholic Church has been unable to provide. Some evidence indicates, however, that they have been more successful in this regard with respect to the first generation of Puerto Ricans. The second generation tends to gravitate back to the Catholic Church and the major Protestant denominations.[117]

The folk medicine aspect of spiritualism is widely used by mainland Puerto Ricans. This is evident from the large number of *botánicas* that are found in such cities as Chicago, New York, and Miami. Often they are also used by other ethnic groups, such as Cubans, Haitians, Dominicans, and West Indians from the Caribbean. Although there is some use made of spiritual mediums, this does not appear to be as widespread among the mainland population as it is in Puerto Rico.

## Language Problems

It used to be that virtually all Puerto Ricans living on the mainland spoke Spanish as their mother tongue. The 1970 census showed that about 92 percent of all people liv-ing in the United States who were of Puerto Rican descent were raised in a family where Spanish was spoken in the home. For the first-generation migrants, the per-centage was 97 percent, whereas for those born on the mainland, the figure dropped to 86 percent.[118] If the Puerto Ricans follow the intergenerational trends displayed by most prior immigrant groups, it can be expected that by the third generation, Spanish will be of much less importance as both social and economic assimilation take place on the mainland. Data from the 1990 Census of Population suggest that this is hap-pening because the percentage of Puerto Ricans who could speak Spanish had declined

81 percent. Comparable figures for Mexican, Cuban, and Dominican Americans are 77 percent, 89 percent, and 94 percent, respectively.[119]

Most mainland Puerto Ricans speak at least some English, but many of the first generation do not speak it fluently. In 1990, one-third of all mainland Puerto Ricans reported that they did not speak English very well. For Mexican, Cuban, and Dominican Americans the comparable proportions were 39 percent, 49 percent, and 60 percent, respectively.[120] Lack of facility with English is a major barrier for the acquisition of managerial and white-collar jobs. Until 1965, a literacy test in English was required before a person was allowed to register to vote in New York City, so most of those who were born in Puerto Rico could not take part in elections until then. The language problems of Puerto Ricans in schools are serious. Millions of dollars are spent each year on bilingual programs in New York City's schools because it has been found that if students learn to read and write well in their native language, then they tend to do better in English as well. In some respects, the language problems that the migrant Puerto Rican students have are greater than was true with some of the immigrant groups who came before them. For instance, when the Italians and Jews were arriving in large numbers in New York City, it was possible for them to leave school at an earlier age, often as early as twelve. The current legal requirement for school attendance until sixteen years of age prolongs the problems with English usage in the schools.[121] In addition, as the occupational mix of New York City has changed, the interrelated problems of language and education make it more difficult for Puerto Ricans to compete for employment opportunities.

Speaking Spanish has become both an emotional and political issue with many Puerto Ricans. The Spanish language is considered to be one of the highest forms of expression of Puerto Rican culture. Communicating in Spanish creates a feeling of security and identity for mainland Puerto Ricans, especially for those belonging to the first generation. Darker-colored Puerto Ricans will sometimes make a point of speaking in Spanish around black Americans to make certain that they are not mistaken as being African Americans. When the United States took over Puerto Rico in 1898, an attempt was made to impose English as the language of instruction in the schools on the island, even though most of the teachers and students did not understand it. Two years later it was decided to use Spanish as the medium of instruction in the first eight grades and to use English from the ninth through twelfth grades. Five years later it was decided again to use English for all grades. The policy was to change back and forth several more times until 1948. In that year it was decided finally to use Spanish as the main language in the schools, with English as a required second language to be taught on a daily basis.[122] Not only was the requirement to speak English a frustrating experience, but it was very much resented by many Puerto Ricans who viewed it as an attempt to destroy the island's culture. In fact, this action is frequently used as evidence by supporters of Puerto Rican independence who predict that if the island becomes the fifty-first American state, its distinctive culture will be lost. Militant students and independence supporters on the mainland also place a heavy emphasis on the use and retention of Spanish as a traditional mark of their identity and cause.

### Attitudes toward Race

The 1990 census of the United States indicated that 46 percent of all mainland Puerto Ricans considered themselves to be white.[123] Another 47 percent said they were a mixture of black and white.[124] Only 6 percent considered themselves to be black. In 1950, about 80 percent of the population living in Puerto Rico was classified as white. It is, therefore, tempting to conclude that the migration stream to the United States has been dominated somewhat less by whites than the population in Puerto Rico. Such a statement, however, would be an oversimplification of the true racial characteristics of the population living in Puerto Rico. In fact, most are a mixture of black and white. As mentioned in the introduction to this chapter, Puerto Ricans range in color along a continuum from being completely white to totally black. Since so many are in between the extremes, the U.S. Bureau of the Census quit distinguishing between blacks and whites on the island after the 1950 census.

Puerto Ricans represent the first large group of immigrants to the mainland who are largely a mixture of blacks and whites. The fact that there has been a great deal of interracial mixing among Puerto Ricans indicates that their attitudes towards social distinctions are far different from those of most Americans. To understand the reasons for this difference in attitude, it is helpful to review briefly the historical background of racial attitudes in Puerto Rico.

The Spaniards first introduced black slaves to Puerto Rico in the early 1500s. Spain had just finished expelling the dark-colored Moors from the Iberian Peninsula at about the same time that Columbus set sail to discover the New World in 1492. As a result of the more than seven-hundred-year Moorish occupation of parts of Spain, the Spaniards had a long experience of living and intermarrying with dark-skinned people before they colonized Puerto Rico. Laws had been developed for the protection of slaves that were somewhat similar to today's international agreements that govern the treatment of prisoners of war.[125] Although these rules did not guarantee civil rights as they are known today, they did serve to soften somewhat the harsh treatment of the slaves in Spanish colonies. Once slavery was established in Puerto Rico, it was common for white men to father children born to black women. Frequently upper-class fathers would legally recognize their illegitimate children by giving them freedom at baptism. It also was common for white men to become *compadres* (godparents) for black children which, as stated earlier in this chapter, created a set of economic and social obligations that were generally taken seriously. This was a relationship that did not exist for black children in the United States.

In 1770, the governor of Puerto Rico declared that all free children, black or white, should be educated. Once slavery was abolished by the Spanish in 1873, the law opened public places to all people, regardless of color. There were no separate drinking fountains, rest rooms, or rear sections of public vehicles for segregated blacks in Puerto Rico, unlike the United States at that time.[126]

Still, blacks on the island have always been overrepresented among the poorer classes of Puerto Ricans. The numbing experience of slavery had deprived many of the blacks of the skills needed to compete in a free society. Nevertheless, it was not impossible for blacks to rise to prominent positions in Puerto Rican society, and there are a few examples of where this happened.

It would be incorrect to assume that there is no consciousness of color among Puerto Ricans. In fact, their awareness is both more subtle and more detailed than that of most Americans. On the mainland a person is usually thought of as being either all white or all black. Rarely are the shades in between recognized. In Puerto Rico, on the other hand, a number of terms have been coined in the vernacular to refer to the specific characteristics of people of mixed origin. To Puerto Ricans living on the island, however, color is only one aspect of class. For instance, there is very little residential segregation based on race in Puerto Rico as there is on the mainland.

The degree of color prejudice that exists varies among Puerto Rico's three major classes. In the lower class, where there is the largest concentration of black features, there is almost no discrimination. Black traits can be completely outweighed by other characteristics, such as a higher income, education, or social standing within the community. Even though there are some blacks among the upper class, they are excluded from a few elite social functions. A small number of social clubs and fraternities still exclude blacks, but most do not. In business and political offices, however, blacks are treated as equals. It is among the middle class that discrimination according to color is most overt, but again it is more subtle and less severe than on the mainland. It is undoubtedly most characteristic of this class because it is here that the people are most upwardly mobile. Although there are many exceptions, this is the Puerto Rican class that tends to be most competitive in trying to achieve higher social and economic status, and some of its members wish to grasp at any possible advantage.[127]

When Puerto Ricans move to the mainland of the United States, they encounter a culture that places a greater emphasis on color. They feel an increase in social pressure for several reasons. First, they find that the intermediate categories recognized in Puerto Rico do not exist on the mainland. They will be classified in American eyes simply as being either black or white. Second, they quickly notice that being perceived as black by Americans hinders their social acceptability. Third, they soon realize that being white has many economic advantages over being black. As a result, the darker-colored Puerto Ricans, especially, try to distinguish themselves from American blacks so they will be recognized as Puerto Ricans. Some emphasize speaking in Spanish, some wear different styles of clothes, and some associate as little as possible with black Americans.

Generally, mainland blacks and Puerto Ricans do not feel that they have much in common. In addition to the friction created by the obvious desire of many Puerto Ricans not to be mistaken for blacks, almost every conceivable type of competition has occurred between these two minorities. They compete for the lowest-paying jobs, the poorest and cheapest housing, public funding for neighborhood projects, and political power. They even compete for the time of doctors and nurses in public health clinics. Some of their youth belong to competitive gangs. Whenever possible they try to segregate themselves residentially, although (as stated earlier) this has been made difficult by scarce housing, slum clearance programs, and public housing projects. Among themselves, most mainland Puerto Ricans appear to treat color differences much the same as they did in Puerto Rico. It is the mainland blacks whom they treat differently. A 1957 study of marriage patterns among Puerto Ricans according to color designation in New York City found that 23 percent were judged to be racially mixed.[128] The author of that study concluded that there was a possibility that, if this pattern continued, the racial intermingling of Puerto Ricans could hasten the integration of the entire white and black populations of those cities where they form a numerically significant minority. However, that was a long time ago, and it is now clear that it was an overstatement. Some scholars predict that, within a generation or two, people of Puerto Rican descent will split into two groups. One will assimilate with white Americans and the other will identify with African Americans. They base this on historical evidence that the children and grandchildren of West Indian blacks who have moved to large American cities have married mostly American blacks.

## CONCLUSION

Clearly, the most important problem facing Puerto Ricans living on the U.S. mainland is the one-third of their population that remains mired in poverty. Well-known anthropologist Oscar Lewis described most Puerto Ricans as living in a culture of poverty during the 1960s. What he said no longer applies to the two-thirds who have emerged as vigorously ambitious members of the American middle class. However, some of his generalizations provide a good summary of what has been said in this chapter regarding the component of the Puerto Rican population that lives below the poverty line.[129]

The culture of poverty is not uniquely characteristic of poor mainland Puerto Ricans because it cuts across ethnic and international boundaries. Still, not all poor people are characterized by the culture of poverty, although being poor is one of its requirements. Lewis suggested that only about 20 percent of the people who lived below the poverty level in the United States in 1965 could properly be said to be living in the culture of poverty. In this category he placed many of this country's poor blacks, Mexican Americans, Indians, and some southern poor whites, in addition to Puerto Ricans.

Lewis called his concept the "culture of poverty" because it can be passed between generations, and the people who belong to it possess a set of recognizable characteristics. Groups that are represented by the culture of poverty lack effective participation and integration in the major institutions of the larger society in which they live. This results from a variety of factors that lessen the group's power, such as lack of economic resources, discrimination, segregation and isolation, and the development of local temporary solutions for problems. These are all characteristics of many members of the poorer class of Puerto Ricans. Although a large share of Puerto Rican workers are members of labor unions, most have been effectively barred from management positions and are generally poorly represented in the union hierarchies. Historically, Puerto Ricans have had low voter registration levels on the mainland and often they have not participated in elections as an effective voting block. This situation is now changing as major efforts have been made in many large American cities to register their Hispanic voting-age populations, including Puerto Ricans (all of whom are American citizens). In the poor Hispanic neighborhoods, the culture of poverty is characterized by a minimum level of organization. The focus tends to be on the nuclear and extended family. Occasionally some informal (usually temporary) organizations emerge, such as youth gangs. More often, however, there are few secondary group associations that are specifically designed to promote the members self-interest. For instance, although there are some exceptions, poor mainland Puerto Rican parents have exhibited low levels of participation at school PTA meetings. The tendency to change residences is frequently one of the major factors that limit group organization in Puerto Rican neighborhoods. The 1970 census indicates that only 33 percent of all mainland Puerto Ricans five years of age or older were living in the same house in 1970 and in 1965.[130] By 1990, this percentage had grown to an even more impressive 50 percent.[131]

On the family level, free or consensual unions are common and illegitimacy rates are often high. It has been estimated that more than one-quarter of all mainland Puerto Rican unions are of the consensual type.[132] Almost half of all live births to Puerto Ricans living in New York City were to women who were not married.[133] In the culture of poverty, free unions often make a lot of sense. Many Puerto Rican women feel that a consensual union gives them a better break because it provides them with some of the free-dom that men have under the double standard that typifies many Latin marriages. By not giving the fathers of their children legal status as husbands, they have stronger claim on their children should they decide to leave their mates. It also gives women exclusive rights to any property they may own.[134]

At the level of the individual, the culture of poverty is characterized by a feeling of marginality, dependence, and frequently fatalistic outlook. A feeling prevails among these people that there is little hope for changing things in their favor. They tend to live for the present and often make little effort to plan for the future. They are quite parochial in their outlook in that they have little knowledge of most areas outside their neighbor-hoods. The mainland Puerto Ricans may be somewhat of an exception to this latter point because of their ties with their homeland in Puerto Rico.

Fortunately, most (two-thirds) mainland Puerto Ricans have been able to escape the culture of poverty, but it is equally important to remember that one-third still live in it. In most cities where they live in sizable concentrations, the poor Puerto Ricans vie with poor black Americans, and other poor Hispanics, for the lowest-paying jobs.

It is not likely that Puerto Ricans will rapidly assimilate soon into American society. At least four major factors have served as major deterrents to the rapid assimilation of Puerto Ricans. One is their notable concentration in the cities of the Northeast, espe-cially in the New York metropolitan area, and in *colonias* in other cities, which makes it easier for them to associate with fellow Puerto Ricans and thus have less contact with Anglos. Second, the cultural infusion that they receive from the continued influx of mi-grants from Puerto Rico also allows them to maintain their cultural ties longer than they might otherwise have. Third, the fact that Puerto Rico has legal status within the juris-diction of the United States makes it easier to keep contact with Puerto Rico for return visits and facilitates arrangements to have relatives and friends follow in the stream to the mainland. A fourth factor that has slowed the assimilation of many Puerto Ricans is their mixed racial lineage.[135] Some researchers have predicted that those who are inter-mediate in color will have the most difficult time assimilating because they will find it hard to be accepted by either white or black Americans.

Although Puerto Ricans historically have not moved as rapidly into the mainstream of American society as Cuban Americans, there is little doubt now that they have begun to do so, especially since the 1980s. There is also little doubt now that the two-thirds that have been able to escape poverty are well on their way toward economic success as they have firmly joined the American middle class. When social scientists speak of a Puerto Rican underclass, they will now be more specifically referring to the unfortunate one-third who still remain in poverty. Furthermore, the Cubans who migrated during the 1960s were much more positively selected than the Puerto Rican migrants in terms of their education, income, and skill levels. Also, as political refugees, they received eco-nomic assistance from the federal government that was not made available to Puerto Ri-cans. Thus, the Cubans were able to establish an economic enclave and numerical dom-inance in Miami that helped absorb future waves of Cuban immigrants. Given their fewer economic resources and the changing occupation and housing conditions of New York City, Puerto Ricans have not had the same chance to develop as rapidly. Neverthe-less, there is no doubt that the two-thirds of them who have escaped the poverty trap are now on their way toward economic integration within mainstream American society.

## NOTES

1. U.S. Bureau of the Census, *Current Population Survey, March 1996*, Internet release, February 3, 1998, Table 1, "Selected Social Characteristics of All People and Hispanic People, by Type of Origin."

2. Population Reference Bureau, *1997 World Population Data Sheet* (Washington, D.C.: Author, 1997).

3. The Cuban population living in the United States also contains very few illegal aliens. However, Cuban Americans are exceptional because the United States Immigration and Naturalization Service has, until recently, accorded them special immigration privileges as a result of the communist takeover in Cuba. For further information on this topic, see chapter 5 on Cuban Americans in this book.

4. Joseph P. Fitzpatrick, *Puerto Rican Americans: The Meaning of Migration to the Mainland* (Upper Saddle River, N.J.: Prentice Hall, 1971), 101–114.

5. Joseph P. Fitzpatrick, "Puerto Ricans in Perspective: The Meaning of Migration to the Mainland," *International Migration Review* 2 (Spring 1968): 7–19.

6. The former Migration Division, originally located within Puerto Rico's Department of Labor, has been reorganized several times since its creation in the early 1950s. It is now located within the Puerto Rican Federal Affairs Administration. This program currently maintains three offices on the U.S. mainland, in New York City, Washington, D.C., and Cleveland, Ohio.

7. Clarence Senior, *Our Citizens from the Caribbean* (New York: McGraw-Hill, 1965), 90–91.

8. Nathan Glazer and Daniel P. Moynihan, *Beyond the Melting Pot* (Cambridge, Mass.: MIT Press, 1970), 109–110.

9. Fitzpatrick, "Puerto Ricans in Perspective," 9.

10. Adalberto Lopez, "The Puerto Rican Diaspora: A Survey," in *Puerto Rico and Puerto Ricans*, ed. Adalberto Lopez and James Petras (New York: Wiley, 1974), 316.

11. Senior, *Our Citizens from the Caribbean*, 77.

12. *Puerto Ricans in the Continental United States: An Uncertain Future* (Washington, D.C.: U.S. Commission on Civil Rights, 1976), 26.

13. Senior, *Our Citizens from the Caribbean*, 76.

14. When Puerto Ricans have been asked why they migrated or planned to move, the vast majority usually respond that they were influenced by economic opportunities. For instance, see C. Wright Mills, Clarence Senior, and Rose Kohn Goldsen, *The Puerto Rican Journey: New York's Newest Migrants* (New York: Harper, 1950), 49–50; and José Hernandez-Alvarez, *Return Migration to Puerto Rico*, Population Monograph Series, No. 1 (Berkeley: Institute of International Studies, University of California, 1967), 91. Several studies that have scientifically investigated the specific economic factors influencing Puerto Rican migration to the United States tend to stress either unemployment or income differentials between the island and mainland. For instance, Fleisher and Maldonado have found the unemployment variable to be most important, whereas Friedlander and Galloway and Vedder place their emphasis on income: Belton Fleisher, "Some Economic Aspects of Puerto Rican Migration to the United States," *Review of Economic and Statistics* 45 (August 1962): 245–253; Rita M. Maldonado, "Why Puerto Ricans Migrated to the United States in 1947–73," *Monthly Labor Review* 99 (September 1976): 7–18; Stanley L. Friedlander, *Labor Migration and Economic Growth* (Cambridge, Mass.: MIT Press, 1965), 125–128; and Lowell E. Gallaway and Richard K. Vedder, "Location Decisions of Puerto Rican Immigrants to the United States," *Social and Economic Studies* 20 (June 1971): 188–197.

15. Gerardo E. Sánchez-Dugergé, Bureau of Economic Analysis, Puerto Rico Planning Board, San Juan, Puerto Rico, April 24, 1998.

16. Francisco L. Rivera-Batiz and Carlos Santiago, *Puerto Ricans in the United States: A Changing Reality* (Washington, D.C.: National Puerto Rican Coalition, 1995), 14.

17. Friedlander lists these three reasons, plus a fourth. The latter was a reduction in the disguised unemployment rate in Puerto Rico, but this no longer appears to be true because of the island's current high rate of unemployment: Friedlander, *Labor Migration*, 160.

18. Francisco L. Rivera-Batiz and Carlos E. Santiago, *Island Paradox: Puerto Rico in the 1990s* (New York: Russell Sage Foundation, 1996), 47.

19. Francisco L. Rivera-Batiz, "The Characteristics of Recent Puerto Rican Migrants: Some Further Evidence," *Migration World* (October 1989): 10.

20. Carlos E. Santiago, "Wage Policies, Employment, and Puerto Rican Migration," in *Hispanics in the Labor Force: Issues and Policies*, ed. Edwin Meléndez, Clara Rodríguez, and Janis Barry-Figueroa (New York: Plenum, 1991), 225–246; and Carlos E. Santiago, "The Migratory Impact of Minimum Wage Legislation: Puerto Rico, 1970–1987," *International Migration Review* 27, no. 4 (Winter 1993): 772–795.

21. Carlos E. Santiago, "The Changing Role of Migration in Puerto Rican Economic Development: Perspective from the Past and a Look to the Future," in *The Commuter Nation: Perspectives on Puerto Rican Migration*, ed. C. A. Torre, H. Rodríguez, and W. Burgos (Río Piedras: University of Puerto Rico Press, 1992).

22. Rivera-Batiz and Santiago, *Island Paradox*, 47.

23. Population Reference Bureau, *1997 World Population Data Sheet*.

24. Nathan Kantrowitz, "Social Mobility of Puerto Ricans: Education, Occupation, and Income Changes among Children of Migrants, 1950–1960," *International Migration Review* 2 (Spring 1968): 53–71.

25. Rivera-Batiz and Santiago, *Island Paradox*, 48.

26. Mills et al., *The Puerto Rican Journey*, 33.

27. Rivera-Batiz and Santiago, *Island Paradox*, 49.

28. Rivera-Batiz and Santiago, *Island Paradox*, 49.

29. José Hernández-Alvarez, "Migration, Return, and Development in Puerto Rico," *Economic Development and Cultural Change* 16 (July 1968): 576.

30. Friedlander, *Labor Migration*, 56–59.

31. Hernández-Alvarez, *Return Migration to Puerto Rico*, 576.

32. Hernández-Alvarez, *Return Migration to Puerto Rico*, 27–28.

33. Rivera-Batiz and Santiago, *Island Paradox*, 49.

34. For examples of this thinking, see the following sources: Clarence Beardsley, "Experto Opina Sangría de Capital Humano de la Economía Puertorriqueña," *El Mundo*, February 23, 1980, p. 1; Elías R. Gutiérrez, "The Transfer Economy of Puerto Rico: Towards an Urban Ghetto," in *Time for Decision: The United States and Puerto Rico*, ed. J. Heine (Lanham, Md.: North-South, 1983), 117–134; Elizabeth Román, "Brain Drain to the Mainland," *Caribbean Business*, September 13, 1990, pp. 1–2; and Andrew Viglucci, "Migration a Fact of Life That Could Be Facilitated," *San Juan Star*, February 6, 1994.

35. Rivera-Batiz and Santiago, *Island Paradox*, 49.

36. Rivera-Batiz and Santiago, *Island Paradox*, 52.

37. Rivera-Batiz and Santiago, *Island Paradox*, 54.

38. Mills et al., *The Puerto Rican Journey*, 47.

39. George C. Myers and George Masnick, "The Experiences of New York Puerto Ricans: A Perspective on Return," *International Migration Review* 2 (Spring 1968): 81–82.

40. Hernández-Alvarez, *Return Migration*, 15–17.

41. This figure was quoted in Joseph P. Fitzpatrick, "Puerto Ricans," in *The Harvard Encyclopedia of American Ethnic Groups*, ed. Stephen Thernstrom (Cambridge, Mass.: Belknap Press of Harvard University Press, 1980), 860.

42. Maldonado, "Why Puerto Ricans Migrate," 13.

43. Rivera-Batiz and Santiago, *Island Paradox*, 55–58.

44. Maldonado, "Why Puerto Ricans Migrate," 13.

45. Myers and Masnick, "The Experiences of New York Puerto Ricans," 88.

46. Maldonado, "Why Puerto Ricans Migrate," 13.

47. Rivera-Batiz and Santiago, *Island Paradox*, 58–62.

48. Fitzpatrick, *Puerto Rican Americans*, 15–19.

49. *Puerto Ricans in the Continental United States*, 5.

50. Fitzpatrick, *Puerto Rican Americans*, 17; and for a more detailed discussion of the relationships between contract labor and Puerto Rican communities in the United States, see Edwin Maldonado, "Contract Labor and the Origins of Puerto Rican Communities in the United States," *International Migration Review* 8 (Spring 1979): 103–121.

51. Fitzpatrick, *Puerto Rican Americans*, 18–19.

52. Sánchez-Duvergé, April 24, 1998.

53. Myers and Masnick, "The Experiences of New York Puerto Ricans," 84.

54. Friedlander, *Labor Migration*, 157–166.

55. U.S. Bureau of the Census, *1990 Census of Population*, Summary Tape File 1A (Washington, D.C.: U.S. Government Printing Office, 1991).

56. For maps showing the distributions of Puerto Ricans by counties for the eight states with the largest Puerto Rican populations, see Angel David Cruz-Báez and Thomas D. Boswell, *Atlas Puerto Rico* (Miami: Cuban American National Council, 1997), 125–128.

57. Gallaway and Vedder, "Location Decisions," 193–197.

58. U.S. Bureau of the Census, *1990 Census of Population*, "Social and Economic Characteristics, United States," 1990 CP-2-1 (Washington, D.C.: U.S. Government Printing Office, 1993), Table 4, p. 4.

59. Population Reference Bureau, *1997 World Population Data Sheet*.

60. Rivera-Batiz and Santiago, *Puerto Ricans in the United States*, 21.

61. U.S. Bureau of the Census, *Census of Population: 1950*, Special Reports, Vol. IV, Part 3, Chapter D, "Puerto Ricans in Continental United States" (Washington, D.C.: U.S. Government Printing Office, 1953), 30–44.

62. Fitzpatrick, *Puerto Rican Americans*, 53–55.

63. Terry J. Rosenberg, *Residence, Employment, and Mobility of Puerto Ricans in New York City*, University of Chicago, Department of Geography, Research Paper No. 151 (Chicago: University of Chicago Press, 1974), 47.

64. Robert T. Novak, "Distribution of Puerto Ricans on Manhattan Island," *Geographical Review* 46 (April 1956): 182–186.

65. *Puerto Ricans in the Continental United States*, 21.

66. J. Hernández-Alvarez, "The Movement and Settlement of Puerto Rican Migrants within the United States, 1950–1960," *International Migration Review* 2 (Spring 1968): 40–51.

67. José Oscar Alers, *Puerto Ricans and Health: Findings from New York City*, Monograph No. 4 (New York: Hispanic Research Center, Fordham University, 1978), 2.

68. Fitzpatrick, *Puerto Rican Americans*, 70–71.

69. Thomas D. Boswell, "Residential Patterns of Puerto Ricans in New York City," *Geographical Review* 66 (January 1976): 92–94.

70. Rivera-Batiz and Santiago, *Puerto Ricans in the United States*, 22.

71. U.S. Bureau of the Census, *1990 Census of Population*, "Social and Economic Characteristics, United States," 1990 CP-2-1 (Washington, D.C.: U.S. Government Printing Office, 1993), Table 173, p. 364.

72. Nathan Kantrowitz, *Negro and Puerto Rican Populations of New York City in the Twentieth Century*, Studies in Urban Geography, No. 1 (New York: American Geographical Society, 1969), 1.

73. Kantrowitz, *Negro and Puerto Rican Populations*, plate 4.

74. Glazer and Moynihan, *Beyond the Melting Pot*, 94–95.

75. Nathan Kantrowitz, *Ethnic and Racial Segregation in the New York Metropolis: Residential Patterns among White Ethnic Groups, Blacks, and Puerto Ricans* (New York: Praeger, 1973), 42, 48, and 52–53.

76. This same pattern of segregation, according to socioeconomic status, has been noted among the Cubans living in Miami; see chap. 5 in this book.

77. U.S. Bureau of the Census, *1990 Census of Population*, "People of Hispanic Origin in the United States," 1990 CP-3-3 (Washington, D.C.: U.S. Government Printing Office, 1993), Table 1.

78. U.S. Bureau of the Census, *1980 Census of Population and Housing*, PHC80-P-53, "Puerto Rico (Preliminary Reports)," February 1981 (Washington, D.C.: U.S. Government Printing Office, 1981), 5.

79. U.S. Bureau of the Census, *Current Population Survey*.

80. U.S. Bureau of the Census, "People of Hispanic Origin in the United States," 1993, Table 1.

81. U.S. Bureau of the Census, *Current Population Survey*.

82. U.S. Bureau of the Census, "People of Hispanic Origin Living in the United States," 1993, Table 3; and U.S. Bureau of the Census, *1990 Census of Population, Puerto Rico*, "Summary Social, Economic, and Housing Characteristics" (Washington, D.C.: U.S. Government Printing Office, 1993), Table 3.

83. U.S. Bureau of the Census, "People of Hispanic Origin Living in the United States," 1993, Table 3; and U.S. Bureau of the Census, *1990 Census of Population, Puerto Rico*, Table 3.

84. Rivera-Batiz and Santiago, *Puerto Ricans in the United States*, 89.

85. U.S. Bureau of the Census, *Current Population Survey*, Table 1.

86. Ronald R. Rindfuss, "Fertility and Migration: The Case of Puerto Rico," *International Migration Review* 10 (Summer 1976): 191–203. Also, see A. J. Jaffe, Ruth M. Cullen, and Thomas D. Boswell, *The Changing Demography of Spanish Americans* (New York: Academic Press, 1980).

87. A. J. Jaffe and Ruth M. Cullen, "Fertility of the Puerto Rican Origin Population—Mainland United States and Puerto Rico: 1970," *International Migration Review* 9 (Summer 1975): 193–209.

88. For examples of this thinking, see Glazer and Moynihan, *Beyond the Melting Pot*, 109–110; and Marta Tienda, "Puerto Ricans and the Underclass Debate," *Annals of the American Academy of Political and Social Science* (January 1989).

89. Linda Chávez, *Out of the Barrio: Toward a New Politics of Hispanic Assimilation* (New York: Basic Books, 1991), 140.

90. Nicholas Lemann, "The Other Underclass," *Atlantic Monthly*, December 1991, 96.

91. Rivera-Batiz and Santiago, *Puerto Ricans in the United States*, 68–69.

92. Rivera-Batiz and Santiago, *Puerto Ricans in the United States*, 65.

93. Rivera-Batiz and Santiago, *Puerto Ricans in the United States*, 64.

94. U.S. Bureau of the Census, *Current Population Survey*, Table 2, "Selected Economic Characteristics of All People and Hispanic People, by Type of Origin: March 1996."

95. These figures have been standardized for the inflation that took place between 1980 and 1990. See Rivera-Batiz and Santiago, *Puerto Ricans in the United States*, Tables 3.2 and 3.3, pp. 28–29.

96. In 1996, both the American black and Hispanic population had poverty rates in the vicinity of 30 percent. U.S. Bureau of the Census, *Current Population Survey*.

97. Rivera-Batiz and Santiago, *Puerto Ricans in the United States*, 35, 48, 50, and 73.

98. Consolidated metropolitan statistical areas (CMSAs) contain two or more metropolitan statistical areas (MSAs). The CMSAs have been designed to capture the essential characteristics of especially large urban areas where several MSAs are in the process of growing together into a single large consolidated conurbation.

99. Rivera-Batiz and Santiago, *Puerto Ricans in the United States*, 35.

100. Rivera-Batiz and Santiago, *Puerto Ricans in the United States*, 48.

101. Fitzpatrick, *Puerto Rican Americans*, 78–80.

102. In 1990, 27 percent of all mainland Puerto Rican households received some form of public assistance income. U.S. Bureau of the Census, "People of Hispanic Origin in the United States," 1993, Table 5.

103. Oscar Lewis, *La Vida* (New York: Random House, 1966), xxxviii–xxxix.

104. Karl Wagenheim, *A Survey of Puerto Ricans on the U.S. Mainland in the 1970's* (New York: Praeger, 1975), 12–13 and 76–77.

105. U.S. Bureau of the Census, *Current Population Reports*, Series P-20, No. 354, "People of Spanish Origin in the United States: March, 1979" (Washington, D.C.: U.S. Government Printing Office, 1980), 41.

106. U.S. Bureau of the Census, "People of Hispanic Origin in the United States," 1993, Table 5.

107. Joseph P. Fitzpatrick and Douglas T. Gurak, *Hispanic Intermarriage in New York City: 1975*, Monograph No. 2 (New York: Hispanic Research Center, Fordham University, 1979), 6.

108. Jaffe et al., *The Changing Demography*, 192–194 and 232.

109. Fitzpatrick and Gurak, *Hispanic Intermarriage*, 86–88.

110. Wagenheim, *A Survey of Puerto Ricans*, 164.

111. Fitzpatrick, "Puerto Ricans," 865.

112. Wagenheim, *A Survey of Puerto Ricans*, 175.

113. Fitzpatrick, "Puerto Ricans," 865.

114. Wagenheim, *A Survey of Puerto Ricans*, 167.

115. Fitzpatrick, *Puerto Rican Americans*, 128.

116. Wagenheim, *A Survey of Puerto Ricans*, 168.

117. Fitzpatrick, *Puerto Rican Americans*, 129.

118. U.S. Bureau of the Census, *Census of Population: 1970*, Subject Reports, Final Report PC(2)-I E, "Puerto Ricans in the United States" (Washington, D.C.: U.S. Government Printing Office, 1973), 32.

119. U.S. Bureau of the Census, "People of Hispanic Origin in the United States," 1993, Table 3.

120. U.S. Bureau of the Census, "People of Hispanic Origin in the United States," 1993, Table 3.

121. Fitzpatrick, *Puerto Rican Americans*, 142.

122. It has been estimated that about 45 percent of all Puerto Ricans living on the island can at least understand some English, even though they may not be comfortable or fluent speaking it. Wagenheim, *A Survey of Puerto Ricans*, 170–173 and 213.

123. These figures on race for 1990 come from a 0.5 percent sample derived by the authors of this chapter from the following source: U.S. Bureau of the Census, *1990 Census of Population and Housing*, "Public Use Microdata Sample, 5 Percent Sample" (Washington, D.C.: U.S. Government Printing Office, 1993).

124. There was a category on the 1990 population census questionnaire for race labeled as "Other." Census Bureau experts assume that most of the Puerto Ricans who checked this category were a mixture of black and white.

125. Fitzpatrick, *Puerto Rican Americans*, 104.

126. Wagenheim, *A Survey of Puerto Ricans*, 162.

127. Sidney W. Mintz, "Puerto Rico: An Essay in the Definition of National Culture," in *The Puerto Rican Experience*, ed. Francesco Cordasco and Eugene Bucchioni (Totowa, N.J.: Littlefield, Adams, 1975), 56–59.

128. Fitzpatrick, *Puerto Rican Americans*, 111–112.

129. Lewis, *La Vida*, xlii–xliii.

130. U.S. Bureau of the Census, *Census of Population: 1970*, 39.

131. Rivera-Batiz and Santiago, *Puerto Ricans in the United States*, 5.

132. Glazer and Moynihan, *Beyond the Melting Pot*, 89.

133. Ian A. Canino, Brian F. Earley, and Lloyd H. Rogler, *The Puerto Rican Child in New York City: Stress and Mental Health*, Monograph No. 4 (New York: Hispanic Research Center, Fordham University, 1980), 41.

134. Lewis, *La Vida*, xlvi.

135. Jaffe et al., *The Changing Demography*, 18–20.

# 7

# American Jews

## Ira M. Sheskin

Despite obvious evidence to the contrary and historical facts, the United States Bureau of the Census classifies Jews only as a religious group. Due in part to the doctrine of the separation of church and state, data on religious preference have not been collected by the Census Bureau since 1957. Thus, unlike most other ethnic groups in this volume, a number of different techniques, all of which have significant drawbacks, have been used to derive estimates of the Jewish population in the United States. These include procedures involving absences from public school on major Jewish holidays, death rate methods, the use of surrogate census variables, random digit dialing survey techniques, and methods using distinctive Jewish names (DJNs).[1]

Since the early 1980s, more than forty-five American Jewish communities have undertaken scientific demographic studies of their own populations.[2] Most of these studies have used a DJN methodology and/or a random digit dialing methodology. Based on these methods, the number of Jews in every United States city containing one hundred or more Jews is reported annually in the *American Jewish Year Book (AJYB)*. In addition, a National Jewish Population Study (NJPS) was completed in 1971[3] and in 1990 (hereafter called NJPS-1990),[4] which provided estimates of the Jewish population of the country as a whole. The *AJYB* estimate of 5.9 million American Jews differs from the NJPS-1990 estimate of 5.5 million. This chapter relies upon NJPS-1990 for estimates of the 1990 Jewish population of the country as a whole and for national demographics but on the *American Jewish Year Book* for local and state population estimates and historical population estimates.[5] This chapter also cites results from local Jewish demographic studies for Jewish community demographics.

## THE NATURE OF AMERICAN JEWISH ETHNICITY

NJPS-1990 showed that only 5 percent of American Jews consider being Jewish solely in terms of being a member of a religious group.[6] Thus, the vast majority of American Jews view themselves as members of an ethnic group and/or a cultural group, and/or a nationality.

The acknowledgment by Jews of the ethnic nature of their identity represents a significant change from the answers one might have received from American Jews during the early part of this century. Jews left European countries in significant numbers during the early part of the twentieth century in large part because they could not be Russians in Russia or Poles in Poland or Bessarabians in Bessarabia, even after centuries of residence in those countries. Jews were viewed (properly) as members of a separate ethnic group who wanted to continue their religious and ethnic traditions. When Jews arrived in the United States, they downplayed the ethnicity of being Jewish in favor of the religious aspect.[7] This was done for three reasons. First, in the United States, as a nation of immigrants, everyone could become an American. Second, while separation of church and state was the goal, it was *American* to have a religion. Third, as a member of an ethnic group, Jews were one of the smaller U.S. ethnic groups, while as a member of a religious group, Jews were the third largest religious group in the United States. This perception clearly led to greater political power for the American Jewish community. Thus, the results from NJPS-1990 show that Jews are now sufficiently comfortable in America, during what some observers have called the "Golden Age of American Jewry," to reassert once again their ethnic identity.

The nature of Jewish identity in the United States is complex and fluid (Table 7.1). The NJPS-1990 found 8.2 million persons in 3.2 million American Jewish households.[8] A Jewish household is defined as a household containing one or more self-defined Jews. These households contained 6.84 million persons of Jewish heritage and 1.35 million Gentiles, including non-Jewish spouses and children and unrelated non-Jews. Thus, almost 17 percent of persons in Jewish households have no Jewish heritage. Examining just the 6.84 million persons of Jewish heritage shows that about 81 percent (about 5.5 million) belong to the "Core Jewish" population. The Core Jewish

**Table 7.1    United States Jewish Population, 1990.**

| Jewish Identity Category | Number | Percent of Jewishly Identified Population | Percent of Total Population in Jewish Households |
|---|---|---|---|
| Born Jews: Religion Judaism | 4,210,000 | 61.6% | 51.3% |
| Jews by Choice—Converts | 185,000 | 2.7% | 2.3% |
| Born Jews: Secular | 1,120,000 | 16.4% | 13.7% |
| Core Jewish Population | 5,515,000 | 80.6% | 67.3% |
| Born Jewish—Switched to Another Religion | 210,000 | 3.1% | 2.6% |
| Adults of Jewish Parentage with Other Current Religion | 415,000 | 6.1% | 5.1% |
| Children Under 18 Being Raised with Other Current Religion | 700,000 | 10.2% | 8.5% |
| Total Jewish Ethnic or Religious Preference | 6,840,000 | 100.0% | 83.4% |
| Gentile Adults Living with Total Jewish Population | 1,350,000 | | 16.5% |
| Total Population in 3.2 Million Jewish Households | 8,200,000 | | 100.0% |

Source: Barry Kosmin et al., *Highlights of the CJF 1990 National Jewish Population Survey* (New York: Council of Jewish Federations, 1991), 6.

population includes three groups. The first group (4,210,000) contains those who were born Jewish and would describe their religion as Jewish. The second group (1,120,000) is composed of those who were born Jewish and would describe themselves as Jewish, but would do so *only* in a secular or ethnic sense. They may be performing religious rituals but are attaching cultural or ethnic reasons to their execution. The third group contains those who have converted to Judaism (185,000). Thus, those of Jewish heritage fall in a number of groups, with various levels of attachment to being Jewish on both religious and ethnic dimensions.

The first part of this chapter examines the migration of Jews. NJPS-1990 shows that American Jews are about twice as mobile as Americans in general and that most of today's Jewish population is the children and grandchildren of immigrants. Thus, an understanding of migration is essential to an understanding of the American Jewish community. First, the chapter traces the international migration of Jews, with a focus on migration to the United States. Second, the significant interurban migration of the Jewish population over the past five decades from cities of the Northeast and Midwest to the West and the South is described, and its implications are discussed. Third, intraurban migration (suburbanization) of the Jewish population is examined. The second part of the chapter contains a brief description of some key elements of American Jewish demography and a discussion of geographic variations in levels of religiosity and ethnic attachment among Jews, the key issue facing the American Jewish community during the twenty-first century.

## INTERNATIONAL MIGRATION: THE CHANGING SPATIAL DISTRIBUTION OF WORLD JEWRY

Table 7.2 shows the changing spatial distribution of the world Jewish population since 1881. The first year (1881) is chosen because it is the year of the assassination of the reformist czar Alexander II, which led to pogroms (anti-Jewish riots) and massive migration out of eastern Europe. The year 1939 is selected because it is pre-Holocaust; 1951 is post-Holocaust and post-Israel independence; 1986 is chosen because it is prior to the dissolution of the Soviet Union; and, finally, 1997 has the latest data available as of this writing. The regions employed in this table are determined by data availability. In some cases, regions had to be combined because of data availability and changes in borders for particular dates. This section examines the worldwide shifts in Jewish population, while the following section examines the migration that has led to the changes shown in Table 7.2 for the Jewish population of the United States.

Significant changes can be seen in the Jewish world over the past 116 years. During this time, the world's Jewish population has increased by only about 36 percent. Even at the rate of natural population increase extant in the world in the late 1890s (1.5 percent), the Jewish population of the world should have more than doubled over the past one hundred years. That it did not is testament to the Holocaust and other massacres of Jews in Europe as well as to assimilation. The 9.6 million Jews in 1881 had increased to more than 16 million by 1939. The Holocaust resulted in a decline to 12 million by 1951. Thirty-five years later (in 1986), the world contained almost 13 million Jews. Since 1951, the world's Jewish population has increased by only about 9 percent. Over the past 150 years, 7.5 million Jews have changed their country of residence.[9]

**Table 7.2    Changes in the Jewish Population of Major World Regions.**

|  | 1881 | 1939 | 1951 | 1986 | 1997 |
|---|---|---|---|---|---|
| United States | 250,000 | 4,500,000 | 5,201,000 | 5,700,000 | 5,700,000 |
| Canada | 16,000 | 165,000 | 208,000 | 310,000 | 362,000 |
| Middle and | | | | | |
| South America | 35,000 | 420,000 | 627,000 | 444,700 | 428,400 |
| Western Europe | 1,074,000 | 1,302,000 | 899,000 | 1,047,700 | 1,038,200 |
| Eastern Europe | | 5,270,000 | 544,000 | 123,200 | 100,000 |
| European FSU | 7,434,000* | 2,800,000 | 1,939,000 | | 499,200 |
| Asiatic FSU | 105,000 | 220,000 | 328,000 | 1,515,000** | 41,100 |
| Other Asia | 277,000 | 350,000 | 173,000 | 34,500 | 19,800 |
| North Africa | 280,000 | 520,000 | 567,000 | 15,200 | 7,800 |
| Rest of Africa | 60,000 | 115,000 | 127,000 | 130,500 | 94,600 |
| Palestine/Israel | 50,000 | 450,000 | 1,330,000 | 3,562,000 | 4,701,600 |
| Oceania | 17,000 | 35,000 | 56,000 | 81,100 | 100,100 |
| Total | 9,598,000 | 16,147,000 | 11,999,000 | 12,963,400 | 13,092,800 |

Sources: 1881 and 1939: Eli Barnavi, ed., *A Historical Atlas of the Jewish People* (New York: Alfred A. Knopf, 1992), 194–195.

1951: Evyatar Friesel, *Atlas of Modern Jewish History* (New York: Oxford University Press, 1990), 132.

1986 and 1997: "World Jewish Population," *American Jewish Year Book* (New York: American Jewish Committee and the Jewish Publication Society, 1988 and 1999), 543–580.

Special Note: Due to clearly erroneous figures for the United States in 1881 in Barnavi's *A Historical Atlas of the Jewish People*, the 1881 estimate for the United States is derived from Jacob Rader Marcus, *To Count a People: American Jewish Population Data, 1585–1984* (Lanham, Md.: University Press of America, 1990), which may be considered a superior source for these data. Note that all figures (except for Israel in 1951, 1986, and 1995 and Canada in 1951) are estimates and that different sources sometimes present widely varying estimates.

*Figure includes Eastern Europe FSU (former Soviet Union).

**Figure includes European FSU and Asiatic FSU.

The spatial pattern found over the past century may be characterized as one of shifting clusters. While Jews are found in almost every country, they are clearly clustered in a small number of countries.[10] Table 7.2 shows the extensive level of clustering as of 1997, when two countries (the United States and Israel) accounted for 79 percent of the world's Jewish population and ten countries contained 95 percent of the world's Jewish population. In fact, the Jewish population was significantly more clustered than was the case in 1930, when two countries (the United States and Poland) contained "only" 47 percent of the world's Jewish population and nineteen countries contained 91 percent of the world's Jewish population.

In 1881, 77 percent of Jews lived in eastern Europe (including those countries that were eventually incorporated into the Soviet Union). Another 11 percent lived in western Europe, and less than 3 percent lived in the United States.

Significant changes occurred in the Jewish world between 1881 and 1939, including large scale migrations (impelled by pogroms throughout eastern Europe) to the United States (which increased to 4,500,000 Jews by 1939), Canada (165,000), Middle and South America (420,000) (the largest numbers to Argentina), and Palestine (450,000). Significant numbers also headed to South Africa, increasing its Jewish population by almost 70,000. This large-scale migration of 3.7 million resulted in a very different distribution of Jews on the eve of World War II. The eastern Europe/European former Soviet Union (FSU) area's share declined from 72 percent to 50 percent, while the share in the United States increased from 10 percent to 28 percent. The actual number of Jews in the United States increased from 250,000 to 4.5 million, but note that the actual number of Jews in the eastern Europe/European FSU actually increased from 7,434,000 to 8,070,000, despite the percentage decline. The absolute number of Jews in Palestine increased by about 400,000 and the percentage increased from 0.5 percent to almost 3 percent.

By 1951, due to the Holocaust and the establishment of the State of Israel, the number of Jews in the world declined significantly, from sixteen million to twelve million, and the spatial distribution also changed dramatically. The percentage of Jews in the United States increased to 43 percent, or about 5.2 million. The percentage in the eastern Europe/European FSU area declined to 21 percent, with an absolute decrease (due to the Holocaust, which exterminated six million Jews, more than one-third of the world total) from more than 8 million to about 2.5 million. The establishment of the State of Israel in 1948, with the concomitant migration of Holocaust survivors and Jews from Arab countries, meant an increase to 1.3 million in Israel, which now contained 11 percent of world Jewry.

While the number of Jews in the United States increased by about half a million between 1951 and 1986, the percentage of Jews living in the United States remained constant at 44 percent. The number in Middle and South America declined, because of assimilation and migration to the United States and Israel. The number and percentage in western Europe increased, in part owing to a large migration from Algeria to France following Algerian independence in the early 1960s. Eastern Europe saw a significant decline from more than 500,000 in 1951 to 123,000 in 1986. The Soviet Union saw an absolute decline from almost 2.3 million to about 1.5 million, partly due to migration to Israel and the United States. In the late 1800s, eastern Europe and the Soviet Union contained 73 percent of the Jews, but by 1986, this area contained a mere 12 percent.

Due in large part to significant migration from the Arab countries, eastern Europe, and the Soviet Union, Israel's Jewish population increased from 1.3 million to 3.6 million between 1951 and 1986. By 1986, more than one in four Jews lived in Israel. Thus, the 1951–1986 period saw the United States' share remain the same and the Israeli share increase, at the expense of most other areas of the world, in particular, eastern Europe and the Soviet Union.

The period from 1986 to 1997 saw a significant decline in the number of Jews in the former Soviet Union, from 1.5 million to 540,000, and a concomitant increase in the number in Israel, from 3.6 million to 4.7 million.

Jews are not the only people to live both in their homeland and in a diaspora.[11] The term *diaspora*, or "dispersion," has now been applied to Armenian, Gypsy, black, Chinese, Indian, Irish, Greek, Lebanese, Palestinian, Vietnamese, and Korean peoples. Chaliand and Rageau suggest that for the dispersion of a people to be called a diaspora, four conditions must be met:

1. There must be a collective forced dispersion, precipitated by a disaster, often of a political nature.
2. Collective memory must transmit both the historical facts that precipitated the dispersion and a cultural and/or religious heritage.
3. The will to survive as a minority by transmitting the heritage must be present.
4. A diaspora must have lasted for enough years to prove that factors 1–3 are at work.

Three significant factors make the Jewish diaspora different from that of the other groups. First, it has lasted for two thousand years. Second, the Jews have been placed in new diasporas at various times in history, as their adopted homelands (with the exception of the United States) have forced or impelled their migration elsewhere. Third, only for the Jews (and the Gypsies) has there been an attempt at genocide. In 1881, 99.5 percent of Jews lived in the diaspora; by 1997, about two-thirds did so. Continued forced and impelled migrations and attempted genocides have changed the Jewish world in the past century and have resulted in even greater clustering of the Jewish population. It has changed from a Europe-oriented world to one dominated by the United States and Israel, which combined contain about 79 percent of world Jewry. The United States' function in the world Jewish community needs to be examined in terms of its role as the leading diaspora nation and indeed in its role (at least for a few more decades) as the nation containing the largest percentage of Jews. While the traditional prayer at the beginning of the *Shabbat* (Sabbath) Torah service states that the "Torah [Jewish law] shall come from Zion, the word of the Lord from Jerusalem," it is also clear that American Jews are making contributions to American, Israeli, and Jewish societies far in excess of their numbers. Yet the ability of the American Jewish community to survive in its current form by "transmitting its heritage" is challenged today. Centers of Jewish life have come and gone over the ages. While the nature of the American governmental and social system probably guards against anti-Semitism of a nature that would lead to a mass migration, assimilation into secular American society endangers the future of the American Jewish community as it exists today.

## INTERNATIONAL MIGRATION: MIGRATION OF JEWS TO THE UNITED STATES

Considerable debate is possible on the issue of identifying the first Jews to inhabit North America. Researchers have conjectured that some Indian tribes were descended from the ten lost tribes of Israel.[12] More likely, the first settlement of Jews in the New World resulted from the Spanish (1492) and Portuguese (1497) Inquisitions, during which time, faced with the decision either to convert to Christianity or to be burned at the stake, many Jews fled to other lands. Many others became *marranos*, persons who outwardly professed Christianity but continued Jewish religious practices in secrecy within their homes. In the same year as the Spanish Inquisition (1492), Columbus arrived in the Caribbean. Some have suspected that Columbus himself was Jewish, perhaps a *marrano*, although the evidence seems scant in support of this thesis.[13] But Columbus did have Jews as members of his crew. Doubtless, *marranos* were among the Spaniards who crossed the Rio Grande in the 1500s. Gross[14] discusses the existence of one hundred Indian families in Venta Prieta, Mexico, who claim they are descendants of sixteenth-century *marranos*.

Between 1492 and 1600, Jews fleeing from Spain and Portugal took refuge in parts of South and Middle America. When the Dutch and the English captured parts of the New World, Jewish communities developed that allowed marranos to emerge as Jews and that attracted Jews from England and Holland. By 1640, Jewish communities had emerged in Brazil from Salvador (Bahia) to São Luis (Maranhao), when the Dutch briefly controlled this area. With the Portuguese reconquest of this area of Brazil, Jews fled to Paramaribo (Dutch Guiana), Cayenne (French Guiana), Tobago, Barbados, Martinique, Curacao, and Kingston (Jamaica).

In addition, Jews fled to New Amsterdam (New York) and Newport, Rhode Island. Some Jews arrived on the east coast of North America in the early 1500s, but their numbers were small and no Jewish communities were ever established. These individuals no doubt intermarried and assimilated into the local societies. It was when the twenty-three Jews left Pernambuco (Recife), Brazil (as a result of the Portuguese reconquest of the area from the Dutch), and arrived at New Amsterdam that the first "Jewish community" was established in what is today the United States. Although Peter Stuyvesant (then the governor of New Amsterdam) was loathe to allow them to remain, they were eventually permitted to stay. Both the manner in which this decision was rendered and the stipulations of the agreement are interesting in that they foreshadow much about the geography of American Jews.

Stuyvesant was a known anti-Semite, having tried to prevent the settlement of Jews in Curacao when he was the principal agent for the Dutch West India Company on that Caribbean island. When two Jews arrived from Holland in 1654, Stuyvesant was apparently unconcerned. When the twenty-three Jews arrived from Brazil, however, Stuyvesant decided to force them to flee. That two Jews would be no problem, but twenty-three would be, presages later events in American Jewish history. Two would be no problem because one could not expect them to do anything but assimilate into the local society and culture. A group of twenty-three, on the other hand, could be expected to form a "community." These feelings of Stuyvesant are consistent with today's reports that anti-Semitic incidents are considerably more prevalent in areas with larger Jewish populations. That the Jewish population will tend to assimilate more in areas of sparse Jewish settlement is also consistent with the findings later in this chapter.

The Jews in New Amsterdam were permitted to stay permanently after the intercession of some wealthy Jews in Amsterdam who were investors in the Dutch West Indies Company. When harassment of Jews continued and worship was banned even in the private homes of individuals, Jews in Amsterdam again intervened. That Jews in one geographic area would come to the aid of Jews in another, that the Jewish community in Europe would continue to influence Jews in the New World, also portended the future.

The agreement allowing the Jews to stay stipulated that "these people may travel and trade in New Netherlands and live and remain there, provided the poor among them shall not become a burden to the Company or to the community, but be supported by their own nation."[15] Thus, Jews were instructed to take care of their own poor and they did so. As shown by NJPS-1990, Jews have continued that tradition. The migration into the United States of ten thousand Soviet Jews above the 1990 quota was permitted by the United States government only if the Jewish community cared for these people. None of these additional admittees would be permitted on welfare.

When permission was granted for Jews to conduct religious services in private, the agreement stated that Jews could "exercise in all quietness their religion within their houses, for which end they must without doubt endeavor to build their houses close together in a convenient place on one side or the other of New Amsterdam."[16] Thus, the first Jewish neighborhood in America was established. Jews would continue to live in a geographically clustered fashion at many different geographic scales, from 1654 to the present day.

Jews moved to the United States during four periods of migration: (1) the Sephardic (1654–1820), (2) the German (1820–1880), (3) the eastern European (1880–1920s), and (4) the modern period (from the 1930s to the present day).[17]

The first period of Jewish migration to the United States was from 1654 until about 1820. Most of this migration, like the original twenty-three, was of Sephardic Jews.[18] Historic estimates of the Jewish population of the United States have been collated by Marcus and form the basis for all estimates in this chapter prior to 1939.[19] By 1776, about 1,000 Jews lived in the United States. Most estimates for 1800 indicate a Jewish population of about 2,000. Estimates for 1820 range from about 2,750 to about 5,000. The earliest synagogues were to be found in New Amsterdam (New York), Newport, Rhode Island, Savannah, Philadelphia, and Charleston. These Jews were mostly shopkeepers and merchants. Not having been allowed to own land in most European countries, Jews did not develop farming skills. They were involved in retail activity in Europe and brought those skills to the United States.

The second period of Jewish migration, from 1820 to 1880, marks the era of German Jewish migration.[20] While Napoleon's message had improved conditions for Jews in Europe and had freed them from the confines of the ghetto in many areas (resulting in the *Haskala* or Enlightenment movement in Jewish history), the end of this era, with the end of the Napoleonic era, made life difficult for Jews in many areas, particularly in Germany. During the first wave of immigration from Germany, from 1820 to 1860, as many as 100,000 Jews immigrated from Germany.[21] Estimates of the number of Jews on the eve of the Civil War ranged from 150,000 to 200,000. Many of these German immigrants were involved in retail trade, particularly in the garment industry. Many began peddling goods from push carts and gradually developed retail outlets. These retail outlets evolved into many of today's major department stores, including Abraham and Strauss, Gimbel's, Bloomingdale's, Lazarus, Macy's, Lord and Taylor, and others. In New York, by 1880, 80 percent of all retail clothing establishments and 90 percent of wholesale clothing establishments were owned by Jews.[22] In other cities, such as Columbus, Ohio, all retail clothing stores were owned by Jews. By 1880, about 250,000 Jews lived in the United States.

The third period of Jewish migration began with the fall of Czar Alexander II in Russia in 1881. Following this change in leadership, pogroms occurred in Russia in 1881 and in Kishinev (Bessarabia, now Moldova) in 1903 and 1905.[23] This led to a significant migration of Jews from eastern Europe to the United States, Palestine, and other locations. This migration was to change the face of American Jewry from one that was dominated by American German Jews, who by 1880 were, because of very high levels of assimilation, well on their way to becoming another Protestant denomination, to one dominated by eastern European Jewish migrants. This large-scale migration increased the Jewish population of the United States to 4.5 million by 1939. More than 90 percent of Jewish migrants during this period were from Russia. In total, 3,715,000 Jews entered the United States between 1880 and 1929. During this period, 8 percent of migrants to the United States were Jewish.[24] The Jewish immigrants came to the United States to stay. The rate of reverse migration was only 5 percent for the Jewish population, compared to 35 percent for the general immigrant population.[25] This difference is probably related to the fact that while "economic opportunity" was a "pull" factor to the United States for all immigrant groups, the "push" factors for Jews to leave Europe were clearly more significant than for most, if not all, other ethnic groups.

At first, the German Jews distanced themselves somewhat from the eastern European group. The German Jews had "made it" and had become quite "Americanized" in the process and had largely adopted Reform Jewish practices. The eastern European arrivals came with an eastern European *shtetl* (small-town) mentality, were poor, spoke Yiddish, and those who were religious followed more traditional practices. Because the rabbis of eastern Europe had opposed emigration to the United States, those with higher incomes and those who were more religious remained in Europe.[26] But in both "look and feel," despite the common heritage, eastern European Jews differed significantly from the German Jews who preceded them. At first, the German Jews wanted to spread the new Jewish immigrants throughout the country. The concept was that if the Jewish population became too geographically clustered, a reaction would occur among non-Jews, resulting in anti-Semitism. This led to the Galveston plan in the early 1900s, which was to divert some of the immigrants headed for northeastern cities, particularly New York, to Galveston, Texas.[27] As any plan would that is at odds with an understanding of the chain migration process, this plan failed: very few Jews could be convinced to move to Galveston. Jews wanted to move to the large northeastern cities that already had large Jewish populations and where they could find a *landsmannschaftan*, a cultural society with membership from their former country, or even their former city.[28]

With the eventual suburbanization of the Jewish population following World War II and the passing of a generation, the distinction between German Jews and eastern European Jews has left the American Jewish psyche. While a revival of interest by many Sephardic Jews in their Sephardic heritage has occurred as a result of the quincentennial of the Spanish Inquisition in 1992, only in isolated cases is there any visible friction between Ashkenazic and Sephardic Jews.[29]

The fourth period of Jewish migration to the United States began in the 1930s. By this time, the First (1921) and Second (1924) Johnson Acts[30] had been passed by Congress, practically halting Jewish (and other eastern and southern European) immigration.[31] Immigration would never return to the high levels that persisted between 1880 and the early 1920s. Unfortunately, this closing of the door to immigration occurred at the worst time for European Jews, as the next two decades saw the rise of Hitler and the extermination of six million Jews in the Holocaust. Jewish immigration from Europe saw a temporary surge from Germany following *kristallnacht* in 1939, the event most historians now agree was the initial event of the Holocaust. A second surge was seen just after World War II, composed mostly of Holocaust survivors. Since the mid-1960s, more than 375,000 Jews have immigrated from the former Soviet Union.[32] As of 1990, 30 percent had settled in New York and 23 percent in California. During the past few decades, significant numbers of Israelis have moved to the United States, resulting in between 90,000 and 193,000 Israeli Jews living in the United States, most in New York and Los Angeles.[33] Smaller numbers have moved from Iran and the Arab world.

## INTERURBAN MIGRATION: THE CHANGING SPATIAL DISTRIBUTION OF AMERICAN JEWRY

This section traces the major changes that have occurred in the distribution of the Jewish population since 1940, during which time the Jewish population moved to the Sunbelt at a much faster pace than is the case for Americans in general. Table 7.3 is a summary of these results.[34]

### 1940 Distribution of the Jewish Population

In 1940, the United States contained about 4.7 million Jews, forming 3.6 percent of the U.S. population. At this point in history, Jews were clearly a Snowbelt population, with

**Table 7.3    Changes in the Regional Distribution of the Jewish Population.**

|  | 1940 | 1960 | 1972 | 1984 | 1998 |
|---|---|---|---|---|---|
| Northeast | 69% | 67% | 63% | 54% | 47% |
| Midwest | 19% | 14% | 12% | 11% | 12% |
| South | 7% | 9% | 12% | 18% | 21% |
| West | 5% | 11% | 13% | 16% | 21% |
| Total | 100% | 100% | 100% | 100% | 100% |
| Index of Dissimilarity at the State Level | 45% | 44% | 44% | 44% | 39% |

Source: *American Jewish Year Book*, 1941, 1961, 1973, 1985, and 1999.
Indices of dissimilarity calculated by author.

69 percent living in the Northeast and another 19 percent in the Midwest. Only 7 percent lived in the South and less than 5 percent in the West.[35] In fact, 46 percent of all United States Jews lived in the state of New York, 9 percent in Pennsylvania, 8 percent in Illinois, 6 percent in Massachusetts, and 6 percent in New Jersey, reflecting the role of New York City, Philadelphia, and Chicago as ports of entry for European Jewish migrants.[36] Note that 75 percent of the Jewish population lived in only five of the then forty-eight states and that 88 percent lived in the top ten states. The only Sunbelt state in the top ten was California. Also note that of the top twenty cities in Jewish population, only one (Los Angeles) was a Sunbelt city.

The index of dissimilarity, often used as a measure of the segregation of an ethnic group,[37] indicates that 45 percent of Jews would have had to change their state of residence for the spatial distribution of Jews among the states to be equivalent to that of the total population.

## 1960 Distribution of the Jewish Population

By 1960, the United States contained about 5.5 million Jews, constituting 3.1 percent of the U.S. population. Jews remained a Snowbelt population, with 67 percent living in the Northeast and another 14 percent in the Midwest. Only 9 percent lived in the South and less than 11 percent in the West. In fact, 46 percent of all U.S. Jews lived in the state of New York (no change from 1940), almost 10 percent in California (accounting for much of the increase in the West Census Division), 8 percent in Pennsylvania, 6 percent in New Jersey, 5 percent in Illinois, and 4 percent in Massachusetts. Note that 75 percent of the Jewish population still lived in only five of the fifty states and, as in 1940, 88 percent lived in the top ten states. Florida and Maryland had joined California as Sunbelt states in the top ten. Of the top twenty cities in Jewish population, three were Sunbelt cities: Los Angeles (which was the second most populous city, with 400,000 Jews), Miami (140,000), and the San Francisco Bay Area (81,000). Little change was seen in the index of dissimilarity, remaining at about 44 percent for the states.

## Changes in the Distribution of the Jewish Population, 1940–1960

The largest absolute increase in the number of Jews occurred in the West Census Division, increasing by 378,578 from 1940 to 1960, most of which occurred in California. The

Northeast gained 368,620 Jews. (Note that while the Middle Atlantic was increasing, New England was decreasing, most of which can be attributed to a decline in Massachusetts.) The Midwest decreased by 149,435, mostly due to a decline in Illinois of 90,000. The Jewish population of the South increased by 156,000, with 90,000 of it in Florida.

Because so few Jews were found in the South and the West in 1940, it is not surprising that the rate of growth of the Jewish population in these two regions outpaced the rate of growth of the total population. During this period, the Jewish population of the West grew by 173 percent; the total population, by 102 percent. In the South, the comparable figures were 47 percent and 32 percent. In the Northeast and the Midwest, the situation was reversed: the Northeast's Jewish population increased by 11 percent; the total population, by 24 percent. The Midwest's Jewish population *decreased* by 16 percent; the total population increased by 29 percent.

The implication of these figures is that the Jewish population in 1960 was still significantly concentrated in the Northeast, but significant declines had begun in the Midwest, and significant increases had started in the West and South, particularly in California and Florida. Thus, although Jews remained a very clustered population, with the vast majority residing in the Northeast and California, significant changes in the spatial distribution of the Jewish population were beginning to occur in the Sunbelt states. An important point is that in 1960 Jews were as "segregated" from the total population as in 1940: the index of dissimilarity remained at about 44 percent at the state level. The index of dissimilarity at the Census Division level was 39 percent, implying that 39 percent of American Jews would have to change the Census Division (Northeast, Midwest, South, and West) in which they lived to be geographically distributed as are all Americans.

### 1972 Distribution of the Jewish Population

In 1972, the United States contained about 6.1 million Jews, forming 2.9 percent of the U.S. population. Jews remained a Snowbelt population, with 63 percent (3,828,810) living in the Northeast. However, unlike 1960, in 1972 the West contained about an equal percentage of Jews (13 percent—808,000) as did the Midwest (12 percent—749,000) and the South (12 percent—723,000). About 42 percent of all U.S. Jews lived in the state of New York (down four percentage points from 1960), almost 12 percent in California, 7 percent in Pennsylvania, 7 percent in New Jersey, 5 percent in Illinois, and 4 percent in Massachusetts and Florida. Note that 72 percent of the Jewish population lived in only five of the fifty states, and 89 percent lived in the top ten states (no real change since 1940). Of the top twenty cities in Jewish population, four were Sunbelt cities: Los Angeles (the second most populous city with 535,000 Jews), Miami (190,000), San Francisco Bay Area (94,000), and Orange County (30,000). Little change was seen in the index of dissimilarity at the state level, remaining at about 44 percent.

### Changes in the Distribution of the Jewish Population, 1960–1972

The largest absolute increase in the number of Jews occurred in the South Census Division, increasing by 49 percent—237,000 from 1960 to 1972, a good portion of which was in Florida (48,000) and Maryland (69,000). The West was the second fastest growing region (35 percent—210,000). The Northeast gained only 146,000 Jews, although unlike the 1940–1960 period, both the Middle Atlantic and New England states showed increasing populations. The Midwest continued its decline, although the decrease was minor (16,000) compared with the 1940–1960 period.

Again, the Jewish population growth in the South and the West outpaced the total population growth. The Jewish population of the West grew by 35 percent; the total population, by 19 percent. In the South, the comparable figures were 49 percent and 23 percent. In the Northeast and the Midwest, the situation was reversed: the Northeast's Jewish population increased by 4 percent; the total population by 11 percent. The Midwest's Jewish population decreased by 2 percent; the total population increased by 11 percent.

The implication is that the Jewish population in 1972 was still significantly concentrated in the Northeast. The continuing decreases in the Midwest and significant increases in the West and South resulted in an almost even distribution of the non-Northeast Jewish population among these three Census Divisions. Thus, even by 1972, the move to the Sunbelt states was significantly affecting the spatial distribution of the Jewish population. An important point is that in 1972 Jews were as "segregated" from the total population as in 1960: the index of dissimilarity remained at 44 percent.

## 1984 Distribution of the Jewish Population

In 1984, the United States contained about 5.8 million Jews, constituting 2.5 percent of the U.S. population. Although Jews remained a Snowbelt population, with 54 percent (3,121,905) living in the Northeast (as discussed later), this represented a significant decline in the predominance of this region. The continuing growth of the South and the West and the decline of the Midwest, noted for the 1960–1972 period, was further amplified. In 1984, the South contained more than 18 percent (1,072,780) of U.S. Jews; the West, more than 16 percent (957,115). In contrast, the Midwest was home to only 11 percent (665,445). About 32 percent of all U.S. Jews lived in the state of New York (down ten percentage points from 1972), 14 percent in California, almost 10 percent in Florida, about 8 percent in New Jersey, and 7 percent in Pennsylvania. Note that 70 percent of the Jewish population still lived in only five of the fifty states but that these five top states included two Sunbelt states: California and Florida. The top ten states still contained 87 percent of U.S. Jews, down only slightly from the 89 percent in 1972. Of the top twenty cities in Jewish population, eight were Sunbelt cities: Los Angeles (500,870), Miami (187,000), San Francisco Bay Area (115,000), Orange County (60,000), Hollywood, Florida (60,000), South Palm Beach County, Florida (45,000), and West Palm Beach (48,000).

Thus, in 1984, Jews were still significantly more concentrated in the Snowbelt than the total population. Little change was seen in the index of dissimilarity for the states, remaining at about 43 percent. For the Census Divisions, however, the index had fallen from 39 percent in 1972 to 33 percent in 1984. Thus, although in 1984 Jews were somewhat more evenly distributed among the Census Divisions than was true twelve years before, the fact that most of the Jewish growth in the South and West occurred in a small number of states (California and Florida, in particular) meant that at the state level of analysis, Jews remained as segregated as ever.

## 1998 Distribution of the Jewish Population

Table 7.3 and Figure 7.1 show the distribution of the Jewish population in 1998, when the United States contained about 6.0 million Jews, constituting 2.2 percent of the U.S.

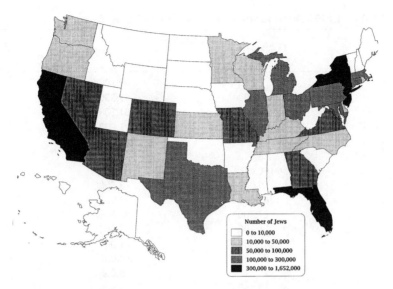

Figure 7.1    Jewish Population, 1998.

population. Although Jews remained a Snowbelt population, with 47 percent (2,813,000) living in the Northeast (as discussed later), this represents a significant decline in the predominance of this region. The continuing growth of the South and the West and the decline of the Midwest, noted earlier, is further amplified by 1998. By 1998, the South contained 21 percent (1,268,000) of U.S. Jews; the West also contained 21 percent (1,260,000). In contrast, the Midwest was home to 12 percent (700,000). About 27 percent of all U.S. Jews lived in the state of New York (down five percentage points from 1984), 16 percent in California, 10 percent in Florida, 8 percent in New Jersey, and 5 percent in Pennsylvania. Note that 66 percent of the Jewish population still lived in only five of the fifty states, the same five states as in 1984, and 83 percent lived in the top ten states. Of the top twenty cities in Jewish population, nine were Sunbelt cities: Los Angeles (519,000), Broward County (Fort Lauderdale; 213,000), San Francisco Bay Area (210,000), Miami (134,000), South Palm Beach County (92,300), Atlanta (80,000), San Diego (70,000), West Palm Beach (74,000), and Orange County (60,000).

Thus, in 1998, Jews were still significantly more concentrated in the Snowbelt than the total population. A significant decline was seen in the index of dissimilarity for the states, from about 44 percent to about 39 percent. For the Census Divisions, however, the index has fallen from 33 percent in 1984 to 27 percent in 1998. Thus, although Jews were somewhat more evenly distributed among the Census Divisions than was true fourteen years earlier, the fact that most of the Jewish growth in the South and West occurred in a small number of states (California and Florida, in particular) means that at the state level of analysis, Jews remained as segregated as ever.

### Changes in the Jewish Population, 1972–1998

Tables 7.3 and 7.4 and Figure 7.2 show changes in the Jewish population from 1972 to 1998. In the South, the growth of the Jewish population over the past two decades has been un-

**Table 7.4    1972 and 1998 Distribution of Jewish Population by State.**

| State | Jewish Population 1972 | Jewish Population 1998 | Absolute Change 1972–1998 |
|---|---|---|---|
| Alabama | 9,260 | 9,100 | (160) |
| Alaska | 300 | 3,500 | 3,200 |
| Arizona | 21,000 | 81,500 | 60,500 |
| Arkansas | 3,340 | 1,600 | (1,740) |
| California | 722,085 | 967,000 | 244,915 |
| Colorado | 26,925 | 68,000 | 41,075 |
| Connecticut | 108,675 | 101,000 | (7,675) |
| Delaware | 9,000 | 13,500 | 4,500 |
| Florida | 269,620 | 628,000 | 358,380 |
| Georgia | 27,700 | 87,500 | 59,800 |
| Hawaii | 1,500 | 7,000 | 5,500 |
| Idaho | 2,680 | 1,000 | (1,680) |
| Illinois | 285,420 | 269,000 | (16,420) |
| Indiana | 25,345 | 18,000 | (7,345) |
| Iowa | 9,455 | 6,500 | (2,955) |
| Kansas | 2,595 | 14,500 | 11,905 |
| Kentucky | 11,380 | 11,000 | (380) |
| Louisiana | 17,340 | 16,500 | (840) |
| Maine | 8,190 | 7,500 | (690) |
| Maryland | 187,110 | 214,000 | 26,890 |
| Massachusetts | 268,775 | 274,000 | 5,225 |
| Michigan | 96,150 | 107,000 | 10,850 |
| Minnesota | 35,475 | 42,000 | 6,525 |
| Mississippi | 5,960 | 1,400 | (4,560) |
| Missouri | 85,170 | 62,000 | (23,170) |
| Montana | 630 | 800 | 170 |
| Nebraska | 9,160 | 7,000 | (2,160) |
| Nevada | 3,380 | 57,500 | 54,120 |
| New Hampshire | 4,830 | 9,800 | 4,970 |
| New Jersey | 420,715 | 465,000 | 44,285 |
| New Mexico | 3,090 | 10,500 | 7,410 |
| New York | 2,540,940 | 1,652,000 | (888,940) |
| North Carolina | 11,495 | 25,000 | 13,505 |
| North Dakota | 1,955 | 700 | (1,255) |
| Ohio | 159,985 | 145,000 | (14,985) |
| Oklahoma | 8,185 | 5,000 | (3,185) |
| Oregon | 9,085 | 22,500 | 13,415 |
| Pennsylvania | 452,120 | 282,000 | (170,120) |
| Rhode Island | 22,570 | 16,000 | (6,570) |
| South Carolina | 9,730 | 9,500 | (230) |
| South Dakota | 2,065 | 350 | (1,715) |
| Tennessee | 18,145 | 18,000 | (145) |
| Texas | 70,950 | 124,000 | 53,050 |
| Utah | 1,900 | 4,500 | 2,600 |
| Vermont | 1,995 | 5,700 | 3,705 |
| Virginia | 42,165 | 76,000 | 33,835 |
| Washington, DC | 15,000 | 25,500 | 10,500 |

**Table 7.4    Continued.**

| State | Jewish Population 1972 | Jewish Population 1998 | Absolute Change 1972–1998 |
|---|---|---|---|
| Washington | 15,990 | 35,500 | 19,510 |
| West Virginia | 5,945 | 2,400 | (3,545) |
| Wisconsin | 35,910 | 28,500 | (7,410) |
| Wyoming | 425 | 400 | (25) |
| Unites States | 6,108,810 | 6,043,248 | (65,562) |

Source: *American Jewish Year Book*, 1973 and 1999.

even. In fact, for 1972–1998, Mississippi (–4,560), West Virginia (–3,545), Oklahoma (–3,185), and Arkansas (–1,740) all declined by more than one thousand. Louisiana, Kentucky, Alabama, South Carolina, and Tennessee all declined by fewer than one thousand. Delaware increased by 4,500, while significant increases occurred in Texas (53,050), Georgia (59,800), Virginia (33,835), and Maryland (26,890). Washington, D.C., increased by 10,500 and North Carolina by more than 13,500. Florida, on the other hand, gained 358,380 Jews over the twenty-six-year period. In fact, 66 percent of the increase in the South's Jewish population occurred within Florida. In addition, within Florida, 82 percent of Jews live in the three-county South Florida area (Miami-Dade, Broward, and Palm Beach Counties).

In the West, only Idaho (–1,680) lost Jewish population between 1972 and 1998, with Wyoming and Montana showing virtually no change. Only a small increase is reported for Utah (2,600), although this more than doubled the state's Jewish population. Somewhat greater increases occurred in Alaska (3,200) and Hawaii (5,500). The most significant increases are shown in California (244,915), Arizona (60,500), Nevada (54,120), Col-

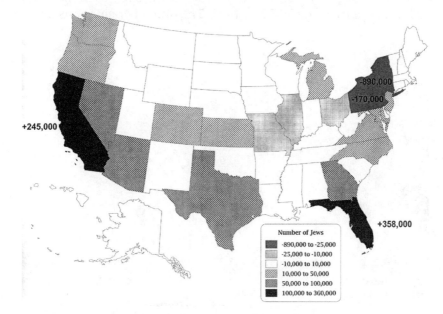

Figure 7.2    Changes in Jewish Population, 1972–1998.

orado (41,075), and Washington (19,510). The bulk (54 percent) of the increase in Jewish population in the West occurred in California. Between 1940 and 1960, the California Jewish population increased by 373,000; 1960–1972, by 192,000; 1972–1984, by 70,000; and 1984–1998, by 244,915. Arizona also represents a growth pole, showing an increase of 60,500 between 1972 and 1998, accounting for another 13 percent of the increasing population of the West. Thus, 67 percent of the increase in Jewish population in the West occurred in California and Arizona.

In the Northeast, 87 percent of the loss in Jewish population may be attributed to a decline in New York of 889,000. Pennsylvania declined by 170,120, Connecticut by 7,765, Massachusetts by more than 5,000, and Rhode Island by 6,570. Maine lost 700 Jews, but Vermont grew by 3,700 and New Hampshire by 4,970. New Jersey gained about 44,000, probably due in part to the migration of New Yorkers across state lines.

In the Midwest, decreases are shown for eight of twelve states, with decreases of about 15,000 for Ohio, 23,000 for Missouri, 16,400 for Illinois, and 7,300 for Indiana. Only Michigan (11,000), Kansas (12,000), and Minnesota (6,500) show significant gains.

In sum, it would appear that the Snowbelt to Sunbelt migration is chiefly one in which a small number of origins (predominantly New York, with a loss of 889,000; but also from Pennsylvania, 170,000; Ohio, 15,000; Missouri, 23,000; and Illinois, 16,000) contribute population to a small number of destinations (predominantly Florida, 358,000; California, 245,000; Arizona, 60,500; and Texas, 53,050). In fact, the clustered nature of the origins and destinations of the Jewish population, herein termed the "limited origin, limited destination" thesis, is even greater, as shown in the next section, than revealed by the state-level data.

## Changes in the Jewish Population of Sunbelt and Snowbelt Cities

Analysis of the data in Figure 7.3 and Table 7.5 reveals the changes in the Jewish population for Jewish communities from 1972 to 1998. The limited origin thesis, forwarded ear-

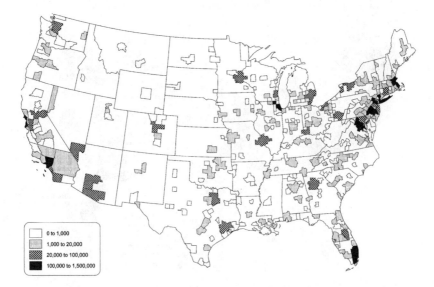

Figure 7.3   Jewish Population by Metropolitan Statistical Area, 1998.

Table 7.5    1972 and 1998 Jewish Populations of 25 Largest Jewish Communities in 1998.

| Community | Jewish Population | | Absolute Change |
| | 1972 | 1998 | 1972–1998 |
| --- | --- | --- | --- |
| New York City, NY | 2,381,000 | 1,450,000 | (931,000) |
| Los Angeles, CA | 535,000 | 519,000 | (16,000) |
| Chicago, IL | 269,000 | 261,000 | (8,000) |
| Boston, MA | 216,000 | 227,000 | 11,000 |
| Broward County, FL | 66,000 | 213,000 | 147,000 |
| San Francisco Bay Area, CA | 101,500 | 210,000 | 108,500 |
| Philadelphia, PA | 325,000 | 206,000 | (119,000) |
| Washington, D. C., and Montgomery and Prince Georges Counties, MD | 112,500 | 165,100 | 52,600 |
| Miami, FL | 220,000 | 134,000 | (86,000) |
| Essex-Morris Counties, NJ | 90,000 | 109,700 | 19,700 |
| Baltimore, MD | 100,000 | 94,500 | (5,500) |
| Detroit, MI | 80,000 | 94,000 | 14,000 |
| South Palm Beach County, FL | 2,000 | 92,300 | 90,300 |
| Bergen County, NJ | 100,000 | 83,700 | (16,300) |
| Rockland County, NY | 25,000 | 83,100 | 58,100 |
| Cleveland, OH | 80,000 | 81,000 | 1,000 |
| Atlanta, GA | 18,000 | 80,000 | 62,000 |
| West Palm Beach, FL | 14,000 | 74,000 | 60,000 |
| San Diego, CA | 14,000 | 70,000 | 56,000 |
| Orange County, CA | 30,000 | 60,000 | 30,000 |
| Phoenix, AZ | 14,000 | 60,000 | 46,000 |
| St. Louis, MO | 60,000 | 54,000 | (6,000) |
| Southern New Jersey | 21,000 | 49,000 | 28,000 |
| Middlesex County, NJ | 27,000 | 45,000 | 18,000 |

Source: *American Jewish Year Book*, 1973 and 1998.

lier, becomes even more evident at this level of analysis. The New York Metropolitan Area (the city of New York, Nassau, Suffolk, and Westchester) lost 931,000 Jews in the twenty-six-year period, accounting for about 87 percent of the total loss of Jewish population in the Snowbelt. Other cities losing significant numbers include Philadelphia (119,000), Miami (86,000), and Bergen County (16,000). Chicago shows a small loss of 8,000 in the same period. Note that certain Snowbelt cities show increases in Jewish population. Essex-Morris Counties and Middlesex County (N.J.) have both shown increases of almost twenty thousand. Rockland County (N.Y.) has increased by fifty-eight thousand.

An examination of the Sunbelt cities from 1972 to 1998 supports the concept of limited destinations. The three-county South Florida area (including Miami, Broward [Fort Lauderdale], South Palm Beach County, and West Palm Beach) accounts for almost 211,000, or 21 percent, of the increased Jewish population of the Sunbelt. Note that while Miami has actually shown a decline, overall South Florida has increased because of explosive growth in the other areas. In California, note that while Los Angeles has lost Jewish population (3 percent), Orange County (a suburb of Los Angeles) increased by 100 percent (30,000). The San Francisco Bay Area increased from about 101,500 to 210,000 during this period. The Washington, D.C., area gained 52,600. Grouping South Florida (211,000 increase), Washington, D.C. (52,600), San Francisco

Bay Area (108,500), Atlanta (62,000), San Diego (56,000), and Phoenix (46,000) accounts for 54 percent of Sunbelt growth in just six metropolitan areas.

In sum, one city (New York) accounts for 87 percent of the loss in the Snowbelt; six metropolitan areas represent 54 percent of the Sunbelt destinations.

## IMPLICATIONS OF THE CHANGES IN THE SPATIAL DISTRIBUTION OF AMERICAN JEWS

This massive shift in the geographic location of the Jewish population has significant implications for the American Jewish community. This section briefly examines four implications: the need to create a sense of community in relatively new Jewish communities, intermarriage and assimilation, geographic dispersion of children from parents and grandparents, and electoral college voting.

### Creating a Sense of Community in Emerging Sunbelt Jewish Communities

A number of articles have commented on the difficulty of involving recent immigrants, particularly retirees in Sunbelt cities, in Jewish communal life, even though these people were involved significantly in the community from which they had moved.[38] Other concerns are expressed in a series of newspaper headlines cited by Goldstein:[39] "Population Shifts Create New Problems for Jewish Federations," "South Dakota's Lone Rabbi Travels Far and Wide to Sell Judaism to All," "Jewish Outposts in Dixie," "A Growing Trend: Jewish Population Moving from Northeast to Sunbelt," and "Being Jewish Where There Is No Community." Thus, this problem is well recognized in the Jewish community. Many Jewish institutions that exist in northeastern and midwestern cities will need to be re-created in southern and western cities. Problems are also created when the Jewish population of a city does not reach the threshold level for the provision of various types of services usually associated with a Jewish community (e.g., Jewish schools, Jewish camping programs, religious institutions, kosher butchers, etc.). Kosmin and Scheckner[40] show that Jews tend to lose their Jewish communal ties as they migrate from one city to another. In total, they estimate that between $10 and $20 million is lost to the Jewish Federation[41] system annually because of migration. Thus, the need to identify new migrants into a community and to integrate those migrants into the community as soon as possible is an important implication of the changing spatial distribution.

In some cases, as Goldstein and Tobin[42] point out, migration to smaller communities outside the core area of Jewish settlement may bring renewed vitality to small Jewish communities, by creating the numbers necessary to reach the threshold needed for Jewish institutions. Yet the overall pattern is that those Jews who move are less well integrated into the community's organized Jewish life.

### Intermarriage and Assimilation

Most important, from a geographical perspective, the extent of attachment to one's Jewish heritage varies significantly by region. For this analysis, households were placed into one of three Jewish Identity Household Types:

1. "Core Jewish Households" are households in which all members are part of the Core Jewish Population (57 percent of interviewed households in NJPS-1990).

2. "Mixed Households" are households in which some members are part of the Core Jewish population, and some, mostly through intermarriage, are not (27 percent of interviewed households).
3. "No Core Jews Households" are households in which no member currently identifies as Jewish, but some (or all) household members are of Jewish descent (16 percent of interviewed households).

Table 7.6 shows the results for the United States Census Divisions with two modifications. In the world of American Jews, Florida is not a southern state, but an exurb of New York. Most of the population is a retirement population that has arrived over the past thirty years from the Northeast. In South Palm Beach County, Florida, for example, 76 percent of the Jewish population is age sixty or over, 52 percent have moved to the area from 1985 to 1995, and about two-thirds moved from the Northeast.[43] Maryland Jews live in Baltimore or the suburbs of Washington and are not southern Jews. Thus, the forces of assimilation which have been at work for centuries in states like the Carolinas and Alabama do not apply to Florida or Maryland. Thus, data are presented for the South without Florida or Maryland.

Overall, 16 percent of households are No Core Jews, 27 percent are Mixed Households, and 57 percent contain only Core Jews. The variations by region are significant. While 65 percent of households in the Northeast are Core Jewish Households, such is the case for only about half of households in the Midwest (49 percent) and the West (52 percent). In the "South," only 38 percent are Core Jewish Households. While only about one-fourth of households in the Northeast (26 percent), the Midwest (25 percent), and the South (29 percent) are Mixed Households, such is the case for almost one-third in the West (32 percent). Perhaps ever more revealing is that only 9 percent of households in the Northeast (which contains almost half of the Jewish population) are No Core Jews households. Such is the case for 16 percent in the West, 33 percent in the South, and 26 per-

**Table 7.6    Jewish Identity Household Types, 1990.**

| Geographic Area | Jewish Identity Household Types | | | |
| --- | --- | --- | --- | --- |
| | No Core Jews | Mixed | Core Jewish | Total |
| Northeast | 9% | 26% | 65% | 100% |
| Midwest | 26% | 25% | 49% | 100% |
| South (ex. Florida and Maryland) | 33% | 29% | 38% | 100% |
| West | 16% | 32% | 52% | 100% |
| New York | 7% | 23% | 70% | 100% |
| California | 13% | 30% | 57% | 100% |
| New Jersey | 11% | 26% | 63% | 100% |
| Florida | 15% | 23% | 62% | 100% |
| Massachusetts | 5% | 32% | 63% | 100% |
| Pennsylvania | 17% | 31% | 52% | 100% |
| Illinois | 17% | 23% | 60% | 100% |
| Maryland | 8% | 25% | 67% | 100% |
| All Other States | 29% | 30% | 42% | 100% |
| Total United States | 16% | 27% | 57% | 100% |

Source: Author, from the 1990 National Jewish Population Survey.

cent in the Midwest. These results clearly reveal that Judaism is strongest in the traditional heartland of the Northeast. As Jews have spread from the Northeast, levels of Jewishness have clearly declined.[44] It may be that "less Jewish" individuals have been most willing to venture forth from the traditional heartland of Jewish settlement or that, once these individuals have migrated, they are faced with a non-Jewish milieu and few choices for Jewish mates and, therefore, assimilate.[45] Probably both forces are at work in most cases. More detail on this issue is provided later.[46]

## Geographic Dispersion of Children from Parents and Grandparents

As a result of the dispersion of the Jewish population, particularly of retirement migration to places like Florida and Arizona, an increasing number of Jewish children are living in different metropolitan areas than those of their parents and grandparents. In South Palm Beach County,[47] for example, only 20 percent of those age forty and over who have adult children who have established their own homes have these adult children living within a ninety-minute drive. In addition, 42 percent of households with married adult children indicated that at least one of their children had intermarried. Thus, just at a time when grandparental influence may be most needed to inculcate Jewish identity in grandchildren of both the in-married and the intermarried, grandparental contact is limited by plane fares and long-distance telephone calls. This is a somewhat paradoxical situation for a group that has prided itself on strong family ties.

## Electoral Voting Patterns

Jewish electoral influence in the United States is in excess of the percentage of Jews in the population (2.2 percent). This is the case for a number of reasons. First, as a relatively well-educated, high-income group,[48] Jews tend to donate to presidential campaigns. Second, as a group with low fertility, Jews constitute a somewhat larger percentage of the voting age population than they do of the total population. Third, Jews tend to register and vote in higher proportions than do non-Jewish Americans.[49]

Fourth, and probably most important, the Jewish population is geographically concentrated in states containing large numbers of electoral votes. In 1940, the ten states that contained 88 percent of the Jewish population controlled 44 percent of the electoral votes. In 1960, the comparable figures were 88 percent and 43 percent; in 1972, 89 percent and 45 percent; in 1984, 87 percent and 41 percent; and in 1998, 84 percent and 46 percent. Thus, over the fifty-eight-year period, while the geographic concentration of Jews has somewhat lessened, Jews remain concentrated in states with a great many electoral votes.

In 1940, Jews formed 16.4 percent (2,206,000) of the population of New York, when New York had forty-seven electoral votes. By 1998, less than 9.0 percent (1,652,000) of New Yorkers were Jewish, but New York had only thirty-three electoral votes. California has seen its Jewish population increase from 157,000 to 967,000 over the fifty-eight-year period, from 2.3 percent to 3.0 percent of the state's population, during which time the number of electoral votes in California increased from twenty-two to fifty-four. Florida has seen its Jewish population increase from 21,000 to 628,000 over the fifty-eight-year period, from 1.1 percent to 4.7 percent, during which time the number of electoral votes in Florida increased from seven to twenty-five.

Thus, while the spatial distribution of the Jewish population has changed significantly during this period, because Jews have tended to "regroup" as they settle areas outside the traditional Snowbelt cities, they have maintained significant geographic concentration in states with significant numbers of electoral votes.

## INTRAURBAN MIGRATION: THE SUBURBANIZATION OF THE JEWISH POPULATION

A geography of American Jews is, of necessity, an urban geography. In 1957, only 4 percent of Jews lived in rural areas, compared to 36 percent of all Americans.[50] In 1986, the largest thirty U.S. metropolitan statistical areas (MSAs) alone contained 90 percent of the Jewish population. NJPS-1990 found that less than 3 percent of the Jewish population lived in nonmetropolitan areas with populations of fewer than forty thousand. And while Jews are just over 2 percent of the American population, they form 17 percent of the population of the West Palm Beach/Boca Raton/Delray Beach MSA, about 11 percent of the population in the New York/Northern New Jersey/Long Island and the Miami/Fort Lauderdale consolidated metropolitan statistical areas (CMSAs), and between 3 and 6 percent of the population in the seven other largest U.S. MSAs (Los Angeles CMSA, Philadelphia CMSA, Chicago CMSA, Boston CMSA, San Francisco CMSA, Washington, D.C., MSA, and the Baltimore MSA).[51] Thus, this section discusses the most important geographic trend among the Jewish population: its continuing suburbanization and dispersion to the nation's suburbs. Despite this suburbanization, certain urban neighborhoods in the United States maintain their Jewish character and may be viewed as American Jewish homelands.[52]

A considerable literature is extant concerning suburbanization and ethnic change within American cities. In his classic work, Nathan Glazer[53] developed a specifically Jewish model of ethnic neighborhood change. He suggests that Jewish communities between the two world wars were composed of rapidly emptying areas of first settlement (slums), rapidly growing areas of second settlement (middle-class apartment houses or two-family houses or, least frequently, single-family dwellings), and areas of third settlement (expensive apartment-house areas or suburban developments of single-family houses).

Glazer suggests that the move from downtown ghetto to the suburbs occurred in stages. Also, in both large and small communities, some affluent families moved to a contiguous area of high-quality housing predominantly occupied by non-Jews. Because Orthodox Jews need to be within walking distance of a synagogue (because of certain religious dictates), the initial movers were the more affluent Reform Jews. Sklare[54] also suggests that such spatial changes reflect increasing levels of socioeconomic mobility and assimilation. For example, both Allen and Turner and Sheskin trace the suburbanization of the southern California Jewish community from Boyle Heights to the Fairfax Avenue area, with the more affluent Reform Jews moving first.[55]

Glazer reports that moves to the suburbs by Jews began during the first twenty years of the twentieth century, particularly between 1910 and 1915, in inland communities. When the number of movers reached a threshold level, synagogues and other Jewish institutions followed. Once the community was so established, other migrants were attracted to the newer area of settlement. In some cases, the synagogues moved in anticipation of the movement of Jewish households. Varady et al.,[56] using the population centroid and standard distance to quantify the trend toward suburbanization and dispersion, present a case study of Cincinnati. The major change in settlement patterns could be explained by sector theory, with Jews expanding away from the central business district, along the Reading Road corridor with abandoned Jewish areas becoming regions of black settlement. This work is continued by Selya and Beyer, who document the continued suburbanization of this population into the 1990s and the problems of moving Jewish institutions to serve this population.[57] Diamond shows that in Toronto, Jews have successfully moved into suburbs and created Jewish neighborhoods.[58]

Mesinger and Lamme[59] suggest that in Cincinnati, Syracuse, and other medium-sized cities, the outward movement of the Jewish community often followed a transportation artery, in a Hoyt-type manner.[60] As socioeconomic status increased, Jews progressively settled and abandoned areas further from the central business district. The abandoned areas often became areas of black settlement. Mesinger and Lamme suggest that this was due either to less resistance to black settlement than in other white areas or to the fact that Jews experienced the same "white flight" as non-Jews.[61] Only in New York City did the area of original settlement (the Lower East Side) maintain much of its original character for many years.[62]

To some extent, these stages of Jewish settlement reflect generational shifts in the Jewish population. The first generation, wishing to cling to tradition, remained within the ghetto area. The second generation, being torn between the old world and the new, migrated from the ghetto to nearby areas of better-quality housing, where they were forced to create specifically Jewish institutions to parallel those from which they were excluded by discrimination. The third generation, being raised in a middle-class American environment, was able to break away even further from the original core area of Jewish settlement.

Yet, even in these areas of second and third settlement, Jews formed new ethnic clusters in more suburban areas. The areas of secondary settlement have been called "gilded ghettos."[63] Although they lacked the low-quality housing, overcrowding, poverty, and Yiddish of the core area and contained many more non-Jews, a Jewish milieu was created by Jewish residential clustering and the presence of Jewish institutions. Gans[64] describes the procedure whereby even Jews in mostly non-Jewish suburbs discover one another and form a Jewish community.

Mesinger and Lamme cite statistics indicating that, from 1957 to 1980, significant Jewish suburbanization occurred in New York. While similar findings have been reported for Chicago, Detroit, Boston, and Minneapolis (where less than 25 percent of Jews live within the city proper),[65] recent evidence in New York City shows some reversal of this trend. The eight-county area covered by UJA-Federation (the umbrella organization of New York Jews) contains about 28 percent of all American Jews. The five counties of New York City showed an overall decline in Jewish population from 1981 to 1991 of about 8 percent (Table 7.7). While (mostly suburban) Queens lost 26 percent of its Jewish population, suburban Nassau lost 22 percent, and suburban Westchester lost 23 percent, Manhattan showed a 15 percent increase. While these findings in New York omit many unstudied suburban New York, New Jersey, and Connecticut counties, they are at variance with the results in most other U.S. Jewish communities.[66]

A number of additional studies have examined intraurban migration of Jews. The existence of Jewish neighborhoods, even in the suburbs, is supported by the work of Lipman and Vorspan,[67] who claim that U.S. cities have become "triple religious ghettos." That is, often groups of Jews, Catholics, and Protestants inhabit a neighborhood with little intermixing or formation of friendship circles with non-co-religionists. Ley[68] states

**Table 7.7    Jewish Population of Metropolitan New York, 1981–1991.**

| County | Number of Jews | | | % of Population that is Jewish | |
|---|---|---|---|---|---|
| | 1981 | 1991 | % Change | 1981 | 1991 |
| **New York City** | | | | | |
| Bronx | 93,700 | 82,000 | −12.5% | 8% | 7% |
| Brooklyn | 409,100 | 371,000 | −9.3% | 18% | 16% |
| Manhattan | 267,800 | 308,000 | 15.0% | 19% | 21% |
| Queens | 313,700 | 233,000 | −25.7% | 17% | 12% |
| Staten Island | 30,300 | 33,000 | 8.9% | 9% | 9% |
| NYC Subtotal | 1,114,600 | 1,027,000 | −7.9% | 16% | 14% |
| **Suburban Counties** | | | | | |
| Nassau | 304,300 | 203,000 | −33.3% | 23% | 16% |
| Suffolk | 103,700 | 98,000 | −5.5% | 8% | 7% |
| Westchester | 119,700 | 92,000 | −23.1% | 14% | 11% |
| Suburban Subtotal | 527,700 | 393,000 | −25.5% | 15% | 11% |
| 8-County Metropolitan Area | 1,642,300 | 1,420,000 | −13.5% | 16% | 13% |

Source: UJA-Federation Jewish Demographic Study as quoted in *The Jewish Week*, January 24–30, 1992, p. 3.

that "the Jewish community has been unusual in that its decentralization has not lessened its spatial clustering . . . the community's regrouping in the suburbs represents a self-conscience attempt to maintain a distinct cultural identity."

Davis[69] presents a study of the changing distribution of Jews in Columbus, Ohio, for 1956, 1972, and 1977. Interestingly, the core area of Jewish settlement did not change over this period, remaining to the south/southeast of the central business district, in and around Bexley. He does note, however, some degree of dispersion of Jews into other areas of the city. A major concern of the Davis work is the juxtaposition of the black and Jewish population.

Local studies completed in Jewish communities around the country confirm the suburbanization of the Jewish population.[70] As one example, in Miami–Dade County, the Jewish population has spread from two original urban "Core Areas" in Shenandoah ( just to the south of the Miami CBD) and South Beach (the southern tip of Miami Beach) and has suburbanized to the south and north. In the late 1920s, there were about eleven hundred Jews in the county, most of whom lived in the first Core Area of Shenandoah. By 1940, about seven thousand Jews lived in the county, with a second Core Area being established in South Beach. By 1950, the Jewish population expanded to forty-seven thousand. The two Core Areas remained strong, with Shenandoah spreading west (to suburban Westchester) and South Beach spreading north. By 1955, eighty thousand Jews lived in the county. Jews began to settle in the suburban city of North Miami. While the two Core Areas still contained 75 percent of the Jewish population, significant numbers were seen for the first time in the Kendall suburb, around U.S. 1 in 1955.

By 1960 (Fig. 7.4), three significant changes occurred as the population grew to 119,500. First, the Shenandoah and Westchester areas declined (from 1955 to 1960), although they were still home to more than twenty thousand Jews. Second, the suburb of North Miami Beach saw significant growth, increasing by more than fifteen thousand Jews. Third, the eastern part of the suburban Kendall area saw significant growth.

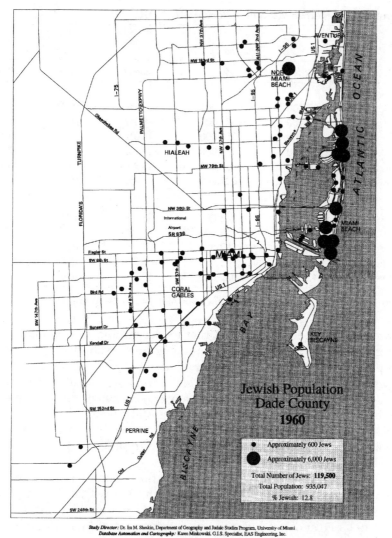

**Figure 7.4    Jewish Population, Dade County, 1960.**

*Study Director:* Dr. Ira M. Sheskin, Department of Geography and Judaic Studies Program, University of Miami
*Database Automation and Cartography:* Karen Minkowski, G.I.S. Specialist, EAS Engineering, Inc.

By 1980 (Fig. 7.5), the Jewish population expanded to 230,000, with the original area of Jewish settlement (Shenandoah) no longer being an important area. Rather, we see Jews moving further from the downtown area toward suburban North Miami Beach and toward suburban west Kendall.

By 1996 (Fig. 7.6), the Jewish population declined to 149,500, with much of the decline occurring both in urban South Beach and suburban North Miami Beach. The suburban Kendall area maintained its Jewish population during this sixteen-year span.

Other local Jewish community studies by Sheskin[71] confirm that this trend toward suburbanization and dispersal in U.S. Jewish communities continues in many American cities. For example, in Broward County (Fort Lauderdale), the years between 1980 and 1997 saw a shift from 57 percent to 77 percent living in the more suburban parts of the county. In Charlotte, North Carolina, 39 percent lived within eight miles of the major

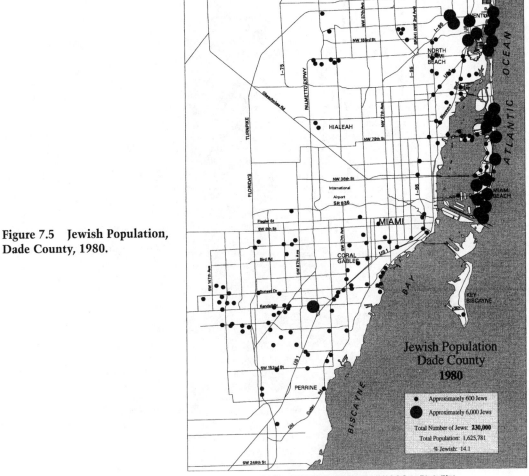

**Figure 7.5   Jewish Population, Dade County, 1980.**

Jewish institutions in 1985, compared to 30 percent in 1997. In Milwaukee, the period from 1983 to 1996 saw a 7 percent shift in Jewish population from the more urban areas to the suburbs, although this period also saw the decline of one suburban neighborhood. In Monmouth County, New Jersey, the years between 1988 and 1998 saw a 36 percent growth in the more suburban western areas of the county, and a 13 percent decline in the more urban eastern areas. In Pinellas County, Florida, the 1980–1994 period showed a 9 percent shift in Jewish population out of St. Petersburg to Clearwater and other parts of the county. In Atlanta, the period from 1984 to 1996 showed stability in the number of Jews in the more urban DeKalb County and Atlanta, with increases of only 5 percent. In contrast, the more suburban areas increased by much greater amounts, including 195 percent in Fulton County (outside Atlanta), 119 percent in Cobb County, and 214 percent in Gwinnett County. In northern Delaware, the more urban Wilmington area showed no change in its Jewish population from 1986 to 1996, while the more suburban Newark area increased by 54 percent.

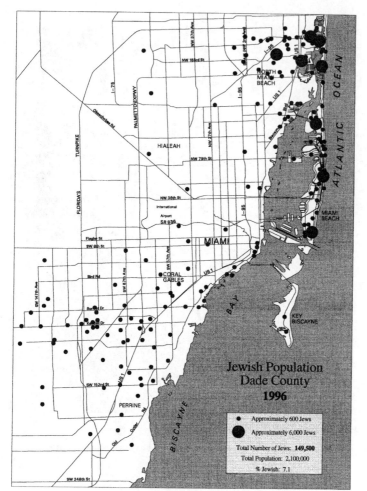

**Figure 7.6   Jewish Population, Dade County, 1996.**

*Study Director:* Dr. Ira M. Sheskin, Department of Geography and Judaic Studies Program, University of Miami
*Database Automation and Cartography:* Karen Minkowski, G.I.S. Specialist, EAS Engineering, Inc.

Finally, Shilhav[72] describes an interesting phenomenon in Jewish settlement patterns: the spatial strategies of the *haredi*, or ultra-Orthodox. Two factors act to segregate this group into distinct and closely settled areas. First, their religious tenets require them to live only with other Jews who follow their interpretations of *halacha* (Jewish law). Second, Jewish law requires that one not carry anything on the Sabbath between public and private domains or between two private domains. To permit observant Jews to carry on the Sabbath, the custom is to symbolically use existing urban barriers (e.g., existing fences) and to string a wire when necessary around a territory to create a space (called an *eruv*) that is one continuous area in which carrying on the Sabbath is permitted. The existence of an *eruv* is a significant advantage to an Orthodox family, and the existence of an *eruv* acts as an attraction for Orthodox Jewish migration. One example of this settlement type in the United States is the village of Kiryas Joel in suburban Orange County New York, forty-five miles northwest of New York City. Here, Hasidic (ultra-Orthodox Jews) have isolated themselves from the world to continue a lifestyle that derives from the mid–eighteenth century and resembles that age. Kiryas Joel's 7,437 residents (1990 census) live in 1,141 households at an average household size of 6.5, 92 percent speak Yiddish at home, and only 3 percent are age sixty-five and over. Several other Hasidic communities are spread throughout the counties to the north of New York City.[73] These represent a unique form of Jewish suburban settlement.

## JEWISH DEMOGRAPHIC STRUCTURE

American Jews differ significantly from other Americans on some demographic dimensions, yet are similar on others.[74] First, Jews have long been older than Americans in general. In 1990, the median age of the Jewish population was 37.3 years, in comparison to 33.6 years for all white Americans. Excluding elderly Jews living in institutions, 17.2 percent of the Jewish population is age sixty-five and over, compared to only 13.3 percent of the white population.[75] This large cohort of persons age sixty-five and over is related to the aging of the relatively young population who migrated during the third period of Jewish migration to the United States described earlier. It should also be noted that the geographic distribution of Jewish elderly is quite different from that of all American Jews.[76]

Second, the percentage of foreign born in the United States Jewish population is now only 9 percent, comparable to that of other Americans. This percentage has declined significantly over the past decades. For example, for Jews in Boston, the percentage of foreign born has declined from 22 to 12 percent to 8 to 9 percent from 1965–1975 to 1985–1995.[77] For Miami, the percentage of foreign-born heads of households declined from 27 percent in 1982 to 22 percent in 1994.[78] Many Jewish demographic studies show that as fewer American Jews have direct memory of the eastern European *shtetl* or are the children of the foreign born, the community becomes more assimilated.[79]

Third, reflecting the significant emphasis on education among American Jews, educational levels among American Jews are much higher than among all Americans. In 1990, among Jews age twenty-five and over, three-quarters had at least some college, and about one-quarter had some graduate education. Thus, the percentage of Jews with a college education is about twice as high as that of American whites, and the percentage with some graduate training was two and a half times as great as for all Americans. Among those age thirty to thirty-nine, 69 percent of Jewish males had graduated college, compared to 31 percent for all white males in this age cohort. These high levels of education are reflected in both the occupational as well as the income achievements of American Jews.

Fourth, both local Jewish community studies and the 1990 National Jewish Population Survey show that Jews are concentrated in the upper ranks of the occupational hierarchy. In 1990, 80 percent of Jewish employed males held white-collar positions, compared to 48 percent for the white male population of the United States. Fully 39 percent of Jewish males were professionals, compared to 16 percent of all employed white males. The percentage employed as managers was similar for the two groups, but Jewish men were more likely to be involved in sales and clerical work than American males in general. It is likely that this concentration of Jews in certain professions and their prominence in the entertainment industry lead many Americans to believe that Jews constitute much more than the 2.2 percent of the American population that they do.

Fifth, in 1990, marital status of the Jewish population almost matched that of the general white U.S. population. Yet, related to the higher levels of attendance at college, only

4 percent of Jewish men age eighteen to twenty-four have been married, compared to 17 percent of the general population. Reflecting greater marital stability, in the Jewish community there are 111 divorced persons per 1,000 currently married persons, compared to a value of 148 for all Americans. Finally, Jewish fertility[80] is well below that of the general population. By ages forty to forty-four, Jewish women averaged only 1.6 children, well below the 2.1 average for all white women in that age group. The very high level of secular education achieved by Jewish women helps explain the low level of fertility.

## SPATIAL VARIATIONS IN LEVELS OF RELIGIOSITY/ JEWISH ETHNIC ATTACHMENT

Currently, a debate among social scientists studying the Jewish community is occurring between those who are "pessimists" and those who are "transformationalists." The former group believes that the Jewish community will gradually assimilate and eventually disappear, except perhaps for some small geographically isolated enclaves of Orthodox Jews. The transformationalists are more optimistic concerning a Jewish future in America, but they believe that the Jewish community will gradually change to meet modern conditions and will survive, albeit in a significantly different form. What the geographer can contribute to this debate is an understanding of the manner in which the evidence for each of these two viewpoints varies geographically.

The 1990 National Jewish Population Survey asked numerous questions about levels of religiosity and Jewish ethnic attachment. Table 7.8 examines just four of these measures for each of the four major census divisions, for the eight states that contain large

**Table 7.8    Jewish Religiosity/Ethnic Attachment by Geographic Area, 1990.**

| Geographic Area | Measure of Religiosity/Jewish Ethnic Attachment | | | |
| --- | --- | --- | --- | --- |
| | Synagogue Member | Always/Usually Attend a Seder | Contribute $100 or More to Jewish Charities | Live in a Very Jewish Neighborhood |
| Northeast | 36.6% | 66.9% | 31.2% | 12.3% |
| Midwest | 39.0% | 57.5% | 29.7% | 5.4% |
| South (excluding Florida and Maryland) | 31.6% | 50.8% | 28.3% | 1.1% |
| West | 21.7% | 50.7% | 20.6% | 4.9% |
| New York | 33.2% | 66.9% | 28.3% | 16.5% |
| California | 20.7% | 53.3% | 20.9% | 5.2% |
| New Jersey | 47.1% | 73.4% | 40.7% | 7.0% |
| Florida | 27.2% | 57.1% | 32.1% | 17.6% |
| Massachusetts | 41.2% | 69.6% | 36.1% | 5.4% |
| Pennsylvania | 33.4% | 63.9% | 29.4% | 7.3% |
| Illinois | 41.6% | 64.0% | 34.1% | 6.5% |
| Maryland | 36.2% | 71.6% | 35.2% | 17.0% |
| All Other States | 32.3% | 49.4% | 26.2% | 3.1% |
| United States | 31.9% | 59.8% | 28.5% | 9.5% |

Source: Author, from the 1990 National Jewish Population Survey.

Jewish populations, and for all other states combined. Note that the South Census Division is modified to omit Florida and Maryland. Synagogue membership is clearly the most important indicator of attachment to the Jewish community. By Census Division, rates are higher in the Northeast (37 percent) and the Midwest (39 percent) than is the case in the South (32 percent) and particularly the West (22 percent). As Jews have moved out of the traditional areas of Jewish settlement in the Northeast and the Midwest, community ties are often severed. The synagogues in the new neighborhoods of the migrants are not the synagogues in which they were raised. Reality dictates that their grandchildren are very unlikely to join them in this new community. Thus, those in newer areas of Jewish settlement are less likely to join a synagogue. By state, California has by far the lowest rate of membership of any of the major states (21 percent). Among the major states, New Jersey (47 percent), Illinois (42 percent), and Massachusetts (41 percent) have the highest rates of synagogue membership.

The contrast in membership rates between New York (33 percent) and New Jersey (47 percent) is instructive. In addition to meeting spiritual needs and the needs for Jewish education, synagogues perform a very important function of socialization. In New York, note that 17 percent of respondents lived in neighborhoods that they described as "very" Jewish, while in New Jersey, only 7 percent lived in such neighborhoods. In New York, people do not need synagogues to "find" Jews for socialization purposes, while in many parts of New Jersey, where Jewish densities are much lower, synagogue membership becomes necessary for many whose level of religiosity would not suggest membership. This is why membership in the "All Other States" category is within range of several of the large states and is almost equal to that of the United States as a whole.

The pattern for always or usually attending a Passover seder is somewhat different from that shown for synagogue membership. Attending a seder (a dinner during which the story of the Jews' exodus from Egypt is related) is the most commonly practiced of all Jewish rituals, but those in the Northeast (67 percent) and the Midwest (58 percent) are much more likely to attend than those in the South (51 percent) and the West (51 percent). Of the major states, rates are lowest in California (53 percent) and Florida (57 percent), states that contain large numbers who have recently inmigrated from other areas. Without the family ties, practice of this ritual declines. The rate of attendance at a seder is highest in New Jersey (73 percent) and Maryland (72 percent). Note that while synagogue membership for "All Other States" was not lower than the national figure, attendance at a seder for this category is significantly lower (49 percent) than the national average (60 percent).

Nationwide, about 29 percent of Jewish households contributed $100 or more to Jewish charities and philanthropies in 1989. This is the case for about 30 percent in the Northeast, Midwest, and South but is true for only 21 percent in the West.[81] Donation rates are highest in New Jersey (41 percent) and are lowest in California (21 percent). Clearly, the Jewish philanthropic network, which is well established in the Northeast and the Midwest, has not been fully transferred to the West. Yet, because many charities can follow their donors via telephone and mail to their new addresses in other parts of the country, the regional influences noted earlier for synagogue membership and seder attendance are not as strong for Jewish philanthropy.[82]

Finally, Table 7.8 examines the results of a question in which respondents were asked about the extent to which the neighborhood they live in has a Jewish population. Overall, about 10 percent of American Jews live in a neighborhood that they would describe as "very Jewish." Such is the case for 12 percent in the Northeast but for only about 5 percent in the Midwest and West and only 1 percent in the South. Three states—New York, Florida, and Maryland—all have about 17 percent of respondents living in areas that are very Jewish. In New York, many still live in the traditional Jewish neighborhoods established by Jewish immigrants of earlier generations. In New York, which is about 13 percent Orthodox, and Baltimore, which is about 20 percent Orthodox, religious requirements (particularly the need to walk to the synagogue on the Sabbath) dictate settlement in dense Jewish neighborhoods. In Florida, Jewish elderly have moved into large adult retirement complexes, such as Century Village, King's Point, Palm Aire, and others, that are often at least 80 to 90 percent Jewish. On the other hand, particularly in the "All Other States" category, most American Jews today do not live in neighborhoods that may be described as "very" Jewish.

## CONCLUSION

The migration of Jews out of the Northeast to other parts of the country at one geographic scale and the suburbanization of Jews within metropolitan areas at another geographic scale both act to weaken ties to the Jewish community. The older age structure, below replacement-level fertility rate, and high rates of intermarriage and assimilation suggest that the demographic base of the Jewish population may well decline in future years. While national numbers will certainly be large enough to sustain national Jewish institutions, some local Jewish communities may find that their population dwindles below the threshold value for the provision of local Jewish goods and services.

Yet, signs of significant strength may also be seen. American Jewish institutions are strong; there is an active Anglo-Jewish press; and significantly increasing numbers of children are attending full-day Jewish parochial schools and informal types of Jewish education, such as Jewish day camps, Jewish sleep-away camps, and teenage Jewish youth groups. Tens of thousands of Jewish college students will be visiting Israel at no cost on the Birthright Israel program during the first years of the new millennium. Increasing numbers of college students are participating in Jewish activities on college campuses. The past few decades have seen the introduction of a multiplicity of Judaic studies programs in American colleges, and philanthropy to Jewish causes continues at a very high level. Thus, while population numbers may decline, this may well be the "Golden Age of American Jewry." An understanding of issues of migration and spatial distribution and their relationship to the maintenance of group identity may prove critical to both maintaining the future size and enhancing the communal quality of this important American ethnic group.

## NOTES

1. For an extensive discussion of the counting of Jewish populations, see Barry Kosmin, Paul Ritterband, and Jeffrey Scheckner, "Counting Jewish Populations: Methods and Problems," in *American Jewish Year Book*, ed. David Singer (New York: American Jewish Committee and the Jewish Publication Society, 1988), 204–241. For a discussion of random digit dialing telephone surveys of Jewish populations, see David P. Varady and Samuel J. Mantel, Jr., "Estimating the Size of Jewish Communities Using Random Telephone Surveys," *Journal of Jewish Communal Service* 59 (1982): 225–234.

2. Barry A. Kosmin, "Jewish Population Studies Conducted since 1975," in *Building an Awareness of a Continental Jewish Community*, Occasional Paper No. 3 (New York: North American Jewish Data Bank, 1987), 25–26. Also see Ira M. Sheskin, *How Jewish Communities Differ: Variations in the Findings of Local Jewish Population Studies* (New York: City University of New York North American Jewish Data Bank, 2000). On the purposes and continuing need for these studies, see Ira M. Sheskin, "Local Jewish Population Studies: Still Necessary after All These Years," *Contemporary Jewry* 15 (1994): 1–3.

3. Fred Massarik and Alvin Chenkin, "United States National Jewish Population Study: A First Report," in *American Jewish Year Book*, ed. Morris Fine and Milton Himmelfarb (New York: American Jewish Committee and Jewish Publication Society, 1973), 264–306.

4. Barry Kosmin et al., *Highlights of the CJF 1990 National Jewish Population Survey* (New York: Council of Jewish Federations, 1991).

5. NJPS-1990 does not provide estimates (either current or historical) of the Jewish population of states or urban areas. The *American Jewish Year Book* is the only source for such data.

6. Kosmin et al., *Highlights*, 28.

7. Howard M. Sachar, *A History of the Jews in America* (New York: Knopf, 1992).

8. Kosmin et al., *Highlights*, 6.

9. Eli Barnavi, ed., *A Historical Atlas of the Jewish People* (New York: Knopf, 1992), 194–195.

10. Antony Lerman, ed., *The Jewish Communities of the World: A Contemporary Guide* (New York: Facts on File, 1989).

11 Gérard Chaliand and Jean-Pierre Rageau, *The Penguin Atlas of the Diasporas* (New York: Viking, 1995).

12. Martin Gilbert, *Jewish History Atlas* (London: Weidenfeld & Nicolson, 1978), 56.

13. Jane Frances Amler, *Christopher Columbus's Jewish Roots* (Northvale, N.J.: Aronson, 1991).

14. David C. Gross, *The Jewish People's Almanac* (New York: Hippocrene, 1988), 416–418.

15. Arthur Hertzberg, *The Jews in America: Four Centuries of an Uneasy Encounter* (New York: Touchstone, 1989).

16. Hertzberg, *The Jews in America*, 24.

17. Max I. Dimont, *The Jews in America: The Roots, History, and Destiny of American Jews* (New York: Simon & Schuster, 1978).

18. Sephardic Jews are those whose ancestors derived from Spain and were expelled in 1492 during the Spanish Inquisition. Many Sephardic Jews migrated to parts of the Ottoman Empire, the Ottoman Sultan having welcomed the Jews who were expelled from Spain. Ashkenazic Jews are those who trace their heritage to other parts of Europe. Today, in general terms, the term *Sephardic* is applied to all Jews except those from (non-Spanish) Europe. Some differences exist in customs and in the worship service between the two major groups. While friction has existed between the two groups at various times and in various places, such friction was relatively rare in twentieth-century America.

19. Jacob Rader Marcus, *To Count a People: American Jewish Population Data, 1585–1984* (Lanham, Md.: United Press of America, 1990).

20. Hertzberg, *The Jews in America*.

21. Hertzberg, *The Jews in America*, 106.

22. Sachar, *A History of the Jews in America*, 86.

23. Naomi Pasachoff and Robert J. Littman, *Jewish History in 100 Nutshells* (Northvale, N.J.: Aronson, 1995), 218–221 and 236–239.

24. Barnavi, *A Historical Atlas*, 194–195.

25. C. Bezalel Sherman, *The Jew within American Society* (Detroit: Wayne State University Press, 1965), 61.

26. Hertzberg, *The Jews in America*, 156–157.

27. Ronald Sanders, *Shores of Refuge: A Hundred Years of Jewish Immigration* (New York: Holt, 1988), 235–240.

28. Ilana Shamir and Shlomo Shavit, *Encyclopedia of Jewish History* (New York: Facts on File Publications, 1986).

29. Ira M. Sheskin, *The Jewish Federation of Greater Monmouth County 1997 Jewish Community Study* (Deal, N.J.: Jewish Federation of Greater Monmouth County, 1998).

30. Sanders, *Shores of Refuge,* 386–387.

31. Evyatar Friesel, *Atlas of Modern Jewish History* (New York: Oxford University Press, 1990), 132.

32. Steven J. Gold, "Soviet Jews in the United States," in *American Jewish Year Book,* ed. David Singer (New York: American Jewish Committee and the Jewish Publication Society, 1994), 3–57; and Sergio DellaPergola, "World Jewish Population," in *American Jewish Year Book,* ed. David Singer (New York: American Jewish Committee and the Jewish Publication Society, 1997), 513–544. See also Mikaella Kagen, "Soviet Jewish Migration to the United States," in *Land and Community: Geography in Jewish Studies,* ed. Harold Brodsky (Bethesda: University Press of Maryland, 1998), 287–295. For results highlighting the acculturation of this group, see Barry A. Kosmin, *The Class of 1979: The "Acculturation" of Jewish Immigrants from the Soviet Union,* North American Jewish Data Bank, Occasional Paper No. 5 (New York: North American Jewish Data Bank, Graduate School and University Center, 1990). For more recent data on this topic, see Ira M. Sheskin, *The Milwaukee Jewish Federation Community Study* (Milwaukee, Wisc.: Milwaukee Jewish Federation, 1996).

33. Steven J. Gold and Bruce A. Phillips, "Israelis in the United States," in *American Jewish Year Book,* ed. David Singer (New York: American Jewish Committee and the Jewish Publication Society, 1996), 51–101.

34. Much of this section is taken from Ira M. Sheskin, "The Changing Spatial Distribution of American Jews," in Brodsky, *Land and Community,* 185–221. The findings in this section are confirmed at the county level by Peter L. Halvorson and William M. Newman, *Atlas of Religious Change in America, 1952–1990* (Atlanta: Glenmary Research Center, 1994), 78–81.

35. For a discussion of early Jewish settlement in the West, see Kenneth Libo and Irving Howe, *We Lived There Too* (New York: St. Martin's/Marek, 1984).

36. Jonathan Mesinger and Ary J. Lamme III, "American Jewish Ethnicity," in *Ethnicity in Contemporary America,* ed. Jesse O. McKee (Dubuque, Iowa: Kendall-Hunt, 1985).

37. The index of dissimilarity is calculated by summing the absolute values of the subtraction of the percentage of the Jewish population residing in each state and the percentage of the total population residing in each state, and dividing by two.

38. Daniel J. Elazar, "Jews on the Move: The New Wave of Jewish Migration and Its Implication for Organized Jewry," *Journal of Jewish Communal Service* 58 (1981): 279–283; Herb Tobin, "The Myth of Community in the Sunbelt," *Journal of Jewish Communal Service* 61 (1984): 44–49; and Ira M. Sheskin, *Jewish Demographic Study* (West Palm Beach: Jewish Federation of Palm Beach County, 1987), 141–162.

39. Sidney Goldstein, "Population Movement and Redistribution among American Jews," *Jewish Journal of Sociology* 24 (1982): 5-23.

40. Barry A. Kosmin and Jeffrey Scheckner. *Federation List Enhancement Resource Guide* (New York: Council of Jewish Federations Research Department, 1995).

41. Jewish federations (which exist in more than two hundred American Jewish communities) act as central coordinating bodies and fund-raising organizations (like the United Way) for local Jewish communities.

42. Sidney Goldstein, "Jews on the Move: Are We a Local or a National Community?" *Moment* 4 (August 1992): 24–29, 49–51. These issues are also discussed by Deborah Dash Moore, "Jewish Migration to the Sunbelt," in *Essays on Ethnicity, Race, and the Urban South,* ed. Randall M. Miller and George E. Pozzetta (Boca Raton: Florida Atlantic University Press). See also Gary A. Tobin, "Issues in the Study of Urban and Regional Distribution of Jews in the United States," in *Papers in Jewish Demography 1989,* ed. Uziel O. Schmetz and Sergio DellaPergola (Jerusalem: Avraham Harman Institute of Contemporary Jewry at the Hebrew University of Jerusalem, 1993), 66–75.

43. Ira M. Sheskin, *1995 Jewish Community Study of South Palm Beach County* (Boca Raton, Fla.: Jewish Federation of South Palm Beach County, 1996).

44. Sydney Goldstein and Alice Goldstein, *Jews on the Move: Implications for Jewish Identity* (New York: State University of New York Press, 1996).

45. For a complete analysis of the effects of migration upon levels of religiosity, see Goldstein and Goldstein, *Jews on the Move;* and Goldstein, "Jews on the Move," 24–30, 49–51.

46. See also Ira M. Sheskin, "Jewish Identity in the Sunbelt: The Jewish Population of Orlando, Florida," in *Contemporary Jewry* 15 (1994): 26–38.

47. Sheskin, *1995 Jewish Community Study.*

48. Kosmin et al., *Highlights,* 19.

49. Ira M. Sheskin, *1994 Jewish Demographic Study of Dade County* (Miami: Greater Miami Jewish Federation, 1995).

50. U.S. Bureau of the Census, "Religion Reported by the Civilian Population of the United States, March 1957," *Current Population Reports,* Series P-20, No. 79, 1958.

51. Jeffrey Scheckner, "Jewish Population in the United States," in *American Jewish Year Book,* 221.

52. Ira M. Sheskin, "Jewish Ethnic Homelands in the United States," *Journal of Cultural Geography* 13 (Spring/Summer 1993): 119-132.

53. Nathan Glazer, *American Judaism* (Chicago: University of Chicago Press, 1957), 82.

54. Marshall Sklare, *America's Jews* (New York: Random House, 1971).

55. James P. Allen and Eugene Turner, *The Ethnic Quilt: Population Diversity in Southern California* (Northridge: Center for Geographical Studies, California State University, 1997), 49–55, 67–70; and Sheskin, "Jewish Ethnic Homelands in the United States."

56. D. P. Varady et al., "Suburbanization and Dispersion: A Study of Cincinnati's Jewish Population," *Geographical Research Forum* 3 (1981): 5–15.

57. Roger Mark Selya and Alysha Beyer, "Where Do We Go Now? Issues in Establishing a Dominant Jewish Neighborhood in Cincinnati, Ohio," in Brodsky, *Land and Community,* 223-244.

58. Etan Diamond, "Sanctifying Suburban Space: Creating a 'Jewish' Bathurst Street in Post-War Toronto," in Brodsky, *Land and Community,* 257–286.

59. Mesinger and Lamme, "American Jewish Ethnicity," 155.

60. Homer Hoyt, *The Structure and Growth of Residential Neighborhoods in American Cities* (Washington, D.C.: U.S. Government Printing Office, 1939).

61. Arthur Goren, "Jews," in *Harvard Encyclopedia of American Ethnic Groups,* ed. Stephen Thernstrom (Cambridge, Mass.: Harvard University Press, 1980).

62. Sklare, *America's Jews.*

63. Judith Kramer and Seymour Leventman, *Children of the Gilded Ghetto* (New Haven, Conn.: Yale University Press, 1961), 11–12.

64. Herbert Gans, "The Origin of a Jewish Community in the Suburbs," in *American Jews: A Reader,* ed. Marshall Sklare (New York: Behrman House, 1983), 149–171.

65. Sidney Goldstein, "American Jewry 1970: A Demographic Profile," in *American Jewish Year Book, 1971,* ed. Morris Fine and Milton Himmelfarb (Philadelphia: Jewish Publication Society), 66.

66. Sheskin, "Jewish Ethnic Homelands in the United States."

67. Eugene J. Lipman and Albert Vorspan, *A Tale of Ten Cities* (New York: Union of American Hebrew Congregations, 1962), 338–342.

68. David Ley, *A Social Geography of the City* (New York: Harper & Row, 1983), 265.

69. Dewitt Davis, Jr., "A Geographic Perspective of Jewish Attitudes towards Neighborhood Transition: A Core Study," *Geographical Perspectives* 45 (1980): 35–45.

70. Ira M. Sheskin, *The Greater Miami Jewish Federation Community Study* (Miami: Greater Miami Jewish Federation, 1995), 28–31; and Ira M. Sheskin, "A Methodology for Examining the Changing Size and Spatial Distribution of a Jewish Population: A Miami Case

Study," in *Shofar*, Special Issue: Studies in Jewish Geography, 17 (Autumn 1998): 97–116. For additional information on Jews in South Florida, see Ira M. Sheskin, "The Jews of South Florida," in *South Florida, Winds of Change* (Washington, D.C.: Association of American Geographers, 1991); and Ira M. Sheskin, "The Miami Ethnic Archipelago," *Florida Geographer* 26 (1992): 40–57.

71. Ira M. Sheskin, *The Jewish Federation of Broward County Community Study* (Fort Lauderdale: Jewish Federation of Broward County, 1997); Ira M. Sheskin, *The Jewish Federation of Greater Charlotte Community Study* (Charlotte, N.C.: Jewish Federation of Greater Charlotte, 1997); Ira M. Sheskin, *The Milwaukee Jewish Federation Community Study* (Milwaukee, Wisc.: Milwaukee Jewish Federation, 1996); Ira M. Sheskin, *The Jewish Federation of Greater Monmouth County Community Study* (Deal, N.J.: Jewish Federation of Greater Monmouth County, 1998); Ira M. Sheskin, *The Jewish Federation of Pinellas County Community Study* (Clearwater, Fla.: Jewish Federation of Pinellas County, 1994); Ira M. Sheskin, Jacob Ukeles, and Ron Miller, *The 1996 Jewish Population Study of Atlanta* (Atlanta: Atlanta Jewish Federation, 1996); and Ira M. Sheskin, Jacob Ukeles, and Ron Miller, *1995 Jewish Population Study of Delaware* (Wilmington: Jewish Federation of Delaware, 1996).

72. Yosseph Shilhav, "Spatial Strategies of the 'Haredi' Population in Jerusalem," *Socio-Economic Planning Science* 15 (1984): 411–418.

73. These Hasidic settlements have been established in an area (often referred to as the "Borscht Belt") whose Jewish character and presence had already been established earlier on a seasonal basis by non-Hasidic groups. See, for example, Stefan Kanfer, *A Summer World* (New York: Farrar Straus Giroux, 1989). For an analysis of these Hasidic communities, see Hune E. Margules, "Housing Aid and the Hasidic Communities in New York," in Brodsky, *Land and Community*, 287–295.

74. The most recent nationwide demographic data for the Jewish population is from the 1990 National Jewish Population Survey. See Kosmin et al., *Highlights*, and Sidney Goldstein, "Profile of American Jewry," in *American Jewish Year Book*, ed. David Singer (New York: American Jewish Committee and the Jewish Publication Society, 1992), 77–173. Results reported in this section are for the Core Jewish population as defined earlier.

75. This greater percentage of elderly among the Jewish population has led to significant interest in the Jewish community in study of the elderly. See Barry A. Kosmin and Jeffrey Scheckner, *The Older Adult Jewish Population of North America*, North American Jewish Data Bank, Information Series No. 1 (New York: Council of Jewish Federations and the Graduate School and University Center, City University of New York, 1987). See also Pnina Zadka, Ira M. Sheskin, and Henry A. Green, "A Comparative Profile of Jewish Elderly in South Florida and Israel," in Schmetz and DellaPergola, *Papers in Jewish Demography 1989*, 154–164.

76. Ira Rosenwaike, "The Geographic Distribution of America's Jewish Elderly," in Schmetz and DellaPergola, *Papers in Jewish Demography 1989*, 145–153.

77. Morris Axelrod, Floyd J. Fowler, and Arnold Gurin, *A Community Survey for Long Range Planning* (Boston: Combined Jewish Philanthropies of Greater Boston, 1967); Floyd J. Fowler, *1975 Community Survey: A Study of the Jewish Population of Greater Boston* (Boston: Combined Jewish Philanthropies of Greater Boston, 1977); Sherry Israel, *Boston's Jewish Community: The 1985 CJP Demographic Study* (Boston: Combined Jewish Philanthropies of Greater Boston, 1987); and Sherry Israel, *Comprehensive Report on the 1995 Demographic Study* (Boston: Combined Jewish Philanthropies of Greater Boston, 1997).

78. Ira M. Sheskin, *The 1994 Jewish Demographic Study of Dade County* (Miami: Greater Miami Jewish Federation, 1995).

79. See, for example, Ira M. Sheskin, *The Jewish Federation of Greater Orlando Community Study* (Orlando: Jewish Federation of Greater Orlando, 1993); Ira M. Sheskin, *The Jewish Community Federation of Richmond Community Study* (Richmond: Jewish Community Federation of Richmond, 1995); and Israel, *Comprehensive Report*.

80. For a discussion of Jewish fertility, see Calvin Goldscheider, "A Century of Jewish Fertility in an American Community: Cohort Trends and Differentials," in Schmetz and DellaPergola, *Papers in Jewish Demography 1989*, 129–144.

81. For a discussion of the diminution of religious practice in the West, see Bruce A. Phillips, "Regional Differences among American Jews," in Schmelz and DellaPergola, *Papers in Jewish Demography 1989*, 104–128.

82. The relationship between geography and ethnic/religious attachment is also shown in Bethamie Horowitz, "Findings from the 1991 New York Jewish Population Study," *Contemporary Jewry* 15 (1994): 4–25.

# 8

# The Japanese in America

*Ines M. Miyares, Jennifer A. Paine, and Midori Nishi*

Once the largest group among Asian populations in the United States, Japanese Americans and Japanese immigrants now rank third in number after the Chinese and Filipinos. Recent changes in Japan's economy, changes in immigration law, and an increased presence of Japanese corporations on the American economic landscape have led to significant growth in the Japanese population over the past two decades. Between 1980 and 1990, the Japanese population in the United States grew by 23.6 percent to 866,160, and has continued to grow rapidly through immigration.

The Japanese are heavily concentrated in two states: California with 37.0 percent of the total and Hawaii with 29.1 percent (Fig. 8.1; Table 8.1). Nine additional states have Japanese populations greater than ten thousand (Colorado, Illinois, Michigan, New Jersey, New York, Ohio, Oregon, Texas, and Washington), and only three states declined in Japanese population between 1980 and 1990 (Louisiana, South Dakota, and Wyoming). In a number of states, the population nearly doubled over that decade, reflecting the impacts of the changing immigrant and economic geographies of the United States.

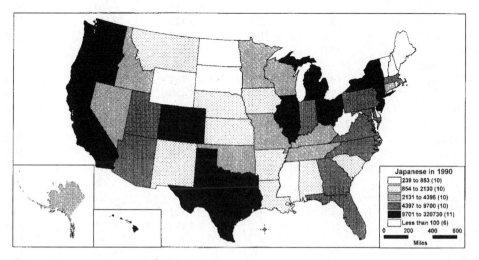

**Figure 8.1   Japanese Population, 1990.**

**Table 8.1    Japanese American Population by States, 1900, 1940, 1980, 1990.**

| | 1900 | 1940 | 1980 | 1990 | Percent Change 1980 to 1990 |
|---|---|---|---|---|---|
| Alabama | 3 | 21 | 1,394 | 1,983 | 42.3 |
| Alaska | n/a | n/a | 1,589 | 2,173 | 36.8 |
| Arizona | 281 | 632 | 4,074 | 6,482 | 59.1 |
| Arkansas | — | 3 | 954 | 1,052 | 10.3 |
| California | 10,151 | 93,717 | 261,817 | 320,730 | 22.5 |
| Colorado | 48 | 2,734 | 9,858 | 12,136 | 23.1 |
| Connecticut | 18 | 164 | 1,864 | 3,869 | 107.6 |
| Delaware | 1 | 22 | 426 | 623 | 46.2 |
| District of Columbia | 7 | 68 | 752 | 1,166 | 55.1 |
| Florida | 1 | 154 | 5,564 | 9,088 | 63.3 |
| Georgia | 1 | 31 | 3,370 | 6,797 | 101.7 |
| Hawaii* | 61,111 | 157,905 | 239,618 | 252,291 | 5.3 |
| Idaho | 1,291 | 1,191 | 2,585 | 2,830 | 9.5 |
| Illinois | 80 | 462 | 18,550 | 22,150 | 19.4 |
| Indiana | 5 | 29 | 2,356 | 4,709 | 99.9 |
| Iowa | 7 | 29 | 1,049 | 1,514 | 44.3 |
| Kansas | 4 | 19 | 1,585 | 1,881 | 18.7 |
| Kentucky | — | 9 | 1,056 | 2,340 | 121.6 |
| Louisiana | 17 | 46 | 1,482 | 1,266 | −14.6 |
| Maine | 4 | 5 | 336 | 788 | 134.5 |
| Maryland | 9 | 36 | 4,805 | 7,307 | 52.1 |
| Massachusetts | 53 | 158 | 4,483 | 8,830 | 97.0 |
| Michigan | 9 | 139 | 5,859 | 10,313 | 76.0 |
| Minnesota | 51 | 51 | 2,790 | 3,708 | 32.9 |
| Mississippi | — | 1 | 687 | 784 | 14.1 |
| Missouri | 9 | 74 | 2,651 | 3,857 | 45.5 |
| Montana | 2,441 | 508 | 754 | 920 | 22.0 |
| Nebraska | 3 | 480 | 1,378 | 1,696 | 23.1 |
| Nevada | 228 | 470 | 2,308 | 4,085 | 77.0 |
| New Hampshire | 1 | 5 | 448 | 701 | 56.6 |
| New Jersey | 52 | 298 | 9,905 | 17,600 | 77.8 |
| New Mexico | 8 | 186 | 1,280 | 2,088 | 63.1 |
| New York | 354 | 2,538 | 24,524 | 36,458 | 48.7 |
| North Carolina | — | 21 | 3,186 | 5,277 | 65.6 |
| North Dakota | 148 | 83 | 230 | 252 | 9.6 |
| Ohio | 27 | 163 | 5,479 | 10,451 | 90.7 |
| Oklahoma | — | 57 | 1,975 | 2,393 | 21.2 |
| Oregon | 2,501 | 4,071 | 8,429 | 11,927 | 41.5 |
| Pennsylvania | 40 | 224 | 4,669 | 6,769 | 45.0 |
| Rhode Island | 13 | 6 | 474 | 611 | 28.9 |
| South Carolina | — | 33 | 1,414 | 1,876 | 32.7 |
| South Dakota | 1 | 19 | 262 | 239 | −8.8 |
| Tennessee | 4 | 12 | 1,657 | 3,221 | 94.4 |
| Texas | 13 | 458 | 10,502 | 15,172 | 44.5 |
| Utah | 417 | 2,210 | 5,474 | 6,585 | 20.3 |
| Vermont | — | 3 | 227 | 396 | 74.4 |
| Virginia | 10 | 74 | 5,207 | 7,738 | 48.6 |

**Table 8.1    Continued.**

|              | 1900   | 1940    | 1980    | 1990    | Percent Change 1980 to 1990 |
|--------------|--------|---------|---------|---------|-----------------------------|
| Washington   | 5,617  | 14,565  | 26,369  | 34,989  | 32.7                        |
| Wisconsin    | 5      | 23      | 2,237   | 2,744   | 22.7                        |
| West Virginia| —      | 3       | 404     | 721     | 78.5                        |
| Wyoming      | 393    | 643     | 600     | 584     | -2.7                        |
| Total        | 85,437 | 284,853 | 700,747 | 866,160 | 23.6                        |

*Japanese Hawaiian population for 1900 and 1940 for the Territory of Hawaii. Source: Andrew W. Lind, *Hawaii's People,* 4th ed. (Honolulu: University of Hawaii Press, 1980), 34.

Sources: United States Bureau of the Census, *1990 Census of the Population,* STF 3A CDROM; *1980 Census of the Population, Supplementary Reports: Race of the Population by States, 1980,* PC 80-S1-3 (Washington, D.C.: U.S. Government Printing Office, 1981); Twelfth Census, *Census of Population: 1900,* Part 1 (Washington, D.C.: U.S. Government Printing Office, 1901); Sixteenth Census, *Census of Population: Inhabitants* 1 (Washington, D.C.: U.S. Government Printing Office, 1942).

The Japanese have experienced a dynamic settlement history, with their initial concentration in the Hawaiian Islands and their pre–World War II distribution primarily in the Pacific region (Figs. 8.2 and 8.3; Table 8.1). This settlement pattern was dramatically altered after the issuance of Executive Order 9066 in February 1942. This order demanded the forced evacuation of all Japanese, even citizens, from California, Oregon, and Washington (Military Zone Number One) to concentration centers and internment camps (Figs. 8.4 and 8.5).[1] During the two years that the order was in effect, the War Relocation Authority assisted a large number of interned Japanese to find employment in eastern and midwestern communities. Although the majority returned to their previous communities in the West after the executive order was rescinded in December 1944,[2] those who remained became the nuclei for a more dispersed settlement pattern.

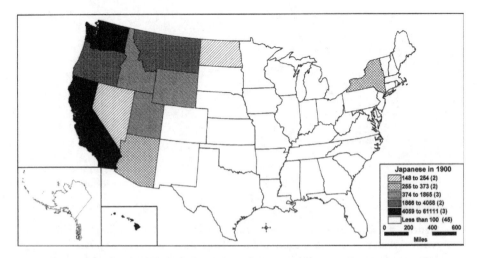

Figure 8.2    Japanese Population, 1900.

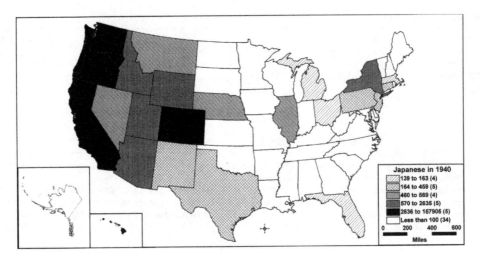

Figure 8.3    Japanese Population, 1940.

## HISTORY OF MIGRATION TO THE UNITED STATES

### The First Emigrants

A number of speculative accounts pertain to the earliest voluntary and involuntary departures from Japan to the Americas. Under the Tokugawa Shogunate, emigration was highly restricted; thus, Japanese did not migrate to the United States in large numbers until the early 1900s. One recorded story was the plight of five fishermen who were cast

Figure 8.4    Distribution of Relocation Centers, 1942–1945. Source: U.S. Army, Western Defense Command and Fourth Army, *Final Report: Japanese Evacuation from the West Coast, 1942* (Washington, D.C.: U.S. Government Printing Office, 1943), 257.

**Figure 8.5    Distribution of Internment Camps, 1941–1946. Note: People of Japanese ancestry were held at other centers in Oklahoma, North Dakota, Tennessee, North Carolina, Maryland, Louisiana, and Alaska. Less information is available on these camps. Source: Michi Weglyn, *Years of Infamy: The Untold Story of America's Concentration Camps* (New York: Morrow, 1976), 176–177.**

adrift in a stormy sea and rescued by an American whaling ship captain who brought one of them, Manjiro Nakahama, to Massachusetts in 1843.[3] Hizoko Hamada, also known as Joseph Heco,[4] was rescued off the shores of Japan in 1850 by a U.S. merchant ship and brought to sojourn in San Francisco.[5] Both men learned sufficient English to return later to their homeland and to stimulate the beginning of United States–Japan relationships during the historic transitional period from the Tokugawa Shogunate rule to the modern period of the Meiji government.

A failed agricultural colony near Gold Hill, north of Sacramento, is commemorated by headstones marking the burial sites of Japanese pioneers. The Watamatsu Tea and Silk colony was an attempt in 1869 by John Henry Schnell, a German who traded in Japan in the late Tokugawa years, to adjust to the changing economic and political situation in Japan. He brought at least twenty-two Japanese to California to establish a silk and tea farming enterprise, but the only lasting marks are the headstones, one of which reads:

In memory of Okei.
Died in 1871.
Age 19 years.
A Japanese girl.[6]

The fall of the Shogunate in the mid–nineteenth century brought an end to the seclusionist policy so vigorously enforced by the Tokugawas, opening the door for Japanese emigration. In 1853 Commodore Perry's arrival in Japan established official diplomatic relations between the United States and Japan, and the United States Immigration Commission lists the first Japanese entrant in 1861 (Table 8.2).[7]

**Table 8.2   Japanese Immigration to the United States, 1861–1990.**

| | |
|---|---:|
| 1861–1870 | 186 |
| 1871–1880 | 149 |
| 1881–1890 | 2,270 |
| 1891–1900 | 25,942 |
| 1901–1910 | 129,797 |
| 1911–1920 | 83,837 |
| 1921–1930 | 33,462 |
| 1931–1940 | 1,948 |
| 1941–1950 | 1,555 |
| 1951–1960 | 46,250 |
| 1961–1970 | 39,988 |
| 1971–1980 | 49,775 |
| 1981–1990 | 47,085 |
| 1991–1994* | 29,175 |

*In October 1991, there was a special visa lottery. 16% of the 40,000 visas were won by Japanese.

Sources: Paul R. Spickard, *Japanese Americans* (New York: Twayne Publishers, 1996), 161; www.ins.usdoj/stas/annual/fy94/744.html.

## Conditions Contributing to Japanese Migration

The Meiji Restoration in 1868 commenced a period of tremendous political, social, and economic change within Japan. Able young Japanese students were encouraged to go to the United States to learn about Western technology and American life. Other young Japanese migrated to escape the military draft. Also, despite its rapidly growing modern industrial economy, Japan experienced severe economic problems and population pressures. Its agricultural sector suffered disproportionately, and early migrants were particularly numerous from extremely poverty-stricken rural areas of southern Japan.

In 1885, the Japanese government began officially permitting its subjects to emigrate. Complete data regarding the origins of early Japanese emigrants are unobtainable from official sources in Japan, but a study made in 1900 included source areas by prefectures from 1899 to 1903.[8] During this brief period, 84,576 persons emigrated, and an estimated 80 percent came to the United States. More than two-thirds of the emigrants were from rural Hiroshima, Kumamoto, Fukuoka, Yamaguchi, and Nagasaki prefectures. Niigata and Wakayama prefectures were also important sources. In contrast, the Kanto (Tokyo) and Kinki (Osaka) industrial districts, now the most densely populated industrialized areas and key immigrant sending areas, had only a small number of emigrants in the early decades.

When news of employment in the United States reached the immigrant's home community, it frequently encouraged others in the neighborhood to make the move overseas. People associated in the same home villages or relatives were likely to assist each other so that the familiarity of the Old World village solidarity and support were translated to the New World settlements.

The burgeoning development of the western United States through the discoveries of gold and other abundant natural resources, the railroad construction boom, and the availability of abundant high-quality agricultural land created an insatiable demand for labor.

Large American companies advertised and offered inducements such as sureties, a demand by the Japanese government under the Emigrants' Protective Law of 1896, to recruit cheap labor.

Passage of the Chinese Exclusion Act of 1882 curbed the large flow of Chinese immigrants and shifted the labor source to Japan. This coincided with the rapid growth of sugar cane plantations in Hawaii and fruit and vegetable farms in California, creating an enormous demand for agricultural labor. Following the signing of a convention between Japan and Hawaii in 1886, thousands came as laborers to work on the plantations.

The 1907 Gentlemen's Agreement that restricted immigration of Japanese laborers to the United States resulted in a sharp decline in male entrants. However, Japanese migrants already living in the United States could send for their relatives in accordance with the agreement. This led to a large influx of Japanese women, many of them "picture brides," wives arranged with the assistance of the home community or marriage brokers.

The National Origins Act of 1924 barred entry of all aliens ineligible for citizenship. As Asians were not allowed to naturalize, this reduced all Asian immigration to a mere trickle. The only exceptions were for merchants and businessmen. Despite subsequent changes in immigration law, the growth of commerce and trade between Japan and the United States made Japanese merchants and businessmen representative migrants.

The McCarran-Walter Immigration and Nationality Act of 1952 ended discrimination by race for immigration and naturalization and allowed a numerical quota of one hundred immigrants from previously barred Asian countries, allowing Japanese and other Asian immigration to increase. The 1965 Immigration Act (Hart-Celler Act) amended the 1952 act by eliminating numerical quotas by national origin, opening the door further for Japanese and other Asian immigration. In recent years, Japanese have benefited from immigrant visa lotteries. Additionally, many Japanese entrants into the United States are on short-term employment visas arranged by Japanese firms in the United States and are not truly immigrants as they are expected to return upon completion of their contracts.

## SPATIAL MOVEMENTS WITHIN THE UNITED STATES

By 1900, the Japanese comprised nearly 40 percent of Hawaii's population. However, an outbreak of bubonic plague in Hawaii in 1900 caused ships loaded with Japanese immigrants to be diverted from Honolulu to San Francisco. San Francisco had been the major port of entry for Japanese immigrants, and newcomers tended to remain in the Bay area. They gradually dispersed throughout the state with major settlements in Los Angeles and several San Joaquin and Sacramento Valley agricultural towns. Outside California, the principal ports of entry were Seattle and Portland. Those who entered via Canada and Mexico tended to drift toward Pacific Coast states where economic opportunities were most favorable. Many of the early settlers worked as laborers on the Santa Fe or Southern Pacific Railroads and became acquainted with the attractive features of southern California, including job opportunities in a new, uncrowded, and steadily growing region. A sudden influx of Japanese to the Los Angeles area occurred following the disastrous 1906 earthquake and fire in San Francisco. According to the 1900 census, 42 percent of the nation's alien Japanese were in California, 23 percent in Washington, 10 percent in Oregon, 21 percent in the intermontane states, and the remainder were widely scattered (Fig. 8.2).

## The Prewar and War Years

Farming and fishing had been leading occupations during the initial Japanese settlement in Hawaii and the West Coast states. As common farm laborers, these hard-working, enterprising people rapidly rose to farm operator or entrepreneur status. In many cases, they acquired poor undeveloped land and transformed it into productive farmland, especially in California. One example is George Shima (Kenji Ushijima), who drained swamplands in the San Joaquin Delta and became widely known as the "Potato King." Kanaye Nagasawa was designated "Samurai of Fountaingrove" for his significant contribution to the state's wine industry.[9] Other important developments were made in rice-growing areas where new productive varieties of rice were introduced. Truck farming, horticulture, and floriculture flourished. In California in 1940, Japanese farmers held a virtual monopoly in acreage of such crops as snap beans, celery, peppers, strawberries, and more than half the acreage of artichokes, cauliflower, cucumbers, tomatoes, spinach, garlic, and other truck crops.[10]

The Japanese also made important contributions to the early successful development of commercial fisheries, canneries, and related activities along the Pacific coast. Bainbridge Island in Puget Sound near Seattle and Terminal Island in the Port of Los Angeles were sites of productive Japanese fishing communities. Because of their sensitive and strategic locations near U.S. Navy yards, the Japanese in those communities were among the first to suffer undue hardship by the evacuation in 1942.[11]

The California Alien Land Laws, enacted in 1913 and later amended in 1920 and 1923, deprived Japanese immigrants of the right to own or lease land. The subsequent decline in land ownership between 1920 and 1940 became the impetus for migration to urban areas. Urban Japanese tended to enter into small businesses in which a considerable degree of independence could be enjoyed. Their rural predominance in growing truck and market crops carried over into wholesale and retail marketing of these crops in nearby cities. In 1940, Japanese employment in wholesale and retail trades ranked second to employment in agriculture in the Pacific Coast states. In the city of Los Angeles, it is estimated that 75 percent of the employed Nisei (U.S.-born Japanese) in 1934 worked in some phase of produce marketing.[12] In Los Angeles County, approximately 75 percent of the retail fruit and vegetable stands were operated by Japanese entrepreneurs.[13] The flower business was also Japanese controlled in Los Angeles County. Although to a lesser extent, this vertical integration was evident in the nursery industry. With their traditional love for nature and their appreciation for beautiful gardens, the Japanese were soon engaged in contract gardening, especially in the Los Angeles area.

Approximately 17 percent of the employed Japanese were engaged in personal services prior to World War II as either domestic day workers or resident workers. They also worked as barbers and beauticians and as employees of cleaning establishments, hotels, and lodging places. Outright discrimination and hostility against the Japanese by white employers both in the public and private sectors, linguistic barriers, and limited capital within the community inhibited entry into many other urban occupations.[14]

By 1940, the distribution of Japanese in the United States was regarded as essentially stabilized (Fig. 8.3). The fertile basins and valleys of the Pacific Coast states were the earliest foci of settlement, and 88.5 percent of the mainland Japanese were located in those areas. California alone accounted for 93,717 or 73.8 percent of the total Japanese population. Areas of greatest concentration were the Los Angeles Basin, the Central Valley, particularly in Sacramento and Fresno, and the San Francisco Bay area. In Washington, the

Puget Sound Lowland, easily accessible to Seattle and Tacoma, became the principal Japanese settlement region, although a large number also settled in the irrigated fruit-growing valleys east of the Cascades. In Oregon, most of them lived in the Willamette Valley proximate to Portland.

In the intermontane states, the Japanese were so widely dispersed that they were only visible in substantial numbers in Denver and Salt Lake City. There were virtually no Japanese in the South, and even New York City, historically an extremely diverse immigrant center, was home to fewer than two thousand Japanese.

During the years 1942–1946, this demographic pattern was completely disrupted. The familiar Pacific Coast agglomerations were broken up, and some 120,000 persons were relocated in temporary assembly centers, ten relocation centers, and more than thirteen internment camps. The relocation centers were located mainly in the intermontane states. The relocation centers were selected based on military necessity and expediency (Figs. 8.4, 8.5). The surrounding lands were generally marginal and devoid of any incentive for permanent settlement. Like temporary army barracks, which were their prototypes, these ugly tar-papered wooden structures were eventually abandoned (Fig. 8.6). Although the majority of Japanese returned to their former communities upon release from the camps, this period of the Japanese experience in the United States resulted in significant social, economic, and spatial changes.

The timetable for the evacuation in early 1942 allowed as little as forty-eight hours, a week, or a few months at the most for preparation to leave homes and businesses. The swift methods employed by the U.S. Army to transport evacuees to assembly and relocation centers prevented the Japanese from adequately disposing of their properties. The economic losses in real property and personal possessions were enormous.

**Figure 8.6   Manzanar Camp. These two 1943 photographs are a grim reminder of the tar-papered barracks, watch tower, and barbed wire of Manzanar, located in the Owens Valley, with the east face of the Sierra Nevada range in the background. The site is now designated a California registered landmark, and a stone monument with a bronze plaque inscribed "Ireito" (Console the Spirit) has been erected on the cemetery grounds. Since 1969, an annual pilgrimage is conducted by Japanese Americans, and special religious ceremonies are performed. Source: Courtesy and permission of Toyo Miyatake, Inc.**

## The Postwar Period

The postwar period led to significant changes in the Japanese experience. Once released from the camps, the majority of Japanese returned to the West Coast. However, the losses of land led to the development of a much more urbanized population. Education, entry into the professions and business, economic changes in the United States, and the growth of Japanese investment in the United States influenced the development of Japanese communities in East Coast cities, the Midwest, and the South. The McCarran-Walter Act of 1952 opened the door for renewed, though limited, Japanese immigration. The Hart-Celler Act of 1965 and concurrent civil rights legislation further expanded Japanese entry and improved treatment of Japanese in the United States.

However, the treatment of the Japanese during the war as a result of Executive Order 9066 could not be ignored. The federal government had made token compensation to the Japanese in 1948, but these reparations were minimal compared to the financial, emotional, professional, social, and cultural losses experienced during the internment. In 1976, responding to pressure from Japanese American political leaders and community groups, President Ford repealed Executive Order 9066 and extended a weak and insufficient apology for the internment. The growing strength of Japanese American political movements led to the formation of the Commission on the Wartime Relocation and Internment of Civilians in 1981. The commission's hearings created national awareness of the treatment of Japanese during the war, and the post–civil rights era mind-set of many Americans supported the call for redress payments. Despite political attempts to prevent the implementation of the commission's recommendations to apologize to and pay reparations to the interned and their families, President Reagan signed the Civil Rights Act of 1988, the legislation that ultimately resulted in redress. In 1990, President Bush established the Office of Redress Administration, and over the next four years, internment camp survivors and their families received payments. This process helped strengthen the Japanese American community and opened the door for Nisei to discuss what had occurred during the war.[15]

## THE "CONTEMPORARY ISSEI"

Like many immigrant groups, the Japanese have formed ethnic clusters particularly in the cities where they have settled. Historically, "Little Tokyos" or "Nihonmachi" (Japantowns) evolved as ethnic islands providing many of the needs and services not available elsewhere. With the emergence of a dominant American-born Japanese community that has more occupational and social mobility than the original Issei (first-generation immigrant Japanese), many Nihonmachi have declined or lost their Japanese identity. The Nisei, Sansei, and Yonsei (second-, third-, and fourth-generation Japanese Americans) reflect a culture that is increasingly "American." However, recent growth in Japanese immigration has resulted in a new wave of Issei, very different from those who arrived a century ago. This is a much more urban professional and diverse cohort, and many are settling in new areas such as the cities of the Eastern Seaboard and the South.

Japanese immigration to the United States increased approximately ten or fifteen years ago, after a long period during which few Japanese immigrated to the United States. While many of the recent immigrants are Japanese businessmen and their families, there is also a new and more diverse group of Japanese immigrants who are settling in core areas of large U.S. cities. The stereotype of Japanese businessmen and their families being representative of the Japanese population in the United States hides great diversity among the Japanese population. The ethnic neighborhood of the East Village in lower Manhattan represents the center of the Japanese immigrant network in New York City and integrates many new immigrants (Fig. 8.7). How these immigrants make the decision to migrate and the factors that pull them to New York City is gender differentiated because of the distinct roles of men and women in Japanese society. Thus, contemporary Japanese immigration is a more complex issue than it appears on the surface.

## Background

The significant increase in the Japanese population in the United States began in the 1980s. The popular press has published many articles about Japanese companies opening offices in the United States and bringing their employees (*chuzaiin*) and their families with them. The Metro North Harlem line commuter train has been nicknamed "the Orient Express," and Yaohan, a Japanese shopping center in Edgewater, New Jersey, has become a tourist attraction for locals who want to experience Japan without leaving home. The Japanese television shows and advertising on New York City's Channel 31, the Japanese restaurants, and services catering to the transferred Japanese businessmen and their families give the impression of homogeneity among the current Japanese population in New York City and elsewhere in the United States. However, this view is misleading.

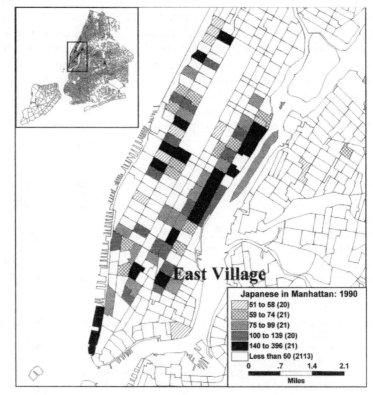

Figure 8.7    Japanese in Manhattan, 1990.

The current stereotype that the Japanese population is made up of *chuzaiin* and their families is only superficially true. *Chuzaiin* are transferred to the United States for two to five years. Most are married and bring their families with them. Outside Hawaii and California, the New York metropolitan area has the highest concentration of Japanese businesses in the United States. Many assume that all Japanese live in Fort Lee, New Jersey, or near Scarsdale in Westchester County, New York. They go to Yaohan to shop; they play golf together; they commute from their suburban homes in New Jersey or Westchester to Manhattan to work in their Japanese offices. Although their children attend public schools, they go to private, after-school schools to prepare them to reenter the Japanese educational system. Most of all, they will return to Japan in a few years. The stereotype is that the Japanese are only fixed-term migrants who live within an expatriate community that they have created here. This re-creation of Japanese society in New York effectively hides a new stream of Japanese migration to New York.

Despite the large numbers of fixed-term Japanese migrants, there are many other types of Japanese migrants. Japanese migration to the United States (Table 8.2) and New York City (Table 8.3) has been increasing over the past ten to fifteen years. This was particularly noticeable between 1989 and 1994. During a special green card lottery in October 1991, the Japanese were the third largest group of applicants and won 16 percent of the forty thousand green cards distributed. Japanese do not contribute a large percentage to Asian immigrants or have a strong presence in absolute numbers in New York City, but their presence is noticeable in the neighborhoods in which they are concentrated. These Japanese immigrants are not the stereotypical *chuzaiin*.

Two common motivations for migration are economic and political. However, the new Japanese immigrants are not choosing to migrate for the usual economic reason of improving their standard of living or for political reasons. The history of Japanese immigration makes this new migration trend all the more noticeable. For the most part, past migration streams from Japan to the United States were precipitated by the desire to improve one's economic status. Generally, contemporary Japanese immigrants choose to migrate for personal lifestyle reasons.

**Table 8.3    Japanese Population by Gender and Nativity, 1990.**

| | Total U.S. | | | California | | | New York[†] | | |
|---|---|---|---|---|---|---|---|---|---|
| Nativity | Percent Male | Percent Female | Total | Percent Male | Percent Female | Total | Percent Male | Percent Female | Total |
| Native-Born: | 49.9 | 50.1 | 584,261 | 49.8 | 52.4 | 221,682 | 45.3 | 54.7 | 7,923 |
| Foreign-Born: Entered prior to 1970* | 18.2 | 81.8 | 84,759 | 23.9 | 76.1 | 33,937 | 24.2 | 75.8 | 3,291 |
| Foreign-Born: Entered 1970–1979 | 32.3 | 67.7 | 43,157 | 37.8 | 62.2 | 17,845 | 24.2 | 75.8 | 3,291 |
| Foreign-Born: Entered 1980–1990 | 48.0 | 52.0 | 153,142 | 47.6 | 52.4 | 45,330 | 50.5 | 49.5 | 20,200 |

*Many of these women are surviving "picture brides."
†The majority of Japanese in New York State reside in New York City.
Source: U.S. Bureau of the Census, *1990 Public Use Microdata Sample of the Census of Population and Housing.*

In Japan, one's life and what path it takes are predetermined by society. It is clear what path one's life is supposed to follow, and society constantly reinforces this message and pressures one into following it. The importance of the group is placed above that of the individual and conformity to the group is stressed.[16] The Japanese proverb "The nail that sticks up is hammered down" still holds some truth about the way in which Japanese society functions, despite its overuse in Japan-bashing books. People are always watching to see whether a person is behaving differently.

These cultural expectations are strongly gender differentiated, especially after graduation from high school. Women in particular have to live up to very rigid expectations and are more restricted in what are acceptable behaviors or lifestyle choices.[17] All members of Japanese society are expected to marry and have children, but there is a stricter timeline for women than for men, and it is unacceptable for Japanese women not to marry. In Japan, marital status defines a woman's status. Regardless of professional success or other accomplishments, women have no status in Japanese society unless they are married.

Men and women also have very different roles in marriage and in their families. As young adults until marriage, women should behave like *ojoosan* (the perfect young Japanese lady). After the wedding, women are known as *okusan* (wife); after the first child, they are known as *okaasan* (mother); after the first grandchild, they are referred to as *obaasan* (grandmother). Along this path, a woman's unique identity is lost, and *okusan* and *okaasan* take over. Not only does the role govern her actions, it also becomes her name. Men, in contrast, are only called *dannasan* or *shujin* (husband) or *otoosan* (father) by their wives or families. These differences in men's and women's lives and roles in society lead to gender-related differences in why Japanese choose to migrate.

Despite changes in the role of women in Japanese society, it is still difficult for them to move beyond their traditional roles. While men may have only a few choices, the opportunities for women are even fewer.[18] It is still common for women who graduate from Tokyo University, the most prestigious university in Japan, to work as secretaries or support staff. After women reach a certain age, typically late twenties or early thirties, companies are reluctant to hire or retain women as employees, believing that they will soon leave to get married and stop working. Many of the companies that hire older women do not want to hire single women who must support themselves; they prefer to hire married women whose pay only supplements their husbands' income. Thus, economically, it can be very difficult for a single woman in her late thirties or forties to support herself because of the difficulty of finding a job at that age. Although the number of women working as professionals is growing, it is still small enough that the United States offers an attractive alternative to Japan as a place to find work to match their capabilities and desires.

Many Japanese immigrants conform to the accepted wisdom that a greater proportion of migrants are young (early to late twenties) and single, with fewer ties to their origination. However, some Japanese female migrants counter this. Cultural conceptualizations of the life course are significant to the organization of these women's migration processes. After a certain age (approximately thirty-five), there is little place in society for single Japanese women. Emigration is the rational choice in a society that has no use for them.

In sum, one might suggest that if a person is willing to follow the "proper" path, it is easy to live in Japan. Otherwise, it is easier to leave than stay. Because of the continuing differences in men's and women's lives and their roles in society, there are more defined motivations encouraging migration based on cultural attitudes toward gender in Japan.

Another factor influencing the decision to emigrate affects both Japanese men and women. In Japan, many forms of American media are available—movies, books, television shows, music, magazines—and in many parts of Japan, the exposure to American culture is widespread. In Tokyo, there is a great awareness of the New York lifestyle and its many similarities to the lifestyle in Tokyo. Thus, many Japanese perceive it to be easy to move to New York and do not expect to experience much culture shock in New York. New York City is a common destination for both tourists and migrants, so many Japanese have relatives or friends who have either visited or lived in New York. Moreover, a well-defined migration stream exists between Tokyo and New York City that makes the decision to migrate easier.

**Manhattan's East Village**

A separate Japanese world exists in New York that very few people can see. One can see it only if one knows what to look for. The Japanese community leaves very few signs on the landscape, but the ones that it does leave give just the barest inkling of what is going on behind closed doors. At first it seems that New York's Japanese community is one of only Japanese businessmen and those associated with them. The East Village in Lower Manhattan also has its own Japan, the Japan that East Village Japanese residents wish existed in reality. Ninth Street and Stuyvesant Street east of Third Avenue are the center of the Japanese ethnic neighborhood. In addition to the usual Japanese restaurants for Americans, there are a Japanese video/newspaper store, Japanese bars, and other small Japanese-owned businesses. There is even a Japanese bakery with beef noodle piroshki and other pastries that are typical Japanese versions of European pastries. In the past few years, Japanese-owned stores and businesses have spread beyond the confines of East Ninth Street to other blocks in the East Village.

There are a few notable exceptions to the restaurants that cater to mainstream society. Village Yoko Cho is a new restaurant and bar right in the central area of concentration (Fig. 8.8). The restaurant is on the second floor of a new building, out of sight from the street level and marked with only a plain green awning with "Village Yoko Cho" lettered on it. The owners explicitly state their attempt to re-create a Japanese cultural landscape. As one walks into the entrance to the stairs, there are photos of the restaurant and bar and the following message: "Village Yoko Cho is created to give you the experience of visiting the hidden side streets of Japan. Here you can find small restaurants, open-air food stands and bars to eat, to drink and to enjoy." Upstairs one finds a very realistic re-creation of the cultural landscape of Japan; the ambience really makes it feel as though one is in Japan.

T.I.C. (Total Information Center) Akean is the center of the Japanese ethnic neighborhood (Fig. 8.9). It has newspapers, videos, and books from home. More important, it is the central hub of the neighborhood Japanese communications network. There is a bulletin board with notices for work opportunities, apartments to rent or share, and many other services. T.I.C. Akean is the only business in the neighborhood that is geared *only* to Japanese customers; it is the only store with a sign completely in Japanese. It functions as part of a chain migration network that is well developed in New York. Many of the signs are not in Japanese at all, but that does not mean that the other signs are not indicators of a cultural landscape (see, e.g., Fig. 8.10). Even in Japan there are many signs only in English (or some version of it); it is trendy and fashionable to have English on

**Figure 8.8    Yoko Cho Restaurant in Manhattan.**

signs and packaging, clothes, and books. In fact, it would be very un-Japanese, at least in the modern portion of Japan, to have a sign exclusively in Japanese. Another cultural pattern is to have bars, restaurants, and clubs without signs or only very small and discreet ones that make it impossible to know what is behind the door unless one already knows. It is an integral part of Japanese culture not to mark location or indicate function. One has to know where something is and how to locate it in order to get there.

Information gathered from personal sources, friends, and family is given a higher regard than that from more impersonal sources. It is well known in Japan that there is a strong and well-developed Japanese community in Manhattan's East Village. Many Japanese receive help from friends who have migrated earlier to New York. They have a place to stay, receive hand-me-down furniture and other household items, get information on all aspects of living in New York, and have a node to plug into the well-established network of the Japanese community in New York. Even without friends in New York, the Japanese community network is much publicized and documented in

**Figure 8.9   T.I.C. (Total Information Center) Akean in Manhattan.**

Japanese guidebooks to the city and in books that give young Japanese all the information they need to go to college in the United States.

The Japanese living in the East Village are not *chuzaiin*. Generally, they are single adults in their twenties or thirties. Many of them work at one of the Japanese restaurants in the neighborhood. Many are or want to be artists, musicians, or filmmakers. The younger Japanese tend to be students at New York University, the New School of Social Research, Fashion Institute of Technology, or Baruch College.

Many Japanese immigrants enter the United States as students because it is relatively uncomplicated to receive a student visa. Few Japanese can qualify to enter the United States through family reunification, due to the small amount of Japanese immigration to United States between the 1920s and the 1970s. The flow of Japanese immigration to the United States was decreased by the Gentlemen's Agreement between the U.S. and the Japanese governments and then completely prevented by the National Origins Quota in 1921. Even after the Hart-Celler Act of 1965 that allowed immigration from Asia once again, Japanese immigration to the United States did not become noticeable until the 1980s. This means that the majority of Japanese Americans have been living in the United States for three or more generations, forestalling new immigrants from entering under family reunification allowances (Tables 8.2, 8.3). Coming to "study" can be either a convenient method of entering the United States or due to a true desire to study a particular subject. Of those who come to study—not just for the visa—there are three subgroups: students of specialized disciplines, traditional students, and women with two-year degrees from Japan.

**Figure 8.10    Business Sign in Both English and Japanese.**

The first subgroup comes to study subjects that do not have well-developed programs of study in Japan or offer only limited opportunities. Some of these disciplines include filmmaking, business, interior design, Western-style art, music, and fashion. Filmmaking and business are two examples of subjects that have no academic presence in Japan. There are no film schools in Japan, so all would-be directors must become apprentices to a film company or leave Japan for training. There are no master of business administration (MBA) programs despite Japan's strong business community. Until recently, young executives have joined corporations with only a bachelor of arts degree from a prestigious university and no training or experience. They received all their training within the company they had joined for life. Many Japanese are now trying to bypass the rigid hierarchy within Japanese companies by receiving MBA degrees in the United States. Or, they are women desiring a professional career.

Japan is one of the leaders in the fashion industry and has many prominent training programs, but there is also a well-developed hierarchy that exists that means that someone may work in fashion for many years before ever designing a single garment. There is a great appreciation for Western-style art in Japan, but little respect for Japanese who create it and have been trained only in Japan. Japanese artists who do not practice traditional art forms will gain respect only after receiving training and recognition in a Western country.

The second subgroup comes to the United States for a college degree after failing to enter a prestigious Japanese university. The rigorous entrance examinations to the best Japanese universities guarantee that many will not be accepted. A degree from a prestigious university ensures a good job after graduation, while a degree from a lower ranked university ensures nothing. Many Japanese believe that receiving a BA from an American university will have higher prestige in Japan than a degree from a mediocre Japanese university, thus improving their chances of finding a good job.

The third subgroup of students is women with degrees from two-year women's colleges in Japan who come to the United States to get a four-year degree from an American university. In Japan, while similar numbers of men and women go on for higher education, 60 percent of women go to two-year institutions compared to only 5 percent of men.[19] In fact, it is easier for a woman with a two-year degree to find a job in an office than a woman with a four-year degree. Managers expect that these women will work for the company for more years than women with four-year degrees, since there is the expectation that all women will be ending their careers at the same age regardless of the kind of degree they received. Men who emigrate to the United States either have a four-year degree or come here with only a high school degree. Women, on the other hand, are just as likely to arrive with a two-year degree as a four-year degree and are less likely to arrive with only a high school degree. In Japan, women are frequently siphoned into two-year women's colleges. Once they have started on that sequence, there is no way to change their life course while remaining in Japan. Thus, many come to the United States to study for the four-year degree they could not get in Japan.

Japanese women have to carry more sociocultural burdens. Women still have the main responsibility to care for elderly parents, and more than one Japanese woman has been obligated to return to Japan to do so. Many Japanese women in the East Village speak of being away from parental or societal pressure in the United States. If their parents are still young and healthy, they come to the United States without guilt. Every time they speak of being free from obligations here, one can hear an unspoken "now" at the end of that statement. In their silence afterward is the knowledge that obligation is just a phone call away.

For younger single women, the initial factor increasing their propensity to migrate may be their career, or the lack of one in Japan. Having to justify being single may not be their primary or even a major reason to migrate, but they have not yet reached the prime pressure years. Younger women with a strong interest in their careers may be discouraged from pursuing them in Japan. They will either migrate to the United States to pursue their career there or may begin on a new path. Some may have the perspicacity to recognize their unsuitability to function within a Japanese workplace and channel themselves to a preferable location. Some women, while existing within their culturally defined role as a woman, may also be representative of a more general type of immigrant.

## CONCLUSION

Whether a Sansei lawyer or businessman in Los Angeles or a contemporary Issei transnational in New York's East Village, ethnic Japanese have been and continue to be an important part of the fabric of the United States. Contributions in agriculture, horticulture, business, foodways, language, and many other areas can be attributed to Japanese immigrants and Japanese Americans. The Japanese community in the United States has also caused the broader population to face up to one of the shameful aspects of U.S. history: the unjust forced migration from their homes to internment camps as a result of prejudice and fear during World War II. The resilience of the Japanese community during the postwar period is a powerful testimony of a population determined to succeed as Americans despite the treatment they received by the government under which they chose to live.

## NOTES

This is a revised version of a chapter originally authored for the first edition of this text in 1985 by Midori Nishi, now deceased.

1. The Pacific military zone included coastal California, Oregon, Washington, and parts of Arizona and included 89.0 percent of the Japanese population in the continental United States.

2. Formal termination of Executive Order 9066 did not take place until February 19, 1976.

3. Isamu Yonekura, "Manjiro: The Remarkable Life of a Fisherman's Son (1)," *East* 12 (May 1976): 17.

4. "Joseph Heco: The First American of Japanese Ancestry," *East* 17 (February 1981): 22.

5. Robert A. Wilson and Bill Hosokawa, *East to America: A History in the United States* (New York: Morrow, 1980), 20.

6. Paul R. Spickard, *Japanese Americans* (New York: Twayne, 1996), 10.

7. Report of the Immigration Commission, *Immigrants in Industries* 23 (Washington, D.C.: U.S. Government Printing Office, 1911), 5.

8. Yosaburo Yoshiba, "Sources and Causes of Japanese Emigration," *Annals of the American Academy of Political and Social Science* 34 (September 1909): 159.

9. Terry Jones, "Samurai of the Wine Country: A Biography of Kanaye Nagasawa," *Pacific Citizen* 81 (December 19–25, 1975): A-1, C-1, 5, 8, 10–12, D-1.

10. Midori Nishi, *Changing Occupance of the Japanese in Los Angeles County, 1940–1950* (Ann Arbor, Mich.: University Microfilms, 1955), 43–44.

11. Some Issei were taken into custody the very night of the Pearl Harbor attack on December 7, 1941, and placed in internment camps without prior notice or forewarning. Some two hundred families were given less that three days' notice to leave the islands.

12. Isamu Nodera, "A Survey of the Vocational Activities of the Japanese in the City of Los Angeles," master's thesis, University of Southern California, Los Angeles, 1936, p. 115.

13. Estimates were made by Sam Minami, business manager, Junior Produce club of Los Angeles, for Tolan Committee, Hearings before the Select Committee Investigating National Defense Migration, Part 31 (Washington, D.C.: U.S. Government Printing Office, 1947), 11724.

14. U.S. Army, Western Defense Command and Fourth Army, *Final Report: Japanese Evacuation from the West Coast, 1942* (Washington, D.C.: U.S. Government Printing Office, 1943), 407, 416.

15. Spickard, *Japanese Americans*, 153–156.

16. Ruth Benedict, *The Chrysanthemum and the Sword: Patterns of Japanese Culture* (Boston: Houghton Mifflin, 1967); Takeo Doi, *The Anatomy of Self: The Individual versus Society* (Tokyo: Kodansha, 1985).

17. Takie S. Lebra, *Japanese Women: Constraint and Fulfillment* (Honolulu: University of Hawaii Press, 1984).

18. From *Ripples of Change*, a documentary film written, directed, and produced by Nanako Kurihara, 1993.

19. Mary C. Brinton, *Women and the Economic Miracle: Gender and Work in Postwar Japan* (Berkeley: University of California Press, 1993), 201.

# 9

# The Chinese in America

*Catherine L. Brown and Clifton W. Pannell*

Chinese have been immigrating to the United States since the mid-1800s. Initially the migration was substantial, encouraged by economic interests in the developing West and other regions to supply labor needs. Public opinion, however, ran against Chinese immigration, and between 1882 and 1943, a series of increasingly severe immigration acts greatly reduced the legal entry of Chinese into the country. After 1943, these restrictions were eased somewhat, but it was not until 1965 that a normal national quota was granted for Chinese immigration. Consequently, and even with the increase in immigration in recent years, the Chinese have never represented more than a small fraction of the total U.S. population.

The Chinese customarily settled in Chinatowns, especially in large cities of the West where the numbers of Chinese were substantial. These ethnic ghettos provided a measure of security and allowed traditional customs and cultural practices to be maintained. The Chinatown ghettos also helped establish the American view and image of the Chinese as thrifty and hardworking but also as clannish and alien, and not particularly good subjects for acculturation into the American crucible.

Over the years, the Chinese have tended to leave these Chinatowns as they have achieved higher levels of education and entered professional fields or have succeeded in commercial endeavors. Even so, Chinatown is only part of the traditional picture of the Chinese in the United States. In many places where Chinese settled, Chinatowns never existed, but social, cultural, political, and economic functions that typified Chinatown were, nevertheless, carried on. Benevolent associations, credit and commercial organizations, and common surname or clan associations all have played a role in helping Chinese maintain some degree of cultural integrity and solidarity, despite the degree of clustering or dispersal of the Chinese community.

The study that follows chronicles the population growth of the Chinese in the United States, and to some extent it emphasizes the smaller communities and groupings as the Chinese dispersed to regions other than the West. The growth and development of the Chinese community in the South is especially a subject of attention and serves to illustrate the special role of the Chinese as another minority in what was until very recently essentially a black/white bicultural society. The chapter, thus, describes and explains the evolution of the Chinese in American society both inside and outside Chinatown ghettos, thereby seeking to present a more complete picture of the evolution of America's Chinese as an ethnic community.

## THE ORIGINS OF PREJUDICE AND ETHNIC SOLIDARITY

### Interaction of Chinese and American Whites

One of the hypotheses of this chapter proposes that racial prejudice, tempered by economic conditions, has greatly influenced the distribution and general characteristics of the Chinese population over time. The idea of the interplay of racial antagonism and the state of the economy on the spatial and socioeconomic patterns of the Chinese is not unique to this study; it is a unifying theme in contemporary literature on the Chinese in America. Miller, in *The Unwelcome Immigrant*, established the origins of the prejudice of Americans against the Chinese.[1] According to Miller, Americans received their first images of China through the accounts of traders, missionaries, and diplomats who had only limited access to the country and who were blinded by ethnocentric beliefs about the innate superiority of northern European racial stock and culture. Miller argued effectively that these three groups of travelers to China were responsible for the development of a negative Chinese stereotype predating the first large-scale immigration of Chinese into the United States in the 1850s. Long before most Americans had made contact with a "genuine Chinaman," they were commonly thought to be, among other things, filthy, debased idolaters given to immoral practices so vile they could barely be discussed by decent men. By the time the Chinese began arriving in America, the image was fixed and reinforced by social Darwinism, a growing pseudoscientific theory of the races that assumed all of the so-called colored races to be naturally inferior to Caucasians. Miller's survey of the national press between 1850 and 1882, the year Congress passed the first Chinese exclusion bill, found that "[t]he general editorial consensus . . . was that while the Chinese were not biologically suitable for the American melting pot, it would be foolish not to exploit their cheap labor before shipping them back to China."[2]

Wu notes in *"Chink,"* his documentary history of anti-Chinese sentiment in the United States, that "racial prejudice gave way temporarily to economic necessity."[3] Kung's discussion of this echoes Wu and others: "The question of economic gain has always been a prime factor in prejudice."[4] Higham in his now classic study of nationalism and ethnic prejudice—or "nativism," as he tagged the complex of ideas represented by the two concepts—closely correlates surges of antiethnic movements in the United States with periods of economic crisis.[5] The implication of this generally accepted theory of racism and economics is that the patterns of Chinese settlement, social interaction, and economic activities in the United States have been dictated by white racism, but the degree to which racist attitudes are acted upon by convention and law is determined by economic stability. In times of plenty, white America is more tolerant of its minority groups than in times of economic instability when money is tight and jobs are scarce.

Another possible explanation for the manner in which the Chinese communities have evolved and sustained themselves is offered by Patterson in *Ethnic Chauvinism*.[6] According to Patterson, "ethnicity is basically a function of economic interest." He documents many Chinese settlements in South America and Asian countries to support his theory but could easily have been describing the Chinese experience in the United States. The typical Chinese immigrant is exemplified by a sojourner who is interested in the host country only for economic gain and fully intends to return home. The sojourner mentality encourages thrift and hard work, but the tendency of sojourners to form exclusive enclaves and cling to their own languages and customs provokes hostility from the host society. The self-imposed segregation of the immigrant group leads to forced segregation, which further isolates them and forces them into greater internal economic cooperation.

Bonacich and Modell discuss this pattern at length in *The Economic Basis of Ethnic Solidarity*, a study of Japanese small independent businesses in the United States.[7] They conclude that hostility from the surrounding society resulted in the promotion of small independent businesses in which Japanese came to occupy a "middleman minority" position in the economic hierarchy. The middleman minority is described as an ethnic group that is an object of discrimination by the host culture but serves as a buffer group between the elites of that society and a subordinated population lower down the social scale. The buffer groups that the middleman minorities represent are usually occupied in trade and services that channel the flow of goods from producers and distributors to the laboring classes. Middlemen are considered *petit bourgeois*, not capitalists, and may come to monopolize certain areas of trade usually through concentrations of numerous small independent businesses.

The middleman concept is especially important to this study. The Chinese have traditionally exploited the middleman position wherever they have settled throughout the world. In the American South, they found marginal acceptance as middlemen merchants, primarily as retail grocers in service to the black community. According to Loewen in his study of the Mississippi Delta Chinese, in the period immediately following the Civil War, white merchants who served blacks were ostracized from white society.[8] Native American blacks, on the other hand, had few acquired skills and no surviving cultural traditions or sources of capital from which to draw to provide services for themselves.[9]

The Chinese came from an area in China with a trading tradition, established their own credit associations (*hui*) that provided capital for members, and were not reluctant to serve the black population.[10] Chinese merchants found a gap in the economic system they could fill with little competition offered from either whites or blacks and without posing a threat to either group's economic position. Loewen feels that the breakdown of the Delta Chinese groups and the outmigration that was taking place by the late 1960s was the result of the breakdown of the segregated social system of the area. Like Bonacich, Modell, and Patterson, Loewen believes that ethnic solidarity was created and reinforced by economic discrimination. Once the economic function of the group was lost, it was no longer necessary or advantageous for individuals to identify with the group.

The main focus of Loewen's study is the change in status undergone by the Mississippi Delta community as their educational attainment and economic success opened their way into white society. When the Chinese first entered the Delta, the desire of the white population to keep color lines clearly defined did not allow for the acknowledgment of a third race without a specific social classification. The following exchange between Loewen and one of his informants sums up the situation and its resolution:

> "You're either a white man or a nigger, here. Now that's the whole story. When I first came to the Delta, the Chinese were classed as nigras." "And now they are called whites?"
> "That's right!"[11]

As a result of this racial definition, a common pattern in the South seems to have been for Chinese to locate in black neighborhoods. Loewen discusses this point, and it is also noted in other studies of Chinese groups in the South. Still, the Chinese maintained social distance from the blacks and preferred to identify with the white community. The Chinese clearly had their own prejudices as well.

### Interaction of Chinese and Blacks

The nature of black and Chinese relations is as important in the case of the South as the nature of Chinese and white relations, although the latter is by far the most studied. Shankman in "Black on Yellow" examines the attitudes toward the Chinese found in the national black press from 1850 to 1935 and finds that in general the black press reflected white journalism in its anti-Chinese bias. Blacks accepted the negative Chinese stereotypes—opium eating, sexual perversion, heathenism—and felt threatened by them on economic grounds because they had often been thrown into competition with immigrant groups for the same types of unskilled labor. As for the South, Shankman notes, the fears of southern blacks over the possible damaging economic consequences of Chinese immigration to the region proved to be unfounded, at least for the black male. The Chinese never entered into competition with the male black wage laborer but chose instead to settle in the large cities and go into business for themselves. Chinese commercial laundries, however, probably took business from black women for whom the home laundry business was an important source of income. A hint that this may have been true of Georgia is provided by Shankman in a reference to an article in an 1892 black Savannah newspaper.[12]

## SOME USEFUL SOURCES OF DATA

Miller's *Unwelcome Immigrant* and Barth's *Bitter Strength* are valuable secondary sources for the early history of Chinese immigration into the United States. Barth's study covers the period 1849–1870, with 1870 witnessing the beginning of the migration of the Chinese from the West Coast to the South and East.[13] Miller carried his study through 1882, the year the first immigration law restricting Chinese immigration was placed into effect. Both of these books contain accounts of the locational shifts of Chinese throughout the country. *The Chinese in America* by Chen is an extremely readable popular history of the Chinese from the mid-1800s to the present. Chen includes an appendix with a discussion of Chinese communities and Chinatowns by region.[14]

Sociology seems to be the only discipline to have exploited the full range of Chinese statistics collected by the U.S. Bureau of the Census since 1860. Two valuable pieces of work in this regard that have contributed to this study are Lee's *The Chinese in the United States of America*[15] and King and Locke's "Chinese in the United States: A Century of Occupational Transition."[16] Lee's study is the first true analysis of the Chinese population in the United States and probably the most cited in the literature. It employs statistical data and historical information to analyze the spatial, social, and economic structure of the aggregate Chinese population and to establish a body of generalizations useful in examining individual Chinese groups.

Much of Lee's statistical analysis is limited to the 1940–1960 period. King and Locke analyze the changes in Chinese occupational structure from 1850 to 1970. Unlike Lee, who emphasizes factors internal to the Chinese community, these authors attribute changes in occupational patterns to institutionalized prejudice by law and custom. King and Locke made some attempt to regionalize the finding, the most significant of which was the high incidence of owner-operated Chinese businesses observed in the South.

## Regional Studies

Specific regional studies of the Chinese are numerous. Examples on the South include Loewen's previously mentioned study on the Mississippi Delta Chinese and an earlier article about the Mississippi group by O'Brien;[17] articles by Farrar[18] and Rhoads[19] on the Chinese in Texas; Liao's[20] thesis about the Chinese in Arkansas; articles by Ken,[21] Law and Ken,[22] and Chiu[23] about the Chinese in Augusta, Georgia; Sieg's[24] account of the Chinese in Savannah, Georgia; Peabody's[25] thesis about the Chinese Labor movement in the South from 1865 to 1970; Krebs's[26] article about the Chinese issue in Alabama in 1870; Cohen's[27] article and book on the introduction of Chinese to Louisiana and surrounding states; and Brown's[28] analysis of the Georgia Chinese.

## Newspapers

Smailes calls the newspaper "perhaps the most potent of all agents in the formulation and propagation of regional opinion on important issues."[29] Newspapers are probably the single most important source of primary information about the Chinese in a given place. Contemporaneous newspaper dispatches provide information about particular events related to a region or state's Chinese and suggest newspapers played a key role in generating and reflecting public opinion about them. Tables and maps compiled from census materials provide a clear illustration of the socioeconomic characteristics and distribution of the Chinese minority, but with the volume of newspaper accounts, the explanation for these patterns would be lackluster and conjectural. Newspapers ranging from San Francisco's *ALTA* and the *New York Times* to the New Orleans *Times-Picayune* and *Augusta Chronicle* all proved useful in this study.

## Chinatown Studies

Although many smaller Chinese communities have never established themselves in ethnic clusters, much scholarly attention has been focused on Chinatowns as concentrated ethnic communities. Some examples from geography are Murphey's[30] study of Boston's Chinatown and a special *Chinatown*[31] edition of the *China Geographer*. However, it is apparent that many of the functional organizations typically found in Chinatowns exist within a dispersed Chinese community at a smaller scale, despite the absence of a clearly definable Chinatown cluster of commercial establishments and residences.

The Chinese community may not always be spatially definable, but the institutional structure commonly found is similar to that of the bounded Chinatowns. For example, institutions such as business, social, and family associations may be found organized under the auspices of a local chapter of the National Chinese Benevolent Association, which is the basic political unit of a typical Chinatown. Although the Chinese communities characteristic of a region, such as the South, may differ in their economic and spatial structure from Chinese settlement patterns elsewhere in the United States, the internal social structure of the southern communities seems to vary only by degree of complexity and the number of people involved from Chinese settlement patterns elsewhere in larger cities in the United States.

This finding, while it supports the hypothesis that the Chinese groups in the South differ from those Chinese groups in other regions, raises the question, Is such a difference a matter of form, function, or some combination of the two? We may answer by suggesting that the Chinese communities in the South traditionally differed based on the roles they played in the segregated societies and the social and economic niches they filled. As the economy and the society of the South has changed in the last half century and created new opportunities for people of all racial and ethnic groups, the role and behavior of the Chinese in the South has changed. In addition, as we shall argue, the new immigration laws of the mid-1960s led to rapid growth in the Chinese population, and this result has been reflected in the South just as in other regions. The combination of these forces has provided both a spatial and structural set of behavioral processes for Chinese in the South that are converging toward the patterns seen in other regions.

Lee developed a theory of Chinatown formation based on city size.[32] According to Lee, for a city to support a Chinatown, it must have a total native population of 50,000 or more, and for a Chinatown to remain viable, it must have at least 260 members. Lee later modified this theory to include Chinese population within a state or service area of a Chinatown—"service area" being loosely defined as any distance Chinese were willing to travel to visit a given Chinatown.[33]

Lee's assumptions are based solely on comparative data for total population of those urban places with Chinatowns indexed to their total Chinese population. She attributes the lack of Chinatowns in the South to smaller city size, but other factors are clearly involved. Historic immigration patterns, nature of the economic base, the biracial culture of South, and the deliberate efforts by some Chinese communities to avoid clustering must all be considered.[34]

More recent studies of Chinatowns in addition to reviewing the historical origins and growth of these ethnic communities have focused on the impact of the remarkable growth of the communities based on the recent changes in the immigration laws and the enormous increase in Chinese populations both legal and illegal.[35] The rapid increase of Chinese populations in recent years has led to an explosion in growth in Chinatowns in some U.S. and Canadian cities such as New York, Toronto, and Vancouver.[36] New economic functions have also appeared and elaborated to include important manufacturing of items such as garments in small factories and shops, and the Chinatowns have become dynamic and vibrant employment centers especially for poorly educated, recent arrivals, some of whom may be illegals. Thus, Chinatown continues its traditional role of offering a place of refugee and solid community while also offering remarkable new economic opportunities all the while expanding its spatial extent and social networks.

## THE CHINESE COME TO AMERICA

The first large-scale immigration of Chinese to the United States began in 1850. Most Chinese entered the country through San Francisco and remained heavily concentrated in California until the late 1860s. The majority of the early Chinese immigrants came from the southern maritime province of Guangdong. They have been variously described as "yeomen farmers," "landless laborers," "petty traders," and "hawkers" "with a tradition of hard work and thrift," and, unlike most Chinese, with a tradition of emigration in response to domestic economic, political, and/or social stress.[37] It was the custom of families who fell on hard times to send their sons abroad to find means by which to support those who remained behind. The young men who left were not considered immigrants but sojourners and were expected to "earn money, save it, and return home as soon as possible."[38] In the mid-1800s, widespread civil and economic disruption in China, coupled with the discovery of gold and stories of "work for all" in California, provided the push and pull mechanism for outmigration.[39] A flow of the sojourners was generated across the Pacific that continued until 1882, when the first of a series of acts restricting Chinese immigration was passed by Congress.

### Trading One Hostile Environment for Another

Prior to 1850, official and unofficial documents show fewer than 800 Chinese in the United States. Between 1850 and 1860, the number rose to 34,933, and by the 1870 census, it was over 63,000 (Table 9.1a and b; Fig. 9.1). The white majority regarded this with alarm. Although the Chinese population was relatively small—less than 1 percent of the total population in 1870—they were a highly visible group who did not conform to the American ideal of the ideal American. Their distinctive physical characteristics, languages, and customs made them appear different in the extreme. Furthermore, the sojourners were clannish and tended to form little enclaves wherever they located, making no great attempt to acculturate because they did not expect to settle permanently. This pattern of settlement put them into direct conflict with the intense nationalism of the period that had among its tenets the belief that national unity depended on a homogenous population with common origins and traditions.[40] "The few years of Chinese occupation leave them as entirely Chinese as when they landed," complained a California correspondent for a New York newspaper, "and a century might pass before any change would be made."[41]

Nativism, ethnocentrism, and xenophobia were all variations of the nationalistic movement. The country was population-hungry and needed labor but was apprehensive about immigration. Immigrants from "superior" northern European racial stocks had been the foundation of the American "breed" and were still welcome as a compatible and assimilable group.[42] But Chinese? For a century before the Chinese immigration began, Americans had been conditioned by the accounts of travelers to China to think of the Chinese as a morally debased, physically and mentally inferior race. This latent image surfaced quickly upon contact, its potential for discord exacerbated by the racism of the nationalistic movement. In 1852 when California's governor denounced the Chinese as "avaricious, ignorant of moral obligations, incapable of being assimilated and dangerous to the welfare of the state," he was only mildly expressing common public opinion.[43]

The hostility toward the Chinese mounted as their numbers increased, but it was tempered by their economic utility to the region. The West had an acute labor shortage. White natives who flooded the region in search of gold created a demand for many personal services, and the capitalists who followed them needed manpower to develop their manufacturing and industrial investments. The Chinese, who were being driven from their mining claims by white prospectors, stepped in to fill the demand for labor. By 1860, Chinese were present in a variety of occupations. Mining companies found them to be a dependable source of inexpensive labor. There were Chinese in construction, agriculture, and manufacturing. Chinese developed California's fishing industry, performed as domestic servants, and opened restaurants, boarding houses, laundries, and small stores.[44] Some were successful and returned home wealthy men. For the majority, however, life in

**Table 9.1a  Chinese Population Change by Region, 1850–1990.**

| | 1850 | 1860 | 1870 | 1880 | 1890 | 1900 | 1910 | 1920 | 1930 | 1940 | 1950 | 1960 | 1970 | 1980 | 1990 |
|---|---|---|---|---|---|---|---|---|---|---|---|---|---|---|---|
| United States (Total) | 758 | 34933 | 63199 | 105465 | 107475 | 89863 | 71531 | 61639 | 74954 | 77504 | 117629 | 237292 | 435062 | 806027 | 1,648,696 |
| **Northeast** | | | | | | | | | | | | | | | |
| Total Population | | | 137 | 1628 | 6177 | 14693 | 11688 | 12414 | 17799 | 19646 | 28931 | 53654 | 115777 | 217730 | 443,866 |
| Absolute Change | | | | 1491 | 4549 | 8516 | –3005 | 726 | 5385 | 1847 | 9285 | 24723 | 62123 | 101953 | 226,136 |
| Percent Change | | | | 1008% | 279% | 138% | (29%) | 6% | 43% | 10% | 47% | 85% | 116% | 88% | 103% |
| **Midwest** | | | | | | | | | | | | | | | |
| Total Population | | | 8 | 813 | 2351 | 3668 | 4610 | 6722 | 8078 | 6092 | 10646 | 18413 | 39343 | 72905 | 129,394 |
| Absolute Change | | | | 805 | 1538 | 1317 | 942 | 2112 | 1356 | –1986 | 4554 | 7767 | 20930 | 33562 | 56,489 |
| Percent Change | | | | 10062% | 189% | 56% | 26% | 46% | 20% | (25%) | 75% | 73% | 114% | 86% | 77% |
| **South** | | | | | | | | | | | | | | | |
| Total Population | | | 218 | 922 | 2116 | 3773 | 3299 | 3900 | 4194 | 4926 | 10468 | 16839 | 34284 | 90616 | 205,373 |
| Absolute Change | | | | 704 | 1898 | 1657 | –474 | 610 | 294 | 732 | 5542 | 6371 | 17445 | 56332 | 114,757 |
| Percent Change | | | | 323% | 206% | 78% | (13%) | 18% | 8% | 17% | 112% | 61% | 104% | 164% | 127% |
| **West** | | | | | | | | | | | | | | | |
| Total Population | 758 | 34933 | 49277 | 102102 | 96844 | 67729 | 51934 | 38604 | 44883 | 46840 | 67584 | 148386 | 245658 | 424776 | 870,063 |
| Absolute Change | | | 14344 | 52825 | –5258 | –29115 | –15795 | –13330 | 6279 | 1957 | 20744 | 80802 | 97272 | 179118 | 445,287 |
| Percent Change | | | 41% | 107% | (5%) | (30%) | (23%) | (25%) | 16% | 4% | 44% | 120% | 66% | 73% | 105% |

Source: United States Bureau of the Census, 1860–1990.

**Table 9.1b  Percent Distribution of Chinese Population by Region, 1850–1990.**

| | 1850 | 1860 | 1870 | 1880 | 1890 | 1900 | 1910 | 1920 | 1930 | 1940 | 1950 | 1960 | 1970 | 1980 | 1990 |
|---|---|---|---|---|---|---|---|---|---|---|---|---|---|---|---|
| Northeast | | | .2 | 1.5 | 5.7 | 16.4 | 16.3 | 20.1 | 23.7 | 25.3 | 24.5 | 22.6 | 26.6 | 27 | 26.9 |
| Midwest | | | .01 | .8 | 2.1 | 4.1 | 6.4 | 10.9 | 10.7 | 7.8 | 9.0 | 7.7 | 9.0 | 9.0 | 7.8 |
| West | 100 | 100 | 99 | 97 | 90.1 | 75.3 | 72.6 | 62.6 | 59.8 | 60.4 | 57 | 62.5 | 56.4 | 52.6 | 52.7 |
| South | | | .3 | .9 | 1.9 | 4.2 | 4.6 | 6.3 | 5.5 | 6.3 | 8.8 | 7.0 | 7.8 | 11.2 | 12.5 |

NOTE: Totals may not equal 100% due to rounding.

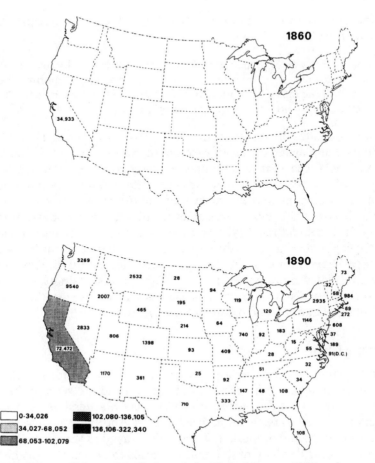

**Figure 9.1    Chinese Population of the United States, 1860 and 1890. Source: U.S. Bureau of the Census, 1860 and 1890.**

the American West became a cycle of hard work and poverty as they eked out meager living for themselves and their families left behind in China.[45]

As long as the Chinese were engaged in occupations that did not bring them into close competition with white labor, anti-Chinese sentiments were held in check. While the Chinese suffered acts of physical aggression during this period, much of the harassment was in the form of what might be termed "codified prejudice"—discriminatory taxes and laws that adversely affected private lives, their business concerns, and stripped them of many constitutional rights. But, in the 1860s as mine production began to drop and the boom-town economy began to flag, the Chinese were made the scapegoats. Among the loudest of the accusers were the Irish, who, by that time, formed a sizable portion of the growing population of white organized labor. They roused public opinion by accusing the Chinese of creating the depression by working for lower wages than "decent" men could accept and sending their earnings out of the country to China.[46]

The West came to regard as sinister the frugality, industry, and strong emotional and family ties the Chinese had with their homeland. Although they were all valued traits in American culture, they were suspect in the Chinese as part of a diabolical plot to deprive white Americans of their rightful jobs and bleed the West of its wealth. In 1869, a California senator offered this opinion:

> It is the duty of every class of men to unite to prevent the introduction of the Chinese. If they come into contact with only the common laborers to-day, tomorrow they will be in competition with the mason, the bricklayer, the carpenter and the machinist, for they are the *most frugal, industrious and ingenious people on the face of the earth.*[47]

The Chinese also made convenient scapegoats for disease, crime, poverty, and the other social problems that plagued the rapidly expanding western cities. Support for this attack came from the social Darwinists, a group who had taken the emotionally held theory of the superiority of the white races and turned it into a popular pseudoscience. Darwin's theory of natural selection and the survival of the fittest was twisted to imply that a biological battle between the white races and the colored races would naturally lead to the elimination of the colored races within a few generations.[48] It was conceded, however, that inferior people such as the Chinese could reap havoc with the natural selection process by their sheer numbers, their penchant for vice, and their superior germs (Asian germs were considered more potent than Western germs); "sinophobes" created a grim scenario in which hoards of immoral, disease-ridden Chinese interbreeding with whites led to the "mongrelization" and decline of the white race.[49]

## Dispersal of the Chinese

Mayhem and murder became the order of the late 1860s and for several decades thereafter as white vigilante committees were organized to rid the West of the "yellow peril." The Chinese responded to the outbreak of violence in several ways. Some returned to China; others relocated outside the United States. Another response was to withdraw from competition in the labor market. Those who stayed in the West clustered for safety in the larger cities, while the Chinese communities in smaller towns and isolated Chinese settlements disappeared.[50] The consensus among researchers is that the anonymity of the city, especially the large city, provided the Chinese an element of protection they did not have in small towns or work camps. Although the urban clusters that grew into Chinatowns lost their invisibility, Chinatown itself became a fortress against outside aggression, and it took on a political, social, and economic life of its own. Chinese who preferred to leave the West but remain in the United States began to migrate eastward. Southern migration was encouraged by a popular movement within the region to secure Chinese contract labor to supplement or replace free black labor. Just about the time the West raised the cry, "The Chinese must go!" the South issued an invitation "Let the Chinamen come."[51]

### Chinese in the South

The Chinese were neither a boon to the South, as some had hoped, nor a burden, as others had predicted. Of the few who remained of the early Chinese laborers, most moved into larger cities. By the 1880s, many southern cities had communities of Chinese who were engaged primarily in trade or personal services as owner operators of small groceries, laundries, and restaurants. The laundries served the white clientele, but the Chinese grocers often functioned as "middlemen" between the white community and blacks and other minority populations—Mexicans and Indians, for example, in the case of Texas and Arkansas.[52]

The Chinese "middlemen" served to fill an economic gap created by the social and economic changes in the post–Civil War era. The antebellum plantation economy had been relatively simple, dominated by an agricultural system that was composed of many self-sufficient plantation and farm units. The diversification of the economy after the war and the growth of urban areas created a need by blacks and whites for a variety of new services.[53] A white merchant class developed, but it had no parallel in the black community. The majority of blacks lacked the capital and skills necessary to establish their own businesses. It has also been argued that the plantation's communal social organization did not allow native blacks to develop a cultural frame of reference that included free enterprise.[54]

The Chinese, on the other hand, had capital, skills, and a cultural background that included commerce and trade.[55] Furthermore, as sojourners only temporarily in the country for economic gain, it has been postulated that they tended to be more frugal than blacks and willing to take risks.[56] In addition to the factors internal to the Chinese community that were conducive to their entry into the grocery trade, there were numerous influences from without—not the least of which was the reluctance of whites to employ Chinese in any capacity other than common labor. But ultimately it was the nature of social relations between blacks and whites in the immediate postwar period that provided Chinese with a means of economic survival in the South. Because whites considered serving blacks to be socially unacceptable and blacks were unprepared at the time to provide necessary services for themselves, there was little competition for the economic position between black consumers and white producers. The Chinese moved in to fill the gap.

Some interesting variations of this pattern include the involvement of Texas Chinese in truck gardening and the development of the dried shrimp industry by Chinese in Louisiana.[57] No doubt many other variations could be cited, but the early records are poor. Given the records that do exist, however, it seems likely that these variations in early occupational representation would have accounted for only a very small percentage of the South's total Chinese population.

## SETTLEMENT AND ACTIVITY PATTERNS OF THE CHINESE

The basic pattern for Chinese settlement in the South and throughout the country where no large concentrations of Chinese were to be found was set by the late 1800s and persisted well into the 1950s. It was characterized by small urban groups engaged primarily in retail food sales (groceries and restaurants) and in the commercial laundry business. There was a Chinatown in El Paso, Texas, until the 1930s, and Lee references a Chinatown in New Orleans sometime prior to 1940, although no mention of such could be found in any historical accounts of the city surveyed in the course of this research.[58]

The Chinese communities in the South, for the most part, typically were dispersed within black neighborhoods.[59] In some southern states, Mississippi, for example, this pattern was enforced by discriminatory laws.[60] In other states, it was enforced by convention. In some cases, as in Georgia, there seems to have been a conscious effort by the Chinese to avoid clustering. Since many of the Chinese who came into the South had been victims of persecution in the West, they preferred to keep a low profile in the community by spreading out.[61] In general, whites made the rules—written and unwritten—that determined the conditions under which Chinese were tolerated within a community, and the Chinese accommodated themselves within those limits. Every community had a slightly different way of dealing with the Chinese among them, and each Chinese group had to adjust itself accordingly. The result, however, was the fairly uniform pattern described.

It is difficult to determine how many of the early Chinese communities faded in and out of existence in the early years. The historical documentation is poor, and even if the censuses were not questionable, small, mobile groups of people can make many changes in location in the intervening years between censuses. Because the Chinese population remained almost exclusively male until the early 1900s and tended to be engaged in easy-entry occupations that required a minimum of investment, they were relatively free to move at will, the successful ones perhaps returning to China and the unsuccessful moving on to find more profitable places to exploit. In the large cities, however, once a social network was established, it seems to have served to maintain community structure even though its members were in a state of flux.

The earliest communities were probably replenished by imported contract laborers who had left their plantation and construction jobs to find more lucrative employment. But as the South's demand for Chinese labor decreased, a small-scale chain migration sprang up between the southern settlements, China, and other Chinese communities in the United States.

### Kinship and the Chinese Community

The extended family or clan was the basic social unit in China, and kinship ties remained important to the sojourning bachelors in the United States. The pattern of migration seems to have been based largely on kinship. This is exhibited in many Chinese communities by the predominance of a few family surnames, although this is not as true of the contemporary period as it was until the 1960s.

It became the common practice for individuals, when well established, to send for relatives and "transfamily relations" (fictive relatives created by blood brotherhood, traditional friendships, surname similarity, geographic proximity, and marriage ties).[62] The newcomers were provided bed and board, employment, and a chance to learn a trade. The store owner was provided cheap labor and the comfort of friends and relatives. Later the original sponsor might help establish an apprentice in a store of his or her own. Had it not been for the persistence of the traditional Chinese family organization in the United States, the original bachelor communities might have quickly died out, but the kinship system kept them alive by the continuous addition of adult males until the early 1900s, when the sex ratio began to normalize and growth by natural increase became possible.

The occupational concentration of Chinese in particular areas has been attributed to the results of this kinship migration and apprenticeship pattern. Liao's analysis of Chinese surnames in Arkansas based on Chinese store ownership in 1949 showed that 66 percent of the stores belonged to families representing four clans. The remaining 34 percent were said to be related in some way to the predominant clans. According to Liao, "a Chinese who runs a store in this region without any relationships with those four clan's families could not survive for a long period."[63] In his analysis of kinship in the Mississippi Delta group, Loewen also identifies several dominant families although clan competition was not indicated.[64] This also proved true of Georgia, but whereas clans may be identified, there was a deliberate effort made, at least by the Savannah Chinese, to put aside clan loyalties for the advantages of internal community cooperation.[65]

## Intraregional Chinese Migration

There is very little data about intraregional Chinese migration, but various studies make reference to the migration of individuals and families within the region.[66] From these references and discussions with Chinese from several southern Chinese communities, the impression is gained that the social networks operating within local communities extend far beyond city and state boundaries. Communication links and intraregional population movement may provide further explanation for the early occupational concentration of southern Chinese in food retailing. For example, Chinese from the Mississippi Delta, who were almost entirely concentrated in the grocery business until the 1950s, were known to have migrated into Arkansas, Houston, Texas, and Augusta, Georgia, where there were high percentages of Chinese-owned groceries at one time. Joe and Woo, which were common surnames in the Delta, were also found to be common in Augusta, thus adding a degree of reinforcement to the theory.

## Prejudice and Hostility

So long as the Chinese remained clustered on the West Coast, the stories of their persecution were reported with a modicum of sympathy by the eastern press. But, when Chinese began appearing in eastern cities, the mood of the press changed from sympathy to antipathy. The South also viewed this voluntary eastward migration with some misgivings. Presumably contract laborers were under the control of their employers, but there could be little control over the number and activities of the Chinese who came to the South as free agents. Besides, after the election of 1876, the South regained its political autonomy and quickly legislated the blacks back into a state of quasislavery, and the Chinese were no longer perceived as economically beneficial.

Most researchers who have examined these surges of anti-Chinese sentiments agree that they were the product of racial prejudice aggravated by economic stress.[67] During times of economic crises, foreigners were regarded at the national level as a threat to unity. Between individuals it was a matter of birthright and competition for scarce jobs and resources. The Chinese—the "ultimate foreigners"—bore the brunt of antiforeign agitation.[68] A general depression between 1873 and 1877 led to the passage of America's first restrictive immigration laws in 1882, the Chinese Exclusion Acts, but only the Chinese were singled out as a nationality to be denied entry into the country.

In 1879, planters in Mississippi and Louisiana made a brief and unsuccessful attempt to revive the Chinese labor movement. The flurry of interest was stirred by a large scale outmigration of blacks to the Midwest territories.[69] The action was significant enough to provoke the *New York Times* into speculating that the national movement for Chinese exclusion would make little political headway as long as the economic interest of the South could be served by Chinese immigration.[70]

National labor problems in the 1880s kept the anti-Chinese movement active even after the first Exclusion Act was passed. The Chinese in the West were subjected to boycotts, lynchings, mass expulsions, and mass murders. Chinese businesses and residences were blown up or burned down with little regard to the fact they might be occupied. Although the agitation was not so intense in the South and East as it was in the West, it was still manifested in some form. Take, for example, an incident in 1882 when a white women in El Paso, Texas, was presented a silver cup for attempting an armed assault on a Chinese laundryman who ventured a complaint about her refusal to pay him for his services. The event occurred in the midst of the national furor over Chinese exclusion and local commotion in El Paso over the Chinese monopoly of the laundry business. When El Paso was a male-dominated frontier town, the Chinese washermen were welcome additions to the city's service sector. As more white women joined the general populace, the Chinese, who had established the commercial laundry business in the city, were accused of unfairly monopolizing an important means of their self-support. Feeling ran so high that a newspaper account of the event suggested that should other "ladies" be encouraged to shoot at Chinese, there would be "no more cups unless they [brought] in scalps."[71]

## The Exclusion Acts

Congress began the Chinese Exclusion Acts with the passage of a single law in 1882, and these continued for more than sixty years with a series of various laws and treaties enacted to deny the entry of Chinese migrants to the United States.[72] The effect of these laws, as has been noted, was profound in restricting the number of Chinese in the United States to a very small and declining fraction of the U.S. population, until the passage of the New Immigration Law of 1965 that eliminated immigration quotas based on national origin.

The total Chinese population of the United States increased by only several thousand between 1880 and 1890, testimony to the effectiveness of the 1882 law excluding Chinese immigration. This small gain has largely been attributed to natural increase.[73] The low birthrate indicated by this figure was the result of an abnormally high ratio of males to females, a characteristic of the Chinese population until the 1940s. The increase in the South, however, was mostly the result of internal population movements. The West lost Chinese population in 1890, both in absolute numbers and its relative share. The Northeast was the recipient of the majority of out migrants from the West, followed by the Midwest and the South (Table 9.1a and b).

For the most part, the South supported the Exclusion Acts. Southern protest raised after the 1882 act came primarily from those who feared the loss of the Chinese foreign cotton market should China choose to register protest against the Exclusion Act by boycotting American goods. China, however, seemed to wish to maintain its southern links, and for a time New York City became a popular courting spot for southern and Chinese economic interests—so much so that the *New York Times* once observed that while antipathy toward blacks remained a powerful force in the South, antipathy for Chinese was conspicuously absent.[74]

This relaxation of negative attitudes toward the Chinese lasted until 1905 when a deterioration in economic well-being generated another antiforeign campaign.[75] This time southern support of the movement was fairly uniform.[76] The South was in agreement with the nation that the new wave of southern European immigrants in the early 1900s was not pure white but tainted by Asiatic bloodstocks. A government official from North

Carolina echoed a spokesman from Alabama when he called the new wave "nothing more than the degenerate progeny of the Asiatic hoards [sic] which, long centuries ago, overran the shore of the Mediterranean."[77] The message was clear: No foreigners need apply, especially Asians and those suspected to be of Asian extraction.

By the turn of the century, the United States had begun to lose total Chinese population. A drop in total numbers in the West reflected the national trend, but the Northeast, Midwest, and South showed both absolute and relative increases due to interregional migration (Table 9.1a and b; Fig. 9.1).[78] The United States continued to show a loss in total Chinese population until 1930 (Fig. 9.2). In the South, the only absolute loss occurred in 1910, but it was accompanied by a small increase in its relative share as the population continued its internal readjustments.

### Changing Attitudes toward the Chinese

Lee's survey of the national press during the 1910s and 1920s determined that by the 1920s, more articles favorable to the Chinese were to be found than in earlier periods. Many of the articles related to this and other Chinese topics written during this period were published in popular periodicals.[79] Throughout this period, the southern press was strangely silent on the Chinese issue. It was not until the 1930s and the advent of World War II (1931–1945) that southerners seem to have again found the Chinese newsworthy. Initially, the hostilities roused by the war were directed toward the Japanese, but it was soon extended to include all Asians. In Georgia, in 1932, a brief flurry arose over a movement to exclude Asians from white schools.[80] In Houston, Texas, there was an effort to drive Chinese grocers out of business.[81] But by the late 1930s, the war efforts of the Mainland Chinese had won the respect of Americans. This new image of China, coupled with the United States–Sino Alliance toward the latter part of the war, resulted in an easing of Chinese immigration restrictions in 1943, when Chinese were also granted rights to naturalization. This action ended the six decades of flagrant discrimination against the Chinese with the recision of the Chinese Exclusion Acts.

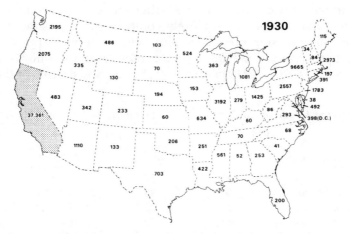

**Figure 9.2    Chinese Population of the United States, 1930. Source: U.S. Bureau of the Census, 1930.**

## Rural–Urban Distribution

Table 9.2 shows the rural–urban distribution of the Chinese population from 1910 to 1970. The percentage urban is high, even for the earlier periods when the general population was primarily rural. According to Lee, the trend toward urbanization of the Chinese began in the 1870s. She provides a national estimate of 23 percent for urban Chinese in 1880 based on a sample of census data for Chinese population in cities and unincorporated places. By 1910, more than half the Chinese in the United States were urban. By region, the Northeast (80 percent) and West (62 percent) had the greatest percent of urban concentration, followed by the Midwest (56 percent) and South (53 percent).[82] By 1990, the Chinese population in the United States had become almost entirely urban (97.7 percent) compared with a U.S. national rate of 75.2 percent (Table 9.3). Of the remaining 2.3 percent, virtually all were in small towns, and only 1,711, or 0.1 percent of the Chinese population, lived on farms. It is clear the Chinese in America today are mainly professionals, small business operators, and workers who reside in cities and generally appear to prefer larger urban places.

## Patterns of National Growth, Dispersal, and Occupational Shift

After 1920, the total Chinese population began showing moderate increases. By 1940, the Northeast had gained 25.3 percent of the national total at the expense of the West, which had declined to a 60.4 percent share despite its large relative increases during the period (Table 9.1a and b). Only 6.3 percent of the nation's Chinese were located in the South. Of the southern group, only 79 percent were reported having urban residences in 1940 as compared to 97 percent in the Northeast, 95 percent in the Midwest, and 88 percent in the West. Data for rural farm and rural nonfarm residence, however, show that the majority of all Chinese in rural areas were designated as rural nonfarm. The assumption is generally made that the rural nonfarm population lived in small towns and had an essentially urban life style (Table 9.3).[83]

Between 1870 and 1930, Chinese occupational statistics are available only for the nation (Table 9.4), but from 1940 through 1970, data are available by regional divisions (Table 9.5). Although the categories in the earlier data sets vary somewhat from the more recent statistics and cannot be too closely compared, it is possible to characterize the 1870–1930 period and concentrated employment in services (including laundry) and trade (including proprietors and employees of retail groceries and restaurants). The significant trends in the 1870–1930 period were the rise and decline of the traditional Chi-

Table 9.2    Percent Urban–Rural Distributions of Chinese by Region, 1910–1970.

|  | 1910 | | 1940 | | 1970 | |
|---|---|---|---|---|---|---|
|  | urban | rural | urban | rural* | urban | rural* |
| Northeast | 80 | 20 | 97 | 2 | 97 | 3 |
| Midwest | 56 | 44 | 95 | 4 | 97 | 3 |
| West | 62 | 38 | 88 | 7 | 97 | 3 |
| South | 53 | 47 | 79 | 18 | 93 | 7 |

*non-farm residence
Source: United States Bureau of the Census, 1910, 1940, 1970.

**Table 9.3    U.S. and Chinese Residents, Urban and Rural Population, 1990.**

|  | Total Population | Urban Total (%) | Rural Total (%) | Rural Farm (%) |
|---|---|---|---|---|
| Chinese | 1,648,696 | 1,610,543 (97.7%) | 38,572 (2.3%) | 1,711 (0.1%) |
| U.S. Population | 248,709,873 | 187,051,543 (75.2%) | 161,658,330 (24.8%) | 3,871,583 (1.6%) |

Source: U.S. Bureau of the Census, *1990 Census of the Population.*

nese hand laundry; the steady increase in those involved in trade; and from 1920 the trend toward representation in the professions.

## 1940–1970

From 1940 to 1970 (Table 9.5), the dominant trend in the changing occupational structure of the Chinese in the United States was growth in professional fields. In 1940, only 3 percent of the nation's Chinese were classified in professional categories; by 1970, the figure had risen to 31 percent. Data for 1980 indicate that the trend was continuing. By region, the Midwest and South led the nation in growth in professional and technical occupations. The South increased from 2 percent to 46 percent between 1940 and 1970; the Midwest, from 3 percent to 51 percent; the Northeast, from 0.4 percent to 29 percent; and the West, from 3 percent to 28 percent. By absolute numbers, however, the West and Northeast surpass the South and Midwest in professional employment. The percentage share for these regions is lower because the New York and San Francisco Chinatowns are principal staging areas for new immigration, which dilutes the population with many unskilled workers.

The South's category of employment is distinguished from the rest of the country by its high percentage of managers and proprietors and relatively low percentage employed in service occupations. Since 1950, the South has shown a proportion of decline in managers and proprietors to other occupations, but for the entire 1940–1970 period, it still showed a higher proportion occupied in this category than any other region. An interesting data set available from the 1970 census shows the percentage of self-employed Chinese in the South at 14.2 percent, with 3.6 percent Chinese reported as unpaid family workers. Self-employed for the other major regional divisions were given as 8.2 percent in the Northeast, 7.8 percent in the Midwest, and 7.5 percent in the West, with the

**Table 9.4    Percent Chinese Employment for the United States for Selected Major Occupational Categories, 1870–1930.**

|  | 1870 | 1900 | 1920 | 1930 |
|---|---|---|---|---|
| Personal services | 41 | 51 | 58 | 48 |
| Laundry | (8) | (25) | (28) | (24) |
| Mining | 40 | 3 | .3 | neg |
| Manufacturing | 8 | 10 | 9 | 8 |
| Agriculture | 8 | 23 | 11 | 7 |
| Wholesale, retail trade | 2 | 10 | 16 | 31 |
| Restaurant | (.4) | (.9) | (10) | (14) |
| Professional services | .7 | .7 | .9 | 2 |

Source: King and Locke, 1980.

**Table 9.5  Percent Chinese Employment by Region for Major Occupational Categories, 1940–1970.***

| | United States | South | Northeast | Midwest | West |
|---|---|---|---|---|---|
| *1940* | | | | | |
| Professional/Technical | 3 | 2 | .4 | 3 | 3 |
| Managers/Proprietors | 20 | 51 | 16 | 30 | 18 |
| Sales | n/a | n/a | n/a | n/a | n/a |
| Clerical | 11 | 15 | 5 | 6 | 16 |
| Craftsmen | 1 | .4 | .7 | 1 | 2 |
| Operatives | 22 | 12 | 37 | 26 | 14 |
| Farmers/Farm Managers | 1 | 1 | .1 | .2 | 2 |
| Farm Labor | 3 | .5 | .1 | .06 | 5 |
| Service | 3 | 15 | 37 | 31 | 27 |
| Domestic | 6 | 2 | 2 | 2 | 10 |
| Labor | 2 | 1 | .5 | 1 | 2 |
| Others | .6 | .5 | .6 | .2 | .6 |
| *1950* | | | | | |
| Professional/Technical | 6 | 7 | 5 | 8 | .6 |
| Managers/Proprietors | 22 | 38 | 18 | 23 | 22 |
| Sales | n/a | n/a | n/a | n/a | n/a |
| Clerical | 11 | 12 | 5 | 5 | 16 |
| Craftsmen | 3 | 2 | 2 | 3 | 5 |
| Operatives | 16 | 9 | 25 | 18 | 12 |
| Farmers/Farm Managers | 1 | 2 | .3 | .4 | 2 |
| Farm Labor | 1 | 3 | .4 | .3 | 2 |
| Service | 32 | 22 | 41 | 36 | 28 |
| Domestic | 2 | 1 | 1 | .5 | 3 |
| Labor | 2 | 4 | 1 | 3 | 2 |
| Others | 1 | 1 | 2 | 1 | 1 |
| *1960* | | | | | |
| Professional/Technical | 18 | 24 | 17 | 32 | 16 |
| Managers/Proprietors | 15 | 29 | 15 | 14 | 13 |
| Sales | 6 | 7 | 8 | 2 | 2 |
| Clerical | 8 | 6 | 10 | 3 | 4 |
| Craftsmen | 7 | 2 | 10 | 3 | 3 |
| Operatives | 13 | 6 | 11 | 11 | 18 |
| Farmers/Farm Managers | .7 | .6 | 1 | .2 | .1 |
| Farm Labor | .4 | .2 | .6 | .2 | .06 |
| Service | 23 | 16 | 19 | 26 | 32 |
| Domestic | .8 | .9 | .9 | .4 | .8 |
| Labor | 2 | 2 | 2 | 1 | .4 |
| Others | 7 | 6 | 5 | 7 | 10 |
| *1970* | | | | | |
| Professional/Technical | 31 | 46 | 29 | 51 | 28 |
| Managers/Proprietors | 15 | 20 | 13 | 10 | 16 |
| Sales | 4 | 3 | 3 | 2 | 5 |
| Clerical | 7 | 5 | 5 | 3 | 9 |
| Craftsmen | 8 | 3 | 4 | 4 | 11 |

**Table 9.5    Continued.**

|  | United States | South | Northeast | Midwest | West |
|---|---|---|---|---|---|
|  |  | 1970 (Continued) |  |  |  |
| Operatives | 10 | 6 | 14 | 5 | 10 |
| Farmers/Farm Managers | .5 | .5 | .1 | .09 | .7 |
| Farm Labor | .2 | .2 | .1 | — | .3 |
| Service | 21 | 15 | 30 | 23 | 17 |
| Domestic | .3 | .1 | .4 | .2 | .2 |
| Labor | 2 | 1 | 1 | .9 |  |
| Others | n/a | n/a | n/a | n/a | n/a |

*Note: Columns do not total 100% due to rounding errors.
Source: United States Bureau of the Census, 1940, 1953, 1960, 1973.

percentage of unpaid family workers a uniform 1.1 percent for each. Conversely, the Northeast showed the highest number of wage earners at 80.6 percent, followed by 75.1 percent in the West, 65.2 percent in the North Central, and 57.8 percent in the South.[84] These 1970 data support the model of the Chinese family-owned business in the South, although they give no information about specific types of self-employment.

The employment data for 1990 (Table 9.6) show the Chinese residents with almost 36 percent of total employment in managerial and professional occupations, much higher than the 26 percent for the whole U.S. population. Of the Chinese total, 8.8 percent were scientists and engineers. Both of these statistics provide strong and consistent evidence of the highly educated, skilled professional workforce among Chinese in the United States as seen in the immigration of educated professionals with technical skills and advanced graduate students, many of whom remain in the United States after completing their degrees. As noted in the earlier employment data, a substantial share (16.5 percent) of Chinese were in service activities, almost all of whom (15.6 percent of total)

**Table 9.6    Employment and Employment Share of Chinese Residents, 1990.**

| Employment Category | Chinese Residents | % Share of Chinese Pop. | Comparison % Share of U.S. Pop. |
|---|---|---|---|
| Managerial & Professional | 293,565 of whom 71,834 (8.8%) were scientists and engineers | 35.8% | 26.4% |
| Technical, Sales & Administrative Support | 255,598 | 31.2% | 31.7% |
| Service Occupations | 135,154 of whom 128,121 (15.6%) were in food services | 16.5% | 13.2% |
| Precision Production & Repairs | 46,042 | 5.6% | 11.3% |
| Operators, Fabricators, etc. | 86,680 | 10.6% | 14.9% |
| Farming, Forestry, Fisheries | 2,893 | .4% | 2.5% |
| TOTAL | 819,932 | (65.9% of those age 16≥ were employed) |  |

Note: % totals do not equal 100% due to rounding.
Source: U.S. Bureau of the Census, 1990 Census of the Population.

were in food services. This evidence supports the importance of entry into the restaurant sector for many Chinese small businesspeople as a relatively reliable point of entry into the U.S. commercial market.

### Effects of the Relaxation of Immigration Restrictions

The 1943 revision of the Chinese Exclusion Acts gave Chinese a token annual immigration quota of 105. Further amendments to this law and other immigration laws that affected Chinese were made in the late 1940s and the 1950s. Finally, in 1965, an act was passed eliminating all discriminatory legislation against Chinese immigration, and the Chinese were allowed the normal national quota of twenty thousand per year.[85] In 1979, the United States officially recognized the People's Republic of China, so an additional quota of twenty thousand per year was added to the twenty thousand already in effect being used by the Republic of China on Taiwan. In addition, Hong Kong was given a minimal quota of six hundred per year, so the total Chinese annual quota was in fact 40,600 after 1979, to which could be added other Chinese who were members of the Southeast Asian Chinese diaspora or Nanyang Chinese. In some years, they had been awarded special quotas to accommodate, for example, boat people refugees from Vietnam who were largely Chinese ethnics or at-risk students studying in the United States or elsewhere following the Tiananmen massacre in June 1989. Thus, the total number of Chinese who have come to the United States following the change in the immigration laws in 1965 has increased substantially. In addition to the legal migrants, there is also a large activity in illegal migration that can be traced mainly to coastal provinces and Taiwan, and some have estimated the illegal migrants found in places such as New York's Chinatown as high as 20 percent of the total Chinese population.[86]

The effect of the relaxation of Chinese immigration restrictions is evident in the 1950–1990 population statistics (Table 9.1a and b). In 1950, absolute gains for all regions were large; the South's total Chinese population increased from 10,486 in 1950 to 16,839 (Fig. 9.3) in 1960. The greatest surge of growth came (Fig. 9.4), however, after 1965 when the last discriminatory laws were repealed. By 1990, the Chinese population in the South had grown to 205,373, placing it third behind the Northeast and West with 12.5 percent of the total Chinese population (Fig. 9.5). The West had regained its growth momentum and climbed to a total of 870,063, over 700,000 of whom were in California alone. Such continuing growth likely results from the Pacific location as well as the large size and employment opportunities available to Asian immigrants in California and its perceived more hospitable social environment for Asians. The Northeast's share of the Chinese population has stabilized around 27 percent, more than 285,000 of whom were concentrated in New York State. Meanwhile, the Midwest region's share has declined to roughly 8 percent of the total (Table 9.1a and b; Figs. 9.2 and 9.3).

Between 1940 and 1970, the urban concentration of Chinese in the United States rose from 91 percent to 97 percent. That trend continued to the point where only 1,711 of the country's Chinese were classified as rural farm in the 1990 census, a share of less than 1 percent of the total Chinese population (Table 9.3). The West, Northeast, and Midwest conform to the national average percentage of urban distribution, with the South showing only 93 percent of its Chinese population in 1970 (Table 9.2) as urban. However, the majority of Chinese having rural residences were reported as rural nonfarm.

Chinese communities in the South underwent many changes in the 1960s and 1970s. Loewen observed the Mississippi groups in the processes of dispersing in the late 1960s

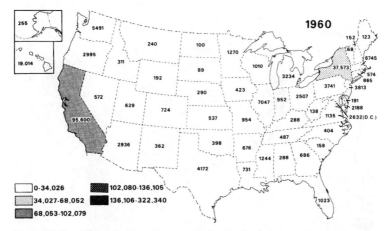

**Figure 9.3    Chinese Population of the United States, 1960. Source: U.S. Bureau of the Census, 1960.**

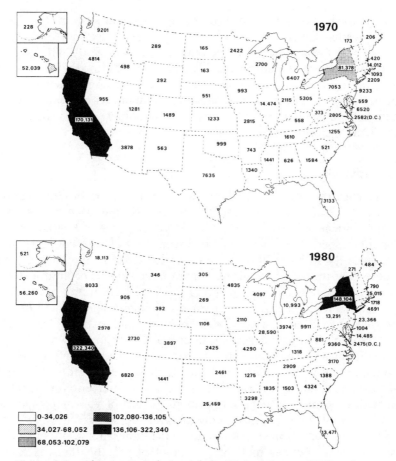

**Figure 9.4    Chinese Population of the United States, 1970 and 1980. Source: U.S. Bureau of the Census, 1970 and 1980.**

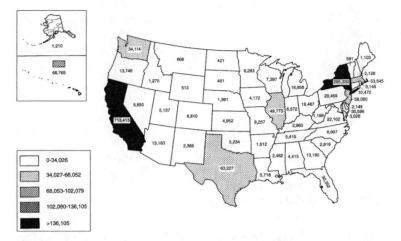

**Figure 9.5    Chinese Population of the United States, 1990. Source: U.S. Bureau of the Census, 1990.**

and attributes it to the breakdown of the segregated social system.[87] In Georgia, where discrimination against Chinese was practiced by custom but not by law, the Chinese communities appear to have begun dispersing in the late 1950s. The general trend has been for the Chinese to move out of black neighborhoods, into white residential areas, and there has been an occupational shift from small business owner-operators to the white-collar professions. These changes have come about as more opportunities for advancement have been opened to the Chinese, and they have gained the education necessary to take advantage of them.

## Change and Dispersals

In recent years with the substantially increased immigration of Chinese to the United States, two social patterns have emerged. The first is composed of low-income immigrants with low educational backgrounds whose knowledge of English is poor. Many of these immigrants, especially in some of the larger cities of both coasts such as San Francisco, Los Angeles, New York, Boston, and Seattle, settle in the large Chinatown communities where they are culturally protected but may often be economically exploited by their fellow countrymen. It is the continuing influx of large numbers of these poorly educated immigrants who help ensure the continuation and rapid growth of the traditional Chinatowns that have been so remarkable in cities such as New York. These are the "downtown Chinese" Kwong[88] describes so compellingly in his work *The New Chinatown*. Here the Chinese form solid communities of recent immigrants with control and protection provided by well-established benevolent societies and/or tongs along with a variety of commercial and industrial enterprises that offer employment but also cutthroat competition within the local Chinatown. Gangs of youths provide enforcement protection for overlords who maintain control, and the community is viewed from the outside as closed and sometimes mysterious. Left to govern and direct itself, these Chinatowns have become replicas of Chinese societies that hearken back to conditions found in China before the revolution. As the populations in Chinatowns have grown so rapidly and real estate prices have become inflated, satellite Chinatowns have emerged in some of the largest cities such as New York.

The second pattern is composed of second-, third-, and fourth-generation Chinese immigrants or those recent migrants with good educational and professional qualifications. These people have either moved away from Chinatown or never lived there. Kwong[89] describes these as the "Uptown Chinese." Generally, they are dispersed residentially in neighborhoods appropriate to their income levels without regard to their race or ethnicity. This dual social pattern is characteristic of the large, older cities with traditional Chinatowns that have persisted along with the recent dispersal. The dispersed pattern is found in cities such as Atlanta or Houston where the bulk of the Chinese population are recently arrived, and most are well-educated professionals with moderate to high incomes. Yet in these large metropolitan areas, the very rapid increase in Chinese immigration has led to the emergence of clustered business areas for Chinese and other Asian-owned commercial establishments such as restaurants and a variety of retail shops and green groceries. Often nearby are found substantial but not exclusive Chinese and Asian residential communities in middle-income suburban areas; these include not only Chinese but Koreans, Vietnamese, and sometimes Filipinos. An example would be the Buford Highway/Chamblee area of northeast Atlanta. Thus, the rapid growth of the Asian and Chinese populations in America's metropolitan and urban areas are creating new communities that are more dispersed but yet represent some intermediate social steps between the enlarged Chinatowns and the previously highly dispersed and better-integrated social patterns of Chinese professionals of the 1970s and 1980s.

## CONCLUSION

The Chinese population in the United States, although historically a small minority among the nation's ethnic immigrant groups, has received a great deal of attention. In the early period of Chinese immigration to the United States, a fearful native public rallied to place obstacle upon obstacle before them to restrict their entry into the country and to make existence difficult for those who had settled. They lived within a mass of contradictions—thwarted at every turn from entering mainstream America and damned because they did not. The press kept anti-Chinese issues circulating long after immigration had all but ceased, in part, perhaps, because the titillating stories about the "evils" of Chinatown sold newspapers. It is no small irony that by the turn of the century, the Chinatowns found tourism to be an important source of income.

Over time, the Chinese began to earn the public's grudging respect. A generation of native-born Chinese grew up with English as a first language, and for the first time the Chinese began writing about themselves. With the barrier to communication down, America was introduced to a different view of Chinese Americans. This fact, coupled with favorable serious academic studies of the Chinese and the effect of the Sino-American alliance of World War II, resulted in a dramatic change in popular opinion.

Several forces have converged to offer a profoundly different picture of the Chinese in the United States today. Following World War II, as noted, the barriers to Chinese immigration began to fall, and these were opened fully to Chinese in 1965 and after. Paralleling the change in immigration laws was the remarkable economic growth of the United States that offered new opportunities for Chinese professionals and those with technical skills. At the same time came the far-reaching changes in civil rights laws and the opening of U.S. society to all following the landmark Supreme Court decision of *Brown vs. The Board of Education* in 1954 and a host of new civil rights laws in the 1960s. All of the forces changed American society in fundamental ways and offered far-reaching new opportunities for Chinese along with other minority groups. The Chinese were quick to avail themselves of these new opportunities and in this manner carved a strong niche in the broader fabric of America's increasingly multiethnic society.

Today Chinese Americans are among the most admired of United States ethnic minorities. They are as a group more educated, better employed, and enjoy higher incomes than the average citizen, and they are often lauded as a prime example of success in the "American Way." Whereas this success story is remarkable witness to the tenacity of the Chinese to overcome extreme odds, it must be remembered that the statistics are based primarily on those who were never isolated in Chinatowns or managed to escape and integrate themselves into general society. For hundreds of thousands of Chinese, Chinatown is still a reality. Because of crowding and poor housing conditions, the incidence of tuberculosis, mental illness, drug abuse, and alcoholism are high; crime is increasing and juvenile street gangs are not uncommon. Chinese in these ghettos still feel the remnants of racial bias from their host cities and believe they are too often left to solve their problems alone. Recent immigrants, often unable to speak English and sometimes here illegally, do not have the same rights and privileges as other Americans and may be abused and exploited by other Chinese who need their inexpensive labor services. Despite the success of many Chinese in the United States, the reality of Chinatown for many of the first generation and recent immigrants is the American dream unfulfilled.

## NOTES

1. Stuart Creighton Miller, *The Unwelcome Immigrant: The American Image of the Chinese 1785–1882* (Berkeley: University of California Press, 1969).

2. Miller, *The Unwelcome Immigrant*, 43.

3. Ching-Tau Wu, *"Chink"* (New York: World, 1972), 2.

4. Shieu-woo Kung, *Chinese in American Life* (Seattle: University of Washington Press, 1962), 167.

5. John Higham, *Strangers in the Land* (New York: Atheneum, 1965).

6. Orlando Patterson, *Ethnic Chauvinism: The Reactionary Impulse* (New York: Stein & Day, 1977), 56.

7. Edna Bonacich and John Moddell, *The Economic Basis of Ethnic Solidarity* (Berkeley: University of California Press, 1980).

8. James W. Loewen, *The Mississippi Chinese: Between Black and White* (Cambridge, Mass.: Harvard University Press, 1971).

9. Thomas Sowell, ed., *Essays and Data on American Ethnic Groups* (Washington, D.C.: Urban Institute, 1978).

10. Colin Greer, *Divided Society* (New York: Basic Books, 1974).

11. Loewen, *The Mississippi Chinese*, unnumbered page.

12. Arnold Shankman, "Black on Yellow: Afro-Americans View Chinese-Americans, 1850–1935," *Phylon* 34 (March 1978): 1–17.

13. Gunther Barth, *Bitter Strength: A History of the Chinese in the U.S. 1850–1870* (Cambridge, Mass.: Harvard University Press, 1964).

14. Jack Chen, *The Chinese in America* (San Francisco: Harper & Row, 1980).

15. Rose Hum Lee, *The Chinese in the United States of America* (Hong Kong: Hong Kong University Press, 1960).

16. Haitung King and Frances Locke, "The Chinese in the United States: A Century of Occupational Transition," *International Migration Review* 14 (Spring 1980): 15–42.

17. Robert W. O'Brien, "Status of Chinese in the Mississippi Delta," *Social Forces* 19 (March 1941): 386–401.

18. Nancy Farrar, "The Chinese in El Paso," *Southwestern Studies*, Monograph No. 23 (El Paso: Texas Western Press and Texas University Press, 1972).

19. Edward Rhoads, *The Chinese in Texas* (Austin: Texas State Historical Society, 1977).

20. P. Y. Liao, "A Case Study of a Chinese Immigrant Community," master's thesis, University of Chicago, 1957.

21. Sally Ken, "The Chinese Community of Augusta, Georgia, from 1873 to 1971," *Richmond County History* 4 (1972): 50–60.

22. Eileen Law and Sally Ken, "A Study of the Chinese Community," *Richmond County History* 5 (1973): 24–43.

23. S. M. Chiu, "The Chinese in Augusta, Georgia," *Bulletin Chinese Historical Society of America* 13 (February 1978): 1–5.

24. Gerald Sieg, "Georgia's Chinese Pioneers," *Atlanta Constitution*, 7 March 1965, p. 18.

25. Etta B. Peabody, "Effort of the South to Import Chinese Coolies 1865–1870," master's thesis, Baylor University, 1967.

26. Sylvia Krebs, "The Chinese Labor Question: A Note on the Attitudes of Two Alabama Republicans," *Alabama Historical Quarterly* 38 (Fall 1976): 214–217.

27. Lucy M. Cohen, "Entry of Chinese to the Lower South from 1865–1870: Policy Dilemmas," *Southern Studies* 17 (Spring 1978): 5–37. See also Lucy M. Cohen, *Chinese in the Post–Civil War South* (Baton Rouge: Louisiana State University Press, 1984).

28. Catherine L. Brown, "A Geographic Analysis of the Chinese in Georgia, 1865–1980," master's thesis, University of Georgia, 1983.

29. A. E. Smailes, "The Analysis and Delimitation of Urban Fields," *Geography* 32 (December 1947): 51–161.

30. Rhoads Murphey, "Boston's Chinatown," *Economic Geography* 28 (1952): 244–255.

31. *The China Geographer*, Special Edition on Chinatowns, 4 (Spring 1976).

32. Rose Hum Lee, "The Decline of Chinatowns in the United States," *American Journal of Sociology* 54 (March 1949): 422–432.

33. Lee, "The Decline of Chinatowns."

34. Sieg, "Georgia's Chinese Pioneers."

35. Peter Kwong, *The New Chinatown*, rev. ed. (New York: Hill & Wang, 1996); Chalsa M. Loo, *Chinatown, Most Time, Hard Time* (New York: Praeger, 1987); Bernard Wong, *Patronage, Brokerage, Entrepreneurship and the Chinese Community of New York* (New York: AMS, 1988); and Gwen Kinkead, *Chinatown: A Portrait of a Closed Society* (New York: HarperCollins, 1992).

36. David Chuenyan Lai, *Chinatowns: Towns within Cities in Canada* (Vancouver: University of British Columbia Press, 1988). See also Kwong, *The New Chinatown*, and Wong, *Patronage*.

37. Francis L. K. Hsu, *The Challenge of the American Dream* (Belmont, Calif.: Wadsworth, 1971).

38. Lee, *The Chinese*.

39. Rose Hum Lee, "Growth and Decline of Chinese Communities in the Rocky Mountains," Ph.D. dissertation, University of Chicago, 1947.

40. Higham, *Strangers in the Land*.

41. "The Chinese," *Alta* (San Francisco), 16 July 1869, p. 1.

42. Higham, *Strangers in the Land*.

43. Miller, *The Unwelcome Immigrant*.

44. Chen, *The Chinese in America*.

45. Lee, *The Chinese*.

46. Barth, *Bitter Strength.*
47. "The Chinese," *Alta* (San Francisco), 1.
48. "The Gothic, African, and Chinese Races," *Debow's Review* (August 1869): 943–945.
49. Miller, *The Unwelcome Immigrant.*
50. Chen, *The Chinese in America.*
51. Barth, *Bitter Strength,* 189.
52. Loewen, *The Mississippi Chinese;* Chiu, "The Chinese in Augusta, Georgia"; Liao, "A Case Study"; and Rhoads, *The Chinese in Texas.*
53. Mildred C. Thompson, *Reconstruction in Georgia* (New York: Columbia University Press, 1915).
54. Sowell, *Essays and Data.*
55. Greer, *Divided Society.*
56. Edna Bonacich. "A Theory of Middlemen Minorities," *American Sociological Review* 38 (October 1973): 583–594.
57. Farrar, "The Chinese in El Paso"; Rhoads, *The Chinese in Texas;* and Federal Writers Project, *Louisiana,* American Guide Series (New York: Hastings House, 1941).
58. Lee, "Growth and Decline."
59. Loewen, *The Mississippi Chinese;* Rhoads, *The Chinese in Texas;* and Brown, "A Geographic Analysis."
60. Loewen, *The Mississippi Chinese;* Ed Ritter and Helen Ritter, *Our Oriental Americans* (St. Louis: McGraw-Hill, 1965).
61. Sieg, "Georgia's Chinese Pioneers."
62. Milford S. Weiss, *Valley City: A Chinese Community in America* (Cambridge, Mass.: Shenkman, 1974), 36.
63. Liao, "A Case Study," 23.
64. Loewen, *The Mississippi Chinese.*
65. *Atlanta Constitution,* 24 July 1960, p. 10.
66. Liao, "A Case Study"; Loewen, *The Mississippi Chinese;* Chiu, "The Chinese in Augusta, Georgia"; and Rhoads, *The Chinese in Texas.*
67. Higham, *Strangers in the Land.*
68. Murphey, "Boston's Chinatown," 249.
69. Vernon Lee Wharton, *The Negro in Mississippi, 1865–1890* (Chapel Hill: University of North Carolina Press, 1947).
70. "Chinese in the South," *New York Times,* 6 May 1879, p. 4.
71. Farrar, "The Chinese in El Paso," 15.
72. An excellent discussion and analysis of the U.S. legal framework constructed to deny Chinese entry into the United States in the late nineteenth century is contained in Charles J. McClain, *In Search of Equality: The Chinese Struggle against Discrimination in Nineteenth Century America* (Berkeley: University of California Press, 1994).
73. Lee, *The Chinese.*
74. "Significant Incident," *New York Times,* 25 February 1899, p. 6.
75. Higham, *Strangers in the Land;* and George E. Possetta, "Foreigners in Florida: A Study of Immigration Promotion, 1865–1910," *Florida Historical Quarterly* 53 (1974–1975): 164–180.
76. Higham, *Strangers in the Land.*
77. Lee, *The Chinese.*
78. Lee, *The Chinese.*
79. Lee, *The Chinese.*
80. Law and Ken, "A Study."
81. Rhoads, *The Chinese in Texas.*
82. Lee, *The Chinese.*
83. Loewen, *The Mississippi Chinese;* Liao, "A Case Study"; and Chiu, "The Chinese in Augusta, Georgia."

84. U.S. Bureau of the Census, *Subject Reports, Nonwhite Population by Race, 1970* (Washington, D.C.: U.S. Government Printing Office, 1973).

85. For a discussion of this legislation, see Kwong, *The New Chinatown*, 21–22.

86. Betty Lee Sung, "Polarity in the Makeup of Chinese Immigrants, " *Sourcebook on the New Immigration* (New Brunswick, N.J.: Transaction, 1980).

87. Loewen, *The Mississippi Chinese.*

88. Kwong, *The New Chinatown.*

89. Kwong, *The New Chinatown.*

**10**

# Mainland Southeast Asian Refugees: Migration, Settlement, and Adaptation

*Christopher Airriess and David Clawson*

During the 1980s and 1990s, Latin America and Asia replaced Europe as the primary source regions for immigrants entering the United States. In the 1990s alone, approximately 37 percent of the twenty million immigrants admitted into the country were of Asian origin. The majority of Asian immigrants, including those from India, the Philippines, Taiwan, China, and South Korea, entered the United States in search of greater economic opportunity. Unlike these voluntary migrants, however, the newest Asian Americans from the mainland Southeast Asian or "Indochinese" countries of Vietnam, Laos, and Cambodia arrived as political refugees after the American withdrawal and subsequent communist takeover of Vietnam in 1975.[1] As a by-product of a failed cold war strategy applied at the regional scale, the U.S. government felt a moral obligation to provide safety for those in harm's way of newly installed communist regimes. Indeed, of the approximately two million refugees who fled these war-ravaged mainland Southeast Asian states between 1975 and 1990, some two-thirds settled in the United States. As political refugees, they entered under special immigrant status and comprised the largest refugee resettlement program in American history.[2]

The four mainland Southeast Asian refugee culture groups are the Vietnamese, lowland Lao, Hmong or highland Lao, and Cambodian or Khmer. Although differing from one another in many cultural particulars, the members of each group shared experiences of physical and/or psychological persecution as well as feelings of isolation and guilt associated with their sudden departure from their homelands, with little chance of repatriation.[3] Their special refugee status and recency of arrival, coupled with their ethnic diversity, warrant an examination of these newest ethnic Asian Americans within the context of the interdependent processes of migration, settlement, and adaptation. Because premigration conditions in their respective homelands are so essential to understanding migration, settlement, and adaptation patterns in the United States, we turn initially to a brief description of the physical and human geography of the region, followed by an examination of the political conflict that determined the refugee status of each ethnic group.

## HOMELANDS AND THE CREATION OF REFUGEE POPULATIONS

Vietnam, Laos, and Cambodia, which comprised the former French colonial possession of Indochina, occupy the eastern half of mainland Southeast Asia, a relatively small, but geographically significant region that separates the Indian subcontinent and China (Fig. 10.1). The region possesses a threefold physiographic structure: highlands dominate much of western Vietnam and much of neighboring Laos, alluvial and coastal plains cover most of eastern Vietnam as well as much of Cambodia, and the alluvial deltas of the Red and Mekong Rivers comprise the northern and southern extremities of Vietnam, respectively. Characterized by a tropical monsoon climate, temperatures are warm to hot throughout the year except in some cooler highland locations. Annual precipitation ranges between forty and eighty inches, with a pronounced dry season in most locations occurring during the months from December through April. Much of the original lowland tropical forest has been cleared for rice cultivation, and the highland forests have been extensively modified through the activities of swidden cultivators and the logging industry. Population distribution and cultural patterns conform to the physical environment.

The plains and alluvial lowlands of each country support relatively dense populations engaged in rice cultivation and fishing. For centuries, these culturally unified lowlanders have constituted the political and cultural cores of their nations, anchored by national capitals and other large urban centers. In contrast to the lowland cores, peripheral highlands were settled by a physically dispersed and culturally diverse array of ethnic groups, each occupying remote pockets of cleared land. Paternalistic French colonial policies reduced the traditional antagonisms between the dominant lowland and adjoining highland cultures, but they simultaneously isolated the latter groups from the rapidly changing world of the lowlands and beyond.

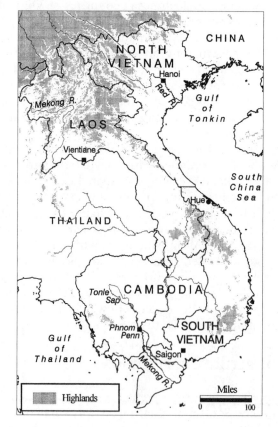

Figure 10.1    Pre-1975 Vietnam, Laos, and Cambodia.

## Vietnam

The cultural core of Vietnam originated as a highly Sinicized and Confucian-based state centered on the northern Red River Valley. By the late 1700s, northern political control and culture diffused to the south and formed a single imperial government based in Hue. Under the pretext of protecting Catholic missionaries that had been active in the region since the 1600s, France ruthlessly invaded Vietnam, capturing the Mekong and Red River deltas by 1867 and 1884, respectively. Having gained complete political control over the elongated-shaped colony by the early 1890s, France proceeded to claim Laos and Cambodia as well, creating the single colonial government of the Union of Indochina. While Vietnam experienced direct colonial occupation, the more remote Laos and Cambodia were controlled indirectly, often through the use of Vietnamese intermediaries. Although sharing a common historical tradition and language, the northern and southern halves of Vietnam came to differ substantially in many respects. As a settlement frontier for northern peasants and as the area most strongly impacted by French colonialism, southern Vietnam has traditionally been more tolerant of political expression, individual initiative, and cultural diversity.[4]

After World War II, the French regained control of Vietnam from the Japanese and waged a protracted war against the nationalist and communist-based Vietminh fighting for independence in the north. By the early 1950s, the French position had substantially deteriorated, and the defeat of French forces concluded with the signing of the 1954 Geneva Agreement, which separated Vietnam into northern and southern halves. As part of the American strategy to contain the spread of communism in Southeast Asia, financial aid was provided to relocate some nine hundred thousand anticommunists from the north to bolster the new pro-Western and capitalist government of South Vietnam. The South Vietnamese leader Diem was Catholic, as were 80 percent of the northern refugees. Many of the upper- and middle-class northerners came to fill important government positions in Saigon and the outlying provinces, while most of the northern peasants were resettled into hundreds of militarily strategic Catholic villages.[5] Although driven in part by humanitarian goals, the American funding of organized refugee movements from north to south was also an expression of its global geopolitical goals. The resultant moral responsibility sensed by the United States toward these refugees was one of the causes of the direct American military intervention initiated in the 1960s.[6]

After 1965, the direct participation of American advisers and troops in the escalating military conflict in the south ushered in a new period of using refugees as a tool to combat communist influence. Because the Vietcong (the southern branch of the Vietminh) had come to influence or control at least half of the villages in the south, U.S. policy focused on winning the hearts and minds of the Vietnamese peasantry so as to rob the Vietcong of local food supplies and manpower. This formal program of "pacification" eventually led to the sponsored relocation of over five million refugees to areas under government control and the funding of a variety of social programs designed to generate political loyalty.[7] By the early 1970s, however, the continued success of communist forces in the south under conditions of an increasingly autocratic South Vietnamese government, together with the waning of both political and popular support for the war in the United States, forced the American government to sign a cease-fire agreement with the government of North Vietnam in 1973. Ignoring protests from the weak and ineffective government of South Vietnam, the U.S. government withdrew all its military forces from South Vietnam that same year. In April 1975, Saigon fell to the victorious communist forces, and Vietnam once again became a politically unified country.

Fear of political, religious, and economic persecution forced some 130,000 "high-risk" Vietnamese directly associated with the American presence to flee their country by the end of 1975. Some of these refugees accompanied the retreating American forces from Saigon under Operation Frequent Wind, while others, over the next few weeks and months, arranged their own evacuation by boat to awaiting rescue vessels offshore. Many of these latter refugees were in fact Catholic fisherfolk and farmers who had participated in the U.S.-sponsored north-to-south refugee transfer programs of 1954. This "first wave" of Vietnamese refugees was followed by a much larger "second wave" between 1977 and 1979. Escaping in overcrowded and often unseaworthy boats originally constructed for river or shallow coastal navigation, these "boat people" experienced almost daily threats from pirates while seeking landfall in Thailand, Malaysia, Indonesia, and the Philippines. Many of the boat people were ethnic-Chinese Vietnamese, fleeing the nationalization of businesses or various forms of persecution that had begun as a result of a border war that broke out between Vietnam and China in 1978. By mid-1979, approximately 300,000 boat people had fled Vietnam, and deaths at sea numbered between 40,000 and 150,000.[8] In response to the rapid outflow of boat people, the United Nations established refugee or transit camps in the previously noted "first asylum" countries to process those selected for admission to the United States and other Western countries. The "third wave," or last major outflow of refugees, occurred under the Orderly Departure Program established in mid-1979 through which the Vietnamese government has allowed the departure of approximately 125,000 persons on commercial or special flights sponsored by the United Nations.[9]

## Laos

Laos provides a classic example of the highland-lowland settlement and culture patterns characteristic of mainland Southeast Asia. Comprising approximately 50 percent of the national population of three million, the politically dominant lowland Lao or "Lao Loum" historically occupied the Mekong River lowlands and engaged in intensive paddy rice agriculture. Dominated by a succession of Buddhist kingdoms dating to the mid-1300s, Laos has long functioned as a vassal state to the more powerful lowland powers based in Thailand, Burma, and Vietnam.[10] The other half of the Laotian population consists of the highland Lao or "Lao Theung," which is composed of some sixty tribal groups speaking either Tai or Mon-Khmer languages and practicing swidden agriculture in combination with some livestock raising. The most numerous of these groups include the Khmu, Tai, and Hmong. This latter group comprised approximately 10 percent of the 1970 national population.[11]

The Hmong were a late addition to the diverse mosaic of highland Lao cultures. For centuries, the Hmong occupied the mountainous provinces of southwestern China, but in response to persecutions by the Chinese government in the mid-1700s, some Hmong gradually migrated southward in search of greater autonomy. They reached mountainous northwestern Vietnam during the early 1800s and subsequently spread to other isolated mountain regions in the remaining present day mainland Southeast Asian states. In Laos, the greatest concentration was in the northeast, where they occupied elevations above three thousand feet, including the much sought-after isolated mountaintops. Inhabiting villages commonly comprised of ten to twenty houses, the Hmong led a seminomadic existence determined by the changing field locations inherent to swidden agriculture. Unlike the Buddhist lowland culture, Hmong are traditional animists, although substantial numbers converted to Protestantism in response to Christian missionary activity beginning in the early 1900s.

Hmong social structure is organized on the basis of families, lineages, and clans. Some twenty major clans or lines of descent exist, and these clans shape political organization, mutual help obligations, marriage rules, and, equally important, migration patterns.[12] Indeed, the Hmong word for "home," *tsev*, connotes no definite geographic location but refers to individual position within family and clan relationships.[13]

The Hmong have strongly influenced the political and military events of Laos for two reasons. First, the Hmong occupy the strategically important mountainous border region between Vietnam and Laos; second, knowledge of such terrain has produced a highly efficient and hardy guerilla force.[14] The Hmong first entered military conflict as allies of the French in the struggle against the communist Pathet Lao who, like the Vietminh, were engaged in armed conflict with the returning French immediately after World War II. Some believe that Vietminh and Pathet Lao reprisals against the Hmong were for providing refuge to French soldiers during the Japanese Occupation, thus forcing the Hmong to ally with the French and the royal Lao government.[15]

Laos was granted independence in 1953 and during the rest of the decade experienced neutralist governments, with factions of both the pro-Western and procommunists sharing political power. Despite substantial amounts of economic development aid and U.S. covert military aid to bolster the Royal Lao Army (RLA), the Vietminh-aided Pathet Lao gradually gained control of ever larger parts of the country. Convinced that the lowland RLA was no longer able to check the spread of communist influence, the U.S. government enlisted the military skills of the Hmong in a CIA-led covert war. The CIA promised the Hmong that if they were victorious, they would be granted an autonomous highland kingdom and, if defeated, a new place to live.[16] By 1969, Hmong mercenaries under the command of General Vang Pao numbered over forty thousand and had become an important bulwark against the military advances of the communists and a tool for disrupting the transport of war supplies from North to South Vietnam along the Ho Chi Minh Trail that straddled the Vietnam-Laos border.

The Hmong homeland in northeastern Laos, however, was eventually overrun by North Vietnamese troops. The U.S. military retaliated with massive bombing sorties, forcing some one hundred thousand Hmong and other highland tribal peoples into U.S. government–funded refugee camps.[17] Although U.S. government support for the secret war in Laos waned as the American withdrawal from Vietnam became imminent, Vang Pao's Hmong troops continued to do battle with the Pathet Lao. The Hmong did not fare well, however, under conditions of a new communist-led coalition government installed in 1973 and the evaporation of covert U.S. aid. Between 1975 and 1979, the forced attendance at political indoctrination camps, loss of land to the state, and eventually genocidal chemical warfare against the Hmong forced up to one hundred thousand people (one-third of the Hmong population in Laos) to engage in an arduous and life-threatening month-long exodus to United Nations refugee camps just across the Mekong River in Thailand. Many died in route because of malnutrition, exhaustion, and Pathet Lao ambushes.[18] Previously, some 17,000 Hmong troops and 50,000 Hmong civilians had died during the war. By 1985, approximately 350,000 Laotians had fled their country.[19]

## Cambodia

Much like Laos, Cambodia too has been the victim of long-term external aggression. Once the center of the powerful twelfth- to fourteenth-century Khmer Empire, which included the magnificent Angkor Wat temple complex, this devoutly Buddhist and culturally homogeneous country sustained by productive lowland rice agriculture was claimed by either its Thai or Vietnamese neighbors until 1863, when it became a French colonial possession.[20] Granted independence in 1953, Cambodia was ruled by a monarchy that remained neutral throughout much of the Vietnam War. The country was drawn into the Vietnam War after the North Vietnamese Army established supply bases in southeastern Cambodia and simultaneously aided the procommunist Cambodian Khmer Rouge guerillas. In response, the U.S. government helped install the pro-American Lon Nol government and commenced in 1970 a covert bombing campaign of communist bases. Bombing sorties increased dramatically during the 1971–1973 period and generated approximately one million internal refugees, most from the free-fire zone of eastern Cambodia. Unlike in Vietnam and Laos, however, the U.S. government provided very little monetary aid to relieve the misery of Cambodian refugees.[21]

After the Americans withdrew from Vietnam, the Cambodian people experienced even greater tragedy. The Khmer Rouge captured Phnom Penh in 1975, instituting a reign of terror that included the systematic murdering of the elite, emptying cities, and forcing the population into collectivized farming or labor camps. Known to the outside world as the country of the "killing fields," Cambodia's population of eight million eventually declined by a fourth.[22]

Further loss of life resulted from the invasion of Cambodia by Vietnamese forces in 1977. The Khmer Rouge and Vietnamese did battle until 1979 when the Khmer Rouge government was overthrown and their forces retreated into the western third of the country. Continued military conflict between the Vietnamese and Khmer Rouge through the mid-1980s created another 250,000 refugees who fled to UN camps in Thailand.[23] In 1989, Vietnamese forces withdrew, and a United Nations cease-fire was arranged in 1991.

## Defining Immigrants and Refugees

Before examining the resettlement process in the United States, a brief description of the differences between refugees and immigrants is warranted because a clearer understanding of this conceptual distinction is critical to the process of resettlement and socioeconomic adaptation in the United States. The issue of choice is the fundamental experiential difference between refugees and immigrants. Immigrants can be classified into the four categories of labor migrants, professional immigrants, entrepreneurial immigrants, and refugees and asylees.[24] Whether legal or illegal, the first three types exit their source countries by choice and are frequently "pulled" to migrate permanently because of employment or educational opportunities. Their long-distance movement possesses predetermined points of origin and destination, is usually planned long in advance of departure, and immigrants have opportunities to return to their source country on short visits if so desired. In addition, when immigration is of the legal variety, the volume is based on quotas established by the receiving country government.

Refugee status, however, confers a very different experience. A refugee is largely a product of "push" forces in the form of life-threatening political, economic, religious, and even environmental circumstances. When exiting the source country, refugees often do not know their final destination, and they do not have the luxury of planning their exit before departure. Although refugees possess a real fear that they will never see their home again, exemption from immigration quotas because of their refugee status facilitates easier entry into a receiving country. Unlike regular immigrants who are granted admission based on a pledge to be financially self-sufficient, refugees are eligible for a package of federal and local assistance monies.[25] This package of financial benefits was formalized with the Refugee Act of 1980, which also included a more coordinated system of admission and resettlement based primary on the goal of repatriating families.

## MIGRATION TO THE UNITED STATES

Between 1975 and 1996, approximately 1.1 million mainland Southeast Asians refugees entered the United States as a country of final residence. The volume of arrivals was not even over time but ebbed and flowed in response to the changing political and military conditions of their homelands (Fig.10.2). The initial flow of refugees across the Pacific consisted primarily of "first wave" Vietnamese who fled the country within a few months of the 1975 fall of Saigon. Although composed largely of the urban educated class

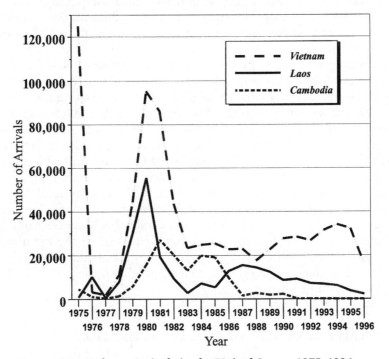

Figure 10.2    Refugee Arrivals in the United States, 1975–1996.
Sources: Rumbaut (1996), 321, for 1975–1992; and *Unpublished Statistics of the Office of Refugee Resettlement* (Washington, D.C.: U.S. Department of Health and Human Services, 1993–1996) for 1993–1996.

that had been closely connected to the American presence, approximately 40 percent of this group consisted of rural Catholics fearful of the new communist regime. This "first wave" also included a much smaller group of pro-Western elites from Laos and Cambodia who, like the Vietnamese, were given priority refugee status by the U.S. government. The number of arrivals for all ethnic groups bottomed out in 1976, but, beginning in 1979, refugee arrivals skyrocketed and continued at high levels through 1983. This four-year period witnessed the arrival of approximately 472,000 "second wave" refugees, with 1980 (166,700) representing the greatest number of refugee arrivals in U.S. history. The flood of Vietnamese refugees during this period coincided with the "boat people" exodus as well as the Orderly Departure Program (ODP). The great number of arrivals was attributable in part to the inclusive nature of those departing under the ODP, which permitted the emigration of close family members left behind after 1975, as well as individuals and their families who had served as employees of the U.S. government and American businesses, former South Vietnamese military personnel, and those who had studied in the U.S. Laotian arrivals consisted largely of those lowland Lao and Hmong who had filled UN camps in Thailand a few years before. Cambodian refugee arrivals represented those UN camps refugees who escaped Pol Pot's "killing fields."

The post-1983 migration period consisted of "third wave" refugee arrivals. From 1984 to 1995, the volume of Vietnamese arrivals remained steady, averaging some 26,500 per year. The source of this rather large number of third-wave refugees is traced to released detainees (and their families) from government indoctrination camps, while others came under the 1980 Refugee Act, which allowed individuals to join family members already residing in the United States. These arrival statistics do not include seventy-one thousand Amerasians who were the discriminated offspring of wartime American and Vietnamese unions. Unlike the Cambodians whose arrivals virtually ended in 1991, the flow of refugees from Laos experienced a substantial increase during the early 1990s. The majority of these refugees were Hmong, who, after many years of refusing sponsorship to resettle in the United States because of the hope of eventually returning to their highland homelands, finally decided to join their cultural kin in the United States. In response to the substantial decrease in the number of Lao and Cambodians seeking refuge in Thai camps, the U.S. government stopped actively interviewing refugees in 1997.

In sum, approximately 1.1 million, or 60 percent of the total number of refugees arriving in the United States between 1975 and 1995, originated from the three mainland Southeast Asian countries of Vietnam, Laos, and Cambodia. Refugees from Vietnam (including Amerasians) accounted for approximately 67 percent of the mainland Southeast Asian refugee population, while those from Laos and Cambodia comprised 20 percent and 13 percent, respectively. The Hmong comprised slightly less than half of the total refugees originating from Laos.[26]

## PRIMARY RESETTLEMENT AND SECONDARY MIGRATION

The geographic patterns of the three waves of mainland Southeast Asian refugee resettlement in the United States have been influenced by a complex set of social and economic factors. In general, the spatial distribution of the four refugee groups has not been uniform, in that some states or regions of the country possess far greater concentrations of refugees than others. Before examining the spatial distribution of each of the four principal refugee groups, we will first assess the geographic factors that impacted the overall resettlement process. In so doing, it is important to recognize that the importance of each factor varies through time from one group to another.

## Primary Resettlement

Unlike earlier waves of immigrant groups, the size of the mainland Southeast Asian communities residing in the United States before 1975 was not sufficiently large to influence the locational decision-making process of the new refugees. During the first half of the 1970s, for example, there were only some fourteen thousand Vietnamese in the United States, and most were semipermanent residents represented by university students, diplomats, and others connected to the U.S. war effort. The combined numbers from Cambodia and Laos were approximately six hundred for the same period.[27] In the absence of substantial preexisting communities, the geography of first-wave resettlement was molded by U.S. government policies to disperse the refugees as widely as possible to prevent the overconcentration of refugees in one region or a handful of regions in the country. An equally important and practical consideration for the dispersal policy was to prevent overburdening the social infrastructure of the states and counties in which the immigrants settled. The policy was also guided by the assumption that assimilation into American society would progress more rapidly if refugees were geographically scattered within the larger host culture.[28]

Also influencing a more geographically balanced pattern of primary resettlement was the administrative vehicle harnessed by the government to disperse refugees. After the U.S. Immigration and Naturalization Service conducted interviews and granted refugees admission into the United States, a number of uncoordinated and autonomous voluntary agencies, or "Volags," representing particular ethnic, religious, and secular interests were authorized to obtain sponsors for the individual refugees and their families across the country. The potential sponsors obtained by the Volags varied from individuals to families, churches, and even civic groups.[29] The most aggressive Volags were Church World Services, Immigration and Refugee Services of America, the International Rescue Committee, United States Catholic Charities, the Lutheran Immigration and Refugee Service, and the World Relief Corporation. Of these, the United States Catholic Conference (USCC) has serviced the greatest number of refugees. With its 119 diocesan refugee offices, the USCC administers a variety of programs to assist in refugee adjustment, particularly in the area of economic self-sufficiency. Because the Volags and their local offices were scattered across the country, the government viewed these volunteer agencies as an ideal mechanism to achieve its goal of refugee dispersion. The dispersion goals for the first-wave Vietnamese refugees were generally achieved, although states west of the Mississippi River received a larger proportion of refugees than eastern states.[30] Indeed, the first-wave refugees were placed in 813 different ZIP code regions in all fifty states, and about 60 percent were resettled in ZIP code areas with fewer than five hundred refugees.[31] Although Volags were able to obtain sponsors in small communities, the tendency was for refugees to settle primarily in urban areas or in settlements that were part of a larger urban area because these volunteer agencies were located in metropolitan communities.[32]

For a handful of reasons, the government goal of refugee dispersion began to breakdown with the arrival of the "second wave" refugees from UN camps during the 1979–1983 period. Most important of these causes was the fact that residents of first-wave communities were now capable of acting as sponsors for these new second-wave refugees, most of whom were relatives of earlier arrivals. By the early 1980s, for example, some two-thirds of the arrivals possessed either close or distant relatives already established in the United States.[33] In recognition of the contribution of kin ties to the successful assimilation of newer refugees, Volag policies were modified to promote the formation of refugee settlement clusters. The third-wave refugees comprising those that were released from indoctrination camps, as well as those arriving under the explicit policy umbrella of family repatriation, exhibited a similar pattern of primary resettlement in locations where relatives functioned as sponsors.

### Secondary Migration

The more recent geographic concentration of refugees in a handful of states or regions has been reinforced by the process of secondary migration. Once settled, however, refugees had the choice either to remain in the location of initial settlement determined by the sponsor or to engage in secondary migration to a more preferred location. In general, the decision to engage in secondary migration is made within the first few years of initial settlement before adjustment to a new environment is complete. By the early 1980s, some 45 percent of 1975 refugees, for example, were living in a state other than the state in which they first settled.[34]

For secondary migrants, the decision to relocate was influenced by environmental, economic, and sociocultural push and pull forces.[35] Environmentally, states with warmer climates appear to attract large numbers of refugees. States that have a substantial Asian or mainland Southeast Asian first-wave community are more likely to draw large numbers of secondary migrants. Also important is the level of state-supported financial and medical assistance available to refugees. States that have eliminated or reduced financial assistance tend to lose refugees over time through secondary migration. Those states with robust or healthy economies also tend to attract greater numbers of secondary migrants. In a mutually reinforcing relationship, healthy economies are also characterized by generous levels of financial assistance. While these push and pull factors have been identified as significant to the general process of secondary migration among all four refugee groups, their relative importance to each group has varied substantially.

## POPULATION DISTRIBUTION

After fifteen years of primary resettlement and secondary migration, the population distribution of refugees and their first-generation offspring is now characterized by substantial concentration. The 1990 census enumerated 984,074 Vietnamese, Lao, Hmong, and Cambodians. While this figure is considered by observers to be below the actual numerical totals, owing to the fact that some 220,000 Vietnamese of ethnic-Chinese extraction from the three countries under study were enumerated as Chinese, the discrepancy does not significantly alter the general spatial distribution of population.[36] Mainland Southeast Asian settlement is now highly concentrated in seventeen states, each of which possess 1 percent or more of the national total (Table 10.1). California alone contains approximately 46 percent of Vietnamese, Lao, Hmong, and Cambodians. When coupled with the states of Washington and Oregon, these three West Coast core states now account for slightly

**Table 10.1    States with Greater Than One Percent of Total Number of Vietnamese, Lao, Hmong, and Cambodians, 1990.**

| State | Number | Percentage |
|-------|--------|------------|
| California | 457,907 | 46.53 |
| Texas | 82,388 | 8.37 |
| Minnesota | 36,763 | 3.73 |
| Washington | 35,734 | 3.63 |
| Massachusetts | 2,498 | 3.30 |
| Virginia | 28,032 | 2.84 |
| Wisconsin | 23,117 | 2.34 |
| Pennsylvania | 22,859 | 2.32 |
| New York | 22,806 | 2.31 |
| Florida | 18,603 | 1.89 |
| Louisiana | 17,887 | 1.81 |
| Illinois | 16,713 | 1.69 |
| Oregon | 14,435 | 1.46 |
| Georgia | 12,710 | 1.29 |
| Colorado | 10,975 | 1.11 |
| Michigan | 10,882 | 1.11 |
| Maryland | 10,629 | 1.08 |
| Total | | 86.81 |

Source: *Census of Population and Housing, 1990, Summary File 3A* (Washington, D. C.: Bureau of the Census, 1990).

more than half of the national total. The second largest regional concentration is in the South Central states, anchored by the second leading state of Texas. Coupled with Louisiana and Florida, this region accounts for 12 percent of mainland Southeast Asians in the country. The third leading regional concentration, with 11 percent of the total, is the Atlantic coast states, from Massachusetts southward to Virginia. The last and smallest settlement core is the Midwest, particularly centered on Minnesota and Wisconsin; these two states account for 80 percent of the region's 9 percent total of mainland Southeast Asians. Some regions are conspicuous by their relative absence of Vietnamese, Lao, Hmong, and Cambodians. With the exception of Georgia, the high economic growth states of the Atlantic Southeast do not have particularly large concentrations. Again, with the exception of Colorado, the Great Plains and Interior Mountain states have not attracted a large number of refugees and their relatives. The spatial distribution of the four individual ethnic groups is also distinctive and based on factors relating to the migration history and the specific sociocultural characteristics of each group.

### Vietnamese

The geographic distribution of Vietnamese is somewhat balanced in the sense that many states now possess relatively sizable communities (Fig. 10.3). There exist, however, identifiable regional cores in the West Coast, South Central, and Northeast states. The most basic explanation for this pattern may be that the reception centers for the initial 130,000 first-wave refugees were established at Camp Pendleton, California; Fort Chafee,

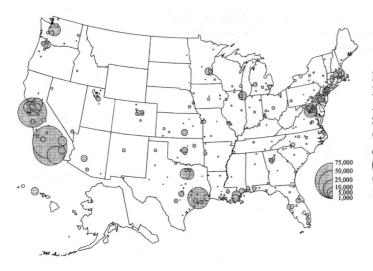

Figure 10.3   Population
Distribution by Counties with
More Than 100 Vietnamese.
Source: U.S. Bureau of the
Census, *Census of Population
and Housing 1990*
(Washington, D.C.: U.S.
Government Printing Office,
1990), Summary File 3A.

Arkansas; Eglin Air Force Base, Florida; and Fort Indiantown Gap, Pennsylvania. Each of these reception centers is now located in the heart of or adjacent to dense present-day regional Vietnamese concentrations. It must also be noted that Volags in the larger urban places of these regions secured numerous sponsors. Functioning as centers of initial settlement, these urban places attracted substantial numbers of second- and third-wave refugee relatives and friends throughout the 1980s. The role of climate as an environmental pull migration factor must be deemphasized because three of the four reception centers were located in Sunbelt states and thus had a direct impact on the initial settlement pattern and subsequent secondary migration process. The factor of a preexisting ethnic community certainly supercedes the environmental factor in explaining secondary migration patterns.

Accounting for some 47 percent of the national total, California has the greatest number of Vietnamese. Two concentrations stand out: four counties of the Los Angeles region account for half of the state's total and one-quarter of all Vietnamese in the entire country. As an economically dynamic and multicultural Pacific Rim urban region, Los Angeles has attracted many ethnic secondary migrants, of which the Vietnamese are but one.[37] The number of Vietnamese in Orange County alone exceeds the total in the state of Texas, the second leading state in terms of ethnic Vietnamese residents. Among recent Orange County home buyers, for example, the common Vietnamese surname Nguyen outnumbered the common English surname of Smith by two to one.[38] The six-county San Francisco Bay region has some 30 percent of the state total, with Santa Clara County and its major urban center of San Jose accounting for 65 percent of the region's ethnic-Vietnamese population. Being one of the most robust regional economies in the country, the much smaller West Coast concentration centered on Seattle and King County provides a good example of the role of economic opportunity in the process of secondary migration.

Much like California, the majority of Texas's ethnic-Vietnamese population of 82,388 are located in the two largest urban areas of Houston and Dallas–Fort Worth; approximately 48 percent of the state total are located in Harris County in the south and

Dallas and Tarrant Counties in the north. The Texas and Louisiana Vietnamese concentrations were first established by first-wave refugees from the Fort Chafee, Arkansas, reception center. Much like other rural states that received first-wave migrants, Arkansas did not retain many of its reception center refugees. Virginia has approximately 28,000 ethnic Vietnamese, with some 55 percent of the state total being residents of the Washington, D.C., suburban county of Fairfax. Coupled with neighboring Arlington and Montgomery Counties in Maryland, this largest of East Coast Vietnamese population concentrations provides a good illustration of the linkages between primary resettlement and increased agglomeration through secondary migration. After being processed at nearby Fort Indiantown Gap, Pennsylvania, many of the first-wave refugees settled in the Washington, D.C., urban region owing to the previous ties of the educated elite to American government and military personnel.[39] Ethnic Vietnamese were only second in number to Salvadorans entering the metropolitan region during the early 1990s.[40]

## Laotians

Totaling 147,375 persons, ethnic Lao represent the third largest group of mainland Southeast Asians in the United States. Although the number of Laotians is substantially fewer than the Vietnamese, their geographic distribution is quite similar in two respects (Fig. 10.4). First, Laotian population distributions are balanced in that many states possess substantial Lao communities. Second, those states and urban regions supporting large Vietnamese communities are the same ones that contain the largest Lao population concentrations. Lao are primarily situated in California, which accounts for some 41 percent of the national population. Although the greater Los Angeles and San Francisco urban regions support substantial Lao communities, the counties of San Diego and the less urbanized Central Valley counties of Sacramento, San Joaquin, Fresno, and Stanislaus con-

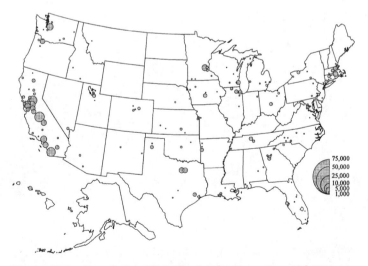

**Figure 10.4    Population Distribution by Counties with More Than 100 Laotians. Source: U.S. Bureau of the Census, *Census of Population and Housing 1990* (Washington, D.C.: U.S. Government Printing Office, 1990), Summary File 3A.**

tain almost half of the state's Lao population. There is no doubt that the presence of a large number of Hmong in these same counties is an example of settlement synergy between these two ethnic populations from the same country. A similar pattern is observed in the Upper Midwest, where Lao and Hmong concentrations are spatially coincident. While Texas supports the second greatest concentration of Lao in the country, the number of Lao in Minnesota and Wisconsin almost equals that of Texas.

## Hmong

Numbering only 94,439 individuals, the distribution of this smallest of the mainland Southeast Asian groups presents an intriguing geographic pattern for two reasons (Fig. 10.5). First, the Hmong population is not widely dispersed but highly concentrated in the states of California, Minnesota, and Wisconsin. Together, these three states are home to 89 percent of the Hmong in the country. California accounts for 52 percent of the national total, while Minnesota and Wisconsin account for 19 percent and 18 percent, respectively. Second, the distribution of the Hmong, with the exception of Minneapolis–St. Paul, is primarily concentrated in small to medium-sized urban regions rather than in large cities. In California, some 60 percent of the Hmong population are located in the smaller urban places of the Central Valley. The medium-sized city of Fresno, often referred to as the "Hmong capital" of the United States, possesses 37 percent of the state's Hmong population and an astounding 19 percent of the country's total. While Minnesota's Hmong population is primarily concentrated in the urbanized Ramsey and Hennepin Counties, the approximately seventeen thousand Hmong in Wisconsin are spread out among seven counties; Milwaukee has 20 percent of the state's total, but 55 percent of Hmong in Wisconsin are located in the lightly urbanized counties of Marathon, La Crosse, Eau Claire, Brown, Sheboygan, and Outagamie.

**Figure 10.5   Population Distribution by Counties with More Than 100 Hmong. Source: U.S. Bureau of the Census, *Census of Population and Housing 1990* (Washington, D.C.: U.S. Government Printing Office, 1990), Summary File 3A.**

Hmong concentrations in these three states, and the tendency for small and medium-sized urban settlement, are directly linked to the deep-seated Hmong desire to preserve a modified clan-based society in the new American context. Clan and family groups were broken up in Laos because of military conflict and were split apart even further while fleeing to Thai camps, and then again upon entry into the United States. The handful of Hmong concentrations in the United States are viewed, then, as the final stage of a long-term reunification process.[41] The earliest Hmong enclaves were in Minnesota and Wisconsin, two states whose citizens have actively functioned as sponsors.[42] Through the process of secondary migration, dispersed individuals and families from elsewhere have joined their fellow clan members and leaders. Throughout the late 1970s and early 1980s, many Hmong entering the country from Thai camps continued on to the Upper Midwest as their initial settlement location.

On the West Coast, Hmong refugees continued to be placed in communities throughout the San Francisco and Los Angeles urban regions. Clan leaders, however, became concerned by the erosion of clan authority and the changing nature of women's traditional roles. In response to these concerns, the clan leader Vang Chao, the nephew of the Hmong military leader Vang Pao and leader of the Vang clan, moved his family to the small San Joaquin Valley community of Merced. Attractive because of its strong agricultural base, it was thought that traditional Hmong cultural life might be better preserved in this slower-paced environment. Other clan leaders were actively recruited to establish satellite enclaves in other small towns of the Central Valley. A Hmong urban archipelago thus emerged that centered on the larger nodes of Fresno and Merced, where secondary migration now accounts for at least 60 percent of the population.

The influence of clan-based secondary migration should not be underestimated. Indeed, because of poor employment opportunities in the San Joaquin Valley, some members of the Vang clan have purchased land in western North Carolina and have attracted a substantial number of clan members to work in newly established poultry-raising facilities. Called Som Thong, this recently founded settlement is named after a major refugee stronghold town in Laos to which many Hmong were forced to migrate after the first communist offensive in the 1960s.

### Cambodians

Totaling 149,047 individuals in 1990, Cambodians are the second largest mainland Southeast Asian group in the country. Their regional distributions are generally similar to the other three groups with strong concentrations in California, but as we have noted with the Vietnamese and Laotians, a relatively balanced dispersion exists (Fig. 10.6). California accounts for some 48 percent of the national total, with 39 percent of the state's total residing in Los Angeles County alone. Additional concentrations comprising another 38 percent of the state's total include, in descending order, the counties of San Joaquin, San Diego, Orange, Santa Clara, and Fresno. Outside the West Coast states, the Cambodians share with the Hmong the distributional trait of a smaller but strong secondary core east of the Mississippi River. Urban centers in Massachusetts, Rhode Island, New York, and Pennsylvania account for approximately 18 percent of the Cambodian national total. Approximately half of the East Coast Cambodian population resides in Massachusetts, where it is highly concentrated in the three counties of Suffolk (Boston), and in the medium-sized cities of the neigh-

**Figure 10.6    Population Distribution by Counties with More Than 100 Cambodians. Source: U.S. Bureau of the Census, *Census of Population and Housing 1990* (Washington, D.C.: U.S. Government Printing Office, 1990), Summary File 3A.**

boring counties of Essex and Middlesex. These concentrations are a result of the "Cambodian Cluster Resettlement Project" of the early 1980s.

## URBAN RESIDENTIAL PATTERNS

Mainland Southeast Asians have settled in a wide spectrum of locations embedded within a larger urban agglomeration. These include traditional downtown immigrant enclaves, transitional residential and commercial zones of the midcity, and more modern and spacious suburban landscapes. The Minneapolis–St. Paul urban region exemplifies a classic ethnic inner-city enclave.[43] Here, not only Hmong but also Vietnamese and Cambodians have concentrated in near-downtown neighborhoods straddling two significant radiating transport corridors. Small pockets of mainland Southeast Asians are also found in selected neighborhoods throughout the city. While mainland Southeast Asians occupy 80 percent of all public housing units, they share the more dispersed low-rent neighborhoods with African Americans, Latin Americans, and whites. The large number of mainland Southeast Asians has created a demand for ethnic business along one of the radiating corridors. Once a prime example of inner-city urban blight associated with economic decline, the ethnic stores have now revitalized the corridor. As an alternative to being employed within the larger economy, many mainland Southeast Asians have opened small grocery stores, restaurants, bakeries, dressmaking shops, and financial service establishments. As is usual with newly arrived immigrants, business owners live in the same neighborhood as both their businesses and co-ethnic customers.

The Hmong enclaves of Fresno provide an instructive example of the persistence of cultural ties to the past.[44] The majority of Hmong live in subsidized Section 8 apartments just on the periphery of downtown (Fig. 10.7). Anchoring this assemblage of non-contiguous Hmong enclaves is a neighborhood commonly referred to as Ban Vinai,

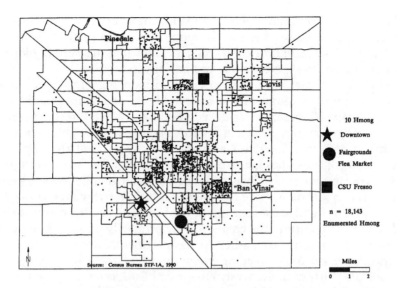

**Figure 10.7    Distribution of Hmong in Fresno, California. Source: Miyares (1996), 105. Copyright permission: Selbstverlag des Instituts für Geographie der Universität Innsbruck.**

named after the largest of the Hmong refugee camps in Thailand. Functioning as an important port of entry for primary migrants who were long-term refugee camp inhabitants, the place name reflects the public assistance or dependency culture that emerged before arrival in the United States. Over time, some Hmong families have also moved to the suburban edge of Fresno into Section 8 housing in Pinedale and Clovis. Many of these Hmong enclaves support grocery stores selling a wide variety of imported foods and sundry goods that are critical to maintaining cultural traditions (Fig. 10.8). Complementing the fixed place commercial establishments are open-air flea markets where a

**Figure 10.8    A Clan-Owned Hmong Grocery Store in Fresno, California. Members of the same clan are expected to patronize their own clan store. Source: Photo courtesy of Ines M. Miyares.**

wide array of common consumer goods are sold, together with Hmong specialty craft goods produced by enclave residents at discount or bargain prices (Fig. 10.9). Foremost among the latter are *pa ndau*, "flowery cloths" and Hmong ceremonial outfits commonly worn during courting, New Year, and burial ceremonies.

Another example of past refugee experiences influencing enclave formation within a large urban community is found in the greater New Orleans metropolitan area where some twelve thousand Vietnamese reside. Approximately five thousand individuals have settled on the eastern suburban fringe in the three contiguous neighborhoods of Versailles Arms (which is a 402-unit Section 8 apartment complex) and the duplex and single-family subdivisions of Versailles Gardens and Village de l'Est.[45] Low occupancy rates in Versailles Arms during a period of local economic slowdown allowed Associated Catholic Charities to reserve apartment space for one thousand first-wave refugees who were also joined by other primary and secondary migrants. Vietnamese now comprise 50 percent of the Versailles Arms population, the balance being primarily African Americans. Through social and economic mobility, Versailles Arms apartment dwellers have moved into the adjacent Versailles Gardens, displacing virtually all of the earlier Anglo and African American residents. Farther to the west, Village de l'Est has become a succession frontier with a mix of Vietnamese and African American residents. This enclave provides a classic example of a refugee "urban village" characterized by a homogeneous cultural world. Some 60 percent of Vietnamese adults originated from the two rural Catholic parishes in northern Vietnam most impacted by the 1954 southward migration of refugees. Much like so many mainland Southeast Asian communities, these enclaves are not just an assemblage of compatriots but a regrouping through secondary migration of relatives, friends, and neighbors from their rural homelands. Lining much of the primary boulevard that separates Versailles Arms and Versailles Gardens are forty-seven commercial establishments, many of which are owned by ethnic-Chinese families who came from the

Figure 10.9   Hmong Flea Market in Fresno, California. The embroidery on the baby backpack is an example of the hand-stitched *pa ndau*. Source: Photo courtesy of Ines M. Miyares.

same rural regions in South Vietnam; the traditional merchant-client relationships have thus been reproduced in a new land. A Saturday morning fresh produce market supplied by enclave vegetable gardens only adds to the enclave's sense of past place in a preexisting American suburban location.

The great size of both the mainland Southeast Asian population and the Los Angeles urban area makes for a yet another settlement pattern. Here, many mainland Southeast Asians, particularly Vietnamese and Cambodians, are located in certain areas of concentration, defined as areal units possessing 3.7 percent or more of that group's population in the five-county Los Angeles urban region.[46] Concentrations of both Vietnamese and Cambodians are found in older central city areas of Los Angeles and Long Beach and in the neighboring Orange County city of Santa Ana. The second zone of concentration consists of older suburban areas; only Vietnamese exhibit this pattern of residence, particularly in Monterrey Park and the Orange County towns of Garden Grove and Westminster just west of Santa Ana. The three concentrations of Santa Ana, Garden Grove, and Westminster possess half of the county's Vietnamese population. Dotted with gleaming malls built with primarily Vietnamese-Chinese investment, Westminister is the Vietnamese commercial and cultural center of the county.[47] With a freeway exit sign marked "Little Saigon," Westminster is perhaps the Vietnamese commercial and cultural capital of the United States as well. Although characteristic of more affluent Asian immigrant groups, these "ethnoburbs" have substantial scale of economies based on local, regional, national, and Pacific Rim ties.[48] The overall settlement pattern is more spatially dispersed, however, than what might be expected. Even during the early years of initial resettlement, for example, some 363 of the 413 census tracts of Orange County possessed Vietnamese residents.[49] While the tendency for newer and poorer immigrants to live within zones of ethnic concentration continues to be strong, the use of automobiles and telephones allowing contact with the zone of ethnic concentration has allowed for greater spatial dispersion of immigrants throughout the larger Los Angeles urban region.[50]

The greater Washington, D.C., urban region was settled primarily by an affluent and educated slice of the first-wave Vietnamese refugees who have scattered throughout the adjacent Virginia and Maryland suburban landscape (Fig. 10.10). The distinct absence of Vietnamese in the District of Columbia is noteworthy; the four Virginia and Maryland suburban counties account for approximately 97 percent of Vietnamese in the metro region. In addition, the relatively even spreads of Vietnamese across many suburban census tracts is equally apparent. In 1990, not one of the Virginia census tracts supported more than 9 percent of the total Vietnamese population, while many were characterized by 1 percent or less. The landscape impact of Vietnamese residential space is thus diffuse as the more affluent have settled in culturally heterogeneous neighborhoods.[51] In the Virginia counties of Arlington and Fairfax, settlement spreads in a leapfrog fashion from the 1920s street car commercial center of Clarendon in Arlington to the automobile suburbs of Falls Church, Tysons Corner, and Annandale.

As in southern California, residence within an enclave is no longer a requirement for individuals and families to be part of the larger ethnic community. To cater to the dispersed population, numerous noncontiguous Vietnamese commercial complexes have emerged along the major roads and highways leading westward from Clarendon. In each case, these strip malls and plazas once catered to the pre-Vietnamese suburban populations and have now been recycled by Vietnamese entrepreneurs to serve a

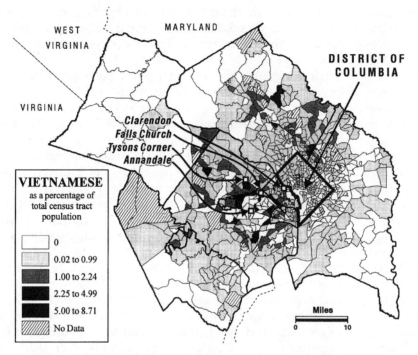

**Figure 10.10    Distribution of Vietnamese by Census Tract in the Greater Washington, D.C., Urban Region. Source: Modified from an unpublished map by Joseph Wood.**

distinct suburban culture group (Fig. 10.11). Often possessing names of shopping districts in Saigon, these commercial complexes form a central place hierarchy that serves daily and weekly automobile-based suburban shoppers, and less frequent Vietnamese visitors from up and down the East Coast.

## SOCIAL ADAPTATION: AGE, RELIGION, AND FOOD HABITS

Lacking significant exposure to Western culture, the majority of refugees have experienced heightened social distress because of problems of "cultural compatibility." One way in which acculturation has proceeded has been through their U.S.-born children who have their feet in both social worlds. At the community level, a host of local Mutual Assistance Associations (MAAs) has also emerged designed to aid in a variety of social and economic adaptation needs. MAAs are generally of five different types: religious, political, self-help, professional, and student.[52] A list of self-help MAAs in the Versailles community in New Orleans, for example, includes committees to collect funds for burials, the construction of fishing boats, aid for new refugee arrivals, a men's club to promote neighborhood safety, and a war-veterans association.[53] Although MAAs have proved helpful in facilitating social adaptation, individuals and families continue to be confronted with numerous inter- and intracultural conflicts, the most important of which we will now address.

**Figure 10.11    Eden Center Shopping Complex in the Seven Corners Area of Fairfax County, Virginia. While serving a diverse economic function, the complex also provides a social place where Vietnamese Americans can act Vietnamese. The yellow- and red-striped flag of former South Vietnam is a common landscape feature of enclaves established by first-wave refugees. Source: Photo courtesy of Joseph Wood.**

## Age: The Elderly and the Young

Social adaptation has proven to be the most difficult to those who arrived in the United States as adults, particularly the elderly. Being wrenched from communities where they long lived, the elderly experience a profound loss of sense of place. Being consumed by thoughts of "past place" often leads to feelings of powerlessness, which in turn may engender various emotional and mental health problems.[54] For example, the elderly generally experience greater difficulty in learning the English language and consequently find it more difficult to function in American society. Simple tasks such as shopping, traveling, reading street signs, applying for social services, visiting the doctor, and phoning police may produce great anxiety.[55]

The loss of superior status traditionally accorded the elderly in their homelands also contributes to a sense of powerlessness as younger adults, with their superior knowledge of American culture and language, become more central to the family decision-making process and traditional familial roles become reversed. One study concludes that if a household has rapidly acculturating teenage children, psychological stress among the elderly is likely to increase because of the attendant intergenerational conflicts.[56] The loneliness and despair created by the loss of place, family status, culture, and absence of language skills are poignantly expressed in the words of an inner-city, apartment-dwelling Hmong grandmother who worries aloud that when her grandchildren speak to each other in English, she loses her "small place in the big city."[57]

At the opposite end of the social adaptation process are the young. This group includes those who became refugees during their first years of life as well as those born in the United States. Members of this so-called 1.5 generation experience a very different adaptation process because they are pulled in the two directions of the past and future worlds and thus are expected to conform simultaneously to the culture of their elders while adapting to the dominant American culture. Occupying this "in-between" cultural position in the adaptation process engenders a substantial amount of conflict and anxiety. Most children of mainland Southeast Asian refugees live with extraordinarily high levels of familial expectation, whether it be of the nuclear or extended variety.[58] These expectations have often expressed themselves through two behavioral patterns that contest the traditional assimilation models explaining conformity to the host society.[59]

The first behavioral pattern stresses the accumulation of traditional social capital through high educational achievement.[60] Adherence to the traditional cultural orientations of strong family bonds, intimate involvement with the ethnic community, and a strong work ethic positively impact educational achievement, which in turn leads to successful adaptation. Those youths who are directed and provided support through the traditional social capital of the community demonstrate individual behavior patterns that allow for greater social and economic mobility within the host society. In this sense, identification with the past has facilitated adaptation and reduced the likelihood that the youth will become part of the host society underclass. Those youths who too rapidly dispose of their traditional culture run the risk of becoming marginal to both the ethnic community and the host society. Becoming too quickly "Americanized" is a symptom of lower educational achievement.[61]

The second behavioral pattern frequently associated with the adaptation of mainland Southeast Asian youth has been close spatial interaction with ethnic peers. Hmong college students in California's Central Valley who live away from their parents have formed their own age-specific and near-campus apartment enclave where a social environment of cultural security and reinforcement is afforded by students sharing apartment space.[62] The spatial separation of the young from their parent's enclaves has in turn created a new Hmong enclave, but with modified cultural attributes. For example, social and sporting events sponsored by the Hmong Student Association are derived from the host culture yet provide opportunities for social networking that occurred in previous generations within the context of the clan or the village. A university education within the context of Hmong tradition causes conflicts for those single women who eschew the Hmong tradition of marrying in their late teens. Often forced to confront tradition, resourceful female college students have participated in an increasingly popular Hmong-based Internet dating service with potential mates in distant enclaves.

## Religion and Adaptation

Given the pervasive role that religion played in the lives of mainland Southeast Asians, it is appropriate that an assessment of religious continuity and change be included in our analysis of social adaptation in the United States. Although research data are still somewhat restricted by the relatively short period of refugee settlement, it is sufficient for us to identify some initial trends and patterns among those whose faiths include Buddhism, Confucianism, Taoism, animism, Catholicism, and Protestantism.

### Increased Religiosity

In studying the religious adaptations of mainland Southeast Asian refugees, it is necessary to recall that a substantial number of Volags were religiously based. As a result, many of the refugees became deeply appreciative of the physical and emotional support extended by these churches, and they either developed higher levels of religious participation than previously had characterized their lives or joined the sponsoring church as new converts. In searching for explanations for the increased levels of individual religiosity reported by the majority of the migrants, we would also do well to remember that the refugee experience itself, with all of its attendant heartache and loss, resulted in intensified feelings of spiritual need among most of the immigrants.[63]

One of the most pronounced examples of the pattern of increased refugee devotion and strictness of religious observance has been the Versailles Vietnamese population of New Orleans, which upon arrival was approximately 87 percent Catholic and 10 percent Buddhist.[64] Ethnic Catholicism has played and continues to occupy such a prominent role in Versailles that the Archdiocese of New Orleans authorized the creation of a new parish to service the community, which now possesses both the new eight hundred–seat Mary Queen of Vietnam church and a second smaller, chapel-like, relic-filled edifice called the Church of the Vietnamese Martyrs (Fig. 10.12).[65] The parish also built a day care and nursery school on the grounds of the larger structure and sponsors a wide range of supplemental activities, including mental health and English-language classes, religious processions, and youth support groups.

**Figure 10.12   A Mosaic on the Wall of Mary Queen of Vietnam Church in the Versailles Enclave of New Orleans. Full of Vietnamese who were instrumental in the spread and maintenance of Catholicism, coupled with its map of Vietnam, this church makes for a place bound to spiritual experience for the faithful. Source: Authors.**

A second example of intensified loyalty and increased religious strictness among Indochinese migrants is the Cambodian community of Boston. Prior to their arrival in the United States, most of the Cambodians were Theravada Buddhists, but some of the elites had converted to Roman Catholicism, and others had joined Protestant denominations. Many of these conversions occurred in Thai refugee camps. Once established in the greater Boston metropolitan area, members of the six Cambodian Protestant congregations became far more dogmatic in doctrine and intolerant of their fellow Cambodians whose beliefs or practices differed from their own.[66] Specifically, the Cambodian Protestants adopted an inflexible stance against the consumption of alcohol and tobacco and music and dancing. Perhaps in part as a reaction to the criticism of their Protestant minority brethren, well over 90 percent of the Boston Cambodians have chosen to retain Buddhism as an expression of their ethnic identity.

### Conversion to New Faiths

While many of the refugees, both Christian and Buddhist, have chosen to adopt an increased level of religiosity as a means of expressing continuing ethnic identity, others have chosen to convert to new faiths as a more dramatic expression of cultural adaptation. Precise counts of the proportion of immigrants who have converted are not available for the refugee population as a whole, but a nationwide telephone survey indicated that 39 percent of respondents had changed their religious affiliation subsequent to their arrival in the United States.[67] This figure is consistent with the 33 percent reported for Hmong conversions to the Mennonite faith in southwestern Ontario and the 36.5 percent for mainland Southeast Asian immigrants residing in Utah.[68] The detailed findings from the Utah study express a widely reported pattern of the majority of refugee conversions being from Buddhism and other East Asian–based faiths to religions of Western origin and identity, rather than vice versa (Table 10.2). Overall, it appears that the Hmong have been the ethnic group most inclined to adopt a new religion in America and the Vietnamese the least likely to do so. Possible reasons for the higher levels of Hmong receptivity to new faiths include the historic persecutions of Hmong minority populations by the dominant lowland Buddhist populations, the establishment of Christian communities among the hill peoples in the early twentieth century, the close political ties in Laos of many Hmong to the U.S. government, and the failure of shamanism to produce desired results in the new American setting.[69]

**Table 10.2    Religious Conversions of Mainland Southeast Asian Immigrants Residing in Utah.**

| Religion | Percent Practicing in Homeland | Percent Practicing in America | Percent Change |
|---|---|---|---|
| Buddhism | 52.1 | 33.7 | −18.4 |
| Traditional* | 28.1 | 18.9 | −9.2 |
| Roman Catholic | 7.3 | 11.6 | +4.3 |
| Protestant | 9.3 | 7.3 | −2.0 |
| Latter-day Saint | 0 | 18.9 | +18.9 |
| None | 2.1 | 8.4 | +6.3 |
| Other | 1.0 | 1.0 | 0 |

*Includes Confucianism, Taoism, and Ancestor Worship.
Source: Modified from Lewis, Fraser, and Pecora, 1988, 276.

Regardless of the ethnic groups or denominations involved, mainland Southeast Asian congregations share a number of common characteristics. Foremost among these is their affiliation with ethnic churches, whose services are conducted largely or entirely in the native language of the worshippers.[70] Not surprisingly, the ethnic congregations are presided over by ethnic pastors, the effectiveness of whose ministries is enhanced not only by their familiarity with the members' native language but also by their understanding of the congregations' culture and values. A second common attribute of the new Christian congregations is, in most instances, their relatively small number of members. Churches with actively participating memberships of fifty to one hundred are common, and it is not unusual to find attendance figures of twenty to thirty. A third characteristic, which is likely attributable at least in part to the modest number of members, is that most of the ethnic congregations meet in somewhat humble physical facilities, frequently consisting of rented units within strip malls and other properties originally developed for commercial purposes. A fourth feature is that the participation levels of women exceed those of men in most congregations. In sum, the ethnic churches provide spiritual support and continuity to their members while simultaneously expressing cultural adaptation to life in a dominant Christian host society.

### Religious Syncretism

The selective blending or mixing of new religious beliefs and practices with old doctrines and customs has often accompanied the mainland Southeast Asian adaptation process. One of the most visible expressions of religious syncretism is the observance of traditional Old World religious holidays. The eighty thousand–strong Vietnamese community of Orange County, California, for instance, has transformed the *Tet* New Year celebration into a huge public event observed at multiple locations.[71] The most important Old World Hmong holiday is the month-long New Year celebration observed during the change of the lunar calendar between late November and late December. In addition to wearing new clothing and offering gifts to parents and elders, the Hmong also travel through the forest from village to village to socialize and arrange marriages for their children. In an interesting adaptation, Hmong communities in the United States, separated in some instances by great distances, have adopted staggered New Year celebration dates to facilitate the perpetuation of traditional holiday travel patterns. Hmong in Minnesota, Wisconsin, and Michigan, for instance, observe the lunar New Year during the American Thanksgiving week, while their counterparts living in Merced and Fresno, California, celebrate the same holiday during American Christmas and New Year. The arrangement allows those who can afford to do so to continue the traditional practices of traveling from one community to another where socializing and the arranging of marriages can occur much as before.[72]

Another expression of religious syncretism is found among the Protestant Hmong community of Kansas City, Kansas.[73] Traditional animistic Hmong cosmology consisted of belief in ancestral and nature spirits. While the Kansas City Hmong continue to believe in the existence of these potentially harmful spirits, they have now embraced the concept that the Christian Trinity is more powerful than the Old World spirit forces. As a result, prayer and massage therapy have replaced shamanistic rituals when members are afflicted with fright illness, and protective neck, ankle, and wrist bands, which were formerly relied on to retain the soul at times of threatened departure, have been discarded. Additional examples of religious syncreticism include the case of a female

Hmong refugee who obtained a leadership role in the women's auxiliary of an ethnic Mennonite congregation but who also continued to function simultaneously as a traditional shaman, and Hmong couples in the Sacramento Valley who choose to be married in Christian ceremonies while wearing traditional dress.[74] Other researchers have observed New World Buddhist community worship services on Sunday, the traditional holy day of most Christian faiths.[75] Lastly, Buddhist monks have abandoned their Asian practice of walking through neighborhoods seeking donations of food and other forms of charity. Such donations are now delivered to the monks by the faithful, much as donations are offered in other Western Christian churches.[76]

### Generational Divergence and Future Prospects

In an attempt to anticipate future religious behavior, it is instructive to note the differences that have appeared between older refugees who fled their homelands as adults and their children who have been reared primarily in the United States or Canada. While it is too early to determine whether the members of this latter group will convert in significant numbers to faiths in which they were not raised, it is clear that the rising generation shows an increased capacity for and desire to adapt culturally to the dominant host society. One of the most common religious manifestations of this tendency has been for members of the younger generation to continue to associate themselves with their parents' faith but to do so in English, rather than their native language. In some instances, young adults from differing (and formerly often adversarial) ethnic and/or national backgrounds are now worshipping together while stressing their common Asian heritage and religious affiliation. For example, the Evergreen Baptist Church in the Los Angeles suburb of Rosemead offers English-language services to its nine hundred members representing seven different Asian groups.[77]

A second possible trend is the emergence of increasing levels of socioeconomic stratification among the churches and congregations serving mainland Southeast Asian refugees and their offspring. For instance, each of the four Buddhist pagodas serving the Vietnamese immigrant population of Montreal has evolved a distinct clientele: one serving an older and more affluent first-wave membership, the second ministering to more recent and economically poorer refugees of largely Chinese ancestry, the third drawing from the intellectual and professional classes, and the fourth acting primarily as an international and religious activities center.[78]

### Food and Dietary Adaptations

Because most refugees were either rural farmers themselves or closely linked to the land through extended family members, it is not surprising that many have continued to engage in some form of agricultural activity after their arrival in the United States. While the specific reasons for the persistence of this activity vary, at least three common motivations can be identified: (1) a desire to provide a familiar diet that serves as an expression of continuity in a time of accelerated change, (2) participation in an emotionally fulfilling avocation, and (3) a means of achieving some degree of economic gain in a setting where a limited knowledge of the English language and a lack of readily marketable job skills restrict most refugees' earning capacities. With their arrival in the United States, most of the Indochinese immigrants found themselves not only living in urban areas but also residing in large apartment complexes with limited access to land. Yet many of the refugees have managed to perpetuate selected components of their agrarian past.

### Provision of a Familiar Diet

The role of traditional foods serving as links to the past and thereby tempering the trauma of residence in a new cultural milieu is widely recognized.[79] Many refugees have no access to land and resort to cultivating herbs in pots and window boxes.[80] When land is available, the most common source of food crops is small gardens. Dooryard or back-yard gardens are found among the Vietnamese in New Orleans and the Hmong and Cambodians in Minnesota and California's Central Valley (Figs. 10.13 and 10.14).[81] Where land for home gardens is not available, some of the immigrants, including the Hmong and other highland Lao of the Central Valley of California and the Hmong of western Montana, have obtained permission to work community gardens.[82]

Regardless of their location, these gardens share four characteristics. The first is their relatively small size, with most averaging only about a hundred square meters of surface area. Second, they are worked very intensively, with Morris's comments that "each plant is watered individually" and "every inch is used efficiently" being typical observations.[83] The third shared feature is that the gardens occupy a semisubsistence niche very similar to the peasant farms of Southeast Asia, with the primary use of the produce being for home dietary needs and the surplus being sold at market. Finally, the gardens exhibit a strong ethnic character, with Old World crops such as bitter cucumber, smooth luffa, ginger, taro, lemongrass, yams, and malabar nightshade being widely cultivated.

**Figure 10.13    A Small-Scale, Fenced-In Kitchen Garden of Apartment-Dwelling Hmong in Fresno, California. The garden contains bananas, Asian pears, and various herbs, condiments, and vegetables. Source: Photo courtesy of Ines M. Miyares.**

**Figure 10.14    An Elderly Vietnamese Versailles Resident Cultivating a Small Backyard Vegetable Garden with Twenty or More Species of Plants. Source: Authors.**

### Gardening as Avocation

The second primary motivation for involvement in agriculture appears to be the emotional and physical benefits that many individuals receive through continued personal contact with the land. The advantages of "hortitherapy" extend to all racial and ethnic groups and include improved health, greater social interaction, and increased self-reliance and self-esteem.[84] Not surprisingly, the gardeners are drawn almost exclusively from the older generation, which has the closest ties to the land and also the greatest difficulty in adjusting to life in the host culture.[85] The age of gardeners in the Versailles Vietnamese community, for example, ranges from fifty-six to eighty-one years.[86]

### Gardening as Economic Gain

While backyard gardening has become the most widely practiced form of mainland Southeast Asian agriculture in the United States, recent years have witnessed the establishment of commercial agriculture in a number of locations. Chief among these is the central San Joaquin Valley of California (Fresno, Merced, San Joaquin, and Tulare Counties), where Hmong and other highland Lao farm thousands of acres of sugar peas, strawberries, cherry tomatoes, and eggplant.[87] Although bitter melon, Chinese long beans, lemongrass, green mustard, and other crops common to traditional diets are cultivated to a lesser extent, the commercial California farms differ markedly from the gardens discussed previously in the fact that their primary consumer market is the Anglo-American rather than the ethnic mainland Southeast Asian community. High-value commercial truck farming on a far more modest scale is also presently found among the Minnesota Hmong, Atlanta Hmong, New Orleans Vietnamese, and Falls Church, Virginia, Vietnamese.[88] In each of these instances, the produce consists mostly of leafy green and tuberous vegetables and squashes that are sold primarily to restaurants, wholesalers, and shoppers at farmer's markets. Another frequently reported characteristic is that the farms tend to be situated on the urban periphery, where undeveloped land is more readily available for renting or leasing. Very few of the farmers actually own their own land. The most common economic transition, then, has been from subsistence gardening in mainland Southeast Asia to urban truck gardening in the United States.

### Future Changes and Generational Issues

Because the members of the younger immigrant generations have adapted more rapidly to the host culture, future demand for ethnic foods among the mainland Southeast Asian population in the United States is likely to diminish steadily.[89] A revealing study related to generational differences in dietary habits of mainland Southeast Asian immigrants discovered a strong preference for traditional Southeast Asian foods among adults and an equally strong shift toward American foods by teenage family members.[90] These changing food consumption patterns, together with the increased educational achievements of the younger generations and their corresponding ability to secure good-paying white-collar jobs, suggest that the present widespread involvement in agriculture, and most especially in ethnic gardening, may gradually decline.

## ECONOMIC ADAPTATION

The contours of social adaptation are intimately intertwined with the processes of economic adaptation. Among the basic quantitative and mutually reinforcing socioeconomic indicators, household income is perhaps the most fundamental to understanding economic adaptation (Table 10.3). Significant income differences exist between the total U.S. population and the four mainland Southeast Asian ethnic groups, as well as between the ethnic groups themselves. It is noteworthy that median family income among the Vietnamese now approaches that of the total U.S. population. This is in part explained by the economic accomplishments of the first-wave refugees who were largely members of the upper and middle classes in South Vietnam. Although most of the first-wave refugees experienced substantial downward economic mobility during their first decade of residence in the United States, owing to their inability to obtain work that matched their prearrival employment status, by the mid-1980s income levels of this group had surpassed the median of the total U.S. population. The myth of the Vietnamese as a "model minority," then, is based solely on the positive economic adaptation experiences of the first-wave cohorts rather than on the population as a whole.[91]

While we recognize that income and employment levels have improved over time, the Hmong and Cambodians continue to be heavily reliant on some form of public assistance.[92] The factors influencing whether a household receives public assistance are complex and include the number of dependent children, which is especially high among the Hmong.[93] Reliance on public assistance may also be a reflection of levels of English proficiency, although linguistic ability has become less important for later arrivals who have been able to obtain employment through preexisting social networks. While English language proficiency does not appear to determine employment levels per se, it does affect wage or income status.

**Table 10.3    Social and Economic Characteristics of Mainland Southeast Asian Groups in the United States, Compared to the Total U.S. Population, 1990.**

|  | U.S. | Vietnamese | Laotian | Hmong | Cambodian |
|---|---|---|---|---|---|
| Total persons | 248,709,873 | 593,213 | 147,375 | 94,439 | 149,047 |
| *Nativity and immigration* | | | | | |
| Born in the U.S. (%) | 92.1 | 20.1 | 20.6 | 34.8 | 20.9 |
| *Age* | | | | | |
| Median Age | 33.0 | 25.6 | 20.5 | 12.7 | 19.7 |
| *Family contexts* | | | | | |
| Fertility (per woman 35–44) | 2.0 | 2.5 | 3.5 | 6.1 | 3.4 |
| *English (persons over 5)*[a] | | | | | |
| Speak English only (%) | 86.2 | 6.2 | 3.2 | 2.6 | 4.0 |
| Linguistically isolated (%) | 3.5 | 42.1 | 51.5 | 59.8 | 54.7 |
| *Education (persons over 25)* | | | | | |
| Less than 5th grade (%) | 2.7 | 11.4 | 33.9 | 54.9 | 40.7 |
| High school graduate (%) | 75.2 | 61.2 | 40.0 | 31.1 | 34.9 |
| College graduate (%) | 20.3 | 17.4 | 5.4 | 4.9 | 5.7 |
| *Employment (persons over 16)* | | | | | |
| In labor force (%) | 65.3 | 64.5 | 58.0 | 29.3 | 46.5 |
| Unemployed (%) | 6.3 | 8.4 | 9.3 | 17.9 | 10.3 |
| *Of those employed* | | | | | |
| White collar (%) | 58.1 | 47.1 | 20.2 | 31.7 | 33.1 |
| Blue collar (%) | 26.3 | 36.6 | 63.7 | 46.0 | 47.2 |
| *Income*[b] | | | | | |
| Median family income ($) | 35,225 | 30,550 | 23,101 | 14,327 | 18,126 |
| Below poverty (%) | 13.1 | 25.7 | 34.7 | 63.6 | 42.6 |
| Receives public assistance (%) | 7.5 | 24.5 | 35.4 | 67.1 | 51.1 |
| Own home | 64.2 | 40.1 | 24.0 | 11.1 | 19.7 |

Source: Modified from Rumbaut, 1996, 324
[a]Fertility: children ever born per woman aged 35 to 44.
[b]Linguistically isolated: a household in which no person age 14 or older speaks English only very well.

Wage levels and job type have also been influenced by employment experiences in the homelands. Unlike the Laotians, Hmong, and Cambodians, who were primarily rural folk with low levels of educational attainment, most Vietnamese had experienced urban life and attained higher levels of education. White-collar employment among the Vietnamese is thus substantially higher than that of the other three groups, and levels of blue-collar employment are substantially lower. Because blue-collar employment is often of the semiskilled or unskilled variety, even a two-worker household often finds it hard to make ends meet. Much like many other Americans living at the poverty level, many Hmong and Cambodian households have chosen to forgo low-wage employment and receive public assistance instead because the latter provides otherwise costly medical coverage.[94]

Public assistance is particularly high among the Hmong, whose largely rural background has made it very difficult to secure nonagricultural employment. For the elderly Hmong cohort, depending on others for employment or receiving public assistance is embarrassing and indeed entails the loss of self-esteem because of the basic self-sufficient nature of their past. A quote from an older Hmong man comparing his past and present situations illustrates this frustration:

> Over there [in Laos] you had to go into the jungle, cut a tree and work very hard in raising chickens and all that just to eat. But even though it is a poor country I could take care of myself there. Here you work day-to-day and year-to-year and you worry too much about your job and you hurt and you're scared. . . . Everything is money here. Over there even if you don't have a job, there is still a lot of land and you can grow potatoes and corn and rice and raise chickens and you are free yourself.[95]

Another important element of the economic adaptation process has been the redefining of traditional gender relationships to better meet the new social and economic circumstances of the host society. For mainland Southeast Asians, alteration of traditional gender relationships has been driven by the basic incompatibility between the Old World–based patriarchal and male-centered family structure and the new American economic environment. Under conditions of low-wage jobs or high unemployment among Vietnamese refugee men, it has been their wives who have assumed a larger role in generating family income.[96] This increased economic role in the United States is simply a magnification of women's roles in wartime Vietnam when many husbands were away at war. The low-paying service jobs in which women are often engaged allow for the continuation of public assistance that is critical for family survival. Where the husband's work is financially remunerative, the wife's income is used either for savings or for unexpected expenses that otherwise would force the family into debt. Whether functioning as a primary or secondary income earner, the wife's heightened economic role has transformed individual familial social roles; through greater economic empowerment, women have been able to challenge male authority. This process, however, does not represent a radical departure from tradition but simply takes place within the context of culturally proscribed gender relationships.[97]

The increased economic prominence among wives is even more heightened among the Hmong.[98] Formerly raised from boyhood to assume the superior roles of leaders and protectors in the Old World patriarchal clan system, adult Hmong men have experienced many more difficulties in adapting to American economic life than have their wives. The greater ability of Hmong women to learn English and consequently to generate more income, coupled with the difficulty of keeping a large extended family intact because of the spatial restrictions of apartment living, has increasingly reduced the role of the older adult Hmong male to a ceremonial figure. The economic relationship between husband and wife among the Lao has been far less contentious.[99] Both men and women, for example, view women's work as necessary to raise the family's level of living. This mutual workload philosophy is explained by the dictates of economic adaptation but is also traced to the premigration experiences of Lao women as petty entrepreneurs, as well as to the role of Theravada Buddhism predisposing men for the religious and political spheres of life.

## CONCLUSION

As the newest layer of America's Asian population mosaic, mainland Southeast Asians arrived not as economic immigrants, but as political refugees from devastated homelands. Because the wartime policies of the U.S. government in many instances purposefully created substantial refugee populations that either were connected to the American presence or would experience ruthless discrimination by the newly installed communist regimes, the United States has provided some one million Vietnamese, Laotians, Hmong, and Cambodians with permanent refuge.

Because primary resettlement locations were largely determined by geographically dispersed Volags and the first-wave reception centers, the initial spatial distribution of mainland Southeast Asian populations was relatively even. The secondary migration process, however, fueled by reunification of family and friends, has created a highly concentrated settlement pattern favoring a handful of states, particularly California. The settlement pattern in urban places has taken many forms, with both suburban enclaves and dispersal being common, particularly among the more affluent Vietnamese and Lao.

Socioeconomic adaptation to the dominant American culture has been extremely challenging to the refugees and varies by time of arrival, age, and gender. While the refugee status of the adult migrants has certainly impacted the adaptation process of their American-born offspring, there is little doubt that the experiences of the 1.5 generation will be significantly less traumatic than those of their parents.

## NOTES

1. Although somewhat cumbersome, the regional label of "mainland Southeast Asian" is a better descriptor than the frequently used term *Indochinese*. The term *Indochina* refers to the former French colonial possessions of Vietnam, Laos, and Cambodia. Not only do refugees not identify with the term *Indochinese*, but no modern political unit exists that is referred to as Indochina. The term *mainland Southeast Asia* is geographically current and includes Vietnam, Laos, and Cambodia, as well as the states of Thailand and Myanmar (Burma). Neighboring Maritime or Insular Southeast Asia is composed of Malaysia, Indonesia, Singapore, Brunei, and the Philippines. The regional label of *mainland Southeast Asia* does not necessarily connote cultural unity, however, owing to the diverse cultural heritages of the refugee population.

2. Rubén G. Rumbaut, "A Legacy of War: Refugees from Vietnam, Laos and Cambodia," in *Origins and Destinies: Immigration, Race, and Ethnicity in America*, ed. Silvia Pedraza and Rubén G. Rumbaut (Belmont, Calif.: Wadsworth, 1996), 316.

3. For definitional and conceptual descriptions of refugees as a type of international migrant, see E. F. Kunz, "Exile and Resettlement: Refugee Theory," *International Migration Review* 7 (1981): 125–146; Leon Gordenker, *Refugees in International Politics* (London: Croom Helm, 1987); Arthur C. Helton, "The Future of U.S. Asylum and Refugee Policy," in *Immigration and Ethnicity: American Society-"Melting Pot" or "Salad Bowl"?*—ed. Michael D'Innocenzo and Josef P. Sirefman (Westport, Conn.: Greenwood, 1992), 257–266.

4. A highly readable description of traditional Vietnamese culture is found in Neil L. Jamieson, *Understanding Vietnam* (Berkeley: University of California Press, 1993), 1–41.

5. H. Hass and B. C. Nguyen, *Vietnam: The Other Conflict* (London: Sheed & Ward, 1971), 40; Jeremy Hein, *From Vietnam, Laos, and Cambodia: The Refugee Experience in the United States* (New York: Twayne, 1995), 11–15.

6. Hein, *From Vietnam*, 12–15.

7. Hein, *From Vietnam*, 15–20.

8. For an excellent account of the experiences of boat people, see Bruce Grant, *The Boat People: An "Age" Investigation* (New York: Penguin, 1979).

9. Hein, *From Vietnam*, 37.

10. For a brief history of precolonial Laos, see Arthur J. Dommen, *Laos: Keystone of Indochina* (Boulder, Colo.: Westview, 1985), 9–23.

11. A good introduction to the diversity of highland Lao culture groups includes Frank M. LeBar and Guy Morechand, "The Many Languages and Cultures of Laos," in *Laos, War and Revolution*, ed. Nina S. Adams and Alfred W. McCoy (New York: Harper & Row, 1970); Frank M. LeBar, Gerald C. Hickey, and John K. Musgrave, *Ethnic Groups of Mainland Southeast Asia* (New Haven, Conn.: Human Relations Area Files Press, 1964).

12. It is from the Chinese that the Hmong have been long referred to as "Miao" or "Meo," meaning "barbarian" or "savage," an indication of deep-seated discrimination by a more politically powerful lowland culture. For an explanation of the term *Hmong* as well as a brief but insightful description of traditional Hmong culture, see Gary Y. Lee, "Cultural Identity in Post-Modern Society: Reflections on What Is Hmong?" *Hmong Studies Journal* 1 (October 1996): 1–28; <http://www.como.stpaul.k12.mn.us/Vue-Benson/HER.html>.

13. Ines M. Miyares, "Changing Perceptions of Space and Place as Measures of Hmong Acculturation," *Professional Geographer* 49 (1997): 214–224.

14. Sucheng Chan, "The Hmong Experience in Asia and the United States," in *Hmong Means Free: Life in Laos and America*, ed. Sucheng Chan (Philadelphia: Temple University Press, 1994), 11.

15. Yang Dao, "Why Did the Hmong Leave Laos?" in *The Hmong in the West*, ed. Bruce T. Downing and Douglas P. Olney (St. Paul: Southeast Asian Refugee Studies Project, Center for Urban and Regional Affairs, University of Minnesota, 1982), 7.

16. Hein, *From Vietnam*, 20.

17. Chan, "The Hmong Experience," 40–41; Hein, *From Vietnam*, 20–21.

18. Dao, "Why Did the Hmong Leave Laos?" 10–18.

19. Chan, "The Hmong Experience," 40; Hein, *From Vietnam*, 35. For a penetrating examination of the systematic abuses perpetrated against the Hmong by the Vietnamese and Lao communist governments, see Jane Hamilton-Merritt, *Tragic Mountains: The Hmong, the Americans and the Secret Wars for Laos 1942–1992* (Bloomington: Indiana University Press, 1993).

20. D. P. Chandler, *A History of Cambodia*, 2d ed. (Boulder, Colo.: Westview, 1996).

21. Hein, *From Vietnam*, 22–24.

22. M. A. Martin, *Cambodia: A Shattered Society* (Berkeley: University of California Press, 1994).

23. Hein, *From Vietnam*, 35.

24. Alejandro Portes and Rubén G. Rumbaut, *Immigrant America: A Portrait* (Berkeley: University of California Press, 1990).

25. Paul J. Rutledge, *The Vietnamese Experience in America* (Bloomington: Indiana University Press, 1992), 8–11; Jacqueline Desbarats, "Indochinese Settlement in the United States," *Annals of the Association of American Geographers* 75 (1985): 524.

26. Office of Refugee Resettlement, *Report to Congress FY1995* (Washington, D.C.: U.S. Department of Health and Human Services, 1996), 35.

27. Rumbaut, "A Legacy of War," 320.

28. Desbarats, "Indochinese Settlement," 526; Hein, *From Vietnam*, 52–54.

29. For an excellent and detailed description of the role of Volags in the refugee resettlement process, see Anne E. Dickinson, "Resettlement of Laotian Refugees in Broome County, New York," *Migration News* 34 (1985): 3–50.

30. Desbarats, "Indochinese Settlement," 526.

31. Rumbaut, "A Legacy of War," 322.

32. For insight into the thinly documented process of refugee resettlement in small towns, see Judith May, "The Vermont Experience: Planned Clusters in Snow County," *Journal of Refugee Resettlement* 1 (1981): 31–35; Dickinson, "Resettlement of Laotian Refugees"; Ken C. Erickson, "Vietnamese Household Organization in Garden City, Kansas," *Plains Anthropologist* 33 (1988): 27–36; Roy Beck, "The Ordeal of Immigration in Wausau," *Atlantic Monthly* 273 (1994): 1–11; <http://www.como.stpaul.k12.mn.us/Vue-Benson/HER.html >.

33. Rumbaut, "A Legacy of War," 322–323.

34. Rumbaut, "A Legacy of War," 322.

35. Desbarats, "Indochinese Settlement," 533–535.

36. Rumbaut, "A Legacy of War," 322.

37. For excellent descriptions of the multiculturalism of the Greater Los Angeles region of which Asians are an important element, see David Reiff, *Los Angeles: Capital of the Third World* (New York: Simon & Schuster, 1991); Barbara A. Weightman, "Changing Religious Landscapes of Los Angeles," *Journal of Cultural Geography* 14 (1993): 1–20.

38. Rumbaut, "A Legacy of War," 323.

39. Alice C. Andrews and G. H. Stopp, Jr., "The Indochinese," in *Ethnicity in Contemporary America: A Geographical Appraisal*, ed. Jesse O. McKee (Dubuque, Iowa: Kendall Hunt, 1985), 217–239.

40. Joesph S. Wood, "Vietnamese American Place Making in Northern Virginia," *Geographical Review* 87 (1997): 58–72.

41. Cheu Thao, "Hmong Migration and Leadership in Laos and the United States," in *The Hmong in the West*, ed. Bruce T. Downing and Douglas P. Olney (Minneapolis: Southeast Asian Studies Center and Center for Urban and Regional Affairs, University of Minnesota, 1982), 99–121.

42. The information on Hmong settlement patterns is taken exclusively from Ines M. Miyares, "To Be Hmong in America: Settlement Patterns and Early Adaptation of Hmong Refugees in the United States," in *Human Geography in North America: New Perspectives and Trends in Research*, ed. Klaus Frantz, Innsbrucker Geographische Studien vol. 26 (Innsbruck: 1996), 97–113.

43. David H. Kaplan, "The Creation of an Ethnic Economy: Indochinese Business Expansion in St. Paul," *Economic Geography* 73 (1997): 214–233.

44. Miyares, "To Be Hmong in America."

45. Christopher A. Airriess, "Creating Landscape and Place in a Vietnamese Community in New Orleans, Louisiana," unpublished manuscript, 1997; Christopher A. Airriess and David L. Clawson, "Versailles: A Vietnamese Enclave in New Orleans, Louisiana," *Journal of Cultural Geography* 12 (1991): 1–15.

46. James P. Allen and Eugene Turner, "Spatial Patterns of Immigrant Assimilation," *Professional Geographer* 48 (1996): 144.

47. Stanley Karnow, "Little Saigon, Where Vietnam Meets America," *Smithsonian* 23 (August 1992): 28–39.

48. Wei Li, "Los Angeles' Chinese Ethnoburb: Evolution of Ethnic Community and Economy," unpublished paper, Association of American Geographers, Chicago, Illinois, 1995.

49. Desbarats, "Indochinese Settlement."

50. Allen and Turner, *Spatial Patterns*, 149.

51. Wood, "Vietnamese American Place Making."

52. Andrews and Stopp, "The Indochinese," 233–234.

53. Airriess and Clawson, "Versailles," 5.

54. Rubén Rumbaut, "Mental Health and Refugee Experience: A Comparative Study of Southeast Asian Refugees," in *Southeast Asian Mental Health*, ed. T. C. Owan (Washington, D.C.: U.S. Department of Health and Human Services, 1985), 433–486.

55. Thanh V. Tran, "Language Acculturation among Older Vietnamese Refugee Adults," *The Gerentologist* 30 (1990): 94–99.

56. Thanh V. Tran, "Family Living Arrangement and Social Adjustment among Three Ethnic Groups of Elderly Indochinese Refugees," *International Journal of Aging and Human Development* 32 (1991): 91–102.

57. Gail Weinstein-Shr and Nancy Z. Henkin, "Continuity and Change: Intergenerational Relations in Southeast Asian Refugee Families," *Marriage and Family Review* 16 (1991): 351–367.

58. Timothy Dunnigan, "Segmentary Kinship in an Urban Society: The Hmong of St. Paul–Minneapolis," *Anthropological Quarterly* 55 (1982): 126–134; T. V. Thanh, "The Vietnamese American Family," in *Ethnic Families in America*, ed. C. H. Mindel, R. W. Habenstein, and R. Wright, Jr. (New York: Elsevier, 1988); Weinstein-Shr and Henkin, "Continuity and Change."

59. Rubén G. Rumbaut and Kenji Ima, *The Adaptation of Southeast Asian Refugee Youth: A Comparative Study* (Washington, D.C.: U.S. Office of Refugee Resettlement, 1988); Rutledge, *The Vietnamese Experience in America*, 143–147.

60. Min Zhou and Carl L. Bankston III, "Social Capital and the Adaptation of the Second Generation: The Case of Vietnamese Youth in New Orleans," *International Migration Review* 28 (1994): 821–845.

61. Rumbaut and Ima, *The Adaptation of Southeast Asian Refugee Youth*.

62. Miyares, "Changing Perceptions," 221–223.

63. Ronald J. Burwell, Peter Hill, and John F. Van Wicklin, "Religion and Refugee Settlement in the United States: A Research Note," *Review of Religious Research* 27 (1986): 356–366.

64. Carl L. Bankston and Min Zhou, "Religious Participation, Ethnic Identification, and Adaptation of Vietnamese Adolescents in an Immigrant Community," *Sociological Quarterly* 36 (1995): 523–534.

65. Airriess and Clawson, "Versailles."

66. Nancy J. Smith-Hefner, "Ethnicity and the Force of Faith: Christian Conversion among Khmer Refugees," *Anthropological Quarterly* 67 (1994): 24–37.

67. Burwell et al., "Religion and Refugee Settlement."

68. Robert E. Pecora, Mark W. Fraser, and Peterson J. Pecora, "Religiosity among Indochinese Refugees in Utah," *Journal for the Scientific Study of Religion* 27 (1988): 272–283; Daphne N. Winland, "Christianity and Community: Conversion and Adaptation among Hmong Refugee Women," *Canadian Journal of Sociology* 19 (1994): 21–45.

69. Lisa L. Caps, "Change and Continuity in the Medical Culture of the Hmong in Kansas City," *Medical Anthropology Quarterly* 8 (1994): 161–177.

70. Pecora, Fraser, and Pecora, "Religiosity among Indochinese Refugees in Utah"; Smith-Hefner, "Ethnicity"; Winland, "Christianity and Community"; Bankston and Zhou, "Religious Participation"; Youngmin Lee, "Vietnamese Immigrants and Buddhism in Southern Louisiana: Ingredients for 'Melting Pot' or for Cultural Diversity," *Journal of the Korean Geographical Society* 31 (1996): 685–698.

71. Weightman, "Changing Religious Landscapes."

72. Miyares, "Changing Perceptions."

73. Caps, "Change and Continuity."

74. Winland, "Christianity and Community"; Jennifer J. Helzer, "Continuity and Change: Hmong Settlement in California's Sacramento Valley," *Journal of Cultural Geography* 14 (1994): 51–64.

75. Louis-Jacque Dorais, "Religion and Refugee Adaptation: The Vietnamese in Montreal," *Canadian Ethnic Studies* 21 (1989): 19–29; Lee, "Vietnamese Immigrants."

76. Edward R. Canada and Phaobtong Thitiya, "Buddhism as a Support System for Southeast Asian Refugees," *Journal of the National Association of Social Workers* 37: 61–67.

77. Weightman, "Changing Religious Landscapes."

78. Dorais, "Religion and Refugee Adaptation."

79. Nancy T. Crane and Nancy R. Green, "Food Habits and Food Preferences of Vietnamese Refugees Living in Northern Florida," *Journal of the American Dietetic Association* 76 (1980): 593–596; Susan Kalcik, "Ethnic Foodways in America: Symbol and the Performance of Identity," in *Ethnic and Regional Foodways in the United States: The Performance of Group Identity*, ed.

Linda K. Brown and Kay Mussell (Knoxville: University of Tennessee Press, 1984), 37–65; Mary Story and Linda J. Harris, "Food Habits and Dietary Change of Southeast Asian Refugees Living in the United States," *Journal of the American Dietetic Society* 89 (1989): 800–803.

80. Miyares, "Changing Perceptions."

81. Sharon Sawyer, "Hmong Gardens: New Additions to Minnesota's Urban Horticulture," *Minnesota Horticulturalist* (October–November, 1986): 232–234; Story and Harris, "Food Habits"; Christopher A. Airriess and David L. Clawson, "Vietnamese Market Gardens in New Orleans," *Geographical Review* 84 (1994): 16–31.

82. Claudia Myers, *Highland Lao Agricultural Activities in California: Small Farms and Community Gardens* (Davis: University of California at Davis, 1986); Carol J. Morris, "Garden Secrets from the Hmong," *Flower and Garden* 33 (1989): 36–38.

83. Morris, "Garden Secrets," 38.

84. Rachel Kaplan, "Some Psychological Benefits of Gardening," *Environment and Behavior* 5 (1973): 145–162; Richard J. Riordan and Craig J. Williams, "Gardening Therapeutics for the Elderly," *Activities, Adaptation, and Aging* 12 (1988): 103–111; Janet F. Talbot and Rachel Kaplan, "The Benefits of Nearby Nature for Elderly Apartment Residents," *International Journal of Aging and Human Development* 33 (1991): 119–131.

85. Helzer, "Continuity and Change"; Miyares, "Changing Perceptions."

86. Airriess and Clawson, "Vietnamese Market Gardens."

87. Myers, *Highland Lao Agricultural Activities*; Miyares, "To Be Hmong"; Pedro Ilic, "Impact of Fresno County Southeast Asian Farmers on the Local Economy," *Small Farm News* (Davis: University of California Cooperative Extension Smallfarm Center, September–October, 1991).

88. Sawyer, "Hmong Gardens"; Elizabeth Kurylo, "Hmong Immigrants Take Root," *Atlanta Constitution*, 3 September 1993, section 3, 1:1; David L. Clawson and Christopher A. Airriess, author field notes, New Orleans, Louisiana, 1997; Walter Nicholls, "Foraging," *Washington Post*, 12 July 1995, section E, 9:3.

89. Airriess and Clawson, "Vietnamese Market Gardens."

90. Story and Harris, "Food Habits."

91. Hein, *From Vietnam*, 135.

92. Office of Refugee Resettlement, *Report to Congress FY1995*, 49.

93. Rubén Rumbaut, "Portraits, Patterns and Predictors of the Refugee Adaptation Process," in *Refugees as Immigrants: Cambodians, Laotians and Vietnamese in America*, ed. David Haines (Totowa, N.J.: Rowman & Littlefield, 1989), 138–182. Although public assistance statistics for the Hmong and Cambodians were not accessible, an example of decreasing public assistance over time is available for Vietnamese refugees. Among those refugee households who arrived in 1990, approximately 20 percent still relied on public assistance as a sole source of income by 1995. Dependency on public assistance as the sole source of household income among those who arrived in 1995 was approximately 28 percent. Office of Refugee Resettlement, *Report to Congress FY1995*, 49.

94. Rumbaut, *A Legacy of War*, 327–328.

95. Hein, *From Vietnam*, 140.

96. Hein, *From Vietnam*, 140–141.

97. Nazli Kibra, "Power, Patriarchy, and Gender Conflict in the Vietnamese Immigrant Community," *Gender and Society* 4 (1990): 9–24.

98. Charles C. Irby and Ernest Pon, "Confronting New Mountains: Mental Health Problems among Male Hmong and Mien Refugees," *Amerasia Journal* 14 (1988): 109–118; Kou Yang, "Hmong Men's Adaptation to Life in the United States," *Hmong Studies Journal* 1 (1997): 1–22; <http://www.como.stpaul.ki2.mn.us/Vue-Benson/HER.html>.

99. Ann M. Rynearson and Pamela A. DeVoe, "Refugee Women in a Vertical Village: Lowland Laotians in St. Louis," *Social Thought* 10 (1984): 33–48.

# RURAL AND URBAN ETHNIC ISLANDS

# The Character and Composition of Rural Ethnic Islands

*Allen G. Noble*

Most immigrants to the United States came in search of economic opportunity. Through the nineteenth century, this often meant the possibility of acquiring land; hence, many sought unoccupied or sparsely settled areas. Some, of course, went to urban centers. The various Homestead Laws of the middle nineteenth century attracted the immigrants toward land heretofore unsettled except for that settled by low numbers of Native Americans. Here they might secure ownership simply by occupying and improving the land, something undreamed of in Europe. Immigration agents for railroads, and even states, facilitated the movement.

The immigrants moved thousands of miles into new and unfamiliar territory. It was only natural that they sought the security, protection, and support of their own cultural group. For example, the Germans, one of the largest foreign national groups to migrate to the United States, sought out existing German settlements or proceeded to establish new ones. A checkerboard pattern of settlement soon emerged in which various ethnic groups clustered together, each maintaining its own identity as far as possible.

Through continued settlement and use of the land, specific groups became identified with certain regions in the United States. Today, many of these cultural areas can still be identified by the character of the landscape. These rural ethnic settlements are generally distinguished as being either *ethnic provinces* or *ethnic islands/folk islands*, depending on their size in terms of population and area. The term *ethnic province* is used to refer to larger areas that frequently contain several thousands or hundreds of thousands of persons. Such identifiable provinces in the United States include African Americans in parts of the rural South, Hispanics in the Southwest, and Native Americans in both Oklahoma and the Southwest. In contrast, ethnic islands are smaller in area and population but are more numerous and include a wider array of ethnic groups. The American Midwest is a good example of an area where numerous ethnic islands appear on the landscape.

Since most of the major groups comprising ethnic provinces are discussed elsewhere in this volume, this chapter will discuss primarily rural ethnic islands. Emphasis will be placed on how the various groups modified the American landscape, particularly with regard to the structures (i.e., houses, barns) they erected. These buildings are what give distinctive character to the landscape.

## CHARACTERISTICS OF ETHNIC ISLANDS ON THE CULTURAL LANDSCAPE

One of the distinguishing characteristics of many European ethnic islands in the United States is the sense of community that persists. It has been so strong within many ethnic groups that the internal divisions that characterized the group in its European setting were established in the New World, even in the face of unfriendly reception from surrounding groups belonging to other nationalities. Peter Munch has shown for Norwegian settlements in Vernon County, Wisconsin, that old country ties remained among the strongest influences affecting later settlements.[1] In Vernon County, although Norwegians are the dominant settlers, at least three substrata can be identified. On Coon Prairie in the northern part of the county, most of the Norwegians came from around Gudbrandsdal and Lake Mjösa in eastern Norway, whereas settlers in the southern part of the county originated in west Norway (Fig. 11.1). Intermediate between these settlements are Norwegians with ties to the southwest coast of Norway. The persistence of the separate identities of the first two groups is all the more interesting because both came in 1850 to Vernon County from a single earlier settlement in Dane County, Wisconsin.[2] Norwegians from the Flekkefjord area did not commence settling Vernon County until about 1880 and hence were forced to those unoccupied lands located between the two earlier Norwegian settlements.

In the nineteenth century and earlier, ethnic communities usually were easy to identify and some were quite well known, but in the latter twentieth century forces of change have been at work. Some communities have dwindled; others have expanded. Some groups found themselves in the path of suburban expansion, and their members sold off the land and turned to urban occupations. The cohesiveness of the ethnic group weakened, and its identity has, in some cases, been lost. Furthermore, strenuous attempts have been made to assimilate the children. Often the immigrant parents enthu-

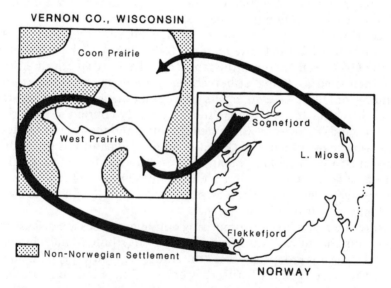

**Figure 11.1   Selective Migration of Norwegians to Vernon County, Wisconsin (after Munch).**

siastically supported the process so that their children might gain the full benefits from complete participation in the affairs of the new country. The rate of assimilation varied, with a number of factors including the difficulties of language, the group's physical accessibility, the strength of opposing institutions (e.g., the presence of ethnic clergymen), and, above all, the size and density of the ethnic community.

In many places, the ethnic identity of the settlers has persisted, even though modified by time. Not everywhere, but in many places, a series of rural ethnic islands can be identified where the original cohesiveness of the group has not been lost. The mosaic of immigrant settlement never has been studied in its entirety, but for restricted regions a few attempts have been made to identify ethnic territories. The literature on the geographic extent of ethnic settlement has been reviewed by geographer Karl Raitz.[3]

The most comprehensive investigation of ethnic territories was made for Wisconsin by George W. Hill using data from 1905.[4] Hill's map, executed at the level of the individual township, attempts to identify every ethnic settlement in the state in a system encompassing twenty-three nationality groups and a "mixed" category when no single nationality reached 80 percent of the total. The pattern revealed by Hill's map is literally one of a checkerboard of ethnic settlements.

The geographer is interested in many aspects of these ethnic islands: the process by which the immigrants chose the place of settlement; the types of areas they sought and those they attempted to avoid; the techniques and systems of cultivation they brought and how these were modified in the new environments; the different perceptions of the environment held by immigrants of other ethnic communities; and, above all, the alterations each immigrant group made to the appearance of the countryside by the structures it erected.

### Buildings within Rural Ethnic Islands

If in sufficient numbers, all ethnic groups stamp their imprint on the land, especially if they are the initial settlers. This idea, called the *concept of initial occupance,* has been used by Fred Kniffen to mean the initial postpioneer, permanent settlement imprint established by migrants in the United States. As Kniffen notes, "the concept is important because it recognizes the initial imprint as long lasting, surviving even where a new ethnic stock has succeeded the original settlers."[5] He restricts the term to migrants coming from eastern seaboard areas, but it applies equally well to those coming directly from overseas, if they come in sufficient numbers and settle in a cohesive fashion.

Because each group followed the guidelines of its traditions, they divided up the land, created settlements, and erected structures as they had learned to do in their countries of origin. Thus, their "islands" of settlement were quite distinct from those of other ethnic groups.

Each group also had different climates to work in and different local resources to utilize or harness. Thus, the early English in New England settled in compact villages organized around a green or commons, separated their fields with stone walls composed of the glacial boulders they had to clear before farming, and sometimes built connected barns to alleviate the rigors of the winter. In contrast, in Appalachia the Scotch Irish settled in dispersed log cabins or at best in tiny hamlets that sprawled up in a valley or hollow. They used split-rail fences if they used any fences at all, and their barns were simple, single-crib structures because the milder climate required only storage for crops, not shelter for animals. Finally, the Germans, at least in Wisconsin, favored a farmstead with a house (often built of brick), a barn, and multiple, small outbuildings built around a roughly defined courtyard. The barn, not only in Wisconsin but almost everywhere Germans settled in the eastern half of the United States, was a conspicuous building that even today identifies the ethnic origins of the community.

The German bank barn is familiar to many Americans because of its widespread distribution as well as its distinctive appearance. Although there are important variations in the basic structure,[6] all German bank barns are at least two stories high and have a distinctive overhanging second-story forebay (Fig. 11.2). Barns of this type are found in great numbers in southeastern Pennsylvania, where German settlement in cohesive groups was first introduced into North America (Fig. 11.3). Elsewhere, the presence of surviving German bank barns indicates either the pathways of German movement from the southeastern Pennsylvania hearth or the location of later German settlements without a direct connection to the earlier hearth. No other nationality built this type of barn, so today it always functions as an indicator of German occupation and original settlement,[7] and the major routes of movement out of southeastern Pennsylvania can be clearly traced by its presence (Fig. 11.3). In parts of the Shenandoah Valley over one-half of all barns are of this type. Another route of migration leads directly west, tying the German settlements of Pennsylvania to those of the Midwest. Independent concentrations of Germans show up in Wisconsin and southern Ontario.

## SOME OTHER ETHNIC ISLANDS

The German bank barn is only one structure that provides a clue to ethnic settlement. Many other nationalities erected distinctive barn types. Dutch, English, and French

**Figure 11.2   A German Bank Barn, Summit County, Ohio. Source: Photo by A. G. Noble, 1976.**

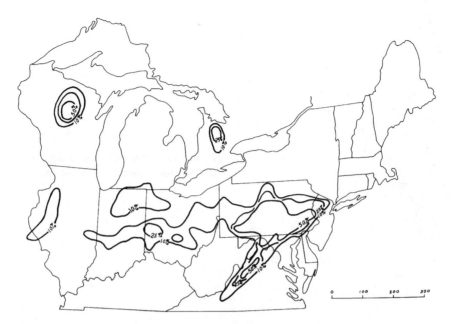

**Figure 11.3     Percentage of German Bank Barns to All Barns, 1975.**

barns are well known. Houses, too, have distinct ethnic connections, although because houses change appearance more frequently than barns, house type connections are more difficult to identify.

The cultural landscapes characterizing some ethnic islands have not been much examined by scholars despite their distinctive character. Such is the case with the Belgian settlements in Door County, Wisconsin (Fig. 11.4).

### Belgians in the Door County Peninsula

French-speaking Walloon settlers began to occupy the heavily forested but fertile soils of the gentle dip slope of the Niagara cuesta in the southern Door peninsula between 1853 and 1857.[8] The dense forest cover, combined with scattered swamps, effectively isolated the Belgian settlement from its neighbors. Although two or three attempts have been made to document the history of this settlement, few serious efforts have been made to examine the distinctive structures that still characterize the area.

In 1979. geographers Charles F. Calkins and William G. Laatsch looked at the outdoor oven.[9] Fifteen surviving ovens are documented in their study. Most were extensions of the summer kitchen, a feature of many Door County Belgian farmsteads. Both the oven and the summer kitchen were normally constructed of blocks of local Niagara limestone. The domed oven was sometimes covered by a wooden roof structure (Fig. 11.5). The baking chamber of the oven was formed of bricks and resembled those of other French-speaking groups.[10] Careful attention was given to the size of the baking chamber, since it governed the effectiveness of the facility. Hence, great uniformity in structural form and size is found in these ovens.[11]

A similar kind of tradition-enforced uniformity also pervades the other Belgian structures, although perhaps with not quite so much exactness. The house dimensions and

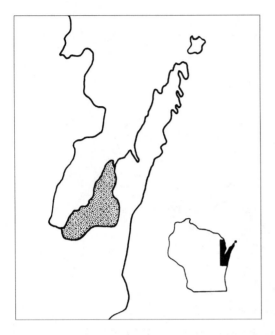

Figure 11.4    Distribution of Belgian Settlement Area in Door County, Wisconsin.

form vary, but all have the unmistakable stamp of Belgian construction (Fig. 11.6). The underlying structure may be of log or timber frame, set on a limestone foundation, but the facing is of brick from local clays. The exterior frequently is ornamented with mortar decorations (large gable-placed stars are popular), stone quoins, window hoods and frames, and even cobblestone panels (Fig. 11.6). The barns, in contrast, are constructed of hewn logs with half notching (Fig. 11.7). Clay chinking keeps out the frigid winds that blow off Green Bay in the winter season. The form of the barns, an elongated rectangle with offset, double wagon doors and a series of smaller man-size doors, is close to that of the Quebec Long Barn of the St. Lawrence Valley.[12] Further study will be necessary to uncover the points of differentiation between these two Gallic areas and peoples.

Figure 11.5    Belgian House, Summer Kitchen, and Outdoor Oven Extension, Door County, Wisconsin. Source: Photo by A. G. Noble, 1980.

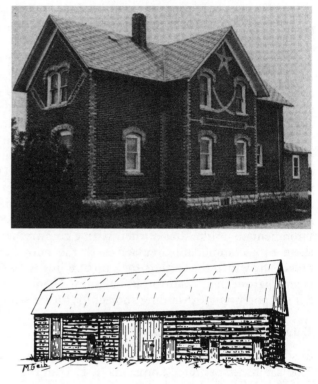

**Figure 11.6    Typical Belgian Brick House, Door County, Wisconsin. Source: Photo by A. G. Noble, 1980.**

**Figure 11.7    Belgian Log Barn, Door County, Wisconsin.**

Even the privy illustrates the architectural distinctiveness of ethnic settlements. In most rural communities, the privy is situated at some convenient distance to the rear of the house, but usually away from other buildings. On the Belgian farmsteads of Door County, the privy usually occupies the ell formed by the bake oven and the rear gable wall of the summer kitchen (Fig. 11.8). Here it takes maximum advantage of the heat radiated by the oven, as well as the shelter afforded from winter winds. A further advantage may be that for most of the way only a single pathway need be shoveled after a snow-

**Figure 11.8    Door County Belgian Farmstead. The privy is snugly fitted into the ell between the outdoor oven and the rear gable wall of the summer kitchen. Note the limestone construction of the latter. Source: Photo by A. G. Noble, 1980.**

storm, thus reducing effort. Both the privy and the summer kitchen/bake oven face in opposite directions, so that despite proximity, functions are kept quite separate.

Another small outbuilding apparently unique to the Belgian community is the diminutive chapel on each farmstead (Fig. 11.9). Just large enough for two or three people to worship, the chapel reflects the strong Roman Catholic heritage of these people. The chapels, which may be frame or stone, measure only about six feet long by four feet wide and are universally covered by a gable roof of shingles or metal. The single door is in the gable, and the diminutive altar and figure of the Virgin rest against the opposite gable wall.

The combination of distinctively decorated brick house, elongated log barn, limestone summer kitchen with bake oven extension, unusual privy location, and the tiny chapel unmistakably mark the Belgian homestead. Unfortunately, no one has yet examined in detail the buildings of this ethnic group, nor have the methods of construction, attitudes toward the structures, or approaches to building been analyzed. Consequently, some intriguing questions remain to be answered. Why did the Belgians seek out an environment so unlike that of their native country? What adjustments were necessary for them to accommodate themselves to the new, harsher surroundings? What was the process by which the settlers took up building with hewn logs, which had not previously been a part of their tradition in Belgium? Obviously the Belgian community in Wisconsin is a potentially rewarding subject for future study.

### Cajuns in Southern Louisiana

In southern Louisiana, another distinctive group occupies a rather large area (Fig. 11.10). The Cajuns first entered Louisiana in 1754 in flight from Acadia (the term *Cajun* is corruption of the word *Acadien*), where they were expelled by the British at the beginning of the French and Indian War.[13] Many of the early Acadians settled to the west of the city of New Orleans. Through time, the Cajuns diffused throughout the lower Louisiana bayous.

The southern Louisiana bayou environment is, of course, quite different from that of the Door County cuesta. Consequently, certain design features are altered in the two locations. Conserving heat, as demonstrated in the Wisconsin Belgian privy location, is not an important consideration, but providing ventilation and protection from dampness and insects is of paramount concern in Louisiana. Hence, houses are raised up on short pillars or piers of cypress wood. This raises the sills of the house from contact with the damp ground, provides a barrier to termites and other pests, and permits circulation of air beneath the floor of the house.

Figure 11.9   Typical Door County
Belgian Farm Chapel. Source:
Photo by A. G. Noble, 1980.

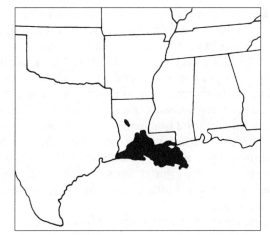

**Figure 11.10   Distribution of French Settlement Area in Louisiana.**

The standard folk house of this area is called "Creole house" despite the fact that most of its builders have been Cajuns.[14] *Creole* is the term applied to the French culture that evolved in Louisiana from the initial settlers who came directly from France or from the St. Lawrence Valley, Florida, or the French Caribbean colonies, especially Santo Domingo. Generally speaking, Creole architecture is associated with established plantation areas, whereas the structures of the Cajuns are those of small scale farmers. In reality, Creole and Cajun building forms are similar enough that a broader term, such as "French buildings," could be applied to both, and it would be appropriate to call the basic or standard house of French Louisiana by the name "grenier house" (Fig. 11.11), thus avoiding the confusion between Cajun and Creole designations. While forms are similar, construction methods are better differentiated, perhaps because of the difference in affluence of the two groups. Cajuns, who lived on the river levees but close to the bayou swamps, used a mixture of Spanish moss, mud, and sometimes calcined seashells called *bousillage* that were used as in-filling between hewn, vertical timbers. As economic levels increased, early Cajuns turned to the abundant resources of the bayous for cypress wood to use as cladding. They found the cypress to be durable, resistant to insects, slow to rot, easy to saw and work with simple hand tools, straight-grained and thus easy to split, unlikely to warp even when used "green," and difficult to burn.[15] A paragon of woods!

**Figure 11.11   The Grenier House.**

Creole builders, while they occasionally employed *bousillage* in the early period, were much more likely to use bricks as wall nogging.[16] Furthermore, their houses might be raised on brick foundations or brick piers, and often in the more elaborate examples, they had full lower stories of brick. Many of the later, and most of the larger, Creole houses had prominent hipped roofs, whereas the Cajun houses employed primarily the gable roof. Both appear to stem from a single New World French building tradition.

The grenier house is the standard French house of rural Louisiana. Its most distinctive feature and the one from which it derives its name is the attic that projects forward over the open, front *galerie* or verandah. Among other early ethnic groups, the front porch is usually clearly an afterthought, tacked on to the main structure and having a separate roof. The grenier, however, is clearly a part of the original design of the French house, as is the verandah. Together they provide a profile that distinctively marks the grenier house.

Knipmeyer has demonstrated by examining typical floor plans that an evolutionary sequence exists among grenier houses from single-room houses with an outside stairway on the verandah to houses of eight to ten rooms with a rear stairway.[17] Ruston has suggested that the former are typical of Cajun buildings, whereas the latter are of Creole origins.[18]

Not quite as common as grenier houses, but nevertheless still important in rural French Louisiana, are shotgun and double shotgun houses. The shotgun house (Fig. 11.12) is as distinctive as the Grenier house but in a much different way. It consists of a single file of rooms, which permits maximum cross ventilation of the house, a desirable feature during the long hot and humid summers of the region. Folk traditions insist that the house derives its name from the fact that the doors of each room are in line, and hence a shotgun fired through the front door would pass through the house and out the back door, despite the fact that many shotgun houses do not possess in-line doors. Folk myths die hard!

Double shotgun houses have been given the name "bungalows," which is unfortunate since it causes confusion with other, rather similar-appearing houses found in other parts of the country, but from much different origins. In French Louisiana, the "bungalow" is a one-story structure derived by placing two single shotgun houses together to achieve a larger building suitable for larger families. That this is its origin is clear from the fact that some double shotgun houses have no interior doorway connecting the two halves of the house, an inconvenience remedied in most later buildings.

Figure 11.12    A Shotgun House near Donaldsonville, Louisiana, 1978. This particular house is somewhat wider than normally found. Source: Photo by A. G. Noble.

The combination of grenier, shotgun, and double shotgun houses differentiates the French agricultural settlements of Louisiana. These house types could never be confused with those of the Wisconsin Belgian farmers. Not only are the houses in Louisiana quite different, but so are the barns and outbuildings, as well as the arrangement of the structures. Barns are small, gable-entry buildings, consisting of a central space with one or two flanking areas.[19] On occasion a rear shed will also be found. The most distinctive feature of the Cajun barn is the recessed entryway (Fig. 11.13). Outbuildings include corn cribs, chicken houses, chicken roosts, and, now and then, an outdoor bake oven.

The farm properties are rectangular, with the house close to the road and the barn and outbuildings behind. Because of the narrow aspects of the farm property, the buildings are not placed to form a barnyard as is frequently the case with the Wisconsin Belgian farmsteads. Both the Wisconsin Belgian and the Louisiana French settlements show adjustments of building design to local environmental conditions that are quite different from one another.

### Finns in the Upper Midwest

Two other quite disparate groups are also found in the Upper Midwest. Of the two groups, Finns and Norwegians, the buildings of the former are the better known. Finns entered the United States in numbers only toward the end of the nineteenth century and at the beginning of the twentieth. Finnish immigration peaked in the 1920s when nearly seventeen thousand emigrated, but their total number of immigrants is considerably smaller when compared to those from Norway. Migration of the Finns was highly localized. One-half of all migrating Finns came from the province of Vaasa, particularly from South Ostrobothnia, and most ended up in the vicinity of Lake Superior (Fig. 11.14).[20] Because they came so late, the Finns found only the poorest land unoccupied. Nevertheless, such land closely resembled what they had left behind, and there was much more of it available and at very low cost. Furthermore, supplemental income was available in logging and mining. The principal difficulty standing in the way of effective settlement was clearing the land of its natural forest cover. Use of pine logs as building material helped in the process of land clearing.

Building with squared, hewn logs is one of eight distinctive features that, according to Mather and Kaups, make up the Finnish cultural landscape of the Lake Superior basin.[21] Other investigators have identified additional characteristics. For example, Alanen and Tishler note that the typical farmstead consists of a cluster of buildings placed in a rough courtyard arrangement.[22] In the earliest of these, all the structures are of log;

**Figure 11.13    A Cajun Barn.**

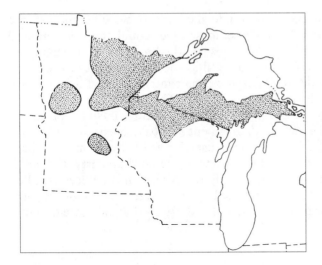

Figure 11.14   Distribution of Finnish Settlement Area in the Great Lakes Region.

but in later farmsteads, houses are built of dimension lumber, but the barns and out-buildings continue to be built of log.

Great variety is found in house design, but a three-rooms-in-line plan (Fig. 11.15) is one of the most common,[23] owing its origins to ancient Baltic center-hearth houses. Finnish settlers often built these houses one or two units at a time, so that sometimes the entire house never was completed. A two-room log house was about as common as the three, even in Finland.[24]

Certain other characteristics identify the Finnish house. Logs are hewn in a quite distinctive fashion, square on both inside and out with the top remaining convex and the bottom hewn concave so that a tight fit of wall logs is achieved. The fit is so close that little or no chinking is required between the logs, a desirable feature in the bitingly cold winters of both Finland and the northern Midwest. In those instances when chinking was required, a layer of moss or a strip of cloth was often used. Also helping produce firmly built walls is the use of corner notching techniques such as the double notch and the full dovetail, both of which permit tight fits.

Figure 11.15   A Finnish Three-Room House. The ladders on the roof and the small enclosed entryway are typically Finnish. Source: Old World Wisconsin Outdoor Ethnic Museum; photo courtesy of Marty Perkins.

Two quite distinctive structures mark the typical Finnish farmstead. One is the sauna and the other is the *riihi* (grain-drying barn). The presence of numerous barns and outbuildings also characterizes the Finnish farmstead.[25] Some barns house livestock; others house hay; still others, such as the *riihi*, have the very specialized function of grain drying and threshing. These barns were never widely built in America because the climate of the northern Midwest was drier than that of Finland, and hence the need for a closed drying facility was eliminated or at least greatly reduced.[26] The most unusual feature of the *riihi* was a large chimneyless stove of brick and stone, in which wood was burned to dry out the grain. The combination of wood burning amid great quantities of easily combustible grain and straw meant that *riihi* fires were always a danger. To reduce the risk, the *riihi* was kept outside the farmstead, away from other buildings.[27]

The sauna, the other distinctive building of a Finnish farmstead, was also a potential fire hazard, and consequently it, too, was built somewhat apart. The log sauna initially was a single-room, windowless structure containing a set of stepped benches and a stove of unmortared field stone. Smoke from the stove, which had no chimney, was allowed to escape through small wall vents or roof flues.[28] The fire was burned primarily to heat igneous and metamorphic rocks piled on the top of the stove. The heated rocks then provided the energy to keep the sauna interior hot for extended periods. Water was ladled onto the rocks to reduce the temperature if it became too hot and at the same time to increase the sensation of heating by increasing humidity.

The original one-room sauna was replaced at an early date on many farms by a larger, two-room structure in which the new room functioned as a dressing area. These structures typically measured eight to ten feet wide by fifteen to eighteen feet long (Fig. 11.16), and builders added both a chimney for ventilation and small windows for interior

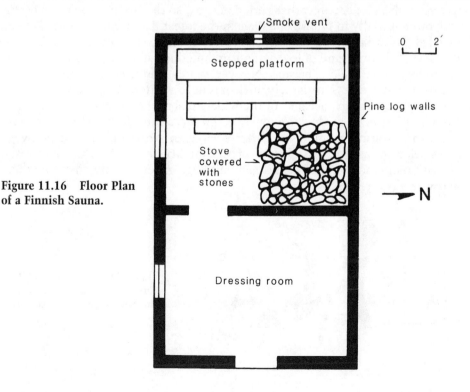

**Figure 11.16    Floor Plan of a Finnish Sauna.**

light. The entrance door remained on the gable but now led into the dressing room rather than into the stove room.

The sauna building received the same meticulous crafting as the Finnish log house. The logs were carefully hewn so as to fit together with virtually no chinking. Double notching or full dovetail notching was employed to ensure the sound, tight structure required to conserve the heat involved. Pine logs were preferred for the sauna because they were little affected by the great temperature changes associated with the sauna.[29] Most important was that the timber be left untreated, neither painted nor even oiled, so that the maximum moisture could be absorbed by the wood.

## The Norwegians in the Midwest

Early Norwegian migration to the United States began in 1825 when approximately fifty Norwegians emigrated. The Norwegian immigration started rather slowly but gathered momentum in the 1860s and continued through the 1920s, with the peak immigration periods occurring in the 1880s and 1900s when slightly fewer than four hundred thousand came to America during these two decades. From 1825 to the present, a total of more than 850,000 Norwegians have migrated to the United States.

After initially forming a colony called the "Kendall Settlement" in Orleans County, New York, Norwegians began moving westward after 1834. The Fox River region, near Ottawa in La Salle County, Illinois, formed the early nucleus of this Norwegian migration. Through time, Norwegians established other settlements in Wisconsin, Minnesota, Iowa, and elsewhere in the Midwest and West.

Norwegians are much more widely scattered than the Finns (Fig. 11.17). They came in greater numbers and at an earlier period of time, so that their farmsteads occupied better land, often initially in prairie openings in the forest. Later on, all of the land on which they settled, toward the West, was treeless prairie. Thus, they were spared part of the rigorous ordeal of clearing land of low agricultural productivity, as the Finns had to do. They built with logs, nevertheless, because Norwegian folk traditions encouraged it and timber was plentiful and cheap. Surprisingly, little has been written about Norwegian vernacular architecture, and, perhaps because of the widely disbursed nature of their ethnic islands, little attempt has been made consciously to preserve their folk architecture. One of the difficulties in locating examples of early Norwegian structures is that Norwegians frequently settled on easily accessible land of high quality, so that in time they prospered and rebuilt with more modern, less traditional buildings. Alternatively, they sold their land to non-Norwegians if prices were right.

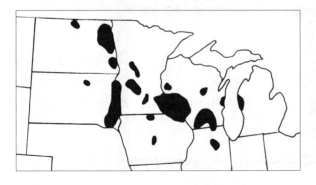

**Figure 11.17  Areas of Greatest Concentration of Norwegians in the Northern Midwest.**

The Norwegians used many of the same log techniques as the Finns. They hewed log walls on both inside and out and hewed each log to be convex on top and concave on the bottom. They further chamfered the top and bottom edges of each log so as to make chinking easier as well as to create a pleasing appearance.

Although definitive evidence is not yet available, it appears that the American Norwegian houses were quite different from those of the American Finnish. Some one-story, three-room houses of the sort that typified the European Baltic Sea basin may have been built. More common, however, was a dwelling that can be called a Norwegian gallery house. Its name is derived from the long, narrow, second-story gallery, or *sval*, which runs along one side of the house (Fig. 11.18). The *sval* is reached by a direct flight of stairs at one end. In many instances, the space beneath the *sval* has been boarded in to create a narrow room on the first floor to complement the two original rooms, which are of unequal size. The first-floor rooms are replicated by two unequal-sized rooms on the second. Sometimes the roof of the house is asymmetrical in order to incorporate the *sval*.[30]

One of the very few detailed descriptions of a Norwegian gallery house in the American Midwest can be found in the works of Richard Perrin.[31] His description of the John Bergen house confirms that these structures are derivations of those found in Norway,[32] as well as in Sweden.[33] Preserved in the Old World Wisconsin outdoor ethnic museum is another Norwegian gallery dwelling (Fig. 11.19), known as the Andrew Kvaale house. The plan of this house is not exactly that of a Scandinavian gallery house, but it is close.[34] The *sval* is incomplete: no outside stairway is present, and the lower level of the

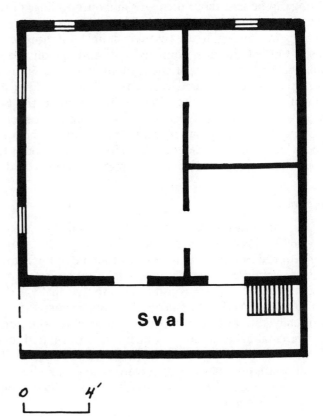

**Figure 11.18    Floor Plan of a Norwegian Gallery House.**

Sval

0        4'

Figure 11.19    A Modified Norwegian
Gallery House. The *sval* is to the
right. Source: Old World Wisconsin
Outdoor Ethnic Museum; photo by
A. G. Noble.

*sval* is partially closed in. However, other features of the structure are faithful to its predecessors: logs are tight fitting, with little or no chinking, hewn in the Scandinavian fashion, and locked at the corners with full dovetail notching. A few other Norwegian gallery houses have been described, mostly in Wisconsin, due to the efforts of the Old World Wisconsin museum staff.[35]

So little research has been attempted on American Norwegian buildings that virtually nothing can be said about the barns and outbuildings of the typical Norwegian farmstead. They are, of course, constructed of logs held in place by saddle notching or half dovetail notching. In contrast, houses employ double notching or full dovetail,[36] much like Finnish houses. One of the more unusual outbuildings on the Norwegian farm is the *stabbur* (granary). As with many of the structures of the Finns and Norwegians, most existing *stabburs* have been covered over with siding or otherwise modified. For this reason, many undoubtedly go undetected. The modifications to the Norwegian *stabbur* at Old World Wisconsin have been better documented than most such structures (Fig. 11.20).

Some ethnic groups are identified primarily on the basis of religious orientation, rather than by language or place of origin. This is true of both the Amish and the Mormons, although their religious history and directions are vastly different from one another.

## The Amish

Amish immigration to America occurred in two peak periods, 1727–1770 and 1815–1860.[37] Because of persecution in Europe, the Amish were reluctant to keep formal records of their members; therefore, official documentation of the arrival date of the first Amish to America remains unknown. However, some may have arrived as early as 1710. Evidence does exist, however, to indicate that in 1727 a ship landed in Philadelphia containing several Amish names on its passenger list.[38] Another ship landed in 1737 that is often referred to as the "first Amish ship" since the numerous families aboard can definitely be established as being Amish.[39] It is estimated that during the eighteenth century, only about five hundred Amish emigrated to America.[40] The early journeys to America were difficult, and many Amish were reluctant to leave their native Switzerland. These early Amish established settlements in Berks, Chester, and Lancaster Counties in southeastern Pennsylvania.

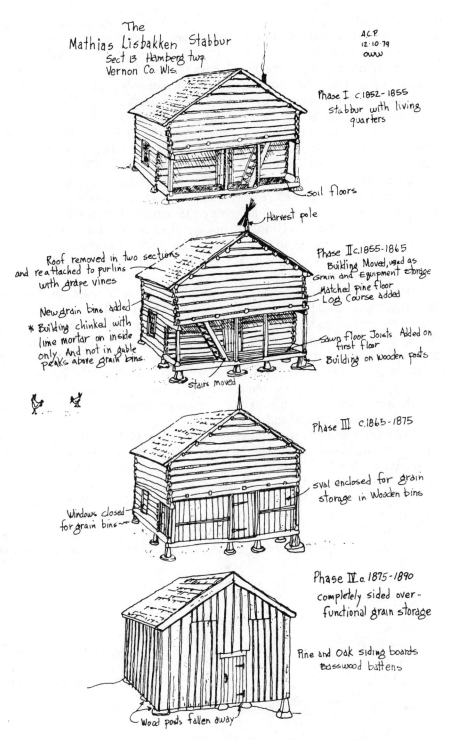

The
Mathias Lisbakken Stabbur
Sect 13 Hamberg twp.
Vernon Co. Wis.

A.C.P
12·10·79
aww

Phase I c.1852-1855
Stabbur with living
quarters

soil floors

Harvest pole

Roof removed in two sections
and reattached to purlins
with grape vines

Phase II c.1855-1865
Building Moved, used as
Grain and Equipment storage
Matched pine floor
Log Course added

New grain bins added
* Building chinked with
lime mortar on inside
only. And not in gable
peaks above grain bins.

Sawn floor Joists Added on
first floor
Building on wooden posts

stairs moved

Phase III c.1865-1875

Sval enclosed for grain
storage in Wooden bins

Windows closed
for grain bins

Phase IV c.1875-1890
completely sided over-
functional grain storage

Pine and Oak siding boards
Basswood battens

Wood posts fallen away

**Figure 11.20    Stages in the Modification of the Lisbakken *Stabbur*. Source: Pope (1980), 3; used by permission.**

During the nineteenth century, the second wave of Amish immigration occurred. Many were from Alsace and Lorraine in France and Bavaria and Waldeck in Germany, and they contributed to the establishment of other communities in North America, such as those in Ohio (Holmes, Stark, Wayne, Geauga, and Fulton Counties); Indiana (Adams, Allen, Daviess, Elkhart, and LaGrange Counties); Illinois (Woodford and Tazewell Counties); Iowa (Henry and Washington Counties); New York (Lewis and Cattaraugus Counties); Maryland (Somerset County); and Ontario, Canada (Waterloo and Perth provinces). Near the end of the nineteenth century, "the 1890 U.S. *Census of Religious Bodies* reported twenty-two Old Order Amish congregations with 2,038 baptized adult members in nine states." Total population in 1890 was estimated to be 3,700. By 1920, the Amish had an estimated population of 14,000; by 1950 the population had grown to 33,000; and as of 1979, there were a total of 85,783 persons.[41] Church districts vary in size, but most are small because distances that can be covered to attend church services by horse and buggy are necessarily limited. In Holmes County, Ohio, the largest districts of Old Order Amish extend for only about six to seven miles. The smallest are barely a mile and a half square. Today the numbers of Amish are approaching 150,000 concentrated in Ohio, Pennsylvania, and Indiana.[42]

These Amish, scattered in a series of ethnic islands from Pennsylvania to beyond the Mississippi River (Fig. 11.21), cling tenaciously to tradition. One consequence is that they continue to need large, two-story barns to house their draft animals as well as other livestock. Barns on all farms are more susceptible to fire than houses, and on Amish farms the risk is even greater because the Amish oppose the use of lightning rods on religious grounds as an interference with God's will.[43] Consequently, barns are replaced much more frequently than houses. Thus, even in the newly settled areas of the Midwest where Amish families have taken over non-Amish properties, the Sweitzer barn gradually defines the Amish cultural landscape.

The Amish traditionally construct Sweitzer barns (Fig. 11.22) of the type built in southern Germany or Switzerland, the area of the group's origin. Newly designed barn types such as pole barns, Wisconsin dairy barns, or round roof barns are noticeably lacking in Amish areas. Furthermore, traditional practices such as stacking straw from threshed grain outside in the barnyard (Fig. 11.22) or shocking of corn and wheat in the fall are maintained. Certain smaller structures found in Amish areas also help contribute to the sense of a traditional landscape. Thus, one finds windmills (Fig. 11.23), because the Amish do not believe in using electrical power; privies, because water normally cannot be made available

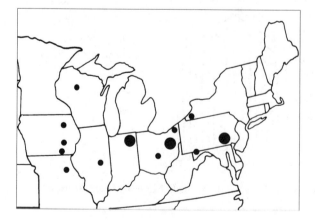

**Figure 11.21   Distribution of Amish Settlements in the Northeastern United States.**

**Figure 11.22   Straw Stack beside a Typical Sweitzer Barn, Holmes County, Ohio, 1981. Source: Photo by A. G. Noble.**

**Figure 11.23   Amish Farmstead in Holmes County, Ohio, 1978. Note the windmill, board fence, and buggy—all typical of Amish landscapes. Source: Photo by A. G. Noble.**

within the house; board fences, often whitewashed; a multiple birdhouse perched high on a pole; and gardens, in front of or close beside the farmhouse rather than behind it. Other typical features closely related to the kitchen garden are the larger "patch" for potatoes and other vegetables consumed in large quantities in the house, and the fruit orchard.

The most typical house associated with the Amish is the four-over-four (Fig. 11.24), a type common in southeastern Pennsylvania. Elsewhere, this house type is less often en-

**Figure 11.24   An Amish Farmstead, Holmes County, Ohio, 1978. Typical elements include the Sweitzer barn, a four-over-four house, the grandfather house, and board fences. Source: Photo by A. G. Noble.**

countered for three reasons. First, the Amish often purchased farmsteads of earlier non-Amish settlers and occupied the existing houses there. Second, the Amish normally have large families and so often build additions to the original houses. With enlargement, the houses are modified so that their original type is sometimes difficult to identify from the outside. Apparently only one floor plan of an Amish house has ever been published.[44] It suggests a structure that has grown by accretion rather than by careful adherence to any preconceived plan traditionally acceptable to the ethnic group.

Finally, on many Amish farmsteads two houses are present (Fig. 11.25). These may be entirely separate structures, the obviously newer one being the smaller of the two. Sometimes the two houses are connected by a closed passageway, or their corners touch. The rationale for two houses on the farmstead lies in the practice among the Amish of retiring from farming at a relatively early age and turning the active direction of the farm over to the youngest son. Upon retirement, the parents move to a newly built house on the family homestead. Sometimes instead of building a separate, or nearly separate, house, the existing dwelling is simply enlarged with a wing to include a private set of rooms for the older generation. When a separate dwelling is built, it is referred to as the "grandfather" or "gross-dawdy" house. Such an arrangement is a strong confirmation of the traditional outlook of Amish society.

### The Mormons

Another group also oriented to religion, but in a quite different fashion, is the Mormons. Beginning just before the middle of the nineteenth century, Mormon settlers occupied a series of desert oases in the intermontane West. Gradually settlement was spread by extending irrigation works until the areas coalesced to form a large Mormon cultural region. Meinig has delimited the Mormon culture region in terms of core, domain, and sphere (Fig. 11.26).[45] The Wasatch Oasis, which extends approximately sixty-five miles in a north-south direction, forms the core of the Mormon settlement area. The central cities of the core are Salt Lake City and Ogden, Utah. Surrounding the core is an area identified as the domain where Mormon culture values are dominant, but Gentile intrusion has occurred, thereby lessening the Mormon homogeneity in the area. In the much wider surrounding sphere, Mormon culture is present, but it is less intense, and Mormons reside as minorities or nucleated enclaves within the region.

Figure 11.25    An Amish Home, Holmes County, Ohio, 1978. The grandfather house is to the left, separate but connected to the older main house by a common porch. Source: Photo by A. G. Noble.

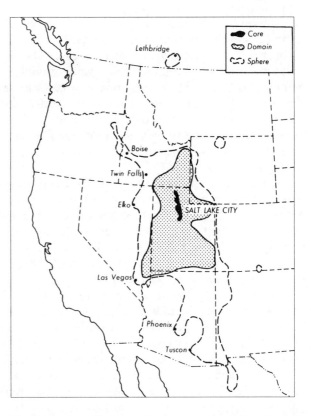

**Figure 11.26    Distribution of the Mormon Cultural Area (after Meinig).**

The Mormons tended to settle in small farm villages rather than on isolated, individual farmsteads. Three reasons probably explain this variance from the usual American practice. First, the apprehension of Indian attack made group settlement sensible. Second, there was a need to organize farmers to construct, maintain, and protect, at the lowest cost possible, the irrigation facilities on which settlement depended. Finally, the clustering of settlers was encouraged by church leaders to maintain the religious discipline and spirit of the Mormons. Thus, the cultural landscape of the Mormons is that of small villages rather than individual farmsteads. Francaviglia has identified ten significant factors that delimit the Mormon village, although other writers suggest a shorter list.[46]

Among the most important and distinctive features are the uniformly very wide streets running at right angles to each other and set in accord with cardinal compass points. They divide each village into spacious, square blocks. Allowing for local idiosyncrasies, the villages have a uniform plan related to that of "the city of Zion" decreed by Mormon church leaders. As Nelson notes, the Mormon village was in part "motivated by a sense of urgent need to prepare a dwelling place for the Saviour at His Second Coming."[47] The large blocks permitted not only the Mormon house but also the farmstead to be located in the village. This combination of house, barn, and outbuildings set on large lots in a spread-out village defines Mormon settlement.

The houses of the Mormons are invariably small, which reflects partly the relatively recent settlement of the area, partly the modest living standards afforded by the desert oases, and partly the frugality and communal quality of Mormon life. That lifestyle requires a large portion of income to be donated to the church and its social welfare work.

One survey of a Mormon village in 1923 showed the mean number of rooms per house to be 4.5 and the median only 3 rooms.[48]

Considerable variety in house types exists, but the most often encountered earlier structure is a two-room, one-story, gable-roofed house with gable chimneys and often a rear extension (Fig. 11.27). Secondary features include very little roof overhang, a general absence of decorations, and sometimes double front doors. A very high percentage of these houses are composed of adobe brick, a logical building material in the dry, unforested lands of the intermontane West. The use of adobe continued in Utah until the construction of rail lines in 1875, making coal deposits easily available as a fuel for producing kiln-fired bricks.[49]

Another group of houses is characterized by central hallways.[50] Regardless of particular type, these houses invariably are done in Greek revival architectural style. A very high percentage of all Mormon houses constructed between 1860 and 1890 adhered to this style, which earlier had been the dominant one in the midwestern and eastern United States when the Mormons left those areas. Thus, the Mormons brought the idea of the Greek revival house to Mormonland, "and their self-imposed isolation kept other styles out until late in the 1800s."[51]

During this period, adobe was superseded by brick as the major building material. Since population was rapidly expanding at this time, predominance of brick structures has come to be recognized as one of the characteristics of the Mormon settlement area.

Very much in contrast to the neat and simple adobe and brick buildings are the rest of the structures, including plank-sided barns (Fig. 11.28), open hay sheds, hay derricks (Fig. 11.29), and rough "Mormon fences" of irregular vertical boards nailed to horizontal rails (Fig. 11.29). All of these features are unpainted and often appear quite ramshackled, giving a strong yet erroneous impression of a relict landscape. Generations of western travelers have remarked on the distinctiveness of the Mormon landscape, a quality probably due to its desert oasis location. Even the trees, planted Lombardy poplars, are a product of the Mormon occupance.[52]

**Figure 11.27   A Mormon House Built of Adobe Brick.**

**Figure 11.28    A Transverse Barn Typical of Mormonland.**

**Figure 11.29    A Hay Derrick, Strawberry Valley, Utah, 1974. This is one of the most**

## RURAL ETHNIC ISLANDS AS DISTINCTIVE CULTURAL LANDSCAPES

The cultural landscapes of other ethnic groups are not quite so easily perceived by casual observers. Nonetheless, they do exist and are important in local areas. Since the settlements of the various ethnic groups are scattered, they form a distinctive checkerboard of ethnic islands strewn across America. Only slowly are the landscapes of these rural ethnic islands becoming appreciated as distinctive and valuable components of the American cultural landscape.

## NOTES

1. Peter A. Munch, "Segregation and Assimilation of Norwegian Settlements in Wisconsin," *Norwegian-American Studies and Records* 18 (1954): 102–140.

2. Munch, "Segregation and Assimilation," 112.

3. Karl B. Raitz, "Ethnic Maps of North America," *Geographical Review* 68 (July 1978): 335–350.

4. George W. Hill, "The People of Wisconsin According to Ethnic Stocks, 1940," in *Wisconsin's Changing Population,* Bulletin of the University of Wisconsin No. 2642 (Madison: University of Wisconsin Press, 1942).

5. Fred B. Kniffen, "Folk Housing: Key to Diffusion," *Annals of the Association of American Geographers* 55 (December 1965): 551.

6. Robert F. Ensminger, *The Pennsylvania Barn* (Baltimore: Johns Hopkins University Press, 1992).

7. Allen G. Noble and Gayle A. Seymour, "Distribution of Barns in Northeastern North America," *Geographical Review* 72 (April 1982): 155–170.

8. Hjalmar R. Holand, *Wisconsin's Belgian Community* (Sturgeon Bay, Wisc.: Door County Historical Society, 1933).

9. Charles F. Calkins and William G. Laatsch, "The Belgian Outdoor Ovens of Northeastern Wisconsin," *Pioneer America Society Transactions* 2 (1979): 1–12.

10. Fred B. Kniffen, "The Outdoor Oven in Louisiana," *Louisiana History* 1 (1960): 20–35; Michel Lessard and Huguette Marquis, *Encyclopedie de la Maison Quebecoise* (Montreal: Les Editions de l'Homme, 1972), 620–625.

11. Calkins and Laatsch, "The Belgian Outdoor Ovens," 4.

12. Eric Arthur and Dudley Whitney, *The Barn: A Vanishing Landmark in North America* (New York: New York Graphic Society, 1972), 114–141.

13. William F. Rushton, *The Cajuns: From Acadia to Louisiana* (New York: Farrar Straus Giroux, 1979), 67–68.

14. William B. Knipmeyer, *Settlement Succession in Eastern French Louisiana* (Ann Arbor: University Microfilms International, 1956), 88.

15. Rushton, *The Cajuns,* 174.

16. Knipmeyer, *Settlement Succession,* 99.

17. Knipmeyer, *Settlement Succession,* 120–123.

18. Rushton, *The Cajuns,* 183–184.

19. Malcolm L. Comeaux, "The Cajun Barn," *Geographical Review* 79 (January 1989): 47–62.

20. Cotton Mather and Matti Kaups, "The Finnish Sauna: A Cultural Index to Settlement," *Annals of the Association of American Geographers* 53 (December 1963): 498–499.

21. Mather and Kaups, "The Finnish Sauna," 500–501.

22. Arnold R. Alanen and William H. Tishler, "Finnish Farmstead Organization in Old and New World Settings," *Journal of Cultural Geography* 1 (Fall/Winter 1980): 66–81.

23. Richard W. E. Perrin, "Log Houses in Wisconsin," *Antiques* 89 (June 1966): 869.

24. Nils E. Wickberg, *Finnish Architecture* (Helsinki: Otava, 1959), 16.

25. Eugene Van Cleef, "The Finn in America," *Geographical Review* 6 (September 1918): 192.

26. Matti Kaups, "A Finnish Riihi in Minnesota," *Journal of the Minnesota Academy of Science* 38 (Spring and Summer 1973): 66.

27. Kaups, "A Finnish Riihi," 69.

28. Matti Kaups, "A Finnish Savusauna in Minnesota," *Minnesota History* 45 (Spring 1976): 15.

29. Kaups, "A Finnish Savusauna," 12.

30. Perrin, "Log Houses in Wisconsin," 870.

31. Richard W. E. Perrin, "John Bergen's Log House," *Wisconsin Magazine of History* 44 (Autumn 1960): 12–14.

32. John Lloyd, "The Norwegian Laftehus," in *Shelter and Society*, ed. Paul Oliver (New York: Praeger, 1969), 33–48.

33. Thomas Paulsson, *Scandinavian Architecture* (Newton, Mass.: Branford, 1959).

34. Alan C. Pape, "Kvaale House: Architectural Analysis Report," unpublished internal report, Old World Wisconsin Outdoor Ethnic Museum, Eagle, Wisconsin, 1980, p. 3.

35. Alan C. Pape, "Lisbakken Stabbur: Architectural Analysis Report," unpublished internal report, Old World Wisconsin Outdoor Ethnic Museum, Eagle, Wisconsin, 1980, p. 3.

36. Lawrence R. Brandt and Ned E. Braatz, "Log Buildings in Portage County, Wisconsin: Some Cultural Implications," *Pioneer America* 4 (January 1972): 37.

37. John A. Hostetler, *Amish Society*, 3d ed. (Baltimore: John Hopkins University Press, 1980), 50.

38. Hostetler, *Amish Society*, 56.

39. Hostetler, *Amish Society*, 56.

40. Hostetler, *Amish Society*, 65.

41. Hostetler, *Amish Society*, 99.

42. Martin B. Bradley et al., *Churches and Church Membership in the United States, 1990* (Atlanta: Glenmary Research Center, 1992).

43. Maurice A. Mook and John A. Hostetler, "The Amish and Their Land," *Landscape* 6 (Spring 1957): 25.

44. Hostetler, *Amish Society*, 178.

45. Donald W. Meinig, "The Mormon Culture Region: Strategies and Patterns in the Geography of the American West, 1847–1964," *Annals of the Association of American Geographers* 55 (June 1965): 191–220.

46. Richard V. Francaviglia, "The Mormon Landscape: Definition of an Image in the American West," *Proceedings of the Association of American Geographers* 2 (1970): 59–61; Richard H. Jackson, "The Use of Adobe in the Mormon Culture Region," *Journal of Cultural Geography* 1 (Fall/Winter 1980): 82.

47. Lowry Nelson, *The Mormon Village* (Salt Lake City: University of Utah Press, 1952), 28.

48. Nelson, *The Mormon Village*, 99.

49. Jackson, "The Use of Adobe," 85.

50. Richard V. Francaviglia, "Mormon Central-Hall Houses in the American West," *Annals of the Association of American Geographers* 61 (March 1971): 65.

51. Richard H. Jackson, "Religion and Landscape in the Mormon Cultural Region," in *Dimensions of Human Geography: Essays on Some Familiar and Neglected Themes*, ed. Karl W. Butzer, Research Paper 186 (Chicago: University of Chicago, Department of Geography, 1978), 113–114.

52. Austin E. Fife, "Folklore of Material Culture on the Rocky Mountain Frontier," *Arizona Quarterly* 13 (Summer 1957): 107.

# ⑫

# Urban Ethnic Islands

*Donald J. Zeigler and Stanley D. Brunn*

American cities have long been destinations for immigrants from all parts of the world. Many early Europeans settled in urban places, and they continue to be the foci for recent ethnic groups arriving from Latin America and Asia. As a result, urban areas in the United States are characterized by a rich diversity of ethnic nationalities, and the mix of ethnic groups has played and continues to play an important role in American history. More recently, the host communities have been suburbs, particularly older neighborhoods filtering down to lower-income populations.

Each large American city contains varying proportions of two or more ethnic nationalities. The total number of cities with English, German, Irish, Italian, Scottish, and Polish ethnic populations is larger than those with Dutch, Portuguese, Japanese, Chinese, and Ethiopian origins. All, however, contribute to the rich diversity of urban America. Mapping the spatial patterns of ethnic groups reveals that some nationalities are spread through urban areas; others exist in two or three concentrations; still others live in small islands. Over the years, the process of acculturation and assimilation has changed the sizes and shapes of these ethnic cores, archipelagos, and islands. Even as they are assimilated, however, they leave behind important contributions to American culture.

This chapter will examine the American concept of ethnicity, historical ethnic settlement processes, urban settlement concentrations, and ethnic mixes in selected cities. In addition, three salient features of individual ethnic groups are investigated: the foreign-language press, foreign-language radio broadcasting, and ethnic festivals and organizations.

## THE THREE WAVES OF IMMIGRATION

The spatial patterning of ethnic minorities, and their cultural attributes, is closely related to the history of United States immigration. This history can be divided into three major immigrant waves that rolled across the American landscape, displacing the Native American population (themselves prehistoric immigrants from Northeast Asia) and forging a new American identity. The first wave of immigrants was composed of peoples from western and northern Europe, most importantly from the British Isles and Germany. This period of immigrant history began with the founding of Jamestown, Virginia, in 1607 and extended until about 1870. It was not until the 1840s, however, that mass immigration began, with economic and political "push factors" in Europe sending more than 1.5 million people, mostly Irish and the German, to the United States. Western and northern European nationalities continued to migrate to the United States throughout the nineteenth and twentieth centuries, but beginning in the 1870s, with the demand for labor in a rapidly industrializing country, eastern and southern Europeans began accounting for a larger share of new arrivals. These new nationalities constituted the second wave of immigrants that by the 1890s accounted for over 50 percent of new arrivals. By the turn of the twentieth century, the growing industrial cities of the Northeast and Midwest were absorbing most of the immigrant stream, with the result that first-generation Americans comprised the majority in many U.S. cities.[1] The 1920 census revealed for the first time that the United States had become an urban nation, with over 50 percent of the population living in urban places. The immigrant wave, however, was decidedly more urban oriented than the nation, with more than eight out of ten arrivals from the Russian Empire, Ireland, Italy, Poland, and Hungary settling in U.S. cities. This was also a period of rural-to-urban migration that brought many second-generation immigrants to the cities in search of jobs.

The second wave ended in 1921 when Congress enacted the first quota system to regulate the overall number of immigrants the nation would accept and the proportions that could originate from any particular country. The quota system in the 1920s, the Great Depression in the 1930s, and World War II in the 1940s put a damper on immigration until the start of the third wave during the 1960s, when the national quota system was replaced with a system more favorable to Latin American immigrants. For the first time, non-European immigrants came to outnumber Europeans: Mexicans, Cubans, Puerto Ricans, and, more recently, Central Americans. Immigration gradually swelled from Asia also. The early dominance of China and Japan gave way during the 1970s to major immigrant streams from Vietnam, the Philippines, and Korea. During the 1970s, 1.4 million Asians immigrated to the United States as compared with 1.8 million Latin Americans and 700,000 Europeans. In the 1960s, Latin American immigrants constituted 39 percent of the immigrant stream and Asian immigrants 13 percent. In the 1980s, Latin America accounted for 47 percent and Asia for 38 percent of new arrivals.

In the 1990s, the geographic source areas have remained focused on countries to the south and west of the United States (Table 12.1), but the diversity of countries supplying immigrants to the United States is remarkable. Seventeen states were dominated by the immigration wave from Mexico in 1995, but there were also states with more Vietnamese, Indian, and Dominican migrants than any other groups.[2] The leading source country for each state is displayed in Figure 12.1 for 1995, when legal immigration totaled 716,000 people. Some of the factors that have led to the diversification of immigration to the United States in the 1990s are the break-up of the Soviet Union and Yugoslavia and the democratization of eastern Europe. This has led to a new "Europeanization" of immigrant streams to many states. Ukraine, Russia, and Poland are now leading sources of immigrants. The second largest immigrant stream to Pennsylvania in 1995 was from Ukraine. To Illinois and Connecticut it was from Poland; and to Missouri, North Dakota, and Vermont it was from Bosnia.

## IDENTIFYING ETHNIC GROUPS

The decennial censuses of population make it possible to determine the country of birth of first-generation immigrants, known as "foreign-born" population. Through

**Table 12.1   Immigration to the United States by Country of Origin, 1995.**

| | |
|---|---|
| Mexico | 86,960 |
| Philippines | 50,962 |
| Vietnam | 41,752 |
| Dominican Republic | 38,392 |
| China | 35,459 |
| India | 34,715 |
| Cuba | 17,932 |
| Ukraine | 17,432 |
| Jamaica | 16,335 |
| Korea | 16,034 |
| Russia | 14,560 |
| Haiti | 13,892 |
| Poland | 13,804 |
| Canada | 12,913 |
| United Kingdom | 12,311 |
| El Salvador | 11,563 |
| Colombia | 10,780 |
| Pakistan | 9,743 |
| Taiwan | 9,374 |
| Iran | 9,178 |

Source: U.S. Immigration and Naturalization Service, reported in "Special Report: Destination USA," *USA Today,* 13 October 1997, p. 11A.

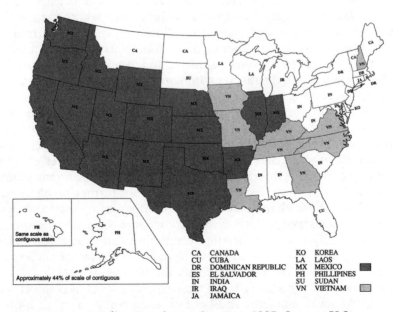

Figure 12.1   Leading Immigrant Streams, 1995. Source: U.S. Immigration and Naturalization Service, reported in "Special Report: Destination USA," *USA Today,* 13 October 1997, p. 11A. United States map produced by the University of Kentucky.

the 1970 census, it was also possible to determine the country of the parents' birth for second-generation immigrants, known as the "native population of foreign or mixed parentage." The fact that foreign nativity data have been collected in so may censuses reflects the importance of ethnicity in American culture. The melting pot hypothesis has been almost institutionalized by the census, which, in essence, has equated the ethnic population of the United States with first- and second-generation immigrants only. Third, fourth, and further generations, as far as the census has been concerned, have not been differentiated from the mainstream of society—that is, until recently.

In the 1980 and 1990 censuses, the foreign-born population remained easy to identify, but not so the "foreign stock" population. Replacing the question about the parents' country of birth was a new open-ended question: "What is your ancestry?" Such a change signals a change in Americans' view of ethnicity. The last two censuses also used a more refined racial classification and singled out populations of Hispanic origin for detailed statistical data. The new racial classification seemed designed to maximize information about the Asian population, and the new questions on Hispanic origin were designed to maximize information about Latinos (but not West Indians from the Anglophone, Francophone, and Dutch-speaking Caribbean). When one considers that two of the six questions asked of everyone had to do with race and Hispanic origin, the importance of immigration and ethnicity in the United States is evident. On the long form, mailed to every sixth household, was the ancestry question, plus questions about place of birth, citizenship status, and language, all of which help paint a portrait of the United States as a multicultural society. Particularly notable among the publications that have flowed from these data is an atlas called *We the People*,[3] which provides a clear picture of the ethnic complexion of an immigrant nation in which, as Sowell notes, there are no real minorities because there is no majority.[4] In the 2000 census, after an intense debate over whether to include a "multiracial" category, it was decided instead to allow people to check more than one of the following groups: American Indian or Alaska Native, Asian, black or African American, Native Hawaiian or other Pacific Islander, white, and Hispanic or Latino.

What do the changes in census questions indicate about American culture? First, they suggest that second-generation immigrants—that is, descendants of original immigrant groups—should not be categorized as foreign stock but as native stock, suggesting, perhaps, that the task of assimilation is easier today than it has been in the past. Second, they illustrate the importance of third-wave immigrants—those from Latin America and Asia and their descendants. Just as previous census questionnaires were designed to maximize information about European immigrant groups, the 1980 and 1990 questionnaires were designed to maximize information about Latino immigrant groups. Third, these changes set the stage for equating ethnicity with origin or ancestry rather than nativity. Both of these concepts span generations, rather than being restricted to only two—the original immigrants and their descendants. Fourth, the census concepts of ethnicity and race have become almost indistinguishable so that individual Americans are able to identify themselves as "black," "Hispanic," and of Cuban ancestry all at the same time. This suggests a level of comfort with our multiracial and multiethnic character and betrays a tendency to think more inclusively about group identity.

The percentage of the population that was identified as first-generation immigrants (i.e., the foreign-born population) increased from 4.7 percent in 1970 to 7.9 percent in 1990 (Table 12.2). Today, almost one out of every twelve people in the United States was born in a foreign country. The national averages, however, mask much regional variation, particularly the contrast between the Sunbelt states and the Snowbelt states of the Northeast. In 1970, only New York, the traditional gateway to America, had more than 10 percent of its population foreign born. By 1990, five states had exceeded 10 percent, and New York's first-place ranking had been usurped by California with a population that was almost 22 percent foreign born. Other states that saw major increases in the foreign-born population were Hawaii, Texas, and Florida. In 1970, fifteen states had 1.5 percent or less foreign born; by 1990, that number had slipped to nine states. Of the states with small first-generation immigrant populations, most are in the South and on the Great Plains. Among this group, the most notable change has taken place in Virginia. In 1970, only 1.5 percent of the Old Dominion's population was foreign born; in 1990, it was 5 percent. A state that had never been a large target of international immigration had suddenly become internationalized. The magnetism of Washington, D.C., was responsible for much of that growth.

**Table 12.2    The Foreign Born Population of the United States.**

| | 1990 Population (in thousands) | 1990 % Foreign Born | 1980 % Foreign Born | 1970 % Foreign Born |
|---|---|---|---|---|
| Alabama | 4,040 | 1.1 | 1.0 | 0.5 |
| Alaska | 550 | 4.5 | 3.9 | 2.5 |
| Arizona | 3,665 | 7.6 | 6.0 | 4.3 |
| Arkansas | 2,350 | 1.1 | 0.9 | 0.4 |
| California | 29,758 | 21.7 | 14.8 | 8.8 |
| Colorado | 3,294 | 4.3 | 3.8 | 2.7 |
| Connecticut | 3,287 | 8.5 | 8.5 | 8.6 |
| Delaware | 666 | 3.3 | 3.4 | 2.8 |
| Florida | 12,938 | 12.9 | 10.9 | 8.0 |
| Georgia | 6,478 | 2.7 | 1.7 | 0.7 |
| Hawaii | 1,108 | 14.7 | 14.0 | 9.8 |
| Idaho | 1,007 | 2.9 | 2.3 | 1.8 |
| Illinois | 11,431 | 8.3 | 7.3 | 5.7 |
| Indiana | 5,544 | 1.7 | 1.9 | 1.6 |
| Iowa | 2,777 | 1.6 | 1.7 | 1.4 |
| Kansas | 2,477 | 2.5 | 2.0 | 1.2 |
| Kentucky | 3,689 | 0.9 | 0.9 | 0.5 |
| Louisiana | 4,220 | 2.1 | 2.1 | 1.1 |
| Maine | 1,228 | 3.0 | 3.8 | 4.3 |
| Maryland | 4,781 | 6.6 | 4.6 | 3.2 |
| Massachusetts | 6,016 | 9.5 | 8.4 | 8.7 |
| Michigan | 9,295 | 3.8 | 4.4 | 4.8 |
| Minnesota | 4,376 | 2.6 | 2.7 | 2.6 |
| Mississippi | 2,575 | 0.8 | 0.9 | 0.4 |
| Missouri | 5,117 | 1.6 | 1.8 | 1.4 |
| Montana | 799 | 1.7 | 2.3 | 2.8 |
| Nebraska | 1,578 | 1.8 | 1.9 | 1.9 |
| Nevada | 1,202 | 8.7 | 6.7 | 3.7 |
| New Hampshire | 1,109 | 3.7 | 4.2 | 5.0 |
| New Jersey | 7,730 | 12.5 | 10.3 | 8.9 |

**Table 12.2    Continued.**

| | 1990 Population (in thousands) | 1990 % Foreign Born | 1980 % Foreign Born | 1970 % Foreign Born |
|---|---|---|---|---|
| New Mexico | 1,515 | 5.3 | 4.2 | 2.2 |
| North Carolina | 6,632 | 1.7 | 1.5 | 0.5 |
| North Dakota | 639 | 1.5 | 2.3 | 2.9 |
| Ohio | 10,847 | 2.4 | 2.7 | 3.0 |
| Oklahoma | 3,146 | 2.1 | 1.8 | 0.8 |
| Oregon | 2,842 | 4.9 | 4.2 | 3.1 |
| Pennsylvania | 11,883 | 3.1 | 3.6 | 3.8 |
| Rhode Island | 1,003 | 9.5 | 8.8 | 7.9 |
| South Carolina | 3,486 | 1.4 | 1.4 | 0.5 |
| South Dakota | 696 | 1.1 | 1.4 | 1.6 |
| Tennessee | 4,877 | 1.2 | 1.0 | 0.5 |
| Texas | 16,986 | 9.0 | 6.0 | 2.8 |
| Utah | 1,723 | 3.4 | 3.5 | 2.8 |
| Vermont | 583 | 3.1 | 4.2 | 4.2 |
| Virginia | 6,189 | 5.0 | 3.2 | 1.5 |
| Washington | 4,867 | 6.6 | 5.8 | 4.5 |
| West Virginia | 1,793 | 0.9 | 1.1 | 1.0 |
| Wisconsin | 4,892 | 2.5 | 2.7 | 3.0 |
| Wyoming | 454 | 1.7 | 1.9 | 2.0 |
| US | 248,718 | 7.9 | 6.2 | 4.7 |

Sources: U.S. Bureau of the Census, *County and City Data Book*, 1994; *1970 Census of Population, Characteristics of the Population*, 1973.

The ancestry question in the 1990 census, which was not limited to a single generation, resulted in over nine hundred different categories of ethnic and national identities. The leading ancestry groups with which Americans identify are listed in Table 12.3. Not a single group constituted more than a quarter of the U.S. population, though the British Isles (including English, Irish, Scottish, and Scotch Irish) and Germany still dominate the ancestry characteristics of the American people, though not to the extent they did during the colonial period of U.S. history. In fact, if ethnic groups that might be classified as white are grouped together, the U.S. population in 1996 would be classified as 73 percent non-Hispanic white. By the year 2050, however, when the total population is likely to be close to four hundred million, the proportion of the population non-Hispanic white is projected to decrease to 53 percent.[5]

## CULTURAL MOSAIC OR MELTING POT?

A classic debate in ethnic geography is whether the U.S. population can best be described as an ethnic mosaic or an ethnic melting pot. The mosaic analogy suggests that immigrant groups, particularly after the start of mass immigration in the 1840s, have had difficulty in becoming part of the mainstream of American culture. According to this school of thought, ethnicity in the United States surfaces as relatively easily identifiable rural and urban ethnic islands of "unmeltable" Americans. The melting pot analogy, on the other hand, suggests that American culture is quick to assimilate newcomers so that

**Table 12.3   Leading Ancestry Groups of the U.S. Population, 1990.**

| Ancestry Group | Total (in thousands) |
| --- | --- |
| German | 57,947 |
| Irish | 38,736 |
| English | 32,652 |
| African-American | 23,777 |
| Italian | 14,665 |
| "American" | 12,396 |
| Mexican | 11,587 |
| French | 10,321 |
| Polish | 9,366 |
| American Indian | 8,708 |
| Dutch | 6,227 |
| Scotch-Irish | 5,618 |
| Scottish | 5,394 |
| Swedish | 4,681 |
| Norwegian | 3,869 |

Source: U.S. Bureau of the Census, *1990 Census of Population, Detailed Ancestry Groups for States* (1990-CP-S-1-2).

in a few generations ethnic Americans are indistinguishable from the population as a whole. According to this school of thought, ethnicity is quickly snuffed out by the business of daily American life. Only selected cultural traits are salvaged from the flotsam of Old World tradition to become a part of popular American culture.

The melting pot idea has been around since the founding of the republic. The clergyman Jedidiah Morse, who defined geography for generations of American schoolchildren in the decades after 1789, postulated an idea that is still being tested by the contemporary generation of social scientists. He noted in his *The American Geography*: "The time . . . is anticipated when the language, manners, customs, political and religious sentiments of the mixed mass of the people who inhabit the United States, shall have become so assimilated, as that all nominal distinctions shall be lost in the general and honourable name of Americans."

What is known today is that the melting pot analogy may pertain to some ethnic groups but not to others, and it may pertain to some traits and not to others. The English language, for instance, has served as a tool of assimilation for centuries. Yet, in terms of race, the United States remains more of a mosaic than a melting pot. In particular, the African American population of the United States, an immigrant group that began arriving in 1619, has not blended into the mainstream the way many European groups have. Religion, until recently, has also proven an impediment to assimilation. The Catholic population of the United States (whether from Ireland or southern or eastern Europe) and the Orthodox population have long been discriminated against because of divergent religious beliefs. Some American ethnic groups, in other words, have been more "meltable" than others. Some have even suggested that rather than a melting pot, American society should be seen as a "stock pot" since neither melting pot nor cultural mosaic seems to accurately describe the nature of ethnic America. According to a 1995 survey, only a slight majority of Americans felt that ethnic groups should adapt and blend into a larger society (Figure 12.2).

If interethnic marriages are the litmus test of the melting pot hypothesis, then ancestry data should provide a first approximation of the extent to which various ethnic groups have melted into the mainstream of American culture. Table 12.4 lists the nationalities that were designated in 1979 as ancestry groups by at least 650,000 Americans. In all, over 179 million Americans reported at least one foreign nationality when asked, "What is your ancestry?" Of those 179 million, 46 percent reported a combination of nationalities. These groups have been arranged in order of descending percentage of mixed ancestry. Almost 89 percent of those listing Scottish as their ancestry listed another nationality as well. So mixed have they become that to speak of Scottish Americans as a single group camouflages the variegated background of most American of Scottish descent. Among blacks, at the other extreme, only 7 percent acknowledged being of mixed parentage. Those groups that are more than one-third of mixed ancestry are all, with the exception of the American Indian, from western and northern Europe. These nationalities represent the first wave of immigrants from Europe. Ancestry groups that are between one-third and two-thirds of mixed ancestry are all from eastern and southern Europe. They represent the second wave of immigration.

Given these two categories, one might conclude that the only correlate of mixed heritage in the United States is the number of generations that have elapsed since the initial immigration. Immigrant groups that arrived first, save African Americans, are "melting pot" Americans, whereas immigrants who arrived later are headed toward "melting pot" status. In the 1990 census, more than one-third of those who reported Irish, Scottish, Welsh, Dutch, and French ancestry reported it as their second line of descent; about one-fifth of those who reported German, Italian, Portuguese, and Greek ancestry reported it as their second line of descent; and less than one-tenth of those who reported Mexican, Puerto Rican, Chinese, Filipino, Vietnamese, or Japanese ancestry reported it as their second line of descent.[6]

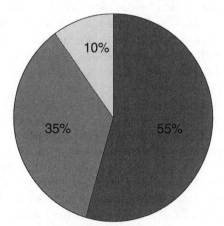

Figure 12.2   Racial and Ethnic Groups. Source: U.S. Immigration and Naturalization Service, reported in "Special Report: Destination USA," *USA Today*, 13 October 1997, p. 11A.

**Table 12.4    Ethnic Groups\* in the United States Reporting Multiple Ancestry, 1979.**

| Ancestry Group | Percent Reporting Multiple Ancestry |
|---|---|
| More than two-thirds of the following groups reported mixed ancestry. | |
| Scottish | 88.6 |
| Dutch | 83.2 |
| Welsh | 82.3 |
| American Indian | 79.3 |
| Irish | 77.7 |
| French and French Canadian | 76.0 |
| Swedish | 75.1 |
| Swiss | 74.6 |
| Danish | 73.8 |
| English | 71.3 |
| Norwegian | 70.1 |
| German | 66.8 |
| Between one-third and two-thirds of the following groups reported mixed ancestry. | |
| Hungarian | 66.5 |
| Austrian | 64.0 |
| Lithuanian | 61.9 |
| Polish | 58.5 |
| Slavic | 58.4 |
| Russian | 56.8 |
| Czechoslovakian | 53.2 |
| Italian | 48.0 |
| Portuguese | 47.9 |
| Greek | 42.7 |
| Less than one-third of the following groups reported mixed ancestry. | |
| Filipino | 31.3 |
| Chinese | 23.4 |
| Japanese | 22.3 |
| Spanish | 21.9 |
| Afro-American | 7.0 |

\*Ancestry claimed by more than 650,000 Americans.
Source: U.S. Bureau of the Census, *Current Population Reports,* 1982.

Among some groups, less than one-third of their members report mixed ancestry. Of those in Table 12.4, the only two that can claim recency of immigration as an explanation for their "purity" are the Spanish, almost all of whom are from Latin America, and the Filipinos. The other groups in this category strongly contradict the melting pot hypothesis. Blacks arrived in the American colonies as early as any European group, yet only a fraction report mixed heritage. Similarly, the Chinese and Japanese who immigrated to the United States by the tens of thousands during the first two decades of the twentieth century have not experienced the same degree of success at melting into the dominant society. The stratification evidenced in Table 12.4 may be understood on the basis of two factors: (1) immigration history, with the earliest arrivals having more opportunities for intermarriage, and (2) race, with black and Asian groups exhibiting the least interethnic marriage.

## URBAN SETTLEMENT PATTERNS

Seventy-five percent of the U.S. population lives in urban places (in the densely populated cores of metropolitan areas or in places over 2,500 regardless of location). Eighty percent of the U.S. population lives in officially designated metropolitan statistical areas, or MSAs (clusters of counties surrounding large urban cores). Thirty-two percent of the U.S. population lives in the central cities of MSAs. It has been common to think of first-generation immigrants as living in ethnic neighborhoods of large cities—that is, highly urbanized in their settlement patterns. Third-generation immigrant groups are commonly thought of as having moved out of the central cities and exhibiting the same settlement patterns as mainstream Americans. The data in Table 12.5 illustrate the degree to which this generalization is true. The most highly urbanized ancestry groups are those that have most recently arrived. Over nine out of ten West Indians, Arabs, Sub-Saharan Africans, and selected Latino and Asian groups are urban, and more than 40 percent of these populations live in the central cities of metropolitan areas. By contrast, more than eight out of ten Americans who claim second-wave ancestries live in urban areas. These

**Table 12.5    Urban Distribution of Ancestry Groups, 1990.**

| Ancestry Group | % Urban | % Central City |
|----------------|---------|----------------|
| Chinese | 97.7 | 53.7 |
| Colombian | 96.7 | 49.9 |
| Iranian | 96.4 | 43.2 |
| Puerto Rican | 96.1 | 70.1 |
| West Indian | 95.6 | 59.7 |
| Indian (Asian) | 95.3 | 39.3 |
| Filipino | 94.9 | 45.3 |
| Brazilian | 94.6 | 47.5 |
| Japanese | 93.6 | 40.5 |
| Arab | 91.1 | 41.1 |
| Sub-Saharan African | 92.7 | 58.3 |
| Mexican | 89.5 | 48.5 |
| Greek | 88.3 | 35.1 |
| Italian | 85.2 | 27.9 |
| Portuguese | 84.6 | 35.3 |
| Hungarian | 83.2 | 28.3 |
| Polish | 81.8 | 27.8 |
| Danish | 74.9 | 26.3 |
| Scottish | 74.4 | 26.1 |
| Swedish | 74.3 | 25.4 |
| Irish | 73.1 | 25.1 |
| French | 71.9 | 25.4 |
| Scotch-Irish | 71.7 | 26.4 |
| Czech | 71.3 | 24.4 |
| Norwegian | 70.8 | 25.5 |
| German | 70.2 | 23.5 |
| US Average | 75.2 | 31.7 |

Source: U.S. Bureau of the Census, *1990 Census of Population, Social and Economic Characteristics: United States.*

include such groups as Greeks, Italians, Portuguese, Hungarians, and Poles. Those Americans who trace their ancestry to first-wave immigrants from northern and western Europe exhibit settlement patterns that mirror national averages. Descendants of people from the British Isles, Germany, France, and Scandinavia are all slightly under the national average of 75 percent urban. Descendents of the second wave of immigrants are also more likely to be concentrated in the central cities than immigrant groups with ancestries in northern and western Europe. Central cities and fringe areas are occupied by varying mixtures of first-, second-, and third-wave immigrant groups. A cross-section of the ethnic populations in any metropolitan area at any time reveals varying residential patterns. Populations that may have existed in the central city in one decade may now have been replaced by a new wave of immigrants in another.

The 1970 Census of Population is the last that made it possible to compare the settlement patterns of first- and second-generation immigrant groups directly. Succeeding censuses collected data only on first-generation immigrants. As revealed in Table 12.6, the foreign stock population has been a decidedly urban population. First- and second-generation immigrants were far more likely to reside in urban settings, urbanized areas, and central cities than the population as a whole. The passage of generations, however, seems to break the grip of central cities on immigrants. Second-generation immigrants (native of foreign or mixed parentage) were not so concentrated in urban settings as were first-generation immigrants (foreign born). More than nine out of ten of the foreign born resided in urban settings as compared with slightly more than seven out of ten of the total population. Likewise, about half the foreign-born population resided in the central cities of metropolitan areas, whereas only 37 percent of the native population of foreign or mixed parentage (second generation) resided in central cities. Of the ethnic groups listed in Table 12.6, the Chinese have the highest percentages residing in central cities.

European, Asian, and Latin American first-generation immigrants exhibited very little variation in their preference for urban settings. More than nine out of ten first-generation immigrants from all three continents lived in urbanized areas or other urban places. Only in terms of the percentage residing in central cities of metropolitan areas do first-generation European ethnic groups differ markedly from Asian and Latin American ethnic groups. Only 48 percent of first-generation European immigrants resided in central cities, whereas 58 and 59 percent of Asian and Latin American groups, respectively, resided in central cities.

European, Asian, and Latin American second-generation immigrants paralleled the first-generation immigrants in their urban settlement patterns, but the second generation in all cases tended to be less concentrated in urbanized areas and central cities than the first generation. Again, second-generation Europeans are less markedly concentrated in central cities than are Asians and Latin Americans. In general, movement toward national averages for the total population seems to have been taking place at the same rate for ethnic groups from all continents. Only Asian second-generation immigrants seemed to be slightly less likely to break the bonds of urban living, with high percentages still residing in urban settings in general and urbanized areas in particular, even among second-generation immigrants.

The ethnic landscape includes a mix of ethnic churches, some of which have long histories in communities. The retention of a specific ethnic label reflects a wish on the part of its adherents to maintain close ties with churches, friends, and family members in their countries of origin. A volume, *Churches and Church Membership in the United*

**Table 12.6   Comparative Urban Settlement Patterns of First and Second Generation Ethnic Groups in the United States: 1970.**

|  | Percent Urban | Percent in Urbanized Areas | Percent in Central Cities |
|---|---|---|---|
| Total Population | 73 | 58 | 31 |
| Native of Native Parentage | 71 | 55 | 30 |
| Native of Foreign or Mixed Parentage | 84 | 74 | 37 |
| Foreign Born | 91 | 83 | 50 |
| First Generation Immigrants: |  |  |  |
| European Nationalities | 90 | 83 | 48 |
| Asian Nationalities | 93 | 84 | 58 |
| Latin American Nationalities | 94 | 87 | 59 |
| Canadians | 85 | 73 | 33 |
| Second Generation Immigrants: |  |  |  |
| European Nationalities | 84 | 74 | 36 |
| Asian Nationalities | 90 | 78 | 46 |
| Latin American Nationalities | 88 | 75 | 49 |
| Canadians | 79 | 64 | 28 |
| First Generation European Immigrants: |  |  |  |
| Greece | 97 | 90 | 62 |
| Italy | 95 | 88 | 52 |
| Ireland | 94 | 90 | 62 |
| U.S.S.R. | 94 | 89 | 61 |
| Poland | 94 | 89 | 60 |
| Lithuania | 93 | 87 | 56 |
| Yugoslavia | 91 | 86 | 53 |
| Hungary | 91 | 86 | 50 |
| France | 89 | 80 | 45 |
| United Kingdom | 88 | 78 | 35 |
| Czechoslovakia | 86 | 79 | 43 |
| Germany | 86 | 76 | 40 |
| Sweden | 82 | 70 | 39 |
| Netherlands | 81 | 70 | 30 |
| Switzerland | 81 | 70 | 33 |
| Denmark | 80 | 67 | 33 |
| Norway | 79 | 66 | 39 |
| First Generation Asian and Latin American Immigrants: |  |  |  |
| Cuba | 99 | 97 | 58 |
| China | 97 | 91 | 72 |
| Japan | 89 | 78 | 50 |
| Mexico | 88 | 74 | 51 |

Source: U.S. Bureau of the Census, *1970 Census of Population*, 1973, Table 97.

*States in 1990* (Glenmary Research Center), lists the number of churches and adherents for several hundred denominations, including sixty counties having Hutterite Brethren, forty-nine counties with the American Association of Latvian Evangelical Church, and forty-eight counties with American Carpatho-Russian Orthodox Greek Catholic Diocese of the USA. There were also thirty-five counties with Romanian Orthodox Episcopate of America, twenty-two with Ukrainian Orthodox Church of America, twenty-one with

Syrian Orthodox Church of Antioch, thirteen with Netherlands Reformed Congregations, and ten with Albanian Orthodox Archdiocese in America. Also noted were Estonian Evangelical Lutheran Churches, Maronite Catholic Churches, and Chaldean Rite Catholic Churches. These churches may serve small numbers but remain part of the vital ethnic fabric of many small communities.

## THE ETHNIC PRESS

Immigrant groups often differ from other Americans in a multitude of cultural traits, especially in terms of their language. In 1990, an estimated thirty-one million people age five and over spoke a language other than English at home, almost 14 percent of the population (Table 12.7). Over seventeen million of these people spoke Spanish. Between one and two million each spoke French, German, Italian, and Chinese; between one-half and one million spoke Tagalog, Polish, Korean, and Vietnamese.[7] Other languages that are among the fifty most frequently spoken "home languages" in the United States are Amharic, Malayalam, Samoan, Syriac, and Danish.

Ethnic islands are very often linguistic islands, and the language of immigrant groups manifests itself in both the spoken and written word.[8] In fact, the appearance of an ethnic press, typically a foreign-language press, has been one of the universal concomitants of immigration to the United States, a country where freedom of the press is guaranteed. Park [9] found in 1922, for instance, that in New York City even the smallest of the immigrant groups had established a periodical of some kind. Roucek,[10] in surveying the status of the press in the 1940s, found that newspapers in the United States were being printed in 39 different tongues. In 1972, Wynar counted 903 ethnic publications, one-

**Table 12.7   Language Other Than English Spoken at Home, 1990.**

| Language | No. of Speakers Age 5 and Over (in thousands) |
| --- | --- |
| Spanish | 17,339 |
| French | 1,702 |
| German | 1,547 |
| Italian | 1,309 |
| Chinese | 1,249 |
| Tagalog | 843 |
| Polish | 723 |
| Korean | 626 |
| Vietnamese | 507 |
| Portuguese | 430 |
| Japanese | 428 |
| Greek | 388 |
| Arabic | 355 |
| Hindu/Urdu | 351 |

Source: *Statistical Abstract of the United States 1997*, p. 53.

third of which were published totally in English and one-fifth of which were Jewish (albeit in several languages).[11] A few years later, a survey of thirteen ethnic groups in Cleveland found that over half of them read more than one ethnic newspaper, and 30 percent read at least one ethnic magazine.[12] The foreign-language press has been called "the best primary source for an understanding of the world of non-English-speaking groups in the United States, their expectations and concerns, their background and evolution as individual communities."[13]

Today, the most vigorous foreign-language press in the United States is the Spanish, with 126 newspapers (some bilingual) published in 19 states and the District of Columbia.[14] Publications in other European languages have made the transition to an ethnic press that is typically bilingual or in English only. These publications appeal to third- and fourth-generation ethnic Americans who operate in an English-speaking world. Publications serving more recent Asian immigrants are more likely to be totally in a foreign language. A survey of *Editor and Publisher International Yearbook* and the *Gale Directory of Publications and Broadcast Media* for 1997 revealed that forty-five ethnic groups in the United States had publications of their own. Examples of America's ethnic press are presented in Table 12.8.

**Table 12.8    Examples of Foreign-Language Publications in the United States, 1997.**

| Ethnic Group | Number of Newspapers, 1997 | Number of Newspapers, 1982 | Newspaper | Place of Publication | Circulation |
|---|---|---|---|---|---|
| Afghan | 1 | 0 | Omaid Weekly | Hayward, CA | 1,700 |
| Albanian | 2 | 0 | Illyria | Bronx, NY | 13,000 |
| Arabic | 4 | 6 | The Syrian-Lebanese Star | Jacksonville, FL | 22,000 |
| Armenian | 6 | 10 | Armenian Reporter Int'l | Fresh Meadow, NY | 5,400 |
| Bulgarian | 1 | 2 | Macedonian Tribune | Fort Wayne, IN | 1,600 |
| Bylorussian | 1 | 1 | Bielarus/The Belarusan | Jamaica, NY | 2,000 |
| Chinese | 16 | 10 | World Journal | Whitestone, NY | 252,500 |
| Croatian | 3 | 2 | Zajednicar | Pittsburgh, PA | 38,000 |
| Czech/Slovak | 1 | 4 | Denni Hlasatel | Berwyn, IL | 5,100 |
| Danish | 2 | 1 | Bien | Burbank, CA | 5,300 |
| Dutch | 1 | 1 | The Windmill Herald | Lynden, WA | 12,900 |
| Estonian | 1 | 1 | Vaba Eesti Sona | New York, NY | 3,800 |
| Filipino | 4 | 0 | Filipino Reporter | New York, NY | 49,000 |
| Finnish | 4 | 4 | Finnish American Reporter | Superior, WI | 3,000 |
| French | 3 | 5 | Journal Français | San Francisco, CA | 30,000 |
| German | 8 | 22 | California-Staats Zeitung | Los Angeles, CA | 19,500 |
| Greek | 8 | 10 | Proini | Long Island, NY | 60,200 |
| Haitian | 1 | 0 | Haiti Progress | Brooklyn, NY | 19,000 |
| Hebrew | 2 | 1 | Haddoar | New York, NY | 4,400 |
| Hungarian | 4 | 8 | Amerikai-Kanadai Magyar Elet | Akron, OH | 16,000 |
| Indian (Asian) | 4 | 0 | India Abroad | New York, NY | 60,200 |
| Indian (American) | 8 | 0 | Chickasaw Times | Ada, OK | 15,000 |
| Irish | 7 | 4 | Irish Voice | New York, NY | 85,000 |

**Table 12.8    Continued.**

| Ethnic Group | Number of Newspapers, 1997 | Number of Newspapers, 1982 | Newspaper | Place of Publication | Circulation |
|---|---|---|---|---|---|
| Israeli | 1 | 0 | Jerusalem Post (Int'l ed.) | New York, NY | 4,200 |
| Italian | 8 | 11 | America Oggi | Westwood, NJ | 60,000 |
| Japanese | 9 | 8 | Japanese Beach Press | Honolulu, HI | 35,000 |
| Jewish (in English) | 84 | * | Tablet | Brooklyn, NY | 85,400 |
| Korean | 4 | 2 | Korea Times | Los Angeles, CA | 45,000 |
| Latvian | 1 | 2 | Laiks | Brooklyn, NY | 10,500 |
| Lithuanian | 7 | 11 | Darbininkas | Brooklyn, NY | 16,000 |
| Norwegian | 2 | 2 | Nordisk Tidende | New York, NY | 5,200 |
| Polish | 18 | 15 | Zgoda | Chicago, IL | 69,800 |
| Portuguese | 5 | 3 | Folha do Brasil | New York, NY | 50,000 |
| Russian | 4 | 4 | Novoye Russkoye Slovo | New York, NY | 53,000 |
| Serbian | 1 | 2 | American Srbobran | Pittsburgh, PA | 12,000 |
| Slovak | 5 | 7 | Jednota | Middletown, PA | 35,000 |
| Slovenian | 3 | 3 | Prosveta | Imperial, PA | 21,200 |
| Spanish | 126 | 22 | La Guia Familiar | Chatsworth, CA | 246,000 |
| Swedish | 4 | 6 | Nordstjernan-Svea | New York, NY | 6,000 |
| Swiss | 2 | 1 | Schweizer Journal | San Francisco, CA | 4,100 |
| Turkish | 1 | 1 | Hurriyet | New York, NY | 5,800 |
| Ukrainian | 4 | 5 | Svoboda Ukrainian Daily | Jersey City, NJ | 13,000 |
| Vietnamese | 1 | 0 | Nguoi Viet Daily News | Westminster, CA | 15,000 |
| Welsh | 2 | * | Ninnau | Basking Ridge, NJ | 21,500 |
| Yiddish | 2 | 4 | Der Yid | Brooklyn, NY | 43,500 |

*Data not available.
Source: *Editor and Publisher International Yearbook,* 1982 and 1997; *Gale Directory of Publications and Broadcast Media,* 1998.

What are the functions of the foreign press accounting for its virtual ubiquity among first-generation immigrant groups and its persistence in a country that is reluctant "to view language and ethnicity as consonant with modern social development"?[15] In general, it serves both to insulate and assimilate successive waves of immigrants into American culture. First, it provides a medium of communication for groups whose native language is not English and whose origins are not in the United States. Even as English is mastered among first- and second-generation immigrants, the language of comfort and security is often the native tongue. Second, it serves to publish news of the home country that would otherwise be unavailable. The Italian press, for instance, gives priority to news from Italy rather than the non-Italian world.[16] Third, it aids the process of assimilation by offering information and advice on lifestyles in a new country. Silverman, for example, has called the Yiddish press one of the two "most powerful Americanizing [agencies] operative on the Jewish scene."[17] The other is the public school. Fourth, it provides a vehicle for promoting social cohesion, ethnic activities, and mutual support networks.

The spatial and temporal dimensions of foreign-language publishing in the United States are closely associated with immigrant history and the settlement geographies of ethnic Americans. The *Media Encyclopedia* lists, by place of publication, thirty-three languages in which newspapers were published.[18] Those states, which served as gateways for immigrants from Europe, Latin America, and Asia, have also become the locus of the majority of foreign-language presses. The *Media Encyclopedia* clearly showed that the New York, Chicago, and Los Angeles metropolitan areas were the capitals of the foreign-language publishing industry in the United States. The American South, the Great Plains, the Northern Rockies, and the Great Basin region, on the other hand, were areas that supported almost no foreign-language newspapers. The maps presented in Figures 12.3, 12.4, and 12.5 focus on the status of immigrant European languages in the 1980s. All three major branches of the Indo-European language family—the Romance, Germanic, and Slavic language groups—accounted for important foreign-language publications.

Although a few newspapers are published in Danish and Norwegian, the Germanic-language press is dominated by the German language itself (Figure 12.3). Today, it is restricted to a handful of major metropolises. It was a German newspaper, however, that initiated foreign-language publishing in the United States. The short-lived *Philadelphia Zeitung* was published by Benjamin Franklin in 1732.[19] Its successor, begun in 1739, attained a circulation of four thousand and served to unite an archipelago of German ethnic islands in New York, Pennsylvania, Virginia, the Carolinas, and Georgia.[20] The first German-language daily in the United States appeared in 1834,[21] and the number of German publications peaked in 1893 at close to eight hundred, when they accounted for over two-thirds of all foreign-language publications in this country.[22] As German Americans and their Scandinavian counterparts have been linguistically integrated into American culture, their patronage of foreign-language newspapers has diminished: what were dailies have become weeklies and monthlies, and publications exclusively in German have given way to bilingual and English-language only.

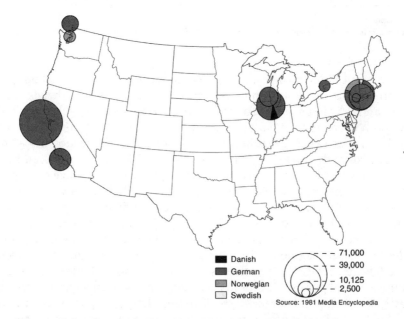

Figure 12.3    Germanic-Language Newspaper Circulation.

The Norwegian press is even smaller than the German press and is restricted to two centers, Seattle and New York, quite distant from the original province of Norwegian settlement in the western North Central states. From 1847, when the first Norwegian daily was founded in Norway, Wisconsin, through the 1870s, Illinois, Wisconsin, and Minnesota spawned a thriving Norwegian press catering to first- and second-generation immigrants. Today the locational pattern reflects two or more recent chapters in Norwegian immigrant history. In the 1880s, the focus of immigration switched to the Pacific Northwest, where both land and opportunities were abundant, and to New York City and other northeastern ports, where Norwegian seamen jumped ship by the thousands. The immigrant communities in Seattle and New York are not as many generations removed from the original immigrants and are now the only major Norwegian-language publishing centers, though the newspapers published in both places are now bilingual.

Slavic-language publications appear to have a larger circulation than Germanic-language publications (Figure 12.4). The Slavic nationalities constituted the second wave of immigration to the United States. Not only did they arrive later than many western and southern European groups, but their full assimilation was hampered by their different cultural, linguistic, and religious traditions. These eastern European nationalities did not start arriving in large numbers until the 1870s and 1880s when the growth centers of the United States were the heavy industrial cities in the northeastern quadrant of the country. Even today, a majority of all Americans who claim Slavic ancestry (and three-quarters of Polish and Slovak Americans) reside in the northeastern quadrant of the United States.[23] Reflecting the persistence of these settlement patterns is the distribution of Slavic publications. That distribution also reflects the predominance of the western Slavic languages, primarily Polish but also including some Czech and Slovak publications. Polish immigration increased dramatically after 1870; during the succeeding decade, Polish-language newspapers appeared to serve ethnic communities in Buffalo, Detroit, Toledo,

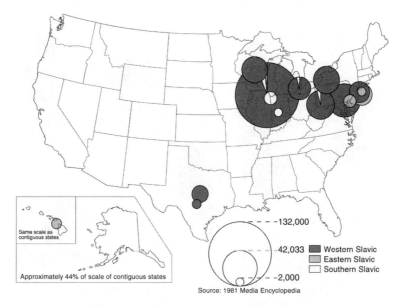

Figure 12.4    Slavic-Language Newspaper Circulation.

Philadelphia, Pittsburgh, and several smaller cities.[24] By 1888, the first successful Polish-language daily had been founded in Milwaukee. The only significant area of Slavic-language publishing outside the Northeast is the Austin and Waco areas of Texas, where several Czech-language newspapers serve the Czech American population of the Texas prairies. The eastern Slavic languages in which ethnic publications appear are Russian and Ukrainian; the southern Slavic languages are Slovenian, Croatian, and Bulgarian.

In the Romance languages, tongues that have descended from Latin (i.e., from "Rome"), publications appear in Spanish, Portuguese, Italian, and French. Of these languages, Spanish dominates. The first Spanish-language newspaper in the United States was published in New Orleans in 1808. Since 1848, there have been 582 Spanish-language newspapers published in the United States.[25] Currently, there are over one hundred in print, some of which are bilingual.[26] One of the major Spanish-language dailies in the United States, *Diario Las Américas*, was founded in Miami in 1953, well before the dramatic growth of south Florida's Hispanic population, and the *Miami Herald* began a Spanish-language section in 1976. New York, Los Angeles, and three cities in Texas—Laredo, Brownsville, and Midland—also have Spanish-language dailies.

The settlement patterns of the Hispanic immigrant wave are reflected in the size and distribution of the proportional circles appearing on the map of Romance-language publications (Figure 12.5). Eleven percent of the U.S. population is Hispanic, and only half of them speak English "very well," facts that help explain the growth of the Spanish-language press through the 1990s. In addition to the Hispanic borderland, two northern metropolises, Chicago and New York, are major foci of Hispanic settlement and Spanish-language publishing. New York's first Spanish-language newspaper began publication in the 1890s and Chicago's in the 1930s.[27]

Like the Spanish press, the Italian and Portuguese presses mirror the settlement patterns of immigrants. Italian newspapers are especially important in the Northeast,

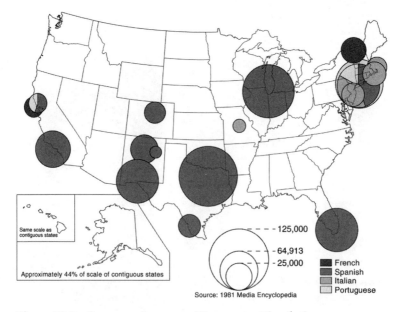

**Figure 12.5    Romance-Language Newspaper Circulation.**

but almost all are now published in bilingual editions or in English alone. Nevertheless, an Italian-language daily was founded in New Jersey in 1988. Overall, however, the number of Italian ethnic newspapers has declined, a reflection of the assimilation of the Italian immigrant wave that arrived around the turn of the century. The Portuguese press reflects the bicoastal settlement patterns of Portuguese (including those from the Azores and Cape Verde Islands) and Brazilian immigrants. Newspapers are to be found in the New York metropolitan area, southern New England, and the San Joaquin Valley area of California. Massachusetts, Connecticut, and Rhode Island are major centers of Portuguese settlement. As the number of Portuguese and Azorean immigrants to this area increased during the 1970s, a Portuguese-language newspaper was founded in New Bedford, Massachusetts, in 1975 and today has a circulation of seventeen thousand. Likewise, as the number of Brazilian immigrants to New York increased in the 1980s, a Portuguese-language weekly began publication in 1991 and today has a circulation of fifty thousand.[28]

Except for the Spanish, the number of Romance-, Germanic-, and Slavic-language publications is declining. As circulation drops off, publication frequency is typically reduced and the publication ultimately terminated. In 1983 for instance, the *Jewish Daily Forward*, published in New York City, became a weekly rather than a daily publication. The *Forward* was the last of the nation's Yiddish dailies. The trend in foreign-language dailies portends a dismal future for many foreign-language presses. Their number declined from seventy-one in 1963 to twenty-four in 1997.[29] In three and a half decades, it dropped by two-thirds. Daily newspaper circulation has historically been confined to urban centers where there is a high density of ethnic Americans. As the density of ethnic Americans thins out, daily newspapers become less practical, and as the number of first- and second-generation immigrants diminishes, as it has for European nationalities, the use of the mother tongue in ethnic publications becomes less readable. The challenge is to make the transition from foreign-language presses to ethnic presses that appeal to Americans who do take pride in their cultural heritage. As the editor of the *Irish American* has stated, "Our readers are losing touch with Ireland as a country and are becoming more attuned to their Irish identity. There are fewer people who have ever been to Ireland, and even fewer who have come from there. I think the press has to adapt itself to this new audience—an audience of third and fourth generation Americans."[30]

Presses serving European immigrants of the first and second waves have also declined, but presses serving Latin American and Asian immigrants have grown. Just as the *Philadelphia Zeitung* provided a medium for the dissemination of news and information to the German ethnic islands of Pennsylvania and surrounding states, the news-oriented Spanish-language press may soon serve the entire Hispanic community in the Unites States. In 1981, the Gannett newspapers acquired *El Diario–La Prensa*, New York's Spanish-language daily that had begun publication in 1913. It has pioneered a nationwide information network serving the Hispanic communities around the country using satellites to transmit full pages of news to any member newspaper of the network.[31] Similarly, the Chinese-language *World Journal* is transmitted via satellite, and Hong Kong's *Sing Tao* is transmitted across the Pacific to the United States and Canada. By taking advantage of modern technology, the emerging ethnic presses may more efficiently serve the needs of a far-flung archipelago of ethnic islands.

Continuing immigration to the United States, narrow-casting trends in communications technology, and the so-called ethnic revival in the United States may contribute to the sustenance of a press serving the needs of American ethnics. In some instances, it may be a totally foreign-language press serving the needs of recent immigrants; in others, it may be an English-language press that sustains the camaraderie of ethnicity long after the native language has disappeared. Whatever the future of the foreign-language press, it has been an important part of American culture although a neglected theme in American cultural geography.

## ETHNIC BROADCASTING

Radio broadcasting targeted at ethnic minorities is another activity that helps map American ethnic islands. Prior to the 1960s, foreign-language broadcasting aimed at European immigrants and Latinos accounted for the bulk of airtime. After the reform of immigration laws in the 1960s, however, Spanish-language and Asian-language programming grew the most rapidly, while many European languages declined, Italian most rapidly (from 609 hours nationwide in 1960 to only 221 in 1997). Since listening to radio does not require the ability to read, its appeal is even broader than the foreign-language press. Ethnic broadcasting serves to create a point of contact with other members of the ethnic community in America and helps preserve ties with the country of origin. Warshauer[32] notes its function as a source of entertainment for linguistic minorities who are geographically isolated from their homeland and culturally isolated from dominant society.

Musical programming has dominated ethnic radio just as it has English-language radio. In fact, some musical formats—polka, tejano, Cajun, Celtic, Soul—are as much a part of the ethnic acoustic landscape as are foreign-language broadcasts. While some of these musical styles fill an ethnic niche, others have found a national audience, as evidenced by National Public Radio's "The Thistle and the Shamrock," a program of Celtic (Irish, Scottish, Breton) music heard nationwide.

In 1941, twenty years after the birth of radio broadcasting, Roucek[33] reported that 205 radio stations in the United States were broadcasting in 26 foreign languages. At that time he predicted the eventual disappearance of foreign-language broadcasting. Twenty years later, in 1960, 1,340 stations were broadcasting in 39 foreign languages, according to data compiled by the Language Resource Project,[34] which also found that the number of stations airing at least a few hours of foreign-language programs had increased at a rate commensurate with radio programming in general. The languages at that time, which accounted for 88 percent of the total broadcast hours, were Spanish, Italian, Polish, German, and French, the most frequently used second languages in the United States.[35] In 1976, radio stations nationwide were broadcasting to at least forty different ethnic groups.[36] In a more detailed field investigation in the 1970s, Grame found radio broadcasts in fifty-six languages.[37] In New York alone, he found thirty-six ethnic groups with programs of their own and in San Francisco he found eighteen.

In 1997, radio stations were broadcasting to at least forty different ethnic groups, sixteen of which commanded "ethnic format" stations of their own because they aired twenty or more hours per week of ethnic programming.[38] Although the vast majority served Hispanics (453 stations) and African Americans (166 stations), eight stations were broadcasting to Native Americans, six to Portuguese Americans, five each to Greek and Korean Americans; and four each to Polish and French Americans (including Cajuns). Other ethnic format stations were targeted to Arabic, Chinese, Filipino, Italian, Japanese, Jewish, Russian, Serbian, and Vietnamese communities. Supplementing these ethnic format stations is an even more extensive archipelago of English-language stations broadcasting up to twenty hours per week of programs, usually in a foreign language, aimed at these same forty groups. "Special programming" in the Spanish language again heads this list, but it is joined by more than two hundred hours per week nationally of Polish, French, Native American, German, and Italian programming all the way down to a mere two hours per week of Turkish, Okinawan, Ethiopian, and Scottish programming.[39]

While the number of hours of radio broadcasting for some European languages is declining, programs appealing to the Asian immigrant stream are increasing. In some American cities, there are growing markets for programs in Filipino/Tagalog, Hindi, Chinese, Japanese, Vietnamese, and Korean (Table 12.9). In 1995, the first Chinese-language news and information radio network premiered in Boston.[40] Nevertheless, Asian radio is a significant advertising magnet in only a handful of major metropolitan markets.

**Table 12.9    Special Radio Programming in Asian, Pacific, and African Languages, 1997.**

| Language | Hours per Week | Broadcast Locations | |
| --- | --- | --- | --- |
| | | States | Cities |
| Filipino | 76 | Alaska | Barrow, Kodiak |
| | | California | Bakersfield, Calexico, Delano, El Centro, Fresno, Los Angeles, Modesto, San Francisco, San Gabriel |
| | | Florida | Indian Rocks Beach, New Port Richy |
| | | Hawaii | Kahului, Lihue, Wailuku |
| | | Illinois | Cicero |
| | | New Jersey | South Orange |
| | | Nevada | Las Vegas |
| | | Washington | Bremerton, Tacoma |
| Hindi/Punjabi/ Asian Indian | 51 | California | San Francisco, Marysville |
| | | Florida | Indian Rocks Beach |
| | | Illinois | Chicago, Highland Park |
| | | Massachusetts | Worcester |
| | | Nevada | Las Vegas |
| | | Ohio | Yellow Springs |
| | | Oregon | Portland |
| | | Pennsylvania | Allentown, Shiremanstown |
| | | Tennessee | Memphis |
| | | Texas | Alvin, Houston, Humble |
| Chinese | 43 | California | Holtville, Los Angeles, San Francisco |
| | | Massachusetts | Cambridge, Quincy, Wellesley |
| | | New York | Stony Brook, Troy |
| | | Texas | Galveston |
| | | Washington | Ferndale |
| Arabic | 37 | Colorado | Denver |
| | | DC | Washington |
| | | Illinois | Evanston, Oak Park |
| | | Kentucky | Murray |
| | | Maryland | Indian Head |
| | | Nevada | Las Vegas |
| | | New Jersey | South Orange |

**Table 12.9    Continued.**

| Language | Hours per Week | Broadcast Locations States | Broadcast Locations Cities |
|---|---|---|---|
| Arabic *(Continued)* | | Ohio | Akron, Cleveland |
| | | Pennsylvania | Allentown |
| | | Texas | Dallas |
| Japanese | 36 | California | Inglewood, San Francisco, Santa Barbara |
| | | Hawaii | Hilo, Wailuku |
| | | Massachusetts | Amherst, Wellesley |
| | | New York | Baldwinsville |
| | | Tennessee | Nashville |
| Vietnamese | 27 | California | Anaheim, Fresno, San Francisco, San Jose, Stockton |
| | | DC | Washington |
| | | Massachusetts | Waltham |
| | | Texas | Galveston |
| | | Wisconsin | Sheboygan |
| Samoan | 27 | California | San Francisco |
| | | Hawaii | Honolulu, Waipahu |
| | | Washington | Bremerton |
| Korean | 20 | California | San Francisco |
| | | Florida | Atlantic Beach |
| | | Hawaii | Honolulu |
| | | Kentucky | Hopkinsville |
| | | New York | Stony Brook |
| Armenian | 11 | California | Inglewood, San Francisco |
| | | Massachusetts | Lowell, Worcester |
| | | New Jersey | South Orange |
| | | Rhode Island | Providence |
| Southeast Asian | 11 | California | Modesto (Hmong), San Gabriel (Thai) |
| | | Wisconsin | Eau Claire, Green Bay (Hmong) |
| Tongan | 8 | Hawaii | Honolulu |
| Farsi/Iranian | 6 | DC | Washington |
| | | Hawaii | Honolulu |
| Turkish | 2 | California | San Francisco |
| Okinawan | 2 | Hawaii | Honolulu |
| Ethiopian | 2 | California | San Gabriel |

Source: *Broadcasting and Cable Yearbook* (1997).

Another growth area is the American Indian market. Carlson tallied only sixteen radio programs targeted at American Indians in 1960 but ninety-four in 1990. The growth in programs parallels the reemergence of America's Indian nations, many of which are using radio programs to promote a sense of separate identity.[41]

Spanish-language radio stations in the Latino borderland and in large cities nationwide account for the vast majority of foreign-language broadcasting in the United States today. While the industry began in the late 1930s, it did not pick up momentum until after World War II.[42] By 1981, 143 radio stations in the United States were listed as Spanish-format stations airing at least twenty hours per week of Spanish-language programs.[43] By 1997, that number had increased to 453.[44] In addition, there are now forty-seven Spanish-language television stations spread across eleven states, and a Spanish-language television program network known as Telemundo with headquarters in Hialeah, Florida. Figure 12.6 depicts the widespread influences of Spanish-language radio and television broadcasting. All but four states have at least some Spanish-language programming even if it is only a few hours per week. The concentration of the Spanish-speaking population is accentuated by the galaxy of radio stations with Spanish-format programming spread over the Hispanic borderland. The first- and second-generation Spanish-speaking populations from Cuba, Mexico, Puerto Rico, and more recently South America (in southern Florida) and Central America (in southern California) have increased in Miami, San Antonio, Phoenix, and Los Angeles. Accompanying the rapid Hispanic growth of these and smaller cities has been an increase in the number of stations and number of hours of Spanish format programming.

Two smaller ethnic archipelagos, with foreign-language broadcasts of their own, are the French and the Portuguese. Of the two, French is the most geographically widespread, with concentrations of Cajun French in Louisiana and French Canadian in southern New England. Portuguese broadcasting is highly concentrated, particularly in California and southern New England. Both languages evidenced healthy rates of growth in broadcast time since 1960: French from 227 hours to over 400 hours per week, and Portuguese from 112 to over 200 hours per week. The map of radio stations tells the story of French and Portuguese culture in the United States (Fig. 12.7).

In 1990, one out of every twenty people, or 5.3 percent of the population, in the United States spoke French at home. One out of every seventy, or 1.4 percent of the population, spoke Portuguese at home. Do not conclude that these are first- or second-generation immigrants from either France or Portugal, however. In fact, the French-speaking population of Louisiana has lived there for centuries as the French-speaking Cajuns, refugees from

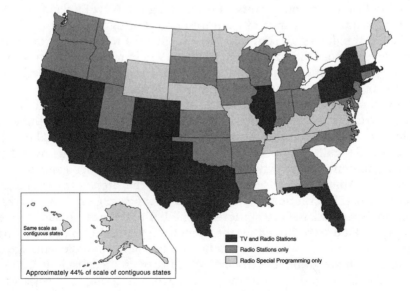

**Figure 12.6    Spanish-Language Broadcast Media, 1997. Source:**
*Broadcasting and Cable Yearbook* (1997).

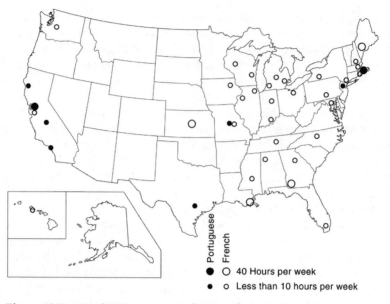

**Figure 12.7    Foreign-Language Radio Broadcasting: French and Portuguese, 1981. Source: *Broadcasting and Cable Yearbook* (1981).**

Acadia on Canada's Atlantic coast. Here the rural isolation of the French ethnic island has preserved the cultural and linguistic heritage longer than in the urban areas where more recent immigrants have settled, such as New England. The French-speaking population of New England has come from Quebec in Canada, originally in search of jobs in the mill towns. The Portuguese-speaking population of the United States has traditionally been concentrated in California and in communities along the New England coast. In the San Francisco–San Joaquin Valley area of California, the Portuguese early established themselves in the dairy industry. In southern New England, a new generation of Portuguese-speaking population from the Azores arrived after 1958 in response to a volcanic eruption, an immigrant stream that continued into the 1970s. More recently, the Portuguese-speaking population of the United States has come from Brazil.

One trend that augurs well for the future of ethnic broadcasting, whether or not it be in a foreign tongue, is the appearance of "narrow-casting," programming aimed at particular audiences. Satellite transmission and extensive land lines make it possible to reach a nationwide audience of ethnic islands, unifying the various overlapping archipelagoes of immigrant groups whose second, third, and further generations have dispersed across the American landscape. According to the *Broadcasting and Cable Yearbook*, the Spanish International Network and three regional networks provided information for Spanish-language stations in the United States. In addition, eleven stations in New England were linked by the French Program Group of New England. The networking of information, whether by radio or television, should encourage ethnic renaissance and accentuate group identity and a feeling of group consciousness among scattered ethnic islands. According to Grame,[45] ethnic broadcasting has "passed through the eye of the storm" into an era when demands for uniformity are giving way to demands for "multiformity."

## ETHNIC FESTIVALS AND ETHNIC ORGANIZATIONS

Festivals of all sorts are a large and growing business in the United States today. Many are devoted to ethnic themes and designed to preserve ethnic cultures, to buttress group identity, and to educate outsiders about the contributions of various nationalities to American culture. Other festivals are extensions of traditional religious and family festivities as they were practiced in the homeland. They often have no function other than to bring members of the group together for a time of social communion. Others seem to depend on an external market and presume the willingness of an ethnic group to expose the best of its culinary, artistic, and musical talents to outsiders. They often depend on a level of mutual respect between the ethnic group and society at large, something that may take many years to develop. For many, ethnic festivals serve as much to revive ethnic customs as to maintain them. They become transient islands of ethnicity that proclaim the importance of holding together. Their locations are often suggested by America's toponymy: the Czech festival in Prague, Oklahoma; the Belgian festival in Ghent, Minnesota; and the Scots Festival in Dunedin, Florida.

An example of a festival that has forged a new ethnic identity out of a multitude of specific and linguistically diverse cultures is the annual West Indian American Day Carnival in New York City's Brooklyn.[46] The festival features steel bands, calypso, parades, and individual masquerades before and during the Labor Day weekend. African Caribbean immigrants to the United States have been drawn like a magnet to New York City. They originate on the many Caribbean islands (e.g., Jamaica, Haiti) and coastal enclaves (e.g., Belize, Guyana) of English-speaking, French-speaking, and even Dutch-speaking cultures. They share an African ancestry. In New York City, a West Indian identity has emerged out of many Caribbean cultures, and the West Indian Carnival has come to symbolize "the emergent collective identity of the African-Caribbean community in New York City."[47] Not only has it buttressed group identity, but it has also forged a new "transnational" ethnic consciousness that unites those from Jamaica, Haiti, Barbados, Trinidad, and other islands under a motto of "all is one." It draws from all over the United States, the Caribbean, and Europe, but the participants are West Indians, not outsiders. The West Indian Carnival illustrates the importance of festivities in the maintenance and creation of group identity.

Many festivals held by European immigrant groups and their descendents have passed through the stage of serving the endogenous needs of the group and are now focused on bringing the group's distinct culture and contributions to a wider audience of Americans. Only in part is the geographic distribution of these ethnic festivals a correlate of immigrant settlement patterns. Most immigrants of Slavic nationalities, for instance, who have settled in the United States exhibit a decidedly urban-oriented settlement pattern. The industrial cities of the northeastern United States, in particular, became the locus of sizable urban ethnic islands. In these settings, however, the number of ethnic festivals is not commensurate with the size of the group's population. Rather, Slavic festivities are usually sheltered within religious or fraternal institutions and are seldom aimed at the larger society. The Slavic groups that established themselves on the frontier during the late 1800s, however, have maintained their identity without the acculturating forces inherent in urban areas. Most Slavic festivals today are found in the plains states from North Dakota to Texas, as depicted in Figure 12.8. Even though these states account for the fewest Czechs and Poles, they have been able to glorify their ethnicity in these rural areas more than have their counterparts in the cities.

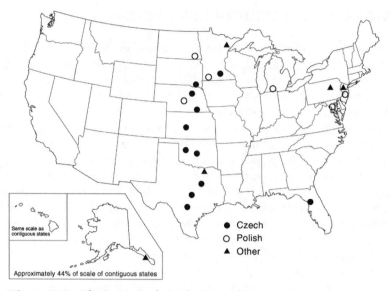

**Figure 12.8    Slavic Festivals in the United States. Source: Wasserman and Morgan (1976).**

Festivals staged by some European ethnic groups have found a secure niche in American culture.[48] For instance, Celtic celebrations have become popular nationwide. Scottish festivals are held in at least twenty-seven large cities and small towns throughout the country. San Diego, Atlanta, St. Paul, Syracuse, and Fairbanks hold them, as do the small towns of Coeur d'Alene, Idaho; Alma, Michigan; Linville, North Carolina; and Dunedin, Florida. Major Irish festivals are held in sixteen places, and, of course, there are the famous St. Patrick's Day parades that are so much a part of urban landscapes nationwide. Yielding a pattern strikingly different from festivals staged by the Slavs and Celts, Scandinavian festivals are held in areas of heaviest initial settlement. Small towns and large cities in Minnesota, Wisconsin, Michigan, Iowa, and the Dakotas are the sites for most of these, though the most famous may be the Danish festival in Solvang, California. Minneapolis and St. Paul, major centers for second- and third-generation Scandinavians, hold Swedish, Norwegian, and Danish festivals annually. Philadelphia, Pennsylvania, and Wilmington, Delaware, the hearth of Swedish culture in North America, both hold Swedish festivals to commemorate their history. Another group that has become noted for its festivals is the Greeks, many of which are sponsored by large, urban Greek Orthodox churches.

In contrast to the large number of festivals sponsored by the aforementioned groups, there are fewer festivals to link smaller ethnic archipelagos and call attention to their accomplishments and cultural contributions. A Syrian-Lebanese festival is held only in Toledo, Ohio; Basque festivals are held in Elko, Nevada, Sun Valley, Idaho, and Snowbird, Utah; Portuguese in six places in Massachusetts and two in California; Hungarian in Los Angeles; and Finnish in St. Paul, Minnesota. Many of these smaller ethnic groups do, however, piggyback on pan-ethnic festivals such as Milwaukee's Holiday Folk Fair, which provides a focal point for large numbers of Germans and Poles as well as small numbers of Dutch Indonesians. Still, many of the smallest ethnic groups have been so successfully absorbed into the mainstream of American society that popular festivals that once drew thousands are now part of history. Luxembourgers, for instance, began the annual Schueberfoer in Chicago in 1904, but it died out in the late 1960s.

An intriguing question that arises in mapping the sites of ethnic festivals and fairs is why so many appear in rural areas. Have rural ethnic islands been able to retain and maintain their sense of ethnicity longer than urban islands? Or are rural farming communities with their seasonal slowdown in activity more suited to festivals than urban communities that run on the same schedule year-round? Perhaps the resurgence of ethnic identification and pride will give rise to more festivals in those metropolitan areas, which have been homes to the majority of Slavic and Scandinavian nationalities. Recent immigrant groups such as the Cubans, Koreans, Vietnamese, and Filipinos are mainly in large cities where some ethnic diversity already exists; many of these same cities have a history of supporting nationalist groups.

The transience of the ethnic festival contrasts sharply with the permanence of ethnic organizations in the United States. Wynar[49] lists seventy-three ethnic groups in the United States that maintain their own organizations, both religious and secular. In 1998, some 150 ethnonational groups were the focus of ethnic and cultural organizations.[50] More than a score of organizations exist to serve Jews, African Americans, American Indians, Poles, Italians, and Chinese. Yet, there are also organizations devoted to Albanian, Cossack, Ecuadorian, Kurdish, Sicilian, Silesian, and Taiwanese culture. Some have large memberships, such as the Ukrainian National Association with sixty-two thousand members. Even the Manx Americans may belong to seven different organizations devoted to the preservation of Manx ethnic identity! New immigrant groups also organize; witness the growth of the Muslim Student Association on college and university campuses since the mid-1970s. The Pakistani Students Association of America and the Organization of Arab Students in the United States and Canada are other examples of student organizations set up along national lines.[51]

Wynar sees ethnic organizations as fulfilling needs of the ethnic group that are not met by established social institutions. They may serve political, social, fraternal, special interest welfare, educational, or scholarly functions within the ethnic system. Wynar maintains that the greater the "cultural disparity" between the immigrant group and society at large, the greater the number of ethnic organizations. He asserts that "the survival of ethnic communities and an ethnic 'life' is largely a result of the continued existence of ethnic organizations and their various activities that insure the continuation of the ethnic society."[52] In addition to organizations set up by and for the groups involved is an increasing number of cultural organizations devoted to research and scholarship about immigrant nationalities in the United States.

The distribution of these ethnic organizations often reflects the distribution of the groups themselves. Seldom are organization locations a perfect mirror of areas of concentration, however. The maps in Figure 12.9 compare the patterns of the Irish, Norwegian, Finnish, and Greek American organizations. New York City appears on all maps and assumes the importance of a capital city for Irish and Greek Americans. Similarly, the District of Columbia has become a major locus of ethnic organizations. Despite the fact that Washington, D.C., has been neither a traditional port of entry nor a major industrial center, it has attracted ethnic organizations because of its role as the major political control point in the United States, just as New York has been the major economic control point. Outside the Northeast, cities that appear on these four maps are located

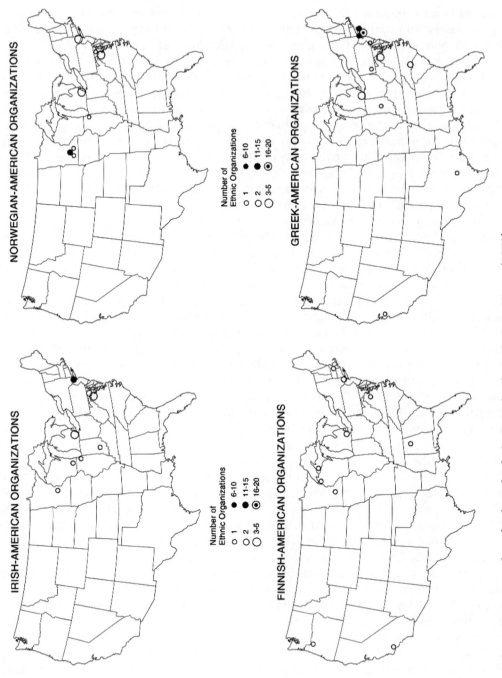

**Figure 12.9  Number of Selected Ethnic Organizations. Source: Wynar (1975).**

primarily in the Midwest. Detroit, Chicago, and Minneapolis–St. Paul appear as major ethnic control points in the American ethnic system. Greek American organizations seem to be most concentrated; Finnish American organizations seem to be most dispersed. Los Angeles and San Francisco, while not major loci for European ethnic organizations, are important control points for immigrant groups from Central America, Southeast Asia, and the Pacific Islands. Los Angeles and Long Beach have ethnic islands of Guamanians, Tongans, and Samoans and serve as sites for the organizations that serve these ethnic islands. These headquarters of ethnic American society provide a focus for ethnic identity at the local, state, and national levels. They serve to give cohesion to increasingly far-flung groups and give many ethnic Americans a visibility that they might not otherwise enjoy.

## ELECTRONIC ETHNIC COMMUNITIES

Another, more recent way that members of ethnic groups maintain contact and solidarity is through electronic communication, especially via listservs. The Internet's arrival in the past five years has provided opportunities for many individuals and groups to have instant, easy, frequent, and inexpensive contacts. Today there are thousands of organizations, businesses, government offices, and individuals scattered throughout the world who use the Internet regularly. Ethnic groups are among those using the Internet to share information about their own heritage in America and also to obtain and disseminate information about the country or countries of their ancestors. That the Internet has achieved global proportions means, for example, that it is just as easy for someone in Warsaw, Poland, to share information with Polish Americans as it is for someone in Chicago to share a piece of community information with relatives living in Poland.

Several ethnic groups in the United States have developed listservs, including the following:

- CEBU-L for Philippine Americans
- LATINO-L for Hispanic Americans
- BALT-L for those from the Baltic states
- SLOVAK-L for Slovak Americans
- POLAND-L for Polish Americans
- HIMNET for those in Pakistan, India, Nepal, Bhutan, and Tibet (China)

There are also listservs for Arab Americans, Haitians, Romanians, Italians, Irish, Argentines, and Hungarians. Several are available for Jews, including BATLUVA, JEWISH, SHABBATSHALOM, PJML (the Progressive Jewish Mailing List), HEWISH-DEAF, and OLAM KATAM (for discussion on the joys, problems, and resources of Jews in rural areas). Some listservs have specific purposes, such as CARIBHAPPENINGS, which promotes itself as a resource for "Caribbeanites" at "home" and the global diaspora; IRL-POL, for discussions on Irish politics; ENVCEE, for the Regional Environmental Center for Central and East Europe, which promotes discussion on a wide range of environmental issues; and SAUDADESDOBRASIL, for views on the music of Brazil. The Koreans in San Francisco have their own listserv, as do Chinese American Christians, whose listserv discusses religious issues, and Bosnians, via the Bosnian Action Coalition. There is one for Adoptive Parents of Vietnamese. Additional ones can be identified by consulting Vivian Neou's "Search of the Lists" at vivian@catalog.com. Some groups, in addition to their listserv, have World Wide Web homepages that describe their organization, history, and activities.

Each listserv contains subscribers who reside in multiple locations in the United States, Canada, Europe, Australia, Asia, Africa, and Latin America. What subscribers have in common is a wish to learn more about the materials shared in daily or weekly electronic mail. That these subscribers can receive the same information at the same time, regardless of location, lends support to the concept of an "electronic community." Subscribers may not know each other or even know who subscribes (or reads) the information, but that they share this electronic medium, focused in this case on ethnic issues, gives them a sense of community. And that community may supplement the communities they share in the places where they live, worship, and participate in festivals.

An analysis of the "electronic traffic" on a listserv during a week reveals a wide variety of information. Some of what is shared is news; other takes on more of the nature of a group conversation, becoming a "discussion group" format. Information is shared about current political, economic, and cultural events from the home country. Specific information may be shared about forthcoming and recent elections, new educational possibilities, international business ventures, and student exchange opportunities. Frequently subscribers share with their relatives and friends overseas information about the United States as well, including costs of living, employment possibilities, tips on adjusting to America, and problems in understanding Americans' lifestyles. Americans making plans to visit their homelands ask for information on available accommodations, living costs, exchange rates, and language instruction tapes and dictionaries. The moderator of a listserv may forward information to subscribers from newspapers in the United States or the home country, often including articles in the native language. The listservs thus provide good opportunities for ethnic group members in the United States to learn how to read and write the language of those living in home countries. But more likely those living outside the United States who have access to the Internet find the exchanges an invaluable way to improve their English skills. Requests are also frequently made on ethnic listservs for information about locations of towns or cities where family members came from, genealogy records, and the origins of family names.

The participation in ethnic listservs varies also. Some subscribers become active members, providing a lot of information and responding to queries. Others post much less information, preferring to be selective in what they request and share with the listserv membership. Others, called "lurkers," only read and never contribute. The importance of these electronic ethnic communities is that they provide a valuable link among members of those with strong, weak, or emerging ethnic identities. That there are more than three dozen such listservs, and the number grows each year, illustrates the wish on the ethnic community's part to be connected to others with similar interests, regardless of location, age, gender, occupation, or interest.

## URBAN ETHNIC GEOMETRIES

The distribution of ethnic groups within a city or metropolitan region may exhibit any number of geometrical forms. Small concentrations or pockets around ethnic churches, schools, clubs, businesses, or organizations may be conceptualized as ethnic "islands." A series of these large and small islands throughout a metropolitan area may be thought of as an "archipelago," with the main islands most often located in the central city and out islands farther away, possibly even in the suburbs. Ethnic groups that grow and remain concentrated over time may occupy so large an area as to be considered a "continent." Linear growth along major thoroughfares radiating out from islands and continents may form "peninsulas" of urban ethnicity.

Agocs has proposed a typology of ethnic communities based on their distinctive geometric patterns within a metropolitan area. Ethnic communities within the central city may be ghettos, immigrant reception centers, urban villages, or more dispersed and integrated residential communities, which she describes as "small islands of ethnic concentration remaining in neighborhoods that had passed to other groups."[53] Immigrant reception centers are described as closely knit, self-contained neighborhoods inhabited primarily by first-generation immigrants, whereas urban villages are described as neighborhoods inhabited primarily by second-generation immigrants and their children. Ethnic communities in the suburban zone, according to Agocs, may be transplanted communities, new suburban settlements, or more dispersed ethnic communities that are more interactional than territorial.

Definitions of ethnic geometries within the city are most easily derived from studies of individual ethnic groups such as the Hasidic Jews of Brooklyn, the Cubans of Miami's Little Havana, San Francisco's Chinatown, and Los Angeles's Little Taipai.[54] To what extent, however, do these ethnic geometries overlap? When ethnic Americans sort themselves out in residential space, do they choose to associate with fellow ethnics, other ethnics, or nonethnics? According to Izaki,[55] few studies have been carried out on the "spatial correspondence of the residential patterns among different groups," probably as a result of limited data and the complexity of a task involving so many variables. The Jones's geographic study on Australian cities is an exception.[56] For examining ethnic patterns within American cities, census tracts provide a useful, albeit less than ideal, geographic base. Unfortunately, data for only the major racial categories (whites, blacks, Asian and Pacific Islanders, etc.) and the Hispanic population are available at the block level, making it difficult to discern small concentrations of ethnic Americans and the intratract overlap among different ethnic groups. Within any one tract there may be one or two dominant groups in combination with any number of minor groups. Detailed large-scale mapping is needed to discern the interdigitation of ethnic groups within a city and whether groups reside side by side, overlap in their cores or on their peripheries, or are completely isolated from other Americans, whether ethnic or not.

Research on ethnic minorities by geographers and other social scientists has revealed a high degree of persistence in the regional patterning of most ethnic groups.[57] Most of this research, however, has focused only on the largest groups, such as the Irish, Germans, Italians, and Polish. It has also tended to center on a few major cities, especially the large cities of the industrial Northeast and Midwest. As a result, a plethora of case studies exists on urban ethnic processes in New York, Philadelphia, Boston, Cleveland, Pittsburgh, and Chicago. Because of the size and regional biases, the largest cities, particularly those in the Northeast, are often used to develop models of ethnic neighborhood development and mobility. Much less is known about the ethnic geographies of most Sunbelt cities and about small and medium-sized metropolitan areas elsewhere in the United States. The latter part of this chapter will focus, therefore, on the ethnic mixes in eight metropolitan areas ranging from 275,000 to 1,400,000 population in 1990, including representative areas from all regions of the United States: Erie, Pennsylvania; Providence, Rhode Island; Norfolk–Virginia Beach, Virginia; Birmingham, Alabama; Omaha, Nebraska; Portland, Oregon; Milwaukee, Wisconsin; and San Antonio, Texas.

Residential segregation has long been used as an indicator of the amount of assimilation that has taken place among ethnic groups over a period of time. Stanley Lieberson's early work on the assimilation of ten ethnic groups in ten northeastern and midwestern cities in 1930 is a case in point. He used the spatial distribution of ethnic groups, citizenship, year of arrival, intermarriage, and ability to speak English. He concluded that "the differential residential segregation of American cities is an important factor in the assimilation of ethnic groups. Segregation is not only a significant dimension of assimilation but, further, the magnitude of a group's segregation appears to influence other aspects of the group's assimilation."[58] In the same study, Lieberson assessed the impact of residential segregation on the occupational composition of eight European groups in 1950. His conclusion supported Hawley's notion that residential dispersion was a prerequisite for assimilation.[59] Segregation and differences were accentuated in these early works with attempts to show how social and spatial assimilation could explain what was happening to the patterns of ethnic groups. Alternative models or conceptual designs based on contrasting rates and patterns of individual groups and their settlement histories were given less importance in explaining segregation and persistence.

The ethnic mosaic of the eight metropolitan areas listed earlier is revealed in the ancestry, race, and ethnicity data available in the 1990 census. Table 12.10 lists the six most identified European ancestry groups (also showing the relative standing of self-identified "Americans") and the six most important Asian and Latino groups (with populations of one thousand and over) in these metropolitan areas. In regard to ancestry mixes, the patterns are not too dissimilar from those associated either with long histories of European ethnic in-migration or those that never had a large ethnic population from Europe or Latin America. Like the nation as a whole, German ancestry is the most frequently cited European ancestry in six of the eight metropolitan areas, and Mexican is the most often cited Latino group in five of the eight. There is much more diversity in the most important Asian groups, with Asian Indians dominating the Asian population in Birmingham and Portland, Hmong in Milwaukee, Koreans in Omaha, Cambodians in Providence, and Filipinos in Norfolk–Virginia Beach and San Antonio.

**Table 12.10   Ethnic Groups in Smaller American Metropolitan Areas, 1990.**

| Metropolitan Area, Population | European Ancestry Groups, Population in Thousands | | Asian and Latino Groups, Population in Thousands | |
|---|---|---|---|---|
| Birmingham, AL 907,810 | "American" | 136 | Mexican | 1 |
| | Irish | 136 | Asian Indian | 1 |
| | English | 119 | Chinese | 1 |
| | German | 97 | Korean | 1 |
| | Scotch-Irish | 33 | | |
| | Scottish | 21 | | |
| Erie, PA 275,572 | German | 113 | Puerto Rican | 2 |
| | Irish | 55 | | |
| | Polish | 40 | | |
| | English | 37 | | |

**Table 12.10  Continued.**

| Metropolitan Area, Population | European Ancestry Groups, Population in Thousands | | Asian and Latino Groups, Population in Thousands | |
|---|---|---|---|---|
| Erie, PA *(Continued)* | Italian | 35 | | |
| | Slovak | 11 | | |
| Milwaukee, WI | German | 693 | Mexican | 29 |
| 1,432,149 | Polish | 215 | Puerto Rican | 15 |
| | Irish | 164 | American Indian | 8 |
| | English | 96 | Hmong | 4 |
| | Italian | 62 | Chinese | 3 |
| | French | 56 | Asian Indian | 3 |
| Norfolk, VA | German | 243 | Filipino | 19 |
| 1,396,107 | English | 217 | Puerto Rican | 9 |
| | Irish | 186 | Mexican | 8 |
| | "American" | 108 | Korean | 3 |
| | Italian | 54 | Chinese | 3 |
| | French | 46 | Vietnamese | 2 |
| Omaha, NE | German | 257 | Mexican | 12 |
| 618,262 | Irish | 131 | Korean | 1 |
| | English | 81 | Japanese | 1 |
| | Swedish | 32 | Filipino | 1 |
| | Danish | 29 | Chinese | 1 |
| | Czech | 28 | Puerto Rican | 1 |
| Portland, OR | German | 399 | Mexican | 31 |
| 1,239,842 | English | 247 | Indian | 12 |
| | Irish | 201 | Chinese | 9 |
| | French | 70 | Vietnamese | 7 |
| | Norwegian | 61 | Japanese | 7 |
| | Swedish | 60 | Korean | 6 |
| Providence, RI | Italian | 157 | Dominican | 9 |
| 654,869 | Irish | 141 | Puerto Rican | 8 |
| | English | 106 | Cambodian | 4 |
| | French | 74 | Guatemalan | 3 |
| | Portuguese | 60 | Mexican | 2 |
| | German | 48 | Filipino | 1 |
| San Antonio, TX | German | 233 | Mexican | 572 |
| 1,302,099 | Irish | 128 | Puerto Rican | 7 |
| | English | 119 | Filipino | 3 |
| | French | 36 | Chinese | 3 |
| | "American" | 31 | Korean | 2 |
| | Scotch-Irish | 30 | Vietnamese | 2 |

Source: U.S. Bureau of the Census, *1990 Census of Population, Social and Economic Characteristics: Metropolitan Areas,* Tables 5 and 26.

## CONCLUSION

With only a few notable exceptions, ethnic minorities in the United States have chosen to reside in the cities that have been ports of entry or centers of economic opportunity. Within these cities, groups have formed conspicuous urban ethnic islands that have developed their own cultural institutions and that support networks to nurture a sense of separateness from the dominant society. The foreign-language press early became a universal concomitant of ethnic settlement in the United States, dating back to 1732. Today, that foreign-language press is becoming an ethnic press that caters to ethnic issues but is published in English. With the advent of commercial radio in the 1920s, foreign-language broadcasting aimed at ethnic audiences experienced an age of growth that for many languages, particularly those most frequently spoken at home, has continued until the present day. Nevertheless, there has been a decline in cohesiveness among many first- and second-wave ethnic groups, now many generations removed from the mother country and the mother tongue. The result has been a diminution of support for many foreign-language newspapers and radio programs. As third-wave immigrants provide the support for new foreign-language publications and broadcasts, older ethnic groups must decide whether their insular identity has been so totally submerged in the mainstream of the dominant society that the need for avenues of ethnic communication is gone.

In popular American culture, the search for individual identity has seen a proliferation of special interest groups, advocacy organizations, and other communities that operate independently of a territorial base. Just because islands of ethnicity disintegrate as territorial entities does not mean that the sense of community must also dissolve. In fact, given the ease of transportation and communication in today's world, even mobile, melting-pot Americans can maintain contact with spiritual cousins of the same ethnic background. This may mean a transition from foreign-language communication to English, but the ethnic press and ethnic radio, supported by regional and national networks, can survive. In essence, nationwide archipelagos of ethnic Americans can take advantage of the trend toward narrow-casting, remain in touch with those of similar interests, and use their ethnic heritage as one of the factors that makes them unique in our pluralistic society.

European, Latin, and Asian Americans continue to be a vital part of American culture and a conspicuous part of the American landscape. When the third wave of immigration will crest or what group will constitute the fourth are open questions, but the future of the United States is as likely to be colored by generations of new immigrants as has its past. What needs to be further investigated is whether third-wave immigrants from Latin America and Asia will conform to the same models as their European counterparts. Another chapter in the ethnic geography of the United States that begs to be written is a treatment of the wave of students that has turned almost all college and university campuses in the United States into mosaics of global cultures. Many of these students remain in the United States to make their own contributions to ethnic America. Those who return home are replaced by new arrivals, guaranteeing at least semipermanent ethnic islands on most campuses. The 1990 census has made available a multitude of statistical data on race, Hispanic origin, nativity, and ancestry that promises decades of fruitful ethnic research. Other data from ethnic organizations and field surveys are needed to provide an understanding of America as a cultural mosaic, as a melting pot, or as a stock pot of ethnic groups.

The evolution of urban ethnic islands is one of many spatial processes that bears watching to see how new immigrants and their descendants sort themselves out between central cities and suburbs and to see whether different forces shape the geometries of ethnic islands in Sunbelt cities versus Snowbelt cities. It may be that residential contrasts will not be as sharp, as demonstrated by previous ethnic groups in northeastern and midwestern cities.[60] Contrasts among regions and among ethnic groups may be so strong as to defy a universal model of ethnic assimilation. Agocs makes a case for pluralistic theories of ethnic evolution when she states:

> There may be little point in hypothesizing uniform patterns of ethnic group development and persistence, or of assimilation.[61] It is more likely that each ethnic community differs from every other in mode and rate of development, under the influences of many different variables, not all which are part of the experience of other groups. Not of the least important of these influences upon ethnic settlement patterns, for example, is historical accident; the timing and circumstances of immigration groups into a particular city, and the locations of their original settlement areas. The pluralistic theoretical perspective that is developing in ethnic and minority studies may sensitize researchers to what is unique in the experience of each ethnic group, as the search for general patterns continues.[62]

Pluralistic theories seem entirely consonant with our multicultural society, and spatial pluralistic theories seem entirely consonant with the renaissance of regionalism in America. The ethnic future will evolve from the conflict between forces encouraging cultural standardization and forces maintaining cultural distinction. At the individual level, the ethnic future will be shaped by our personal decisions to cast off the cultural baggage of our immigrant forebears, to maintain the practices and values of our ethnic heritage, or to resurrect an ethnic identity that individuals may never have known, even as children.

## NOTES

1. David Ward, "Immigration: Settlement Patterns and Spatial Distribution," *Harvard Encyclopedia of American Ethnic Groups* (Cambridge, Mass.: Belknap Press of Harvard University Press, 1980), 496–508.

2. U.S. Immigration and Naturalization Service, reported in "Special Report: Destination USA," *USA Today*, 13 October 1997, p. 11A.

3. James Paul Allen and Eugene James Turner, *We the People: An Atlas of America's Ethnic Diversity* (New York: Macmillan, 1988).

4. Thomas Sowell, *Ethnic America: A History* (New York: Basic Books, 1981).

5. Jorge del Pinal and Audrey Singer, "Generation of Diversity," *Population Bulletin* 52 (October 1997): 14–15.

6. U.S. Bureau of the Census, *1990 Census of Population, Detailed Ancestry Groups for States,* 1990-CP-S-1-2 (Washington, D.C.: U.S. Government Printing Office, 1991).

7. U.S. Bureau of the Census, *Statistical Abstract of the United States 1997* (Washington, D.C.: U.S. Government Printing Office, 1997), 53.

8. Donald J. Zeigler, "Printing in Tongues: The Foreign-language Press in the United States," paper presented at the annual meeting of the Association of American Geographers, Denver, Colorado, 26 April 1983, ERIC Reports, ED 236 281.

9. Robert E. Park, *The Immigrant Press and Its Control* (New York: Harper & Row, 1922).

10. Francis J. Brown and Joseph Roucek, eds., *One America* (New York: Prentice Hall, 1945).

11. Labomyr R. Wynar, *Encyclopedic Directory of Ethnic Organizations in the United States* (Littleton, Colo.: Libraries Unlimited, 1975).

12. Leo W. Jeffres and K. Kyoon Hur, "The Forgotten Media Consumer—The American Ethnic," *Journalism Quarterly* 57 (1980): 10–17.

13. Sally M. Miller, *The Ethnic Press in the United States* (New York: Greenwood, 1987), xii.

14. Editor and Publisher, *Editor and Publisher International Yearbook* (New York: Editor and Publisher, 1997), II-96–98.

15. Joshua A. Fishman, *Language Loyalty in the United States* (The Hague: Mouton, 1966).

16. Charles Jaret, "The Greek, Italian and Jewish American Ethnic Press," *Journal of Ethnic Studies* 7 (1979): 47–70.

17. David W. Silverman, "The Jewish Press: A Quadrilingual Phenomenon," in *The Religious Press in America*, ed. M. E. Marty et al. (New York: Holt, Rinehart & Winston, 1963), 123–172.

18. Beverly J. Fike, ed., *The Media Encyclopedia: Working Press of the Nation* (Chicago: National Research Bureau, 1981).

19. Carl Wittke, *The German Language Press in America* (New York: Haskell House, 1973).

20. Park, *The Immigrant Press*, 254.

21. Park, *The Immigrant Press*, 252.

22. Wittke, *The German Language Press*, 282.

23. U.S. Bureau of the Census, *Statistical Abstract of the United States 1997*, p. 53.

24. Jan Kowalik, *The Polish Press in America* (San Francisco: R & E Research Associates, 1978), 4.

25. Robert B. Kent and Maura E. Huntz, "Spanish-Language Newspapers in the United States," *Geographical Review* 86 (July 1996): 446–456.

26. Editor and Publisher, *Editor and Publisher International Yearbook*, II-96–98.

27. Kent and Huntz, "Spanish-Language Newspapers," 449, 452.

28. Editor and Publisher, *Editor and Publisher International Yearbook*, II-93–95.

29. Editor and Publisher, *Editor and Publisher International Yearbook*, II-93–99.

30. Nina Kessler, "Ethnic Newspapers Speak to Interests of Their Readers," *Advertising Age*, 22 September 1980.

31. Andrew Radolf, "Gannet Acquires El Diario–La Prensa," *Editor and Publisher*, 5 September 1981, pp. 10 and 29.

32. Mary Ellen Warshauer, "Foreign Language Broadcasting," in *Language Loyalty in the United States*, ed. J. A. Fishman (The Hague: Mouton, 1966), 75–91.

33. Joseph Roucek, "Foreign Language Broadcasts," in *One America*, ed. Brown and Roucek, 384–391.

34. Warshauer, "Foreign Language Broadcasting."

35. Warshauer, "Foreign Language Broadcasting."

36. Paul Wasserman and Jean Morgan, eds., *Ethnic Information Sources in the United States* (Detroit: Gale Research, 1976).

37. Theodore C. Grame, *Ethnic Broadcasting in the United States* (Washington, D.C.: Library of Congress, 1980), 73, 109–130.

38. *Broadcasting and Cable Yearbook* (New Providence, N.J.: Bowker, 1997).

39. *Broadcasting and Cable Yearbook*.

40. Todd Hyten, "Asian Radio Network Debuts in Boston," *Boston Business Journal*, 28 April 1995, p. 1.

41. Alvar W. Carlson, "A Geographical Analysis of America's Ethnic Radio Programming," *Social Science Journal* 34 (1997): 285–296.

42. Carlson, "A Geographical Analysis."

43. *Broadcasting/Cable Yearbook* (Washington, D.C.: Broadcasting Publications, 1981 and 1982).

44. *Broadcasting and Cable Yearbook*.

45. Grame, *Ethnic Broadcasting*.

46. Remco van Capelleveen, "The 'Caribbeanization' of New York City" in *Feasts and Celebrations in North American Ethnic Communities*, ed. Ramon A. Gutierrez and Genevieve Fabre (Albuquerque: University of New Mexico Press, 1995), 159–171.

47. van Capelleveen, "The 'Caribbeanization' of New York City," 167.

48. Wasserman and Morgan, *Ethnic Information Sources*.

49. Wynar, *Encyclopedic Directory*.

50. *Encyclopedia of Associations* (Detroit: Gale Research, 1998).

51. *Encyclopedia of Associations.*

52. Wynar, *Encyclopedic Directory,* xviii.

53. Carol Agocs, "Ethnic Settlement in a Metropolitan Area: A Typology of Communities," *Ethnicity* 8 (1981): 137.

54. Mark Abrahamson. *Urban Enclaves: Identity and Place in America* (New York: St. Martin's, 1996).

55. Yoshiharu Izaki, "The Residential Correspondence Between Japanese and Other Ethnic Groups in San Francisco," *Geographical Review of Japan* 54 (1981): 115.

56. L. F. Jones, "Ethnic Concentration and Assimilation: An Australian Case Study," *Social Forces* 45 (1967): 412–423.

57. Ward, "Immigration," 496–508.

58. Stanley Lieberson, "The Impact of Residential Segregation on Ethnic Assimilation," *Social Forces* 40 (1961): 57.

59. Amos H. Hawley, "Dispersion versus Segregation: Apropos of a Solution of Race Problems," *Papers, Michigan Academy of Science, Arts, and Letters* 30 (1944): 674.

60. Stanley Lieberson, "Suburbs and Ethnic Residential Patterns," *Journal of Sociology* 67 (1962): 673–681; N. Kantowitz, *Ethnic and Racial Segregation in the New York Metropolis* (New York: Praeger, 1973); Avery M. Guest and J. Weed, "Ethnic Residential Segregation: Patterns of Change," *American Journal of Sociology* 81 (1976): 1088–1111; Avery M. Guest, "The Suburbanization of Ethnic Groups," *Sociology and Social Research* 64 (1980): 497–513.

61. A. M. Greeley, *Ethnicity in the United States: A Preliminary Reconnaissance* (New York: Wiley, 1974); W. M. Newman, *American Pluralism: A Study of Minority Groups and Social Theory* (New York: Harper & Row, 1973).

62. Agocs, "Ethnic Settlement," 146.

# Index

*Page numbers in italic refer to figures or tables.*

# About the Contributors

**Christopher A. Airriess** is an associate professor of geography, Ball State University. His teaching and research interests include cultural–historical landscapes, ethnic geography, social and economic development, and Southeast and East Asia. Recent research publications appear in *Geography, Journal of Cultural Geography, Tideschrift voor Economische en Sociale Geografie, Geographical Review,* and *Indonesia*. Much of his work in ethnic geography has been with the Vietnamese American community in New Orleans, Louisiana.

**Daniel D. Arreola** was born and raised in Los Angeles but has resided in and professed at universities in three of the four U.S. borderland states. He is coauthor of *The Mexican Border Cities: Landscape Anatomy and Place Personality* (1993) as well as numerous papers about the cultural geography of Mexican Americans. He is a professor in the Department of Geography at Arizona State University.

**Thomas D. Boswell** was born and raised in the suburbs of Los Angeles. He received his Ph.D. from Columbia University in New York City, then he worked for one year at the Research Institute for the Study of Man in New York City and thereafter taught for four years at the University of Florida before moving to the University of Miami. His research specialties are demography and ethnic geography, with particular emphasis on Hispanic Americans and immigrants living in the United States who have come from the Caribbean Islands.

**Catherine L. Brown** is the director of planning, Department of Planning and Development, Chicopee, Massachusetts. She received her master's degree from the University of Georgia and wrote her thesis on the Chinese in Georgia.

**Stanley D. Brunn** (Ph.D., Ohio State) is a professor of geography at the University of Kentucky. During the past three decades, he has published articles and books on a variety of themes related to racial and ethnic issues, social problems, and political geographies at local and global scales. His current research addresses the nature of "electronic ethnic communities, diasporas and networks"—that is, those connected by e-mail, listservs, and the World Wide Web. He would eventually like to be able to utilize DNA data to unravel questions of "who we really are" and human migrations of our past and present.

**David L. Clawson** has taught cultural geography for more than twenty years at the University of New Orleans. His research has focused on tropical agroecosystems and the geography of religions/belief systems, in both Latin America and Southeast Asia. He is the author of *Latin America and the Caribbean: Lands and Peoples* (2d ed., 2000) and editor of *World Regional Geography: A Development Approach* (7th ed., 2001). He and Professor Christopher A. Airriess have collaborated on two previous articles on Vietnamese settlement in New Orleans that appeared in the *Geographical Review* (1994) and the *Journal of Cultural Geography* (1991).

**Angel David Cruz-Báez** was born in Cayey, a municipio in central Puerto Rico. He received his M.S. and Ph.D. from the University of Wisconsin at Madison. He received two faculty fellowships to conduct research with the National Aeronautics and Space Administration (NASA) during the summers of 1988 and 1989. He is coauthor of several books and numerous articles written in Spanish about Puerto Rico. He and Dr. Boswell were recent coauthors of the *Puerto Rico Atlas*, a bilingual atlas published by the Cuban American National Council in Miami in 1997.

**James M. Goodman**, professor emeritus at the University of Oklahoma, now lives in Santa Fe, New Mexico. He served as geographer-in-residence at the National Geographic Society, 1993–1995. His research and teaching focuses on American Indian lands and resources, physical environments, and teacher education. He is the author and coauthor of numerous scholarly works on Native Americans and other topics. He has been a consultant or adviser on several videotapes, multimedia shows, and educational posters.

**Douglas Heffington** (Ph.D., University of Oklahoma) is an associate professor of geography at Middle Tennessee State University. He has served as chair for the American Indian Specialty Group and the American Ethnic Specialty Group within the Association of American Geographers. He works closely with NASA exploring sustainable development among native peoples of Costa Rica, and his most recent article was entitled "Ethnicity: Lessons from the Field" in *Pathways*, a publication of the National Council for Geographic Education.

**Jesse O. McKee** is a professor of geography at the University of Southern Mississippi. His areas of research and teaching have concentrated on cultural, ethnic, population, and historical geography. He has authored several articles and book chapters and received numerous research grants. Some of his books include *The Choctaws: Cultural Evolution of a Native American Tribe*, *The Choctaw*, and *Mississippi: Portrait of an American State*.

**Ines M. Miyares** is an associate professor of geography at Hunter College–CUNY. Her teaching and research interests have focused on population, migration and ethnicity, political geography, and geographic education. She has numerous publications, particularly on refugees, and has served as chair of the American Ethnic Specialty Group of the Association of American Geographers.

**Allen G. Noble** is distinguished professor of geography and planning at the University of Akron. He is the author of the two-volume *Wood, Brick and Stone: The North American*

*Settlement Landscape;* coauthor of *The Old Barn Book;* editor of *To Build in a New Land: Ethnic Landscapes in North America;* and coeditor of *Barns of the Midwest.* He is currently researching and writing on the Amish community in Ohio.

**Jennifer A. Paine** received her M.A. degree from Hunter College–CUNY and is a Ph.D. candidate in the Department of Geography at Ohio State University. Her research interests have focused on ethnic and population geography, geographic perspectives on women, and Vietnam.

**Clifton W. Pannell** (Ph.D., University of Chicago) is a professor of geography and the associate dean of the Franklin College of Arts and Sciences at the University of Georgia. His areas of research and teaching have always focused on the urban and economic geography of China and Taiwan. His publications include a book (with L. Ma) on China's geography and development, numerous articles, chapters, and reviews, and he has recently been involved in a funded research project on urbanization in small cities and towns in China. Pannell has a long-term interest in the Chinese diaspora, and especially the North American Chinese population and Chinese communities in the Southeast.

**Harold M. Rose** is distinguished professor emeritus in the Department of Geography at the University of Wisconsin–Milwaukee. His teaching and research interests have focused on urban spatial structures, urban social geography, and population geography. Much of his recent research has concentrated on aspects of black homicide. He has served as president of the Association of American Geographers and has numerous publications in such journals as the *Annals Association of American Geographers, Economic Geography, Urban Geography,* and the *Urban Affairs Annual Review.*

**Ira M. Sheskin** is an associate professor of geography at the University of Miami. He has completed community studies for eighteen American Jewish communities and is a member of the National Technical Advisory Committee of the United Jewish Communities, which is responsible for the decennial National Jewish Population Survey. He is the editor of *Florida Jewish Demography,* the author of numerous publications on American Jews, and is currently writing a book entitled *Jewish Geography.*

**Donald L. Zeigler** (Ph.D., Michigan State University) is a professor of geography at Old Dominion University. His teaching and research interests have focused on the geography of ethnicity, global ethnoregionalism, political geography, and the Middle East. He has served as president of the National Council for Geographic Education and has numerous publications.